Mass
Media
Law

PEMBER BOOKS AND ARTICLES

Books   Pember, Don R. *Privacy and the Press*. Seattle: University of Seattle Press, 1972.

Pember, Don R. *Mass Media in America*. Chicago: Science Research Associates, 1974; Second Edition, 1977.

Articles   Pember, Don R. "The Pentagon Papers Decision: More Questions than Answers," 48 *Journalism Quarterly* 403 (1971).

Pember, Don R. "The Smith Act as a Restraint on the Press," 10 *Journalism Monographs* 1 (1969).

Pember, Don R., and Teeter, Dwight L. "Privacy and the Press Since Time, Inc., v. Hill," 50 *Washington Law Review* 57 (1974).

Pember, Don R. "The Broadcaster and the Public Interest: A Proposal to Replace an Unfaithful Servant," 4 *Loyola of Los Angeles Law Review* 83 (1971).

Teeter, Dwight L., and Pember, Don R. "The Retreat from Obscenity: Redrup v. New York," 21 *Hastings Law Journal* 175 (1969).

Teeter, Dwight L., and Pember, Don R. "Obscenity, 1971: The Rejuvenation of State Power and the Return to Roth," 17 *Villanova Law Review* 211 (1971).

Don R. Pember

University of Washington, Seattle

Mass
Media
Law

Wm. C. Brown Company Publishers
Dubuque, Iowa

Copyright © August 1977 by Wm. C. Brown Company Publishers

Library of Congress Catalog Card Number: 76-42593

ISBN 0–697–04309–6

Third Printing, 1978

Printed in the United States of America

Contents

Preface

This is a book about mass media law. Mass media law is that particular body of law which regulates the mass media. The law of libel and invasion of privacy, copyright regulation, and administrative and statutory rules affecting broadcasting and advertising are some of the topics which are discussed in this book.

There are several things you should know about this book and about mass media law before you begin your reading. First of all, the law, all law, is a living thing. Law is not, as many believe, chipped in granite or marble, to remain indelible throughout the centuries. Some laws, because they have lasted so long, seem to be permanent. The First Amendment to the United States Constitution, for example, seems to have remained unchanged for nearly two centuries. But you will discover, after you have read this book, that appearances can be deceptive. While the words of the First Amendment have remained unaltered for almost two hundred years, the meaning of those words (as interpreted by the courts) has changed many times.

Because the law is a living thing, it is difficult to write a book about the law. The author faces the problem that between the time the manuscript is completed and the book reaches the hands of the reader the law will have changed. Indeed, in the months between the completion of this manuscript and the beginning of production on the book, three important changes in the law occurred. In two decisions by the Supreme Court of the United States, the meaning of the First Amendment was explained to include hitherto unprotected rights. In *Nebraska Press Association* v. *Stuart*, the high Court ruled that in most circumstances it is unconstitutional for judges to bar the press from reporting information about criminal trials, even if the publication of that information may in some way make it more difficult for the defendant to receive a fair trial. In *Virginia State Board of Pharmacy* v. *Virginia Citizens Consumer Council,* the Supreme Court ruled that commercial speech, advertising for example, enjoys the protection of the First Amendment. In addition to these two decisions, the Congress of the United States adopted the first major revision of the copyright laws since 1909.

Both the author and the publisher have made every effort possible to bring to you the most up-to-date book. The developments in the law just mentioned are all discussed in this book. Students should be alert to other changes in the law as they are announced in the press, on television or radio, or better yet, in many of the professional magazines published by and for mass media practitioners.

Mass Media Law is not a book for lawyers or law students. It is not really a law book. I like to consider it instead a journalism or mass media book *about* the law. As such, the book is not written like a law book. It is not what is called a case book—a collection of excerpts from cases with comments by the author. Nor is it filled with footnotes and citations which lawyers and law students use to substantiate their legal arguments.

This book was prepared as a synthesis. At the end of each chapter is a substantial bibliography. In these books, articles, and cases can be found the documentation for the synthesis presented in the chapter. The book is prepared in a narrative style, and I have strived to make the book readable. An attempt has been made to organize the law in an understandable and meaningful manner. This organization is based on my experience in teaching mass media law to more than four thousand students over the past seven years. The book is written to help practitioners and students solve their problems with the law, to answer their questions about the law, and to prepare them to work within legal boundaries as journalists, editors, broadcasters, and advertising and public relations specialists. As such, I believe that substantial documentation within the text is immaterial and distracting.

Whenever possible the law has been simplified to make it more understandable to nonlawyers and to journalism students and practitioners. In no instance, however, has the law been distorted or bent out of shape for the sake of clarity. There are times when I have been forced to speculate, based on existing law, on how the courts or other governmental agencies might react to fresh problems. This is educated speculation and proper warning is always provided in the text. In other cases there are conflicting opinions about existing law, differing court opinions, for example, on the same problem. I, like a judge or a lawyer, have selected what I believe to be the most authoritative decision or opinion for guidance.

Because I believe that examples are important teaching tools, I have used them whenever possible in the text. When real cases exist, they are used to illustrate the point. But in those instances in which no case law exists (or is known to the author), imaginary examples are used. These are clearly labeled as being fictional and are used simply to give readers a means of better understanding a legal point. To facilitate this I make extensive use of fictional characters and institutions, including John Smith, Jane Adams, and the *River City Sentinel.*

Finally, *Mass Media Law* is undoubtedly biased toward the press and the mass media. My background as a journalist and a teacher of journalism preclude any other attitude. I have made every attempt to be fair, honest, and objective. Many people helped in putting this book together. It was Dick Crews of Wm. C. Brown who originally pushed the idea of this book on a somewhat hesitant author. He now has my gratitude. Thanks also must go to others at Wm. C. Brown, Natalie Gould and Julie Kennedy. Many of my colleagues at the School of Communications of the University of Washington helped, especially Jerry Baldasty and Roger Simpson. Many of my students have contributed ideas and support. Finally, my family deserves recognition for putting up with me while work on the book was completed. To Diann, Alison, and especially Brian, a little man who was born just about the same time the idea for the book was generated and probably who had the most difficult time understanding why Daddy often couldn't be bothered, goes my love and thanks.

D. R. P.

CHAPTER 1

The American Legal System

Probably no nation is more closely tied to the law than the American Republic. From the 1770s, when in the midst of a war of revolution we attempted to legally justify our separation from the motherland, to the 1970s, when a dissatisfied people used the law as a wedge to drive a president from office, and during the nearly two hundred years between, the American people have showed a remarkable faith in the law. One could write a surprisingly accurate history of this nation using reports of court decisions as the only source. Beginning with the sedition cases in the late 1790s which reflected the political turmoil of that era, one could chart the history of the United States from adolescence to maturity. As the frontier expanded in the nineteenth century, citizens used the courts to argue land claims and boundary problems. Civil rights litigation in both the midnineteenth and midtwentieth centuries reflects a people attempting to cope with racial and ethnic diversity. Industrialization brought labor unions, workmen's compensation laws, and child labor laws, all of which resulted in controversies that found their way into the courts. As mass production developed and large manufacturers began to create most of the consumer goods used, judges and juries had to cope with new laws on product safety, honesty in advertising, and consumer complaints.

Americans have protested nearly every war the nation has fought—including the Revolutionary War. The record of these protests is contained in scores of court decisions. The prohibition and crime of the twenties and

The Bibliography at the end of each chapter supplies additional information about the sources and legal cases cited in the text. An explanation of how to locate a given case using its citation is provided on page 6.

the economic woes of the thirties both left residues in the law. In the United States, as in most other societies, law is a basic part of existence, as necessary for the survival of civilization as are economic systems, political systems, cultural achievement, and the family.

This chapter has two purposes: to acquaint readers with the law and to present a brief outline of the legal system in the United States. Students who study mass media law frequently face the serious difficulty of studying a special area of law without having an understanding of the law or the court system in general, a situation somewhat like a medical student studying neurosurgery before taking work in anatomy, basic medicine, and surgical techniques. While this chapter is not designed to be a comprehensive course in law and the judicial system—such material can better be studied in depth in an undergraduate political science course—it does provide sufficient introduction to understand the remaining eleven chapters of the book.

The chapter opens with a discussion of the law, giving consideration to the five most important sources of the law in the United States, and moves on to the judicial system including both the federal and state court systems. Judicial review is discussed, and finally there is a brief explanation of how lawsuits, both criminal and civil, are started and proceed through the courts.

THE LAW

There are almost as many definitions of law as there are people who study the law. Some people say that law is any social norm, or any organized or ritualized method of settling disputes. Most writers on the subject insist that it is a bit more complex, that some system of sanctions is required before law exists. John Austin, a nineteenth-century English jurist, defined law as definite rules of human conduct with appropriate sanctions for their enforcement. He added that both the rules and the sanctions must be prescribed by duly constituted human authority. Roscoe Pound, an American legal scholar, has suggested that law is really social engineering—the attempt to order the way people behave. For the purposes of this book it is probably more helpful to consider the law to be a set of rules which attempt to guide human conduct and a set of sanctions which are applied when those rules are violated.

Scholars still debate the genesis of "the law." A question that is more meaningful and easier to answer is, What is the source of American law? There are really five major sources of law in the United States: the common law, the law of equity, the statutory laws, the Constitution, and the rulings of various administrative bodies and agencies. Historically we can trace American law to Great Britain. As colonizers of much of the North American Continent the British supplied Americans with an outline for both a legal system and a judicial system. In fact because of the many similarities between British and American law, many people consider the Anglo-American legal system to be a single entity.

The Common Law

The common law, which developed in England during the two hundred years after the Norman Conquest in the eleventh century, is one of the great legacies of the British people to colonial America. During those two centuries the crude mosaic of Anglo-Saxon customs was replaced by a single system of law worked out by jurists and judges. The system of law became common throughout England; it became the common law. It was also called the common law to distinguish it from the ecclesiastical (church) law prevalent at the time. Initially, the customs of the people were used by the king's courts as the foundation of the law, disputes were resolved according to community custom, and governmental sanction was applied to enforce the resolution. As such, the common law was, and still is, considered "discovered law." It is law that has always existed, much like air and water. When a problem arises, the court's task is to find or discover the proper solution, to seek the common custom of the people. The judge doesn't create the law; he merely finds it, much like a miner finds gold or silver.

This, at least, is the theory of the common law. Perhaps at one point judges themselves believed that they were merely discovering the law when they handed down decisions. As legal problems became more complex and as the law began to be professionally administered (the first lawyers appeared during this era and eventually professional judges), it became clear that the common law reflected not so much the custom of the land as the custom of the court—or more properly, the custom of the judges. While judges continued to look to the past to discover how other courts had decided, given similar facts (precedent is discussed in a moment), many times judges were forced to create the law themselves.

This common law system was the perfect system for the American colonies. Like most Anglo-Saxon institutions, it was a very pragmatic system aimed at settling real problems, not at expounding abstract and intellectually satisfying theories. The common law is an inductive system of law in which a legal rule is arrived at after consideration of a great number of specific instances of cases. (In a deductive system the rules are expounded first and then the court decides the legal situation under the existing rule.) Colonial America was a land of new problems for British and other settlers. The old law frequently didn't work. But the common law easily accommodated the new environment. The ability of the common law to adapt to change is directly responsible for its longevity.

Fundamental to the common law is the concept that judges should look to the past and follow earlier court precedents. The Latin expression for the concept is this: *Stare decisis et non quieta movere* ("to stand by past decisions and not disturb things at rest"). *Stare decisis* is the key phrase: let the decision stand. A judge should resolve current problems in the same manner as similar problems were resolved in the past. When Barry Goldwater sued publisher Ralph Ginzburg for publishing charges that the conservative Republican Senator was mentally ill, was paranoid, the judge most certainly looked to past decisions to discover whether in previous cases such a charge had been considered defamatory or libelous. There are ample precedents for ruling that a published charge that a person is mentally ill is libelous, and Senator Goldwater won his lawsuit (*Goldwater* v. *Ginzburg*, 1969).

At first glance one would think that under a system which continually looks to the past the law can never change. What if the first few rulings in a line of cases were bad decisions? Are we saddled with bad law forever? Fortunately, the law does not operate quite in this way. While following precedent is the desired state of affairs (many people say that certainty in the law is more important than justice), it is not always the proper way to proceed. To protect the integrity of the common law, judges have developed several means of coping with bad law and with new situations in which the application of old law would result in injustice.

Imagine for a moment that the newspaper in your hometown publishes a picture and story about a twelve-year-old girl who gave birth to a seven-pound son in a local hospital. The mother and father do not like the publicity and sue the newspaper for invasion of privacy. The attorney for the parents finds a precedent (*Barber* v. *Time*, 1942) in which a Missouri court ruled that to photograph a patient in a hospital room against her will and then to publish that picture in a news magazine is an invasion of privacy.

Now does the existence of this precedent mean that the young couple will automatically win their lawsuit? that the court will follow the decision? No, it does not. For one thing, there may be other cases in which courts have ruled that publishing such a picture is not an invasion of privacy. In fact in 1956 in the case of *Meetze* v. *AP*, a South Carolina court made just such a ruling. But for the moment assume that *Barber* v. *Time* is the only precedent. Is the court bound by this precedent? No. The court has several options concerning the 1942 decision.

First, it can accept the precedent as law and rule that the newspaper has invaded the privacy of the couple by publishing the picture and story about the birth of their child. Second, the court can modify or change the 1942 precedent by arguing that *Barber* v. *Time* was decided almost forty years ago when people were more sensitive about going to a hospital since a stay in a hospital was often considered to reflect badly on a patient, but that hospitalization is no longer a sensitive matter to most people. Therefore, a rule of law restricting the publication of a picture of a hospital patient is unrealistic, unless the picture is in bad taste or needlessly embarrasses the patient. Then its publication is an invasion of privacy. If not, the publication of such a picture is permissible. In our imaginary case, then, the decision turns on what kind of picture and story the newspaper published—a pleasant picture which flattered the couple? or one that mocked and embarrassed them? If the court rules in this manner, it modifies the 1942 precedent, making it correspond to what the judge perceives to be contemporary life.

As a third option the court can argue that *Barber* v. *Time* provides an important precedent for a plaintiff hospitalized because of disease—as Dorothy Barber was. But that in the case before the court the plaintiff was hospitalized to give birth to a baby, a different situation: Giving birth is a voluntary status; catching a disease is not. Consequently the *Barber* v. *Time* precedent does not apply. This practice is called *distinguishing the precedent from the current case*, a very common action.

Finally, the court can overrule the precedent. In 1941 the United States Supreme Court overruled a decision made by the Supreme Court in 1918 regarding the right of a judge to use what is called the summary contempt power (*Toledo Newspaper Co.* v. *U.S.*, 1918). This is the power of a judge to charge someone with being in contempt of court, to find him guilty of contempt, and then to punish him for the contempt—all without a jury trial. In *Nye* v. *U.S.* (1941) the high court said that in 1918 it had been improperly informed as to the intent of a measure passed by Congress in 1831 which authorized the use of the summary power by federal judges. The 1918 ruling was therefore bad, was wrong, and was reversed. (Fuller explanation of summary contempt as it applies to the mass media is given in chapter 6.) The only courts that can overrule the 1942 decision by the Missouri Supreme Court in *Barber* v. *Time* are the Missouri Supreme Court and the United States Supreme Court. Judges in other states can just ignore the *Barber* v. *Time* precedent if they believed it to be a poor decision.

Obviously in the preceding discussion the judicial process is oversimplified. Rarely is a court confronted with but a single precedent. And numerous other factors must be taken into account in addition to past case law. In fact, many people talk about the "hunch theory" of jurisprudence which suggests that judges decide a case on the basis of their instincts and then seek to find rational reasons to explain the decision. The imaginary invasion-of-privacy case just discussed demonstrates that the common law can have vitality, that despite the rule of precedent a judge is rarely bound tightly by the past. There is a saying, Every age should be the mistress of its own law. This saying applies to the common law as well as to all other aspects of the legal system.

It must be clear at this point that the common law is not specifically written down someplace for all to see and use. It is instead contained in the hundreds of thousands of decisions handed down by courts over the centuries. Many attempts have been made to summarize the law. Sir Edward Coke compiled and analyzed the precedents of common law in the early seventeenth century. Sir William Blackstone later expanded Coke's work in the monumental *Commentaries on the Law of England.* More recently, in such works as the massive *Restatement of Torts* the task was again undertaken, but on a narrower scale. Despite these compilations, in the eyes of some European attorneys the common law remains "the law nobody knows" because it isn't spelled out neatly in a statute book or administrative edict.

Courts began to keep records of their decisions centuries ago. In the thirteenth century unofficial reports of cases began to appear in Year Books, but they were records of court proceedings in which procedural points were clarified for the benefit of legal practitioners, rather than collections of court decisions. The modern concept of fully reporting the written decisions of all courts probably began in 1785 with the publication of the first British Term Reports.

While scholars and lawyers still uncover the common law using the case-by-case method, it is fairly easy today to locate the appropriate cases through a simple system of citation. The cases of a single court (such as the United States Supreme Court or the federal district courts) are collected in a single case reporter (such as the *United States Reports* or the *Federal Supplement*). The cases are collected chronologically and fill many volumes. Each case collected has its individual citation which reflects the name of the reporter in which the case can be found, the volume of that reporter, and the page on which the case begins. For example, the citation for the decision in *Adderly* v. *Florida* (a freedom-of-speech case) is 385 U.S. 39 (1966). The letters in the middle (U.S.) indicate that the case is in the *United States Reports,* the official government reporter for cases decided by the Supreme Court of the United States. The number 385 refers to the specific volume of the *United States Reports* in which the case is found. The last number (39) gives the page on which the case appears. Finally, 1966 provides the year in which the case was decided. So, *Adderly* v. *Florida* can be found on page 39 of volume 385 of the *United States Reports.*

If you have the correct citation, you can easily find any case you seek. Locating all citations of the cases apropos to a particular problem—such as a libel suit—is a different matter and is a technique taught in law schools. A great many legal encyclopedias, compilations of the common law, books, and articles are used by lawyers to track down the names and citations of the appropriate cases.

There is no better way to sum up the common law than to quote Oliver Wendell Holmes (*The Common Law*, published in 1881):

> The life of the law has not been logic; it has been experience. The felt necessities of the time, the prevalent moral and political theories, intuitions of public policy, avowed or unconscious, even the prejudices which judges share with their fellow-men, have had a good deal more to do than syllogism in determining the rules by which men should be governed. The law embodies the story of a nation's development through many centuries, and it cannot be dealt with as if it contained only the axioms and corollaries of a book of mathematics. In order to know what it is, we must know what it has been, and what it tends to become. . . . The very considerations which judges most rarely mention, and always with an apology, are the secret root from which the law draws all the juices of life. I mean, of course, considerations of what is expedient for the community concerned.

The Law of Equity   The common law is not the only legal legacy the British provided the American people. The law of equity, as developed in Britain beginning in the fourteenth and fifteenth centuries, is also a remnant of our British heritage and is the second basic source of the law in the United States. Equity was originally a supplement to the common law and developed side by side with the common law. During the 1300s and 1400s the king's courts became rigid and narrow. Many persons seeking relief under the common law for very real grievances were often turned away because the law did not provide a suitable remedy for their problems. In such instances the disappointed litigant could take his problem to the king for resolution, petitioning the king to "do right for the love of God and by way of charity." According to legal scholar Henry Abraham (*The Judicial Process*), "The king was empowered to mold the law for the sake of 'justice,' to grant the relief prayed for as an act of grace." Soon the chancellor, the king's right-hand man, set up a special office or court to settle the kinds of problems which the king's common law courts could not resolve. At the outset of the hearing the aggrieved party had to establish that he had no adequate remedy under the common law and that he needed a special court to hear his case. The office of the chancellor soon became known as the Court of Chancery. Decisions were made on the basis of conscience or fairness or "equity."

British common law and equity law were American law until the Revolution in 1776. After independence was won, the basic principles of common law in existence before the War of Revolution were kept because the cases remained acceptable precedent. After some hesitation, equity was accepted in much the same way. While present-day United States courts can consider decisions made in British courts after the Revolution, they are not bound by these decisions. For example, when the law of privacy is discussed, it will be seen that the decisions of British courts were often cited by American judges in the early development of privacy law, but were rarely fully accepted.

Initially there was a separate court of equity, or chancery, in Great Britain. But today in Great Britain and the United States, the same court hears cases both in equity and under the common law. Depending upon the kind of judicial relief sought by the plaintiff, the judge applies either the common law or the rules of equity.

The rules and procedures under equity are far more flexible than those under the common law. Equity really begins where the common law leaves off. Equity suits are never tried before a jury. Rulings come in the form of judicial decrees, not in judgments of yes or no. Decisions in equity are (and were) discretionary on the part of judges. And despite the fact that precedents are also relied upon in the law of equity, judges are free to do what they think is right and fair in a specific case.

Equity provides another advantage for troubled litigants—the restraining order. A judge sitting in equity can order preventive measures as well as remedial ones. An individual who can demonstrate that he or she is in peril, or about to suffer a serious irremediable wrong, can usually gain a legal writ such as an injunction or a restraining order to stop someone from doing something. Generally a court issues a temporary restraining order until it can hear arguments from both parties in the dispute and decide whether an injunction should be made permanent.

In 1971 the federal government asked the federal courts to restrain the *New York Times* and the *Washington Post* from publishing what have now become known as the Pentagon Papers (this case is discussed in greater detail in chapter 2). This case is a good example of equity law in action. The government argued that if the purloined documents were published by the two newspapers the nation would suffer irremediable damage; that foreign governments would be reluctant to entrust the United States with their secrets if those secrets might someday be published in the public press; that the enemy would gain valuable defense secrets. The federal government argued further that it would do little good to punish the newspapers after the material had been published since there would be no way to repair the damage. The federal district court temporarily restrained both newspapers from publishing the material while the case was argued—all the way to the Supreme Court of the United States. After two weeks of hearings the high Court finally ruled that publication could continue, that the government failed to prove that the nation would be damaged (*New York Times* v. *U.S.*, 1971).

Statutory Law

Americans were bound also by laws adopted by the British Parliament before the Revolution since they were British subjects then. Of course, after the Revolution this was no longer true. Instead of parliamentary laws Americans were bound by the laws of their own legislatures. Legislation is therefore the third great source of United States law.

Actually, Americans were bound by the rules of American legislatures long before the Revolution. State assemblies, town councils, and other similar bodies passed rules which ordered the lives of citizens for more than a century before the battle at Lexington and Concord. In fact, many authorities argue that if the British had simply allowed the American colonists more discretion in governing themselves the Revolution would never have occurred.

Today there are legislative bodies of all shapes and sizes. The common traits they share are that they are popularly elected and that they have the authority to pass laws. In the beginning of our nation, legislation, or statutory law, really didn't play a very significant role in the legal system. Certainly many laws were passed, but the bulk of our legal rules were developed from the common law and from equity law. After 1825 statutory law began to play an important role in our legal system, and it was between 1850 and 1900 that a greater percentage of law began to come from legislative acts than from common law court decisions. Today, most American law comes from various legislatures: Congress, state legislatures, city councils, county boards of supervisors, township boards, and so forth. In fact, legislative action is the most important source of American law in the 1970s.

Several important characteristics of statutory law can best be understood by contrasting them with common law. First, statutes tend to deal with problems affecting society or large groups of people, in contrast to common law, which usually deals with smaller, individual problems. (Some common law rulings affect large groups of persons, but this occurrence is rare.) It should also be noted in this connection the importance of not confusing common law with constitutional law. Certainly when judges interpret the Constitution they make policy which affects us all. However, it should be kept in mind that the Constitution is a legislative document voted upon by the people and is not "discovered law" or "judge-made law."

Second, statutory law can anticipate problems, and common law cannot. For example, a state legislature can pass a statute which prohibits publication of the school records of a student without prior consent of the student. Under the common law the problem could not be resolved until a student's record has been published in a newspaper or broadcast on television and the student brings action against the medium to recover damages for the injury he or she incurs.

Third, the criminal laws in the United States are all statutory laws—common law crimes no longer exist in this country and haven't since 1812. Common law rules aren't precise enough to provide the kind of notice needed to protect a criminal defendant's right to due process of law.

Fourth, statutory law is collected in codes and law books, instead of in reports as is the common law. When a proposal or bill is adopted by the legislative branch and approved by the executive branch, it becomes law and is integrated into the proper section of a municipal code, a state code, or whatever. However, this does not mean that some very important statutory law cannot be found in the case reporters.

Passage of a law is rarely the final word on the subject. Courts become involved in the process of determining what that law means. While a properly constructed statute usually needs little interpretation by the courts, judges are frequently called upon to rule upon the exact meaning of ambiguous phrases and words. The resulting process is called a statutory construction and is a very important part of the law. Even the simplest kind of statement often needs interpretation. For example, a prohibition stating "it is illegal to distribute an obscene newspaper" is filled with ambiguity. What does *distribution* mean? Can an obscene newspaper be sent through the mail? distributed from house to house? passed out on street corners? Are all of these actions prohibited? What constitutes a newspaper? Is any printed matter a newspaper? Is any printed matter published regularly a newspaper? Are mimeographed sheets and photocopied newsletters considered newspapers? Of course implicit is the classic question with which courts have wrestled in this country for nearly a century, What is obscenity?

Usually a legislature tries to leave some kind of trail to help a judge find out what the law means. For when judges rule on the meaning of a statute, they are supposed to determine what the legislature meant when it passed the law (the legislative intent), not what they think it should mean. Minutes of committee hearings in which the law was discussed, legislative staff reports, and reports of debate on the floor can all be used to help a judge determine the legislative intent. Therefore when lawyers deal with statutes, they frequently are forced to search the case reporters to find out how the courts interpreted a law in which they are interested.

Constitutional Law   Great Britain does not have a written constitution. The United States does have a written constitution and it is an important source of our law. In fact, there are many constitutions in this country: the federal Constitution, state constitutions, city charters, and so forth. All of these documents accomplish the same ends. First, they provide the plan for the organization of the government. Next, they outline the duties, responsibilities, and powers of the various elements of government. Finally, they usually guarantee certain basic rights to the people, such as freedom of speech and freedom to peaceably assemble.

One Supreme Court justice described a constitution as a kind of yardstick against which all the other actions of government must be measured to determine whether the actions are permissible. The United States Constitution is the supreme law of the land. Any law or other constitution which conflicts with the United States Constitution is unenforceable. A state constitution plays the same role for a state: a statute passed by the Michigan legislature and signed by the governor of that state is clearly unenforceable if it conflicts with the Michigan constitution. And so it goes with all levels of constitutions.

While constitutions tend to be short and infrequently amended, the process of determining what specific areas of these documents mean and whether a specific law or government action violates a certain constitutional provision is a laborious one, usually taking hours and hours and days and days of court time. Consequently, with the exception of the bare-bone documents themselves, the case reporters are once again the repository for the constitutional law which governs the United States.

Twenty-six amendments are appended to the United States Constitution. The first ten of these are known as the Bill of Rights and provide a guarantee of certain basic human rights to all citizens. Included are freedom of speech and freedom of the press, rights you will come to understand more fully in future chapters.

Constitutions are an important source of the law in the United States, especially law involving the mass media.

Administrative Agencies

By the latter part of the nineteenth century in the United States, not only had the simple idyllic life of the eighteenth century slipped away, but also the job of governing had become much more complex. Congress was being asked to resolve questions going far beyond such simple matters as budgets, wars, treaties, and the like. Technology created new kinds of problems for the Congress to resolve. Many such issues were complex and required specialized knowledge and expertness which the Congress lacked and could not easily acquire, had it wanted to. Federal agencies were therefore created to deal with these problems.

For example, the flow of natural gas through long pipelines which traversed the nation created numerous disputes. Since questions concerning use of these pipelines fell within the commerce power of the Congress, that deliberative body was given the task of resolving this complex issue. But pipeline regulation involved serious technical matters and competent regulation required a high level of expertise. To deal with these problems, Congress created the first administrative agency, the Interstate

Commerce Commission (ICC). This agency was established by legislation and funded by Congress. Its members were appointed by the president and approved by the Congress. Each member served a fixed term in office. The agency was independent of the Congress, the president, and the courts. Its task was (and is) to regulate commerce between the states, a matter which concerned pipelines, shipping, and transportation. The members of the board presumably were somewhat expert in the area before appointment and of course became more so during the course of their term.

Today hundreds of such agencies exist at both federal and state levels. Each agency undertakes to deal with a specific set of problems which are too technical or too large for the legislative branch to handle. Typical is the Federal Communications Commission (FCC) which was created by Congress in 1934. Its task is to regulate broadcasting in the United States, a job which Congress has really never attempted. Its members must be citizens of the United States and are appointed by the president. The single stipulation is that at any one time no more than four of the seven individuals on the commission can be from the same political party. The Senate must confirm the appointments, which was a fairly routine matter until recently when former President Richard Nixon had difficulty getting some of his political appointees confirmed by the upper house.

Congress sketched the broad framework for the regulation of broadcasting in the Federal Communications Act of 1934, and this act is used by the agency as its basic regulatory guidelines. The agency also creates much law itself in administration of the 1934 Act. In interpreting provisions, handing down rulings, developing specific guidelines, and the like, the FCC has developed a sizable body of regulations which bind broadcasters. For example, the Federal Communications Act of 1934 states that broadcasters must operate in the public interest, convenience, or necessity. The FCC holds that one aspect of operation in the public interest is to air all sides of a controversial issue to make certain that the audience has access to the full range of opinion on the topic. This general rule gradually emerged during the past forty years as the fairness doctrine, a full-blown set of rules created by the FCC which carry the force of law. Broadcasters who fail to live up to these rules can be fined or (rarely) have their license to broadcast taken away.

The courts get into the question, but on a limited basis. Persons dissatisfied with rulings by the FCC can go to court and seek a reversal of the commission action. But courts are strictly limited in their power when reviewing decisions by administrative agencies, and can overturn a commission ruling or any other action by an administrative agency in only these limited circumstances: (1) if the original act which established the commission is unconstitutional, (2) if the commission exceeds its authority, (3) if the commission violates its own rules, or (4) if there is no evidentiary basis whatsoever to support the ruling. The reason for these limitations is simple: These agencies were created to bring expert knowledge to bear on complex problems, and the entire purpose for their creation would be defeated if judges with no special expertise in a given area can reverse an agency ruling merely because they have a different solution to a problem.

The case reporters contain some law created by the administrative agencies, but the reports which each of these agencies themselves publish contain much more such law. These reports are also arranged on a case-by-case basis in chronological order. A citation system similar to that used for the case reporters is used in these reports.

As the problems which governments must deal with become more complicated and more numerous, administrative agencies seem to proliferate, and more and more of our law comes from such agencies.

There are other sources of American law. Executives—a governor, a president, a mayor—have the power to make law in some circumstances through executive order. The five sources just discussed—common law, law of equity, statutory law, Constitutional law, and administrative agencies—are the most important, however, and are of most concern in this book. First Amendment problems fall under the purview of constitutional law. Libel and invasion of privacy are matters generally dealt with by the common law and the law of equity. Obscenity laws in this country are statutory provisions (although this fact is frequently obscured by the hundreds of court cases in which judges attempt to define the meaning of obscenity). And of course the regulation of broadcasting and advertising falls primarily under the jurisdiction of administrative agencies.

While this section provides a basic outline of the law and is not comprehensive, the information is sufficient to make upcoming material on mass media law understandable.

THE JUDICIARY

This section gives an introduction to the American court system. Since the judicial branch of our three-part government is the field upon which most of the battles involving communications law are fought (if not settled!), an understanding of the judicial system is essential.

It is technically improper to talk about the American judicial system. There are fifty-one different judicial systems in the United States, one for the federal government and one for each of the fifty states. While each of these systems is somewhat different from all the others, the similarities among the fifty-one systems are much more important than the differences. Each of the systems is divided into two distinct sets of courts, trial courts and appellate courts. Each judicial system is established by a constitution, federal or state. In each system the courts act as the third branch of a common triumvirate of government: a legislative branch which makes the law, an executive branch which enforces the law, and a judicial branch which interprets the law.

Common to all judicial systems is the distinction between trial courts and appellate courts, and it is important to understand this distinction. Each level of court has its own function: basically, trial courts are fact-finding courts and appellate courts are law-reviewing courts. Trial courts are the courts of first instance, the place where nearly all cases begin, usually because the law says that they are where cases shall begin. Juries sit in trial courts, but never in appellate courts. Trial courts are empowered to consider both the facts and the law in a case. Appellate courts consider only the law. The difference between facts and law is significant. The facts are what happen. The law is what should be done about the facts.

The difference between facts and law can be emphasized by looking at an imaginary libel suit. The *River City Sentinel* publishes the following story on the front page of its Sunday edition.

Ineffective Medications Given to Ill, Injured
**SANDRIDGE HOSPITAL OVERCHARGING
PATIENTS ON PHARMACY COSTS**

Scores of patients at the Sandridge Hospital have been given ineffective medications, a three-week investigation at the hospital has revealed. In addition, many of those patients were overcharged for the medicine they received.

The *Sentinel* has learned that many of the prescription drugs sold to patients at the hospital had been kept beyond the manufacturer's recommended storage period.

Many drugs stored in the pharmacy (as late as Friday) had expiration dates as old as six months ago. Drug manufacturers have told the *Sentinel* that medication used beyond the expiration date, which is stamped clearly on most packages, may not have the potency or curative effects that fresher pharmaceuticals have.

Hospital spokesman deny giving patients any of the expired drugs, but sources at the hospital say it is impossible for administrators to guarantee that none of the dated drugs were sold to patients.

In addition, the investigation by the *Sentinel* revealed that patients who were sold medications manufactured by _____ Pharmaceuticals were charged on the basis of 1975 price lists despite the fact that the company lowered prices significantly in 1976.

The Sandridge Hospital sued the newspaper for libel. When the case got to court, the first thing that had to be done was to establish what the facts were—what happened. Both the hospital and the newspaper presented evidence, witnesses, and arguments to support its version of the facts. Several issues had to be resolved. In addition to the general questions of had the story been published and had the hospital been identified in the story, the hospital had to supply evidence that its reputation had been injured, that its good name had been damaged, and that the newspaper staff had been negligent. The newspaper relied on the truth as its defense. It presented evidence to document its charges that the hospital overcharged patients, that the medications were stale, that expired medicine is less effective than fresh medicine, and that patients did receive the stale medicine.

All this testimony and evidence establishes the factual record—what actually took place at the hospital. When there is conflicting evidence, the jury decides whom to believe (in the absence of a jury, the judge makes the decision). Suppose that the evidence presented by the newspaper convinced the jury that the hospital did possess expired drugs, that patients were charged 1975 prices for some medications, and that most authorities do regard expired medication to be less beneficial than fresher drugs. Given the factual record of the case, what is the law? Had the newspaper really proved its charges against the hospital? Had it proved the truth? A simple explanation is that in order to successfully use the defense of truth (defense of truth is discussed further in chapter 3) the newspaper must prove the substance of its charges, the heart of its allegations. In this case, a judge would probably rule that the newspaper had not proved the substance of its charges: there was no evidence that any patients had been given expired medication. Therefore, the hospital wins the suit. If the newspaper is unhappy with the verdict, it can appeal.

In an appeal, the appellate court does not reconsider the factual record. No more testimony is taken. No more witnesses are called. The factual record established by the jury at the trial stands and cannot be reconsidered. What the appellate court can do is to decide whether the law has been applied properly in light of the facts. It is possible that in this case the appellate court would rule that in establishing that the drugs were stored in the hospital pharmacy the newspaper has in fact established the substance of its charge—that it is inconceivable that patients had not received the expired medicine and that the trial judge erred in applying the law. Perhaps the judge erred in allowing certain testimony into evidence, or he refused to allow a certain witness to testify. Nevertheless, in reaching an opinion the appellate court considers only the law; the factual record established at the trial stands.

What if new evidence is found or a previously unknown witness comes forth to testify? If the appellate court believes that the new evidence is important, it can order a new trial. However, the court itself does not hear the evidence. These facts are given at a new trial.

The important differences between trial and appellate courts have now been pointed out. Other differences will undoubtedly emerge as the specific structure of each court system is discussed.

In the discussion that follows, the federal court system and its methods of operating are considered first, and then some general observations about state court systems are given, based on the discussion of the federal system.

The Federal Court System

The Congress has the authority to abolish every federal court in the land save the Supreme Court of the United States. The United States Constitution calls for but a single federal court, the Supreme Court. Article III, Section 1 states: "The judicial power of the United States shall be vested in one supreme Court." The Constitution also gives Congress the right to establish inferior courts if it deems these courts to be necessary. And Congress has, of course, established a fairly complex system of courts to complement the Supreme Court.

The jurisdiction of the federal courts is also outlined in Article III of the Constitution. The jurisdiction of a court is its legal right to exercise its authority. Briefly federal courts can hear the following cases:

1. Cases that arise under the United States Constitution, United States law, and United States treaties
2. Cases that involve ambassadors and ministers, duly accredited, of a foreign country
3. Cases that involve admiralty and maritime law
4. Cases that involve controversies when the United States is a party to the suit
5. Cases that involve controversies between two or more states
6. Cases that involve controversies between a state and a citizen of another state (we must remember that the Eleventh Amendment to the Constitution states that a state must give its permission before it can be sued)
7. Cases that involve a controversy between citizens of different states

While special federal courts have jurisdiction which goes beyond this broad outline, these are the circumstances in which a federal court may normally exercise its authority. Of the seven categories of cases just listed, categories one and seven account for most of the cases getting to federal court. For example, disputes which involve violations of the myriad federal laws and disputes which involve constitutional rights such as the First Amendment are heard in federal courts. Also, disputes between citizens of different states—what is known as a diversity of citizenship matter—are heard in federal courts. It is very common, for example, for libel suits and invasion of privacy suits against publishing companies to start in federal courts rather than state courts. If a citizen of Arizona should be libeled by *Time* magazine, the case would very likely be tried in a federal court in the state of Arizona, rather than in a state court. The magazine would look at the tribunal as a more neutral court. But the federal court would still follow Arizona law when hearing the case.

The Supreme Court of the United States   The Supreme Court of the United States is the oldest federal court, having been in operation since 1789. The Constitution does not establish the number of justices who will sit on the high Court. That task is left to the Congress. In 1789 the Congress passed the first judiciary act and established the membership of the high Court at six: a chief justice and five associate justices. This number was increased to seven in 1807, to nine in 1837, and to ten in 1863. The Supreme Court had ten members until 1866 when Congress ruled that only seven justices would sit on the high tribunal. Since 1869 the Supreme Court has had eight associate justices and the Chief Justice of the United States. (Note the title: not Chief Justice of the Supreme Court, but the Chief Justice of the United States.)

No attempt to change the size of the Court has occurred since the 1930s when President Franklin Roosevelt, unhappy about the manner in which it treated some of his New Deal legislation, proposed enlarging the Court. Publicly, Roosevelt argued that serving on the Court was arduous and that the work load for the older judges had become onerous. He sought the power to appoint one new justice for every justice over seventy years of age, to a limit of fifteen justices on the high Court. A bill giving him this power was beaten in the Senate by a large vote, but the Supreme Court responded to this pressure and began to treat the new economic legislation with more deference. In the end Roosevelt appointed nine men to the high court, more than any President except Washington.

The Supreme Court exercises both original and appellate jurisdiction. Under its original jurisdiction the Court is the first court to hear a case and acts much like a trial court in ascertaining facts and deciding the law. By the middle of this century the court had exercised its original jurisdiction only one hundred twenty-nine times. The Supreme Court has the authority to exercise this jurisdiction in only certain instances. In cases between two or more states, for example, the Supreme Court is the only court which can hear the matter and has exclusive jurisdiction. In cases involving foreign ambassadors and ministers the Supreme Court can exercise original jurisdiction, but Congress has given federal district courts jurisdiction in these matters as well. While there are a few other situations in which the high court can exercise original jurisdiction, as a practical matter it rarely does so. Consequently this power is not very important.

The appellate jurisdiction of the Supreme Court *is* important, for it is under this jurisdiction that much of the law in the United States is ultimately made or reviewed. Basically, under appellate jurisdiction a case gets to the Supreme Court in one of two ways: by direct appeal or by writ of certiorari. The third way, by certification, is rarely used—so rarely that the Court hears even fewer cases by certification than under original jurisdiction.

Under appeal, the aggrieved party (the aggrieved party is the appellant; the answering party is the appellee or respondent) has a statutorily granted right to carry an appeal to the Supreme Court. When does the right to appeal exist? Following are some examples of this right:

1. When a federal circuit court says that a state statute violates the United States Constitution or that it conflicts with a federal law or a federal treaty and is invalid, the state has the right to appeal the decision to the Supreme Court.

2. When a federal court declares an act of Congress to be unconstitutional, the United States has the right to appeal the matter to the Supreme Court.

3. When a state court rules that a United States law is unconstitutional or that one of the state's own laws violates the United States Constitution, the right of appeal to the United States Supreme Court exists.

These are just some instances of when technically the Supreme Court must accept jurisdiction and hear an appeal. The word *technically* is important to note because over the years the Court has constructed a vast loophole to escape from hearing cases under direct appeal. The Court can reject even a statutorily granted appeal if the case lacks "a substantial federal question." That is, if the Court feels that an issue is unimportant, that an issue has been decided previously by other courts, or that an issue isn't as important or as pressing as other issues, the Court can simply refuse to hear the case.

Despite the right to appeal, many litigants are turned away from the high Court without a hearing. Generally, the Supreme Court is concerned more with construction of law than with ensuring every citizen in the land his or her full measure of justice. The high Court is a policy-making court. If it heard every case in which a litigant claimed he or she was treated unfairly, it would have no time to do anything else. The Supreme Court looks for cases which raise important points of law, issues which are ripe for decision, issues which are troubling lower courts, issues which need a final resolution. Sometimes a citizen who has been denied justice by the lower courts finds the Supreme Court unwilling to set things right just because it is too busy.

Only about nine percent of the Supreme Court's business comes to it through direct appeal. The much more common way for a case to reach the nation's high Court is via a writ of certiorari. No one has the right to such a writ. It is a discretionary order issued by the Court when it feels that an important legal question has been raised. Litigants using both the federal court system and the various state court systems can seek a writ of certiorari. The most important requirement which must be met before the Court will even consider issuing a writ is that a petitioner exhaust all other legal remedies. While there are a few exceptions, this generally means that if a case begins in a federal district court, the trial level court, the petitioner must first seek a review by a United States court of appeals before bidding for a writ of certiorari. The writ can be sought if the court of appeals refuses to hear the case or sustains the verdict against the petitioner. All other legal remedies have then been exhausted. In state court systems every legal appeal possible must be made within the state before seeking a review by the United States Supreme Court. This usually means going through a trial court, an intermediate appeals court, and finally the state supreme court.

But occasionally the law provides for limited appeal and sometimes for no appeal at all—to wit, the case of Shufflin' Sam and the city of Louisville, Kentucky. Sam Thompson was an itinerant soul who made his way through life the best he could on the streets of Louisville. He may have been a vagrant, but he was harmless and rarely got into trouble. Sam's name was added to American legal history because he liked music and he liked to dance. Since he didn't have a radio or record player of his own, he frequently stood in the doorway of cafés and restaurants and shuffled his feet to the beat of the jukebox music playing inside. He was arrested one day during a spell of shuffling and charged with loitering and disorderly conduct. At police court he was convicted and received a small fine. The public defender felt that the law under which Sam was tried was too vague and therefore sought an appeal of the ruling. But there was no provision in the law for appeal—the lowly police court was the highest and only court which could hear the matter. Sam had exhausted all the state remedies. The next step was the United States Supreme Court. A writ was granted. In 1960 the high Court overturned the conviction and ruled that the city had presented no evidence that Sam had violated the law, and that to convict a man without evidence was a violation of the Fifth Amendment to the Constitution (*Thompson v. Louisville*, 1960). This is a rare event in United States legal history—

not every litigant can go from police court to Supreme Court and win. But it can happen!

When the Supreme Court grants a writ of certiorari, it is ordering the lower court to send the records to the high Court for review. Each request for a writ is considered by the entire nine-member court, and an affirmative vote of four justices is required before the writ can be granted. The high Court rejects most of the petitions it receives. Again, work load is the key factor. Certain important issues must be decided each term, and the justices do not have the time to consider thoroughly most cases for which an appeal is sought. Term after term suggestions to reduce the court's work load are made. Chief Justice Burger has on several occasions argued that a second high court, a court just below the Supreme Court, is needed to screen out less important cases. Theoretically, the Supreme Court would then have more time to deliberate on really important matters, while the second-level court would arbitrate less cosmic problems.

But such plans have got a cool reception from attorneys, Congress, and the public. All citizens believe that they should have the right to appeal to the Supreme Court—even if the appeal will probably be rejected, and even if the court may never hear the case, the right to make the appeal should remain.

Hearing a Case   While it is impossible to go into detail about each court considered here, it is important to understand the manner in which the Supreme Court operates.

The first thing the Court does is to decide whether it will hear a case, either on appeal or via a writ of certiorari. Once a case is accepted, the attorneys for both sides have the greatest burden of work during the next few months. Oral argument on the case is scheduled, and both sides are expected to submit briefs—their legal arguments—for the court to study before the hearing. The greatest burden at this point is on the party seeking appeal since he or she must provide the court with a complete record of the lower court proceedings in the case. Included are trial transcripts, lower court rulings, and all sorts of other material. Getting multiple copies of all the records is time-consuming and, more important, is quite costly.

Arguing a matter all the way to the Supreme Court takes a long time, often as long as five years—sometimes longer—from initiation of the suit until the Court gives its ruling. James Hill brought suit in New York in 1953 against Time, Inc., for invasion of privacy. The United States Supreme Court made the final ruling in the case in 1967 (*Time* v. *Hill*, 1967). Even at that the matter would not have ended had Hill decided to go back to trial, which the Supreme Court said he must if he wanted to collect damages. He chose not to.

After the nine justices study the briefs (or at least the summaries provided by their law clerks), the oral argument is held. For a generation schooled on Perry Mason and Owen Marshall, oral argument before the Supreme Court (or indeed before any court) must certainly seem strange. For one thing, the attorneys are strictly limited as to how much they may say. Each side is given a brief amount of time, often no more than an hour or ninety minutes, to present its arguments. In important cases "friends of the court" (amici curiae) are allowed to present briefs and to participate for thirty minutes in the oral arguments. For example, the American Civil Liberties Union often seeks the friend status in important civil rights cases. The attorneys' arguments are carefully planned and often scripted, to make full use of the allotted hour or so. The justices often destroy these plans by their questions and comments to participants on both sides of the issue. Sometimes the justices get into small disputes among themselves during an attorney's oral argument and use up valuable time. In some instances the justices can be downright rude as the legal advocates attempt to make their argument. For example, during oral argument on a case involving a Florida law which required newspapers to allow political candidates space to respond to editorial attacks upon them (*Miami Herald* v. *Tornillo*, 1974; this case is discussed in chapter 2, where the complete citation is also provided) former Justice William O. Douglas opened and slammed shut law books on the desk in front of him. Such behavior is a trifle disconcerting at best.

After the oral argument, which of course is given in open court with visitors welcome, is over, the members of the high Court move behind closed doors to undertake their deliberations. No one is allowed in the discussion room except members of the Court itself—no clerks, no bailiffs, no secretaries. The discussion, which often is held several days after the arguments are completed, is opened by the Chief Justice. Discussion time is limited, and by being the first speaker the Chief Justice is in a position to set the agenda, so to speak, for each case—to raise what he thinks are the key issues. Next to speak is the justice with the most seniority, and after him, the next most senior justice. The Court usually has an average of seventy-five items or cases to dispose of during one conference or discussion day; consequently brevity is valued. Each justice has just a few moments to state his thoughts on the matter. After discussion, a tentative vote is taken and recorded by each justice in a small, hinged, lockable docket book. In the voting procedure the junior justice votes first; the Chief Justice, last. The Court normally works from 10 A.M. to 5:30 P.M. on conference days in an attempt to get through all the matters before it.

Under the United States legal system, which is based so heavily upon the concept of court participation in developing and interpreting the law, a simple yes-or-no answer to any legal question is hardly sufficient. More important than the vote, for the law if not for the litigant, are the reasons for the decision. Therefore the Supreme Court and all courts which deal with questions of law prepare what are called opinions in which the reasons, or rationale, for the decision are given. At the Supreme Court this is a complex task. One of the justices voting in the majority is asked to write what is called the court's opinion. If the Chief Justice is in the majority, he selects the author of the opinion. If he is not, the senior associate justice in the majority makes the assignment. Either the Chief Justice or the senior associate justice can write the opinion himself.

Opinion writing is a difficult task. Getting five or six or seven people to agree to yes or no is one thing; getting them to agree upon why they say yes or no is something else. The opinion must therefore be carefully constructed. After it is drafted, it is circulated among all Court members, who make suggestions or even draft their own opinions. The opinion writer incorporates as many of these ideas as possible into the opinion to retain its majority backing. While all this is done in secret, historians have learned that rarely do court opinions reflect solely the work of the writer. They are more often a conglomeration of paragraphs and pages and sentences from the opinions of several justices. Henry Abraham, in his book *The Judicial Process*, writes that former Chief Justice Earl Warren wrote, circulated, and rewrote his opinion in the case of *Brown* v. *Board of Education* (1954) for nearly two years in an attempt to get a unanimous court with a single opinion. (This was the case in which the court ruled that segregation in the schools in Topeka, Kansas, violated the Constitution.)

A justice in agreement with the majority who can't be convinced to join in backing the court's opinion has the option of writing what is called a concurring opinion. This means that the justice agrees with the outcome of the decision, but does so for different reasons than those of the majority. The late Justice Hugo Black and former Justice Douglas frequently joined in writing concurring opinions in freedom-of-expression cases. While other members of the Court often agreed that in a particular case government censorship was not appropriate, Black and Douglas often wrote opinions in which they argued that government censorship is *never* permissible.

Justices who disagree with the majority can also write an opinion, either individually or as a group, called a dissenting opinion. Dissenting opinions are very important. Sometimes, after the Court has made a decision, it becomes clear that the decision was not the proper one. The issue is often litigated again by other parties who use the arguments in the dissenting opinion as the basis for a legal claim. If enough time passes, if the composition of the Court changes sufficiently, or if the Court members change their minds, the high Court can swing to the views of the original dissenters. This is what happened in the case of *Nye* v. *U.S.* (noted earlier) when the high Court repudiated a stand it had taken in 1918 and supported instead the opinion of Justice Oliver Wendell Holmes, who had vigorously dissented in the earlier decision.

Finally, it is possible for a justice to concur with the majority in part and to dissent in part as well. That is, the justice may agree with some of the things the majority says, but disagree with other aspects of the ruling. This kind of stand by a justice, as well as an ordinary concurrence, frequently fractures the Court in such a way that in a six-to-three ruling only three persons subscribe to the Court's opinion, two others concur, the sixth concurs in part and dissents in part, and three others dissent. From 1957 until 1973 the high Court found it extremely difficult to get a majority of the Court to subscribe to a single definition of obscenity. Concurrences were common, and as a result the law was in considerable confusion.

The Supreme Court can dispose of a case in two other ways. A per curiam ("by the court") opinion can be prepared. This is an unsigned opinion drafted by one or more members of the majority and published as the Court's opinion. There are probably several good reasons for the publication of unsigned opinions, but these opinions normally succeed only in creating confusion among Court watchers and other persons who study decisions of the high Court. Per curiam opinions are not common, but they are not rare either.

Finally, the high Court can dispose of a case with a memorandum order—that is, it just announces the vote without giving an opinion. Or the order cites an earlier Supreme Court decision as the reason for affirming or reversing a lower court ruling. This device is quite common today as the work load of the high Court increases. In cases with little legal importance and in cases in which the issues were really resolved earlier, the Court saves a good deal of time by just announcing its decision.

One final matter in regard to voting remains for consideration: What happens in case of a tie vote? When all nine members of the Court are present, a tie vote is technically impossible. However, if there is a vacancy on the Court, only eight justices hear a case. Even when the Court is full, a particular justice may disqualify himself from hearing a case. For instance, when William Rehnquist was named an associate justice a few years ago, before the Court were several cases on which he had worked as a member of the justice department before being appointed to the Court. It would not have been fair for him to act as a judge in these matters. Former Justice Douglas also had a slight conflict of interest in cases involving Grove Press, Inc. Grove Press publishes much erotic literature and is frequently in court on charges of violating obscenity laws. Douglas was paid a small sum for writing an article for one of the Grove Press publications. However tenuous, this was said to give him an interest in the case, and he was forced to sit out several cases involving Grove Press. This situation shows that a tie vote is possible. What happens? Nothing. A tie means that the opinion of the lower court is sustained or affirmed. No opinion is written. It is almost as if the high Court had never heard the case.

During the circulation of an opinion justices have the opportunity to change sides, to change their vote. The number and membership in the majority may shift. It is not impossible for the majority to become the minority if one of the dissenters writes a particularly powerful dissent which attracts support from members originally opposed to his opinion. This event is probably very rare. Nevertheless, a vote of the Court is not final until it is announced on decision day, or opinion day. The authors of the various opinions—court opinions, concurrences, and dissents—publicly read or summarize their views. Printed copies of these documents are handed out to the parties involved and to the press. In the past opinion day was always on Monday, and three Mondays during each month were set aside for this public reading. But on some opinion days when the Supreme Court handed down several important rulings, important cases were often overlooked by both the press and the public. Suggestions were made that the Court hand down opinions on other days as well. And that is the practice today—any day of the week can be a decision day, but it is usually Monday.

After the Decision   Are lower courts bound to follow United States Supreme Court decisions? The answer to that is yes and no. Since the Supreme Court is the supervisor of the federal courts, lower federal courts are bound closely by the high Court rulings. Still, occasionally lower federal courts are reluctant to follow the lead of the high Court.

The Supreme Court is not empowered to make a final judgment when it reviews a state court decision. All it can do, as Henry Abraham writes in *The Judicial Process*, is "to decide the federal issue and remand it to the state court below for final judgment 'not inconsistent with this opinion.'" However, new issues can be raised at the lower level by the state courts, and the opportunity to evade the ruling of the Supreme Court always exists. One study undertaken by the *Harvard Law Review* showed that of one hundred seventy-five cases remanded to state courts between 1941 and 1951, twenty-two of the litigants who won at the high Court level ultimately lost in the state courts following the high Court ruling. As pointed out earlier, because courts operate on a case-by-case basis the opportunity for defiance beyond the instant case is real.

Finally, the Supreme Court itself has no real way to enforce decisions and must depend upon other government agencies for enforcement of its rulings. The job normally falls to the executive branch. If perchance the president decides not to enforce a Court ruling, no legal force exists to compel him to do so. If former President Nixon, for example, had chosen to refuse to turn over the infamous Watergate tapes after the Court ruled against his arguments of executive privilege, no other agency could have forced him to give up those tapes.

At the same time, there is one force which usually works to see that Supreme Court decisions are carried out—public opinion. Political scientists frequently use the concept of "legitimacy" in connection with public opinion to describe how those "nine old men" can wield such immense power in the nation. People believe in the high Court; they have an immense amount of faith that what the Supreme Court does is probably right. This doesn't mean that they always agree with the decision. But they do agree that this is the proper way to settle disputes, and that when the Supreme Court speaks, its opinions become the rule of law. The Court helps engender this spirit or philosophy by acting in a temperate manner. It generally avoids answering highly controversial questions in which an unpopular decision could weaken its legitimacy. It calls such disputes "political questions," nonjusticiable matters. When it senses that the public is ready to accept a ruling, the Court may take on a controversial issue. Desegregation is a good example. Many people think that *Brown* v. *Board of Education* (1954) came out of the blue. Of course this isn't true. There had been almost a decade of desegregation decisions and executive actions prior to the *Brown* case. The nation was prepared for the decision, and it was generally accepted, even by the South which continued to fight desegregation tooth and nail for nearly ten years more. The high Court will continue to enjoy its legitimacy so long as it avoids rushing headlong into unsettled issues which the people consider important. Caution is the byword. This is not to say however that the high Court is conservative. It isn't, or at least it was not during the fifties and sixties, and early years of the seventies. The Court frequently leads both the Congress and the executive branch in forging new social policy. It can be argued, however, that this situation reflects not the radical policy of the Court, but rather the Stone-Age thinking of Congress and the executive branch.

In summary it can be safely said that the Supreme Court of the United States is unique, that there is no other institution in the world like it, and that it plays a role in our government probably not envisioned by the drafters of the Constitution nearly two hundred years ago. In this role, it adds an important element to our democratic system. In addition, the Court gives the law and the legal process high visibility in this nation and is at least partially responsible for the stability of our democratic Republic during the past two centuries.

Other Federal Courts

The United States Supreme Court is the most visible, perhaps the most glamorous (if that word is appropriate), of the federal courts. But it is not the only federal court nor even the busiest. There are two lower echelons of federal courts, plus various special courts, within the federal system. These special courts, such as the Court of Military Appeals, Court of Claims, Customs Court, and so forth were created by the Congress to handle special kinds of problems.

The United States District Court   Most business in the federal system begins and ends in the district court. This court was created by Congress by the Federal Judiciary Act of 1789, and today there are nearly one hundred such courts in the United States. Every state has at least one United States district court. Some states are divided into two districts: an eastern and western district or a northern and southern district. Individual districts often have more than one judge; sometimes many more than one. The Southern District of New York (a veritable hotbed of litigation), for example, has two dozen judges at work full time. Other metropolitan areas frequently have six or eight district judges.

When there is a jury trial, the case is heard in a district court. It has been estimated that about half the cases in United States district courts are heard by a jury.

The United States Court of Appeals   At the intermediate level in the federal judiciary are the United States courts of appeals. Until thirty years ago these courts were called circuit courts of appeals, a reflection of the nation's early history when members of the Supreme Court "rode the circuit" and presided at circuit court hearings. The court of appeals was also created by the Federal Judiciary Act of 1789. Today the nation is divided into eleven circuits, and there are eleven courts of appeals. Ten of the circuits are numbered (the Second Circuit comprises Connecticut, New York, and Vermont; the Seventh, Illinois, Indiana, and Wisconsin, for example). The eleventh unnumbered circuit is the District of Columbia Court of Appeals in Washington, a very busy court which has the added responsibility of hearing direct appeals of decisions made by many of the federal regulatory agencies such as the Federal Communications Commission.

The courts of appeals are appellate courts, which means that they hear appeals from lower courts and other agencies exclusively. These courts are the last stop for nine out of ten cases in the federal system. Normally each circuit has nine judges. While all nine judges can hear a single case—sitting en banc it is called—more commonly three judges hear a case. It is possible for two judges to hear a case, but this is unusual. In a case of extraordinary importance all nine judges hear the case, as in the Pentagon Papers case, when in both the Second Circuit Court and the District of Columbia Circuit, all nine members of the court heard the appeals from the two district courts.

The Three-Judge District Court   The one special court deserving attention is the three-judge district court because for a time, at least, this court heard a great many First Amendment cases. This court was provided by statute to hear special kinds of cases—most commonly cases in which someone seeks to restrain the enforcement of a state or federal law on the grounds that the law violates the United States Constitution.

The three-judge panel is normally made up of two district court judges (from the district in which the case arises) and one judge from the court of appeals. While the statute providing for such a court is old, three-judge panels were relatively rare until the civil rights struggles of the fifties and sixties. In 1965 in *Dombrowski* v. *Pfister* the Supreme Court urged that three-judge panels be assembled to aid civil rights workers frequently harassed by local authorities who arrested them in violation of their constitutional rights. The use of three-judge panels did blunt the attack upon civil rights workers in the sixties, upon war protesters in the seventies, and upon others in danger of being denied basic civil liberties. In fact, the special courts worked so well that their use put a strain on the judicial system: judges from district courts and courts of appeals spent so much time on the special panels that their case loads backed up. After months of pressure from Chief Justice Warren Burger, the Supreme Court ruled that a special three-judge court should not be used unless failure to call the tribunal would result in irremediable harm to the aggrieved party (*Younger* v. *Harris*, 1971). Temporary denial of a constitutional right—such as freedom of expression—is not necessarily considered irremediable damage. This ruling generally eclipsed the use of the special courts.

Then in the summer of 1976, Congress finished the job that the Supreme Court started in *Younger* v. *Harris*. Federal law was amended to severely limit the use of the three-judge panels. Under the new section 2284 of Title 28 of the United States Code, the three-judge courts can only be convened "when otherwise required by an Act of Congress, or when an action is filed challenging the apportionment of congressional districts or the apportionment of any statewide legislative body." Instances in which Acts of Congress call for the use of such a panel are rare, but include laws such as the Civil Rights Act of 1964 and the Voting Rights Act of 1965. Under this new law the panels would not be convened to hear cases involving First Amendment rights.

Federal Judges   All federal judges are appointed by the president and must be confirmed by the Senate. The appointment is for life. The only way a federal judge can be removed is by impeachment. Nine federal judges have been impeached. Four were found guilty by the Senate, and the other five were acquitted. Impeachment and trial is a long process and one rarely undertaken. The most recent consideration of impeachment was in connection with former Judge Otto Kerner, a judge of the United States court of appeals and a former governor of Illinois. He was found guilty of income tax evasion and sentenced to jail. At first Judge Kerner was reluctant to resign his judgeship, and the question as to whether income tax evasion is an impeachable offense was raised. Kerner finally resigned from the bench and saved the Congress considerable trouble.

Political affiliation plays a distinct part in the appointment of federal judges. Democratic presidents usually appoint Democratic judges, and Republican presidents appoint Republican judges. Nevertheless, it is expected that nominees to the federal bench be competent jurists. This is especially true for appointees to the courts of appeals and to the Supreme Court. The Senate must confirm all appointments to the federal courts, a normally perfunctory act in the case of lower court judges. More careful scrutiny is given nominees to the appellate courts. The Senate has rejected twenty-one men nominated for the Supreme Court either by adverse vote or by delaying the vote so long that the appointment was withdrawn by the president, or the president left office and the new chief executive nominated a different individual. Recently the upper house turned down two nominees of former President Richard Nixon. Judge Clement Haynsworth was rejected ostensibly because of possible conflicts of interest regarding personal finances, and Judge G. Harrold Carswell was turned down on the basis of demonstrated insensitivity toward blacks early in his judicial career. Both were judges of the court of appeals; both were judicial conservatives. These men were the first appointees to the Supreme Court to be rejected by the Senate since 1930.

American presidents have used various schemes to select justices to the Supreme Court, but normally most presidents ask the American Bar Association to approve a list of potential nominees. In selecting a justice to the high Court the president obviously seeks a person who reflects some of his personal philosophy. Because so many different kinds of issues confront the Court, to find someone who is both "right" on all the issues and professionally competent is virtually impossible. A potential nominee may have the same philosophy on law and order issues, but take a stance opposite the president on labor matters and antitrust law.

While a district judge must live in the community in which he or she works and is therefore clearly sensitive to some public pressure, judges of the courts of appeals and the justices of the Supreme Court are quite isolated from public pressure. Hence, philosophy can change when an individual reaches the court; judges and justices mature or change in many directions. Liberal President John Kennedy named Justice Byron White to the Supreme Court, but Justice White more often than not takes the conservative position in recent years. On the other hand conservative President Dwight Eisenhower appointed former Chief Justice Earl Warren and Justice William Brennan, two of the court's most outstanding liberals in the last half of the twentieth century. It is difficult to predict just which way an appointee will move after reelection or reappointment is no longer a factor.

The State Court System

The constitution of every one of the fifty states either establishes a court system in that state or authorizes the legislature to do so. The court system in each of the fifty states is somewhat different from the court system in all the other states. There are, however, more similarities than differences between the fifty states.

The base of each judicial system are its trial courts (or court). At the lowest level are usually what are called courts of limited jurisdiction. Some of these courts have special functions, like a traffic court which is set up to hear cases involving violations of the motor vehicle code. Some of these courts are limited to hearing cases of relative unimportance, such as trials of persons charged with misdemeanors or minor crimes or civil suits where the damages sought fall below $1,000. The court may be a municipal court set up to hear cases involving violations of the city code. Whatever the court, the judges in these courts have limited jurisdiction and deal with a limited category of problems.

Above the lower level courts normally exist trial courts of general jurisdiction similar to the federal district courts. These courts are sometimes county courts and sometimes state courts, but whichever they are, they handle nearly all criminal and civil matters. They are primarily courts of original jurisdiction; that is, they are the first court to hear a case. However, on occasion they act as a kind of appellate court when the decisions of the courts of limited jurisdiction are challenged. When that happens the case is retried in the trial court—the court does not simply review the law. This proceeding is called hearing a case de novo.

A jury is most likely to be found in the trial court of general jurisdiction. It is also the court in which most civil suits for libel and invasion of privacy are commenced (provided the state court has jurisdiction), in which prosecution for violating state obscenity laws starts, and in which many other media-related matters begin.

Above this court may be one or two levels of appellate courts. Every state has a supreme court, although some states don't call it that. In New

York, for example, it is called the Court of Appeals, but it is the high court in the state, the court of last resort. Formerly a supreme court was the only appellate court in most states. As legal business increased and the number of appeals mounted, the need for an intermediate appellate court became evident. Therefore, in most of the more populous states there is an intermediate court, usually called the court of appeals. This is the court where most appeals end. In some states it is a single court with three or more judges. More often numerous divisions within the appellate court serve various geographic regions, each division having three or more judges. Since every litigant is normally guaranteed at least one appeal, this intermediate court takes much of the pressure off the high court of the state. Rarely do individuals appeal beyond the intermediate level.

State courts of appeals tend to operate in much the same fashion as the United States courts of appeals, with cases being heard by small groups of judges, usually three at a time.

Cases not involving federal questions go no further than the high court in a state, usually called the supreme court. This court—usually a seven- or nine-member body—is the final authority regarding the construction of state laws and interpretation of the state constitution. Not even the Supreme Court of the United States can tell a state supreme court what that state's constitution means. Some years ago a group of citizens protested the use of public money to pay for crossing guards and safety devices to protect students walking to parochial schools. They sued in federal court to have the support stopped on the grounds that it violated the First Amendment to the United States Constitution which guarantees the separation of Church and State. The United States Supreme Court ruled that the First Amendment did not prohibit a state from giving money to church-sponsored schools to pay for safety materials and crossing guards. So the citizens brought suit in state court and argued that the payments violated a similar provision of the state constitution which ensures the separation of Church and State. This time they won; the state supreme court ruled this was indeed a violation of the state constitution. The decision was final. The United States Supreme Court could not overrule it because what was involved was interpretation of the state constitution, not of the federal Constitution.

State supreme court judges—like most state judges—are usually elected. Normally the process is nonpartisan, but because they are elected and must stand for reelection periodically, state court judges are generally a bit more politically motivated than their federal counterparts. In some states the judges or justices are appointed, and a few states have experimented with a system which both appoints and elects. Under this scheme, called the Missouri Plan, the state's high court judges (and sometimes all judges) are appointed to the bench by the governor from a list supplied by a nonpartisan judicial commission. After a one-year term the judge must stand before the people during a general election and win popular support. The voter's ballot says "Shall we retain Judge Smith yes (   ) no (   ) check one." If Judge Smith wins support his next term is usually a long one, up to twelve years. If support is not forthcoming, a new person is selected to fill the seat for one year, and at the end of the term must seek voter approval.

The advantages of the Missouri Plan are appointment of a qualified person initially and eventual citizen participation in the selection process.

The Power of Judicial Review

One of the most important powers of courts and at one time one of the most controversial is the power of judicial review—that is, the right of any court to declare any law or official governmental action invalid because it violates a constitutional provision. We usually think of this in terms of the United States Constitution. However, a state court can declare an act of its legislature to be invalid because the act conflicts with a provision of the state constitution. Theoretically, any court can exercise this power. The Circuit Court of Lapeer County, Michigan, can rule that the Environmental Protection Act of 1972 is unconstitutional because it deprives citizens of their property without due process of law, something guaranteed by the Fifth Amendment to the federal Constitution. But this action isn't likely to happen because a higher court would quickly overturn such a ruling. In fact, it is rather unusual for any court—even the United States Supreme Court—to invalidate a state or federal law on grounds that it violates the Constitution. Only about one hundred federal statutes have been overturned by the courts in the nearly two-hundred-year history of the United States. During the same period less than eight hundred state laws and state constitutional provisions have been declared invalid. Judicial review is therefore not a power which the courts use excessively. In fact, a judicial maxim states: When a court has a choice of two or more ways in which to interpret a statute, the court should always interpret the statute in such a way that it is constitutional.

Early in the history of our nation the power of the courts to undertake judicial review was questioned. After all, the federal Constitution does not give the federal courts the power to overrule laws legally enacted by the representatives of the people. Of course, the Constitution doesn't deny the courts that power. The idea was debated during the Constitutional Convention of 1787, but nothing was written into the charter about it. Little is known about what went on during that closed meeting in Philadelphia, but it is known that many delegates—maybe even a majority—favored the idea of judicial review.

The federal courts began to use the power of judicial review sparingly shortly after George Washington took office in 1789. However, many authorities consider the 1803 decision by the United States Supreme Court the fountainhead of judicial review in the Republic. This was the famous case of *Marbury* v. *Madison* (1803), whose beginnings were in the politics of the era, not in the law. John Adams and the Federalist Party were voted out of office in November of 1800. The loss of both the presidency and the Congress by the Federalists hurt Adams, and he therefore attempted to ensure some continued power for the party by filling the judicial branch with Federalist appointees.

During the time between the election and Thomas Jefferson's inaugural in March of 1801, Adams and the Federalist-controlled Congress created numerous new judicial positions. Then Adams set about appointing loyal Federalists to fill these jobs. Adams signed all the appointments and sent them to his Secretary of State, John Marshall, to affix the Great Seal of the United States and deliver them to the appointees. Marshall, by the way, was also the nation's chief justice. A Virginian, Marshall didn't march to the same quickstep drummer of the New Englander Adams, and therefore failed to deliver all of the commissions. When Thomas Jefferson took office, some of the Federalist office seekers who knew they had been appointed to the federal bench and who also had not received their appointment sought to obtain the official documents. Jefferson refused to surrender them. He did not intend to add to his political troubles by finishing a job his political opponents failed to complete. William Marbury, who had been appointed justice of the peace, went to court to force the new president to give him his commission. Citing a 1789 statue in which Congress organized the federal judiciary, Marbury sought relief directly from the United States Supreme Court. The 1789 law stated that under its original jurisdiction the Supreme Court could issue a writ of mandamus against persons holding office under the authority of the United States. Marbury's suit was brought against James Madison, Jefferson's secretary of state. If the court issued the writ, Madison was legally bound to deliver the signed appointment papers to Marbury.

Chief Justice Marshall found himself in a difficult position. A Federalist, he certainly favored Marbury's claim. But the chief justice knew that if the high Court ruled that Madison must deliver the commission Jefferson and Madison would ignore the ruling. There was no power short of force that could persuade Jefferson to honor the decision. Such behavior would severely damage the young court. Marshall appeared to be stuck—but only for the moment.

In his decision, Chief Justice Marshall neatly avoided answering the question altogether. He said that the statute under Marbury sought the writ of mandamus, the 1789 law, was unconstitutional because it expanded the original jurisdiction of the Supreme Court, and Congress couldn't constitutionally do that. Therefore, Marshall wrote, there is no way that this court can force the Secretary of State to deliver the commission. At the same time that he delivered this decision to Marbury, however, Marshall attacked the Jeffersonians for being petty and unfair and said that there was no doubt that Mr. Marbury deserved the commission and was entitled to the commission.

While *Marbury* v. *Madison* remains a monumental ruling, it was a most unusual ruling for a judge to make. First, one might think that Marshall should have disqualified himself from hearing the case. After all, he had affixed the Great Seal to Marbury's commission and had been assigned the job of delivering it—only a slight conflict of interest! Second, Chief Justice Marshall could have interpreted the statute as not applying to Madison, that he was not a person holding office "under the authority of the United States," that he was a political appointee, a temporary cabinet officer. Third, the chief justice probably could have construed the statute in a constitutional manner as well. Instead, he went right to the heart of the law, ruled it invalid, and breathed life into the concept of judicial review.

Judicial review is one of the most interesting aspects of American government and one of the most unusual as well. It is extremely important when matters concerning regulations of the mass media are considered. Because the First Amendment prohibits laws which abridge freedom of the press and freedom of speech, each new measure passed by the Congress, by state legislatures, and even by city councils and township boards must be measured by the yardstick of the First Amendment. Courts have the right, in fact have the duty, to nullify laws or executive actions or administrative rulings which do not meet the standards of the First Amendment. While many lawyers and legal scholars rarely consider constitutional principles in their work and rarely seek judicial review of a statute, attorneys who represent newspapers, magazines, broadcasting stations and motion-picture theaters constantly deal with constitutional issues, primarily those of the First Amendment. The remainder of this book will illustrate the obvious fact that judicial review, a concept at the very heart of American democracy, plays an important role in maintaining the freedom of the American press, even though the power is not included in the Constitution.

THE LAW SUIT   The final topic which needs to be understood before mass media law itself is considered is what happens in a law suit. The brief discussion of the process which follows is simplified as much as possible. Many good books on the subject are available for persons interested in going further into the intricacies of law suits (some are listed in the Bibliography at the end of the chapter).

The party who commences a civil action is called the plaintiff, the person who brings the suit. The party against whom the suit is brought is called the defendant. In a libel suit the person who has been libeled is the plaintiff, and he starts the suit against the defendant—the newspaper, the magazine, the television station, or whatever. To file a civil suit is a fairly simple process. A civil suit is usually a dispute between two private parties. The government offers its good offices—the courts—to settle the matter. A government can bring a civil suit such as an antitrust action against someone, and an individual can bring a civil action against the government. But normally a civil suit is between private parties. (In a criminal action, the government always initiates the action.)

To start a civil suit the plaintiff first picks the proper court, one which has jurisdiction in the case. Then the plaintiff presents the charges in the form of a complaint. The plaintiff also summons the defendant to appear in court to answer the charges. If the defendant chooses not to answer the charges, he or she normally loses the suit by default. After the complaint is filed, a hearing is scheduled. Then the plaintiff prepares a more detailed set of charges and arguments called pleadings, a very formal, written statement of the charge and the remedy sought. Usually the remedy involves money damages.

The defendant then prepares his or her own set of pleadings which constitute an answer to the plaintiff's charges. If there is little disagreement at this point about the facts—what happened—and that a wrong has been committed, the plaintiff and the defendant might settle their differences out of court. The defendant might say, "I guess I did libel you in this article, and I really don't have a very good defense. You asked for $15,000 in damages, would you settle for $7,500 and keep this out of court?" The plaintiff might very well answer yes because a court trial is costly, and takes a long time, and the plaintiff can also end up losing the case. Smart lawyers try to keep their clients out of court if possible and settle matters in somebody's office.

If there is disagreement, the case is likely to continue. A common thing the defendant does at this point is to file a motion to dismiss, or a demurrer. In such a motion the defendant says this to the court: "I admit that I did everything the plaintiff says I did. On June 5, 1975, I did publish an article in which he was called a socialist. But your honor, it is not libelous to call someone a socialist." The plea made then is that even if everything the plaintiff asserts is true the plaintiff is not legally wronged. The law cannot help the plaintiff. The court might grant the motion, in which case the plaintiff can appeal. Or the court might refuse to grant the motion, in which case the defendant can appeal. If the motion to dismiss is ultimately rejected by all the courts up and down the line, a trial is then held. It is fair play for the defendant at that time to begin argument of the facts, in other words, to deny that his newspaper published the article containing the alleged libel.

Before the trial is held, the judge may schedule a conference between both parties in an effort to settle the matter before starting the formal hearing or at least to narrow the issues so that the trial can be shorter and less costly. If this move fails, the trial goes forward. If the facts are agreed upon by both sides and the question is merely one of law, a judge without a jury hears the case. There are no witnesses and no testimony, only legal arguments before the court. If the facts are disputed, the case can be tried before either a jury or, again, only a judge. Note that both sides must waive the right to a jury trial. In this event, the judge becomes both the fact finder and the law giver. Now, suppose that the case is heard by a jury. After all the testimony is given, all the evidence is presented, and all the arguments are made, the judge instructs the jury in the law. Instructions are often long and complex, despite attempts by judges to simplify them. Instructions guide the jury in determining guilt or innocence if certain facts are found to be true. The judge will say that if the jury finds that X is true and Y is true and Z is true, then it must find for the plaintiff, but if the jury finds that X is not true, but that R is true, then it must find for the defendant.

After deliberation the jury presents its verdict, the action by the jury. The judge then announces the judgment of the court. This is the decision of the court. The judge is not bound by the jury verdict. If he or she feels that the jury verdict is unfair or unreasonable, the judge can reverse it and rule for the other party. Needless to say this happens rarely.

If either party is unhappy with the decision, an appeal can be taken. At that time the legal designations change. The person seeking the appeal becomes the appellant. The other party becomes the appellee or respondent. The name of the party initiating the action is listed first in the name of the case. For example: Smith sues Jones for libel. The case name is *Smith* v. *Jones*. Jones loses and takes an appeal. At that point Jones becomes the party initiating the action and the case becomes *Jones* v. *Smith*. This change in designations often confuses novices in their attempt to trace a case from trial to final appeal. If Jones wins the appeal and Smith decides to appeal to a higher court, the case again becomes *Smith* v. *Jones*.

The end result of a successful civil suit is usually awarding of money damages. Sometimes the amount of damages is guided by the law, as in a suit for infringement of copyright in which the law provides that a losing defendant pay the plaintiff the amount of money he might have made if the infringement had not occurred, or at least a set number of dollars. But most of the time the damages are determined by how much the plaintiff seeks, how much the plaintiff can prove he or she lost, and how much the jury thinks the plaintiff deserves. It is not a very scientific means of determining the dollar amount. In chapter three in the discussion of libel damages we will see that considerable hocus-pocus is involved.

A criminal case is like a civil suit in many ways. The procedures are more formal, are more elaborate, and involve the machinery of the state to a greater extent.

The state brings the charges, usually through the county prosecutor. The defendant can be apprehended either before or after the charges are brought. In the federal system persons must be indicted by a grand jury, a panel of twenty-one citizens, before they can be charged with a serious crime. But most states do not use grand juries in that fashion, and the law provides that it is sufficient that the prosecutor issue an information, a formal accusation. After the defendant is charged, he or she is arraigned. An arraignment is the formal reading of the charge. It is at the arraignment that the defendant makes his formal plea of guilty or not guilty. If the plea is guilty, the judge then gives the verdict of the court and passes sentence, but usually not immediately, for presentencing reports and other procedures must be undertaken.

If the plea is not guilty, a trial is then scheduled. Some state judicial systems have an intermediate step called a preliminary hearing or preliminary examination. The preliminary hearing is held in a court below the trial court, such as a municipal court, and the state has the responsibility of presenting enough evidence to convince the court—only a judge—that a crime has been committed and that there is sufficient evidence to believe that the defendant might possibly be involved. There is no need to convince the judge that the defendant is guilty, only that he or she might be guilty. The trial is then held in much the same fashion as is a civil trial. A jury may or may not be used—this decision is up to the defendant. The evidence is presented, the verdict is announced, the judgment is read, the sentence is imposed, and the appeals are undertaken.

In both a civil suit and a criminal case, the result of the trial is not enforced until the final appeal is exhausted. That is, a money judgment is not paid in a civil suit until the defendant exhausts all of his or her appeals. The same is true in a criminal case. Imprisonment or payment of a fine is not required until the final appeal. However, if the defendant is dangerous or if there is some question that the defendant might not surrender himself when the final appeal is completed, bail can be required. Bail is money given to the court to ensure appearance in court. When the defendant surrenders the bail money is returned. But if bail is set and the defendant cannot afford to raise the amount needed, then he is kept in jail until the appeals are finally over.

As stated at the outset, this chapter is designed to provide a glimpse, only a glimpse, of both our legal system and our judicial system. The discussion is in no way comprehensive, but it provides enough information to make the remaining eleven chapters meaningful. The chapter is not intended to be a substitute for a good political science course in the legal process. Students of communications law are at a distinct disadvantage if they don't have some grasp of how the systems work and what their origins are.

The United States legal and judicial systems are old and tradition bound. But they have worked fairly well for these last two hunderd years. In the final analysis the job of both the law and the men and women who administer it is to balance the competing interests of society. How this balancing act is undertaken comprises the remainder of this book. The process is not always easy, but it is usually interesting.

BIBLIOGRAPHY

Here is a list of some of the sources that have been helpful in the preparation of chapter 1.

Books   Abraham, Henry. *The Judicial Process.* New York: Oxford University Press, 1962.

Abraham, Henry. *The Judiciary: The Supreme Court in the Governmental Process.* 3rd ed. Boston: Allyn & Bacon, 1973.

American Law Institute. *Restatement of the Law of Torts.* St. Paul, Minn.: American Law Institute, 1939.

Blackstone, William. *Commentaries on the Laws of England.* Edited by St. George Tucker. Philadelphia: W. Y. Birch and Abraham Small, 1803.

Franklin, Marc A. *The Dynamics of American Law.* Mineola, N. Y.: The Foundation Press, 1968.

Holmes, Oliver Wendell. *The Common Law.* Boston: Little, Brown & Co., 1881.

Mayers, Lewis. *The American Legal System.* 2nd ed. New York: Harper & Row, 1964.

Pound, Roscoe. *The Development of the Constitutional Guarantees of Liberty.* New Haven: Yale University Press, 1957.

Roche, John P. *Courts and Rights.* 2nd ed. New York: Random House, 1966.

Cases   *Barber* v. *Time,* 159 S.W. 2d 291 (1942).

Brown v. *Board of Education,* 347 U.S. 483 (1954).

Dombrowski v. *Pfister,* 380 U.S. 479 (1965).

Goldwater v. *Ginzburg,* 414 F. 2d 324 (1969).

Marbury v. *Madison,* 1 Cranch 137 (1803).

Meetze v. *AP*, 95 S.E. 2d 606 (1956).
New York Times Co. v. *U.S.*, 403 U.S. 713 (1971).
Nye v. *U.S.*, 313 U.S. 33 (1941).
Thompson v. *Louisville*, 360 U.S. 199 (1960).
Time v. *Hill*, 385 U.S. 374 (1967).
Toledo Newspaper Co. v. *U.S.*, 242 U.S. 402 (1918).
Younger v. *Harris*, 401 U.S. 32 (1971).

CHAPTER 2

The Freedom of the Press

When a man reaches the final years of his life he often ponders how people will remember him. What aspects of his character and his contributions to society will people cherish? What will be quickly forgotten? So too is it with nations. Historians outline the important contributions made by ancient Greece and Rome, by Imperial Spain, and by the British Empire. What will historians consider the outstanding contributions of America and Americans? William O. Douglas, former associate justice of the Supreme Court of the United States, suggests that United States technology will not be the most memorable aspect of the nation's life. Instead, it will be our experiment with freedom of expression, an experiment shared with other Western democracies. Freedom of speech and freedom of the press—they are the achievements people will look upon with awe in eons to come.

No one knows whether Justice Douglas will be right. Clearly the attempt by Western democracies during the past three centuries to construct societies based upon the freedom to speak, the freedom to publish, and the freedom to criticize the government is a remarkable effort. Perhaps even more remarkable is that the experiment has worked so well. The guarantee of freedom of expression can be found in the constitution of nearly every nation. Only in a few countries such as the United States, however, are the people and the government dedicated to making the ideal come true.

The purpose of this chapter is to sketch a broad outline of the meaning of freedom of the press in the United States today. Freedom of the press is an element in all aspects of mass media—libel, invasion of privacy, obscenity, regulation of broadcasting and so forth. While certain specific guarantees did evolve from the First Amendment, they embody a broader concept, or at least define freedom of the press in more general terms, than originally conceived in the Amendment. It is that broader concept which is considered in this chapter.

Before freedom of the press can be defined, however, a brief look at the roots of the idea, roots which wind through many centuries, is necessary. Freedom of the press is not, and was not, exclusively an American idea. We did not invent the concept—in fact, no one invented it. Like Topsy, it just grew from crude beginnings which can be traced back to Plato and Socrates. The concept developed more fully during the past four hundred years. The modern history of freedom of the press really began in England during the sixteenth and seventeenth centuries as printing developed and grew. Today the most indelible embodiment of the concept is the First Amendment to the United States Constitution, forged in the last half of the eighteenth century by the men who built upon their memory of earlier experiences. To understand the meaning of freedom of the press and freedom of speech, it is necessary to understand the meaning of censorship, for viewed from a negative position freedom of expression can be simply defined as the absence of censorship. To understand censorship it is necessary to look first at the experience of the British who fought to be free from the yoke of censorship more than four centuries ago.

THE BRITISH EXPERIENCE

When William Caxton set up the first British printing press in Westminster in 1476 his printing pursuits were restricted only by his imagination and ability. There were no laws governing what he could or could not print—he was completely free. For five centuries Englishmen and Americans have attempted to regain the freedom that Caxton enjoyed, for shortly after he started publishing the British crown began the control and regulation of printing presses in England. Printing developed during a period of great religious struggle in Europe and it soon became an important tool in that struggle. Printing presses made communication with hundreds of persons fairly easy and in doing so gave considerable power to small groups or individuals who owned and/or could use a printing press. These facts make the printing press unique in the development of mass communication since it became a weapon in the fight for the minds of men. To understand the importance implied here, consider how other modern mass media developed. Motion pictures began as an entertainment device, radio was considered only a gadget until its commercial possibilities became evident, and television also developed as a commercial device, a twentieth-century electronic medicine show.

The British government soon realized that unrestricted publication and printing could dilute its power seriously. Information is a powerful tool in any society, and the individual or individuals who control the flow and content of the information received by a people exercise considerable control over those people. The printing press broke the crown's monopoly of the flow of information, and therefore control of printing was essential.

In his study of censorship of the British press during the three hundred years between establishment of printing in England and the American Revolution, Fredrick Siebert (*Freedom of the Press in England*) lists several means used by the crown to limit or restrict what today is called freedom of the press. Criticism of the government or of the king or the great men of the realm was called "sedition" or "seditious libel" and considered a serious crime. Whether the criticism was truthful was immaterial. In fact, for many years British courts considered truthful criticism of the government more harmful than untruthful criticism since untruthful criticism was easier to deny. Truthful criticism could more easily stir the people to dissatisfaction and anger. Hence the maxim which was the law in Britain for decades: The greater the truth, the greater the libel, that is, the more truthful the criticism, the more serious the crime.

In England, the press was licensed as well until the 1690s. Licensing meant prior censorship since all printers were forced to get prior approval to publish from the crown or the Church. Bonding ensured that printers followed the rules. Printers were required to put up large sums of money before they were allowed to print. If they violated the law or failed to assist the government in enforcing the law, they forfeited the money and were out of business until they raised another bond. The British government granted patents and monopolies to certain printers in exchange for their cooperation in publishing only acceptable material and for their assistance in locating printers who broke the law by printing without permission or printing seditious material. For their help these printers were granted exclusive rights to publish various categories of books such as spellers, Bibles, and grammar books.

These restraints were just some of the means the British used between 1476 and 1776 to control printing, and they are considered by most authorities to have been effective in controlling the press. While control was fairly effective, it did not go unchallenged. Men of ideas—writers, philosophers, even statesmen—argued for the rights of free British subjects to enjoy freedom of expression: the right to print without prior restraint and the right to criticize the government and the Church without punishment. The basic elements of what is called today the natural rights philosophy come from the ideas of these men. The natural rights philosophy asserts that man is a rational, thinking creature and must be free to plot his destiny. Men may have to sacrifice some natural rights in order to live in harmony with other men in society, but basic rights such as the freedom to think, the freedom to speak, and the freedom to publish can never be denied.

The men who drafted the Constitution were well acquainted with these ideas as well as with British censorship and control of the press. In addition, the founding fathers could draw upon first-hand experience of British control of the press in the American colonies.

THE AMERICAN EXPERIENCE

There were laws in the United States restricting freedom of the press for almost thirty years before the first newspaper was published. As early as 1662 statutes in Massachusetts made it a crime to publish anything without first getting prior approval from the government, twenty-eight years before Benjamin Harris published the first—and last—edition of *Publick Occurrences*. The second and all subsequent issues of the paper were banned because Harris failed to get permission to publish the first edition, which contained material construed to be criticism of British policy in the colonies, as well as a report that scandalized the Massachusetts clergy because it said the French king took immoral liberties with a married woman (not his wife).

Despite an inauspicious beginning, the American colonists seemed to have had a much easier time getting their views into print than their British counterparts. There was censorship, but when the British prosecuted offenders, American juries were reluctant to convict. Also, the colonial government was less efficient, and the British had less control over the administration of its colonies in North America, making criticism of the government somewhat easier for publishers.

The British attempted to use sedition laws to control the press in America, but did not attempt to organize guilds or printing monopolies. Licensing, which died in England in 1695, continued until the 1720s in the colonies. In 1723 the government of Massachusetts forbade printer James Franklin to publish the *New England Courant* or any similar newspaper or pamphlet without government supervision. Franklin, who was Benjamin Franklin's older brother, angered officials by charging in his newspaper that the colonial government was ineffective in protecting coastal communities from raids by bands of pirates. This restraint was the dying gasp of licensing in America.

The few taxes on the press were legitimate taxes levied to raise revenues, not to censor the press. The taxes were generally ignored by publishers and printers. The most widely known tax, the Stamp Act of 1765, succeeded only in increasing disgust toward and hatred of Parliament and the king. The stamps were poorly distributed, not being available in many communities. Newspaper publishers, who were supposed to buy the stamps and affix one to each copy of papers printed and sold, devised a multitude of schemes to avoid the tax. Some publishers removed the nameplate (the name of the paper) from the first page and declared they no longer published newspapers, but pamphlets, which were not subject to the tax. Others defied the law with little fear of retribution.

The John Peter Zenger Case

American law is fairly rife with cases that are very famous, but not very important. The Pentagon Papers case, which will be discussed shortly, is a contemporary example. Little law was made in the 1971 ruling. The case of John Peter Zenger probably falls into this category also, and is cited when sedition is discussed possibly because scholars are still unsure of the legal impact of the case upon freedom of the press in the American colonies.

The *Zenger* case was a case of sedition, but was not the first sedition trial in America. One of the nation's leading scholars on colonial freedom of the press, Prof. Harold L. Nelson, reports that at least four sedition cases occurred prior to the widely publicized trial of Zenger (*American Journal of Legal History*, 1959). Nelson found no record of subsequent sedition trials in justice courts after the Zenger case, but he did find at least four other instances in which charges of seditious libel were brought against colonists by colonial legislatures.

In the *Zenger* case, the defendant, an immigrant printer, was prosecuted because in the newspaper he published, the *New York Weekly Journal,* he printed statements which the royal governor of New York, William Cosby, believed to be critical of both him and the government. The *Zenger* case became famous in all likelihood because some of the participants wanted to make it famous. At the time freedom of expression was an important issue both in the colonies and in Great Britain, and the results of the trial, as well as a short book about the trial, were widely circulated. The case is also well known because it has all the elements needed to become well known: a noble cause, a proper villain, and a truly eloquent advocate as spokesman for freedom of the press.

Zenger's newspaper was sponsored by political opponents of Governor Cosby, who was unpopular since Cosby apparently saw his position as a means to acquire great wealth. His chief opponent was Lewis Morris, a wealthy politician who also had his eye on the money to be made from land speculation in the colony. Lewis Morris enlisted an associate, James Alexander, to publish a newspaper opposing the governor in hope of political gain. Zenger printed the newspaper and thereby became embroiled in a political dispute not of his making.

The first edition of the *New York Weekly Journal* appeared on November 5, 1733. The attacks on Cosby in subsequent editions were relentless, and in November of 1734 Zenger found himself in jail, accused of printing and publishing seditious libels which "tended to raise factions and tumults in New York, inflaming the minds of the people against the government, and disturbing the peace." Since Zenger was one of only two printers in the colony (the other printed a progovernment newspaper), Morris and Alexander had to get him out of jail if they were to continue publication of the *Journal*. Although Alexander was a lawyer, he could not defend Zenger because he was disbarred for attacking the authority of two members of the Supreme Court.

A court-appointed attorney, John Chambers, prepared to defend Zenger as the trial opened in August 1735. He was ably assisted by Andrew Hamilton, a fifty-nine-year-old Scots attorney and a renowned criminal lawyer whose interest in the case led him to come from Philadelphia to participate in the defense. Prof. Stanley Nider Katz, an authority on the Zenger trial, writes in Alexander's *A Brief Narrative on the Case and Trial of John Peter Zenger*, "Armed with years of courtroom experience and a well-prepared brief, speaking with the daring of one indifferent to the local political contests, Hamilton made short work of convincing the sympathetic jury of Zenger's injured innocence." Defying both British law and tradition with regard to seditious libel, Hamilton urged the jury to find Zenger innocent if they believed that his criticism of the government was truthful and fair. This impassioned plea caught the fancy not only of the thousands who read about the trial, but also of the members of the jury. A verdict of not guilty was returned and Zenger was freed.

Despite its fame the *Zenger* case did not, as lawyers like to say, make any "new law." The law before the trial was that truth is not a defense in a prosecution for seditious libel and remained the law after the trial. In addition, the jury was prevented by British law from determining whether the criticism of the government was seditious. The judge made such determinations. All the jury could rule upon was whether the defendant had in fact printed or published the work. The *Zenger* case did not change that law, either. The verdict was simply a case of jury revolt. The freemen on the jury ignored the law and found Zenger innocent.

The debate continues as to whether the Zenger trial really matters to American law. Legally, it probably does not. Politically, it is probable that the trial suggested strongly to colonial governors that future prosecutions for sedition before colonial juries were likely to fail. Historically, it is one of the best publicized instances in colonial America in which a ringing defense of freedom of the press carried the day. As such, the case is fondly remembered by most journalists and civil libertarians.

After Zenger's trial, government strategy changed. Rather than haul printers and editors before juries often hostile to the State, the government hauled printers and editors before legislatures and state assemblies which were usually hostile to journalists. The charge was not sedition, but breach of parliamentary privilege, or contempt of the assembly. There was no distinct separation of powers then, and the legislative body could order the printer to appear, question him, convict him, and penalize him. The same kinds of criticism which previously provoked a sedition trial now resulted in a trial before a colonial assembly. Only the basis of the charge was changed. In a contempt hearing the printer was accused of questioning the authority of the assembly, detracting from its honour, affronting its dignity, or impeaching its behavior, rather than of arousing general dissatisfaction among the people. Professor Nelson estimates that probably a large number of persons were brought before legislatures on such charges, but much more research is needed before all that happened during that period is known. We do know that repression of this kind was powerful and quite common. The press was as free as the colonial legislatures and assemblies permitted it to be.

The belief of many persons that freedom was a hallmark of society in colonial America ignores history. Political scientist John Roche (*Shadow and Substance*) writes persuasively that in colonial America the people and their representatives simply did not understand that freedom of thought and expression means freedom for the other fellow also, particularly for the fellow with hated ideas. Roche points out that colonial America was an open society dotted with closed enclaves—villages and towns and cities—in which citizens generally shared similar beliefs about religion and government and so forth. Citizens could hold any belief they chose and could espouse that belief, but personal safety depended upon the people in a community agreeing with a speaker or writer. If they didn't the speaker then kept quiet or moved to another enclave where the people shared his ideas. While there was much diversity of thought in the colonies, there was often little diversity of belief within towns and cities, according to Roche.

Patriots and Tories   The propaganda war which preceded the Revolution is a classic example of the situation. In Boston, the Patriots argued vigorously for the right to print what they wanted in their newspapers, even criticism of the government. Freedom of expression was their right, a God-given right, a natural right, a right of all British subjects. Many people, however, who did not favor revolution or separation from England—who are often forgotten—were also Americans. Such people were called Tories. Tories believed in their right to publish newspapers which advocated remaining a British colony and which defended the government. The right may have existed, but after 1770 in cities such as Boston expressing sentiments critical of the patriots was often difficult. Printers who published such newspapers frequently did so at their peril. Printers were attacked, their shops were wrecked and their papers were destroyed. Freedom of the press was a concept with limited utility in Boston for colonists who opposed revolution once the Patriots had moved the populace to their side. In other cities the Tories held the upper hand, and colonists seeking independence published in fear for their safety.

Many small towns in the United States still operate in much the same way. There is no governmental censorship, but social censorship makes certain that alien ideas don't often find their way into the community. Many activists on both the right and the left who scream the loudest about freedom deny that freedom to their political or economic opponents without hesitation.

Freedom is often fragile, and in the United States, as well as in other countries, the government is not always the most powerful censor. The community or social pressure, sometimes violent social pressure, is often a greater villain than the law in stifling freedom of expression. The First Amendment, which is the next subject at hand, affords little protection for the publisher or speaker in these kinds of cases.

THE FIRST AMENDMENT

As stated previously, the men who built the legal structure of this nation drew upon their colonial experience (just recounted here) in establishing a government. Freedom of expression was clearly not a new idea. British subjects both in England and in colonial America fought for this right for nearly two centuries. The basic belief that men can best serve themselves and their society when they are exposed to a full range of opinion was an idea with broad support in all levels of society, although it was not universally accepted in colonial America.

Even before the end of the Revolution, the government of this new nation drafted its first constitution, the Articles of Confederation. The Articles provided for a looseknit confederation of the thirteen colonies, or states. It was a weak government system and unworkable in many ways since the separate states retained most of the power and were frequently reluctant to work in concert to solve problems which affected the entire nation. Many persons criticized the national charter because it did not contain a single article which ensured citizens the freedom of conscience, freedom of the press, or any of the other rights which Americans had insisted the British respect. The Articles of Confederation did not contain such provisions because the men who drafted the Articles did not believe such guarantees necessary. The states remained sovereign and independent under our first constitution. The national government had little power. There was no need to forbid the national government from interfering with freedom of expression. It had no power to do so in the first place. With regard to the power of the states, most states had guarantees of freedom of expression in their state constitutions.

Virginia was fairly typical. In June 1776, nearly a month before the Declaration of Independence was written, a new constitution containing a declaration of rights or a bill of rights was adopted. The document, written by George Mason, guaranteed citizens that the state could never impose excessive bail, that the state could never use cruel or unusual punishment, that an accused person would enjoy a speedy trial, that an accused person would not have to testify against himself, and that freedom of religion would be preserved. Section 12 of that document states: "That the freedom of the press is one of the great bulwarks of liberty and can never be restrained except by despotic governments." Other states soon followed Virginia's lead and declarations of rights could be found in the charters of most of the new states by 1785.

The weaknesses in the confederated system of government soon became intolerable. As many of the citizens of the new nation desired to see the states retain sovereignty and power in the new alliance called the United States of America, it soon became obvious that a loose collection of states could not survive. A stronger alliance was needed, an alliance that would create a nation. In the hot summer of 1787 each state sent a handful of delegates to Philadelphia to revise or amend the Articles of Confederation. It was a remarkable group of men; perhaps no such group has gathered before or since. The members were merchants and planters and professional men and none were full-time politicians. As a group these men were by fact or inclination members of the economic, social, and intellectual aristocracy of their respective states. These men shared a common education centered around history, political philosophy, and science. Some of them spent months preparing for the meeting—studying the governments of past nations. Professor Robert Rutland (*The Birth of the Bill of Rights*) reports that John Adams outlined the history of scores of past nations and tried to determine the governmental defects which led to their ultimate downfall. While some members came to modify the Articles of Confederation, many others knew from the start that a new constitution was needed. In the end that is what they produced, a new governmental charter. The charter was far different from the Articles in that it gave vast powers to a central government. The states remained supreme in some matters, but in other matters they were forced to relinquish their sovereignty to the new federal government.

No official record of the convention was kept. The delegates deliberated behind closed doors as they drafted the new charter. However, some personal records remain. We do know, for example, that inclusion of a bill of rights in the new charter was not discussed until the last days of the convention. The Constitution was drafted in such a way as not to infringe upon state bills of rights. When the meeting was in its final week George Mason of Virginia indicated his desire that "the plan be prefaced with a Bill of Rights. . . . It would give great quiet to the people," he said, "and with the aid of the state declarations, a bill might be prepared in a few hours." Few joined Mason's call. Only one delegate, Roger Sherman of Connecticut, spoke against the suggestion. He said he favored protecting the rights of the people when it was necessary, but in this case there was no need. "The state declarations of rights are not repealed by this Constitution; and being in force are sufficient." He said that where the rights of the people are involved Congress could be trusted to preserve the rights. The states, voting as units, unanimously opposed Mason's plan. While the Virginian later attempted to add a bill of rights in a piecemeal fashion, the Constitution emerged from the convention and was placed before the people without a bill of rights.

Opposition to the proposed national charter sprung up immediately. Opponents of the charter are remembered as the anti-Federalists. Their primary complaint was that the new Constitution gave the federal government too much power. They had many other complaints, one of which was that the document lacked the guarantee that the federal government would not interfere with the rights of citizens such as freedom of expression, freedom of religion, and so forth. Thomas Jefferson, who was in France, wrote a letter to James Madison complaining about the lack of a bill of rights. The anti-Federalists argued that the new constitution would be the supreme law of the land, and that state declarations of rights were of little good in the face of the new powerful charter. They pointed out that the new charter gave the Congress the power to do anything necessary and proper to carry out its responsibilities under the Constitution. Congress was given the right to make war. What if Congress decided that curtailing freedom of speech was necessary and proper to making war? What was to stop Congress from undertaking such a restriction?

Supporters of the Constitution, the Federalists, worked diligently to win passage of the new charter. As part of this campaign, John Jay, James Madison, and Alexander Hamilton published a series of letters in a New York newspaper. These eighty-five letters, known today as *The Federalist* papers, were an eloquent argument for adoption of the new Constitution in which the authors attempted to refute the arguments of the opposition. In letter eighty-four Alexander Hamilton argued that a bill of rights was not needed. Specifically, Hamilton asked in respect to a provision which guaranteed the liberty of the press, "Why, for instance, should it be said that the liberty of the press shall not be restrained, when no power is given by which restrictions may be imposed?" He then added:

> What signifies a declaration that "the liberty of the press shall be inviolably preserved?" What is the liberty of the press? Who can give it any definition which would not leave the utmost latitude for evasion? I hold it to be impracticable: and from this I infer that its security, whatever fine declarations may be inserted in any constitution respecting it, must altogether depend upon public opinion, and on the general spirit of the people and the government.

When the states finally voted on the matter, the Constitution was approved, but only after the Federalists had promised several states, such as Virginia, that the first Congress would add a bill of rights.

Adoption of the First Amendment

James Madison was elected from Virginia to the House of Representatives, defeating James Monroe for the House seat only after promising his constituents to work toward adoption of a declaration of human rights. When Congress convened, Madison worked diligently toward keeping his promise. He first proposed that the new legislature incorporate a bill of rights into the body of the Constitution, but the idea was later dropped. That the Congress would adopt the declaration was not a foregone conclusion. There was much opposition, but after several months, twelve amendments were finally approved by both houses and sent to the states for ratification. Madison's original amendment dealing with freedom of expression states: "The people shall not be deprived or abridged of their right to speak, to write or to publish their sentiments and freedom of the press, as one of the great bulwarks of liberty, shall be inviolable." Congressional committees changed the wording several times, and the section guaranteeing freedom of expression was merged with the amendment guaranteeing freedom of religion and freedom of assembly. The final version is the version we know today:

> Congress shall make no law respecting an establishment of religion, or prohibiting the free exercise thereon; or abridging the freedom of speech, or of the press; or the right of the people peaceably to assemble, and to petition the Government for a redress of grievance.

The concept of the "first freedom" has been discussed often. Historical myth tells us that because the Amendment occurs first in the Bill of Rights it was considered the most important right. In fact, in the Bill of Rights presented to the states for ratification the Amendment was listed third. Amendments one and two were defeated and did not become part of the Constitution. The original First Amendment called for a fixed schedule that apportioned seats in the House of Representatives on a ratio many persons thought unfair. The Second Amendment prohibited senators and representatives from altering their salaries until after a subsequent election of representatives. Both amendments were rejected, and amendment three became the First Amendment.

Passage of the last ten amendments didn't occur without struggle. Not until two years after being transmitted to the states for approval did a sufficient number of states adopt the amendments for them to become part of the constitution. Connecticut, Georgia, and Massachusetts didn't ratify the Bill of Rights until 1941, a kind of token gesture on the one hundred fiftieth anniversary of its constitutional adoption. In 1791 approval by these states was not needed since only two-thirds of the former colonies needed to agree to the measures.

The First Amendment in the Eighteenth Century

What did the First Amendment mean in 1790? What was the accepted definition of freedom of expression at that time? There is no easy answer to these questions. One theory, held by most scholars until about twenty years ago, is that freedom of expression includes at least the right to criticize the government and the right to be free from prior restraint, or from prior censorship.

Freedom from prior restraint was supposedly guaranteed to all British subjects, as well as to American subjects, even before the Revolution. As has been noted, licensing of printers came to an end in England in the 1690s and in the colonies sometime in the 1720s. Between 1765 and 1769 Sir William Blackstone, the first professor of English law at Oxford University, published four volumes summarizing the common law at that time. In *Commentaries on the Law of England* Blackstone noted that liberty of the press was essential to the nature of a free state, and defined freedom of expression as "laying no previous restraints upon publication." The law professor asserted, however, that if something improper or mischievous or illegal is printed the publisher must then take the consequences. This obligation he said, is necessary for the preservation of peace and good order and is the only solid foundation of civil liberty. The First Amendment contained at least the prohibition against prior censorship.

American legal scholars, however, contended until recently that it contained more. They argued that one of the reasons for the Revolution was to rid the nation of the hated British sedition law. Americans, they argued, fought for the right to criticize their government and their governors. The First Amendment is a guarantee of the unrestricted discussion of public affairs. A second theory was proposed by Prof. Leonard Levy of Brandeis University in a book, *The Legacy of Suppression*, published in 1960. He argues that the common definition of freedom of the press in 1790 includes only freedom from prior restraint. The crime of seditious libel, Levy asserts, remained intact following the adoption of the First Amendment. There had been no intent to abolish it. Levy bases his arguments largely on philosophical tracts and a few court opinions. These, he argues, demonstrate that Americans did not believe unrestricted discussion of government to be one of their rights.

Levy's book provoked a good deal of comment and research. At the University of Wisconsin, for example, scholars examined Levy's thesis in light both of how juries operated between the Revolution and 1800 and of what newspaper editors printed and wrote during the same period. The conclusions drawn from this evidence are that discussion of government, including sharp criticism at times, was robust and relatively free and uninhibited and that editors published such discussion with little retaliation from the State. The few trials which did result often ended in acquittal for the publisher or pamphleteer. This seems to suggest that while many of the political philosophers and judges of the era believed that sedition should be punished most editors, pamphleteers, and citizens favored a more liberal definition of freedom of expression.

A third theory on the meaning of the First Amendment in 1790 probably makes more sense than any of the others: In 1790, the First Amendment meant different things to different people—just as it does today. The states insisted that a bill of rights be included in the national Constitution. The men who wrote the Constitution as well as the Bill of Rights were above all pragmatists. The last thing they wanted was a fight over whether the Constitution guaranteed this or guaranteed that—fights which could delay adoption. The same was true of the Bill of Rights. Hence, they presented the people with an eloquently vague document and appended to it an eloquently vague Bill of Rights. The First Amendment meant almost anything a citizen wanted it to mean. Had definition of each right been spelled out in great detail, the states might not yet have adopted the Bill of Rights.

This is not to say that there was no definition of freedom of expression in 1790. On the contrary, there were probably many definitions. There was probably little consensus on the exact meaning of the concept, even among the Congressmen who drafted the First Amendment. There is little consensus today on the meaning of the First Amendment. Were it not for the Supreme Court, which periodically defines the First Amendment, the law would be in a terrible state. One is not being facetious to say that in the 1970s the First Amendment means what the Supreme Court of the United States says it means—no more and no less. It should come as no surprise that many people, sometimes a majority of the people, disagree with the high Court's definition of freedom of expression. One man says it means freedom to publish anything, another man says it means the freedom to publish anything but obscenity, and a third man qualifies it even more and says it means freedom to print anything but obscenity or material which will hurt the nation. And so it goes.

The Supreme Court had barely begun operation in 1790, and the nation was thus denied its wisdom concerning the meaning of the First Amendment. In fact the high Court has taken nearly two centuries to offer, in its case-by-case approach, a comprehensive definition of the meaning of freedom of expression in the United States. Even today some questions remain unanswered completely. For example, does the First Amendment and freedom of the press guarantee the right of the press to gather news and information for publication? The Supreme Court has never fully answered this question.

The best practical definition of freedom of expression in 1790 is the one Professor John Roche gives, which we noted earlier. In 1790 freedom of the press meant that one could publish anything the community would tolerate. If a person's beliefs fit nicely with majority sentiment, freedom of expression was broad indeed. If a person was a political or religious heretic, freedom was narrow and tenuous, and the best solution was to find another place to live, a community whose people agreed with his ideas.

The First Amendment Today

While considerable debate over the meaning of the First Amendment when it was adopted nearly two hundred years ago remains, its meaning today is probably a little clearer. The Supreme Court has diligently attempted to define freedom of expression for more than fifty years. The high Court has drawn a fairly complete, if not altogether consistent, set of boundaries for freedom of the press. The chart has changed as the philosophical bent of the high Court changed from decade to decade. The Court has also had a lack of success in defining some of the limits of freedom of expression. Nevertheless, the working journalist has fairly good guidelines which outline, for example, what the First Amendment allows and what the Court forbids.

It should be obvious by now that the First Amendment does not really mean what it says—that Congress shall pass NO law. The argument that there can be no restrictions whatsoever on freedom of the press and freedom of speech is held by a few persons today. The most prominent person to hold that view in recent years was the late Associate Justice Hugo Black. Justice Black argued for years that there can be no restrictions upon freedom of expression, that any restriction at all violates the First Amendment. But Justice Black was always in the minority on this issue. He was joined often by former Associate Justice William O. Douglas, but two was the greatest number of court members ever subscribing to this theory. As attractive as it is—absolutes are always attractive because of their simplicity—the theory has few adherents even among people in the mass media. Because of the great power of the mass media today to flood the nation with false, as well as truthful, statements, few Americans— even journalists—are willing, for example, to forgo their right to sue for libel, when their reputation has been damaged. Of course, libel law is a serious restriction upon the press. At the same time, few editors and publishers believe in a completely unrestrained press when the publication and sale of obscenity are in question. Nearly all favor some kind of restriction.

The most common theory about the First Amendment expounded by jurists today is that freedom of expression is one right among many and may be exercised freely until it comes into conflict with another social value or human right. At that point the right of free expression must be weighed against the other value or right, and a decision on which takes precedent must be made. This process is called balancing. The right of a free press, for example, is balanced against the right of an individual to protect his or her reputation which might be damaged by publication of falsehoods. Or the right of a state to protect itself from revolution or riots is balanced against the right of freedom of the press. Interests must be balanced and decisions reached as to which is more important. This is what the Supreme Court has done since about 1918. But a handful of freedom-of-expression cases reached the high Court before that time.

Balancing is a highly pragmatic approach: rights and liberties are defined on a case-by-case basis. Each time a new situation occurs, the values are reweighed and a new balancing takes place. The law is somewhat unpredictable because a new Court sometimes tosses new elements on the scale. In obscenity law, for example, the high Court for years weighed how supposedly obscene material affected children and used this basis to determine its acceptability to the general public. Then in 1957 the high Court changed its mind and ruled that obscenity is determined by the affect of the matter on average adults, rather than on children. A new element was added to the balancing formula and changed the law.

Consideration of the charts—the maps—prepared by the courts so that citizens can use freedom of the press confidently makes up the remainder of this book, starting with the final sections of this chapter in which a few important general dimensions of freedom of the press are outlined.

Five basic aspects of freedom of expression included in the First Amendment are considered: (1) the right to oppose the government, in which sedition is considered, (2) the right to freedom from prior censorship, or prior restraint, (3) the right to freedom from unfair taxation, (4) the right to freedom from unfair licensing laws, particularly as they affect distribution, and (5) the right to freedom of expression in the schools.

Finally, a fundamentally new interpretation of the First Amendment which emerged about thirty years ago—an interpretation that is likely to persist for many years despite rejection by the Supreme Court—is discussed.

THE RIGHT TO OPPOSE THE GOVERNMENT

The right to oppose the government is the heart of freedom and democracy. Without this right a government by the people is a mockery indeed. Exercise of the right is using freedom of expression for a specific purpose: to alert fellow citizens to unfair government practices, to urge change of leadership, and even to advocate a new form of government. Freedom of expression becomes a means to an end, which is exactly the kind of freedom Professor Levy argues the First Amendment did not guarantee because the colonists accepted the British notions on sedition.

Whether the new government officials actually believed British sedition law to be intact after adoption of the Bill of Rights, they acted as though they did in 1798 when Congress approved a wide-ranging law which severely curbed citizens' rights to comment upon the government or governmental leaders.

Sedition in the Eighteenth Century

Some basic history is needed to put the affair in perspective. In 1798 John Adams was in the third year of his presidency. As Washington's successor to the high office, Adams was also the head of the nation's first political party, the Federalist Party, the party of the Constitution. It was the party which favored a strong national government. It was the party of Alexander Hamilton and Timothy Pickering and John Marshall. Arrayed against the Federalists was the party of Thomas Jefferson, variously called the anti-Federalists, the Republicans, the Democratic-Republicans, and the Jeffersonians.

The young nation was experiencing policy difficulties with the French in 1798. Some persons—usually Federalists—said that war with France was imminent. The impact of democratic ideas generated by the French Revolution clearly stirred some segments of the American population, but the stories of French espionage and plots against the United States government were largely rumors. Nevertheless, antagonism to the French and French aliens ran high in many Federalist districts. The feud with France was fueled by the Republican press, which rarely missed an opportunity to attack Adams or the Federalists. Many Republican editors were French sympathizers, and a large number were aliens, some French aliens. Journalism was not as we know it today. Newspapers were tied closely to political parties and sought to interpret news and events in terms of political affairs. Editorials in 1798 were editorials, not tame explanatory "comment" so often present in the press today. Editors were outspoken and wrote in polemical terms—they were vicious, they were vitriolic. In many instances the papers were funded either by the government or by the political party out of power.

No one will ever know whether John Adams really feared war with France and sought to stifle dissent in order for the nation to present a united front to Europe, or whether the trouble with France was a convenient excuse to muzzle some of his political enemies. In either case Adams approved of the efforts of some extremists in the Federalist Party to curb the power of the aliens, the Republicans, and the Republican press. In 1798 the Federalist Congress passed four laws know today as the Alien and Sedition Acts of 1798. The first three acts dealt with aliens: the period of residence for naturalization was extended from five to fourteen years, and the President was given the power to apprehend, restrain, and deport aliens whom he deemed to be dangerous. The sedition law was aimed directly at the Jeffersonian press. It forbade false, scandalous, and malicious publications against the United States government, the Congress, and the president. It said nothing about scandalous and malicious writing against the vice-president because Thomas Jefferson was vice-president, and the last thing the Federalists wanted to do was silence criticism of their number one political enemy. The new law also punished persons who sought to stir up sedition or urged resistance to federal laws. The punishment was a fine of as much as $2,000 and a jail term of not more than two years.

Truth was a defense in a prosecution brought under the new law, and the jury was given the power to determine whether the words were seditious. However, these safeguards proved ineffective. The courts insisted that the defendant had to prove that his statements or opinions were true. This was a reversal of the normal criminal law presumption of innocence in which the state must prove that the words are false and scandalous. Since the trials were normally held in communities dominated by Federalists, both the judge and jury were highly sensitive to criticism of the Federalist government.

The fifteen prosecutions under the law ranged from ludicrous to absurd. Speaking for the Republican Party were five major newspapers in Philadelphia, Boston, New York, Richmond, and Baltimore. The editors of four of the five newspapers were prosecuted, as well as the editors of four lesser Republican newspapers. Even Congressmen did not escape. Matthew Lyon, a Republican member of Congress from Vermont, was prosecuted for publishing an article in which he asserted that under President Adams, "every consideration of the public welfare was swallowed upon in a continual grasp for power, in an unbounded thirst for ridiculous pomp, foolish adulation and selfish avarice." He also printed a letter written by a friend that suggested the president be committed to a madhouse. For these offenses against the government Congressman Lyon was fined $1,000 and spent four months in jail. While he was in jail he was reelected to Congress.

In Massachusetts two residents erected liberty pole, a kind of 1798 billboard, which carried this inscription: No Stamp Act, No Sedition, No Alien Bill, No Land Tax; downfall to the tyrants of America, peace and retirement to the President. The two men were indicted for this crime. One recanted, saying that he really didn't mean it, that he loved his president. He was sentenced to spend six hours in jail and fined five dollars—the lightest punishment any defendant received. His associate refused to recant and was fined $400 and sentenced to eighteen months in jail. When he couldn't pay the fine, he spent two years in jail.

The low comedy of the entire episode was furnished by the government prosecution of Luther Baldwin, a Newark tavern lounger who was elevated to the status of Republican hero overnight after the government prosecuted him for a drunken remark made against President Adams. The president was traveling through Newark on the way to his home in Massachusetts for summer vacation. Newark celebrated the event as a festive occasion; flags were everywhere, as was the local militia. As the church bells pealed and the town cannon fired a salute to the passing president, Baldwin struggled to get to the local dramshop. As Adams passed along the street, the cannon positioned several yards beyond the president nevertheless fired in the direction the presidential party moved. One drunken soul standing outside the tavern noted, "There goes the President and they are firing at his ass." To which Luther Baldwin loudly replied, "I don't care if they fire through his ass." This remark was seditious to the Federalists in the crowd, and Luther was indicted and convicted of violating the 1798 law. He was fined $150 and spent several days in jail until money to pay his fine was raised.

Baldwin became a martyr, as did the other citizens prosecuted under the punitive and repressive law. Far from striking down dissension, Adams succeeded only in generating dissension among many persons who were formerly his supporters. The constitutional issues raised by the law never reached the Supreme Court, although the validity of the measure was sustained by Federalist judges and by three Federalist Supreme Court justices hearing cases on the circuit. In this case, however, the people acted as a kind of court and voted Adams out of office in 1800, replacing him with his Republican foe Thomas Jefferson. Other factors prompted public dissatisfaction with the Massachusetts nationalist to be sure, but unpopularity of the alien and sedition laws cannot be underestimated. The Sedition Act expired in 1801. Jefferson pardoned all persons convicted under it, and Congress eventually repaid most of the fines.

Several lessons emerge from the experience under that set of laws. Foremost is the proposition that the First Amendment does nothing, in and of itself, to guarantee freedom of expression. The people and the courts must support the proposition before it becomes workable. In 1798 the courts were staffed with Federalists who were basically sympathetic to the law, and juries sympathetic to the Federalist cause could also be drawn quite easily. In 1798 the defense of truth didn't help much if it was framed in such a way as to force the defendant to prove the truth of his assertions. This principle remains true today in civil libel cases. Truth is not a very effective defense because convincing a jury of the truth of a statement or of an allegation is often very difficult. More about that later.

We discovered that in 1798 there was little consensus on what freedom of the press really means. Some of the best writing ever on the topic was published during this period as the Republicans attempted to define free expression in a way which tolerated a broader range of governmental criticism. Tracts by men like Tunis Wortman, forgotten by most scholars for more than one hundred fifty years, have emerged in the second half of the twentieth century and offer legal scholars profound insight into how freedom of expression and stability of the government can be balanced.

Another lesson is that the nation's first peacetime sedition law left such a bad taste that another peacetime sedition law was not passed until the Smith Act of 1940.

Our brief consideration also shows that Americans (to their probable chagrin) were not really so different from their colonial forebearers on the issue of free expression, that an American president and a Congress could be as ignorant of the importance of freedom of speech as a British king and parliament.

While the last three years of the eighteenth century in the United States can be considered a period of political repression, the period clearly was no Dark Ages for freedom of expression, as some authorities assert. In fact, the period might be better called a Renaissance because during this period difficult questions for which there seemed to be few answers were asked. The period marked the rebirth of the entire concept of freedom of expression and its meaning, and a few halting first steps toward understanding were taken. Indeed, discussion of the meaning of freedom of expression continues today.

Sedition in the Nineteenth Century

The issue of freedom of expression was not dormant for the next one hundred fifteen years, but neither was it at the forefront of public discussion as in 1800 and at the approach of World War I. Debate on freedom of expression arose again during the period in which abolitionist publishers worked to end slavery in the United States. Somewhere between 1830 and 1840 both the states and the members of the federal government made serious efforts to stop the circulation of abolitionist newspapers on the grounds that they tended to incite slave revolt. The legal moves were defeated in northern states, and the Congress, instead of bowing to President Andrew Jackson's request to ban these publications from the United States mail, insisted that local postmasters had to deliver all mail, even if it contained abolitionist sentiments. Informal pressure was far more effective in stifling publication and circulation of abolitionist newspapers. This was especially true in the South where community pressure was a far more effective censor, despite the existence of laws in a few states making circulation of some abolitionist tracts punishable by death. During the antebellum period freedom of expression in most of the South meant freedom to discuss or publish only the views with which a community did not disagree.

In the North the issue of liberty of the press received a substantial airing during debates over censorial statutes in many state legislatures. However, because slavery did not touch the lives of many Northerners, persons living north of the Mason-Dixon line found it easier to stand behind a more expansive definition of freedom of expression.

Freedom of expression was an issue during the Civil War also. Some newspapers were temporarily closed in the North. The government effectively screened most war news published in the press, and Lincoln showed little sensitivity to civil liberties on some occasions. Still, the war was a national crisis of unprecedented proportions, and one way or another most persons were intimately involved in the war. Freedom of the press paled somewhat when placed next to the life-and-death struggle many persons suffered.

The right to criticize the government did not become a serious issue in this nation again until after the turn of the century when the political "isms" of the late eighteen hundreds (socialism, anarchism, syndicalism) fused with the war in Europe. The safety of the nation appeared to be at stake, and repression once again seemed to be the proper answer.

In the late nineteenth century hundreds of thousands of Americans began to realize that democracy and capitalism were not going to bring the prosperity promised by some obscure national compact. The right to pursue happiness did not assure that one would find it. The advancing rush of the new industrial society left many Americans behind, and they were unhappy. Some of the more dissatisfied persons wanted to do something about the situation and proposed new systems of government and advanced new economic theories. The spectre of revolution arose in the minds of millions of Americans. Emma Goldman, Big Bill Haywood, and Daniel DeLeon represented salvation and hope to their tens of thousands of followers, but they represented a violent change in the comfortable status quo to many other thousands of Americans. Hadn't the radicals caused a riot in 1886 in Chicago? Hadn't they killed President McKinley in 1902? Hadn't they planted bombs along the West Coast and in the Northwest? Didn't they advocate general strikes? Didn't they want to take over the plants and factories and let the workers control production? With this threat lurking in the background, the United States found a real live bogeyman in 1918 when the nation went to war against the Hun—to win the war that would make the world safe for democracy.

Sedition in the Twentieth Century

The history of sedition law in the United States during and since World War I centers upon the struggle by courts at all levels to fashion some kind of test which permitted the government to protect itself from damaging criticism without stifling expression which is protected by the First Amendment. Beginning with cases which grew out of dissent against the war in Europe through cases in the early 1970s, federal courts, especially the Supreme Court, have made numerous attempts to develop a satisfactory test or formula. In the following section these attempts are outlined through a discussion of many of the major cases which raised this difficult problem. But before the cases can be discussed, it is necessary to look briefly at the period which many regard as the most repressive in the history of the nation, the World War I era.

World War I

World War I is probably the most unpopular war this nation fought until the Vietnam conflict of the sixties and seventies. The war was a replay of the imperial wars of the seventeenth and eighteenth centuries in Europe, except that it was fought with more deadly new weapons. Patriots were thrilled that the United States was finally asked to fight in the big leagues. Farmers and industrialists saw vast economic gains. The military believed that no more than six months or so were needed to clean up what many called at the outset "that lovely little war." So most of the ins liked the idea of going to war. But most of the outs hated it because they had to fight the war, because many were born in nations now our enemies, and because a war always signals the beginning of a period of an internal political repression for the outs. When persons who opposed the war in an organized way spoke out against it, their opposition became just another excuse for suppression, fines, and jail.

Suppression of freedom of expression reached a higher level during World War I than at any other time in our history. Government prosecutions during the Vietnam War, for example, were minor compared to government action between 1918 and 1920. Vigilante groups were active as well, persecuting when the government failed to prosecute.

Two federal laws were passed to deal with persons who opposed the war and United States participation in it. In 1917 the Espionage Act was approved by the Congress and signed by President Woodrow Wilson. The measure dealt mostly with espionage problems, but some parts were aimed expressly at dissent and opposition to the war. The law provided that it was a crime to willfully convey a false report with the intent to interfere with the war effort. It became a crime to cause or attempt to cause insubordination, disloyalty, mutiny, or refusal of duty in the armed forces. It also became a crime to willfully obstruct the recruiting or enlistment service of the United States. Punishment was a fine of not more than $10,000 or a jail term of not more than twenty years. The law also provided that material which violated the law could not be mailed.

In 1918 the Sedition Act, an amendment to the Espionage Act, was passed, making it a crime to attempt to obstruct the recruiting service. It was criminal to utter or print or write or publish disloyal or profane language which was intended to cause contempt of or scorn for the federal government, or of the Constitution, or the flag, or of the uniform of the armed forces. Penalties for violation of the law were imprisonment for as long as twenty years and/or a fine of $10,000. Approximately two thousand offenders were prosecuted under these Espionage and Sedition laws, and nearly nine hundred were convicted. Offenders who found themselves in the government's dragnet were usually aliens, radicals, publishers of foreign-language publications, and other persons who opposed the war.

In addition the United States Post Office Department censored thousands of newspapers, books, and pamphlets. Some publications lost their right to the government-subsidized second-class mailing rates and were forced to use the costly first-class rates or find other means of distribution. Entire issues of magazines were held up and never delivered, on the grounds that they violated the law (or what the postmaster general believed to be the law). Finally, the states were not content with allowing the federal government to deal with dissenters, and most adopted sedition statutes, laws against criminal syndicalism, laws which prohibited the display of a red flag or a black flag, and so forth.

While the Congress adopted measures making it a crime to oppose the government or to oppose the recruiting service, the courts were given the task of reconciling these laws with the guarantee of freedom of expression in the First Amendment. The courts, ultimately the Supreme Court, had to specifically define what kinds of words were protected by the First Amendment and what kinds of words were outside the range of protected speech.

Courts continually face the determination of whether speech is permissible or criminal. In the past sixty years the Supreme Court has adopted various tests or definitions or formulas for solving the dilemma. Justice Black's absolutist formula was noted earlier (pp. 52-53); that great liberal believed that Congress cannot forbid any utterance, that all words are protected. The First Amendment provides absolute protection to speakers and to the press. The high Court frequently uses what most authorities call the balancing test, a very pragmatic approach in which two competing interests—freedom of expression and another value or right—are weighed to determine which deserves protection in a specific instance (see also p. 53). For example, is it more important that the recruiting service undertake its work unimpeded by criticism or that people are allowed the right to criticize this governmental agency? Which takes precedence: the right of the defendant in a criminal case to a fair trial? or the right of the press to inform the public about the suspect and the trial? A third test which can be used is the "preferred freedom doctrine" (see p. 78) which, briefly, is a type of balancing in which freedom of expression is given special priority unless the government can justify limiting the freedom of speech or the freedom to print.

In 1917, the Philadelphia Socialist Party authorized Charles Schenck, the general secretary of the organization, to publish 15,000 antiwar leaflets. They were distributed through the party's bookshop and mailed directly to young men who had been drafted. The publication urged the young inductees to join the Socialist Party and work for the repeal of the selective service law, told the young men that the law was a violation of the Thirteenth Amendment which abolished slavery, and told the draftees that they were being discriminated against because certain young men (Quakers and clergymen) didn't have to go to war. The pamphlet also described the war as a cold-blooded and ruthless adventure propagated in the interest of the chosen few of Wall Street. Schenck and other party members were arrested, tried, and convicted of violating the Espionage Act. The Socialist appealed to the high Court, asserting that the law denied him the right of freedom of speech and freedom of the press. Justice Oliver Wendell Holmes wrote the opinion in this important case (*Schenck* v. *U.S.*, 1919). Holmes initially asserted that the main purpose of the First Amendment is to prevent prior censorship, although he conceded that the Amendment might not be confined to that. In ordinary times, such pamphlets might have been harmless and considered protected speech. "But the character of every act depends upon the circumstances in which it is done. . . . The question in every case is whether the words used, are used in such circumstances and are of such a nature as to create a clear and present danger that they will bring about the substantive evils that Congress has a right to prevent. It is a question of proximity and degree."

In translation, this is what Holmes' proposition means. Congress has a right to outlaw certain kinds of conduct which can be harmful to society. Words, as in publications or public speeches, which can result in persons undertaking the illegal conduct can also be outlawed, and publishers or speakers can be punished without infringing upon First Amendment rights. How great must be the connection between the forbidden conduct and the words? Holmes said the words must create a "clear and present danger" that the illegal activity will result.

Needless to say, the requisite clear and present danger of obstructing the recruiting service existed in the Schenck case, and the conviction was upheld. In two other Espionage Act cases also decided in the spring of 1919, Holmes wrote the opinion for the Court and used the clear and present danger test to affirm the convictions of Jacob Frohwerk, editor of a German-language newspaper (*Frohwerk* v. *U.S.*, 1919) and Eugene V. Debs, leader of the American Socialist Party during World War I (*Debs* v. *U.S.*, 1919). The requisite clear and present danger existed in both cases, Holmes said.

Many authorities consider Oliver Wendell Holmes to be one of the great civil libertarians to sit on the Supreme Court. Consequently, it is often erroneously assumed that Holmes' "clear and present danger" test was a truly liberal test designed to afford maximum protection for freedom of expression. The assumption is incorrect. Holmes seemed to admit as much later in 1919 in an important dissent he wrote in *Abrams* v. *U.S.* During the summer of 1919 civil libertarians criticized rulings of the Supreme Court in the *Schenck*, *Frohwerk*, and *Debs* cases. Many distinguished students of the law including friends of Holmes sharply attacked the clear and present danger test. In an interesting article in the *Journal of American History* (1971) Professor Fred D. Ragan states that Holmes was aware of the criticism and during that summer became convinced that the freedom of expression established by the First Amendment was far broader than championed in his spring decisions.

In November 1919 when the court decided its first appeal of conviction under the Sedition Act, Holmes shifted dramatically to the left. In *Abrams* v. *U.S.* (1919) the high court upheld the convictions of five young radicals who protested the movement of American troops into the Soviet Union and called for a general strike to stop the production of munitions and arms. In writing for the majority Justice John Clarke wrote that the leaflets published by the defendants "obviously intended to provoke and to encourage resistance to the United States in the war." Whether they intended to hurt the United States was not at issue. "Men must be held to have intended, and to be accountable for, the effects which their acts were likely to produce." As Professor Ragan notes: "Thus Clarke employed criteria used by Holmes earlier in the year . . . to sustain the conviction."

Holmes, on the other hand, joined his colleague Louis Brandeis in a dissent and wrote one of the most stirring defenses of freedom of expression of the twentieth century. The jurist wrote that the ultimate good desired is better reached by free trade in ideas, that the best test of truth is the power of a thought to get accepted in the marketplace. "That, at any rate, is the theory of our Constitution," he wrote. Holmes then argued that nobody could seriously believe that the silly leaflet published by the five defendants would hinder the war effort. He turned his back on notions of probable or indirect interference with the prosecution of the war. To be guilty of resistance meant direct and immediate opposition to some effort by the United States to prosecute the war. There was no evidence of that here, Holmes concluded.

Holmes' change of heart did not spell the demise of the clear and present danger test. It was used in other sedition cases by the high Court. However the only instances in which a majority of the high Court subscribed to the test were to uphold convictions under various sedition laws. Holmes and Brandeis used the test often to argue that the requisite clear and present danger was missing, that the utterances or published materials were protected by the First Amendment. These arguments, it should be noted, were in dissenting opinions.

The Keystone Case   Many civil libertarians argue, correctly no doubt, that the most important civil rights case of the twentieth century is *Gitlow* v. *New York* (1925), the case in which the defendant lost his appeal before the Supreme Court. Benjamin Gitlow and three other persons were arrested, tried, and convicted of publishing and distributing a pamphlet which, the state of New York argued, advocated the violent overthrow of the government—a violation of the New York Criminal Anarchy Law. The pamphlet, the *Left Wing Manifesto*, was a dreadfully dull thirty-four-page political tract on revolution and social and economic change. In his book *Free Speech in the United States*, Zechariah Chafee, a renowned legal scholar of Harvard University, accurately notes, "any agitator who read these thirty-four pages to a mob would not stir them to violence, except possibly against himself. This manifesto would disperse them faster than the riot act." Nevertheless Gitlow was sentenced to ten years in prison. In his appeal to the high court he argued that the state criminal anarchy statute violated his freedom of expression guaranteed by the

United States Constitution. In making this plea, Gitlow was asking the Court to overturn a ninety-two-year-old precedent.

Some important historical information is now needed if we are to understand the significance of Gitlow's argument. In the early 1830s the city of Baltimore, Maryland, undertook to pave its streets and in doing so diverted several streams from their natural course. A man named Barron owned a wharf in the city, and when the streams were diverted, deposits of sand and gravel built up near his wharf. The water around the dock became shallow, and boats could not use the dock. The wharf became useless. Barron sued the city arguing that the diverting action deprived him of use of the wharf and was a violation of the Fifth Amendment to the United States Constitution which forbids the taking of private property (the wharf) for public use (the streets) without just compensation. The city disagreed and argued that the United States Constitution applies only to actions by the United States government, not to actions by cities and states. The Supreme Court agreed. Chief Justice John Marshall ruled that the people of the United States established the United States Constitution for their government, not for the government of the individual states. The limitations of power placed upon government by the Constitution applied only to the federal government, not to cities or states (*Barron* v. *Baltimore,* 1833).

In terms of the First Amendment this decision means that while the United States cannot interfere with freedom of the press the United States Constitution does not prohibit New York or Detroit or Florida from interfering with freedom of the press. Only the constitution of New York or Michigan or Florida can validly protect the rights of citizens in those states from infringement by state and local governments. That was the law in 1925 when the *Gitlow* case reached the Supreme Court and was the rule that the convicted anarchist hoped to overturn.

Gitlow's attorneys, especially Walter Heilprin Pollak, did not attack the rule directly; instead they went around it. Pollak constructed his argument upon the Fourteenth Amendment to the Constitution which was adopted in 1868, thirty-five years after the decision in *Barron* v. *Baltimore.* The attorney argued that the general agreement was that the First Amendment protected a citizen's right to liberty of expression. The Fourteenth Amendment says in part "no state shall deprive any person of life, liberty or property, without due process of law. . . ." Pollak asserted that included among the liberties guaranteed by the Fourteenth Amendment is liberty of the press as guaranteed by the First Amendment. Therefore, a state cannot deprive a citizen of the freedom of the press which is guaranteed by the First Amendment without violating the Fourteenth Amendment. By jailing Benjamin Gitlow for exercising his right of freedom of speech granted by the First Amendment, New York State denied him the liberty assured him by the Fourteenth Amendment. Simply, then, the First Amendment as applied through the Fourteenth Amendment prohibits states and cities and counties from denying an individual freedom of speech and press.

The high Court had heard this argument before, but apparently not as persuasively as Mr. Pollak presented it. In rather casual terms Justice Edward Sanford made a startlingly new constitutional pronouncement: "For present purposes we may and do assume that freedom of speech and of the press—which are protected by the First Amendment from abridgement by Congress—are among the fundamental personal rights and 'liberties' protected by the due process clause of the Fourteenth Amendment from impairment by the states."

Despite this important ruling, Gitlow lost his case. Justice Sanford said that the New York law was warranted and did not violate the First Amendment nor the Fourteenth Amendment. Sanford then went on to outline his own rather novel interpretation of Holmes' clear and present danger test. He said that in passing the Espionage Act, the Congress forbade certain deeds—interference with the recruiting service, for example. In such instances when the defendant is charged with using words to promote the forbidden deeds, the courts must decide whether the language used by the accused creates a clear and present danger for bringing about the forbidden deeds. In other words, does the defendant's pamphlet create the danger that persons will in fact interfere with the recruiting service?

However, in this case, Sanford said, the New York legislature outlawed certain words—that is, advocating violent overthrow of the government is forbidden. The clear and present danger test doesn't apply, he said. The only issue the court has to decide is, Do the words in question, in this case the *Left Wing Manifesto*, fall within the class of forbidden words, words that advocate violent overthrow of the government? The court has no power to determine in such a case if in fact the defendant's pamphlet creates the danger of a violent revolt. It is sufficient that the state has outlawed such words. Only if the judgment of the legislature is completely without foundation can the court interfere. In this case the legislature's action is warranted: Gitlow's pamphlet falls within the category of proscribed words—ten years in jail!

Holmes and Brandeis vigorously dissented, arguing that it was absurd to think that Gitlow's small band of followers posed any danger at all to the government. "It is said that this manifesto was more than a theory," Holmes wrote, "that it was an incitement. Every idea is an incitement. . . . The only difference between the expression of an opinion and an incitement in the narrower sense is the speaker's enthusiasm for the result." The argument was to no avail. After three years in prison Gitlow was pardoned by Governor Alfred Smith.

The importance of the *Gitlow* case is that the high court acknowledged that the Bill of Rights places limitations upon the actions of states and local government as well as upon the federal government. The *Gitlow* case states that freedom of speech is protected by the Fourteenth Amendment. In later cases the Court placed freedom of the press, freedom of religion, freedom from self-incrimination, and freedom from illegal search and seizure under the same protection. Today, virtually all of the rights outlined in the Bill of Rights are protected via the Fourteenth Amendment from interference by states and cities as well as by the federal government. The one outstanding exception is the guarantee in the Fifth Amendment that a person must be indicted by a grand jury before he or she can be called to trial for a serious crime. The federal criminal justice system still uses grand juries in such cases, which is an expensive system. Most states use a far simpler process in which the public prosecutor files an information against a suspect, that is, places a charge against him. In the federal system placing charges is the function of the grand jury. The Supreme Court has been reluctant to apply this part of the Fifth Amendment against the states because of the burden and cost of winning grand jury indictments in all serious cases. The importance of the *Gitlow* case cannot be underestimated. It truly marked the beginning of attainment of a full measure of civil liberties for the citizens of the nation. It was the key which unlocked an important door.

Whitney v. California

The Sanford interpretation of the clear and present danger test was next used two years later when the Supreme Court reviewed the prosecution by California of sixty-year-old philanthropist Anita Whitney for threatening the security of the state, (*Whitney v. California*, 1927). Miss Whitney, the niece of Justice Stephen J. Field who served on the Supreme Court from 1863 to 1897, joined the Socialist Party in the early 1920s. At a convention in Chicago the chapter to which Miss Whitney belonged seceded from the Socialist Party and formed the Communist Labor Party. The Communist Labor Party held a convention in Oakland to which Miss Whitney was a delegate. She worked hard as a delegate to ensure that the new Party worked through political means to capture political power, but the majority of delegates voted instead for the Party to dedicate itself to gaining power through revolution and general strikes in which the workers would seize power by violent means. After this convention Miss Whitney was not active in the party, but she was nevertheless arrested three weeks after the Oakland convention and charged with violating the California Criminal Syndicalism Act which prohibited advocacy of violence to change the control or ownership of industry or to bring about political change.

Following her conviction she appealed to the high Court, arguing that the law violated the guarantees of freedom of expression. Justice Edward Sanford, writing for the majority, again ruled that the clear and present danger test did not apply, that the California state legislature outlawed certain kinds of words which it deemed a danger to public peace and safety, and that the court could not hold that the action was unreasonable or unwarranted. There was therefore no infringement upon the First Amendment.

This time Holmes and Brandeis concurred with the majority, but only Brandeis said because the constitutional issue of freedom of expression had not been raised sufficiently at the trial to make it an issue in the appeal. In his concurring opinion, Brandeis disagreed sharply with the majority regarding the limits of free expression. In doing so he added flesh and bones to Holmes' clear and present danger test. Looking to the *Schenck* decision, the justice noted that the court had agreed that there must be a clear and imminent danger of a substantive evil which the state has the right to prevent before an interference with speech can be allowed. Then he went on to describe what he believed to be the requisite danger:

> To justify suppression of free speech there must be reasonable ground to fear that serious evil will result if free speech is practiced. There must be reasonable ground to believe that the danger apprehended is imminent. There must be reasonable ground to believe that the evil to be prevented is a serious one. Every denunciation of existing law tends in some measure to increase the probability that there will be violation of it. Condonation of a breach enhances the probability. Expressions of approval add to the probability. Propagation of the criminal state of mind by teaching syndicalism increases it. Advocacy of law-breaking heightens it further. But even advocacy of violation, however reprehensible morally, is not a justification for denying free speech where the advocacy falls short of incitement, and there is nothing to indicate that the advocacy would be immediately acted on. The wide difference between advocacy and incitement, between preparation and attempt, between assembling and conspiracy, must be borne in mind. In order to support a finding of clear and present danger it must be shown either that immediate serious violence was to be expected or was advocated, or that the past conduct furnished reason to believe that such advocacy was then contemplated.

Brandeis concluded that if there is time to expose through discussion the falsehoods and fallacies, to avert the evil by the process of education, the remedy to be applied is more speech, not enforced silence.

This truly is a clear and present danger test that even the most zealous civil libertarian can live with. And this is the test that many mistakenly confuse with Holmes' original pronouncement. Unfortunately, this version of the clear and present danger test has never found its way into a majority opinion in a sedition case.

The First Reversal

Before the last two important sedition cases decided during this century are discussed, it should be noted that in 1927 the Supreme Court first struck down a state sedition conviction because the defendant's federal constitutional rights had been violated (*Fiske* v. *Kansas,* 1927). In Kansas a man named Fiske was arrested, tried, and convicted of violating that state's criminal anarchy statute. He was an organizer for the International Workers of the World (IWW), a radical union group. The evidence the state used against him was the preamble to the IWW constitution which discussed in vague terms the struggle between workers and owners and the necessity for workers to take control of the machinery of production and to abolish the wage system. No mention was made of violence, but the state supreme court upheld the conviction on the grounds that despite the lack of specific reference to violence it was possible for the jury to read between the lines in light of the reputation of the IWW. The United States Supreme Court reversed the conviction because there was no evidence on the record to support the conviction. There was no suggestion in the testimony that Fiske used anything but lawful methods, and thus the conviction was "an arbitrary and unreasonable exercise of the police power of the state, unwarrantably infringing upon the liberty of the defendant." While this was a terribly small victory and no major liberal interpretation of the First Amendment was announced, as Zechariah Chafee (*Free Speech in the United States*) notes, "the Supreme Court for the first time made freedom of speech mean something."

The Smith Act

The Congress adopted the nation's first peacetime sedition law in 1798 and approved the second law in 1940 when it ratified the Smith Act, a measure making it a crime to advocate the violent overthrow of the government, to conspire to advocate the violent overthrow of the government, to organize a group which advocates the violent overthrow of the government, or to be a member of a group which advocates the violent overthrow of the government.

When the Sedition Act of 1918 was repealed in 1921 (the Espionage Act is still on the books but is applicable only during wartime), the United States Justice Department and the military sought a replacement for the Act. From the early 1920s to 1940 numerous attempts were made to pass such a bill, but were always unsuccessful because labor unions, civil rights groups, farm organizations, and even the United States press sent representatives to Washington to work against the law. But in 1940,

America's second peacetime sedition law, buried in an innocuous omnibus bill called the Alien Registration Act, quietly wormed its way through Congress and was signed by the president. There is no doubt that the times were different. Hitler had won stunning victories in Europe and had recently forced the French to surrender. In the Far East, rumblings of war became louder each day, and rumors were rife that the Japanese would attack Indochina momentarily.

The Smith Act, which was aimed at the Communist Party, was drafted by Congressman Howard Smith of Virginia and Congressman John McCormack of Massachusetts. It received little publicity, and many months elapsed before civil libertarians realized that the act had been passed. Among others Zechariah Chafee (*Free Speech in the United States*) writes, "Not until months later did I for one realize this statute contains the most drastic restriction on freedom of speech ever enacted in the United States during peace."

While the government suggested during hearings on the measure that Congress best act quickly, lest the Communists take over the nation, the first prosecution of Communists under the Smith Act did not take place until eight years later. A small band of Trotskyites, members of the Socialist Workers Party, were prosecuted and convicted in 1943, but not until 1948 did a federal grand jury indict twelve of the nation's leading Communists for advocating the violent overthrow of the United States government. The trial began in January 1949 and lasted nine months. Eleven defendants (one became sick during the trial and was excused temporarily) were convicted, including Eugene V. Dennis, one of the Party leaders in the United States. The trial judge, Harold Medina, who was presiding at his first criminal trial after being appointed a federal district judge, told the jury that the statute did not prohibit discussing the propriety of overthrowing the government by force or violence, but "the teaching and advocacy of action for the accomplishment of that purpose by language reasonably and ordinarily calculated to incite persons to such action." In other words, the Smith Act prohibited the teaching or advocacy of action aimed at the violent overthrow of the government.

The convictions were appealed all the way to the Supreme Court, and in *Dennis* v. *United States* (1951) the high Court once again had the opportunity to decide the limitations in our democracy upon persons who oppose the government. The clear and present danger test was raised by the defense, which argued that the law violates the First Amendment. Chief Justice Vinson could have used the original Holmes test or Brandeis' brilliant exposition of the test in his concurrence in *Whitney*. Vinson chose instead to take a middle course far more close to Holmes than to Brandeis.

Vinson first insisted that the evil involved in the case (the evil which Congress has the right to prevent) was a substantial one, the overthrow of the government. That was the professed aim of the Communists, no doubt, but it wasn't actually very realistic. That doesn't matter, Vinson wrote. We reject the contention that success or probability of success is the criterion. "Certainly an atempt to overthrow the Government by force, even though doomed from the outset because of inadequate numbers or power of the revolutionists, is a sufficient evil for Congress to prevent. The damage which such attempts create both physically and politically to a nation makes it impossible to measure the validity in terms of the probability of success, or the immediacy of a successful attempt." However Vinson equated advocacy of overthrow with actual attempt at overthrow. It could be asked, how likely is it that the words spoken or written by the defendants would lead even to an attempted overthrow? Vinson's opinion was a far cry from Justice Brandeis' statement in *Whitney*. Recall Brandeis' words: "But even advocacy of violation (of the law), however reprehensible morally, is not a justification for denying free speech where the advocacy falls short of incitement and there is nothing to indicate that the advocacy would be immediately acted upon. The wide difference between advocacy and incitement, between preparation and attempt, between assembling and conspiracy, must be borne in mind."

Vinson outlined the test used by court of appeals Judge Learned Hand when that court sustained the conviction of the eleven Communists. "In each case [courts] must ask whether the gravity of the 'evil,' discounted by improbability, justifies such invasion of free speech as is necessary to avoid the danger." Vinson said, "We adopt this statement of the rule."

The clear and probable danger test really says little more than the original Holmes clear and present danger test if Holmes' exposition in the Debs, Frohwerk, and Schenck cases are added to the five-word rule. If the gravity of the evil is considered, Holmes said that the evil must be substantive or serious. Hand said that the probability of what might occur must be considered. What might occur? Might the overthrow succeed? Might the overthrow be attempted? Might the words lead someone to attempt an overthrow? What kind of danger are we trying to avoid? The issue is so unclear.

One could speculate that if the clear and present danger test as articulated by Justice Brandeis had been applied in this case the convictions would have gone out the window. The danger wasn't clear, nor was it present. However, in the atmosphere of 1951 such was not likely. We were in the midst of both a cold war with the Soviet Union and a hot war with the North Koreans and Communist Chinese, and as was said, previously, the Supreme Court (all courts for that matter) are political bodies at least to some extent.

Chief Justice Vinson made one additional far more important observation than his exposition of the clear and probable danger test. Almost in passing, he noted that the Smith Act is aimed at advocacy, not at discussion. Judge Medina said the law is aimed at advocacy of action or the teaching of action aimed at violent overthrow. Justice Vinson said the law is aimed at advocacy, and that is all.

After the government's success in the *Dennis* case, more prosecutions were initiated against Communists in the United States. Seven separate prosecutions were started in 1951, three in 1952, one in 1953, and five more during the next three years. One trial begun in late 1951 involved the top Communist leadership on the West Coast. At the trial after hearing both sides, Judge William C. Mathes told the jury that any advocacy dealing with the forcible overthrow of the government and presented with a specific intent to accomplish the overthrow is illegal under the Smith Act. This is about what Vinson said in the *Dennis* case, but is far different from the standard used by Judge Medina in the *Dennis* trial. The defendants appealed their conviction and six years later, in 1957, the Supreme Court voted five to two to reverse the convictions (*Yates* v. *U.S.*, 1957). On what grounds? Several factors influenced the reversal in *Yates* v. *U.S.*, but the basic reason is that Judge Mathes failed to distinguish between the advocacy of forcible overthrow as an abstract doctrine and the advocacy of action aimed at the forcible overthrow of the government. The Smith Act reaches only advocacy of action for the overthrow of government by force and violence, Justice John Marshall Harlan wrote for the court. "The essential distinction," Harlan notes, "is that those to whom the advocacy is addressed must be urged to do something now or in the future, rather than merely to believe in something." How specific must this advocacy of action be? It does not have to be immediate action; it can be action in the future. But it must be an urging to do something: form an army, blow up a bridge, prepare for sabotage, train for street fighting, and so forth.

The government was unprepared to meet this new burden of proof. Far more evidence is needed to prove that someone has urged people to do something than to prove that someone has merely urged them to believe something. All but one of the cases pending were dismissed. The defendants in the single case that was tried were set free on an evidentiary issue (*Bary* v. *U.S.*, 1957) and were never retried. In fact, there has not been a single successful prosecution for advocacy of violent overthrow since the *Yates* decision. One successful prosecution under the membership clause of the Smith Act has occurred, but it was in 1961 (*Scales* v. *U.S.*, 1961).

To his credit, Justice Harlan did not attempt to apply either the clear and present danger test or the clear and probable danger test. This consideration wasn't necessary since the constitutionality of the law is not the heart of the appeal in the *Yates* case as it is in *Dennis*. Still, the temptation to take a crack at defining that catchy little phrase must have been great.

Few sedition trials have occurred since 1957. In 1969, the Supreme Court once again looked at a state sedition law in *Brandenburg* v. *Ohio* (1969). In this case a Ku Klux Klan leader was prosecuted by Ohio for advocating unlawful methods of terrorism and crime as a means of accomplishing industrial and political reform. The high Court voided his conviction on the grounds that the Ohio law failed to distinguish between the advocacy of ideas and the incitement to unlawful conduct. In its per curiam opinion the Court said, "the constitutional guarantees of free speech and free press do not permit a State to forbid or proscribe advocacy of the use of force or of law violation except where such advocacy is directed to inciting or producing imminent lawless action or is likely to incite or produce such actions." This opinion came close to how Louis Brandeis outlined the clear and present danger test in 1927 in the Whitney case.

The famous Holmes test is not dead by any means. It still lives, for example, in criminal contempt law where the high Court has fashioned it into a workable test to protect both courts and defendants from the interference of the mass media in the judicial process. If it is not dead, the test is certainly lifeless with regard to sedition law, partly because sedition law is not nearly so robust as it was forty years ago. The Communists long since ceased to be a threat in this nation. In fact one author suggests that the Party is currently alive only because it is subsidized by the United States government. Indeed, political scientist John Roche (*Shadow and Substance*) asserts that if the many undercover FBI agents who are members of the Party were to withdraw their membership and stop paying dues the Party would collapse.

More seriously, the federal government chose not to use sedition laws in prosecuting protestors and dissidents during the Vietnam War. Instead the government used rather exotic conspiracy laws and still enjoyed little success. The Smith Act is still on the books, and it probably could have been used against some antiwar leaders. But it was not. The law is not popular today. Sedition laws are not popular today. When people feel little direct threat to their well-being, they are willing to exercise a remarkable range of tolerance of unpopular ideas and suggestions. Unpopular or unorthodox speakers and writers are written off as kooks, which in many cases they are. However, should there occur another serious war, a deep depression which causes loss of confidence in the government, or other situation in which people feel threatened, what could happen is difficult to predict.

Today, in the last quarter of the twentieth century, Americans probably enjoy as much right to oppose their government as do citizens in any other nation in the world, and more of this freedom is enjoyed now than at any other time during this century, perhaps during the lifetime of the Republic. If the legal tests used to measure the danger of words seem really to be silly little word games devised by grown men to fill their time, the outlook is in some respects correct. However, the games are devised more in desperation than for any other reason, for democracy has not yet solved the problem of determining how far to go in allowing dissent which attacks the system of government itself. Scholars continue to argue about using this test or that "definitional balancing" as opposed to "clear and probable danger." Judges and legal scholars continue to look for the correct formula, the key which will provide both maximum freedom and maximum safety. The key probably does not exist. But it is man's nature to continue to search.

PRIOR RESTRAINT

People who are prosecuted for opposing the government generally are punished after they have said something or written something or published something. There are, however, times when freedom of expression is limited even before something is written or published. This action is called prior restraint and in its purest form means that the government prohibits the publication of certain words or prohibits the distribution of pamphlets containing certain ideas. Prior restraint is a matter not of punishing someone after he speaks or publishes, but of stopping him before he has the chance to do so.

In the United States the Supreme Court and the lower courts have considered scores of different versions of prior restraint in defining the limits of freedom contained in the First Amendment. In a few instances the cases are simple prior restraint in which the government seeks to stop the publication of certain material. Other instances are more complicated and involve special taxes against newspapers or the right of people to distribute matter already published. Let us look first at the basic problem of freedom to publish.

Near v. *Minnesota*

Earlier it was said that the great compiler of the British law William Blackstone defined freedom of the press in the 1760s as freedom from "previous restraint" or prior restraint. Most people take it for granted that the First Amendment protects freedom of the press at least to that extent.

An individual might ultimately be punished for what he says, but he certainly has the right to say it. The Supreme Court first considered the question of prior restraint in 1931 in the case of *Near* v. *Minnesota.* City and county officials in Minneapolis, Minnesota, brought a legal action against Jay M. Near and Howard Guilford, publishers of the *Saturday Press,* a small weekly newspaper. Near and Guilford were reformers whose purpose was to clean up city and county government in Minneapolis. In their attacks upon corruption in city government they used language which was far from temperate and defamed some of the town's leading government officials. Near and Guilford charged that Jewish gangsters were in control of gambling, bootlegging, and racketeering in the city and that city government and its law enforcement agencies did not perform their duties energetically. They repeated these charges over and over again in a highly inflammatory manner.

At that time in Minnesota there was a state law which empowered a court to declare any obscene, lewd, lascivious, malicious, scandalous, or defamatory publication a public nuisance. When such a publication was deemed a public nuisance, the court issued an injunction against future publication or distribution. Violation of the injunction resulted in punishment for contempt of court.

In 1927 County Attorney Floyd Olson initiated an action against the *Saturday Press.* A district court declared the newspaper a public nuisance and "perpetually enjoined" publication of the *Saturday Press.* The only way either Near or Guilford would be able to publish the newspaper again was to convince the court that their newspaper would remain free of objectionable material. In 1928 the Minnesota Supreme Court upheld the constitutionality of the law, declaring that under its broad police power the state can regulate public nuisances, including defamatory and scandalous newspapers.

The case then went to the United States Supreme Court which reversed the ruling by the state supreme court. The nuisance statute was declared unconstitutional. Chief Justice Charles Evans Hughes wrote the opinion for the court in a narrow five-to-four ruling, saying that the statute in question was not designed to redress wrongs to individuals attacked by the newspaper. Instead, the statute was directed at suppressing the *Saturday Press* once and for all. The object of the law, Hughes wrote, was not punishment but censorship—not only of a single issue, but also of all future issues—which is not consistent with the traditional concept of freedom of the press. That is, the statute constituted prior restraint, and prior restraint is clearly a violation of the First Amendment.

One maxim in the law holds that when a judge writes an opinion for a court he should stick to the problem at hand, that he shouldn't wander off and talk about matters that don't really concern the issue before the court. Such remarks are considered dicta, or words that don't really apply to the case. These words, these dicta, are never really considered an important part of the ruling in the case. Chief Justice Hughes' opinion in *Near* v. *Minnesota* contains a good deal of dicta.

In this case Hughes wrote that the prior restraint of the *Saturday Press* was unconstitutional, but in some circumstances, he added, prior restraint might be permissible. In what kinds of circumstances? The government can constitutionally stop publication of obscenity, the government can stop publication of material which incites people to acts of violence, and it may prohibit publication of certain kinds of material during wartime. Hughes admitted, on the other hand, defining freedom of the press as the only freedom from prior restraint is equally wrong, for in many cases punishment after publication imposes effective censorship upon the freedom of expression.

The exceptions to freedom from prior restraint listed by Hughes have vexed the mass media for nearly fifty years. Despite the fact that these remarks were dicta, Hughes' statement that obscenity can be censored is used time and again in defending decisions proscribing the publication of erotic material.

The *Near* case nevertheless remains an important pronouncement in favor of a broadly based freedom of the press. Despite the closeness of the five-to-four ruling, the proposition that in most instances prior censorship, or prior restraint, is a violation of the First Amendment exists today as a strong part of the foundation of freedom of expression.

Organization for a Better Austin v. *Keefe*

Two important Supreme Court decisions since 1931 reinforce this ruling to some extent. Both decisions were handed down in 1971. The first case involved the attempt of a real estate broker to stop a neighborhood community action group from distributing pamphlets about him (*Organization for a Better Austin* v. *Keefe*, 1971). The Organization for a Better Austin was a community organization in the Austin suburb of Chicago. Its goal was to stabilize the population in the integrated community. Members were opposed to the tactics of certain real estate brokers who came into white neighborhoods, spread the word that blacks were moving in, bought up the white-owned homes cheaply in the ensuing panic, and then resold them at a good profit to blacks or other whites. The organization received pledges from most real estate firms in the area to stop these blockbusting tactics. But Jerome Keefe refused to make such an agreement. The community group then printed leaflets and flyers describing his activities and handed them out in Westchester, the community in which Keefe lived. Group members told the Westchester residents that Keefe was a "panic peddler" and said they would stop distributing the leaflets in Westchester as soon as Keefe agreed to stop his block-busting real estate tactics. Keefe went to court and obtained an injunction which prohibited further distribution by the community club of pamphlets, leaflets, or literature of any kind in Westchester on the grounds that the material constituted an invasion of Keefe's privacy and caused him irreparable harm. The Organization for a Better Austin appealed the ruling to the United States Supreme Court. In May 1971 the high court dissolved the injunction. Chief Justice Warren Burger wrote, "the injunction, so far as it imposes prior restraint on speech and publication, constitutes an impermissible restraint on First Amendment rights." He said that the injunction, as in the *Near* case, did not seek to redress individual wrongs, but instead sought to suppress on the basis of one or two handbills the distribution of any kind of literature in a city of 18,000 inhabitants. Keefe argued that the purpose of the handbills was not to inform the community, but to force him to sign an agreement. The Chief Justice said this argument was immaterial and was not sufficient cause to remove the leaflets and flyers from the protection of the First Amendment. Justice Burger added:

> Petitioners [the community group] were engaged openly and vigorously in making the public aware of respondent's [Keefe's] real estate practices. Those practices were offensive to them, as the views and practices of the petitioners are no doubt offensive to others. But so long as the means are peaceful, the communication need not meet standards of acceptability.

The *Keefe* case did a good job of reinforcing the high court's decision in *Near* v. *Minnesota*.

New York Times Co. v. *U.S.*

While it is more famous, the second 1971 decision is not as strong a statement in behalf of freedom of expression as either *Near* or *Keefe*. This is the famous Pentagon Papers decision (*New York Times Co.* v. *U.S.*, *U.S.* v. *The Washington Post*, 1971). While the political implications of the ruling are very important, the ruling itself is legally quite unsatisfying. As many remember, the case began in the summer of 1971 when the *New York Times*, followed by the *Washington Post* and a handful of other newspapers, began publication of a series of articles based on a top-secret forty-seven-volume government study entitled "History of the United States Decision-Making Process on Vietnam Policy." The day after the initial article on the Pentagon Papers appeared, Attorney General John Mitchell asked the *New York Times* to stop publication of the material. When the *Times'* publisher refused, the government went to court to get an injunction to force the newspaper to stop the series. A temporary restraining order was granted as the case wound its way to the

Supreme Court. Such an order was also imposed upon the *Washington Post* after it began to publish reports based on the same material.

At first the government argued that the publication of this material violated federal espionage statutes. When that assertion didn't satisfy the lower federal courts, the government argued that the president had inherent power under his constitutional mandate to conduct foreign affairs to protect the national security, which includes the right to classify documents secret and top secret. Publication of this material by the newspapers was unauthorized disclosure of such material and should be stopped. This argument didn't satisfy the courts either, and by the time the case came before the Supreme Court the government argument was that publication of these papers might result in irreparable harm to the nation and its ability to conduct foreign affairs. The *Times* and the *Post,* consistently made two arguments. First, they said that the classification system is a sham, that people in the government declassify documents almost at will when they want to sway public opinion or influence a reporter's story. The press also argued that an injunction against the continued publication of this material violated the First Amendment. Interestingly, the newspapers did not argue that under all circumstances prior restraint is in conflict with the First Amendment. Defense attorney Professor Alexander Bickel argued that under some circumstances prior restraint is acceptable, for example, when the publication of a document has a direct link with a grave event which is immediate and visible. Former Justice William O. Douglas noted that this is a strange argument for newspapers to make—and it is. Apparently both newspapers decided that a victory in that immediate case was far more important than to establish a definitive and long-lasting constitutional principle. They therefore concentrated on winning the case, acknowledging that in future cases prior restraint might be permissible.

On June 30 the high Court ruled six to three in favor of the *New York Times* and the *Washington Post*. The court did not grant a permanent injunction against the publication of the Pentagon Papers, but the ruling was hardly the kind which strengthened the First Amendment. In a very short per curiam opinion the majority said that in a case involving the prior restraint of a publication the government bears a heavy burden to justify such a restraint. In this case the government failed to show the court why such a restraint should be imposed upon the two newspapers. In other words, the government failed to justify its request for the permanent restraining order.

The decision rested upon a First Amendment doctrine called the preferred position doctrine. Normally, when a legislature passes a law, or the government takes some action based upon a law, it is presumed that these laws or actions are constitutional. In other words, the laws or actions do not violate the constitution. Therefore when the constitutionality of a law or a government action is challenged, the court presumes constitutionality, and the challenger bears the burden of proof to show that the law or action is not constitutional. For example, if someone challenges the constitutionality of laws making it a crime to transport dangerous drugs across state lines on the grounds that Congress has no power to regulate such material, it is up to the challenger to prove that Congress in fact has no power. All the government technically has to do is say that Congress does have the power. The challenger must prove that it does not. This principle is called the presumption of constitutionality.

However, when the issue involved is freedom of expression, the presumption of constitutionality does not apply. In 1938 in a case entitled *United States* v. *Carolene Products Co.,* Justice Harlan Fiske Stone suggested obliquely that when the government passes a law or takes an action involving basic civil liberties, when it does something which appears on the face to be prohibited by the Bill of Rights, the government bears the burden of justifying its action. The citizen should not have to prove that what the government did is unconstitutional. This principle is called the preferred position doctrine, and while it applies to all rights guaranteed by the first ten amendments to the Constitution, the doctrine has been fully developed with regard to the First Amendment.

Applying that doctrine in *New York Times Co.* v. *U.S.,* the Supreme Court simply said that the government failed to show the court why its request for an injunction was not a violation of the First Amendment. The Court did not say that in all similar cases an injunction would violate the First Amendment; it did not even say that in this case an injunction was a violation of the First Amendment. It merely said that the government had not shown why the injunction was not a violation of freedom of the press. The decision is not what you would call a ringing defense of the right of free expression.

In addition to the brief unsigned opinion from the majority, the Chief Justice and each of the eight associate justices wrote short individual opinions. They were not very instructive, but should be noted anyway.

Justices Black and Douglas clung to their absolute position and argued that they could conceive of no circumstance under which the government can properly interfere with freedom of expression. Debate on public questions must be open and robust, Justice Douglas wrote. Justice William Brennan echoed the court's opinion: there was no proof that the publication of the papers would damage the national security or the nation. Justice Potter Stewart agreed and attacked the notion of classifying public documents and excessive secrecy in government. "For when everything is classified," he wrote, "then nothing is classified, and the system becomes one to be disregarded by the cynical or the careless, and to be manipulated by those intent on self-protection or self-promotion."

Justice Byron White supported the notion that the government lacked the evidence needed to sustain an injunction. But Justice White added that he believed the publication of the material would damage the national interest, and if the government chose to bring the newspapers back to court for criminal prosecution for violating an espionage statute, he could surely support a conviction. These last remarks are another example of dicta. The last member of the majority, Justice Thurgood Marshall, said he did not believe the president has the right to classify documents in the first place, that Congress has consistently rejected giving the executive this power, and that consequently the court should not support such questionable authority.

All three of the dissenters, Chief Justice Burger, Justice John M. Harlan, and Justice Harry Blackmun, complained that there had not been sufficient time to properly consider the case. The issues were too important for such a rush to judgment, Justice Burger said, noting his dissent was not based upon the merits of the case. Harlan and Blackmun did dissent on the merits. Harlan argued that foreign relations and national security are both concerns of other branches of the government and the court should accept the government's assertions in this case—even without evidence—that disclosure of the material in the Pentagon Papers would substantially harm the government. Justice Blackmun wanted to send the case back to the trial courts for fuller exposition of the facts and to allow the government more time to prepare its case.

What many people at first called the case of the century certainly fizzled at the end, at least with regard to developing First Amendment law. The Pentagon Papers case, *New York Times Co.* v. *U.S.*, left the law on prior restraint pretty much where it was after *Near* v. *Minnesota.* Events happened too quickly for this to be a great case. There was no time to develop and present important constitutional arguments. The case was frightening in some respects. Both the *New York Times* and the *Washington Post* were prevented for fifteen days—while the case was in court—from printing the Pentagon Papers series, the first time this has happened to two such important newspapers. One cannot be reassured by reading the opinion of each of the justices. A single ringing defense of freedom of the press can hardly be found among them. The exceptions are the opinions of justices Black and Douglas, one of whom has since died and the other retired from the high Court.

Knopf v. *Colby*

As if to emphasize the fragile nature of the Pentagon Papers decision, in 1974 and 1975 in an unusual case federal courts ruled that a former employee of the Central Intelligence Agency (CIA) had waived his First Amendment rights and restrained the former agent from publishing material from classified documents in a book (*Knopf* v. *Colby*, 1974). When he joined the Central Intelligence Agency in 1955, and again when he resigned in 1969, Victor Marchetti signed agreements that he would not reveal information learned during his employment. In 1971 when Marchetti and John D. Marks decided to publish a book about the spy agency, the federal government went to court to enforce the agreements Marchetti had signed. In reviewing the original manuscript the CIA deleted almost three hundred forty passages. In negotiations with the authors which followed the government agreed to trim its requests to one hundred sixty-eight passages.

Marchetti and Marks went to court, and a federal district judge reduced the number of deletions to twenty-six. The government then appealed and won an injunction from Judge Clement Haynsworth of the Fourth Circuit Court of Appeals, who restored the one hundred sixty-eight deletions desired by the CIA. The judge ruled that Marchetti effectively relinquished his First Amendment rights "by his execution of the secrecy agreement and his entry into the confidential relationship." The court ordered the former deputy director of the agency to submit all his future writing about the CIA to the agency for prepublication censorship. In May 1975 the Supreme Court refused to hear an appeal by Marchetti and Marks, leaving the Fourth Circuit Court order to stand (*Knopf* v. *Colby*, 1975).

Marchetti's book, *The CIA and the Cult of Intelligence*, was published with blank spaces representing the CIA deletions. This is clearly an unusual case. Few citizens have signed the kind of agreements Marchetti signed. Nevertheless, none of these court proceedings made much sense in respect to the fragile nature of freedom of expression and the devastation which blanket prior restraint can wreak.

There are many different kinds of prior restraint, some of which are obvious as in the cases just discussed and some of which are subtle and hidden. When the Congress passed the Federal Election Law placing a limit upon the amount of political advertising a candidate can buy, the Supreme Court said the action amounts to prior restraint (*Buckley* v. *Valeo*, 1976). When a state passes a statute which prohibits the press from publishing the name of a rape victim, even when the name is included in a public trial of the accused rapist, the action amounts to prior restraint (*Cox Broadcasting Corp.* v. *Cohn*, 1974). The kinds and varieties of prior restraint are simply too numerous to consider in this short chapter, but the following general definition can probably be used as a guideline. If it can be proved that a law or rule or regulation in fact constitutes a prior restraint upon the press, and if the rule or law does not fall under one of the categories listed by Chief Justice Hughes in the *Near* case (obscenity, incitement to violence, and publication of dangerous material during wartime), ninety-nine times out of one hundred a court will declare that rule or law unconstitutional.

FREEDOM FROM UNFAIR TAXATION   In addition to permitting opposition to the government and prohibiting prior restraint in most instances, the First Amendment also guarantees that the press shall be free from unfair and discriminatory taxes which have an impact upon circulation, or distribution. In this area the classic case concerns a United States senator from a southern state and the daily press of that state (*Grosjean* v. *American Press Co.,* 1936).

During the late 1920s and early 1930s the political leader of Louisiana was Huey P. Long. Long was a demagogue by most accounts and in 1934 held his state in virtual dictatorship. He controlled the legislature and the state house and had a deep impact upon the judicial branch as well. Long started his career by attacking big business—Standard Oil of California, to be exact. He became a folk hero among the rural people of Louisiana and was elected governor in 1928. In 1931 he was elected to the United States Senate and many people believe that he would have attempted to win the presidency had he not been assassinated in 1935.

In 1934 the Long political machine, which the majority of the big-city residents had never favored, became annoyed at the frequent attacks by the state's daily newspapers against the senator and his political machine. The legislature enacted a special 2 percent tax on the gross advertising income of newspapers with a circulation of more than 20,000. Of the 163 newspapers in the state, only 13 had more than 20,000 subscribers, and of the 13, 12 were outspoken in their opposition to Long. The newspapers went to court and argued that the tax violated the First Amendment as well as other constitutional guarantees. The press won at the circuit court level on other grounds, but the state appealed. Then in 1936 the Supreme Court ruled in favor of the newspapers squarely on First Amendment grounds.

The state of Louisiana argued that the English common law, which it claimed the American courts had adopted after the Revolution, conferred the right to tax newspapers and license them if need be upon the government. Justice George Sutherland, who wrote the opinion in this unanimous Supreme Court decision, said however that such taxes upon newspapers were the direct cause of much civil unrest in England and one of the chief objections Americans had to British policy—objections which ultimately forced independence.

The justice wrote:

> It is impossible to concede that by the words "freedom of the press" the framers of the amendment intended to adopt merely the narrow view then reflected by the law of England that such freedom consisted in immunity from previous censorship. . . . It is equally impossible to believe that it was not intended to bring within the reach of these words such modes of restraint as were embodied in . . . taxation."

Sutherland asserted that the tax not only restricted the amount of revenue the paper earned but also restrained circulation. Newspapers with less than 20,000 readers would be reluctant to seek new subscribers for fear of increasing circulation to the point where they would have to pay the tax as well. The justice added that any action by the government which prevents free and general discussion of public matters is a kind of censorship. Sutherland said that in this case even the form in which the tax was imposed was suspicious—was levied against a distinct group of newspapers. He then wrote:

> The tax here involved is bad not because it takes money from the pockets of the appellees [the newspapers]. If that were all, a wholly different question would be presented. It is bad because, in the light of its history and of its present setting, it is seen to be a deliberate and calculated device in the guise of a tax to limit the circulation of information to which the public is entitled in virtue of the constitutional guaranties. A free press stands as one of the great interpreters between the government and the people. To allow it to be fettered is to fetter ourselves.

Therefore in *Grosjean* v. *American Press Co.*, the Supreme Court struck down a discriminatory tax against the press. An interesting footnote to the case concerns the opinion. Justice Sutherland's opinion is one of the most eloquent ever penned in defense of free expression. The Justice was not normally such an articulate spokesman. What happened in this case? Speculation is that Sutherland's opinion incorporates a concurring opinion by Justice Benjamin Cardozo, perhaps the greatest writer to ever serve on the Court, and the eloquence of the *Grosjean* opinion is really Cardozo's, not Sutherland's.

Despite the fact that Justice Sutherland specifically noted in his opinion that the ruling in *Grosjean* did not mean that newspapers are immune from ordinary taxes, some newspaper publishers apparently did not read the opinion that way, but saw it instead as a means of escaping other kinds of taxes. After *Grosjean*, for example, unsuccessful attempts were made to have a sales tax in Arizona declared inapplicable to newspapers because it was a restriction on freedom of the press (*Arizona Publishing Co.* v. *O'Neil, 1938*). Since 1953 when the United States Supreme Court refused to hear a appeal from a California decision affirming the constitutionality of a general business tax on newspapers, the matter has been fairly well settled. The California case involved the *Corona Daily Independent* which challenged a business tax imposed by the city of Corona. A license tax of thirty-two dollars had been levied for many years against all businesses. In 1953 the newspaper refused to pay the levy on the grounds that the tax violated its First Amendment rights to freedom of expression. The *Grosjean* case prohibited such taxation, lawyers for the publication argued. The trial court ruled in favor of the newspaper, but the California Appellate Court disagreed and reversed the ruling (*City of Corona* v. *Corona Daily Independent,* 1953). Justice Griffin wrote that there is ample authority to the effect that newspapers are not made exempt from ordinary forms of taxation. Justice Griffin said that the newspaper had not shown that the amount of the tax was harsh or arbitrary, that the tax was oppressive or confiscatory, or that the tax in any way curtailed or abridged the newspaper's right to disseminate news and comment:

> We conclude that a nondiscriminatory tax, levied upon the doing of business, for the sole purpose of maintaining the municipal government, without whose municipal services and protection the press could neither exist nor function, must be sustained as being within the purview and necessary implications of the Constitution and its amendments.

The United States Supreme Court refused to review the ruling in *City of Corona* v. *Corona Daily Independent,* and most people believed the refusal signaled concurrence with the opinion of the California court.

The basic rule of First Amendment law regarding taxes on the press is this: Newspapers, broadcasting stations, and other mass media must pay the same taxes as any other business. Taxes which are levied only against the press and tend to inhibit circulation or impose other kinds of prior restraints (such as very high taxes which keep all but very wealthy people from publishing newspapers) are unconstitutional.

FREEDOM FROM UNFAIR DISTRIBUTION LAWS

In addition to the subtle form of censorship applied as discriminatory taxation of the press, another restraint against freedom of expression, placing a limitation upon the distribution of pamphlets or leaflets or other types of mass communications, has been tried at times. While there seems to be very little difference between a discriminatory law which taxes the press and a law which requires a license before distribution of a publication, these two kinds of restraints are placed in separate categories.

The preeminent judicial ruling on the question of the validity of licensing laws is the case of *Lovell v. Griffin* decided by the nation's high Court in 1938. The city of Griffin, Georgia, had an ordinance which prohibited the distribution of circulars, handbooks, advertising, and literature of any kind without first obtaining written permission from the city manager. Under the law, the city manager had considerable discretion as to whether he gave permission. Alma Lovell was a member of the Jehovah's Witnesses religious sect, an intense and ruggedly evangelical order which suffered severe persecutions in the first half of this century. But the Witnesses doggedly continued to spread the Word, passing out millions of leaflets and pamphlets and atempting to proselytize anyone who would listen. Laws like the distribution ordinance were common in many communities in the United States and were directed at stopping the distribution of material by groups such as the Witnesses.

Alma Lovell didn't even attempt to get a license before she circulated pamphlets, and she was arrested, convicted, and fined fifty dollars for violating the city ordinance. When she refused to pay the fine, she was sentenced to fifty days in jail. At the trial the Jehovah's Witnesses freely admitted the illegal distribution, but argued that the statute was invalid on its face because it violated the First Amendment guarantees of freedom of the press and freedom of religion.

On appeal the Supreme Court agreed that the law did indeed violate freedom of the press. Chief Justice Charles Evans Hughes wrote, "We think that the ordinance is invalid on its face" because it strikes at the very foundation of freedom of the press by subjecting it to license and censorship. The city argued that the First Amendment applies only to newspapers and regularly published materials like magazines. The high Court disagreed, ruling that the amendment applies to pamphlets and leaflets as well: "These indeed have been historic weapons in the defense of liberty, as the pamphlets of Thomas Paine and others in our own history abundantly attest. The press in its historic connotation comprehends every sort of publication which affords a vehicle of information and opinion."

Lawyers for Griffin also argued that the First Amendment was not applicable because the licensing law said nothing about publishing, but only concerned distribution. Again the high Court disagreed, noting that liberty of circulation is as essential to freedom of expression as liberty of publishing. Chief Justice Hughes wrote, "without the circulation, the publication would be of little value."

Lovell v. *Griffin*, then, seemed to explicitly forbid laws which place an unreasonable limitation upon freedom of circulation or distribution.

This case did not, however, end the question, for it is a problem with many dimensions.

Nineteen months after the *Lovell* decision the Supreme Court decided a second distribution case, a case which involved licensing laws in four different cities. The four cases were decided as one (*Schneider* v. *New Jersey*, 1939). A Los Angeles ordinance prohibited the distribution of handbills on public streets on the grounds that distribution contributed to the litter problem. Ordinances in Milwaukee, Wisconsin, and Worcester, Massachusetts, were justified on the same basis—keeping the city streets clean.

An Irvington, New Jersey, law was far broader, prohibiting street distribution or house-to-house calls unless permission was first obtained from the local police chief. The police department asked distributors for considerable personal information and could reject applicants the law officers deemed not of good character. This action was ostensibly to protect the public against criminals.

Justice Owen Roberts delivered the opinion of the Court which struck down each of the four laws. Justice Roberts said that a city can enact regulations in the interest of public safety, health, and welfare, but not regulations which interfere with the liberty of the press or freedom of expression. He then gave some examples of what he meant, examples which have proved most helpful in framing such ordinances. Cities, he said, have the responsibility to keep the public streets open and available for the movement of people and property, and laws to regulate the conduct of those who would interfere with this legitimate public problem are constitutional:

> For example, a person could not exercise this liberty [of free expression] by taking his stand in the middle of a crowded street, contrary to traffic regulations, and maintain his position to the stoppage of all traffic; a group of distributors could not insist upon a constitutional right to form a cordon across the street and to allow no pedestrian to pass who did not accept a tendered leaflet; nor does the guarantee of freedom of speech or of the press deprive a municipality of power to enact regulations against throwing literature in the streets.

These kinds of activities, Roberts said, bear no relationship to the freedom to speak, write, print, or distribute information or opinion. The justice closed by saying that the high court characterized freedom of speech and freedom of the press as fundamental personal rights and liberties: "The phrase is not an empty one and was not lightly used. . . . It stresses, as do many opinions of this Court, the importance of preventing the restriction of enjoyment of these liberties."

A somewhat different dimension of this same problem arose in a Connecticut case in which, again, members of Jehovah's Witnesses faced criminal prosecution under an ordinance which limited the solicitation of funds (*Cantwell v. Connecticut*, 1940). Jesse Cantwell and his two sons attempted to carry their religious message along the streets of a heavily Catholic neighborhood in New Haven, Connecticut. They were arrested for violating a state law which prohibited the solicitation of money by a religious group without first gaining approval from the local public official whose job it was to decide whether the religious cause in question was a "bona fide object of charity" and whether it conformed to "reasonable standards of efficiency and integrity." The Supreme Court tossed out the law as a violation of the First Amendment. For the unanimous Court, Justice Roberts wrote that the state could, in order to protect its citizens from fraudulent solicitations, require strangers in the community to establish identity and authority to act for the cause he purports to represent before permitting any solicitation in the community. And the state could pass rules setting reasonable regulatory limits on the time of day solicitations could be made (no solicitations before 9 A.M. or after 10 P.M., for example).

> But to condition the solicitation of aid for the perpetuation of religious views or systems upon a license, the grant of which rests in the exercise of a determination by state authority as to what is a religious cause, is to lay a forbidden burden upon the exercise of liberty protected by the Constitution.

In 1943, three years after the decision in *Cantwell v. Connecticut* the high Court voided another distribution ordinance, this one from Struthers, Ohio, which prohibited door-to-door distribution of handbills, circulars, or other advertising material (*Martin v. Struthers*, 1943). The law also barred anyone from ringing doorbells to summon householders for the purpose of distributing literature or pamphlets. Justice Hugo Black wrote the opinion for the majority in the divided Court. He said the arrest of Thelma Martin, another Jehovah's Witness, for ringing doorbells in behalf of her religious cause was a violation of her First Amendment rights. Door-to-door distributors can be a nuisance or even be a front for criminal activities, Justice Black acknowledged. Further, door-to-door distribution can surely be regulated, but it cannot be altogether banned. It is a valuable and useful means of the dissemination of ideas and is especially important to those groups which are too poorly financed to use other expensive means of communicating with the people. Black said a law which makes it an offense for a person to ring the bell of a householder who has appropriately indicated that he or she is unwilling to be disturbed would be lawful and constitutional. However, the city of Struthers cannot by ordinance make this decision on behalf of all its citizens—especially when such a rule clearly interferes with the freedom of speech and of the press. "The right of freedom of speech and press has broad scope. The authors of the First Amendment knew that novel and unconventional ideas might disturb the complacent, but they chose to encourage a freedom which they believed essential if vigorous enlightenment was ever to triumph over slothful ignorance."

Nearly ten years later, in 1951, the high Court was confronted with still another case of door-to-door solicitation. This case, however, concerned solicitation of subscriptions for nationally circulated magazines (*Breard v. Alexandria,* 1951). The Alexandria, Louisiana, ordinance in question prohibited door-to-door solicitation for sale of goods, wares, or merchandise without the prior consent or invitation of the homeowner. Jack H. Breard, who was employed by a Pennsylvania magazine subscription company, appealed his conviction all the way to the Supreme Court on the grounds that the law violated his First Amendment rights. This time the divided Court ruled against the solicitor, stating that the restriction was not a violation of the First Amendment.

Justice Stanley Reed distinguished the early cases from the *Breard* case by arguing that *Breard* was a case of door-to-door sale of wares, not of propagation of ideas or religious faith. "This kind of distribution is said to be protected because the mere fact that money is made out of the distribution does not bar the publications from First Amendment protection. We agree that the fact that periodicals are sold does not put them beyond the protection of the First Amendment. The selling, however, brings into the transaction a commercial feature," Reed wrote. He added that there are many other ways to sell magazines besides intruding upon the privacy of a householder through door-to-door techniques. Justices Black, Douglas, and Vinson disagreed with Justice Reed, arguing that the high Court turned its back on earlier free expression decisions. "The constitutional sanctuary for the press must necessarily include liberty to publish and circulate. In view of our economic system, it must also include freedom to solicit paying subscribers," Black wrote. The jurist added that homeowners could themselves place the solicitor on notice by using a sign that they do not wish to be disturbed.

The difference between the decisions in *Martin* v. *Struthers* and *Breard* v. *Alexandria* probably rests upon the fact that something is sold in the latter case, that is, the commercial aspects of the solicitation in *Breard* versus the religious aspects of the door-to-door canvassing in *Struthers.*

What do all these cases mean? With regard to the mere propagation of ideas, as opposed to solicitation for funds, cities and states cannot completely prohibit the distribution of handbills or pamphlets, they cannot set up licensing systems which discriminate between one group or one kind of group and another group, and they cannot limit distribution or regulate distribution of material in an unreasonable manner such as banning all street distribution because it contributes to the litter problem. On the other hand, cities and states can legitimately regulate the time such distribution takes place and can regulate distribution in a reasonable manner to protect the safety of the people or the welfare of the public such as prohibiting distribution in the middle of a busy intersection or blocking a sidewalk by distributors. Concerning solicitation connected with distribution, communities have all the rights just listed, plus they can ask solicitors to first check in with local authorities to determine the legitimacy of the solicitor. That is, if someone solicits for Church of Divine Trinity, local officials have the right to establish that there is such a church and that the solicitor in fact represents that church. If the church is phony or the solicitor is not an authorized representative, the solicitation can be denied. However, solicitation cannot be denied on the ground that the local officials don't like the church or what it stands for.

Of course, when it comes to solicitation for commercial items, the community has broader latitude to pass rules defining the rights of door-to-door salesmen (see chapter 10).

FREEDOM OF EXPRESSION IN THE SCHOOLS

While freedom of expression has been considered a basic right for the press in this country for nearly two hundred years, this right was not articulated for college and high school newspapers until quite recently. Until the sixties, college or high school editors enjoyed about as much freedom of expression as the newspaper's adviser or the high school principal or the college dean was willing to allow. Freedom of expression in the schools was something vigorously discussed and defended in class, but often denied in practice. Then in 1967 a federal district court in Alabama ruled that schools had better begin to practice what they preached (*Dickey* v. *Alabama*, 1967). The editor of the newspaper at Troy State College, Gary Dickey, prepared an editorial in support of the president of the University of Alabama who was under fire from state legislators for his refusal to censor a University of Alabama student publication dealing with world revolution. The adviser to the school newspaper instructed Dickey not to publish the editorial because it violated a rule prohibiting the publication of editorials critical of the governor or the Alabama state legislature. Laudatory editorials only were permissible. Dickey published the editorial anyway and was suspended from school for insubordination. The federal court overturned the suspension and ruled that the First

Amendment did apply to school children and students insofar as unreasonable rules are concerned. What kinds of rules are permissible?

> State school officials cannot infringe on their students' right of free and unrestricted expression as guaranteed by the Constitution of the United States where the exercise of such right does not "materially and substantially interfere with requirements of appropriate discipline in the operation of the school."

Judge Johnson said the school could not punish Gary Dickey for exercising rights given to him under the Constitution by cloaking his expulsion in the robe of insubordination. This did not disguise the fact that he was suspended for exercising his right of free expression.

The *Dickey* rule—censorship of school papers is allowed only when the exercise of freedom of speech interferes materially and substantially with the requirements of appropriate discipline and order in the school—is the law today. The rule has been upheld in numerous cases involving both college and high school students, and the Supreme Court adopted this rule in 1969 in *Tinker* v. *Des Moines School District*. There must be some reasonable forecast of substantial disruption of or material interference with school activities before censorship can be undertaken. While this standard may be something less than the freedom enjoyed by publications in the real world, it is a far cry from the old standards based on timidity of school officials.

AN EMERGING INTERPRE-TATION OF THE FIRST AMENDMENT

This chapter on First Amendment rights cannot be closed without a short discussion of another definition of freedom of the press which has emerged during the past ten years. Other aspects of this subject will be touched upon in the discussion of right of reply and retraction statutes in libel law and the fairness doctrine in broadcasting regulation. It is important, however, to outline a little of the origin behind this First Amendment concept before moving to other topics.

The First Amendment simply says that government cannot interfere with freedom of the press. We have seen that there are many ways in which various governments attempted to restrain press freedom, normally without success. Many people ask, however, if this is really a sufficient measure of freedom of the press. Is freedom from government censorship a meaningful kind of freedom of the press in the 1970s?

A look back to the 1940s will indicate the genesis of these questions. In the mid-1940s a private commission, the Commission on Freedom of the Press, was set up to study freedom of the press in the United States. The two-year investigation was funded primarily by Time, Inc., and its founder Henry Luce. The study was organized by the University of Chicago and the panel of investigators included philosophers, economists, historians, theologians, professors of law, and others. While no one from the media was on the commission, many media people were interviewed in the process of information gathering.

The conclusions of the Commission on Freedom of the Press were somewhat surprising, at least to the press. The commissioners found that freedom of the press, that is, as it is traditionally defined as freedom from government restraint, was fairly secure at mid twentieth century in the United States. However, because of changing economic patterns within the mass media, because of the concentration of control of newspapers and broadcasting stations in fewer and fewer hands, freedom of the press wasn't very secure for the average citizen. The average American has little chance to use his or her freedom of the press because they cannot afford to own a newspaper or a broadcasting station. The traditional definition of freedom of the press, freedom from government control, does not mean very much to most of us since we have no means of publishing or broadcasting anyway.

The reports of the privately funded Commission on Freedom of the Press were neatly filed in libraries across America and were read occasionally by students and scholars. But the ideas were not publicized by the media, and the recommendations of the Commission were soon forgotten.

Then in the late sixties a few legal scholars began to assert the same kind of contrary First Amendment doctrine. Led by Professor Jerome Barron at the George Washington University Law School, these writers and researchers fashioned a fairly substantive legal philosophy upon which to base a call for what they referred to as the right of access to the media.

The philosophy can be summarized fairly briefly. The traditional definition of freedom of the press is a negative kind of freedom—it is freedom from government control. As such, the definition implies that keeping the press free from the restraints of government is an end in itself and and is the purpose of the First Amendment.

Many argue that it is a fairly valueless freedom. The press must be free from government control in order to accomplish something. Freedom of the press is really a means to an end. The men who drafted both the Constitution and the First Amendment believed that a popular democracy could be best served if widespread debate on all public issues is allowed, that is, if all interested persons have an opportunity to speak their piece on a subject. Full public discussion of issues is the goal or the end which freedom of the press serves.

In 1790 this was a fairly attainable goal. Most large communities had several newspapers representing various points of view. Most communities were small enough that a person could use handbills and posters to effectively circulate ideas excluded from the popular press. Finally, starting a newspaper was a costly and risky venture, but something which many citizens could reasonably undertake. Succeeding with a newspaper was another question, however.

Times have changed. Most communities in America are served by but a single daily newspaper and a handful of small circulation weeklies. There is little difference among the newspapers which are published; most of the mainstream press tends to represent a fairly conservative "business" point of view. At the same time the content of newspapers has changed since the eighteenth century. Today, the press provides "objective news," advertising, features, and small amounts of commentary or opinion. Two hundred years ago there was little advertising, some news, and mostly comment and opinion. Newspapers were not frightened by controversy and controversial ideas in the eighteenth century since the people who read a newspaper generally agreed with the bias of the newspaper. Today, there are fewer newspapers, and they try to reach all readers. Not wanting to alienate large groups, the press tends to shy away from controversy. It is difficult for a person with novel, innovative, crazy, or controversial ideas to have them published in the daily press today. The number of letters to the editor printed are few and are screened.

Because many cities are so large today, persons cannot effectively communicate their ideas through handbills or leaflets except in the smallest towns. And the cost of getting into the publishing industry is very high. Millions of dollars are required to start a daily newspaper in a large city, and the chance of success is small because most advertisers seem to prefer single newspapers serving many persons rather than many newspapers each serving a smaller segment of the community.

In this very real situation, the right of freedom of the press has very little meaning to the average man or woman. While it is significant that the government will not interfere with the freedom of the press, just where does the average man use his freedom of the press? Where can he publish his thoughts about government, economy, foreign policy, school taxes, and the like? As it was once graphically pointed out, it is useless to tell a man that he is free to walk without first determining whether he has legs.

Using this basic rationale (the Bibliography at the end of the chapter provides information for those interested in a fuller treatment of the arguments), advocates of the right of access move in somewhat different directions in search of a solution. Some argue that newspapers should be required to publish statements from community groups which represent a considerable segment of the people. Others feel that the press should be obligated to present all sides of controversial issues not only in news stories, but also in editorials written by advocates. Some proponents believe that the press should be required to publish more letters to the editor. Numerous other ideas are also advocated. All arguments assume that someone, presumably the government, will ensure that the press lives up to these responsibilities or requirements. But isn't this government interference with the press? Doesn't this violate the First Amendment? No, say the right-of-access advocates. If the First Amendment is conceived of as a means to an end, and if broad public discussion is the goal of freedom of the press, a law which forces the press to provide a forum for broad public discussion is not then in violation of the First Amendment. Such a law enhances freedom of the press and makes freedom of the press meaningful for persons who don't own a newspaper or aren't traditional newsmakers.

In 1974 the Supreme Court had the opportunity to consider this argument in a case involving an all-but-forgotten Florida law passed not in the sixties, but more than sixty years earlier (*Miami Herald* v. *Tornillo,* 1974). The state statute in question provided that if a newspaper attacks the personal character or the official record of a candidate for public office, the newspaper must, upon request of the candidate and without cost, permit the injured party the right to publish a reply to the charge. If the newspaper refuses to comply, it is guilty of a crime.

In September of 1972 the *Miami Herald* attacked Pat Tornillo, a candidate for the Florida State legislature. Tornillo was president of the local Classroom Teachers Association and led teachers in a strike against the school system when salary demands and other issues were not resolved. In two separate editorials the newspaper attacked Tornillo and charged that he failed to file a list of contributors to his campaign as required by law, that he had led an illegal strike, and that the Classroom Teachers Association was really a powerful special-interest group which had little concern for the public welfare.

Tornillo requested space to reply, and the *Herald* refused his request. The local trial court held that the law was in violation of the First Amendment and refused to enforce the law. However, the Florida supreme court reversed the lower court ruling in a six-to-one decision (*Tornillo* v. *Miami Herald,* 1973).

The Florida high court said that the election of public officials is the basic precept upon which our democracy rests and that while the press has the right to publish without government restraint, "we emphasize that there is a correlative responsibility that the public be fully informed." An informed electorate is one of the basic pillars of the democracy. People must be able to find out what is going on, what the issues are, and where the candidates stand on the issues. The law in question was designed to add to this flow of information. It does not interfere with what the newspaper must publish: it simply requires that in special circumstances additional information must be published. The per curiam opinion then said:

> Freedom of expression was retained by the people through the First Amendment for all the people and not merely for a select few. The First Amendment did not create a privileged class which through a monopoly of instruments of the newspaper industry would be able to deny to the people the freedom of expression which the First Amendment guarantees.

The court concluded by saying that the state law does not abridge the right of expression of anyone; it merely assures that more persons will be able to take advantage of this constitutional right.

The *Miami Herald* appealed the decision to the United States Supreme Court, and in June of 1974 the high Court unanimously reversed the Florida supreme court ruling.

In his opinion for the court Chief Justice Warren Burger basically agreed that there is a need for citizens to have a right of access to the media, that freedom of the press isn't very meaningful without access to the press. He also said that no matter how valid these arguments are the implementation of a remedy in which the government forces the press to provide such access brings about direct confrontation with the First Amendment: "A responsible press is an undoubtedly desirable goal, but press responsibility is not mandated by the Constitution and like many other virtues it cannot be legislated."

Burger said that those who argued that the right of reply statute did not penalize the newspaper were wrong. Publication of such replies cost the newspaper time and space, and even if there is no penalty, this law still interferes with the function of the editors.

> The choice of material to go into a newspaper, and the decisions made as to limitations on the size of the paper, and content, and treatment, of public issues and public officials—whether fair or unfair—constitutes the exercise of editorial control and judgement. It has yet to be demonstrated how governmental regulation of this crucial process can be exercised consistent with First Amendment guarantees of a free press as they have evolved to this time.

The high Court, then, refused to accept the argument that fuller public discussion is the real meaning of the First Amendment and that a law which worked toward this expanded debate cannot be in violation of freedom of the press. The ruling in *Miami Herald* v. *Tornillo* was a blow to the right-of-access activists who, while not expecting a clear victory, at least assumed some support from a few members of the Supreme Court.

The ideas, the philosophy, behind the arguments for a right of access are not dead, however. This theory of the First Amendment, clearly more in tune with the realities of the twentieth century than the romantic notions inherent in the traditional "freedom from" theory expounded by Justice Burger, will not go away simply because of the Tornillo decision. In the future such cases will be litigated, and just as the high Court gradually came to accept that the First Amendment means a good deal more than mere freedom from prior restraint, it may someday also accept the notion that the right of access is inherent in freedom of the press.

BIBLIOGRAPHY

These are some of the sources that were helpful in the preparation of chapter 2.

Books   Alexander, James. *A Brief Narrative on the Case and Trial of John Peter Zenger.* Edited by Stanley N. Katz. Cambridge, Mass.: Harvard University Press, 1963.

Chafee, Zechariah. *Free Speech in the United States.* Cambridge: Harvard University Press, 1941.

Fellman, David. *The Limits of Freedom.* New Brunswick, N. J.: Rutgers University Press, 1959.

Gerald, J. Edward. *The Press and the Constitution.* Minneapolis, Minn.: University of Minnesota Press, 1948.

Jensen, Merrill. *The Articles of Confederation.* Madison, Wis. University of Wisconsin Press, 1966.

Jensen, Merrill. *The Making of the American Constitution.* New York: Von Nostrand Reinhold Co., 1964.

Levy, Leonard. *Freedom of Speech and Press in Early American History.* New York: Harper & Row, Harper Torchbooks, 1963.

Miller, John C. *Crisis in Freedom.* Boston: Little, Brown & Co., 1951.

Peterson, H. C., and Fite, Gilbert. *Opponents of War, 1917-1918.* Seattle, Wash.: University of Washington Press, 1957.

Roche, John P. *Shadow and Substance.* New York: Macmillan Co., 1964.

Rutland, Robert. *The Birth of the Bill of Rights.* Chapel Hill, N. C.: University of North Carolina Press, 1955.

Siebert, Fredrick. *Freedom of the Press in England, 1476-1776.* Urbana, Ill.: University of Illinois, 1952.

Smith, James Morton. *Freedom's Fetters.* Ithaca, N. Y.: Cornell University Press, 1956.

Articles   Barron, Jerome. "Access to the Press—A New First Amendment Right," 80 *Harvard Law Review* 1641 (1967).

Nelson, Harold. "Seditious Libel in Colonial America," 3 *American Journal of Legal History* 160 (1959).

Pember, Don R. "The Pentagon Papers Decision: More Questions Than Answers," 48 *Journalism Quarterly* 403 (1971).

Pember, Don R. "The Smith Act as a Restraint on the Press," 10 *Journalism Monographs* 1 (1969).

Ragan, Fred D. "Justice Oliver Wendell Holmes, Jr., Zechariah Chafee, Jr., and the Clear and Present Danger Test for Free Speech: The First Year, 1919," 53 *Journal of American History* 24 (1971).

Cases *Abrams* v. *U.S.*, 250 U.S. 616 (1919).

Arizona Pub. Co. v. *O'Neil*, 22 F. Supp. 117, affd 304 U.S. 543 (1938).

Barron v. *Baltimore*, 7 Peters 243 (1833).

Bary v. *U.S.*, 248 F.2d 201 (1957).

Brandenburg v. *Ohio*, 395 U.S. 444 (1969).

Breard v. *Alexandria*, 341 U.S. 622 (1951).

Buckley v. *Valeo*, 96 S. Ct. 612 (1976).

Cantwell v. *Connecticut*, 310 U.S. 296 (1940).

City of Corona v. *Corona Daily Independent*, 252 P2d 56 (1953).

Cox Broadcasting Corp. v. *Cohn*, 95 S.Ct. 1025 (1975).

Debs v. *U.S.*, 249 U.S. 211 (1919).

Dennis v. *U.S.*, 341 U.S. 494 (1951).

Dickey v. *Alabama*, 273 F. Supp. 613 (1967).

Fiske v. *Kansas*, 274 U.S. 380 (1927).

Frohwerk v. *U.S.*, 249 U.S. 204 (1919).

Gitlow v. *New York*, 268 U.S. 652 (1925).

Grosjean v. *American Press Co.*, 297 U.S. 233 (1936).

Knopf v. *Colby*, 502 F.2d 1362, cert. den. 95 S.Ct. 1555 (1975).

Lovell v. *Griffin*, 303 U.S. 444 (1938).

Martin v. *Struthers*, 319 U.S. 141 (1943).

Miami Herald Co. v. *Tornillo*, 287 S.2d 78 (1973), revd. 94 S.Ct. 2831 (1974).

Near v. *Minnesota*, 383 U.S. 697 (1931).

New York Times Co., v. *U.S.*, 713 U.S. 403 (1971).

Organization for a Better Austin v. *Keefe*, 402 U.S. 415 (1971).

Scales v. *U.S.*, 367 U.S. 203 (1961).

Schenck v. *U.S.*, 249 U.S. 47 (1919).

Schneider v. *New Jersey*, 308 U.S. 147 (1939).

Tinker v. *Des Moines School District*, 393 U.S. 503 (1969).

Whitney v. *California*, 274 U.S. 357 (1927).

Yates v. *U.S.*, 354 U.S. 298 (1957).

CHAPTER 3

Libel

Defamation, or libel, is probably the most common legal problem most journalists face in the 1970s. Not that there are a great many libel suits. There are not. Reporters and newspapers and broadcasting stations are rarely sued for libel. Still, the potential for libel exists with virtually every story that is published or broadcast. Consequently, libel is an ever-present, if not always obvious, danger in the newsroom.

Probably considerably more defamation is published and broadcast than editors like to imagine. Still, a lawsuit is rare. The chances of success in winning a libel suit are often very low. Many attorneys advise their clients that a lawsuit often only publicizes the original defamation far beyond the original audience. A defamatory falsehood published in a small gossip magazine or obscure newspaper column has a limited audience. A lawsuit based on such publication draws attention to the defamation, and many persons who did not originally see the story are drawn to it. Other lawyers argue that the truth rarely catches up with a lie, and it is best just to ignore the defamation because the public will soon forget it. Finally, while many defamatory statements may be partially false, they may be partially true as well. The injured person may be reluctant to admit that a portion of the defamation is true in order to prosecute the untrue portion in a lawsuit.

Hesitancy to sue, however, is sometimes offset by the possibility and hope of a large money judgment. To the press losing a major libel suit, or sometimes even winning one, can be financially devastating. In past years libel judgments amounting to hundreds of thousands of dollars have not been uncommon. In a few cases more than one million dollars has been awarded. Time, Inc.—which has had nearly twenty major libel suits since 1969—can afford to pay a $500,000 libel judgment. The *Texas Observer* and the *New Times* cannot. Judgments like this can kill small publications. Even if the publication wins, victory can be costly. Drew Pearson's biography asserts that he was sued for libel approximately 275 times for a total of $200 million during the years that he wrote the column "Washington Merry-Go-Round." Pearson won all suits but one, which he settled out of court for $40,000. At the same time, however, he paid out hundreds of thousands of dollars in legal fees to defend himself in these suits. Small publications cannot afford such fees. In the face of such enormous libel judgments and costly legal fees the great temptation for the editor is to pull back, to not take the chance, to censor his own publication or news broadcast. This situation is discussed more fully at the end of the chapter.

Many lawyers are often troubled by libel because of the immense inconsistencies in the law. The roots of libel law are in the common law. In some states libel law is codified, and statutes have been approved by various state legislatures. Regardless, differences exist from state to state. Even within states many areas of the law remain unsettled. Libel attorney and author Paul Ashley writes in his handbook *Say It Safely*:

> Significant segments of the law of libel are unique—dissimilar from legal rules with which lawyers and judges are most familiar. Libel cases are relatively few in number. Judges are not ordinarily experienced in the practical application of the esoteric concepts of privilege and fair comment essential to the preservation of freedom of speech and, in turn, of a free society. And so it is that here and there will be found maverick decisions which distort the law of libel.

No editor wants his newspaper to become the victim of one of these maverick decisions. The impetus toward self-censorship is strong.

Libel, therefore, remains a very important consideration for publishers and broadcasters. Despite the libel protections for the press which have evolved in the past few years through constitutional law, the threat of a libel suit still works against the kind of free and robust communication system envisioned by many philosophers of the First Amendment.

HISTORY OF LIBEL

The law of defamation is ancient; its roots can be traced back several centuries. Initially the law was an attempt by government to establish a forum for persons involved in a dispute brought about by an insult or by what we today call a defamatory remark. One man called another a robber and a villain. The injured party sought to avenge his damaged reputation. A fight or duel of some kind was the only means of gaining vengeance before the development of libel law. It was obvious that fights and duels were not satisfactory ways to settle such disputes, so government offered its "good offices" to solve these problems. Slowly the law of defamation evolved. Today the process of going to court to avenge one's honor is highly institutionalized.

In other parts of the world different schemes are used to accomplish similar ends. In continental Europe libel suits are uncommon. When a newspaper defames a person, that person has a right—under law—to strike back, using the columns of the same newspaper, to tell his side of the story, so to speak, to blast the writer or the editor. This right is called the right of reply and exists in the United States in a far less advanced form, as is noted near the end of this chapter. Many people favor the notion, that is, letting the parties fight it out in print or by broadcast. They say it is far better to set out after the truth in this fashion than to rattle the chains on the courthouse door every time an insult is flung in the public press.

Over the centuries the law of defamation has become very complex and very confusing. Parts of the law, however, do not really concern journalists. In this chapter the discussion of the law of libel is generally confined to those areas of the law which are important to reporters, editors, and broadcasters and some aspects of libel law are not included. For example, the law of defamation regarding private communications as opposed to public communications differs somewhat. What a newspaper can legally do is somewhat different from what an employer writing a job evaluation for an employee can legally do. Defamation contained in personal letters, credit reports, job evaluations—a whole range of relatively private communications—is treated somewhat differently in the eyes of the law. The focus of this chapter is defamation in the mass media, that is, public communication libel.

Another complex problem in the law has to do with whether a communication is a libel (written defamation) or a slander (an oral defamation). The law in many states distinguishes between the two. The problem was simple one hundred years ago. Because of the state of technology, a public communication, one meant for a wide audience, was a printed communication—a newspaper, magazine, or handbill. Therefore a law which dealt with libel more harshly than with slander made sense: libel caused more severe damage. A libel lasted longer than a slander since a libel was printed, more people saw it, and it was generally considered to be planned defamation, not words accidentally spoken in the heat of argument. Film, radio, and television have made these distinctions meaningless. If Johnny Carson defames someone on "The Tonight Show," despite the fact that the defamation is not printed it still has immense impact and is heard by millions. A great many states continue to wrestle with the problem of whether defamatory radio and television broadcasts are libel or slander. We are going to take the position—supported by several authorities—that a published defamation, whether it is in a newspaper, on radio or television, in the movies, or what have you, is a libel. And libel rules apply.

The purpose of this chapter is to give journalists guidance and rules to apply in the process of gathering, writing, and publishing and broadcasting the news. People who want to learn to litigate a lawsuit should go to law school. This author's goal is to keep reporters and broadcasters out of libel suits or at least to keep them from losing a libel suit.

The chapter is divided into two basic parts. The first section deals with the nature of a defamation suit: definitions of libel, what a plaintiff must prove in a libel suit, words that tend to be defamatory, and so forth. The second section outlines the various defenses—legal excuses for publishing defamatory matter—for a libel suit. A developing First Amendment defense for libel suits is also discussed here.

LIBEL DEFINED   There are lots of definitions of defamation, and they are all about the same. A few typical definitions follow.

In their book *Libel* Phelps and Hamilton include this definition:

> Defamation is a communication which exposes a person to hatred, ridicule, or contempt, lowers him in the esteem of his fellows, causes him to be shunned, or injures him in his business or calling.

The legal encyclopedia *Corpus Juris* defines libelous words as follows:

> . . . words which have a tendency to disgrace or degrade the person or hold him up to public hatred, contempt, ridicule or cause him to be shunned and avoided; the words must reflect on his integrity, his character, and his good name and standing in the community. . . . The imputation must be one which tends to affect the plaintiff in a class of society whose standard of opinion the court can recognize. It is not sufficient, standing alone, that the language is unpleasant and annoys and irks plaintiff and subjects him to jests or banter, so as to affect his feelings.

The new edition of the *Restatement of Torts,* a compilation by the American Law Institute of what it thinks the common law says, defines libel this way:

> . . . a communication which has the tendency to so harm the reputation of another as to lower him in the estimation of the community or to deter third persons from associating with him.

Here's a shorter definition: Defamation is any communication which holds a man up to contempt, hatred, ridicule, or scorn.

When the preceding four definitions are read, the common and important elements of defamation become obvious. First, defamation is an action which damages the reputation of a person, but not necessarily his or her character. Character is what you are. Your reputation is what people think you are. And reputation is what the law protects. If there were but a single soul on this planet, he or she would have no reputation. Reputation is what other persons think of you. Second, the words don't have to actually damage a reputation. They just must be capable of causing damage or have a tendency to do damage. However, unless the injured party can prove that his or her reputation has incurred some actual harm, the court will not allow a recovery. Being able to establish the defamatory nature of a statement does not always mean that a plaintiff will also be able to recover damages, as is discussed more fully in the section later in the chapter.

Third, at least a significant minority of the community must believe that the plaintiff's reputation has been damaged. However, the group cannot be an unrepresentative minority. Imagine that the *River City Sentinel* calls Jane Adams a bank robber.* Such a charge is defamatory in the eyes of nearly everyone except perhaps of other bank robbers. But if the *Sentinel* characterizes Ms. Adams as a woman "living" with her boyfriend, a large percentage of people would not think any less of her. Still, a larger percentage of readers probably are contemptuous of such behavior. Consequently, the statement is defamatory.

What about a story suggesting that Jane Adams takes a drink now and then, not that she is a boozer, but merely a social drinker? Most people won't think any less of her. Some religious sects forbid drinking, and members of those sects might scorn Ms. Adams because of her habit. Those groups do not constitute a significant representative minority. To add a complicating factor, suppose the newspaper says Ms. Adams is a social drinker, and she is a member of a religious sect which frowns on such a habit. It is quite possible (but not necessarily probable) that Ms. Adams can recover damages if she can offer sufficient evidence to the court to demonstrate that her relationship with her friends in this sect has been severely harmed or that other persons not in the sect think significantly less of her because she does not live up to the religious creed she professes. The point that must be made is simply this: the defamatory communication must be capable of lowering a person's reputation

---

*Jane Adams, John Smith, Frank Jones, Professor LeBlanc, KLOP, the *River City Sentinel, Scam* magazine, and the like, are my fictional creations and are used to illustrate specific points I wish to make when actual case law either does not exist or is unknown to me.

in the eyes of a significant number of people, and unless unusual circumstances exist, these people must reflect fairly representative views.

Some authorities include in their definition of libel that the charges or statements must be false. The point is worthy of a brief discussion here, even though it is discussed more fully later. At issue is really only a problem of semantics. Some people say that a truthful statement cannot be defamatory; others say that it can be defamatory, and the fact that it is true is a defense against a libel suit. In either case when talking about truth in a libel suit we are talking about what the defendant— the defamer—can prove is true. A few states have statutes declaring that even a truthful statement can be actionable if it is not published with the proper motives. That is, if John Smith is a thief he can be called a thief if the purpose is to alert others to his antisocial tendencies, but he can't be described as a thief for the purpose of being nasty or of hurting him. Such motives are wrong. This is old law, and one by one these statutes fall by the wayside as courts rule that such regulations violate the First Amendment (see *Farnsworth* v. *Tribune Co.*, 1969). Probably the simplest rule to remember is that if a statement can be proved to be truthful it may be safely published.

Fourth, the words must tend to cause hatred, contempt, scorn, ridicule, and so forth (these words are examples of libelous words, not the *only* libelous words). The nature of defamatory words is explored more thoroughly momentarily, and it is sufficient here to remember that if the words used lower the reputation of the person involved they are defamatory whether or not they cause the person to be hated, scorned, or ridiculed.

NATURE OF A CIVIL LIBEL SUIT

Injury Due to Libel

Persons can be injured through a libel in numerous ways. The statement may simply hurt their reputations, or it may be that lowering their reputation deprives them of their right to enjoy social contacts, which is a fancy way of saying that their friends don't like them any more or their friends want to avoid them. A man or woman's ability to work or hold a job or make a living may be injured. A person need only be injured in *one* of these three ways to have a cause of action for libel. If the plaintiff can show actual harm in any one of these areas chances are good he or she will recover some damages. That is one of the reasons libel law exists—to compensate the plaintiff for injury. There are other reasons. A libel suit can help vindicate the plaintiff, help restore his or her reputation. A victorious plaintiff can point his finger at the newspaper or television station and say "See, they were wrong, they lied, they made an error." A damage judgment is also considered punishment for the defendant. Hopefully, having to pay a sum of money will remind the editor or broadcaster to be more cautious in the future. It can stand also as an example to other journalists to avoid such behavior.

Any living person can bring a suit for civil libel. If a dead person is libeled, relatives cannot sue in the name of the deceased. However, as noted in the last section of this chapter, it is possible (but highly improbable) for the state to bring a criminal libel action against the publisher of a defamation against a person who has died. A business corporation can sue for libel, as can a nonprofit corporation if it can show that it has lost public support and contributions because of the defamation. There is a division in judicial opinion about whether unincorporated associations like labor unions and political action groups can sue for libel. Some court rulings say no, others say yes. Find out what the law is in your state or play it safe. Cities, counties, agencies of government, and governments in general cannot bring a civil libel suit. This question was decided years ago and is settled law (See *City of Chicago v. Tribune Co.*, 1923). Nevertheless, every now and then an angry public official brings an action against the media in the name of his city or state rather than suing as an individual. In 1970 *Life* magazine reported that organized crime strongly influenced the government of Louisiana. The governor of the state brought an action against *Life* in the name of the state. The case was quickly thrown out by a state appeals court which ruled that a government is composed of temporary representatives and has no cause of action for defamation (*State* v. *Time, Inc.*, 1971). Neither can relatives of defamed persons sue simply because they are relatives. If you call John Smith a fraud, John's brother Homer cannot sue just because he is related to John. It is a different story if Homer can show that the libel reflects on him. For example, if you call John Smith illegitimate, the charge reflects directly on his parents, and they can sue.

Proof of Libel

In a libel case it is up to the plaintiff to prove several elements even before the defendant is faced with erecting a defense. The plaintiff must prove that the communication was published, that he or she is the person referred to in the libel, that the statement is defamatory, and that the publisher of the defamation was negligent. Each of the four elements is discussed separately since they comprise the bulk of a libel suit. The place to start is with proof of publication because it is the simplest requirement.

Publication

Before the law recognizes a statement or a comment as a civil libel (criminal libel is different) the statement must be published. In the eyes of the law publication occurs when one person, in addition to the writer

and the person who is defamed, sees or hears the material.* Think of the situation as a kind of triangle. The writer or broadcaster (ultimately the defendant) is at the first point, the subject of the defamatory statement (ultimately the plaintiff) is at the second point, and a third person is at the third point. All three are necessary for a libel suit. The issue of publication becomes a real problem in defamation via private communications. You send a nasty letter to someone and his secretary opens it first by mistake. Is that publication? You dictate the letter to your secretary. Is that publication? (In both instances the law answers with a resounding "it depends.") In defamation by the mass media publication is virtually presumed, however. In fact, some cases are on record in which courts ruled that if a statement is published in a newspaper or broadcast over television it is presumed that a third party saw it or heard it (see *Hornby* v. *Hunter,* 1964). There are some other aspects of the publication question with which the journalist should be familiar. A chain libel suit is likely to result when several different publications or broadcasting stations publish the same defamatory statement at the same time. Imagine that the Associated Press (AP) reports that John Smith was arrested and charged with murder in Sacramento. Four hundred thirty-seven American newspapers carry that story. It is not true. Theoretically, Smith can sue the Associated Press and every newspaper that carried the story. A newspaper or broadcasting station is responsible for the AP material it publishes or broadcasts. Some states place limitations on this kind of suit. In Florida, for example, a newspaper is not legally responsible for wire service stories it carries (see *Layne* v. *Tribune,* 1933). The Massachusetts legislature passed a statute that bars a plaintiff from recovering damages in Massachusetts if he or she has already recovered damages elsewhere on the basis of the same libelous remarks. This law is unique, although some states allow the defense to introduce evidence that the plaintiff has won damages elsewhere in an attempt to reduce the damage award.

*This statement may confuse some people who see it as a contradiction of an earlier statement that to be defamatory something must lower an individual's reputation in the eyes of a significant minority of the community. It is not a contradiction. Publication is what is being discussed here: how many people must see something before the law considers it to have been published. The earlier remark refers to damage to an individual: how many people must think less of a person upon hearing or reading the statement. It is necessary for the plaintiff to convince the court that a significant number of people in the community think less of him because of the libelous remark, but it is not necessary that the plaintiff show that these people have actually seen the libelous remark, only that they would think less of him if they had seen it.

It should be noted that the law may be changing (or may have already changed) on this point. Recently the Supreme Court insisted that before a plaintiff can collect damages for a libelous remark he or she must prove that the defendant was negligent in publishing or broadcasting the remark (*Gertz* v. *Robert Welch Inc.*, 1974). (More about this rule shortly.) Some persons argue that it is extremely difficult for a plaintiff to convince a judge or jury that an editor or broadcaster was negligent in publishing a seemingly truthful report from a reputable and normally trustworthy news source such as the Associated Press or United Press International. This new requirement placed on the plaintiff may spell an end to the chain libel suit (see *Washington Post* v. *Keogh,* 1966).

Every republication of a libel is a new libel. Judge Leon Yankwich (*It's Libel or Contempt If You Print It*) wrote more than two decades ago:

> In brief, the person who repeats a libel assumes responsibility for the statement and vouches for its truth as though it had been of his own making or on his own information, no matter how emphatically the qualifying words show that the statement is made on the basis of a source other than the writer himself.

If the *River City Sentinel* is being sued for libel for calling John Smith a Communist and the *Ames Daily Gazette* informs its readers about the suit and notes that the *Sentinel* called Smith a Communist, the *Gazette* has republished the libel. A more common problem under republication has to do with one of the great myths of American journalism called attribution. Somebody somewhere along the line started the rumor that a publication is not responsible for a libelous statement so long as the statement is attributed to a third person. Everybody knows that it is libelous for a newspaper to say that John Smith shot and killed his wife's lover, but for a newscaster to report that "according to the police" Smith shot and killed his wife's lover or that the police said or Capt. Jack Jones said or Prosecutor Webley Webster said that Smith shot and killed his wife's lover is somehow OK. This is absolutely not true. Attribution does not help one whit. The newscaster has republished the libel, and the law treats the bearer of tales in the same manner that it treats the author of tales.

Because of the republication rule nearly everybody in the chain of production of a news story is liable in a law suit. The reporter is liable: he wrote the story and published it when he gave it to the editor. The editor passes it along after checking it (another publication); the copy editor does the same. The story goes to the composing room, and the printers and the delivery boys—every one of them—are technically republishing the libelous remark. Nobody ever sues the kid who delivers the paper, or the copy editor, or the city editor, or the compositor. The

Identification

law releases vendors of publications from liability unless it can be shown they had knowledge of the defamatory contents. The other people at the newspaper really aren't worth suing; they don't have any money to speak of. So the publication is sued. Sue the big money. Sometimes the reporter is also named as a defendant, but rarely does he have to pay anything.

The second element in a libel suit is identification: the injured party must be identified. All sorts of nasty things can be published about anonymous people, but as soon as someone is named, or identified in some other way, a libel suit can result. Not all readers have to recognize the person about whom you write. Not even the majority of readers need know to whom you refer. Some authorities say for only a single person to identify the subject of your story is sufficient.*

A person can be identified in a number of ways. He can be named; the Knave of Hearts stole the tarts. A photograph without a name is considered identification. A person can be identified by his pen name, by his nickname, by his initials, and even by a pencil or pen drawing. Circumstances can sometimes point the finger at someone. Several years ago a New York gossip columnist wrote, "Palm Beach is buzzing with the story that one of the resort's richest men caught his blond wife in a compromising spot the other day with a former FBI agent." A man named Frederick Hope sued the Hearst Corporation (for whom the columnist worked) for libel. Hope, who was a former member of the Federal Bureau of Investigation (FBI), convinced the jury that the article identified him. He had recently joined the county attorney's staff and had been given considerable local publicity. His background as a former FBI man was given special prominence. He was also able to show that he was the only former G-man who ran with Palm Beach high society. Hope claimed that many of his friends would put these two facts together and know that the columnist referred to him. Hope won a $58,000 judgment (*Hope* v. *Hearst Corp.*, 1961).

It is also possible to put two stories together to make an identification. Imagine that this story was broadcast on Monday: "A fugitive, wanted by the FBI for bank robbery, was injured today when the automobile in which he was riding was struck by a train." No name appears

---

*This situation should not be confused with damage to the plaintiff. Only one person has to see a story for it to have been published. Some authorities (e.g., Phelps and Hamilton) also say that only one person has to identify the plaintiff. However, when a judge and jury consider whether the material is defamatory and damaging to the plaintiff, they must decide whether the statement can lower the plaintiff's reputation in the eyes of a significant minority of the community.

here, so there is no problem. Tuesday's story appears to be safe as well: "John Smith who was severely injured yesterday when the automobile in which he was riding was struck by a train. . . ." Smith can put two stories together and claim that he has been identified as the fugitive and bank robber.

If the statement does not on its face explicitly refer to the plaintiff, the plaintiff then has the burden of proving that it does refer to him, which is not usually an insurmountable burden. Extreme care must be exercised in identification when affiliations, especially business affiliations are included in a story. Comments about an executive of a corporation, the president, for example, may reflect on the prestige of the firm, and give rise to cause of action by the corporation. The corporation must prove, however, that the comments about the management discredit the business in some way.

One of the most common problems in libel is careless identification which results in a case of mistaken identity. Years ago the *Washington Post* ran a story about a District of Columbia attorney named Harry Kennedy who was brought back from Detroit to face charges of forging a client's name. The attorney charged was Harry P. L. Kennedy, a man who used his middle initials when he gave his name. The *Post* left out the middle initials. Harry F. Kennedy, another District of Columbia attorney who did not use his middle initial in business, sued the newspaper and won a substantial judgment (*Washington Post* v. *Kennedy*, 1924). This was sloppy journalism.

Most journalists learn early that complete identification is required when an individual in a news story is discussed. The identification should include the name, John Smith; the address, 2185 Pine Street; the age, 34; and if possible the occupation, carpenter. This complete identification clearly separates your John Smith from any other John Smith in the area. The number of suits which result from mistaken identity is high and most are preventable. One thing a young reporter should learn immediately is to not take anyone's word for an identification. If the police tell you they have arrested John Smith of Pine Street, you should double-check their statement. Numerous means of checking are available: city directories, utility company records, and so forth. Newspapers, broadcasting stations, and magazines are responsible even for errors which result from official blunders because they compound the error.

The most troublesome question regarding identification is group identification. Can the members of a group sue when the group as a whole is libeled? The answer to this question is not completely clear. If the group is massive—let's say the charge is that all lawyers are thieves—

there can be no suit. The group is too big for the comment to reflect on any single member of the group. If the group is small—the three-man zoning board is corrupt—each member can sue. The group is small enough so that each member can be clearly identified. What about the middle-sized group. The *Restatement of Torts* says this:

> One who publishes defamatory matter concerning a group or class of persons is subject to liability to an individual member of it, but only if (A) the group or class is so small that the matter can reasonably be understood to refer to the individual or (B) the circumstances of publication reasonably give rise to the conclusion that there is particular reference to him.

According to the *Restatement*, publication of defamatory statements about groups having more than twenty-five members are safe. However, at least one case of a group with sixty members—the University of Oklahoma football team—suing because of derogatory statements is on record. The members of the team successfully sued *True* magazine after it charged that some members of the team used drugs (*Fawcett Publications* v. *Morris*, 1962). Other authorities put the number at one hundred. If the group is smaller, there can be trouble.

Circumstances and what is said play a big part in this question. Several years ago employees of Neiman-Marcus department store in Dallas sued the publisher of a book entitled *USA Confidential* for statements in the book about the store's sales staff and models. The author of the book charged that the models and salesgirls were call girls and that most of the salesmen in the men's wear department were homosexual. Only nine models were employed in the store, and that suit was uncontested. The store had twenty-five men's wear salesmen. The article said most were "fairies," and the court allowed recovery for several individual salesmen. However, there were more than three hundred salesgirls in the store, and the federal court said the group was too large. "No reasonable man would take the writer seriously and conclude from the publication a reference to any individual saleswomen," the judge ruled (*Neiman-Marcus* v. *Lait*, 1952).

Caution must be exercised even when a very large group is dealt with if only a small number of that group lives in the community. If the charge is made that all astrologers are frauds and there is but one astrologer in the community, the remark can be dangerous. Saying "all" members of a group are corrupt is worse than saying "most" members of a group are corrupt. Saying "most" is worse than saying "some," and saying "some" is worse than saying "a couple of." The entire question remains a gray area: There are no definitive answers (as in many areas of libel). In a suit the decision is in the hands of a judge and jury who may not look at the situation in the same way the journalist does, or even in the way most judges and juries might look at the situation. Caution is urged.

Defamation

The third element in the plaintiff's case are the words themselves. There are two kinds of defamatory words. The first kind are words which are libelous on their face, words which obviously can damage the reputation of any person. Words like *thief, cheat* and *Communist*—there is no question that they are defamatory.

The second kind of words are innocent on their face and become defamatory only if the reader or viewer knows other facts. To say that Jane Adams had a baby appears safe enough. But if the reader knows that Ms. Adams isn't married, then the words are libelous.

The distinction between these two kinds of words used to be more important than it is now. Time was when the plaintiff had to prove he or she was harmed by the words in the second category. Damage was presumed from words that were libelous on their face. But the law has changed.

Now the plaintiff must show harm in both cases. This change is explained more fully in the discussion on damages. In addition, because the plaintiff must now prove negligence, the possibility also exists that the defendant can completely escape liability in the case of words which are innocent on their face. Presumably, unless the plaintiff can show that the publisher of the words was somehow negligent because he or she did not know about the existence of the facts which turned the otherwise harmless words into libel there can be no recovery.

The definition of words that are libelous is codified (by statute) in most states. These laws are most general, however, describing kinds of words (words which hold someone up to ridicule, hatred, scorn, etc.) rather than specific words. Only by looking at the numerous court decisions in libel law can one get a fairly good picture of the specific kinds of words which can be libelous. Even then the process is imprecise. The common law is a lot like a connect-the-dot picture. Connect the dots from one to fifty and you make a picture. That is what we do when we make generalizations about libel—draw lines between the various cases to make a picture. This procedure is fine so long as there are enough dots. If there aren't enough dots, the picture takes on a rather nebulous shape and is often hard to distinguish. Some parts of libel have lots of dots and are consequently well defined. Other parts don't have enough dots, and the picture is fuzzy.

There is another problem. The picture frequently changes. The meanings people attach to words change over time. Socialists were once feared and hated, and the word was defamatory. It is doubtful that calling someone a Socialist today would be libelous. Labeling someone a Communist was and is defamatory, except during the period between 1942 and 1945 when Communists were our allies in World War II. The term *slacker* seems harmless enough today, but in World War I *slacker* had a derogatory meaning: the word described someone who sought to avoid military service. Today in various subcultures in the United States some ordinary words have special meanings. Street language is a language all its own, and when a Black Panther leader proclaimed several years ago that the president should be "killed," the term *killed* had a different meaning for his audience than for the population.

At a libel trial a judge and a jury are supposed to consider words in light of their ordinary meaning unless the evidence is persuasive that the defendant meant something else when he published the statement. It is for the judge to decide whether an ambiguous statement can convey a defamatory meaning and for the jury to decide whether in fact the statement does convey that meaning. A judge can dismiss a suit without a trial if he or she believes the words cannot be considered defamatory. By letting a case go to the jury the judge is only ruling that a jury could find that the words are defamatory.

A person may be defamed in any number of ways. Simply saying that Robert Smith is the illegitimate child of John and Mary Smith is defamatory. The parents have been defamed. Implication can be used: John and Mary Smith have been married for six years and have a seven-year-old son named Robert. Some journalists think that if they don't spell a situation out, just drop subtle hints, they are on safe ground. In Massachusetts a libel case resulted when a newspaper reporter thought he smelled a rat and tried to say so subtly. Here is part of the story:

> The Veterans' Hospital here suspected that 39-year-old George M. Perry of North Turo, whose death is being probed by federal and state authorities, was suffering from chronic arsenic poisoning.
>
> State police said the body of Perry, and his brother, Arthur, who is buried near him, would probably be exhumed from St. Peter's Cemetery in Provincetown.
>
> George Perry died in the VA hospital last June 9, 48 hours after his 10th admission there. . . . His brother, who lived in Connecticut and spent two days here during George's funeral, died approximately a month later. About two months later, in September, George's mother-in-law, 74-year-old Mrs. Mary F. Mott, who had come to live with her daughter, died too. Her remains were cremated.

While the story lacked a good deal in journalistic clarity, an Ellery Queen or a Perry Mason isn't needed to get the gist of what the reporter was saying. Mrs. Perry murdered her husband, her brother-in-law, and her mother. Lizzie Borden strikes again! The insinuations are that Arthur died after visiting the plaintiff's home and that the mother had "died too." Isn't it too bad that her remains were cremated. This story cost the Hearst Corporation, publishers of the *Boston Record*, $25,000 (*Perry v. Hearst Corp.*, 1964).

A libel suit cannot be based on an isolated phrase wrenched out of context. The article as a whole must be considered. A story about baseball's legendary base stealer Maury Wills might contain the sentence "Wills might be the best thief of all time," referring to his base-stealing ability. Wills can't sue on the basis of that single sentence. The story itself makes it clear the kind of thievery the writer is discussing. Nevertheless, a libelous remark in a headline—even though it is cleared up in the story which follows—can be the basis for a libel suit. Also, a headline cannot go beyond the story and say more than the story says. "Police Nab Killer of Jane Adams" the headline proclaims. The story merely says that the police arrested John Smith and charged him with the Adams' murder. The headline goes too far.

Recently a federal court in Seattle ruled that reader habits can also be material in a libel case. Suit was brought against the *Seattle Post-Intelligencer* for a story it published about the redemption of a home mortgage by a local attorney. The headline and the first four or five paragraphs suggested that the attorney had done something illegal or unethical. The remainer of the story—which was about fifty paragraphs long and jumped from page to page after leaving the front page—explained that what the attorney had done was not illegal or unethical, that his actions were fair and aboveboard. The court admitted expert testimony on reader habits which indicated that people tend not to finish such long stories, that many people stop reading as soon as the story is continued on the inside pages of a newspaper. The plaintiff argued that in the minds of most readers the libelous opinion created by the first part of the story was not corrected since they did not finish the story. The jury awarded the attorney $100,000 in damages (*McNair v. Hearst Corp.*, 1975).

Factual statements can obviously be defamatory. What about an opinion? "I think John Smith is a rotten actor." Is that statement defamatory? Such an opinion statement clearly would have been defamatory until only a few years ago in nearly all jurisdictions. It probably remains defamatory today in many states. But because of recent Supreme Court decisions, which will be noted later in this chapter, many authorities believe that statements which contain only opinion are not actionable. The newest draft revision of the Restatement of Torts states that an opinion statement can only be defamatory if "it also expresses, or implies the assertion of a false and defamatory fact which is not known or assumed by both parties to the communication." Other experts suggest the same rule. Only time will tell if courts accept this argument and writers should use caution in publishing defamatory opinions.

The next one hundred pages could be a kind of Sears Roebuck catalog of defamatory words, but such an enumeration here is a waste of time. Instead, we will consider specific examples of the kinds of words which in the past were held to be defamatory. These examples should permit you to generalize about specific remarks. Simply ask this question when you evaluate whether something is defamatory: Will the people in the community think less of this person after I publish this story than they do before I publish it? If the answer is yes, then the statement, remark, or comment is probably defamatory.

Criminal Imputation   Probably, the category of words, more than any other, responsible for the greatest number of libel suits pertains to crime and criminal acts. Any imputation that a man or woman has done something illegal—from murder to jaywalking—is libelous. The statement can be a straightforward charge: John Smith is an arsonist or John Smith was convicted of arson. The imputation can be indirect: John Smith makes his living using matches and gasoline. The statement might note only that John Smith has spent much of his life in jail because fire fascinates him. A description might be used: John Smith went to the Fuddle Paint Company, poured gasoline on an outside wall, and then lit a match. Maybe John has a nickname—John the Torch. Each of these statements and many more which you can think of accomplish the same end: they defame poor John Smith.

It is also libelous to call John an "alleged arsonist," which points out another great myth of journalism. According to the dictionary, to allege means "to assert without proof." The police assert that John is an arsonist, and by calling him an alleged arsonist the journalist republishes the libel the police officer uttered. Republication of a libel is a new libel.

A serious problem faced by the reporter who writes or broadcasts about crime is lack of knowledge about the meaning of criminal terms. Not every killing is a homicide or murder. When John Smith kills his wife he might be acting in self-defense. Calling him a murderer creates a problem. Be certain the term used does not go beyond the action.

Sexual Slurs   It has been said that the United States is a nation overly concerned with sex. Sexual references, comments about sexual morality, sexual abnormality, and so forth, all constitute bases for libel suits. Supposedly, we are in the midst of a sexual revolution, but many people are not aware of the fact. For a woman to be sleeping with a man to whom she is not married may be perfectly normal in some parts of our society, but is still not acceptable behavior in other parts of our society. If such a charge were made against a woman, a libel suit would probably stand. Woman's virtue is strongly protected by our courts via the libel suit. In the past to merely mention that a women worked at a place where women of loose morals usually worked, like a dance hall or a saloon, was held to be defamatory. Standards are somewhat less rigid today, but any charge made in any fashion that a woman may be unchaste or may not be virtuous is dealt with harshly by a court. Charges of rape come within this category as well.

Similarly, comments about sexual abnormality are dangerous. John is gay or John is queer, Jane is a lesbian, Frank is an exhibitionist: all are defamatory remarks. Again, while we are supposedly in the throes of a new maturity with regard to homosexuality, bisexuality, trisexuality, autosexuality, and so forth, to most Americans—at least those found on most juries—such sexual behavior is repugnant and a charge of such conduct is very damaging. Caution must be exercised as well in stories about less exotic sexual concerns: calling a man impotent can be libelous. Charges of wife swapping and failure to fulfill "marital obligations" are also defamatory. Why newspapers, broadcasters, and magazines get into discussion of these topics is a mystery to many persons. When it happens be careful!

About Personal Habits and Characteristics   Much of a person's reputation is concerned with his personal habits. Is he honest, ethical, and kind? Does he pay his bills on time or is he a deadbeat? Is she clean, does she drink too much liquor, does she use dope, does she smoke pot? Statements regarding all such behavior have been and will continue to be the subject of libel suits. To call a man dishonest is defamatory. Likewise are charges that he is unkind to his children and unethical in the way he conducts his financial affairs. She drinks too much, she's a drunkard, she is always potted or smashed, she is an alcoholic, she is a member of Alcoholics Anonymous, she is on the juice, she was arrested for drunken driving: all of these charges are libelous. The same is true of statements regarding the use of drugs and marijuana. A good credit rating is very important today, therefore any charge that reflects on financial standing—the Smiths live beyond their means, they are broke, they don't pay their bills, they owe money all over town—is defamatory.

Reporters must be wary of many other aspects of personal characteristics. Imputation that a person has a certain kind of disease can be dangerous. What kinds of disease? Not a cold or the flu: anyone can have these disorders. Syphilis and gonorrhea—euphemistically called social diseases—suggest a kind of loose sexual behavior and uncleanliness frowned upon by many people. Any disease which causes a person to be shunned—contagious diseases such as smallpox and infectious hepatitis—are examples. One of the ways in which a plaintiff can prove damage to a reputation is by demonstrating that he or she has lost the ability to have personal contact with friends and other people. Mental illness is another dangerous area. To say that someone is crazy or insane or nuts is defamatory. We are becoming a bit more sophisticated in this area. While fifty years ago the charge that someone had a nervous breakdown was probably defamatory, today such a charge is probably safe unless the plaintiff can prove that the charge caused him or her some special harm such as the loss of a job. The gray area between a specific charge of insanity—he is schizophrenic—and the imputation of a nervous breakdown is broad and largely uncharted. Smith goes to a psychiatrist. Libel? Possibly. Smith has mental problems. Smith acted very strangely—Smith stood on top of a table in the cafeteria and read the Declaration of Independence. All can be problem statements. As in all areas of libel, the greatest difficulty lies in the land between clearly defamatory and clearly not defamatory. A judge decides whether the words can be considered damaging to a reputation; a jury considers whether they did damage the reputation.

About Religious Beliefs and Political Affiliations If a person professes to belong to a specific faith, a charge which reflects on his or her commitment to or acceptance by that faith can be defamatory. To say that a Catholic was denied the right of Holy Communion is a serious charge, for to most people it suggests some ghastly kind of behavior by the excommunicant. The same rule applies to political and patriotic affiliations. To charge that a person had been stripped of his or her citizenship is defamatory. Charging someone with being a traitor or a spy or with urging sedition or anarchy or revolution are all defamatory statements. Political and patriotic values change the most rapidly of all matters regarding reputation. In 1965 some persons regarded statements urging American troops to be pulled out of Vietnam almost as traitorous. (It is doubtful, however, that being labeled such an advocate would have stood as cause of action for a libel suit without proof of special harm.) Seven or eight years later almost everyone advocated that exact idea. To call someone pro-German in 1918 and 1943 was a serious and defamatory charge. It is perfectly safe to make the same charge today. What about derogatory nationalistic references? John is a Polack or a spik or a dago. These terms are probably not libelous. However, in some backwater regions of the United States to mistakenly identify a white person as being a black is still probably considered libelous. No suits of the opposite nature—a black suing for being called a white—are on record.

A person's affiliations frequently suggest a good deal about the person. Consequently, a person can be defamed by merely naming him a member of a certain group. Adams is a member of the Ku Klux Klan, the

Nazi Party, the Weather Underground, the Communist Party, or any group currently thought to be repugnant. In some cases judgments were awarded when the charge was simply that the plaintiff was employed by a group. In the 1940s the *Readers' Digest* was successfully sued because it published that an attorney was a legislative representative for the Communist Party, not that he was a Communist, but that he was employed by the Party. The court ruled that this subtle distinction was meaningless to most readers who would assume that the attorney espoused Communist beliefs (*Grant* v. *Reader's Digest Association,* 1945).

It can be libelous to ridicule someone, to make him appear foolish. Ridicule is a difficult area to describe because not all ridicule is defamatory. Many humorous stories about people have been ruled to be safe. Newspapers are frequently the victims of false obituaries, and generally courts rule that such stories are not libelous to the person alleged to have died (*Cohen* v. *New York Times,* 1912). In one case the false obituary had the deceased lying in state in a saloon (*Cardiff* v. *Brooklyn Eagle,* 1948). Other humorous kinds of accounts are generally protected.

Ridicule which can be libelous is that which makes the plaintiff appear to be uncommonly foolish, which carries a kind of sting that hurts. Everyone must die and therefore a false obituary really says nothing derogatory about the plaintiff. It is just a joke at his expense. But a story in a New England newspaper about a man so thrifty that he built his own casket and dug his own grave was ruled to be libelous ridicule. The story made the man appear to be foolish, weird, and unnatural. A fifty dollar judgment was awarded (*Powers* v. *Durgin-Snow Publishing Co.,* 1958). How can reporters tell the difference between the two kinds of stories? The distinction is often very difficult. Extreme care is needed to avoid problems.

About Business Reputation   Thus far the kinds of charges that can injure almost any person, hurt his reputation, cause him to lose friends, have been discussed. The law goes beyond these limits in protecting individuals; it goes to the point of protecting both men and women in their business or occupation. Any comment which injures a person's ability to conduct a business or occupation successfully can be considered defamatory. For example, comments about business ethics can be defamatory. Sid, the butcher, sells tainted meat. Archie, the mechanic, overcharges his customers. Similarly, statements about competence to do a job can be defamatory. Milton lacks the skill to be an architect. Doris, the nurse, can't tell a bedpan from a baby bottle. Comments about honesty, about the financial solvency of a businessman—anything which tends to impair an individual's means of making a livelihood or discredits him in his business or profession—can be the basis for a successful libel suit.

Professional people, people whose integrity is very important to their job, can be defamed more easily than, for example, an auto mechanic or switchboard operator. Saying that a switchboard operator is almost illiterate is not nearly so damaging as saying a teacher or a doctor is almost illiterate. Calling a physician a quack, a charlatan, a butcher, or an incompetent is clearly defamatory. Reporting that a surgeon operated unnecessarily on a patient suggests either incompetence or lack of ethics. Referring to an attorney as a shyster or an ambulance chaser is equally dangerous. Teachers, doctors, journalists, businessmen, lawyers, and many other persons are very easily defamed by comments about their business or occupation. The law does provide some exceptions. For example, the law does not presume that people think that business or professional people are perfect. Therefore, to report that a professional person or a business person has made an error is not always defamatory. It depends upon how the statement is made. If the statement merely suggests that the individual made an isolated mistake—Dr. John Smith operated on Jane Adams yesterday to remove a sponge he failed to remove during an earlier operation on Ms. Adams—it is probably not libelous. However, if the published comment suggests a pattern of incompetence—this is the fifth time in the past two years Dr. Smith had to operate a second time to remove a surgical tool left in a patient—the statement clearly is defamatory. Be careful in this area. Recourse to this rule is never an excuse for clumsy or careless journalism. This rule (called by some the single mistake rule) is not constructed upon an unassailable foundation.

Also, if a person practices his profession *illegally* reference to him as unskilled or incompetent is not defamatory. A person who practices medicine without a license can be called a quack with little danger. Finally, a journalist can be critical of a person who engages in an *illegal* occupation. If John Smith is a hit man for the local crime syndicate, it is not libelous to call him an *incompetent* hit man, a lousy killer, or whatever.

One other kind of "businessmen" can sue if they are improperly criticized: government officials and politicians. It is much harder to libel government officials and candidates for elective office than, say, doctors. Nevertheless charges of corruption, bribery, vote buying, gross dereliction of duty, and graft can all stand as the basis for a successful libel action. Accusing a judge of being biased and unfair, accusing the head of the street department of improperly maintaining the public roads, and accusing a public official of selling out to the mob are all defamatory charges.

While a person's general reputation is fairly nebulous, the individual's right to earn a living, practice a profession, successfully operate a business, and so forth, are quite specific. Courts are prone to protect them from unwarranted attack. Journalists and broadcasters must exercise caution in dealing with such subjects lest they inadvertently damage that right.

About a Business   In addition to damaging a person, a defamatory statement can injure a business or corporation. A corporation can maintain a lawsuit when it believes its credit has been damaged or its reputation has been hurt. The same kinds of words that can defame an individual can also defame a corporation or business. Any assertion that the corporation has engaged in criminal activity, is dishonest, has ties to organized crime, lacks integrity, fails to pay its bills on time, and so forth, can be libelous. Corporations can be hurt in other ways as well.

An assertion that the corporation makes unsafe products—not that the products are unsafe, but that the corporation deliberately produces unsafe products to cut costs—can result in a libel suit. Statements which reflect on the company's labor policies—management runs a real sweatshop, takes advantage of its workers, violates labor laws—are libelous. Attacks on fiscal integrity (better not buy a car from Acme Motors because chances are good that the company won't be around next year to fix the car when it breaks) are defamatory. An assertion that DooDad Industries does not maintain safe working conditions, or that the company makes illegal political contributions, or that it cheats its customers is libelous to that business.

Some authorities assert that making derogatory statements about persons who manage a business, who work at a business, or who are customers of a business can also be used as the basis for a defamation suit. The law is not settled in this area. Publishing nasty things about the president and vice-president of DooDad Industries will not give the corporation the right to sue unless it can be proved that such statements actually damaged the reputation of the company. Reporting that DooDad employes are "a bunch of louts" might also serve as the basis for a damage suit if the company can prove that the charge somehow reflects on the corporation's ability to hire the proper people.

There is little chance, however, that a corporation can sue merely because of actions or behavior of its customers. Several years ago Louis Stillman sued Paramount Pictures for the remark in the motion picture *Country Girl* that punch-drunk fighters frequented Stillman's Gym in New York City. Stillman argued that the remark reflected upon him and his business. The court disagreed (*Stillman* v. *Paramount Pictures,* 1957). Proprietors of public businesses have no control over the kinds of persons who use their establishments. Therefore, readers should not think anything less of Stillman because punch-drunk fighters might be training in his gym. Another example of the problem is a story that for the second time in two weeks a fight broke out at a local tavern last night. Again, the proprietor does not have much control over who drinks in his tavern and what happens when they drink. Any implication that the owner of the place encourages this kind of behavior, condones it, fails to call authorities after it starts, and so forth, will, of course, change the nature of the remark and can be libelous.

What about remarks concerning a private club? There is no good answer to this question. There is clearly more danger in discussing a private club which can control membership than in reporting about a public club which cannot. Probably the nature of the remark is what counts. The danger of libel lurks here.

About a Product   Criticism of a product falls into a different legal category called disparagement of property. While such cricicism is often called trade libel, it is not really libel at all but product disparagement. What is the difference? A plaintiff finds it significantly harder to win a trade libel case than to win a garden-variety libel suit. First, consider some examples of trade libel. Bango Rifles fail to eject empty cartridges. Crumo Bread gets stale in one day. DooDad Motorcycles fail to stop within a safe distance. The remarks are aimed at the products, not at the companies. There is no implication that the manufacturer intentionally makes a bad product, tries to cheat customers, or conducts its business fraudulently. DooDad may make the best motorcycles it can make; they just turn out to be unsafe.

Since the company itself is not presumed to be hurt, the law raises some stiff barriers to a successful trade libel suit. First, the plaintiff, the manufacturer of the product, must prove that the statement is untrue. Proof is difficult, but not too difficult for the kinds of statements just given. If DooDad is able to demonstrate to the court that some of its motorcycles brake to a stop within a safe distance, the company then shows the falsity of the charge. It is much safer to refer to individual products. For example, rather than say that DooDad Motorcycles don't stop safely, report that of the ten motorcycles tested none stopped safely, or that of the Bango Rifles tested none ejected cartridges properly. The manufacturer will then have to refute this evidence, not merely find examples of his product which are in good working order.

Next, the plaintiff will have to show special damage—actual monetary loss because of the comments. Loss of orders attributable to the unfavorable report is such evidence, and testimony from potential customers who failed to purchase the maligned product because of the comment can be used to support the damage claim. Finally, the plaintiff has to prove what is called malice (malice is discussed in some depth later in the chapter). For the time-being, malice can be defined as ill will, bad feeling, and gross carelessness. The plaintiff can prove malice if he can show that the negative remarks were published "to get him" and that the writer doesn't like him. The plaintiff might also be able to show malice by demonstrating that the writer was grossly negligent in checking the truth of the statement. Before the plaintiff can collect for trade libel he must prove all three charges: falsity, damage, and malice.

Evaluate the following three statements on the basis of the foregoing discussion of trade libel:

1. DooDad autos are superior to Acme cars.
2. Acme cars stop running after about one year.
3. Acme cars stop running after about one year because the company has a plan to force customers to buy a new car every year.

Is statement one libelous? It contains no libel, no disparagement, no anything. Nothing negative was said about Acme; only a positive statement about DooDad cars was made. Statement two? This statement is trade libel, an attack upon the product. Statement three? Here we have garden-variety libel. The comment states that Acme purposefully sells automobiles that break down after one year and reflects upon the integrity of the business itself.

About Banks and Insurance Companies   One other point should be made before we leave this topic. In addition to the protections businesses and corporations have against libel, many states have laws which prohibit critical and untrue comments about banks, insurance companies, and other such organizations. What these laws are designed to do is to protect such organizations from attack upon their fiscal integrity to avoid turning customers against them and destroying them. After all, a bank has only its fiscal integrity and other people's money to sell.

Suits under such statutes are rare, but occasionally they do occur. And then the newspaper or broadcasting station soon discovers that the many protections the press enjoys in a libel suit often do not apply when a suit is brought under such a law. Check the insurance laws and the banking laws in your state. If such laws exist, find out how the courts interpreted the laws. This check might save a lot of grief some time in the future.

Negligence

Until 1974 defamation law was governed by the doctrine of strict liability, which meant that in a libel suit all the plaintiff needed to prove was that the material was published, that he or she was identified, and that the comment or story was defamatory. In most other areas of tort law plaintiffs were bound to prove negligence on the part of the defendant before damages could be collected. This was not true in libel. When publication, identification, and defamation were proved, regardless of how the defendant prepared his story and of how many checks for accuracy he made, and no matter how cautious he was, the defendant was held responsible and could defeat the lawsuit only if there was a defense (such as truth or fair comment) for publication of the libel.

New Fault Requirement In 1974 the Supreme Court ruled that a plaintiff cannot win a libel suit unless there is evidence of negligence on the part of the defendant. This ruling was made in *Gertz* v. *Welch,* a decision which had a major impact upon the law of libel in many ways. (Discussion of the facts and other aspects of the ruling in this case is postponed until a later section of the chapter where it is more appropriate. However, the curious will find a discussion of *Gertz* v. *Welch* on page 149.) The Supreme Court reinforced its ruling in *Gertz* early in 1976 in *Time, Inc.* v. *Firestone* when it sent a Florida case back for trial on the negligence question. It became clear in the *Firestone* case as well that the high Court considers negligence to be a question of fact, a question to be determined by juries (or by judges if they are the fact finders in nonjury trials), not a question of law to be determined by judges.

A plaintiff can seek to prove negligence in many ways. For example, a plaintiff can attempt to show that there was negligence in publication: the story was erroneously published; it was meant to be thrown in a wastebasket and instead found its way into a stack of copy. The publisher might have been negligent in attempting to determine the truth or falsity of the publication. He might have been negligent in evaluating the defamatory nature of the words. The negligence might have been mechanical, a typographical error that someone should have caught. The negligence might have been in identification, a case of mistaken identity due to lack of a good description of the real subject of the story.

One of the questions yet to be resolved following *Gertz* regards the standard of fault or negligence which the Supreme Court determined should be used. Justice Lewis Powell made no real mention of this question in his opinion for the Court. Negligence is defined in the law as conduct which creates an unreasonable risk of harm. The standard of conduct used as the yardstick is the conduct of a reasonable person. What would a reasonable person do in the same circumstances as the defendant? Are there reasonable grounds to believe the story to be true? Did the defendant act reasonably in not checking this detail? What would another newspaper editor or broadcast news reporter do in the same circumstances?

It is assumed that most states will use this kind of negligence standard in determining fault. The state of Washington, for example, has adopted a "reasonable care" standard which says that in publishing the statement the defendant in the exercise *of reasonable care* should have known that the statement was false or would create a false impression (*Taskett* v. *King Broadcasting*, 1976).

According to the 1974 Supreme Court decision negligence is a minimum fault standard. States can require plaintiffs to meet a more rigorous standard. For example, a state can insist that a plaintiff prove that the defendant was grossly negligent in publishing the material, which is a more unreasonable conduct than the simple negligence or reasonable care standard just described. A state can require that the plaintiff prove that the defendant acted in reckless disregard of the plaintiff's rights, that the defendant entertained serious doubts as to the truth of the matter or entertained serious doubts as to whether the story referred to the plaintiff or to another person with the same name.

States may also choose to adopt a variable fault standard, that is, require proof of negligence in cases involving stories about private affairs, but a higher standard of fault in cases based upon stories dealing with matters of public concern or of public importance. As of September 1976 the following states have adopted a variable fault standard: Maryland (*General Motors* v. *Piskor,* 1975), Colorado (*Walker* v. *Colorado Springs Sun, Inc.,* 1975), Indiana (*AAFCO Heating and Air Conditioning* v. *Northwest Publications,* 1974), New York (*Commercial Programming Unlimited* v. *CBS,* 1975), and Arizona (*Peagler* v. *Phoenix Newspapers, Inc.,* 1976). In these five states plaintiffs bringing libel suits based upon stories which deal with issues of public concern or public importance must prove that the defendant knew the statements were false when he or she published them or had serious doubts as to the truth or falsity of the material. This standard is called actual malice (examined in greater depth when the First Amendment libel defense is discussed shortly). All other libel plaintiffs in those five states, that is, persons bringing suit based on material which has no public concern or public interest, must prove only simple negligence—that the defendant did not exercise reasonable care in determining the truth or falsity of the material. For example, if an Indiana newspaper mistakenly published that John Smith was arrested for blocking construction of a nuclear power plant, Smith has to prove actual malice—the defendant knew the story was false or had serious doubts as to whether it was true. But if the same newspaper mistakenly wrote that John Smith was overdue in payment of several bills, Smith need only prove negligence. A purely private matter is in question here, and the story contains nothing of public importance. The states are beginning to decide which kinds of standards they want to apply to libel plaintiffs. Students should discover what the courts in their state have decided on this important question.

What kinds of measures are used to determine negligence? What is reasonable care? These questions remain largely unanswered at this time. Despite the constant claim that journalism is a profession, it has few professional standards. Its few codes of ethics, promulgated by such groups as the American Society of Newspaper Editors and the Society of Professional Journalists, are vague and have no sanctions. At best journalism can be called a craft, and its standards vary from medium to medium and among individual units within a medium. The *New York Times* probably has higher standards than most American newspapers. The television network news departments probably have higher standards than do news departments at most local stations. The situation is due partly to wealth: the richer media can afford to do more checking. A magazine editor has more time to check a story than a daily newspaper editor has. A television documentary team has more time to verify details than does the producer of the nightly news. The question becomes this: The standard of conduct will be that of reasonable care. But what is reasonable journalistic care? What standards do we use? Perhaps the courts will measure the conduct of media defendants against the conduct of other persons in the same medium—the stories of one magazine editor against those of another, the films of one television documentary team against those of another team. Courts will probably use expert testimony to evaluate some of these matters, but there is little agreement on matters in some areas. In law, for example, the lawyer is obligated to investigate if he thinks his client's claim in a lawsuit is fraudulent. Furthermore, the lawyer has the time to investigate. What about the editor who, the day before an election, gets a report—attested to by two independent sources—that a candidate for mayor has taken bribes? Does he publish the story? Should he check it further? What is the editor's obligation to the candidate? What is the editor's obligation to the public? to the voters? What is reasonable care? Only time can help define these standards as courts try lawsuits using the new negligence rules.

Impact of New Fault Requirement   The new fault requirement will obviously have some impact upon the law of libel. How much remains to be seen. Some authorities argue that the impact will be minimal. Older judges, who are used to the strict liability doctrine, will not like the new rules and will define negligence in a way exceedingly simple for the plaintiff to prove. Other authorities argue that if they believe a plaintiff has been harmed juries will find publishers guilty regardless of whether evidence of negligence is sufficient. There may be a tendency to infer negligence if a defamatory falsehood has been published. It is not yet known whether a finding of negligence is a "constitutional fact," as is the finding of reckless disregard, and subject to appellate review. If it is not, and if the finding of fault by the jury is final, this new requirement may indeed not have as great an impact as some journalists now hope. One commentator, writing in the *Brooklyn Law Review,* states:

> A jury's propensity for punishing objectionable opinion may in practice undermine the court's insistence on a fault standard of liability for media defamation; via the flexibility of the negligence concept itself, a jury may easily find the publisher has failed to act reasonably in printing such a libel. The defendant, therefore, may yet be liable in damages not for harm done to the plaintiff on a valid complaint, but rather, for defendant's expression of an unpopular view.

The initial aspects of the plaintiff's case have now been considered. To this point the burden of proof has been on the plaintiff, who must prove publication, identification, defamation, and negligence. If the plaintiff is unable to prove any of the preceding charges, the suit ends. The defendant then normally asks that the case be dismissed, and the judge normally complies if the requisite evidence is lacking.

DEFENSE OF CIVIL LIBEL

The defendant does not automatically lose the lawsuit even though the plaintiff has established a case, that is, met his burden of proof. The defendant has the opportunity to convince the court that he or she had a legally acceptable reason for publishing the defamation, has what is called a defense. There are two kinds of libel defenses: common law defenses and constitutional defenses. Under common law defenses are defense of truth, privilege of the reporter, fair comment, and one or two minor defenses. The First Amendment is the only constitutional defense. Before the substantive defenses for libel are considered, it is appropriate to consider one other defense which offers publishers complete immunity in a libel action—the statute of limitations.

Statute of Limitations

For nearly all crimes and most civil actions there is a statute of limitations. Courts don't like stale legal claims. They have plenty of fresh ones to keep them busy. Prosecution for most crimes except homicide and kidnapping must be started within a specified period of time. For example, in many states if prosecution is not started within seven years after an armed robbery is committed, the robber cannot be brought to trial. He or she is home free. (However, the robber can still be prosecuted for failing to pay income tax on money taken from a bank, but that is another story.)

The statute of limitations for libel differs from state to state, varying from one to five years. In most states the limitation is two or three years, which means the lawsuit must be started (not completed, just started) within two or three years. Assume the following events take place in a state whose statute of limitations is two years. *Scam Magazine* libels Jane Adams in its October 1975 edition. Ms. Adams must bring suit before October 1977 or the statute of limitations will preclude her suing. The republication rule plays a part here. What happens if somebody visits the *Scam* offices in August of 1977 and buys a back issue, the October 1975 issue, of the magazine? In many states buying a back issue is considered new publication, and the statute of limitations starts over. More and more jurisdictions have rejected this rule and substituted the single publication rule. This rule states that the entire edition of a newspaper or magazine is a single publication and that isolated sales in the months or years to come do not constitute republication. Therefore the statute of limitations starts on the day the edition hit the newsstands and ends two or three or five years later. The statute cannot be reactivated by a later sale. About half the states have this progressive rule. Find out if your state does.

Common Law Defense

Truth

A truthful statement does not stand as a cause of action for libel. It is true that in a handful of states the law says that only truthful statements published for justifiable ends or with good motives are protected. As we have noted, appellate courts are overturning these laws as being in violation of the First Amendment. Such a law was declared null and void in Illinois, for example, in 1969 (*Farnsworth* v. *Tribune Co.*).

The words may be defamatory, they may harm the reputation of the plaintiff, but the injured party will lose his or her case if the statement is true. Sounds nice, doesn't it? But hold on a minute. In a libel suit the law presumes that the libelous statement is false, that it is not true. It is up to the defendant to convince the jury that what he or she has published is the truth. Truth of the statement is not something that the plaintiff must refute. If the plaintiff can demonstrate there was a libel, there was publication, there was identification, and there was negligence, the defendant has to prove the truth of the statement. And that is not always easy to do. What is provable in court is often far less than what a reporter knows to be true. Judge Leon Yankwich (*It's Libel or Contempt If You Print It*) once wrote, "Libel lurks in vague general charges and inferences. Easy to make, they are the most difficult to prove." A specific charge—John stole a car—is often far easier to prove than a general statement—John is a thief. The problem of proving the truth is more complex than this, however.

Many people who are willing to tell a reporter something in confidence are frequently reluctant to repeat the charge in public. They may fear for their safety or their job. Often to reveal the truth publicly may compromise their reputation. Some people make bad courtroom witnesses. People with criminal records or other stains upon their past are often easily impeached as witnesses by clever attorneys for the plaintiff. Sometimes witnesses cannot be found; they have left the community or have died. What the reporter has seen and heard himself or herself is usually persuasive testimony. But remember, the plaintiff may tell the jury a different story, and the case can come down to which party is the more credible witness. Libel defendants therefore don't often rely on truth. Many other better defenses, defenses easier to use in court are available. Nevertheless it is important to know the dimensions of this defense.

To prove the truth the evidence presented in court must be as broad as the libelous charge. The proof must be direct and explicit; it must go to the whole charge. If there is conflicting evidence, the judge or the jury (whichever is the fact finder) decides who is telling the truth. If the *River City Sentinel* publishes that John Smith operates a fraudulent business, proving that Smith once cheated a customer will likely not convince a court of the truth of the libelous charge. The published charge suggested a pattern of cheating or continuous cheating. Similarly, if a broadcaster asserts that Mayor Smith is a wife beater, evidence that he once slapped her in a fit of rage probably will not establish the truth of the assertion.

You are not required to prove every word of the defamatory charge, just the main charge, the part that carries the sting or the gist of the libel. John Smith is a violent man, you report. He likes to beat people, to hit them with clubs and chains and rocks. It will not damage your argument if you can't prove that Smith hit people with rocks so long as you can prove that he hit them with chains and clubs.

Similarly, extraneous errors will not destroy the defense. A newspaper reports that Jane Adams was arrested by city police last night about nine o'clock while driving a stolen 1976 Buick on Main Street.

The fact that Ms. Adams was arrested at ten o'clock while driving a stolen 1976 Pontiac on Elm Street will probably not materially affect the defense. The gist of the charge—that she was arrested while driving a stolen car—can be proved.

How does the court evaluate whether the defendant successfully proved the truth of the charge. The jury does this with guidance from the judge. The judge will probably give the jury a test to use in evaluating the evidence against the defamatory charge. One of the commonly used tests comes from a 1934 New York case, *Fleckstein* v. *Friedman.* Defendant Benny Friedman, a former all-star professional football player, charged that some of the players in the National Football League were sadists and bullies. Friedman named names in his *Collier's* magazine story, and one of the players identified, William Fleckstein, sued.

In attempting to prove the truth of the charge, Friedman demonstrated some of the tactics used by these rough players. In instructing the jury in this case, the judge said:

> . . . a workable test of truth is whether the libel as published would have a different effect on the mind of the reader from that which the pleaded truth would have produced. When truth is so near to the facts as published that fine and shaded distinctions must be drawn and words pressed out of their ordinary usage to sustain a charge of libel, no legal harm has been done.

In simpler terms this is what the court said: After reading the article, readers were left with a certain opinion of William Fleckstein, a negative opinion since he was called a bully and a sadist in the story. Now, if persons who had not seen the story had a similar opinion of Fleckstein after seeing the evidence Friedman presented in court, Friedman then succeeded in proving his charges. The point here is a lot simpler than it sounds, but it is something which should be understood. The proof must be as broad as the charge; the evidence presented in court must leave the reader with the same impression of the plaintiff as did the defamatory charge.

One more point should be stressed about truth. Correctly quoting someone or accurately reporting what someone else has told you does not constitute proof of the truth of the charge. Imagine that John Smith tells a reporter that the police chief changes arrest records of certain prisoners to simplify their getting bail and winning acquittal. This charge, attributed to John Smith, is contained in the reporter's story which is subsequently published. The police chief sues for libel. It is not sufficient for the reporter to prove merely that the statement in his story was an accurate copy of what Smith said. Even if the reporter's story contained an exact duplicate of Smith's charge, truth can be sustained only by proving the substance of the charge, that the police chief has altered arrest records. A newspaper or broadcasting station is responsible for proving the truth of a libelous charge, not merely of the accuracy of the quote in the story. Accuracy, then, is not always the same thing as truth.

Privilege of the Reporter

Traditionally in the United States we value robust debate as a means of discovering those elusive truths which we continually pursue. The law takes pains to protect this debate, making sure that speakers are not unduly punished for speaking their minds. Article 1, Section 6, of the federal Constitution provides that a member of the Congress is immune from suit based on his or her remarks on the floor of either house. This is called a privilege. The statement in question is referred to as a privileged communication.

Today, privilege attaches to a wide variety of communications and speakers. Anyone speaking in a legislative forum, congressmen, senators, state representatives, city councilpersons, and so forth, enjoy this privilege. Even the statements of witnesses at legislative hearings are privileged. Similarly, the privilege attaches to communications made in judicial forums—courtrooms, grand jury rooms, and so forth. Judges, lawyers, witnesses, defendants, plaintiffs, and all other persons are protected so long as the remark is uttered during the official portions of the hearing or the trial. Finally, persons who work in the administrative and executive branches of government enjoy privilege as well. Presidents, mayors, governors, department heads—official communications or official statements by these kinds of persons are privileged. In 1959 in *Barr* v. *Mateo* the Supreme Court suggested that the privilege applies to any publication by a government official which is in line with the discharge of his or her official duty. This case involved a press release from a department head explaining why two federal employees had been fired. "A publicly expressed statement of the position of the agency head," the Court ruled, "announcing personnel action which he planned to take in reference to the charges so widely disseminated to the public was an appropriate exercise of the discretion which an officer of that rank must possess if the public service is to function effectively."

This is an absolute privilege. The speaker cannot be sued for defamation on the basis of such a remark.

A similar kind of a privilege applies also to certain kinds of private communications. Discussions between an employer and an employee are privileged; the report of a credit rating is privileged; a personnel recommendation by an employer about an employee is privileged. These kinds of private communications remain privileged so long as they are not disseminated beyond the sphere of those who need to know. For example, an employer can write a negative evaluation about your job skills and pass that along to another prospective employer if asked to do so. The evaluation is privileged. But the employer cannot show that evaluation to others in the office or publish it in the company newsletter. Such action destroys the privilege.

The privilege goes far beyond the absolute immunity granted to speakers at public and official meetings and the conditional immunity applied to certain types of private communication. The press is granted a qualified or conditional privilege to report what happens at official governmental meetings and other meetings open to the public. This is how the privilege is outlined in the newly adopted second edition of the *Restatement of Torts*:

> The publication of defamatory matter concerning another in a report of any official proceeding or any meeting open to the public which deals with matters of public concern is conditionally privileged if the report is accurate and complete, or a fair abridgement of what has occurred.

This means that a libel suit premised upon such a publication will not stand. While technically the press has no special privileges in the law of defamation, in actual operation of the law this privilege is invoked so infrequently on behalf of anyone other than the press that it is generally regarded to be a privilege of the press. In fact, this privilege is sometimes called the privilege of the reporter, as opposed to the absolute immunity noted earlier which is referred to as the privilege of the participant.

There is much to discuss about this privilege. Perhaps the most important point which needs to be made is that it is a *conditional* privilege. That is, the privilege of the reporter works as a defense in a libel suit only if certain conditions are met. First, the privilege applies only to reports of certain kinds of meetings, generally meetings of governmental bodies, public meetings on issues of public importance, and other public proceedings. Second, the privilege applies only to reports which are a fair and accurate or truthful summary of what occurred at the meeting. Third, publication of a report cannot be motivated by malice such as ill will. Extreme carelessness in preparation of the report can also defeat the privilege. However, if the meeting is the kind covered by the privilege, if the report is a fair and true summary of what took place at the meeting, and if there is no malice in the report, the conditional privilege then provides absolute protection for the press. It will totally defeat a libel suit.

The defendant bears the burden of proving that the privilege applies to the libelous material. The court determines whether the particular occasion (meeting or proceeding) is privileged. The jury determines whether the defendant's story is a fair and accurate report. Each of these elements needs closer scrutiny. Let us, therefore, focus now on meetings and proceedings said to be privileged.

The privilege applies at the very least to a report of all official proceedings of a governmental agency. Some authorities contend that it also applies to all public meetings at which matters of public concern are discussed (more on this in a moment). The qualified privilege applies to official proceedings of the legislative branch of government, to the judicial branch, and to the executive branch. Let's look at each briefly.

Legislatures   Quite obviously, the privilege applies to meetings of organizations like Congress, state legislatures, city councils, county councils, and so forth. The privilege also applies to the reports of meetings of committees of such organizations, as well as to stories about petitions, complaints, and other communications received by these bodies. The only requirement which must be met in regard to this aspect of the privilege is that the official body, such as a city council, must officially receive the complaint or petition before the privilege applies. If the Citizens for Cleaner Streets bring a petition charging the street superintendent with incompetence and various and sundry blunders in his job to a city council meeting, publication of these charges is privileged as soon as the city council officially accepts the petition. Nothing has to be done with the document. It must merely be accepted.

Whether the privilege applies to stories about the news conferences of members of a legislative body following a session, to stories about what was said during a closed meeting by the body, and to what was said during an informal gathering of legislators before or after the regular session remains somewhat unclear. Robert Phelps and E. Douglas Hamilton in their book *Libel* suggest that if what is said or what occurs during these kinds of events is of great public interest and there is a compelling public need to know the privilege then likely applies. This contention rests more upon "educated" common sense than upon case law, and caution should be exercised in reporting what occurred at closed meetings, informal meetings, and press conferences.

The Courts   The privilege of the reporter also applies to actions which take place in judicial forums: testimony of witnesses, arguments of attorneys, pronouncements of judges, and so forth. Stories about trials, decisions, jury verdicts, court opinions, judicial orders and decrees, and grand jury indictments are all protected by the privilege.

Probably the most serious problem a reporter on the court beat has to face is what to do when a lawsuit is initially filed. Under our legal system a lawsuit is started when a person files a complaint with a court clerk and serves a summons on the defendant. The complaint is filled with charges, most of which are usually libelous. Can a reporter use that complaint as the basis for a story?

This is a tricky question. In most states the complaint is not privileged until a judge takes action on the suit. Scheduling a hearing is sufficient. Oliver Wendell Holmes, later Justice Holmes, wrote in 1884, "It is enough to mark the plain distinction between what takes place in open court, and that which is done out of court by one party alone, or more exactly, as we have already said, the contents of a paper filed . . . in the clerk's office." This makes good sense. John Smith doesn't like Jane Adams, so he files a phony lawsuit against her in which he charges her with defrauding him of $10,000. The paper publishes the charges, and the next day Smith withdraws his suit. The only reason he filed the suit was to have his phony charges publicized. In most states the initial complaint in a civil suit is not privileged until some judicial action has been taken.

In a few states this is not the rule; the complaint is privileged as soon as it is placed on file with the clerk and the summons has been served.

One further word of caution. The privilege applies only to reports of what is said and done during the official proceeding—during the trial, for example. What the judge tells the reporter in the hallway after the trial is not privileged. Similarly what an attorney tells the journalist over a brew at the local pub is not protected either.

Stories about those parts of the judicial process which are closed to public view are also not protected by the privilege. Frequently, court sessions for juveniles and divorce proceedings are closed in order to further a public policy. The legislature or the courts feel obligated to discourage publicity about what occurs during such hearings. A few years ago the *New York Daily News* published a series of articles about a sensational divorce case, one in which the wife accused the husband of keeping a harem of women in a private plane which he used for business (and pleasure?) trips. When the husband sued the newspaper for libel, the *Daily News* argued that it had taken its report directly from court records and trial testimony.

In New York, however, divorce proceedings are closed to the public. The state's high court ruled that the legislature deemed it to be in the public interest to close divorce proceedings to public scrutiny (*Shiles* v. *News Syndicate Co.*, 1970):

> Since, then, such matrimonial actions were and are not proceedings which the public had the right to hear and see, it follows—and it has been consistently held—that the privilege generally accorded to reports of judicial proceedings is unavailable to reports of matrimonial actions.

Governmental Executives and Administrators Reports of the statements and proceedings conducted by mayors, department heads, and other persons in the administrative and executive branches of government are generally privileged. The law lacks the clarity here, however, that it has with regard to legislatures and courts. Some authorities suggest there is a broad privilege for the published accounts of the actions, statements, and reports of government officials. Others say the privilege is limited. Probably the best guideline is that the privilege is confined to stories about actions or statements which are official in nature, the kinds of things which are substantially "acts of state." By law administrators are required to prepare certain reports and to hold certain hearings, and the privilege certainly covers stories on these activities. Although not required by law, other actions are unmistakably part of the job. Reports on these affairs are undoubtedly protected as well. Questions arise when the executive or administrator gets off into places where he probably doesn't belong. A mayor is supposed to do many things, but he is not the public prosecutor. Therefore, a statement by the mayor at a press conference that John Smith runs a fraudulent insurance business is probably not privileged.

Reports of police activities also fall under the heading of executive actions, but the privilege is applied sparingly here. It is fairly well settled that a report that a person has been arrested and charged with a crime is privileged. The arrest and charge is a public kind of event. All the additional information the police and prosecutor are wont to give the press—how the crime was committed, statements by witnesses, circumstances surrounding the arrest—is clearly not protected by the privilege. The police really go beyond their authority in making such statements and frequently defame the suspect in the process. Remember, the police never arrest an innocent person, and they think that what they tell you is the truth. If that were the case, we wouldn't need trials. The suspect is presumed to be innocent until proved guilty. A statement published by a newspaper or broadcast over a television station that the defendant "shot and killed the bank manager, according to police" is libelous and practically indefensible if the defendant is acquitted of the crime. You have to prove what the state cannot, that the plaintiff who is suing you is a killer.

The law is somewhat benevolent with the press when it comes to problems involving official actions which have all the appearances of legality, but which turn out to be illegal: a hearing that is improperly conducted and turns out to be illegal, a trial in which the presiding judge lacks jurisdiction, an arrest that is illegally made, and so forth. Journalists are not expected to know more than the public officials about whom they write, and consequently reports of such activities remain privileged, despite the fact the proceeding or the event turned out to be less than official.

Other Public Concerns   The privilege of the reporter is not confined only to those instances of reporting official government proceedings. How far beyond such proceedings the privilege does apply is by no means settled. Books published no more than ten or fifteen years ago declared quite authoritatively that the privilege was limited to reports about official governmental proceedings. There were a few court decisions to the contrary. In 1956, for example, an Idaho court ruled that the privilege applied to a story about a meeting called by citizens to protest the actions of a judge. It clearly was not an official meeting, but concerned important public business, the conduct of a public official. The court said, "There is a general doctrine that what is said at a public meeting, at which any person of the community or communities involved might have attended and heard and seen for himself, is conditionally privileged for publication" (*Borg* v. *Boas,* 1956). That might have been a general doctrine in Idaho in 1956. It was not a general doctrine in most of the nation.

Since then the authorities—those mysterious beings who tell us what the law says—have moved much closer to the Idaho position. The *Restatement of Torts,* which traditionally takes a conservative position on the law, says flatly that reports of what occurs at meetings open to the public at which matters of public concern are discussed are privileged. Paul Ashley, libel authority and author of *Say It Safely,* (1976), says that the privilege probably applies to a public meeting even though admission is charged, so long as everyone is free to pay the price. "By supplying them with information about public events," Ashley writes, "the publisher is acting as the 'eyes and ears' of people who did not attend."

In such a circumstance, the report of a public meeting, the key element undoubtedly is the subject of debate. Was it of public concern? Was it of limited public concern? Was it a purely private matter? Using the standard of public concern, we can look at some kinds of nonofficial public meetings and try to determine whether the privilege applies.

1. Meeting of local Rotary Club: probably of private concern; not privileged
2. Meeting of board of directors of United Fund: of public concern; privileged
3. Meetings of local bar association or medical society: of limited public concern; privileged
4. Meeting of stockholders of General Motors Company: about private business and of private concern; not privileged
5. Meeting of county Democratic party: of public concern; privileged

At this point how far the privilege will extend in protecting nonofficial public meetings cannot be said. Traditionally each state handles this problem differently, and therefore you should seek guidance from local statutes and court decisions. The privilege is clearly being extended to gatherings outside the official governmental sphere.

Abuse of Privilege Whether the privilege applies to a particular story is only part of the problem. There is also the question of whether the privilege was abused.

A jury might find that abuse occurred in one of two ways: (1) the publisher used the privilege as a shield in order to attack the plaintiff or (2) the story was not really a fair and accurate account of what took place at the meeting, was not a fair summary of the court's ruling, or did not give a fair and accurate account of the conclusion of the official report.

The first type of abuse is called malice. The purpose of the privilege is to foster public understanding of what is happening, to allow wide public exposure of what takes place at a public meeting, in a public trial, or at a public session of the legislature. If fostering public understanding was not the primary purpose of the publication, if the publisher or broadcaster instead sought to harm the person defamed at the hearing or trial or in the report, and if publication was motivated by ill will and not by serving the public good, the privlege was then abused. Once the defendant has successfully convinced the court that the privilege should apply, it is up to the plaintiff to show its abuse. This is not an easy task, but it can be done. By showing previous ill will on the part of the publisher, the plaintiff might be able to establish an "evil" state of mind and convince a jury that publication was made to hurt him, not to inform the public. There are other ways as well. In some instances gross negligence (not simple negligence, which was discussed earlier) was used to demonstrate abuse of the privilege. In other words, extreme carelessness, gross carelessness, in preparing the story might destroy the privilege.

What if the defendant knew that the charges in the privileged story were false? At a city council meeting, for example, Councilwoman Jane Adams charges that the Acme Construction Company is cheating the city in its current road repair work. The publisher of the local newspaper, John Smith, knows the charge is false, having investigated the same allegations himself. If he nevertheless quotes Jane in his story about the city council meeting, will he be abusing the privilege? Most authorities say no, that the public has a right to hear the charge, false or not. But there are some cases on record in which courts have ruled otherwise, that publication of a knowingly false statement is malicious and destroys the privilege.

The privilege can also be destroyed if the story in question is not a fair and accurate or true report of what took place. *Fair* means balanced. If at a public meeting speakers both attack and defend John Smith, the story should reflect both the attack and the defense. A story which just focuses on the charges is not fair, and the privilege will have been abused. Similarly, if the story concerns a continuing kind of an affair, a legislative hearing, a trial, and so forth, in which testimony is given for several days, the press is obligated to publish stories about each day's events if the privilege is to be used. If in the first day of the trial four witnesses come forth and say that John Smith raped Jane Adams, and two days later defense witnesses appear who challenge those charges, reports of both days' testimony are required before fairness can be obtained. Another way of accomplishing the same thing is to report what happened at the first day's session and include within that story comments from the defendant or his attorney which give the other side of the dispute. There has to be balance. If a story about a civil suit based upon the charges listed in the complaint is prepared, it is important to get the defendant's response as well. Balance is the key.

An accurate or true report means just that: it should honestly reflect what took place or what was said. John Smith testifies before a Congressional committee that Professor LeBlanc is a *radical*. If in the story the reporter writes that Smith called LeBlanc a *Communist*, the story is inaccurate and goes substantially beyond the charge the witness made. As with truth, little errors will not destroy the privilege. The news story says Smith testified in the morning and actually he testified in the afternoon and the story says Smith spoke extemporaneously and actually he used notes, are minor mistakes and do not have impact upon the privilege. So long as the error has nothing to do with the basic defamation there is no problem. It must be remembered that the story must be substantially true. If it is an untruthful report, the privilege is lost.

The story must also be in the form of a report. If the defendant fails to make it clear that he or she is reporting something that was said at a public meeting or repeating something that is contained in the public record, the privilege is lost. The law says the reader should be aware that the story is a report of what happened at a public meeting or at an official hearing or is taken from the official record. The reader must be aware that he or she could have attended the proceeding or can get a copy of the document. It must be plain that the reporter is merely a transmission belt for conveying information about what was said in an official proceeding, at a public meeting, or in a government report or a jury verdict. These facts should be noted in the lead and in the headline if possible.

At City Council Session
MAYOR BLASTS CONTRACTOR WITH CHARGES OF FRAUD

Mayor John Smith during a city council meeting today charged the Acme Construction Co. with fraudulent dealings.

The writer should also beware of adding material to a story about a privileged meeting or hearing. The court adjourns and the reporter prepares a fair and accurate story about what took place during the day's testimony, but at the end of the piece he or she notes that informed sources in the prosecutor's office have reported that charges are about to be brought against John Smith for attempting to bribe a police officer. Obviously these last remarks are not privileged. Only that part of the story which deals with the trial is protected by the privilege. The extraneous matter added at the end must stand on its own.

The privilege of the reporter is a very important defense and protects the press in a large percentage of the stories which are printed or telecast. Privilege is much easier to use than truth since all the defendant must prove is that the event, meeting, or report was in fact a privileged occasion and the story was a fair and true report.

Fair Comment   Fair comment is another kind of privilege. It permits the journalist to express defamatory opinions on matters of public interest. The key words are *opinions* and *public interest*. Once again the law allows the press valuable protection when it concerns itself with matters of importance to readers and viewers.

By its very nature an opinion is not subject to proof or to test by evidence. An opinion is a subjective statement which reflects the speaker's tastes, values, or sensitivities. As such, the defense of truth is worthless. The privilege of the reporter just discussed is also limited by the kinds of proceedings and reports which fall under its ambit. British courts long ago recognized the need for some means of permitting critical views and opinions to be aired. Lord Ellenborough nicely summed up the basis for the defense of fair comment in the early nineteenth century (*Tabart* v. *Tipper,* 1808):

> Liberty of criticism must be allowed, or we should have neither purity of taste nor of morals. Fair discussion is essentially necessary to the truth of history and the advancement of science. That publication, therefore, I should never consider as a libel which has for its object not to injure the reputation of any individual, but to correct misrepresentations of fact, to refute sophistical reasoning, to express a vicious taste in literature or to censure what is hostile to morality.

As Professor Harry Kalven noted, "One cannot be too solemn about the distinction between fact and opinion, and undoubtedly in practical operation the privilege of fair comment serves to protect not only what are clearly statements of opinion, but also a kind of twilight zone of fact."

Requirements   Fair comment is also a conditional privilege. As for the privileges discussed earlier, the writer or broadcaster who plans to use fair comment to defend his work is expected to meet certain requirements.

| *Legitimate public interest*   The first requirement is that the comment must concern something of legitimate public interest. The courts have granted a wide range of topics that are fair game for comment. Educational, charitable, and religious institutions are eligible for comment, as are quasi-public organizations such as bar associations, medical societies, and other professional groups. Manufacturers who place products on the market must expect criticism; businesses which cater to the public such as restaurants, theaters, and galleries are subject to the same treatment. Any solicitation for public support such as an advertisement is fair game, as are artistic and creative efforts such as movies, plays, operas, books, paintings, recitals, comic strips, and television and radio programs. The work of journalists and broadcasters may be commented upon. The performances of those who seek to entertain the public—actors, musicians, athletes, and the like—are also considered legitimate targets for fair comment. In the 1930s a football coach sued a newspaper for its criticism of his team and his coaching abilities. The court found little sympathy for the plaintiff (*Hoeppner* v. *Dunkirk Printing Co.,* 1930):

> When the plaintiff assumed the position of . . . coach to the football team of the Dunkirk High School he was no exception to the habits and customs which have become a part of the game. His work and the play of his team were matters of keen public interest; victories would be heralded, defeats condemned. The same enthusiasm which welcomed the home-coming of the Roman conqueror now finds expression in the plaudits of the bleachers and the grandstand. The conquered now appear not in chains, but what may be far worse, amidst ridicule and derision—the boos of the crowd.

A broad range of subjects, then, come under the purview of the privilege.

As a kind of a corollary to the rule that the comment must concern something of public interest, the comment must also focus upon the public aspects of the subject. That is, while Elvis Presley's performances may be legitimate targets of criticism, his private life is not. Similarly, while a book might be the fair subject even of scathing critical analysis, fair comment is no license to undertake scathing criticism of the author or the author's life. A very old case makes the point best. The plaintiff was a lecturer and teacher named Oscar Lovell Triggs. After a series of lectures by Triggs in New York the *New York Sun* editorially attacked Triggs' public performance and his public pronouncements. These were fair game. But the newspaper went further and criticized the plaintiff because he and his wife took a year to name their baby. This attack was upon his personal life and could not be excused as a fair comment (*Triggs* v. *Sun Printing and Publishing Association*, 1904). To quote Lord Ellenborough about another case (*Carr* v. *Hood*, 1808), "Every man who publishes a book commits himself to the judgment of the public and any one may comment upon his performance. If the commentator does not step aside from the work, . . . he exercises a fair and legitimate right."

Another requirement of the privilege is that the opinion expressed by the writer or broadcaster be his or her true opinion. It doesn't have to be the right opinion or the majority opinion. The jury does not have to agree with the opinion of the defendant. It just must be the author's honest opinion. Several years ago *Look* magazine wrote an article about baseball star Orlando Cepeda, who was at that time playing with the San Francisco Giants. The article noted that the Giant management was critical of Cepeda. Management said that he was not a team man, that when things went wrong he tended to blame others and not himself, that he was underproductive, and so forth. Cepeda sued, and *Look* attempted to erect the privilege of fair comment as a barrier. But the court did not allow the defense, for the opinions expressed in the articles were not those of the writer, but of other persons quoted by the writer. If Cepeda had brought suit against the Giant's management, fair comment would have applied to them, but not to the writer of the article. Similarly, if the writer had expressed these opinions himself rather than quote others, the defense of fair comment would have undoubtedly held up (*Cepeda* v. *Cowles Magazine, and Broadcasting, Inc.*, 1964).

The opinion does not need to be temperate. As a federal court once noted, an opinion can be good, bad, or indifferent, immature, premature, or ill founded. A newspaper in Alaska once called the late Drew Pearson "the garbage man of the Fourth Estate." The court permitted this comment (*Pearson* v. *Fairbanks Publishing Co.*, 1966). Decades ago the *Des Moines Leader* published this review of a vocal trio, the Cherry Sisters (*Cherry* v. *Des Moines Leader*, 1901):

> Effie is an old jade of 50 summers, Jessie is a frisky filly of 40, and Addie, the flower of the family, a capering monstrosity of 35. Their long skinny arms, equipped with talons at the extremities, swung mechanically, and anon waved frantically at the suffering audience. The mouths of their rancid features opened like caverns, and sounds like the wailing of damned souls issued therefrom. They pranced around the stage with a motion that suggested a cross between the danse du'ventre and fox trot—strange creatures with painted faces and hideous mien. Effie is spavined, Addie is stringhalt, and Jessie, the only one who showed her stockings, has legs with calves as classic in their outlines as the curves of a broom handle.

This review was also considered fair comment.

Factual basis   In addition to an honest opinion upon a subject of public interest, the writer or broadcaster who expects to use the defense of fair comment must also publish some facts along with the opinion, facts which are truly stated and which allow the reader opportunity to determine whether to agree with the critic's remarks. To wit: an imaginary review in the *River City Sentinel:*

> John Smith came to town last night and bombed at the Civic Auditorium. It was probably the worst performance I've seen all year. We should all get our money back; better yet, we should pass an ordinance barring that bandit from our town. When they write a history of musical performances at the Auditorium, last night's show has got to go in the chapter entitled "Flops and Ripoffs."

This is strong comment. The writer does not, however, give any facts to allow readers to judge for themselves. Fair comment does not apply here. However, if the writer follows that paragraph with this one, the defense will work:

> First of all, the show started 45 minutes late. The scrub band that Smith hired to keep us all entertained for the first half hour played off key most of the time. Then the "man" came out after intermission (which was the best part of the evening—the popcorn was warm and the Coke was cold) and regaled us with a medley of contemporary songs, none of which he has recorded, and most of which don't fit his style. He sang for 50 minutes, refused to come out for an encore, and showed his ultimate disregard for his audience by stationing big, burly bodyguards around his door to keep away the few well-wishers who sought to thank him. What a bummer.

OK, there are some facts, and hopefully they are truly stated, for the defense can be lost just as easily when the facts are wrong as when no facts exist.

How many facts are needed to support an opinion? The courts have had difficulty in deciding this question. In some states, New York, for example, courts ruled years ago that it is sufficient if the facts upon which the criticism is based are merely referred to, provided that they have been fairly extensively published beforehand. For example, in 1975 within the span of about three weeks two attempts were made on the life of President Gerald Ford. In editorial comments the press was critical of both Ford and the Secret Service. In this case the facts were well known and had been widely publicized before the comment. It was sufficient for the editor to merely remind readers of what had happened. If the story is more obscure, and the details less widely known, the writer has the obligation to present the facts fairly extensively. This requirement is not settled law by any means. Some courts will insist upon a fuller explanation of the facts than other courts. From a journalist's standpoint it makes good sense to provide this context, whether or not the law requires it. This policy is more fair to readers and viewers who have lots of things on their mind and often forget the details of even important events and happenings.

Criticism of the arts and of public institutions must be treated in the same way. Readers and viewers should be given opportunity to come to a judgment on their own, and information—facts—is needed before they can do that.

~~Lack of malice~~   Finally, as for the privilege of the reporter, the comment of the writer cannot be motivated by malice or ill will. It cannot be published solely to hurt someone. It may in fact hurt someone: Critics have closed Broadway shows, ended politicians' careers, torpedoed advertising campaigns. The harm is not important. What is important is whether the comment was made for the purpose of hurting someone, not for the purpose of enlightening the public, educating readers and viewers, or warning consumers or theatergoers.

Fair comment is a valuable privilege, and writers and broadcasters must be most cautious when ascertaining the facts. The comment may be fair, but if the subject of the criticism can sustain a libel suit because the facts are untrue, the defense helps very little.

Before the constitutional defense in libel suits is discussed, it is appropriate to consider two additional common law defenses, as well as common law malice. Both defenses have been used on occasion to successfully ward off a libel suit, but their foundations are tenuous. They have been accepted in some courts, and rejected in other courts. Reliance upon either of them as the only defense is therefore not advised. However, both make excellent backup defenses, to be used with privilege or fair comment. The two defenses are consent and right of reply.

Consent   As one authority notes, an otherwise actionable defamation may be privileged if the plaintiff consented to its publication. Imagine that Frank Jones, a reporter for the *River City Sentinel*, hears rumors that John Smith is a leader of organized crime. Jones visits Smith and tells him that he has heard these rumors. Then Jones asks Smith if he cares if the rumors are published in the newspaper. Smith says it is OK with him, and Jones writes and publishes the story. In this instance Smith consented to publication of the defamation.

Now, this event is not too likely to happen, is it? Cases of consent are extremely rare. Courts insist that the plaintiff either know or have a good reason to know the full extent of the defamatory statement in advance of its publication before consent can be said to exist.

At least one authority (Phelps and Hamilton) has suggested that while the kind of direct consent just noted is difficult to obtain, indirect consent is a viable defense. Indirect consent means that the individual was informed of the defamatory charges against him or her and was asked to comment upon the charges. The logic behind this defense is that if the newspaper publishes the response to the charges it must publish the charge as well.

For example, let's look at Smith and Jones again. Frank Jones tells John Smith that the police have called Smith "a big-time gangster." Jones says he is going to print the charge, and then asks Smith, "Would you care to comment on the charge." Smith denies the charge and claims that he is a legitimate businessman. He calls the man who made the charge a liar. Again, the logic of the defense suggests that if Smith's denial is printed the charge which he denies must also be printed.

This reasoning may be logical, but few courts have accepted it. On record are one or two cases in which this kind of indirect consent by itself worked to defeat a libel suit (*Pulverman* v. *A. S. Abell Co.*, 1956). A very imaginative judge is needed to accept these arguments.

This does not mean, however, that it is not good policy to get a comment from the defamed party before the story is published. The facts may be wrong and the subject of the story can then point out errors and save the newspaper from a suit. Even if the story isn't incorrect, the reporter's attempt to get both sides of the story, to discover the truth, will impress a jury if a suit does result. His efforts will demonstrate that he was not malicious in printing the story, that he honestly sought the truth, and that the plaintiff was given a chance to explain the charges. This policy is far more effective than giving the plaintiff the chance to reply after he has been defamed. At that point, the offer looks like an afterthought. Similarly, even if the subject of the story can't be reached, it is good policy for the journalist to tell readers that he tried to contact the person or that the person refused to comment. A reporter can have no worse experience than to testify in a libel suit that he made no attempt to contact the plaintiff before printing the story. "You mean you didn't even try to find out from the plaintiff whether the charges were true or not? You didn't have the decency to make a simple phone call?" the plaintiff's attorney will ask as the jury sits up attentively.

Indirect consent can help in a defense, but it is rare indeed for it to defeat a libel suit when standing by itself.

Right of Reply

Right of reply is a better defense than consent, is used more often, and is somewhat more substantial. The basis of right of reply is simple: The one who has been libeled may answer in kind. John Smith calls

Steve Wilson a cheat, a fraud, and a common thief. Wilson has the right
to answer Smith in kind. He can defame Smith in response.

The right of reply is based on the broader concept of self-defense;
in fact, it is often referred to as *the* self-defense. As in self-defense, right
of reply does have limitations. If a woman walks down the street and
someone begins to pepper her with a peashooter, she has the right to stop
her assailant, to protect herself. She does not have the right to pull out
a .44-magnum pistol and pump three or four slugs into her attacker. Her
defense then far exceeds the threat of the original attack. The same is
true in a libel case. If a woman has been defamed, she may respond in
kind. She may defame her attacker, but her reply cannot exceed the provocation: she cannot hit back harder than she was hit.

In a famous lawsuit two American journalists assailed one another in
print. Newsman Quentin Reynolds suggested that columnist Westbrook
Pegler once called a third journalist, Heywood Broun, a liar. This bothered Broun, Reynolds wrote, to the extent that he couldn't sleep. Broun
became ill and finally died. Pegler was incensed by this comment, claiming it charged him with moral homicide. So he attacked Reynolds, calling
him sloppy, a sycophant, a coward, a slob, and a four-flusher. Pegler accused Reynolds of public nudism, of being a war profiteer, and of being
an absentee war correspondent. Pegler also attacked the deceased Broun,
calling him a liar and someone who made his living by controversy.

In the libel suit that followed Pegler raised the defense of right of
reply. The court agreed that Pegler's comments about Broun bore a resemblance to a reply, but that the columnist had gone too far in his attack on Quentin Reynolds. This portion of the article had no conceivable relationship to a reply. Reynolds was awarded $175,000 from Pegler,
the *New York Journal-American,* and the Hearst Corporation (*Reynolds
v. Pegler,* 1955).

The right of reply works. Where does the press fit in? Many authorities argue that the press has the right to carry the reply and remain immune from suit. In several cases it was held that where the plaintiff's
charge was made in a newspaper the newspaper was privileged to carry
the defendant's reply (*Fowler* v. *New York Herald,* 1918). Otherwise
the right of reply is of no avail to the defendant; no one would be able
to see or read the reply if he were denied use of the press. Similarly, it
was held that the reply can even be carried in a newspaper or a medium
different from the medium used for the attack.

In *Cases and Materials on Torts* law professor Harry Kalven writes:

> The boundaries of this privilege are not clearly established and
> it gives rise to questions amusingly reminiscent of those raised in
> connection with self-defense: How vigorous must the plaintiff's orig-

inal aggression have been? Must the original attack itself have been defamatory? What if it (the original attack) is true or privileged? How much verbal force can the defendant use in reply? Can he defend third parties?

Questions like these continue to reduce the true effectiveness of the defense of right of reply. Most authorities agree that the original attack must be defamatory in order to defend a defamatory reply, and many authorities argue that the defendant can in fact defend third parties in a reply. There are so few reported cases in which this defense either stood or fell on its own accord that its substance as a defense remains quite tenuous. It is useful as a second defense, to back up either the privilege of the reporter or of fair comment, perhaps. Beyond this use its value is limited, at least at this point.

Common Law Malice

The final aspect of the common law defenses which needs to be considered is common law malice. Every one of the common law defenses, with the exception of truth, can be swept aside by a plaintiff who has evidence of common law malice. That is, the privilege of the reporter, the privilege of fair comment, consent, and right of reply are all lost if the defendant acted maliciously in preparing or publishing the defamatory material.

What is common law malice? It really has two aspects. The first deals with the defendant's state of mind and the second with his conduct in publishing the story. Consider the state of mind first.

State of Mind Ill will is the key to this element of common law malice. If the plaintiff can prove that the defendant had ill will toward him or her, common law malice then exists. Ill will can be proved in many ways. For example, if the plaintiff can show that there had always been bad blood between him and the defendant, he has proved ill will. Personal grudges, feuds, and even physical violence between the two are evidence of ill will. Many years ago in Boston the mayor and a leading newspaper publisher got into a brawl on a city street. When he was bested in the fight, the publisher retreated to his newspaper and published a defamatory editorial cartoon about the mayor. The mayor brought criminal libel action against the publisher, and the state easily proved malice by recounting how the mayor had whipped the newspaper man in a street fight prior to the publication. The cartoon was revenge.

Continued publication of libelous matter, even after the publisher is informed that it is untrue and libelous—can also be interpreted as ill will. As Phelps and Hamilton note in their book *Libel,* the theory is that repetition of published statements of a similar character shows a continuing state of mind on the part of the publisher or a continuing purpose or intent to injure.

Still another way to prove common law malice is to demonstrate that the motive behind the libel is not to inform the people but to harm the plaintiff. John Henry Faulk's suit against Laurance Johnson and Vincent Hartnett in the 1950s contains a classic example of this kind of ill will. Johnson and Hartnett labeled Faulk a Communist after he attacked their right-wing anti-Communist crusade. In awarding Faulk a $550,000 judgment the New York appellate court ruled: "The proof in support of the plaintiff's case was overwhelming. He conclusively established that the defendants planned to destroy his professional career through the use of the libelous publications directed to the places where they would do him the most harm" (*Faulk* v. *Aware, Inc.,* 1956).

The defendant's state of mind, then, is very important. Any evidence at all that the publication of the libel was not made with the highest of motives can be damaging.

Conduct   The aspect of malice which deals with the conduct of the defendant is far less clear. If the plaintiff can prove gross negligence or gross carelessness, he or she can prove common law malice. What is gross negligence? Supposedly, it is a greater degree of negligence than simple negligence, but falls considerably short of knowledge of falsity or reckless disregard for the truth. Making a simple error like leaving out the middle initial of a man's name which results in a case of mistaken identity is *not* gross negligence. It is a minor error at best. In reality gross negligence is what a judge decides it is, and is what a jury is ready to accept. The law has always lacked precision, for it depends upon human judgments rather than upon statistical measurements for its decisions. Therefore, concepts like gross negligence and simple negligence take on meanings which reflect the time and place of the trial, the judge, and the jury and the circumstances of the case. Perhaps when a substantial body of case law defining simple negligence is amassed, a better picture of gross negligence will also result.

The best advice is that any effort at all by reporters to verify a charge or to substantiate a story will probably help reduce the risk of being found guilty of gross negligence. Similarly, wholesale abandonment of general journalistic and reportorial standards in preparing a story will undoubtedly assist plaintiffs in building a case of gross negligence.

Common law malice is very important. In some ways it is the key to successful use of the common law defenses. A reporter should never use his or her position in the press to settle a personal score. Of course, care in gathering, reporting, and writing the news must be journalistic by words.

Constitutional Defense

If this were 1963 this section on libel defense would be pretty much complete, for in 1963 in most states the common law defenses were the only means available to the press to ward off libel plaintiffs. In 1964 the

Supreme Court of the United States added an important new defense—the First Amendment—to the media's arsenal. Variously called the First Amendment defense and the *New York Times* rule, this constitutional defense grew so rapidly that it has almost dominated libel defenses during the past decade and one half. The First Amendment is far easier to use than the defense of truth and is a much stronger defense than the other common law protections.

In the discussion of this constitutional defense that follows, the principal features of the defense are outlined. The *development* of the *New York Times* rule, while fascinating to study, is beyond the scope and purpose of this book. It seems like only yesterday that the high Court first announced this defense, but the decision is actually legal history now, and the *Gertz* case, which has been mentioned so frequently, is but one chapter in that history. In this section the discussion focuses on the practical aspects of the *New York Times* rule: when the rule can be used, when it can be defeated by the plaintiff, and its scope and its limitations.

*Libel and the
First Amendment*

Until 1964 the First Amendment guarantee of freedom of the press and speech had never been held to be a bar to a civil libel suit. A civil libel suit, after all, was an action by a private individual against another private individual. There was no action by the government to censor the press. In addition, a man's reputation was valuable; society lost little by allowing the injured party to seek compensation for the damage.

In the years shortly before 1964, however, the American legal climate began to change. The concept of "state action" developed a new meaning during the civil rights struggles of the fifties and sixties. It became obvious that when a court enforced the rights of a private party in a lawsuit such as upholding the right of a restaurant owner to refuse to serve blacks the state itself was enforcing discrimination. Similarly, in a libel suit when a court forced a newspaper to pay a $500,000 judgment to a plaintiff the state was punishing the newspaper for publishing defamatory remarks. Clearly the government was involved in a kind of censorship of the press.

In the years preceding 1964 the legal evolution of this idea was coupled with the realization that while for all practical purposes the law of sedition was impotent in the last half of the twentieth century lawsuits by government officials could accomplish much the same thing as sedition trials: quieting criticism of government. Important segments of the press were politically active in the sixties, taking a strong stand in support of the passage and enforcement of strong civil rights laws. Such a stand resulted in retaliation in at least one state, Alabama, where in a series of libel suits five government officials sued the *New York Times* for $3 million.

The material upon which the suits were based was not even a news article; it was an editorial advertisement (an advertisement which promotes an idea rather than a product or commercial service). A civil rights group, the Committee to Defend Martin Luther King and the Struggle for Freedom in the South, had placed the advertisement. In the narrative part of the full-page advertisement charges were leveled at various Alabama government leaders. While it was basically true, the advertisement was nevertheless peppered with small factual errors. These errors proved to be the downfall of the *Times* in an Alabama state court where the newspaper lost the first suit brought by Montgomery, Alabama, Police Commissioner L. B. Sullivan. Sullivan won a $500,000 judgment—all that he asked for—and this ruling was affirmed by the state supreme court. One must remember that as much as anything the case against the *Times* allowed Alabamians to vent their pipes which had been filling with steam ever since that (according to prevailing Southern thought) "damned, liberal (radical, Communist) New York scandal sheet" had taken a leadership role in seeking passage and enforcement of federal civil rights guidelines in the South. The political implications of this case are beyond the scope of this text, but should not be overlooked.

The *New York Times* appealed the decision to the Supreme Court of the United States and won a unanimous reversal of the judgment. In reversing the Alabama state courts in the case of *New York Times Co.* v. *Sullivan* (1964), the Supreme Court changed the law of libel forever.

Before significance of the high Court's decision in this case is explained it is important to explain first why the Court made the ruling, or at least the reasons the justices gave for their decision, for this rationale remains today the basic foundation of the important First Amendment libel defense.

Only with the benefit of hindsight is it possible to get at what the Supreme Court said in the 1964 *Sullivan* ruling, and some points still remain less than crystal clear. Under the traditional law of libel the newspaper was in serious trouble. There had been publication and identification, and the words were clearly defamatory. (The negligence standard did not apply at this time.) The *Times* could not use truth as a defense; the publication contained numerous errors. The advertisement did not enjoy any kind of privilege. The newspaper was clearly responsible.

But Justice William Brennan and his eight colleagues on the high Court did not apply the traditional law of libel. Sullivan was not a typical plaintiff, he was a government officer. The defamation did not concern his private life; it focused on his role as police commissioner. While the action rode under the colors of a civil libel suit, many recognized it as sedition—punishment for criticism of the government. The high Court ruled therefore that because of the nature of this suit, because of the immense First Amendment implications, plaintiff Sullivan was forced to carry an added burden of proof. He had to show that the publication of the advertisement was made with actual malice. Actual malice was defined as knowledge of falsity or reckless disregard of whether the story was truthful. Sullivan, then, had to show that the *New York Times* published the advertisement with knowledge that some of its charges were false, or that the newspaper exhibited reckless disregard as to whether the charges were true. (Don't worry now about what reckless disregard is; it is discussed in detail in a moment.)

Why did the Court make such a ruling? When the Sullivan case itself is looked at, three explanations appear. Each deserves brief consideration. First, and perhaps least important in the long run although it appeared important initially, is the notion that this was in fact a kind of sedition case, a case of punishment of government criticism. One is hard pressed to deny that it was such a case, but that is hardly sufficient reason for rearranging the law of libel in the way the Court did via the *Sullivan* ruling. There are other ways to cope with sedition that are far less traumatic to the law.

Second, and this is a philosophical justification, the court was concerned that these kinds of lawsuits might have an impact upon debate about political issues. Quoting numerous earlier high Court opinions, Brennan wrote (*New York Times Co.* v. *Sullivan*, 1964):

> The general proposition that freedom of expression upon public questions is secured by the First Amendment has long been settled by our decisions. The constitutional safeguard, as we have said, "was fashioned to assure the unfettered interchange of ideas for the bringing about of political and social changes desired by our people. . . ." The maintenance of the opportunity for free political discussion to the end that government may be responsive to the will of the people and that changes may be obtained by lawful means, an opportunity essential to the security of the Republic. . . . The First Amendment, said Judge Learned Hand, "presupposes that right conclusions are more likely to be gathered out of a multitude of tongues, than through any kind of authoritative selection."

Thus, Brennan wrote, this case is considered against the background of a profound national commitment to the principle that debate on public issues should be uninhibited, robust, and wide open.

Turning to the fact that there were errors in the publication, Brennan asserted, "Erroneous statement is inevitable in free debate, and it must be protected if the freedoms of expression are to have the 'breathing space' that they need . . . to survive." Whatever is added to the field of libel, the associate justice noted, is taken from the field of free debate. This concept—traditional concern with maintaining free debate—formed the philosophical basis for the decision.

The third rationale for the ruling probably appeared least important at the time, but has since emerged as perhaps equal to the philosophical justification. As a public official, a government leader, Sullivan voluntarily took a position for which criticism was common, usual, and, indeed, expected. As a servant of the public one must expect to be criticized, sometimes quite strongly. In a way, he had asked for criticism. Also, as a public official and a politician he had easy access to the press to respond to criticism. Whereas a private person whose reputation has been damaged may have no recourse but to go to court to win vindication, Sullivan could give as good as he got. He could deny the charges in the public press; he could make countercharges. In short, he had access to an effective means of rebuilding his damaged reputation without relying upon a libel suit which, as we have noted, can have a serious impact upon the freedom of expression.

These reasons are the pillars upon which the *Sullivan* decision rested. In taking this stand the high Court followed a course of action which a handful of other states adopted years earlier. In 1908 the Kansas Supreme Court ruled that public officials and candidates for public office must carry a more rigorous burden of proof than private citizens to sustain a libel judgment in order to preserve the immense public benefit gained from free and robust debate (*Coleman* v. *MacLennan*, 1908). The *Sullivan* case amplified and extended this ruling to every state in the Union. Henceforth, public officials had to prove actual malice in order to sustain a civil libel suit.

Kansas Rule

After *New York Times Co.* v. *Sullivan* two very practical questions remained for journalists seeking to apply the new libel defense to their work. The first question was, What kinds of people will have to prove actual malice? That is, to whom and under what conditions does the First Amendment defense apply? The second question was no easier to answer: What is actual malice? More specifically, what is reckless disregard for the truth? During the nearly fifteen years since 1964 the Supreme Court and various lower courts have fashioned answers to these questions. These court decisions, plus the opinions of libel experts, which form the bases for the outline of how the First Amendment defense can be applied, follows.

Who Must Prove Actual Malice?

Public Officials   In *New York Times* v. *Sullivan* Justice Brennan ruled that all public officials must prove actual malice when suing for defamation. Who is a public official? L. B. Sullivan was a high city official, the police commissioner, in the city of Montgomery. In almost anyone's mind he clearly met the requirements of Justice Brennan's definition of public official. But clearly all government employees are not public officials. Two years later the high Court added precision to its description of a public figure. "It is clear," Justice Brennan wrote, "that the 'public official' designation applies at the very least to those among the hierarchy of government employees who have or appear to the public to have substantial responsibility for or control over the conduct of governmental affairs" (*Rosenblatt* v. *Baer,* 1966). The Court added that the person must hold a position that invites public scrutiny of the person holding it, entirely apart from the scrutiny and discussion occasioned by the particular charges in the controversy.

Elected officials certainly meet this definition, as do many appointed officials. Context is an important aspect of this problem as well. Detective Lt. John Smith may not have a position that normally invites public scrutiny. However, if Smith is assigned to head the investigation of the assassination of Mayor Frank Jones or if he takes charge of the hunt for a sexual psychopath who has murdered fourteen young women in the area in the past six months, this special assignment brings with it closer public scrutiny. In such a case a strong argument can be made that Smith is a public official for purposes of the *New York Times* rule. The courts have held that judges, senators, state legislators, mayors, school board members, deputy sheriffs, city tax assessors, and many others are public officials and must prove malice under the provision of the *Times* rule.

American courts continue to develop philosophies and strategies to determine who is and who is not a public official under the terms of the *Sullivan* ruling. There will of course be differences from state to state. Some courts are reluctant to rule that an ordinary police officer is a public official, but a superior court in Seattle recently ruled that because police officers have the power of life or death over citizens in the community they must be considered public officials in the eyes of the law.

A very important aspect of the who-is-a-public-official question is often overlooked. It is this: Just because an individual is a public official does not mean that he will necessarily have to prove actual malice in every defamation suit he brings against a newspaper, magazine, or broadcasting station. The only circumstances for which public officials must prove actual malice are when the defamatory comments or statements concern (1) their *official conduct,* that is, actions taken in an official capacity or actions while they undertake their public official role and (2) their general fitness for public office.

The second category is the most troubling. Suppose the mayor is drunk when he presides at a meeting of the city council. In this case a personal habit directly affects his fitness for office. The fact that the mayor was drunk clearly reflects upon how well he can conduct the public's business. What if the mayor's drinking problem doesn't interfere with his work? What if he is arrested for drunken driving once, and the newspaper mistakenly reports that this is his third arrest for drunken driving? Does he have to prove actual malice? Does this behavior speak to his general fitness for office? That question is much tougher. In stories like this extra caution must be exercised.

Public Figures   Public officials must prove actual malice. Persons who are considered to be public figures must also prove actual malice. While to some people a public figure is a public figure, defining a public figure or public person is not simple.

The language in some of the court decisions is quite instructive in determining who is and who is not a public figure, and examples are also helpful.

A lower federal court first defined "public figure" in 1966 in the case of *Pauling* v. *Globe-Democrat.* The plaintiff was Linus Pauling, Nobel Prize-winning physicist who was active in the movement to ban atmospheric testing of nuclear weapons in the United States in the early sixties. The *St. Louis Globe-Democrat* incorrectly published that Pauling had been convicted of contempt of Congress. In the libel suit that followed the federal court agreed with the newspaper that Pauling must prove actual malice because, although he was not a public official, he was a public figure.

> Professor Pauling, by his public statements and actions, was projecting himself into the arena of public controversy and into the very vortex of the discussion of a question of pressing public concern. He was attempting to influence the resolution of an issue which was important, which was of profound effect, which was public, and which was internationally controversial.

A look at this description of Pauling's activities suggests several aspects or elements of the definition of a public figure. First, Pauling was involved in an important public controversy, the key words being *important* and *public*. Next, he had voluntarily injected himself into this controversy. He had initiated the movement into the public spotlight himself. He sought to influence the resolution of an issue. Finally, the question was controversial, and controversial questions usually draw considerable public comment. Hence, he probably knew what he was getting into.

This statement of criteria for defining a public figure was widely used in lower courts between 1967 and 1974. In 1967 in the cases of *Curtis* v. *Butts* (1967) and *AP* v. *Walker* (1967), the Supreme Court for all intents and purposes adopted the rule that public figures have to prove actual malice. While Justice John Marshall Harlan's opinion talked about "highly unreasonable conduct constituting an extreme departure" from responsible reporting standards, for practical purposes most authorities accepted that this decision applied the actual malice standard. The high Court added little to the definition of a public figure in these rulings, however.

It wasn't until 1974 that the Supreme Court began to shape what has become a fairly precise definition of a public person or a public figure. *Gertz* v. *Welch,* which changed the law in many different ways, gave Justice Lewis Powell an opportunity to explore the meaning of the public-figure concept. Gertz is a Chicago attorney very prominent in civil rights disputes in that city. He is the author of several books and articles and has served on many commissions and committees in Chicago, Cook County, and Illinois. Elmer Gertz represented the family of a young man who was slain by a police officer. The policeman had been tried and convicted of murder in the shooting, and the deceased lad's parents retained Gertz to bring a civil action for damages against the police officer. Gertz was a peripheral player in the drama surrounding the death and murder trial. *American Opinion* magazine, a publication of the John Birch Society, attacked Gertz, charging falsely that he was a Communist fronter, a Leninist, and an architect of the frame-up against the police officer, and alleged that he had a criminal record. Gertz sued for libel.

The Supreme Court found for the plaintiff in the case, ruling that he was not a public figure and did not have to prove actual malice. Justice Powell said that there are two kinds of public figures. "In some instances an individual may achieve such pervasive fame or notoriety that he becomes a public figure for all purposes and in all contexts," Powell wrote. While the justice did not give examples of such a person, people like Jacqueline Kennedy Onassis and perhaps Ralph Nader come to mind. More commonly, Justice Powell wrote, "an individual voluntarily injects himself or is drawn into a *particular* [author's emphasis] public controversy and thereby becomes a public figure for a limited range of issues. In either case such persons assume special prominence in the resolution of public questions."

This second kind of public figure, the limited public figure, is the typical public figure. Justice Powell clarified the status of this individual even more when he wrote, "It is preferable to reduce the public figure question to a more meaningful context by looking to *the nature and extent of an individual's participation in the particular controversy giving rise to the defamation* [author's emphasis]." Here is the key phrase: An individual must play a prominent role in the particular controversy giving rise to the defamation, the controversy which is the subject of the defamatory article or broadcast. In the *Gertz* case there was no question that Elmer Gertz was a limited public figure in regard to the civil rights movement in Chicago and Cook County. Had he been defamed in an article about that subject, Powell suggests that Gertz would have to prove actual malice. But the defamatory story was about another subject, the murder of a young man and the subsequent trial of a police officer. Gertz was not an important participant in that controversy.

To emphasize this ruling the high Court decided in 1976 that a socially prominent Palm Beach woman was not a public figure with regard to the divorce action in which she was involved. The case, *Time, Inc.* v. *Firestone,* resulted from a short notice published in *Time* magazine that Russell Firestone was granted a divorce from his wife on grounds of extreme cruelty and adultery. Firestone was in fact granted a divorce from his wife, but on grounds that neither member of the couple was "domesticated." Mary Alice Firestone sued *Time* for libel, claiming she had been called an adultress. *Time* argued that her prominence in the Palm Beach community made her a public figure. On the record she clearly appeared to be a public figure, a leading member of "Four Hundred of Palm Beach society," an "active member of the sporting set," a person whose activities attracted considerable public attention. She even maintained a clipping service to keep track of her publicity. The divorce case became a *cause célèbre* in the community, prompting forty-three articles in a Miami newspaper and forty-five stories in the Palm Beach newspapers. She held several press conferences during the course of the seventeen-month legal dispute. Nevertheless, the Supreme Court refused to acknowledge that Mary Alice Firestone was a public figure in the context of the divorce case, the subject of the *Time* article which was defamatory. Justice William Rehnquist wrote:

> Respondent did not assume any role of especial prominence in the affairs of society, other than perhaps Palm Beach society, and she did not thrust herself to the forefront of any particular public controversy in order to influence the resolution of the issues involved in it.

Time argued that because the trial was well publicized it must be considered a public controversy and Mary Alice Firestone a public person. "But in doing so," Justice Rehnquist wrote, "petitioner seeks to equate 'public controversy' with all controversies of interest to the public." The Justice said that a divorce proceeding is not the kind of public controversy referred to in *Gertz.* While there was public interest in the proceedings, the case was not an important public question.

Rehnquist also pointed out that Mrs. Firestone was not a voluntary participant in the divorce proceeding. She was forced to go into public court to dissolve her marriage. Whether the individual has voluntarily thrust himself or herself into the public spotlight is probably not a controlling issue in most cases. But Justice Powell did write in the *Gertz* decision, "it may be possible for someone to become a public figure through no purposeful action of his own, but the instances of truly involuntary public figures must be exceedingly rare. For the most part those who attain this status have assumed roles of especial prominence in the *affairs of society* [author's emphasis]."

From these cases it is possible to distill some tentative rules about who is and who is not a public figure.

First, certain kinds of people are for all purposes public figures because of their extreme fame and notoriety. These kinds of people are not common. It must also be remembered that even these kinds of public figures retain parts of their life which are not public. Comment on the private part of even a public figure's life is not protected by the First Amendment defense. Assume that Ralph Nader is such an all-purpose public figure. A story about Nader's romance with an old school friend would not be protected by the *New York Times* rule. Nader would not be required to prove actual malice in a libel suit based on this story.

Second, limited public figures are more common and are protected more fully by the law. The only stories written about these kinds of public figures protected by the First Amendment are stories about public controversy in which the plaintiff is an important participant. The president of the Lockheed Aircraft Corporation became a public figure with regard to the recent scandals involving payoffs by that company to foreign governments. A defamatory story about such payoffs is protected by the First Amendment, but if a newspaper erroneously publishes that the president of Lockheed was arrested for shoplifting, the *New York Times* rule does not apply.

Finally, the court seems to be fixing its sights upon the kind of public controversy which focuses upon governmental matters or matters important to society such as environmental problems, public health and safety and energy conservation. Although sensational crimes and sexual escapades are of interest to the public, such occurrences are probably not public controversies as defined by Justice Powell and Justice Rehnquist. As stated earlier, while it is possible, it is "exceedingly rare" for someone to be an involuntary public figure.

This definition is relatively narrow. Some authorities think it pulls back from the broader definition enunciated in the *Pauling* case and in other lower court rulings. Probably it is just a fuller definition of a concept which remained quite vague for about seven years.

Public officials and public figures must prove actual malice in libel actions in all states, and in a few states other persons must prove malice as well.

Persons Involved in Public Controversy   For about three years between 1971 and 1974 the law of the land extended application of the *New York Times* rule beyond public officials, beyond public figures, to any person involved in public controversy or question of public concern, including private persons. As with the public figure rule, the defamatory remarks had to concern the public controversy in which the individual had become involved.

For example, John Smith is taken hostage by Calabrian terrorists who seek the government of Calabrise to change the color of the national flag from green to mauve. In a story about the incident the newspaper defames poor Smith. Under the rule which existed between 1971 and 1974 Smith, who may have been completely anonymous the day before, had to prove malice. Why? Because the terrorist kidnapping is a matter of great public concern. Smith just happened to get drawn into the affair, but freedom of debate is more important.

This rule came from the 1971 Supreme Court decision in *Rosenbloom* v. *Metromedia.* In defending it Justice Brennan wrote:

> If a matter is a subject of public or general interest, it cannot suddenly become less so merely because a private individual is involved, or because in some sense the individual did not "voluntarily" choose to become involved. The public's primary interest is in the event; the public focus is in the conduct of the participant and the content, effect, and significance of the conduct, not the participant's prior anonymity or notoriety.

Despite the fact that the rule precluded a successful libel suit for a large number of the persons defamed by the press, many people felt it was a good rule, that the rule made sense, that public concern is about the event and not about the people involved, and that public concern should be the factor determining use of the *Times* rule.

Between 1971 and 1974 the membership of the Court changed, and so did support for the so-called *Rosenbloom* rule. In the *Gertz* case in 1974 five members of the high Court voted to strike down that rule. The protection of the *Times* malice rule again applied only to public officials and public figures as before the *Rosenbloom* decision.

But it isn't as simple as that. Remember that libel law is basically state law. The United States Supreme Court generally gets involved only because of the constitutional standards involved with the First Amendment. The majority rule of the high Court in the *Gertz* case was that the First Amendment does not require that states apply the *Times* malice standard in libel suits where private persons become involved in matters of public concern or in public controversies. The only thing the Constitution requires, Justice Powell wrote, is that the *Times* rule be applied in suits involving public figures or public officials. However, the court noted that states can, if they want, continue to use the *Rosenbloom* rule. It is their choice. The First Amendment does not mandate the action, but a state can set any standard it wants in its own libel law.

Consequently, today the law varies from state to state. At this writing the courts in at least five states, Colorado, Indiana, New York, Arizona, and Maryland indicate a desire to continue to use the *Rosenbloom* rule and require all plaintiffs who bring libel suits based on stories or broadcasts about matters of general public concern, regardless of their station in life or their status as celebrities, to prove actual malice. Other states have reverted to the public official-public figure rule. Most states haven't decided what to do. (Only thirteen states had decided by September, 1976.) You should find out the rule in your state as soon as possible since it can be very important in the manner in which you handle stories about persons other than public officials and about figures who become involved in matters of public concern.

Actual Malice Defined

Defining actual malice is somewhat easier than defining who is and who is not a public figure or public official. In *New York Times Co.* v. *Sullivan* Justice Brennan defined actual malice as "knowledge of falsity or reckless disregard of whether the material was false or not." The two parts of this definition should be considered separately.

Knowledge of Falsity   Knowledge of falsity is a fancy way of saying *lie*. If the defendant lied, and the plaintiff can prove it, actual malice has then been shown. But plaintiffs are rarely in a position to show that the defendant lied. Furthermore, not many defendants, at least not many mass media defendants, lie. On at least two occasions libel plaintiffs have in fact demonstrated knowledge of falsity. In 1969 Barry Goldwater was able to convince a federal court that Ralph Ginzburg published knowing falsehoods about him during the 1964 presidential campaign in a "psychobiography" carried in Ginzburg's *Fact* magazine. Ginzburg sent questionnaires to hundreds of psychiatrists asking them to analyze Goldwater's mental condition. Ginzburg published only those responses that agreed with the magazine's predisposition that Goldwater was mentally ill and changed the responses on other questionnaires to reflect this point of view. Proof of this conduct plus evidence of other kinds of similar practices led the court of appeals to conclude that Ginzburg had published the defamatory material with knowledge of its falsity (*Goldwater* v. *Ginzburg*, 1969; see also *Morgan* v. *Dun & Bradstreet, Inc.*, 1970).

Reckless Disregard for the Truth   A few months after the initial decision in the *Sullivan* case, the Supreme Court defined reckless disregard in a criminal libel action (*Garrison* v. *Louisiana*, 1964) as "a high degree of awareness of probable falsity" of the material or statements. In 1968, in *St. Amant* v. *Thompson,* the high Court said that before a court can conclude that reckless disregard for the truth exists "there must be sufficient evidence to permit the conclusion that the defendant in fact entertained serious doubts as to the truth of his publication."

Both are good definitions of reckless disregard for the truth, but they are not much help to the working journalist who needs a more practical measure of reckless disregard. The Supreme Court has, to an extent, provided that as well. Look at *New York Times Co.* v. *Sullivan,* for example. All that was required to check the truth of the charges made in the advertisement that ultimately became the basis for the libel suit was for someone to compare the assertions in the advertisement with clippings in the newspaper's files, a simple matter. Yet the Court in that case did not indicate that such a check was really called for. There was no reason for the advertising staff to doubt the veracity of the claims in the document. The newspaper had every reason to believe that the charges contained in the advertisement were true.

A better practical definition of reckless disregard evolved from the cases of *Curtis Publishing Co.* v. *Butts* and *AP* v. *Walker.* In developing the criteria that follow Justice Harlan said he was attempting to determine whether the plaintiffs in these cases had seriously departed from the standards of responsible reporting. He did not call his opinion a definition of reckless disregard. Some of the other members of the court did, however, refer to these standards as a measure of reckless disregard, and so have many lower federal and state courts.

These two appeals came before the Supreme Court at about the same time and were joined and decided as one case. In the first case Wally Butts, the athletic director at the University of Georgia, brought suit against the *Saturday Evening Post* for an article it published which alleged that Butts and University of Alabama football coach Paul "Bear" Bryant had conspired prior to the annual Georgia-Alabama football game to "fix" the contest. The *Post* obtained its information from a man who said that while making a telephone call he had been accidentally plugged into a phone conversation between Butts and Bryant. George Burnett, who had a criminal record, told the *Post* editors that he had taken careful notes. The story was based on these notes.

In the other case Major General (retired) Edwin Walker, a political conservative and segregationist from Texas, brought suit against the Associated Press (AP) and a score of publications and broadcasting stations for publishing the charge that he led a mob of white citizens against federal marshals who were attempting to preserve order at the University of Mississippi during the crisis over the enrollment of James

Meredith. The AP report, which was wrong, was filed by a young AP correspondent on the scene.

The court ruled that in the *Butts* case the *Post* had exhibited highly unreasonable conduct in publishing the story, but that in the Walker case no such evidence was present. Again, it is important to note that while Justice John Marshall Harlan did not call the conduct reckless disregard at the time, most authorities accept these cases as good indicators of what the court means by reckless disregard. Look at the details of each case.

In the *Butts* case the story was not what would be called a hot news item. It was published months after the game occurred. The magazine had ample time to check the report. The source of the story was not a trained reporter but a layman who happened to be on probation on a bad-check charge. The *Post* made no attempt to investigate the story further, to screen game films to see if either team made changes in accord with what Bryant and Butts supposedly discussed. Many persons were supposedly with Burnett when he magically overheard this conversation, and none were questioned by the *Post*. The magazine did little, then, to check the story, despite evidence presented at the trial that one or two of the editors acknowledged that Burnett's story needed careful examination.

In the Walker case different circumstances were present. It was a hot story, one that had to get out on the wires right away. It was prepared in the "heat of battle" by a young, but trained, reporter who in the past gave every indication of being trustworthy. All but one of the dispatches from the correspondent said the same thing: Walker led the mob. So there was internal consistency. Finally, when General Walker's previous actions and statements are considered, the story that he led a mob at Ole Miss was not terribly out of line with his prior behavior. There was nothing to cause AP to suspect that the story was wrong as, for example, a report that the Archbishop of New York led a mob down Fifth Avenue. A red light should signal those kinds of instances which should suggest further checking because the story doesn't sound very likely.

Sorting all this out, we find that three key factors emerge. Was publication of the story urgent or was there sufficient time to check it fully? How reliable was the source? Was it a trained journalist? Finally, was the story probable or was it a tale which suggested the need for further checking?

These factors make up a fairly good operational definition of reckless disregard and are the kinds of considerations a court might take a close look at in determining the reasonableness of the conduct of an editor or broadcaster.

By combining the two conceptual definitions from *Garrison* and *St. Amant* and the practical guidelines from *Butts* and *Walker,* you should have a pretty good idea of the meaning of actual malice. The standard from *St. Amant,* the requirement of evidence that the defendant in fact entertained *serious* doubts as to the truth of the material, is a significant burden for the plaintiff to overcome. In addition, in bringing forward evidence to prove to the jury that the defendant did "entertain serious doubts," the plaintiff must meet a rigorous burden of proof. The normal evidentiary test in civil suits—the plaintiff must prove with a preponderance of evidence—has been abandoned in cases involving the *Times* rule. Instead the plaintiff must prove with "convincing clarity," must bring forth "clear and convincing evidence," that there was reckless disregard. If there is doubt in the juror's mind, he or she must vote for the defendant. This standard strengthens the *Times* rule additionally.

The *New York Times* actual malice rule is a potent defense in warding off many kinds of libel suits. It places an immense burden on public officials and public figures who hope to sue for defamation. There is no question that at present the Court is badly fractured with regard to the extent of use of the rule. Even the *Gertz* case, which effectively overturned the more liberal *Rosenbloom* rule, was really only subscribed to by four justices: Powell, Rehnquist, Marshall, and Stewart. Justice Blackmun's concurrence was reluctant. He said he preferred the *Rosenbloom* test but saw an overriding need for a definitive ruling. Hence he joined the other four justices to make a majority of five.

Regardless of the disagreements upon the Court, reporters can be assured that the *Times* rule means at least this: A plaintiff who is a public official and sues because of a story about his official conduct or other acts which have an impact upon how he conducts the public business or his fitness for office will have to prove actual malice. Similarly, a public figure who sues because of a story about an important public matter or a public controversy in which he or she has an important part, will also have to prove actual malice. In some states, just a few now, any person who brings a libel suit based upon a story about a matter of public or general interest has to prove actual malice. Actual malice, remember, is defined as knowledge that the charges or statements were false or reckless disregard of the truth or falsity of the charges.

DAMAGES   The *Gertz* case, about which I am certain you are tired of hearing, also drastically changed the law regarding libel damages. In the past in a libel case where no defense existed the plaintiff always collected some money, whether he could prove he had been damaged or not. Such damages are called general or presumed damages. Sometimes the award was only six cents, and sometimes it was a great deal more. The plaintiff had no responsibility to bring forth evidence of injury. He merely had to allege injury and ask for a fitting sum—let's say $100,000.

Those days are gone. The aftermath of *Gertz* makes it apparent that there are four kinds of damage claims which the plaintiff can make, and each requires the plaintiff to prove either injury or actual malice.

Actual Damages

In present-day law the basic element in damages is what are called actual damages, or damages for actual injury. The plaintiff has to convince the jury that he or she has suffered actual harm. What kind of harm? Not physical harm, obviously. The best definition of actual damages (as they are now defined) comes from the *Gertz* case. Justice Powell wrote that actual injury is not limited to out-of-pocket loss or money loss, which is how many authorities defined actual damages prior to this decision. Powell said, "Indeed, the more customary types of actual harm inflicted by defamatory falsehood include impairment of reputation and standing in the community, personal humiliation, and mental anguish and suffering." This statement is a very broad definition of actual damage. How can someone prove that he has suffered mental anguish? What is evidence of personal humiliation? These are very hard questions to answer. Libel damages have never been precise, and the new formulation doesn't promise additional precision. The plaintiff will have to bring evidence of some kind, and as in the past, the jury will be the key factor in making the determination of how much harm and how much damage.

Special Damages

Special damages are specific items of pecuniary loss caused by published defamatory statements. Special damages must be established in precise terms, much more precise terms than those for the actual damages just outlined. If a plaintiff can prove he lost $23,567.19 because of the libel, that amount is then what he can ask for and what he will likely get if he can convince the jury of his case. Special damages represent a specific monetary, and only monetary, loss as the result of the libel. Most plaintiffs don't seek special damages. However, in some cases special damages are all that can be sought. In trade libel, for example, the only award a plaintiff can get is special damages.

Presumed Damages

Presumed damages are damages that a plaintiff can get without proof of injury or harm. The only way a plaintiff may be awarded presumed or general damages is if actual malice, knowledge of falsity, or reckless disregard of the truth is proved.

Punitive Damages

Lawyers used to call punitive damages, or exemplary damages, the "smart money." Punitive damage awards are usually very large. The other kinds of damages just discussed are designed to compensate the plaintiff for his injury. Punitive damages are designed to punish the defendant for his misconduct and to warn other persons not to act in a similar manner. The only way a plaintiff can win punitive damages is if he can prove actual malice—knowledge of falsity or reckless disregard for the truth.

One point should be made clear about damages. When defenses were discussed earlier, it was pointed out that only public officials and public figures (and in some states private persons involved in matters of general concern) have to prove actual malice to win their case. But all plaintiffs can attempt to prove actual malice in the hope of getting punitive and presumed damages, and it is only if they meet this burden that they can collect the smart money.

RETRACTION

The phrase "I demand a retraction" is common in the folklore of libel. What is a retraction? A retraction is both an apology and an effort to set the record straight. Let's say you blow one as an editor. You report that Jane Adams was arrested for shoplifting, and you are wrong. In your retraction you first tell readers or viewers that Jane Adams was not arrested for shoplifting, that you made a mistake. Then you might also apologize for the embarrassment caused Ms. Adams. You might even say some nice things about her. At common law a prompt and honest retraction is usually relevant to the questions of whether the article was published with malice and whether the plaintiff's reputation was actually harmed. After all, you are attempting to reconstruct that part of her reputation which you tore down just the day before. She might have difficulty proving actual harm.

A good example of correction, or retraction, occurred about two years ago and involved of all things *Playboy's Book of Wines.* The slick-paper wine book erroneously charged on page 63 that a leading Italian winery, Bolla Vineyards, doctored its wine. As one writer noted, "All hell broke loose" when the American distributor of Bolla wines saw the reference. Playboy Press reached an agreement with the vintners in which it called back all five thousand copies of the book already distributed, sliced the two offending pages out of those copies and replaced them with two new pages containing flattering references to Bolla, stopped publication of the book until corrections could be made, and issued multiple apologies. These were extreme measures, but they prevented a lawsuit.

Statutes

In the several states which have retraction statutes, a plaintiff must give the publisher an opportunity to retract the libel before a suit may be started. If the publisher promptly honors the request for a retraction and retracts the libelous material in a place in the newspaper as prominent as the place in which the libel originally appeared, the impact will reduce and in some instances cancel any damage judgment the plaintiff might later seek in a lawsuit. Failure to seek a retraction limits the plaintiff's right to bring a lawsuit against the publisher.

About twenty-four states have retraction laws of one kind or another. In one state, Nevada, the editor must publish a denial or correction within a specified period of time or face a penalty of up to $1,000 or six months in jail. It should be noted that at this writing the Nevada law has not been tested in respect to the Supreme Court ruling in *Miami Herald* v. *Tornillo* (1974). In light of that decision the Nevada law might be unconstitutional because of the criminal penalty attached.

Retraction laws make good sense. It is the truth we seek, after all; a successful libel suit results in lining the plaintiff's pocket, but it is not very effective in correcting the errors in people's minds resulting from publication of the defamation.

CRIMINAL LIBEL

Since this book is for persons in the media or persons who plan to work in the media, there is really little reason to spend time discussing criminal libel. But it is there and is difficult to ignore. So here are a few well-chosen words on the subject.

The bulk of this chapter deals with civil libel—one person suing another for defamation. In most states, however. libel can be a crime as well. That is, there are criminal libel statutes, laws which make certain kinds of defamation a crime. For the most part these laws go unused today. They are relics of the past. In some states, in the South especially, recent instances of criminal libel prosecutions have occurred. In the 1970s most states are not very interested in taking on someone else's troubles and suing for libel. A prosecutor has very little to gain from such an action. In fact, he would probably be roundly criticized for instituting criminal libel charges. In an age when people are mugged, robbed, raped, and murdered with increasing frequency, damage to an individual's reputation, or even to the reputation of a large number of persons, somehow does not seem too serious. Moreover, individuals who have been harmed already have recourse—a civil suit. Several years ago in New York a judge stated this proposition very well (*People* v. *Quill*, 1958):

> The theory, in simplest terms, is that when an individual is libeled, he has an adequate remedy in a civil suit for damages. The public suffers no injury. Vindication for the individual and adequate compensation for the injury done him may be obtained as well in the civil courts. Thus the rule has always been, that the remedy of criminal prosecution should only be sought where the wrong is of so flagrant a character as to make a criminal prosecution necessary on public grounds.

Despite the fact that they are not used, criminal libel statutes remain on the books in most states. The California statute proclaims:

> . . . a libel is a malicious defamation, expressed either by writing, printing or by signs or pictures, or the like, tending to blacken the memory of one who is dead, or to impeach the honesty, integrity, virtue, or reputation or publish the natural or alleged defects of one who is alive, and thereby expose him to public hatred, contempt, or ridicule.

In Louisiana the law is defined in this manner:

> Defamation is the malicious publication or expression in any manner, to any one other than the party defamed, of anything which tends:
> (1) To expose any person to hatred, contempt, ridicule or to deprive him of the benefit of public confidence or social intercourse; or
> (2) To expose the memory of one deceased to hatred, contempt or ridicule; or
> (3) To impair any person, corporation or association of persons in his or their business occupations.
> Whoever commits the crime of defamation shall be fined not more than $3,000 or imprisoned for not more than one year or both.

As you can see, the crime of defamation is very similar to the tort of defamation: a person can get into trouble in both instances by doing about the same thing. It can be seen from the statutes quoted that it is possible to criminally libel a dead person. Since the deceased can't sue to protect his own good name it only makes sense to allow the state to intercede. Criminal libel differs from civil libel in several other ways as well.

First, in a few states criminal libel is tied to causing or potentially causing a breach of the peace. This charge used to be quite common. If a publication, speech, or handbill so provoked the readers or listeners that violence became possible or did in fact occur, criminal libel charges might result. In 1966 the United States Supreme Court undermined most of the "breach of the peace" statutes as well as the actions of those states that brought criminal libel actions under the common law. The case was *Ashton* v. *Kentucky* and involved a mining dispute in Hayard, Kentucky. An agitator was arrested for circulating a pamphlet which contained articles attacking the chief of police, the sheriff, and a newspaper editor, among others. At the criminal libel trial the judge defined the offense as "any writing calculated to create a disturbance of the peace, corrupt public morals or lead to any act, which when done, is indictable."

The Supreme Court reversed the conviction. Writing for a unanimous court Justice William O. Douglas said the crime as defined by the trial court is too general and indefinite. It left the standard of responsibility— whether something is illegal or not—wide open to the discretion of the judge. Also, Douglas noted, the crime is determined not by the character of the man's words, not by what he says or writes, but rather by the boiling point of those who listen to him or read his pamphlet. The law makes a man a criminal simply because his neighbors have no self-control and cannot refrain from violence.

This decision was an important factor, but only one factor, in the passing of "breach of the peace" as an aspect of criminal libel. It is extremely rare for such a case to occur today.

It is also possible to criminally libel a large group or race of people. The Supreme Court upheld such a law in 1952, a law which made it a crime to libel any race, color, creed, or religion. The case originated in Illinois where a white racist named Joseph Beauharnais distributed insulting literature at a time when blacks were attempting to integrate the white Chicago suburb of Cicero. Beauharnais's words were strong at a time when police and other officials had their hands full keeping the peace. He was arrested, tried, and fined $200 for his pamphleteering.

He argued that his conviction violated the First Amendment. In a five-to-four vote, the Court upheld the conviction on the grounds that libelous utterances are not within the protection of the First Amendment. Justice Felix Frankfurter wrote that if an utterance directed at an individual may be the object of criminal penalties the high Court could not then deny the right of a state to make such utterances aimed at a well-defined group criminal as well (*Beauharnais* v. *Illinois*, 1952).

The rationale for this decision was eroded by the *New York Times* decision: Libelous utterances are protected by the First Amendment in an increasing number of instances, and the Beauharnais case is also certainly weakened. One would be hard pressed to predict what the Court might do with such a case today.

The high Court has heard one criminal libel case since the **Sullivan** ruling. The high Court ruled in *Garrison* v. *Louisiana* that when the defamation of a public official is the basis for a criminal libel suit the state has to prove actual malice on the part of the defendant, that is, knowledge of falsity or reckless disregard for the truth or falsity of the matter. Justice Brennan wrote that the reasons which persuaded the court to rule that the First Amendment protected criticism of public officials in a civil libel suit applies with equal force in a criminal libel suit. "The constitutional guarantees of freedom of expression compel application of the same standard to the criminal remedy," he added. However, the question of what the court would do with a group libel suit of the kind it faced in 1952 is still not answered.

Criminal libel is not a real problem for journalists and broadcasters. Within the few criminal libel cases on record since World War II, cases in which the media were the defendant can be counted on one hand.

Normally the action is brought against the writer of the article or the speaker of the words, not against the medium publishing the comments.

As was noted at the beginning of this chapter, libel is probably the most common legal problem most journalists and broadcasters face today. Unlike difficulties with courts and problems in getting information from the government, which occur infrequently, libel is something the press lives with day in and day out. Virtually every story contains the potential for a libel suit.

The press is much better protected today than it was thirteen years ago before the *New York Times* decision. The *Sullivan* ruling has helped the press in many ways. In the past plaintiffs with only the remote possibility of victory were lured to court by the possibility of a large windfall judgment. Recent cases have made the smart money tougher to get. Also, infusion of good, solid First Amendment idealism and logic into the law has made judges at all levels far more sensitive to the needs of the press. These events have been very helpful. While "freedom of the press" may be legally vague, a judge or jury who thinks about the First Amendment is likely to be more receptive to the arguments of the defense.

Some persons fear that the broad freedoms won in the days of the Warren Court have already begun to erode, that the Burger Court is not as sensitive to the First Amendment freedoms as its predecessor. The *Gertz* decision was the first sign of a rollback, they argue. In a recent edition of the *Brooklyn Law Review* a commentator noted:

> There is a danger . . . that the *Gertz* decision may in fact exacerbate rather than eliminate self-censorship. Since publishers tend to "steer far wider of the unlawful zone," a rule allowing recovery on the basis of negligence may cause them simply to refrain from printing articles on sensitive subjects, in lieu of attempting to anticipate a jury's view of reasonableness of prepublication decisions. It is precisely discussion of such controversial issues that the First Amendment was designed to secure, "since speech which arouses little emotion is little in need of protection."

Negligence and the reasonable man are the focus of many of the worries expressed by some authorities today. Professor Harry Kalven once remarked that there may be no place in the scope of the First Amendment for the reasonable man. And Justice Douglas added that with such continued erosion of the First Amendment protection the reasonable man may well be the one who refrains from speaking at all.

The problem about which these people speak is not only censorship by the courts, but also self-censorship by the press itself. Professor David Anderson (*"Libel and Press Self-Censorship"*) of the University of Texas Law School wrote recently:

> The *Times* privilege has failed to prevent self-censorship primarily because it does little to reduce the cost of defending against libel claims. Instead, it perpetuates a system of censorship by libel lawyers— a system in which the relevant question is not whether a story is libelous, but whether the subject is likely to sue, and if so, how much it will cost to defend.

Anderson estimates that the cost of defending a full-fledged libel suit begins at about $20,000. In *Rosenbloom* v. *Metromedia* noted earlier, Metromedia, which won the case, spent $100,000 in defense costs.

The Texas Observer, a bright little weekly newspaper in the Lone Star State was fighting for its very life as this chapter was written. The *Observer* was being sued for libel. While the paper had a strong case, defending the legal challenge was stripping the publication's financial reserves.

In August 1974 the journalism review *MORE* informed its readers that certain passages in one edition were deleted from a story for fear publication would result in a legal action. *MORE* said it had consulted its lawyers, who advised that the review would probably win the libel suit. ". . . but that the cost of defending it might easily bankrupt the magazine. After a good deal of agonizing . . . we decided the risk was not worth it," the editor noted.

Cost is a terrible problem for much of the press in the United States today, for the smaller, less financially strong media. These newspapers and magazines, often the most interesting and often the most outspoken, have the least ability to fight a libel suit. One partial solution is for courts to regularly assess unsuccessful plaintiffs for the costs accumulated by the defendant. This practice would make a plaintiff think twice before suing and would also make a newspaper less hesitant about publishing libelous material which it thinks is defensible. Unfortunately most judges do not follow this practice, and there is little prospect presently for a change.

A reporter's knowledge of the law, then, becomes more important both in avoiding libel suits and in knowing what the law allows to be published. Except for the largest papers and broadcasting stations, attorneys who advise and defend the press in libel suits are not especially skilled or qualified in this area of the law. Few lawyers specialize in communications law. Most attorneys who represent the media rarely see more than two or three libel suits a year and few of these go to trial. Professor Anderson (*Texas Law Review*) writes, "One may doubt whether the nature of these lawyers' practice will give them either the time or the inclination to contemplate seriously the subtle constitutional and societal interests at stake in libel litigation."

In many instances, the task falls to reporters themselves, which is perhaps the prime reason so many pages in this books are given over to the law of libel.

BIBLIOGRAPHY
Here are some of the sources that have been helpful in the preparation of chapter 3.

Books American Law Institute. *Restatement of the Law of Torts Second.* Tentative Draft No. 21, Division Five—Defamation. Philadelphia, Pa.: American Law Institute, 1975.

Ashley, Paul. *Say It Safely.* 5th ed. Seattle, Wash.: University of Washington Press, 1976.

Gregory, Charles O., and Kalven, Harry, Jr. *Cases and Materials on Torts.* 2d ed. Boston: Little, Brown & Co., 1969.

Hansen, Arthur. *Libel and Related Torts.* New York: Publishers Association Foundation, 1969.

Phelps, Robert, and Hamilton, Douglas. *Libel.* New York: Macmillan Co., 1966.

Prosser, William L. *Handbook of the Law of Torts.* St. Paul, Minn.: West Publishing Co., 1964.

Thomas, Ella Cooper. *The Law of Libel and Slander.* Dobbs Ferry, N. Y.: Oceana Publications, 1963.

Yankwich, Leon R. *It's Libel or Contempt If You Print It.* Los Angeles: Parker & Sons Publications, 1950.

Articles Anderson, David A. "Libel and Press Self-Censorship," 53 *Texas Law Review* 422 (1975).

"Defamation Law in the Wake of *Gertz* v. *Welch, Inc.*," 69 *Northwestern University Law Review* 960 (1975).

Frakt, Arthur N. "Evolving Law of Defamation: *New York Times Co.* v. *Sullivan* to *Gertz* v. *Robert Welch, Inc.,* and Beyond," 6 *Rutgers Camden Law Journal* 471 (1975).

"Torts: Libel," 41 *Brooklyn Law Review* 389 (1974).

Cases *AAFCO Heating and Air Conditioning* v. *Northwest Publications,* 321 N.E. 2d 580 (1974).

Ashton v. *Kentucky,* 384 U.S. 195 (1966).

Barr v. *Mateo,* 360 U.S. 564 (1959).

Beauharnais v. *Illinois,* 343 U.S. 250 (1952).

Borg v. *Boas,* 231 F. 2d 788 (1956).

Cardiff v. *Brooklyn Eagle,* Inc., 75 N.Y.S. 2d 222 (1948).

Carr v. *Hood,* 1 Campbell 355 (1808).

Cepeda v. *Cowles Magazine & Broadcasting, Inc.,* 328 F. 2d 869 (1964).

Cherry v. *Des Moines Leader,* 86 N.W. 323 (1901).

City of Chicago v. *Tribune Co.,* 139 N.E. 86 (1923).

Cohen v. *New York Times,* 138 N.Y.S. 206 (1912).

Coleman v. *MacLennan,* 98 P. 281 (1908).

Commercial Programming Unlimited v. *CBS,* 367 N.Y.S. 2d 986 (1975).

Curtis Publishing Co. v. *Butts, AP* v. *Walker,* 388 U.S. 130 (1967).

Farnsworth v. *Tribune Co.,* 253 N.E. 2d 408 (1969).

Faulk v. *Aware, Inc.,* 155 N.Y.S. 2d 726 (1956).

Fawcett Publications v. *Morris,* 377 P. 2d 42 (1962).

Fleckstein v. *Friedman*, 193 N.E. 537 (1934).

Fowler v. *New York Herald*, 172 N.Y.S. 423 (1918).

Garrison v. *Louisiana*, 379 U.S. 64 (1964).

General Motors v. *Piskor*, 340 A 2d 767 (1975).

Gertz v. *Robert Welch, Inc.*, 94 S. Ct. 2997 (1974).

Goldwater v. *Ginzburg*, 414 F. 2d 324 (1969).

Grant v. *Reader's Digest Association*, 151 F. 2d 733 (1945).

Hoeppner v. *Dunkirk Printing Co.*, 172 N.E. 139 (1930).

Hope v. *Hearst Corp.*, 294 F. 2d 681 (1961).

Hornby v. *Hunter*, 385 S.W. 2d 473 (1964).

Layne v. *Tribune Co.*, 146 So. 234 (1933).

Miami Herald v. *Tornillo*, 94 S. Ct. 2831 (1974).

Morgan v. *Dun & Bradstreet, Inc.*, 421 F. 2d 1241 (1970).

McNair v. *Hearst Corp.* (1975).

Neiman-Marcus v. *Lait*, 13 F.R.D. 311 (1952).

New York Times Co. v. *Sullivan*, 376 U.S. 254 (1964).

Pauling v. *Globe-Democrat*, 362 F. 2d 188 (1966).

Peagler v. *Phoenix Newspapers, Inc.*, 547 P. 2d 1074 (1976).

Pearson v. *Fairbanks Publishing Co.*, 413 P. 2d 711 (1966).

People v. *Quill*, 177 N.Y.S. 2d 380 (1958).

Perry v. *Hearst Corp.*, 334 F. 2d 800 (1964).

Powers v. *Durgin-Snow Publishing Co.*, 144 A 2d 294 (1958).

Pulverman v. *A. S. Abell Co.*, 228 F. 2d 797 (1956).

Reynolds v. *Pegler*, 223 F. 2d 429 (1955).

Rosenblatt v. *Baer*, 383 U.S. 75 (1966).

Rosenbloom v. *Metromedia*, 403 U.S. 29 (1971).

St. Amant v. *Thompson*, 390 U.S. 727 (1968).

Shiles v. *News Syndicate Co.*, 261 N.E. 2d 251 (1970).

State v. *Time, Inc.*, 249 So. 2d 328 (1971).

Stillman v. *Paramount Pictures*, 147 N.E. 2d 741 (1957).

Tabart v. *Tipper*, 1 Camp. 350 (1808).

Taskett v. *King Broadcasting*, Dockett #43702, Washington Supreme Court, Feb. 11, 1976.

Time, Inc. v. *Firestone*, 96 S. Ct. 958 (1976).

Triggs v. *Sun Printing & Publishing Association*, 71 N.E. 739 (1904).

Walker v. *Colorado Springs Sun, Inc.*, 538 P. 2d 450 (1975).

Washington Post v. *Kennedy*, 3 F. 2d 207 (1924).

Washington Post v. *Keogh*, 365 F. 2d 965 (1966).

CHAPTER 4

Invasion of Privacy

Privacy is a commodity which seems to be in shorter and shorter supply each day. Every person seems to give up a little more privacy as one year passes into the next. Full participation in our buy now—pay later, opinion-research-oriented, full-insurance, credit-card, big-government society without giving up additional privacy becomes harder and harder every day. It is still possible for an individual to withdraw from this kind of society, to live in a cabin in some remote wilderness, but few persons are willing to give up the comforts that modern life provides.

**PRIVACY
DEFINED**

Privacy is a very difficult concept to define. It has many meanings. One individual may say that he believes in the right of privacy, but also believes that the police have the right to wiretap telephone conversations. A shopkeeper may assert that she stands behind the right of privacy, but is reluctant to give up the television cameras which scan every nook and cranny of the shop in an effort to discourage shoplifting. The government is supposed to help citizens protect their privacy; yet government at all levels seriously invades our privacy by gathering massive amounts of data on private citizens for a variety of reasons, good and bad.

In 1888 in *Treatise on the Law of Torts* Thomas M. Cooley defined privacy as "the right to be let alone." More recently privacy was defined as the right of an individual to control information about himself. The right of privacy was first proposed as a narrow legal right in 1890. However, as Prof. Edward J. Bloustein writes in "Privacy as an Aspect of Human Dignity," "What began at the turn of the century as a limited private right to prevent undue and unreasonable publicity concerning private lives has now developed into an extraordinarily broad constitutional right, the limits of which are still not clear."

Today invasion of privacy encompasses a wide range of behavior which includes wiretapping, illegal surveillance, misuse of information by retail credit agencies, use of two-way mirrors in department store dressing rooms, and collection of private information by researchers, banks, and government agencies. The mass media are also frequently accused of invasion of privacy. This chapter is about invasion of privacy by the press, by radio and television, and by the motion-picture industry.

The chapter opens with a brief history of the law of privacy. Then each of the four ways in which the media can run afoul of the law for invasion of privacy is discussed and the defenses for each kind of invasion of privacy are outlined. It is important to remember this point. Invasion of privacy by the media really involves four distinct legal wrongs: (1) appropriation of an individual's name or likeness for commercial purposes without first getting consent, (2) intrusion upon a person's solitude, (3) publication of private information about a person, and (4) publication of false information about a person, or putting someone in a false light. Each area has defenses which the press may erect in an effort to ward off a plaintiff's lawsuit. The defenses that work for one kind of invasion of privacy suit are generally not effective in defending another kind of suit for invasion of privacy. The defense of newsworthiness, for example, can be used to stop a suit for the publication of private information, but the defense won't work in a suit based upon appropriation of a likeness or name. It is best to think of invasion of privacy as four separate legal problems, each with its own defenses.

**HISTORY OF
LAW OF
PRIVACY**

Despite its apparent similarity to libel, the law of privacy is far less mature than its older tort cousin. In fact, from the standpoint of the centuries-old common law system, privacy is downright modern. Unlike most other areas of the law, we can say specifically that a legal remedy for invasion of privacy was first advocated less than one hundred years ago.

The concept of privacy is old, but the law of privacy is young, growing out of the dramatically changing social conditions of the late nineteenth century, the era which spawned present-day urban United States. The Industrial Revolution brought crowded cities and reduced space to a premium, and at the same time the American press changed profoundly. In the fight for circulation the mass press of the big cities undertook new schemes to attract readers. It is perhaps an understatement to note that this was not journalism's finest hour.

While privacy was something which people enjoyed and sought, it was not something with which our legal system could cope. There was no legal right to privacy, no law which guaranteed the right to be left alone. In 1890 two young lawyers proposed in the *Harvard Law Review* ("The Right to Privacy") that such a law should exist. One of the pair, the prominent Boston attorney Samuel D. Warren, was annoyed at what he described as the gossipy, snoopy Boston press which frequently focused on the social activities of the Warren family. Warren sought the aid of his former law partner, former Harvard Law School classmate and close friend, Louis D. Brandeis, in preparing a plea for the legal recognition of the right to be let alone.

The pair argued, "Instantaneous photographs and newspaper enterprise have invaded the sacred precincts of private and domestic life; and numerous mechanical devices threaten to make good the prediction that 'what is whispered in the closet shall be proclaimed from the house-tops.'" Warren and Brandeis said they were offended by the gossip in the press, which they said has overstepped in every direction the obvious bounds of propriety and decency.

> To satisfy a prurient taste the details of sexual relations are spread broadcast in the columns of the daily papers. To occupy the indolent, column upon column is filled with idle gossip, which can only be procured by intrusion upon the domestic circle. . . .
> The common law has always recognized a man's house as his castle, impregnable, often, even to its own officers engaged in the execution of its commands. Shall the courts thus close the front entrance to constituted authority, and open wide the back door to idle or prurient curiosity?

To stop this illicit behavior the two young lawyers proposed that the courts recognize the legal right of privacy, that is, citizens should be able to go to court to stop such unwarranted intrusions and also secure money damages for the hardship they suffered by such prying and publication of private material about them.

To a modern observer, the Boston press doesn't appear to be nearly so scandalous as the charges by Warren and Brandeis suggested. One gets the distinct impression that Mr. Warren was an overly sensitive individual.

The article also appears to have been Warren's idea. He sought help from Brandeis, who was indeed a legal scholar. Brandeis later went on to have a distinguished career as a jurist. Finally, despite the eloquence of their plea, the Warren and Brandeis proposal fell on somewhat deaf ears. Thirteen years passed before any state recognized the legal right of privacy. In 1903 New York passed a privacy statute which guaranteed its citizens protection from invasion of their privacy, but the statute contained a far different concept of privacy than that proposed in 1890. What the New York law did was prohibit commercial exploitation of the name or picture of any citizen.

From these rather humble beginnings more than seventy years ago, privacy law has grown until today it is an important segment of our legal rights. It has also become a serious problem for the mass media. As of today the courts in nearly four-fifths of the states and in the District of Columbia have recognized the legal claim of invasion of privacy. Five of these states (California, New York, Oklahoma, Utah, and Virginia) accomplished this via state statute; the remaining jurisdictions recognized the right through the common law. In three states, Nebraska, Wisconsin, and Rhode Island, the courts say that no such right exists within their jurisdiction. And the courts in Idaho, Maine, Minnesota, North Dakota, Washington, Vermont, and Wyoming have yet to make up their minds about the protection of the right of privacy. It would be foolish, however, given the public attitude toward privacy and the growing recognition of the legal right, for anyone to deny that with the proper case the courts in any one of the states are very likely to acknowledge the existence of the legal remedy for invasion of privacy.

While the law has grown, it has not grown in exactly the way Warren and Brandeis proposed. In fact, today much of the law bears no resemblance at all to the plan put forth in 1890. Like Topsy, the law of privacy just grew—in all directions. Today legal scholars, like the late William Prosser, argue that invasion of privacy really encompasses not just one, but four legal wrongs. Let's briefly summarize the four and then study each in depth.

Appropriation

The first kind of invasion of privacy is called appropriation and is defined as taking a person's name, picture, photograph, or likeness and using it without his permission for commercial gain. Imagine you are a photographer and shoot a great picture of your neighbor skiing down a mountainside. You put the photograph in a local display, and a representative of Acme Skis sees it and wants to use it in an advertising campaign. You sell the picture for $500, and Acme puts it in an advertising poster which is circulated throughout the nation. Both you and Acme are guilty of appropriation, and your neighbor can seek (and will probably get) money damages and an injunction to stop distribution of the poster. Of course, if your neighbor gives you permission to sell the picture and permission for the ski company to use it, no legal wrong has then been committed.

This is technically the only right of privacy which is guaranteed in the five states which have privacy statutes. The laws are limited to outlawing this one kind of behavior. But as a matter of fact, judicial construction of these laws has allowed them to encompass many of the other aspects of invasion of privacy as well.

Intrusion

Intrusion is the second type of invasion of privacy, an area of the law growing rapidly today, and is what most people think of when invasion of privacy is mentioned. Intrusion upon the solitude and into the private life of a person is prohibited. While this area of the law is growing rapidly, it has not had much of an impact upon the mass media. Newspapers and broadcasting stations don't usually wiretap telephones, bug rooms, make illegal searches, or break into private files. While it has brought out the best in the press, the current popularity of "investigative reporting" has also brought out the worst in some reporters. Therefore intrusion must be discussed.

Publication of
Private Information

The law prohibits publication of private information—truthful private information—about a person. What is truthful private information? Gossip, substance of private conversations, and details of a private tragedy or illness have all been used as the basis of a suit. Because this area of the law prohibits communication of truthful comments, the courts have been quite reluctant to impose a liability upon the press. Instead, a range of defenses that nearly suffocate the legal remedy have been constructed. It is very hard for a person to collect damages for publication of private information. Usually only when good taste and good sense are totally abandoned will the press be in trouble.

Publication of
False Information

The publication of any false information about a person can result in a privacy suit, whether the material is defamatory or not. The fourth area of the law is an outgrowth of the first, the appropriation area. Maybe both should be in a single category, but they are probably easier to understand when they are considered separately.

Some people have said that a law of privacy is really not needed. Several years ago law professor Frederick Davis ("What Do We Mean by Right to Privacy?") wrote, "Indeed, one can logically argue that the concept of a right of privacy was never required in the first place, and that its whole history is an illustration of how well-meaning but impatient academicians can upset the normal development of the law by pushing it too hard."

One can make a persuasive argument that Davis is right. The appropriation area of the law really deals with a property right and would probably fit more comfortably as part of the law of literary property, product disparagement, trademarks, and the like. Intrusion is really more akin to the law of trespass. False information is very close to defamation. Publication of private information—the only truly unique aspect of the law—has enjoyed such limited success that it might be abandoned altogether with little loss. Control of this kind of behavior might better be left to public opinion and the conscience of reporters and editors, as Prof. Zechariah Chafee once suggested.

Regardless of whether it is legally logical, the law of privacy does exist; it is a part of our legal system. Persons in the media must be constantly aware of it. The number of privacy suits seems to increase a little each year. A considerable number of cases are settled in favor of the plaintiff. For better understanding of the law each of the four types or kinds of invasion of privacy is discussed at length in the pages that follow.

APPROPRIATION   Appropriation is the oldest and in many ways the least ambiguous of the four types of invasion of privacy. Two of the earliest cases remain good examples of this area of the law.

1. In 1902 young Abigail Roberson of Albany, New York, awoke one morning to find her picture all over town on posters advertising Franklin Mills Flour. Twenty-five thousand copies of the advertisement were placed in stores, warehouses, saloons, and other public buildings. Abigail said she felt embarrassed and humiliated, that she suffered greatly from this commercial exploitation, and she therefore sued for invasion of privacy. But she lost her case, and the state's high court ruled (*Roberson v. Rochester Folding Box Co.*, 1902):

> . . . an examination of the authorities leads us to the conclusion that the so-called "right of privacy" has not yet found an abiding place in our jurisprudence, and, as we view it, the doctrine cannot now be incorporated without doing violence to settled principles of law by which the profession and the public have long been guided.

Following this decision a great controversy arose in New York, led by the press, much of which was outraged by the way the court had treated Abigail. The controversy settled on the state legislature which during the following year, 1903, adopted the nation's first privacy law. The statute was very narrow: that is, it prohibited a very specific kind of conduct. Use of an individual's name or likeness without his consent for advertising or trade purposes was made a minor crime. In addition to the criminal penalty, the statute allowed the injured party to seek both an injunction to stop the use of the name or picture and money damages. This was the first privacy statute.

2. Two years later Georgia became the first state to recognize the right of privacy through the common law. Paolo Pavesich, an Atlanta artist, discovered that a life insurance company had used his photograph in newspaper advertisements. Pavesich's photograph was used in a before-and-after advertisement to illustrate a contented, successful man who had bought sufficient life insurance. A testimonial statement was also ascribed

to the artist. He sued for $25,000 and won his case before the Georgia Supreme Court which ruled (*Pavesich* v. *New England Life Insurance Co.,* 1905):

> . . . the form and features of the plaintiff are his own. The defendant insurance company and its agents had no more authority to display them in public for the purpose of advertising the business . . . than they would have had to compel the plaintiff to place himself upon exhibition for this purpose.

Compensation

Before the ramifications of this aspect of the law are discussed, let us ask the question, For what are plaintiffs compensated in an invasion of privacy suit? What is their damage? In a libel case the reputation is damaged, a fairly invisible injury. But in a privacy suit the damage is even more invisible: the damage is the humiliation, embarrassment, and general bother that an ordinary person might experience from invasion of privacy. In other words, the damage is personal. The right of privacy is a personal right.

In the other three areas of the law of privacy such damage probably makes sense. Intruding into a person's privacy by bugging or wiretapping, publishing details of a private matter, and publishing untruthful statements about a person certainly would cause anguish to most persons. But many people believe that in appropriation the humiliation and embarrassment are minimal. What the plaintiff should be compensated for is the use of his or her name or his or her picture—something which he or she owns—to assist someone else to make money. In other words, a business or an advertiser makes commercial gain from something which belongs to the plaintiff. If you write a book and someone steals it and publishes it, you can sue to compensate for your loss. If someone sets up a business on your land and makes a fortune, he has appropriated something which belongs to you without paying you for its use. The same logic applies to your name and face. If a successful advertising campaign is based on your smile, or if people buy Acme Corn Flakes because the manufacturer tells customers that you eat this cereal every morning, something that belongs to you is used by somebody else to make money.

Until recently the law was content to live with the myth that plaintiffs are rewarded in appropriation cases for psychological damage. In 1953 a distinguished jurist, Jerome Frank, exposed this myth when he wrote in a case involving baseball bubble gum cards and professional athletes that the issue in most appropriation cases is not the right of privacy but what he called the right of publicity, the right of a person to control the commercial exploitation of his name or likeness (*Haelan*

Laboratories, Inc. v. *Topps Chewing Gum,* 1953). Other legal scholars joined Judge Frank, but to no avail. The myth remains.

Recently, however, a refreshing honesty has crept into some court decisions, and in two of the cases involving athletes like Arnold Palmer and Jack Nicklaus and stars of professional baseball, courts ruled that a person has the right to enjoy the fruits of his own industry free from unjustified interference, and that a celebrity has a legitimate proprietary interest in his public personality (*Palmer* v. *Schonhorn Enterprises,* 1967, and *Uhlaender* v. *Henricksen,* 1970). One judge added that the celebrity's "identity, embodied in his name, likeness, statistics and other personal characteristics, is the fruit of his labors and is a type of property." In New Jersey a court ruled that even the unfamous, the unknown Mr. and Mrs. Average American enjoy a property right in their identities (*Canessa* v. *J. I. Kislak, Inc.,* 1967). A real estate company used the Canessa family's name and pictures in some advertisements. "However little or much plaintiff's likeness and name may be worth," the judge wrote, "defendant, who has appropriated them for his commercial benefit, should be made to pay for what he has taken. . . ."

Regardless of whether it is the right of privacy or the right of publicity that is protected, the law remains pretty much the same and is fairly clear in this area. If a person's name or likeness is appropriated without his permission and used for commercial purposes, and if the thief is caught, he will probably lose the case and have to pay. There are few ifs, ands, or buts. The important aspects of appropriation are the dimensions of such terms as likeness, advertising and trade purposes, and consent.

Everybody knows what a name is, and it is therefore unnecessary to dwell on that term. It should be noted, however, that stage names, pen names, pseudonyms, and so forth, count the same as real names in the eyes of the law. If the name of rock star Elton John is used in an advertisement for dental floss without his permission, the suit cannot be defended on the basis that since Elton John's real name is Reginald Kenneth Dwight his "name" was not appropriated illegally. It should also be noted that the law of privacy protects only people's names. Company names, trade names, and corporate names are not protected. Only people enjoy the right of privacy. Businesses, corporations, schools, and other "things" are not protected under the law. However, the use of a trade name like Kodak or Crest can create other serious legal problems.

Likeness

What is a likeness? Obviously a photograph, a painting, and a sketch—anything that suggests to readers and viewers that the plaintiff is pictured—are likenesses.

Trade and Advertising Purposes

What are advertising and trade purposes? While minor differences exist among the states—especially among the five states with statutes—a general guideline can be set down: advertising or trade purposes are commercial uses, that is, someone makes money from the use. Here are examples of the kinds of actions which clearly are commercial use:

1. Use of a person's name or photograph in an *advertisement* on television, on radio, in newspapers, in magazines, on posters, on billboards and so forth
2. Display of a person's photograph in the window of a photographer's shop to show potential customers the quality of work done by the studio
3. A testimonial falsely suggesting that an individual eats the cereal or drives the automobile in question

Newspapers and Magazines

What about this argument? A newspaper runs a photograph of John Smith on the front page after his car rolled over several times during a high-speed police pursuit. Smith sues for invasion of privacy, arguing that his picture on the front page of the newspaper attracted readers to the paper, resulted in the sale of newspapers, and therefore was used for commercial or trade purposes. Despite the arguments of many persons—even today—courts have consistently rejected this claim.

This plea was first made in 1907 by a New Yorker who objected to having his picture appear on the front page of the *New York World*. The state supreme court rejected the argument, noting that surely the intent of the state legislature was not to prohibit a newspaper or magazine from publishing a person's name or picture in a single issue without his consent (*Moser* v. *Press Publishing Co.*, 1908). Two years later another New York court reiterated this stand, ruling that advertising and trade purposes referred to commercial use, not to the dissemination of information (*Jeffries* v. *New York Evening Journal*, 1910). The United States Supreme Court has ruled that the fact that newspapers and books and magazines are sold for profit does not deny them the protection of liberty of expression. So the rule is, use of a person's name or likeness to inform as opposed to sell is protected (*Time, Inc.* v. *Hill*, 1967).

The law of privacy, like all law, contains narrow exceptions to general rules, and this is one of them. Despite what has just been said, there is a category of advertisements in which use of a person's name or picture without consent is not an invasion of privacy. These are advertisements for media—newspapers, television, and magazines—which are otherwise protected by freedom of expression. The use of a person's name or picture in such an advertisement will not result in liability provided that the picture or name was used earlier in a news or information story. Here is an example from a real case.

The controversy which sparked this rule involved actress Shirley Booth. She was photographed in Jamaica, and the picture was published in a feature story in *Holiday* magazine. *Holiday* then used the same picture to advertise the magazine itself. The full-page advertisement told readers that the picture was typical of the material appearing in *Holiday* magazine and urged people to advertise in the periodical or subscribe **to** *Holiday*. Ms. Booth did not object to her photograph in the feature story, only to its use in the subsequent advertisement. The courts, however, refused to call the use an invasion of privacy. The New York Supreme Court ruled that the strength of a free press depends upon economic support from advertisers and subscribers, and hence a publication or broadcasting station must promote itself. Since the picture in this case was first used in an information story, its subsequent use in a promotion for the magazine was really only "incidental" to its original use and was merely to show the quality and content of the magazine. The picture was not used to sell spaghetti or used cars. Hence the use did not constitute an invasion of privacy (*Booth* v. *Curtis Publishing Co.*, 1962).

In advertisements promoting itself a newspaper can republish stories and photographs which contain the names and pictures of people—private citizens as well as celebrities. A television station can put together a montage of news clips from stories it has broadcast and use the montage as a promotion. The advertisements must be for the medium itself—"self ads" as they are sometimes called. A commercial firm cannot republish a news story in its advertising without liability. If there was a fire at the Acme Furniture Store, and the local newspaper wrote a long story about it which contained the names of firemen, employees, witnesses, and so forth, Acme could not republish this story in its Fire Sale advertisements unless it first deleted the names of the persons mentioned and covered up the faces of any persons identifiable in the photographs. The exception to the general rule applies only to advertisements for the mass media which contain pictures or names previously used in informational or news stories.

Television   It has been established that use of a name or likeness in a news story or informational story is not appropriation, and that use of a name or likeness in a commercial advertisement is appropriation. In newspapers and magazines, column rules separate the advertisements from the news. What about television where nearly all programs are sponsored? Tastee Bread Brings You the News With John Smith. Is the inclusion of a person's name or photograph in a sponsored newscast an invasion of privacy? No. In a case decided more than twenty years ago the Appellate

Division of the New York Supreme Court ruled (*Gautier* v. *Pro-Football, Inc.*, 1952):

> The unique necessities of radio and television . . . require that in large part programs appear under the sponsorship of commercial advertisers. To hold that the mere fact of sponsorship makes the use of an individual's name or picture on radio or television a use "for advertising purposes" would materially weaken the informative and educational potentials of these still developing media.

The court added that in the absence of exploitation of a name or picture in the commercial announcement or in direct connection with the product itself use for commercial purposes does not exist.

Consent as Defense

The law prohibits only the unauthorized use of a name or picture. In those states that have privacy statutes the law specifically requires that the consent be a written authorization from the subject. In the remainder of the states the law is more ambiguous on the question. Nevertheless, the defendant is forced to prove he or she has consent if and when a lawsuit arises, and therefore it only makes sense to obtain written consent. An example of a standard consent or release form is on page 178.

The problems which can arise from the defense of consent are numerous, and in each case they are more severe when written consent has not been obtained. For example, it is always possible for the person to withdraw consent after it has been given. Columbia Broadcasting System prepared a fictional television drama about the kidnapping of Jackie Gleason. Gleason played himself in the story, and an actor played the part of Gleason's manager. The manager's real name was used in the script. Suddenly the man decided after the program was filmed that he did not want his name included in the program. Despite the fact that he had worked on the play for many weeks, planning and writing, a New York court said that inclusion of the plaintiff's name in the film against his will constituted an invasion of privacy (*Durgom* v. *CBS*, 1961). While this suit falls under category four of invasion of privacy, the rules are the same for both appropriation and falsehood. Columbia Broadcasting was therefore forced to write the plaintiff out of the script and reshoot part of the production.

Had the network gained written consent from the subject, and had it paid the plaintiff for using his name in the play, he would have found it much harder—if not impossible—to revoke consent at the last minute. Written consent has a distinct advantage. The safest rule is to always get written consent. Photographers especially are advised to carry copies of a standard model release form in their gadget bags so that when that once-in-a-lifetime picture comes along, the one they are certain to sell for $10,000, they can obtain written consent from the subject on the spot.

There are times when even written consent does not work as a defense, and the media must be aware of such situations.

1. Consent given today may not be valid ten years hence, especially if it is gratuitous oral consent. In Louisiana a man named Cole McAndrews gave permission to the owner of a health spa to use his before-and-after pictures in advertisements for the gym. But the owner, Alvin Roy, waited ten years to use the photographs, and in the interim McAndrews' life had changed considerably. He sued Roy, who argued that it was McAndrews' responsibility to revoke the consent if he no longer wanted the pictures used. But a Louisiana court of appeals agreed instead with the plaintiff. Judge Robert D. Jones wrote (*McAndrews* v. *Roy*, 1961):

> We are of the opinion that it would be placing an unreasonable burden on the plaintiff to hold he was under duty to revoke a gratuitous authorization given many years before. As the defendant was the only person to profit from the use of the pictures, then, under all the circumstances, it seems reasonable that he should have sought renewal of the permission to use the old pictures.

Reauthorization is needed when a name or photograph is used many years after consent was first given.

2. Some persons cannot give consent. A teenage girl is perfect to appear in an Acme Shampoo advertising campaign. She agrees to pose and signs a release authorizing use of her picture in the advertisements. The pictures are great, the advertisements are great, everything is great— until notice arrives that the model is suing for invasion of privacy! But she signed the permission form. Right. But she was only sixteen years old, and under the law minors cannot give consent. Parental consent is required in such instances.

Other people are unable to give consent as well, as Frederick Wiseman discovered when he filmed the documentary *Titicut Follies*. Wiseman shot the film at the Massachusetts Correctional Institute at Bridgewater, a facility housing insane persons charged with crimes. Most of the sixty-two inmates filmed were not legally competent to give consent, and the state refused to give permission to Wiseman for the inclusion of those persons in the documentary. Instead, Massachusetts obtained an injunction which restricted the showing of the film to professional persons (correctional officers, psychologists, students, etc.) only (*Commonwealth* v. *Wiseman*, 1969).

It is important to know that the person from whom consent is obtained is legally able to give consent.

3. Finally, consent to use a photograph of a person in an advertisement or on a poster cannot be used as a defense if the photograph is

materially altered or changed. Several years ago a well-known and well-paid New York fashion model posed for pictures to be used in an advertising campaign for a bookstore. After the photography session model Mary Jane Russell signed this standard release form:

> The undersigned hereby irrevocably consents to the unrestricted use by Richard Avedon [the photographer], advertisers, customers, successors, and assigns, of my name, portrait, or picture for advertising purposes or purposes of trade, and I waive the right to inspect or approve such completed portraits, pictures, or advertising matter used in connection therewith.

It sounds as though she signed her life away, and with regard to the pictures Avedon took she did. However, the bookstore sold one of the photographs to a maker of bed sheets. The bedding manufacturer had a reputation for running sleazy advertising and consequently had trouble getting first-class models to pose for advertising pictures. The manufacturer substantially retouched the Avedon photographs, changing the context. Mary Jane Russell sued for invasion of privacy, but the manufacturer answered her by telling the court that the model had given irrevocable consent for anyone to use those pictures, that she had waived her right to inspect the completed pictures and the advertising, and so forth.

The court agreed with the cotton mill: Mary Jane had given up her right of privacy with regard to the pictures Avedon took. But the picture used by the sheet maker in its advertising was not the same picture taken by Avedon. It had been altered. Justice Matthew Levy of the New York Supreme Court wrote (*Russell* v. *Marboro Books,* 1959):

> If the picture were altered sufficiently in situation, emphasis, background, or context, I should think that it would no longer be the same portrait, but a different one. And as to the changed picture, I would hold that the original written consent would not apply and that liability would arrive when the content of the picture has been so changed that it is substantially unlike the original.

What is substantial alteration? It probably means something other than minor retouching, but how much retouching is permissible before a privacy suit can accrue is difficult to say. This is one of the few cases on this legal point. Persons who want to retouch a photograph should be careful, even when they have written consent. They might change the picture sufficiently so that the consent would not apply.

In some respects the appropriation category of invasion of privacy is the simplest and easiest to understand. Use of a person's name or picture without consent for commercial purposes is an invasion of privacy. If a lawsuit results, it will probably be successful. The only defense is consent. If it can be proved that the plaintiff consented to the use of his name or picture the suit will then fail. The problems with the defense of consent were noted previously.

Right of Publicity

Another aspect of the appropriation problem deserves brief mention at this point. In some jurisdictions judges have been reluctant to recognize appropriation claims made by well-known, publicity seeking plaintiffs. In a few lawsuits courts rejected the plaintiffs' claim on the ground that their complaint really was that their "right of publicity" had been violated, not that their privacy had been invaded. When comedian Pat Paulsen announced his candidacy for president in 1968, unauthorized campaign posters of the comedian were published. Paulsen sued, claiming appropriation of his likeness (*Paulsen* v. *Personality Posters*, 1968). In a similar case a musician who stepped onto the stage at Woodstock and played the mess call on his flügelhorn sued when the producers of the movie *Woodstock* filmed the incident and included it in the movie without getting his permission (*Man* v. *Warner Bros.*, 1970). In both instances the New York courts noted that the plaintiffs were professional entertainers who in the last analysis really had not sought privacy. The real complaint in both cases, the court noted, was that the entertainer had not been paid for the use of his photograph on a poster and for his 45-second appearance in the movie. The law is not able to redress such wrongs, the New York court suggested, no matter how justified the complaints may be. While the courts and legislatures and legal scholars sort out the subtleties of this aspect of appropriation, the professional communicator is urged to play it safe and get consent, regardless of whether the performer appears to seek publicity.

The news side of the media is rarely affected by appropriation suits. Persons in advertising and entertainment are more acutely in danger of legal error. It should be remembered that the inadvertent error can still constitute an invasion of privacy. The negligence standards which have been applied in libel via the *Gertz* case have not as yet been applied in privacy law by any court in the land. When the composing room accidentally puts the wrong picture in a testimonial advertisement and city councilwoman Doris Smith is shown endorsing Acme sponges instead of home economist Joan White, the mistake is an invasion of privacy, albeit an accidental one. There is little a newspaper can do to compensate for the embarrassment and humiliation caused by such a mistake. Beware and be careful.

INTRUSION

Intrusion is what most people think of when they think of invasion of privacy: supersleuths sneaking about tapping telephones, planting bugs, listening at doors, or maybe Peter Graves and the *Mission Impossible* gang violating constitutional rights here and there by pilfering files and safes, stealing private papers, and so forth. The recent surge in electronic excesses has resulted in an increasing number of lawsuits for intrusion. While lawsuits for intrusion are common today, they rarely involve the mass media. The press doesn't often go in for this kind of snooping or at least doesn't get caught very frequently. Until the mid-sixties there were but one or two cases in which the media was charged with intrusion. In 1926 a reporter for the *Washington* (D.C.) *Herald* stole a picture from the home of Mrs. Louise Peed, who had nearly died from asphyxiation when a gas jet was carelessly left open in the home of a friend she was visiting. The court held the newspaper responsible because it had published the plaintiff's picture, not because it had stolen the picture (*Peed* v. *Washington Times Co.*, 1927). A similar suit in Los Angeles a few years later failed altogether (*Metter* v. *Los Angeles Examiner*, 1939).

The *Peed* case points out a very important aspect of intrusion in invasion of privacy. In appropriation cases and in cases based upon publication of private information or publication of falsehoods, the legal wrong occurs when the picture or story is published. It must be published. A photographer who takes the picture of a pretty girl, enlarges it to eight-by-ten inches, and hangs it on his kitchen wall has not invaded the girl's privacy. If he were to publish the picture in an advertisement, for example, appropriation, an illegal invasion of privacy then occurs. If a newspaper reporter uncovers private information about a teacher's life but keeps the information to himself, no invasion of privacy occurs. Only when he publishes this information might a lawsuit succeed.

In intrusion, however, the legal wrong is committed as soon as the intrusion takes place, whether or not the fruits of the intrusion are published. If your home is bugged, someone intrudes upon your privacy. Invasion of privacy occurred regardless of whether the contents of the overheard conversations are published. If a reporter breaks into a private office and copies information from a private file, his act would probably be considered an invasion of privacy, an intrusion.

The press has not often been involved in intrusion cases because it normally conducts its information-gathering processes without bugging rooms or breaking into offices. But with the recent push for "investigative journalism" some reporters have become as comfortable with hidden cameras and microphones as they are with pencil and paper. Another reason the press has not often been sued for intrusion is that when the intrusion is carried out properly the injured party is unaware of it. Awareness does not usually result until after the fruits of the intrusion are disseminated via the mass media, and then the injured party normally finds it easier to bring a suit based on the publication of the material than on the acquisition of it.

Because of the paucity of case law not many guidelines can be provided at this time. There are a few important ones which should help you avoid trouble (or perhaps recognize trouble when you have gotten into it).

In two cases in the late sixties federal courts in Washington, D. C., established the principle that a news medium which publishes material obtained via intrusion by someone not connected with the medium cannot be held liable for the intrusion. In the two instances the late newspaper columnist Drew Pearson obtained documents from private files of the Liberty Lobby, a right-wing public-interest group in Washington, and from the files of former Connecticut Senator Thomas Dodd. Employees of both Dodd and Liberty Lobby took the files from the private offices, made copies of them (which were given to Pearson), and then returned the purloined files. In both cases the court ruled that the publishers could not be held responsible for the actions of the intruders (*Liberty Lobby* v. *Pearson*, 1968; *Pearson* v. *Dodd*, 1969).

Judge J. Skelly Wright wrote in the *Dodd* case:

> If we were to hold appellants liable for invasion of privacy on these facts, we would establish the proposition that one who receives information from an intruder, knowing it has been obtained by improper intrusion, is guilty of a tort. In an untried and developing area of tort law, we are not prepared to go so far, . . .

There is another aspect of intrusion of which you should be aware. First, in some circumstances the injured party may be successful in another kind of suit, one based on property law rather than on invasion of privacy. The ancient doctrine of conversion and trover could have been applied had the original files, not mere copies, been given to Pearson. Both Dodd and Liberty Lobby attempted to sue for conversion, but the court in both instances said that since the original files were still in the possession of the owners, that is, they had not been deprived of their property, no conversion had taken place. (Conversion equals converting what belongs to someone else to your use.) But this area of the law is very immature. Tommorrow a different court might reach the opposite conclusion and hold the publisher of the documents responsible.

In California the publisher and a reporter of the *Los Angeles Free Press* were found guilty of possession of stolen goods after they bought a list of names of undercover narcotic agents stolen from the attorney general's office. Art Kunkin and Robert Applebaum were freed upon appeal to the state's high court, but only because there was insufficient evidence to prove that they knew the list was stolen when they purchased it (*People* v. *Kunkin,* 1973). If the state could have adduced any evidence at all that the pair had knowledge that the list was stolen, the conviction would have stood. As it was, the thief was a former employee of the attorney general's office, and Kunkin and Applebaum said they thought he still worked for the attorney general. The thief also asked that they return the list to him after it was copied, presumably to return it to the proper file, the two journalists said.

This whole area of the law is gray. Of course, if an employee of the publication is the intruder, liability might result, depending upon whether he acted on his own or at the employer's suggestion. In any case, intruders are always liable if they are caught, regardless of what use is made of the purloined material.

Journalists should ask tough questions of their sources of documents and files. Did you steal it? Did you copy it illegally? If a jury can be convinced that the journalist knew it was obtained illegally, or should have known it was obtained illegally (secret files, for example, can normally only be obtained illegally), a suit based on property law, not on privacy, might then in fact hold up.

While reporters may not engage in stealing or breaking and entering, they may undertake other kinds of intrusions. These intrusions are harder to define, and generally involve the use of snooper aids, that is, hidden cameras, telephoto lens, and hidden microphones.

Photography

No broad, general proposition can be stated here, and we must rely instead upon examples. Hopefully, as more and more cases are litigated, the gaps will be filled and a rule formulated. Reporters probably have the right to photograph persons in public places, even when they don't know they are being photographed. These people are present in a public, not a private, place and are visible to anyone who passes by. It is hard to make a case that by being photographed they have had their privacy invaded.

On record is a case in which harrassment, not invasion of privacy, was charged. In another state the case might have been a privacy case, but New York does not recognize this kind of invasion of privacy. The photographer was Ron Galella, whose whole life seemed to revolve around taking pictures of Jacqueline Kennedy Onassis. He went everywhere she went, blocked her path, made a general nuisance of himself. When he wasn't around Mrs. Onassis, he followed the Kennedy children. In one instance his penchant for getting close almost resulted in a serious accident for young John Kennedy when the horse he was riding bolted after being frightened by Galella. The Secret Service, which guards the Kennedy children and Mrs. Onassis, went to court to stop Galella. A federal court enjoined the photographer from coming within twenty-four feet of Mrs. Onassis and within thirty feet of the children, from blocking their movement in any way, from doing anything which might put them in danger or might harass, alarm, or frighten them, and from entering the children's play area at school (*Galella* v. *Onassis,* 1973). This is truly a rare case. The average photographer does not have to worry about such injunctions. Nevertheless, the case does show how the law is empowered to protect citizens.

Hidden Devices

When the photographer snoops, however, another question is at hand. No case law on this topic yet exists. Given the present propensity of the courts to protect privacy, one can think of situations in which an intrusion suit might stand up in court.

1. Using a telephoto lens to take pictures from a hill of a person sunbathing in an enclosed (and presumably private) backyard might be seen as an intrusion since most people behave differently when they think they are alone.

2. Sneaking around the outside of a home taking pictures through cracks between the draperies would probably be an intrusion.

3. Using a hidden camera and not revealing one is a reporter can be an intrusion.

An instance similar to example three was ruled an intrusion in a California lawsuit. The plaintiff was a disabled veteran and journeyman plumber named A. A. Dietemann who practiced healing using clay, minerals, and herbs. Dietemann practiced his strange version of medicine in his home. It was there that two *Life* magazine reporters who had agreed to work with Los Angeles law enforcement people visited the healer. Jackie Metcalf and William Ray pretended they were married, and Ms. Metcalf complained of a lump in her breast. Dietemann diagnosed the ailment as due to rancid butter she had eaten eleven years, nine months, seven days previously. While the "doctor" examined Ms. Metcalf, Ray photographed him with a secret camera. The conversation between the reporters (who never revealed that they were reporters) and the healer was also broadcast via a hidden microphone to investigators waiting in a car outside.

Dietemann was arrested weeks later and charged with practicing medicine without a license. *Life* photographers took more pictures at the time of the arrest, and in an article on medical quackery included those pictures with pictures taken by the hidden camera. Dietemann sued for invasion of privacy. *Life* magazine said the pictures were informational and newsworthy and were protected. The court agreed that the pictures were indeed newsworthy, but ruled that they had been obtained by intruding upon Dietemann's privacy. The magazine had a right to publish the pictures; publication did not constitute an invasion of privacy. It was the use of the secret camera and microphone that constituted the invasion of privacy. Whether they were published or destroyed, the legal wrong was committed when the two reporters invaded the healer's premises and secretly photographed him and recorded his conversations.

The magazine protested saying the story was simply an example of good investigative reporting. Judge Shirley Hufstedler was unimpressed (*Dietemann* v. *Time, Inc.*, 1971):

> Investigative reporting is an ancient art; its successful practice long antecedes the invention of miniature cameras and electronic devices. The First Amendment has never been construed to accord newsmen immunity from torts or crimes committed during the course of news gathering.

Lawyers call the Dietemann case *sui generis*—one of a kind. No other similar cases have yet occurred. Consequently, the questions which remain after the case are numerous and serious.

One gets the impression from reading the decision that Judge Hufstedler based her ruling on the facts that the two reporters were in the man's home and that they used a hidden camera and a concealed microphone. What if Dietemann had had an office with outside signs (there was no advertising on his home for his healing business) inviting people in for examination? Would this fact have made a difference?

More important to the press, would the judge have ruled the same way if there had been no hidden gadgets? if the two reporters had merely pretended to be man and wife, getting the examination, returning to the magazine to write their story from memory, and taking no photographs save one of the outside of the house? Journalists have been pretending they are somebody else to get a story for more than a century. It is hard to believe that a court would now make such conduct liable on grounds that it constitutes an intrusion and invasion of privacy. There is not the slightest indication in the *Dietemann* case that the courts are now prepared to do that, but there is also not the slightest assurance that they are not.

Another recent development should be noted at this point. There have been instances in which trespass suits have been brought against reporters and photographers who entered private property to gain information for a story. In Florida, a photographer and reporter were invited by police and fire officials into a house that had been gutted by fire. The owner of the house, who was not on the premises at the time of the fire, later brought suit for trespass against the newspaper. The Florida

Supreme Court in *Florida Publishing Company* v. *Fletcher* ruled that since the homeowner did not object at the time (she was not there), and since it was common custom for the press to inspect private premises after a serious fire or a crime, that the press was not guilty of a trespass in this case. The common custom constituted a kind of indirect consent. However, the court noted that if the homeowner had been on the premises at the time and had objected to the reporter and photographer coming on the property, then an action for trespass would stand. But the case should stand as a warning. Reporters and photographers have always tagged along with policemen and firemen. But policemen and firemen carry badges and conduct official investigations. A press pass may get a reporter free seats at a circus, but it is probably not a badge authorizing trespass on private property.

Public Interest as Defense

While the public interest is the key to defending most privacy suits, it has very little to do with intrusion. In the eyes of the law, whether Aunt Minnie's personal diary (which has absolutely no public value) or Senator Jones' personal papers which graphically demonstrate that he takes bribes (which have great public value) are stolen, the theft is the same. The intrusion and invasion of privacy are the same also. Public furor may be considerably less in the latter case, but the legal wrong is the same. Similarly, using a hidden camera to photograph a criminal (but private) act in a man's own home is no different from using a concealed camera to photograph a legal act in the same place. After all, Dietemann broke the law when he examined, diagnosed, and prescribed for Metcalf and Ray. Public interest, therefore, isn't really a controlling factor in these cases. The chances are pretty good that if the government hadn't so badly botched the Ellsberg case Daniel Ellsberg would have been held responsible for purloining the Pentagon Papers.

Because intrusion is such a new area of the law, no good defenses have been developed. A heavy burden rests upon the plaintiff to prove that the behavior by the reporter or cameraman was in fact an intrusion, an invasion of privacy. If invasion of privacy can be established, there are no good "legal excuses" with which to defend this behavior. In addition to the legal problems involved, members of the press themselves have begun to raise ethical questions about such behavior. Defending illegal behavior on the grounds that it is in the public interest is an excuse which the American people seemed to reject when the members of the Nixon White House used it in 1973 and 1974. There are few causes that are "good enough" to justify illegal intrusion upon the privacy of others. Intrusion as an aspect of invasion of privacy should really not be a problem to journalists who conduct their business in an ethical fashion. Still, the paucity of good guidelines at this time can be somewhat frightening.

Until there is more law to guide the press, journalists are advised to be guided by the common sense, conscience, and integrity one normally expects from responsible adults.

PUBLICATION OF PRIVATE INFORMATION

Probably the most controversial aspect of the right of privacy in the current decade is that aspect of the law which prohibits the publication of private information about a person. This, of course, is the kind of privacy protection that Warren and Brandeis sought in 1890. Strangely, as we will see shortly, American courts have been most reluctant to curb this kind of journalism, for it touches at the very foundation of our long-held notions about freedom of the press. This aspect is what makes invasion of privacy controversial, for even today many commentators argue that the press goes too far sometimes in publicizing the lives of persons who attempt to stay out of the public spotlight. They would limit the protection of the press to that coverage which deals with "governing affairs," or information citizens need to vote and discuss public issues.

The courts have been reluctant to prescribe this limitation. Starting in 1895 American judges have granted the press a broad protection to publish whatever it wants about people—within very broad boundaries—so long as there is some evidence of public interest in the topic. There are probably two explanations for this attitude of the courts. First, truth is not a defense in a suit brought for the publication of private information. If the material is of an intimate nature, its truth or nontruth is immaterial. This fact is difficult for many persons to accept, including judges who have for centuries ruled that truth is a good, solid defense in a libel suit. By creating a liability for the publication of truthful material, one opens all sorts of doors, doors which are then difficult to close. If the journalist can be held responsible for publishing truthful, intimate reports, the historian can then be held liable as well. Courts have also been reluctant to impose liability for truthful personal reports because of the hesitancy to become social engineers. When a judge rules that a medium cannot publish a story, he is also saying that people cannot read it. (This implication became obvious in the regulation of obscenity.) Judges do not like to wear the cloak of social censor, evaluating (and thereby structuring) the reading interests and behavioral habits of the population. In a famous privacy suit more than thirty years ago Judge Charles E. Clark wrote that like it or not people enjoy reading about the problems, the misfortunes, and the troubles of their neighbors and other people in the community. "When such are the mores of the community," he noted, "it would be unwise for a court to bar their expression in the newspapers, books, and magazines of the day" (*Sidis* v. *F-R Publishing Co.*, 1940). One often senses in the criticism of court decisions which allow publication of the gory details of crime and tragedy or the intimate details of misfortune or calamity that critics do not really mean that the press should not publish such material, but instead that the people should not read about such affairs. Such judgment is called social engineering.

The dimensions of this kind of invasion of privacy are fairly specific: publication of private information. First, there must be publication, and publication here means far more than the "third-person rule" in libel. Generally it is assumed that the publication must reach many people; that is, some sort of mass medium is required.

Second, the information must be private, or of a personal nature. It must be something that people don't generally know. Of course, the subject of the report cannot sue if he has published the material first. There was a case in Tennessee in which the plaintiff complained that a magazine published certain intimate details about his life. The material had appeared earlier in another publication, and the plaintiff brought an action for libel. He attached a copy of the objectionable article to his complaint, and of course the entire matter became part of the public record. In the succeeding privacy suit the court ruled that the plaintiff could hardly complain about the magazine publishing "intimate details" which the subject himself had placed upon the public record for all who wished to see (*Langford* v. *Vanderbilt University,* 1956).

Newsworthiness as Defense

The primary defense in this kind of suit (where, remember, truth is not a defense) is the argument that the published material is newsworthy, that it has wide public or general interest. In chapter 3 on defamation the First Amendment defense of actual malice was discussed. Public officials or persons who thrust themselves into the public spotlight cannot sue for defamation unless they can prove actual malice. The privacy rule is much broader, but at the same time it is not based solely on the First Amendment (or it was not when it emerged about seventy years ago). From nearly the beginning of privacy litigation judges realized that to restrict the publication of truthful comments clearly interfered with both the function of the press and the reading habits of the public. A kind of "newsworthiness formula" emerged in which the nature of the story, the status of the subject, the intimacy of the revelations, and the degree of embarrassment to the plaintiff were all weighed against each other. This formula is the basis for the defense of newsworthiness today.

As has been noted earlier, the defense of newsworthiness has generally overwhelmed plaintiffs suing for invasion of privacy on the grounds that private facts about their lives were published. The easiest way to understand the kinds of private information which can and cannot be legally published is to understand how the courts apply the defense of newsworthiness. If the information is newsworthy it is protected; it can be published. Discussion of each of the four basic elements of news-worthiness illuminates the subject.

Nature of the Story
Factual stories, reports or broadcasts which have great public interest, have generally been protected in invasion of privacy suits. The courts have been really quite liberal in defining public interest not as something people should read about (the social engineer role), but as something they do read about, something in which people are interested.

Over the years a vast array of subjects have been declared to be of interest to the American public. Women exercising in gymnasiums (*Swee-nek* v. *Pathe-News*, 1936), the details of a divorce case (*Berg* v. *Minne-apolis Star & Tribune*, 1948), photographs of the victim of a tragic accident (*Kelley* v. *Post Publishing Co.*, 1951), a twelve-year-old girl who gave birth to a baby (*Meetze* v. *AP*, 1956), the erroneous arrest of an innocent man (*Williams* v. *KCMO Broadcasting Co.*, 1971), the suffocation of two children in an old refrigerator (*Costlow* v. *Cuismano*, 1970), and so forth. The courts have been most generous to the press in their understanding of American reading and viewing habits. With the exception of a handful of cases, important cases, one could say that the press itself pretty much determines what subjects are of public interest by virtue of including them in newscasts and newspapers.

Even the way a story is presented is normally not a factor: sensationalism and sensational treatment generally do not remove the protection of newsworthiness. Concerning the story of the suffocation of the two young children, the parents found the sensational treatment of the story as objectionable as the story itself. However, the court ruled that the manner in which the article was written was not relevant to whether the article was protected by the constitutional guarantees of free speech and free press—which, by the way, it was. In another case a Boston newspaper published a horrible picture of an auto accident in which the bloodied and battered body of one of the victims was clearly visible and identifiable, and the court rejected the plaintiff's claim. The Massachusetts Supreme Court noted, "Many things which are distressing or may be lacking in propriety or good taste are not actionable" (*Kelley* v. *Post Publishing Co.*, 1951).

What the story is about, then, is an important aspect of determining whether it is newsworthy. American readers, viewers, and listeners are believed to have a wide range of interests which often focus on grotesque events and the tragedy, unhappiness, and misfortune of other persons.

Subject of the Story
Under the *New York Times* rule in libel whom the story is about is very important: the First Amendment standard applies only to public officials and persons who choose to be public figures by thrusting themselves into the public spotlight. The standards in privacy are somewhat

wider. Clearly publication of information about public officials is protected, whereas publication of the same kind of information about private citizens might not be. The fact that Mayor John Smith has a serious drinking problem might qualify as newsworthy; the fact that Bill Brown the druggist has the same problem is not newsworthy.

Courts have also recognized that reports about "voluntary public figures—entertainers, labor leaders, sports personalities, even some journalists and broadcasters—normally qualify as newsworthy. The law of privacy also recognizes an additional kind of public figure, called by many courts the "involuntary public figure," a person who has fame thrust upon him by an act he commits or by something that happens to him. Since the decision in *Gertz* v. *Welch,* the First Amendment has not been an acceptable defense in most states for libelous comments published about involuntary public figures. Many people wonder whether the *Gertz* case spelled the demise of the involuntary public figure rule in privacy as well. The Supreme Court hasn't answered the question yet, but the best guess is that the *Gertz* ruling will not impact privacy law. The so-called involuntary public figure rule in libel was initiated with a plurality opinion (not a majority opinion) in the case of *Rosenbloom* v. *Metromedia* in 1971. The rule was overturned in *Gertz* three years later. The involuntary public figure rule in privacy law was initiated more than fifty years ago and today has what might be called an abiding place in the fabric of the law. It would be difficult for a court to void the rule now. In libel we are concerned with untruthful comments, inaccuracies, and falsehoods. Society loses little (it loses something but not much) by forbidding such expression. Privacy law involves truthful comment, and society can lose much when prohibitions are placed upon this kind of expression. As of the spring of 1977, there is no indication by any court that it wants to follow the *Gertz* libel precedent and eliminate the involuntary public figure rule in privacy cases.

Who is an involuntary public figure under the law of privacy? In 1929 the Kentucky Supreme Court gave this definition (*Jones* v. *Herald Post Co.,* 1929):

> The right of privacy is the right to live one's life in seclusion, without being subjected to unwarranted and undesired publicity. In short, it is the right to be let alone. . . . There are times, however, when one, whether willing or not, becomes an actor in an occurrence of public or general interest. When this takes place he emerges from his seclusion, and it is not an invasion of his right of privacy to publish his photograph with an account of such occurrence.

The court later noted that private citizens can become "innocent actors in great tragedies in which the public has a deep concern." The scope, therefore, of the rubric involuntary public figure is wide. In Kansas City not too long ago a young man was arrested by police outside the local courthouse on suspicion of burglary. Local television news cameramen filmed the arrest and it was broadcast on television that night. The young man, however, had been released by police who admitted they arrested the wrong man. An invasion of privacy suit followed, but the courts rejected it, stating that the plaintiff must show a serious, unreasonable, unwarranted, and offensive invasion of private affairs before recovery can be allowed (*Williams* v. *KCMO Broadcasting Co.*, 1971):

> In the case at bar, plaintiff was involved in a noteworthy event about which the public had a right to be informed and which the defendant [television station KCMO] had a right to publicize. This is true even though his involvement therein was purely involuntary and against his will.

In a similar case nearly twenty years ago the plaintiff argued that the television station had an obligation to get the facts right before broadcasting a story. In that case the Florida Supreme Court came to the same conclusion as the Kansas court: no liability on the part of the broadcaster. Then the court added what amounts to almost a classic defense for the press in such a case (*Jacova* v. *Southern Radio-Television Co.*, 1955):

> It should be remembered that a television newscaster must, like a newspaper reporter, attempt to get before the public "today's news today". . . . This court judicially knows that it frequently takes a legal tribunal months of diligent searching to determine the facts of a controversial situation. When it is recalled that a reporter is expected to determine such facts in a matter of hours or minutes, it is only reasonable to expect that occasional errors will be made. Yet, since the preservation of our American democracy depends upon the public's receiving information speedily . . . it is vital that no unreasonable restraints be placed upon the working news reporter or the editorial writer.

Persons who are thrust, even unwillingly thrust, into the public spotlight lose some of the protection of their right of privacy. How much privacy is lost? Probably only the privacy which protects that part of their life which has come into focus because of the event or incident. This line is not easy to draw. Imagine that John Smith, publisher of *The Daily Sentinel*, is arrested for violating the state unfair labor practices act. Under the guise of his status as an involuntary public figure how far into his life can the press go? Can it report his extramarital affairs? that he has a gun fetish? that he cheats at cards? All these questions are hard to answer. Probably the answers depend upon the status of the person involved, the magnitude of the event, the scope of public interest, and so forth.

Sometimes the people who are close to public figures also lose some of their privacy. In 1971 in Pennsylvania the state high court ruled that the *Saturday Evening Post* was not liable for the publication of the names of the children of an entertainer in a story relating that the entertainer, Lillian Corabi, was accused of masterminding a complex burglary (*Corabi* v. *Curtis Publishing Co.*, 1971). The court said that "Tiger Lil" Corabi was a public figure and that anyone could legitimately publish her biography without consent and could include the names of the members of her family. Other courts made similar rulings in connection with suits based on stories about the spouses of Hollywood stars. One judge wrote, "People closely related to such public figures . . . to some extent lose their right to the privacy that one unconnected with the famous or notorious would have" (*Carlisle* v. *Fawcett Publishing Co.*, 1962).

Lapse of Time

A great number of privacy suits have resulted from both published and broadcast stories about people who were formerly in the public eye. In these cases the plaintiffs have consistently argued that the passing of time dims the public spotlight, and a person stripped of privacy because of great notoriety regains the protection of privacy after several years. Courts have not accepted this argument very often. The general rule is that once a person becomes a public figure he pretty much remains a public figure, despite attempts to avoid publicity. Two kinds of stories fall into this category: (1) stories that merely recount a past event (fourteen years ago today Walter Denton jumped off the Golden Gate Bridge and survived) and don't tell readers what the subject of the story does today, and (2) stories that recount a past occurrence and attempt to focus as well on what the participant does today (fourteen years ago Walter Denton jumped off the Golden Gate Bridge and survived and today he is principal of Madison High School).

With the exception of a few aberrant cases in California (we will talk about privacy in California), the law has been fairly consistent in permitting the first kind of story, the historical account. Courts have considered the story just that—history—and have been reluctant to limit discussion about people and events which are part of the heritage or background of a community.

The second kind of story can be a problem. While courts have gone on record permitting the where-are-they-now kind of story (again, except for California one is hard pressed to find a ruling against the press in such suits), judges have nevertheless indicated that stories aimed at humiliating or purposely embarrassing a person because of his past conduct might not be tolerated under all circumstances (see *Kent* v. *Pittsburgh*

Press, 1972; *Sidis* v. *F-R Publishing Co.*, 1940; *Bernstein* v. *NBC*, 1955).
A real risk is run in broadcasting a story about a local banker which mentions that twenty years ago he was arrested for car theft. However, if the banker is running for public office the situation is different. Also, a story saying that here is a man who was down and out twenty years ago, but now see what he has accomplished would probably pass muster. However, it would be best to first get the banker's approval. Stories which for no good reason purposely dig into a person's past in search of indiscretions are the ones likely to cause problems.

*Intimacy of the
Revelations*

We have discussed the nature of the story: whether it is of public or general interest. We have talked about the subject of the story: public officials and public figures. The third part of the formula has to do with the intimacy of the information or revelations. Courts have not spoken as much about this aspect as about the first two aspects of newsworthiness. They have, however, provided a few guidelines, the most important of which is that privacy suits cannot be based on publication of information which is part of the public record. What is a public record? The public record is discussed in some length in chapter 12, "Access to Information." For our purposes here, however, a public record can probably be defined as the same records that are considered privileged in libel law: legislative records, certain police records, court records, and so forth. Public records are those records that citizens can walk in from the street and legally see. No liability can result from merely republishing what is already on view to the public.

For years four states—Georgia, Wisconsin, South Carolina, and Florida—prohibited publication of the name of a victim of rape. This was a noble goal and a practice many responsible newspapers throughout the country undertook voluntarily. Nevertheless, many persons questioned the legitimacy of such a law. After all, in any trial which followed rape the victim's name was sure to be made public and become part of the public record. Nevertheless, in 1963 a federal court of appeals upheld the constitutionality of the South Carolina statute in a case involving the rape of two young state workers identified in a television newscast (*Nappier* v. *Jefferson Standard Life Insurance Co.*, 1963). In 1972 WSB-TV in Atlanta, Georgia, was sued for the broadcast of the name of Cynthia Cohn who had been raped and murdered. The television reporter obtained the victim's name from the grand jury indictments and from the trial proceedings. State courts ruled in favor of the plaintiffs, the victim's parents, but in 1975 the United States Supreme Court reversed the Georgia court ruling and said that the press cannot be held liable for invasion of privacy for reporting information already part of the public record. Justice Byron White noted that most persons depend upon the mass media for information about the operations of the government via public meetings and the public record. Judicial proceedings are an important part of our governmental system, and something in which the public has always expressed a great interest. By making judicial records and proceedings public, the state of Georgia must have concluded that the public interest was being served (*Cox Broadcasting Co. v. Cohn*, 1975):

> We are reluctant to embark on a course that would make public records generally available to the media but forbid their publication if offensive to the sensibilities of the supposed reasonable man. Such a rule would make it very difficult for the press to inform their readers about the public business and yet stay within the law. The rule would invite timidity and self-censorship and very likely lead to the suppression of many items that would otherwise be put into print and that should be made available to the public.

Quoting the latest revision of the *Restatement of Torts*, which attempts to summarize the law of torts, the court said, "There is no liability when the defendant merely gives further publicity to information about the plaintiff which is already public. Thus there is no liability for giving publicity to facts about the plaintiff's life which are matters of public record."

The single danger journalists face with regard to the public record question is that they must be certain that the document quoted is a public record and the meeting reported is a public meeting. Several years ago in Florida the *Tampa Tribune* published what really amounted only to a legal notice that a woman named Virginia Patterson had been committed to a state hospital as a narcotic addict. When Ms. Patterson sued for invasion of privacy, the newspaper argued that it obtained the information from the court progress docket, which is a public record. The paper was unaware that the legislature had passed a law specifically restricting the inspection of the records of narcotic commitment proceedings. Such records are not public records. The newspaper asked how was it to know that this part of the progress docket was not a public record, since the court clerk hadn't stopped the reporter from looking at it. This argument was unpersuasive. The Florida Supreme Court said it was the responsibility of the newspaper to know the law and not to compound the error of the court clerk (*Patterson v. Tribune Co.*, 1962). Reporters should make certain they are quoting a public record. Asking the court clerk or person at the desk is not always the best way to find out. Most newspapers retain or have access to legal counsel. If there is a question, call the lawyer.

Degree of Embarrassment   The last element of the newsworthiness formula concerns the degree of embarrassment the story creates for the subject. How humiliated does the subject feel? Obviously, some people are more easily hurt than others.

But the law is not designed to protect oversensitive, easily embarrassed persons. The publication must be offensive to persons of ordinary sensibility before liability is likely to accrue. Judges, perhaps more than most people, are aware that we live in a society which while valuing privacy does not permit a great deal of it. A quarter of a century ago Judge Leon Yankwich, a respected jurist, noted ("It's Libel or Contempt If You Print It," 1950), "whether we like it or not we have no more privacy than the proverbial goldfish. If we participate in any manner in the life of a community, we live in public. What is news is a matter of place and circumstance."

There is really no place for hypersensitive persons in public life. Perhaps the most difficult aspect of life for a new public official or for someone just stepping into the public spotlight is to develop tolerance for publicity, often inane publicity, publicity in bad taste, erroneous and harmful publicity. The new president of a university, who has always maintained good relationships with the student press while at the lower echelons of administration, suddenly finds himself in the spotlight and doesn't like it. The performer who finds success after long years of struggle suddenly is besieged by the media. The government worker who testifies before Congress on cost overruns she discovered in her department's procurement of weapon systems finds herself harassed by reporters. Few people defend this kind of happening. Yet it is part of the way of life in the last quarter of the twentieth century. As is so often the case, the cure—placing restrictions on such publicity—is undoubtedly worse than the illness.

While perhaps not consciously, judges and juries generally weigh the four factors just outlined when determining whether a truthful, informational report crosses the bounds of propriety and is an invasion of privacy. In the weighing process if the story or broadcast has public interest, if it is about a public official or public figure, or if it comes from the public record, embarrassment to the plaintiff probably will not create a liability. In the short history of the law, as noted earlier, courts have shown great concern for protecting the freedom of expression from incumberances. Few instances in which a publisher was liable for the publication of a truthful, factual report have occurred. Those instances in which liability resulted seem to have some factors in common. These cases generally involved involuntary public figures, private people thrust unwillingly into the public spotlight. The stories seemed to be of low public value—not public interest, but public value. The world would not have ceased to revolve had the stories been scrapped rather than published. The stories were not what some people call "hard news." Finally, the subject of the stories was greatly embarrassed, as any person of ordinary sensibility would have been. Here are two of the cases.

1. Several years ago a woman with a rather unusual disease—she ate constantly, but still lost weight—was admitted to a hospital. The press was tipped off and descended upon her room, pushed past the closed door, and took pictures against the patient's will. *Time* magazine ran a story about the patient, Dorothy Barber, whom in inimitable *"Time* style" it called "the starving glutton." Mrs. Barber sued and won her case. The judge said the hospital is one place people should be able to go for privacy (*Barber* v. *Time, Inc.,* 1942). More than the privacy of hospitals influenced the decision because there are scores of decisions in which persons in hospitals have been publicized and courts have ruled there was no invasion of privacy. Look at the ingredients of the newsworthiness formula for a moment. Although public curiosity may have been a factor, Mrs. Barber was the most involuntary of public figures. Her embarrassment was great, and the revelations were highly intimate. All these factors combined to produce a verdict of guilty.

2. A Georgia housewife took her two sons to the county fair and finally succumbed to their pressure to be taken through the fun house. As she left the building an air jet blew Mrs. Flora Bell Graham's dress up over her head, and she was exposed from the waist down except for her underclothing. As fate would have it a local photographer was nearby and captured the moment on film. The picture was featured in the Sunday edition of the local newspaper as a publicity piece for the fair. Mrs. Graham sued. By logical analysis one could suggest that she shouldn't have won. The event took place in public. Many people saw her. She couldn't be readily identified in the picture because her dress was over her head. Persons who knew the children, who were also in the picture, could make the connection between mother and children. Regardless, Mrs. Graham did win (*Daily Times Democrat* v. *Graham,* 1962). She suffered an immense amount of embarrassment from the most intimate kind of revelation, and the public value of the photograph was extremely low.

The newsworthiness formula probably sounds more scientific than it really is. What we have really discussed is judicial intuition and various important factors that cause judges to decide whether a story is an invasion of privacy.

In most jurisdictions today there is really little danger of invasion of privacy suits from the publication of private information. The courts are not very receptive to such claims. The press itself is somewhat responsible because most journalists and broadcasters don't publish pictures and stories about hospital patients or about women who are embarrassed in a carnival fun house. By sticking to the news and information business, the press protects itself from successful lawsuits. Also, the plaintiff is at a distinct disadvantage in this kind of suit because the alleged damage is so difficult to demonstrate. In most tort cases the plaintiff has a broken arm or a wrecked car to show the court. Even in a libel case it is possible to get witnesses to testify: "Yes, I used to like Frank, but because of this story I don't trust him and won't let him handle my insurance any more."

In appropriation cases the injured party can produce an advertisement or poster with his name on it; in intrusion there are the secret pictures or rifled files as evidence of damage. But in private information cases all the plaintiff can do is say "Yes, the story is true, and its publication bothers me greatly." Such evidence just doesn't have the impact of crutches, of an arm in a sling, or even of a smiling face in an advertisement for shaving cream.

California and Social Value Test

While the law of privacy is still not recognized in every state, the law has grown rather consistently in those states which have adopted it. The state of California is the exception to this general rule. California adds an element to the newsworthiness test which distinguishes the state from all other states at this time and also creates a far greater risk of liability for the press than anywhere else in the United States. It is the element of social value, or social utility. California first recognized the law of privacy via the state constitution rather than by statute or through the common law. (California does have a privacy statute which was adopted in 1974 and is modeled after the New York statute.) The courts in the state were confronted with an extraordinary case. The plaintiff, Mrs. Gabrielle Darley Melvin, was formerly a prostitute. She had also been charged with first-degree murder, but was acquitted after a lengthy trial. After the trial she reformed, married, and started a new life. About six years later during the boom years of the twenties in Hollywood a small movie company filmed a biography of Mrs. Melvin's earlier life including her scrapes with the law. The plaintiff's real name was used in the movie which was heavily advertised as the true story of Gabrielle Darley. She sued.

It was the first privacy case to find its way into a California courtroom, and the jurists were somewhat perplexed. With the benefit of more than forty years of hindsight, we now find it easy to see what should have been done. Obviously, the woman deserved some kind of help. The court should have (for the sake of the orderly development of the law) recognized invasion of privacy via the common law, much like Georgia, and declared the film to be a commercial venture using the plaintiff's name without her consent. (The film was at least partly fictional, and as we will see in the next section that constitutes commercial or trade use.) Instead, the court rejected the notion that the right of privacy was inherent under California common law and grounded the law in the state constitutional provision which guaranteed citizens the right to pursue happiness and obtain safety and happiness.

In ruling in behalf of the plaintiff Judge Emerson Marks said the film did constitute an invasion of privacy, for despite the fact that it was based on a true story (a story, by the way, which was clearly a part of a public trial record), the filmed account had no social utility. In fact, it had a harmful impact upon society because it negated all of Mrs. Melvin's efforts at rehabilitation.

Courts in other jurisdictions rejected the social utility rule in this case, *Melvin v. Reid* (1931), as bad law. The Delaware Supreme Court said, "Such a rule would in reality subject the public press to a standard of good taste—a standard too elusive to serve as a workable rule of law" (*Barbieri v. News Journal Publishing Co.*, 1963). The California courts have tended to continue to use this social value test however.

Recently the *Reader's Digest* was subjected to a suit for publishing a story which incidentally revealed the criminal past of a man named Marvin Briscoe. The story was about truck hijacking, and to make its point the *Digest* recalled the case of Marvin Briscoe who with a friend hijacked a truckload of bowling pin spotters, was caught after a shoot-out with police, and subsequently spent several years in prison. The magazine did not inform readers that the incident occurred some eleven years earlier.

Briscoe sued, but both the trial court and the intermediate California appellate court ruled that the magazine had published a truthful, newsworthy account of an event which was clearly a part of the public record. No liability. The Supreme Court disagreed, however, and applying the social value test, the Court ruled that the case should be returned for trial so that a jury could determine whether the story had social utility or social value. Briscoe claimed that since being released from prison he had led an exemplary life and the revelations in the magazine article destroyed his new life. The Supreme Court opinion said (*Briscoe v. Reader's Digest Association*, 1971):

> Plaintiff is a man whose last offense took place eleven years before, who has paid his debt to society, who has friends and an 11-year-old daughter who were unaware of his early life—a man who has assumed a position in "respectable" society. Ideally his neighbors should recognize his present worth and forget his past life of shame. But men are not so divine as to forgive the past trespasses of others, and plaintiff therefore endeavored to reveal as little as possible of his past life. Yet as if in some bizarre canyon of echoes, petitioner's past life pursues him through the pages of *Reader's Digest*, now published in thirteen

languages and distributed in one hundred nations, with a circulation in California of almost 2,000,000 copies.

In a nation built upon the free dissemination of ideas it is always difficult to declare that something may not be published. But the great general interest in an unfettered press may at times be outweighed by other great social interests. As a people we have come to recognize that one of these societal interests is that of protecting an individual's right to privacy. The right to know and the right to have others not know are, simplistically considered, irreconcilable. But the rights guaranteed by the First Amendment do not require total abrogation of the right to privacy. The goals sought by each may be achieved with a minimum of intrusion upon the other.

However, before a jury trial could begin, *Reader's Digest* had the case removed to federal court in California on diversity of citizenship grounds, and there, a federal judge granted the magazine's motion for a summary judgment. No opinion was written.

In other privacy suits in California which have been tried in federal court, judges have indicated unhappiness with the social value standard. When two young Californians brought suit against *Life* magazine for publishing a story about their existence in a cave on the Mediterranean island of Crete, the federal district court in northern California for all intents and purposes ignored the social value standard and based its ruling for the magazine instead upon the degree of public interest in a report on the activities of disenchanted young American expatriates (*Goldman* v. *Time, Inc.*, 1971).

The disadvantages of court tests which put judges in the position of social censors or social engineers were discussed earlier. The same arguments apply to the social value test. It is hardly within the robust spirit of the First Amendment for writers to be forced to consider whether a social good will result from their writing, and whether in fact a great social purpose may be stalled or even thwarted. To carry the social value idea to its logical extreme one could argue that criticism of any social program or any governmental scheme might lack social utility and should be prohibited. Clearly this interpretation is not what the California courts had in mind. Nevertheless the social value test remains a serious problem to persons who see the First Amendment as encompassing the right to publish truthful comments and reports on matters of public interest and about persons who are or who have been in the public eye.

The social value test is presently confined to California. Courts in other states have recently seemed to reject the test in light of the U.S. Supreme Court ruling in *Cox* v. *Cohn*. It is difficult to believe, in light of the decision in the *Cox* case, that the California courts could punish as an invasion of privacy the publication of a story based on open court records, the source of the Briscoe story. Still, the test may be applied to a wide range of stories which are founded upon material other than court records, or other public records.

PUBLICATION OF FALSE INFORMATION

What does publication of false information, or of a falsehood, have to do with invasion of privacy? This question is frequently asked by persons who study the law of privacy. If invasion of privacy is conceived of solely as snooping, digging into a person's past, and bugging bedrooms, publication of false information about a person then seems totally out of line with the law of privacy. This area of the law does make some sense, however, when the first category of invasion of privacy—appropriation of a person's name or likeness for commercial purposes—is recalled. The fourth category of the law of privacy is really a hybrid of the first category.

History

What are the origins of falsehood law? You will recall that the law of privacy began as a means to stop commercial exploitation of persons in advertising and for trade purposes. Commercial exploitation was a key in early privacy litigation. In the 1920s a film producer made a travelogue about New York City. All of the film was shot in the city and showed real people walking along the streets, selling their wares, and riding in cars just as in a true documentary travelogue. To make the movie a bit more interesting the producer hired actors and wrote a script. What had been an ordinary documentary travelogue about New York became a documentary in which two fictional New York teachers escorted two fictional out-of-town teachers on a tour of the city. Miriam Blumenthal, a bread peddler, was photographed and appeared in the film for six seconds as she hawked her baked goods near Washington Square. When the motion picture was released, Mrs. Blumenthal sued for invasion of privacy. The logic of her argument was this. The law prohibits the use of a person's name or likeness for commercial or trade purposes. When the producer fictionalized certain aspects of the documentary travelogue, he transformed the movie from an informative film (which is protected because it is newsworthy) into an entertainment film. When a film entertains it has been created for trade purposes; the producer hopes to make a profit by entertaining people. Hence, Miriam's likeness was used for a trade purpose and was an invasion of privacy (*Blumenthal* v. *Picture Classics*, 1933).

From these propositions the following corollaries emerge. If a story is fictional, it is an item of trade or commerce rather than a news item. When a true story is somehow fictionalized by the addition of dialogue or other changes, it becomes a fictional piece. Falsehoods in an otherwise true story remove the protection of newsworthiness because the piece is then a fictional piece. Consequently we have reached the point today in which many privacy suits are brought for publication of false information or for publishing material which puts someone in a false light. An amazingly large number of these suits are successful.

Before the specifics of the law in this area are considered, this very important fact must be emphasized. The false report aspect in invasion of privacy grew in a very ragged fashion. That is, there are contradictory court rulings: action that is illegal in one state is not in another. The guidelines presented here are tentative because the law remains tentative. The distressing factor is that false report suits occur more frequently today and may become increasingly more common because of the new libel restrictions requiring plaintiffs to show negligence before they can collect damages. Although some questions still need to be answered by the Supreme Court (as will be noted shortly), injured parties today may find it easier to sue for invasion of privacy than for defamation when they are the subject of an untruthful report.

Types of False Reports

Suits for publication of falsehoods generally fall into one of two categories: (1) fictionalization or (2) false light. Fictionalization occurs when an otherwise true story is embellished with little falsehoods. Examples include making up dialogue, adding drama when none exists and changing the setting of the story to make it more interesting. False light is simpler to define and means merely to give readers a false impression by publishing facts which are not true about a person. While fictionalizing an otherwise true story generally puts someone in a false light, the reverse is not necessarily true. The simplest means of distinguishing between the two categories is to remember that fictionalization is a purposeful act, something the writer does intentionally, and false light can result from an unintentional error, an unplanned inaccuracy.

Fictionalization

Radio and television writers who dramatize true stories are the most common victims of fictionalization suits. A few years ago the *National Broadcasting Company* dramatized the heroism of a naval officer who, as a passenger on a flight from Honolulu to California, was responsible for saving many lives when the plane crash-landed at sea. The drama stuck to the hard facts of the story, but of course dialogue between passengers and crew was added. In addition, the naval officer was somewhat humanized: he smoked a cigarette and prayed before the crash. The court which heard the officer's privacy suit ruled that these embellishments constituted fictionalization and resulted in an invasion of privacy (*Strickler* v. *NBC*, 1958).

Newspapers and magazine writers have been caught when they dramatized true stories in the same manner by adding dialogue, changing the scene slightly, and so forth. A writer for a Philadelphia newspaper uncovered an interesting divorce suit involving a teenage couple. The boy married the girl only to spite her parents who didn't like him. The newspaper story described the couple as they secretly planned the marriage, as they walked to the justice of the peace, and so forth. Dialogue between the couple was invented. A suit resulted, and the newspaper lost the case because the story was written "in a style used almost exclusively by writers of fiction" (*Acquino* v. *Bulletin Co.*, 1959). Note, the court didn't say that the story was fiction because it wasn't. The basic facts were true, but were presented in a fictional style.

Such opinions are not always the rule. Other courts in other cases have said that minor fictionalization, the creation of dialogue, does not constitute invasion of privacy in an otherwise true story (*Carlisle* v. *Fawcett*, 1962).

The foregoing examples point up the confused state of the law in this area noted earlier.

The style of the fiction writer—a heavy emphasis on descriptive detail, the use of dialogue, narrating a story from the subject's point of view rather than the writer's point of view—is being used increasingly today by some journalists. Writers such as Gay Talese, Tom Wolfe, Jimmy Breslin, Joan Didion, and Norman Mailer are leading the way in the exploration of stylized nonfiction writing, often called New Journalism. Nonfiction novels like Truman Capote's *In Cold Blood* and Joseph Wambaugh's *The Onion Field* demonstrate the journalistic power of this style. Yet, these writers clearly open themselves to lawsuits unless extreme care is taken.

The simplest way to avoid a suit for fictionalization, if the truth is embellished in any way, is to change the names of the characters in the story. This strategy will work in every case except in those stories which are about a specific person. It doesn't make much sense to do a character sketch about Mick Jagger if you must refer to him throughout the piece as John Smith because parts of the story are embellished or fictionalized.

On the opposite side of the fictionalization coin is the problem of using the name of a real person in what is clearly a work of fiction.

What happens when a novel is about a fictional character named Judy Splinters and a real Judy Splinters exists? Can the real Ms. Splinters sue for invasion of privacy? The first point to remember is that the little notice in the front of the book—all characters in this book are fictional and any resemblance to persons living or dead is purely coincidental—doesn't help much. It is impossible to escape liability by merely saying you are not liable. If a man commits an illegal act, he is responsible for his action, regardless of the notices he may have published. If someone trips on a broken piece of cement in a sidewalk, it matters not that the owner of property has a sign on his lawn declaring that he takes good care of his property and that he is not responsible for the injuries to other persons.

Does Judy Splinters have a case? If only her name is used, she does not. The names of many people get into works of fiction. Such occurrences are coincidental. Liability doesn't accrue unless Judy can convince a jury that in fact she is the character in the book. She can do this by showing that more than her name was used, that other aspects of her identity were used as well. For example, suppose both the fictional and the real Judy are in their mid-twenties. Both are waitresses. Both were born in Michigan and moved to San Francisco. Both like fast cars and tall men. Both were the victims of brutal rape. As the similarities mount a juror would have to be either dishonest or a fool to believe in coincidence. Judy's identity was taken, and invasion of privacy did occur. One case is on record in which an author wrote about a real person, but changed her name. The author was sued and lost the case. The character was an extraordinary one, and many persons recognized her, even though her name was changed (*Cason* v. *Baskin,* 1947).

False Light

False light doesn't refer to lights that aren't there, but to false impressions. The late William Prosser, called the dean of torts by some authorities, is responsible for this concept, and it is a useful one. Many courts agree that a false impression of a person, even though the impression is not unfavorable, is an invasion of privacy. In a recent case a writer for a national newspaper told his readers that a mystery surrounded the suicide death of a mother. The woman killed herself after murdering her children, and the writer said police, family, and friends were baffled because she had been a happy, normal woman. Her husband sued, charging false light. He was able to show that the woman had a history of psychiatric care and mental illness. She was quite despondent before the incident, and her death was really not a mystery at all. The court ruled that the publication had put the woman in a false light (*Varnish* v. *Best Medium,* 1969).

Photographs are a more common source of false light cases than are stories. The late, great *Saturday Evening Post* seemed to have a penchant for false light cases, most of which involved photographs. Years ago the magazine published a picture of a little girl who was brushed by a speeding car in an intersection and lay crying in the street. The girl was the victim of a motorist who ignored a red traffic light, but in the magazine the editors implied that she caused the accident herself by darting into the street between parked cars. The editors simply needed a picture to illustrate a story on pedestrian carelessness and plucked this one out of the files. The picture was totally unrelated to the story except that both were about people being hit by cars.

Eleanor Sue Leverton sued the *Post* and won. Judge Herbert F. Goodrich ruled that the picture was clearly newsworthy in connection with Eleanor's original accident (*Leverton* v. *Curtis Publishing Co.,* 1951):

> but the sum total of all this is that this particular plaintiff, the legitimate subject for publicity for one particular accident, now becomes a pictorial, frightful example of pedestrian carelessness. This, we think, exceeds the bounds of privilege.

Just before the *Post* succumbed it faced another suit for the same action. This time the magazine used a picture taken at a gambling club in the Bahamas to illustrate a story about organized crime infiltrating the casinos on the islands. The caption said: "High rollers at Monte Carlo [the name of the club] have dropped as much as $20,000 in a single night. The U. S. Department of Justice estimates that the Casino grosses $20 million a year, and that one-third is skimmed off for American mafia families." Included in the picture was one James Holmes, neither a high roller nor a Mafioso. He sued, claiming that the photograph and article put him in a false light (*Holmes* v. *Curtis Publishing Co.,* 1969).

Sometimes an error simply occurs and there is nothing anyone can do about it. One simple precaution can be taken to avoid false light suits: refrain from using unrelated pictures to illustrate news stories. When the annual Christmas story warning readers to be wary of shoplifters in department stores is prepared, control the impulse to pull from the files a picture of people shopping and run it as artwork with the story. When a story warning older men to be wary of overexertion as they shovel the first snow lest they fall victim to a heart atack is published, don't use the file picture of a sixty-year-old man clearing his driveway. In both cases the juxtaposition of the story and the photograph implies a relationship which is not necessarily true.

A suit for invasion of privacy brought for publishing a false report can be defended in two ways. The first defense is obvious—prove the truth of the report. If the truth can be established, the suit will fail.

The second defense is the First Amendment. Since 1967 and the case of *Time, Inc.,* v. *Hill,* the First Amendment guarantee of freedom of the press has been applicable as a defense in an invasion of privacy suit based upon false report.

First Amendment as Defense

The First Amendment can be used as a defense in a libel suit, as was established in chapter 3. The so-called *New York Times* malice rule states that before public officials and public figures can collect damages for publication of a defamatory falsehood they must prove that the statement was published with actual malice, that is, the publisher knew the story was false when he published it or exhibited reckless disregard for the truth of the story.

The case in which the New York Times malice rule was applied to invasion of privacy was the first mass media—invasion of privacy suit ever heard by the U.S. Supreme Court. In the early 1950s the James Hill family were held captive in their home for nearly twenty-four hours by three escaped convicts. The fugitives were captured by police shortly after leaving the Hill home. The incident became a widely publicized story. A novel, *The Desperate Hours,* was written about a similar incident, as was a play and a motion-picture script. *Life* magazine published a feature story about the drama, stating that the play was a reenactment of the ordeal suffered by the James Hill family. The actors were even taken to the home in which the Hills had lived (but now vacant) and photographed at the scene of the original captivity.

James Hill sued for invasion of privacy. He complained that the magazine used his family's name for trade purposes, and that the story put the family in a false light. *The Desperate Hours* did follow the basic outline of the Hill family ordeal, but contained many differences. The fictional Hilliard family, for example, suffered far more physical and verbal indignities at the hands of the convicts than did the Hill family.

After the family won money damages in the state courts, the Supreme Court vacated the judgment and remanded the case to the state court for a new trial. (The trial never did take place because the Hills were sick of the entire mess.) The high Court tossed out the trade purposes portion of the complaint, reminding all concerned that despite the fact that newspapers and magazines are published for profit informative material contained in these publications is protected by constitutional guarantees of freedom of expression.

Then Justice William Brennan, who had written the decision in *New York Times* v. *Sullivan,* wrote that the standards which apply to false publication in libel suits must also apply in invasion of privacy suits based on a false report (*Time, Inc.,* v. *Hill,* 1967). Hence, the Hill family must show that the editors of *Life* magazine knew that the play was not a reenactment of the family's siege with the convicts, or that the editors displayed reckless disregard as to whether their story was true or false. In all likelihood the Hills, who chose not to continue the suit, could have proven malice.

Much as in the original *New York Times* ruling, the decision in *Time, Inc.,* v. *Hill* left many questions unanswered. While the high Court and various lower courts have had numerous opportunities to clarify many of the libel questions, the courts have not had much opportunity, or have not taken the opportunity, to clear the muddy waters of privacy law. Therefore, discussion of the impact of *Time, Inc.,* v. *Hill* on privacy law must be somewhat tentative.

If the problem is approached in the same manner in which libel was considered, the first question to be asked is, Who must prove malice? Obviously, only plaintiffs suing for publication of false reports need prove malice. Application of the First Amendment to privacy law in the *Hill* case sensitized judges to the implications of freedom of expression in all privacy actions involving the mass media, but the so-called malice rule applies only to suits based on the publication of falsehoods.

Do all plaintiffs suing for false report have to prove malice? This question is unanswerable at this time. It seems clear that the courts will apply the standard at least to public officials, to voluntary public figures, and probably to involuntary public figures. In several lower court rulings including some which have ultimately found their way to the high Court, persons thrust into the public spotlight against their will have had to prove malice; the innocent gambler in the *Saturday Evening Post* picture is one example (*Holmes* v. *Curtis,* 1969); the woman and her children whose husband and father was killed in a terrible bridge accident (*Cantrell* v. *Forest City Publishing Co.,* 1974); the husband of a suicide victim (*Varnish* v. *Best Medium,* 1968); the long-time convict released from prison because a court ruled that during his trial his constitutional rights were violated (*Kent* v. *Pittsburgh Press,* 1972). There are others. Each person was an involuntary public figure. For that matter, James Hill was an involuntary public figure, also.

In 1975 the high Court noted in a case that it had not yet been asked to consider whether the constitutional standard announced in *Time, Inc.,* v. *Hill* applies to all false light cases or whether a state can use a more relaxed standard in cases brought by private individuals. To the present time, the experience is that such persons in most instances are considered involuntary public figures, and the high Court seems to want these people to prove malice. It should be noted that while the comment from the court just quoted followed the *Gertz* decision many of the involuntary-public-figure cases noted preceded the 1974 libel ruling. While *Gertz* is expected to have little impact on privacy suits based on public disclosure of private facts, its impact on false report cases, which parallel libel so closely, could be greater. Final determination of this question may take a few more years.

MALICE AND PRIVACY

To determine just what the plaintiff needs to prove under the malice standard, one should look directly at the law of libel. The standards are the same; the definitions of malice the same; the burden of proof the same. The *St. Amant* rule that the plaintiff must show that the defendant entertained serious doubts as to the truth of the story is the law in privacy as well. The standards in *Curtis* v. *Butts* and *Walker* v. *AP* concerning breaking news versus less urgent news, concerning experienced reporters versus rookies, and concerning internal consistency of reports all apply to privacy as well. Here is how the malice rule was applied in three privacy suits.

1. In 1967 a bridge across the Ohio River between West Virginia and Ohio collapsed, killing forty-three people. Reporter Joe Eszterhas wrote a feature story about the family of one of the victims for the *Cleveland Plain-Dealer*. A year later Eszterhas revisited the scene of the tragedy and wrote a story about how the family managed without their husband and father. The story contained several inaccuracies about the family's poverty and other matters. In addition Eszterhas implied that he had seen and talked to the widow, described her, and told readers she said she refused money from people in town and was reluctant to talk about the tragedy. In fact the woman was not at home when the reporter made his second visit, and he did not see her. The Supreme Court said that evidence of these "calculated falsehoods" was sufficient proof of actual malice (*Cantrell* v. *Forest City Publishing Co.*, 1974). The reporter must have known, Justice Stewart wrote, that a number of statements in his story were untrue.

2. Sixty-seven-year-old James Kent was released from prison after twenty-seven years of incarceration on a murder charge. He had won a new trial, and the state chose not to reprosecute. Therefore, in the eyes of the law, Kent was innocent of the murder he had been charged with. A story in the *Pittsburgh Press* on prison reform made a single-sentence reference to Kent as a man who had taken a life. He sued for publication of a false report, arguing that had the reporter checked with the prison officials he would have discovered the facts—that Kent's conviction for murder had been overturned. The federal district court said that the story was not reckless disregard for the truth, it was not malice (*Kent* v. *Pittsburgh Press*, 1972):

> Obviously if Grochot [the reporter] had checked the court records relating to Kent, he could have discovered the reason for his release. Obviously too, however, he had no reason in the circumstances to entertain any doubts, quite apart from serious doubts, as to the matter of Kent's release.

3. In a case mentioned earlier, a young mother killed her three children and then took her own life. In the *National Enquirer* story about the incident the victim was pictured as "the happiest mother" with no apparent reason to commit suicide. The newspaper published what it

called a "cryptic" suicide note giving no hint as to the reason for the murder-suicide. The victim's husband, Melvin Varnish, sued the weekly newspaper for publishing a false report. He proved that the reporter had access to records which indicated that Mrs. Varnish was depressed and despondent before the incident. He also proved that the reporter had a copy of the entire suicide note, of which the paper published only a portion, and that the entire note clearly explained the reasons for the murder-suicide. The federal court of appeals ruled that this evidence was sufficient to support a finding of reckless disregard for the truth (*Varnish* v. *Best Medium*, 1968).

While many plaintiffs in false report cases may have an increased burden of proof, the burden of proof is not insurmountable. In light of *Gertz,* we might speculate that in the future it is a burden that some plaintiffs will not have to meet at all.

Before the discussion of the right of privacy comes to an end, we need to recall a few points. First, remember that only people have the right of privacy. Corporations, businesses, and governments do not enjoy the legal right of privacy as such. Second, unlike libel, the law of privacy does provide that the plaintiff may seek an injunction to stop an invasion of privacy. This action is in addition to the right to seek money damages. However, it is difficult for a plaintiff to get an injunction. Courts are very hesitant to enjoin tortious conduct unless the plaintiff can show that the action will cause irreparable injury and that the tortious conduct will likely be continued. Such was the case in the *Galella-Onassis* suit. A plaintiff is far more likely to get an injunction in either an intrusion or an appropriation case than in a private facts or false report suit. Normally courts refuse to grant injunctions because they believe an adequate legal remedy is available or because they belive that the injunction could constitute prior censorship in violation of the First Amendment. The plaintiff bears an immense burden in convincing a court that prior restraint is called for. While it is possible to get an injunction, it is difficult.

Third, it is impossible to civilly libel a dead person, but in some states it is possible for an heir to maintain an action for invasion of privacy.

Although privacy law is not well charted as libel law, and although there are fewer privacy cases, suits for invasion of privacy are a growing menace to journalists. If journalists stick to the job of responsibly reporting the news, they may rest assured that the chance for a successful privacy suit is slim.

BIBLIOGRAPHY

Here are some of the sources that were helpful in the preparation of chapter 4.

Books Pember, Don R. *Privacy and the Press.* Seattle: University of Washington Press, 1972.

Articles Bloustein, Edward J. "Privacy as an Aspect of Human Dignity: An Answer to Dean Prosser," 39 *New York University Law Review* 962 (1964).

Davis, Frederick. "What Do We Mean by Right to Privacy?" 4 *South Dakota Law Review* 1 (1959).

Pember, Don R., and Teeter, Dwight L. "Privacy and the Press Since Time, Inc., v. Hill," 50 *Washington Law Review* 57 (1974).

Prosser, William L. "Privacy," 48 *California Law Review* 383 (1960).

Warren, Samuel, and Brandeis, Louis D. "The Right to Privacy," 4 *Harvard Law Review* 193 (1890).

Cases *Acquino v. Bulletin Co.*, 190 Pa. Super. 528 (1959).

Barber v. Time, Inc., 159 S.W. 2d 291 (1942).

Barbieri v. News-Journal Publishing Co., 182 A 2d 773 (1963).

Berg v. Minneapolis Star & Tribune, 79 F. Supp. 957 (1948).

Bernstein v. NBC, 232 F. 2d 369 (1955).

Blumenthal v. Picture Classics, 261 N.Y. 504 (1933).

Booth v. Curtis Publishing Co., 11 N.Y. 2d 907 (1962).

Briscoe v. Reader's Digest Association, 483 P. 2d 34 (1971).

Canessa v. J. I. Kislak, Inc., 235 A 2d 62 (1967).

Cantrell v. Forest City Publishing Co., 95 S. Ct. 465 (1974).

Carlisle v. Fawcett Publishing Co., 210 Cal. App. 2d 733 (1962).

Cason v. Baskin, 159 Fla. 131 (1947).

Cohen v. Marx, 94 Cal. App. 2d 704 (1949).

Commonwealth v. Wiseman, 249 N.E. 2d 610 (1969).

Corabi v. Curtis Publishing Co., 273 A 2d 899 (1971).

Costlow v. Cuismano, 311 N.Y.S. 2d 92 (1970).

Cox Broadcasting Co. v. Cohn, 95 S. Ct. 1029 (1975).

Daily Times-Democrat v. Graham, 162 So. 2d 474 (1962).

Dieteman v. Time, Inc., 449 F. 2d 245 (1971).

Durgom v. CBS, 214 N.Y.S. 2d 752 (1961).

Florida Publishing Co. v. Fletcher, #48,372, Florida Supreme Court, Oct. 7, 1976.

Galella v. Onassis, 487 F. 2d 986 (1973).

Gautier v. Pro-Football Co., 304 N.Y. 354 (1952).

Goldman v. Time, Inc., 336 F. Supp. 133 (1971).

Haelan Laboratories, Inc., v. Topps Chewing Gum, 202 F. 2d 866 (1953).

Holmes v. Curtis Publishing Co., 303 F. Supp. 522 (1969).

Jacova v. Southern Radio-Television Co., 83 So. 2d 34 (1955).

Jeffries v. New York Evening Journal, 124 N.Y.S. 780 (1910).

Jones v. Herald Post Co., 18 S.W. 2d 972 (1929).

Kelley v. Post Publishing Co., 327 Mass. 275 (1951).

Kent v. Pittsburgh Press, 349 F. Supp. 622 (1972).

Langford v. Vanderbilt University, 199 Tenn. 389 (1956).

Leverton v. Curtis Publishing Co., 192 F. 2d 974 (1951).

Liberty Lobby v. Pearson, 390 F. 2d 489 (1968).

McAndrews v. Roy, 131 So. 2d 256 (1961).

Man v. Warner Bros., 317 F. Supp. 50 (1970).

Meetze v. *AP*, 95 S.E. 2d 606 (1956).

Melvin v. *Reid*, 297 P. 91 (1931).

Metter v. *Los Angeles Examiner*, 95 P. 2d 491 (1939).

Moser v. *Press Publishing Co.*, 109 N.Y.S. 963 (1908).

Nappier v. *Jefferson Standard Life Insurance Co.*, 322 F. 2d 502 (1963).

Palmer v. *Schonhorn Enterprises, Inc.*, 232 A 2d 458 (1967).

Patterson v. *Tribune Co.*, 146 So. 2d 623 (1962).

Paulsen v. *Personality Posters*, 299 N.Y.S. 2d 501 (1968).

Pavesich v. *New England Mutual Life Insurance Co.*, 122 Ga. 190 (1905).

Pearson v. *Dodd*, 410 F. 2d 701 (1969).

Peed v. *Washington Times Co.*, 55 Wash. Law Rep. 182 (1927).

People v. *Kunkin*, 100 Cal. Rep. 845 (1972), revd. 107 Cal. Rep. 184 (1973).

Roberson v. *Rochester Folding Box Co.*, 171 N.Y. 538 (1902).

Russell v. *Marboro Books*, 183 N.Y.S. 2d 8 (1959).

Sidis v. *F-R Publishing Co.*, 113 F. 2d 806 (1940).

Strickler v. *NBC*, 167 F. Supp. 68 (1958).

Sweenek v. *Pathé News*, 16 F. Supp. 746 (1936).

Time, Inc., v. *Hill*, 385 U.S. 374 (1967).

Uhlaender v. *Henricksen*, 159 F. Supp. 1277 (1970).

Varnish v. *Best Medium*, 405 F. 2d 608 (1968).

Williams v. *KCMO Broadcasting Co.*, 472 S.W. 2d 1 (1971).

CHAPTER 5

The Law of Copyright

When a person builds a house or a chair or makes a lamp or a new shirt, it is fairly obvious who owns those goods. The person who built the house lives in it, rents it, or sells it—in any case there is a deed, and ownership can be proved. The same is true of other material goods. The owner can possess them and guard them from theft.

But take a look at the book on the corner of your desk. Who owns that? Well, if you bought the book you own it. At least, you own the paper and cardboard and fabric used for binding. But who owns the words? Is it possible for someone to own words? Doesn't language belong to everybody? Sure it does. The words in that book, however, are not just a random selection of entries from a dictionary. Somebody has spent a lot of time organizing those words in a specific pattern so that they tell you something, give you new information, make you laugh, or maybe make you cry. Or they might tell you the way to do something, or help you understand some deep philosophical problem. The answer to the question, Who owns the words? therefore is, the author owns the words or at least owns the way the words are organized in this instance.

Copyright is an area of the law which deals with immaterial property, property that a man can't put his hands on, that can't be felt or touched or locked in a safe. Some examples of this kind of property are inventions, ideas, writing, painting, music, and drama. In this chapter the rights of authors, composers, artists, inventors, and playwrights are discussed. This area of the law seems at first glance to be terribly complicated, but when the facts are sorted out, copyright law is really not too difficult to understand.

People who work in the mass media don't need to become copyright and patent attorneys in order to avoid lawsuits in the 1970s. But writers and broadcasters should know both how to protect their own work from theft and how to avoid illegally taking the work of someone else.

Until 1976, when the Congress passed a major revision of the copyright law, this nation suffered under a statute that had been adopted in 1909 and became out of date soon afterward. Beginning in the midfifties, the Congress began work on revision of the 1909 law. It seemed as though each time the revision was completed new technology such as cable television and photocopying made the proposal obsolete. In addition, special interest groups lobbied long and hard to have the law framed in a way favorable to them. Publishing groups, librarians, jukebox operators, and cable television operators are just some of the kinds of interest groups which put pressure on the Congress.

The new law covers a great many aspects of copyright which fall outside the scope of this book, which is law affecting the mass media. Hence, we will focus on a narrow range of subjects within the broader measure. First, the conditions creating the need for copyright laws and development of the law are discussed. Second, the kinds of works that may be copyrighted and the kinds that may not are considered. Third, how authors may protect their own work is discussed. Finally, the precautions which should be taken to avoid stealing the work of other persons, either inadvertently or advertently, are outlined.

As with any new law, many questions in regard to the meaning of words and phrases within the statute will arise. How the courts answer these questions, of course, will determine the ultimate meaning of the new law. The measure was signed by the president in October 1976, literally days before this book went to press. Consequently, we have no court cases to help determine what the ambiguous sections of the new law really mean. However, many sections of the new law are similar or nearly identical to parts of the 1909 measure. The courts will probably rely heavily upon cases in which sections of the old statute were interpreted to help them understand similar sections of the 1976 law. Judges normally behave in this fashion. Therefore, we will use the same cases to clarify some of the more difficult portions of the new law (more about this later). First a brief look at our British legal heritage to uncover the roots of the law of copyright is necessary.

BRITISH HERITAGE

Law professor Paul Goldstein writes in the *Columbia Law Review* (1970), "Copyright is the uniquely legitimate offspring of censorship." British history from the late fifteenth century through the early eighteenth century partially substantiates this assertion. It is naive, however, to think of copyright as solely a limiting force on the production of written works. Protection of the rights of an author, after all, can give impetus to authors to write and publish more. There were really few legal problems in protecting literary property prior to the development of mechanical printing. Each hand-copied manuscript was the result of the labor of a copyist. It was an individual entity, a specific creation. As such, it was protected by the law of personal property. But the printing press, which permitted mass production of exact copies of a written work changed the situation. The press produced both a piece of physical property—the book itself— and an immaterial property—the arrangement and organization of the words or ideas. The immaterial property was called literary property and was not protected by British law.

As noted in chapter 2, printing created many problems for the king. The crown was fearful of the power of the press to rouse the passions of the people against the government. Therefore, in the sixteenth century the government sanctioned and supported the grant of printing privileges to certain master printers in exchange for loyalty and assistance in ferreting out antigovernment writers and publishers. In *The First Copyright Statute* Harry Ransom writes:

> The privilege had its origins in the Crown's patronage of specific printers. Warrants granting rights to print books or a specific book, usually for a certain term—two years, ten years, or the lifetime of the printer—were a natural outgrowth of the system of appointing King's printers. The grant was a recognition of confidence in his printing and a protective guarantee of his right in copy. It was a means of extending royal control of the press through official choice of printers to be encouraged by patronage.

The first recorded privilege or royal grant was given in 1518 according to Professor Ransom. About forty years later the Stationers' Company was founded for much the same purpose. This was an organization of master printers chartered by the government to control, regulate, and protect printing. The company had sufficient power to regulate who did the printing and what was printed. The crown cooperated with this guild because it served as a useful tool for censorship. Some of the basic rudiments of copyright law were developed by the Stationers' Company. The company required printers to record the publication of their works in a registration book. While this device was used originally to keep track of what printers published, the registration book later became evidence in lawsuits over printing privileges. Registration of a book prior to publication of a pirated version substantiated a claim of ownership. It was in 1586 that a court first accepted the registration book as evidence of ownership.

Note that the protection of the rights of printers is all we have discussed thus far. What about the rights of authors, the persons who wrote the books published by the printers? In the sixteenth century authors had few rights. Generally when an author sold his manuscript to a printer or a bookseller he sold all rights with it for a single fee. If the book sold well, the bookseller might further compensate the author, but the additional compensation stemmed from generosity, not from legal obligation. Ransom reports that many sixteenth-century authors were jailed for nonpayment of debt, others went hungry, and most had to undertake some kind of additional labor to keep body and soul together. If the author printed the work himself, he retained rights which would provide him a royalty, or he might make an agreement with a printer or bookseller to gain part of the proceeds of sales. Such arrangements were uncommon, and there was no organized royalty system.

In the seventeenth century litigation over the ownership of books increased, and with the increased litigation certain common law principles developed. A decree by the Star Chamber in 1637 asserted that all books which were published had to be registered in the Stationers' registration book, that the name of the printer or bookseller must appear in the published book, and that there was to be no infringement on the publishing rights of persons who held the printing privilege, that is, no theft of another person's work. In 1649 the government passed a law which provided a penalty—a fine—for anyone found guilty of reprinting works entered in the Register.

More laws were passed and more cases tried in the second half of the seventeenth century. It soon became obvious, however, that problems of authors—who were becoming quite angry—and of booksellers and printers as well could not be solved by any measure short of a comprehensive law. Petitions began to appear at Parliament urging legislation to protect the rights of authors. In 1710 Parliament passed the first British copyright law: "An Act for the Encouragement of Learning, by Vesting the Copies of Printed Books in the Authors or Purchasers of Such Copies, during the Times therein mentioned." The law was passed in the eighth year of the reign of Queen Anne and hence became known as the Statute of Eight Anne.

The law gave the legal claim of ownership of a piece of literary property to the person who created the work or to a person who acquired the rights to the work from the author. The claim of ownership lasted for only fourteen years. The copyright could be renewed for fourteen more years, but after twenty-eight years the work fell into the public domain and could be copied by anyone. The copyright owner had to give nine copies to the government for use in libraries and had to register the book with the Stationers' Company. The most important aspect of this law was not the specific legal provisions, but the recognition by the British government that writers or authors should enjoy a right of ownership in their creations. This concept is very important, for without it we might find ourselves with far less to read today. While most authors are motivated by a desire to inform and entertain, they must also subsist. By providing them the right of ownership in their work, authors are compensated in such a way as to encourage them to continue to write.

Clearly any law giving authors the right of ownership automatically limits copying and use of the literary property. This limitation is what Professor Goldstein means when he talks of censorship. A copyright law does in fact act as censorship since it restricts the right to republish or copy books, articles, photographs, and any work that is copyrighted.

The Statute of Eight Anne did not go unchallenged. Booksellers were angered by the limit on ownership. (The law provided that the ownership in any work created before the statute was adopted would terminate in twenty-one years.) Publishers rushed into print with works the law ruled were in the public domain, but which booksellers still claimed as literary property. The booksellers sought injunctions to stop what they called pirating. They argued that under the common law their ownership of a book was perpetual—it lasted forever. The Parliament could not take this away from them, they said. This dispute finally came before Britain's highest court, the House of Lords, in 1774. The House of Lords ruled that it was true that at common law the right of first printing and publishing lasted forever, but that the statute superseded the common law, revoked the common law copyright in perpetuity for published works. The common law no longer applied. Twenty-eight years were the maximum for ownership of published literary property.

This case, *Donaldson* v. *Beckett,* established a very important point in copyright law: that the law treated an unpublished work differently from a published work. Eight Anne specifically applied to works which had been published. The House of Lords ruled that limited ownership applied to such works. However, the law did not embrace unpublished works, and hence the common law rule of ownership in perpetuity remained in force.

COPYRIGHT IN AMERICA

While our copyright laws are direct descendants of the British law, the British law had little impact in the colonies. The colonies had no separate copyright statute, but printing and publishing original books and pamphlets was not an active business prior to the Revolution. After the Revolution, of course, the British law did not apply.

Our first constitution, the Articles of Confederation, made no mention of the protection of literary property. Congress did, however, recommend that the states adopt legislation to protect the rights of authors. Several states did before our present Constitution was adopted in 1789. In Article I, Section 8, of that document lies the basic authority for modern United States copyright law:

> The Congress shall have the power . . . To promote the Progress of Science and useful Arts, by securing for limited Times to Authors and Inventors the exclusive Right to their respective Writings and Discoveries.

This provision gives the Congress the power to legislate on both copyright and patent. The Congress did in 1790 by adopting a statute similar to that of Eight Anne. The law gave authors who were United States citizens the right to protect their books, maps, and charts for a total of twenty-eight years—a fourteen-year original grant plus a fourteen-year renewal. In 1802 the law was amended to include prints as well as books, maps, and charts. In 1831 the period of protection was expanded by fourteen years. The original grant became twenty-eight years with a fourteen-year renewal. Also, musical compositions were granted protection. Photography was given protection in 1865 and works of fine art were included five years later. Translation rights were added in 1870.

A major revision of the law was enacted in 1909, and as was previously noted, our current law was adopted in 1976.

WHAT MAY AND MAY NOT BE COPYRIGHTED

The law of copyright gives to the author, or the owner of the copyright, the sole and exclusive right to reproduce the copyrighted work in any form for any reason. Before a copyrighted work may be printed, broadcast, dramatized, translated, or whatever, the consent of the copyright owner must first be obtained. The law grants this individual exclusive monopoly over the use of that material.

What kinds of works are protected? The federal statute lists a wide range of items which can be copyrighted:

1. Literary works
2. Musical works, including any accompanying words
3. Dramatic works, including any accompanying music
4. Pantomimes and choreographic works
5. Pictorial, graphic, and sculptural works
6. Motion pictures and other audiovisual works
7. Sound recordings

To quote the statute specifically, copyright extends to "original works of authorship fixed in any tangible medium of expression." The Congress has defined *fixed in a tangible medium* as that work which is "sufficiently permanent or stable to permit it to be perceived, reproduced or otherwise communicated for a period of more than a transitory duration." Extemporaneous speeches or improvised sketches are good examples of materials which are not fixed in a tangible medium and are not protected by the law. However, these kinds of works are undoubtedly protected by common law copyright.*

Original Works   Can all books and motion pictures be copyrighted? Not really. The law specifically says that only "original" works can be copyrighted. What is an original work? In interpreting this term in the 1909 law, courts ruled that the word *original* means that the work must owe its origin to the author. In 1973 a court reporter, an employee of the court who transcribes the proceedings, attempted to claim copyright over a transcript he made of some of the proceedings during the investigation of the death of Mary Jo Kopechne. This young woman drowned when a car driven by Senator Edward Kennedy went off a bridge and into a creek near Chappaquiddick, Massachusetts. In *Lipman* v. *Commonwealth* (1973), a federal judge ruled that the transcript could not be copyrighted. "Since transcription is by very definition a verbatim recording of other persons' statements, there can be no originality in the reporter's product."

The work must be original. Must it be of high quality or be new or novel? The answer to both questions is no. Even common and mundane works are copyrightable. Courts have consistently ruled that it is not the function of the legal system to act as literary or art critics when applying copyright law. In 1903 Justice Oliver Wendell Holmes wrote in *Bleistein* v. *Donaldson Lithographing Co.*, "It would be a dangerous undertaking for persons trained only to the law to constitute themselves final judges of the worth of pictorial illustrations, outside of the narrowest and most

---

*Under the 1909 law the United States had two kinds of copyright protection: common law copyright and statutory copyright. Much as it did in eighteenth century England, the common law protected any work which had not been published. Common law protection was automatic; that is, the work was protected from the point of its creation. And it lasted forever—or until the work was published. In order to protect published works, the author, photographer, or composer had to register the book or picture or song with the United States government and place a copyright notice on the work. The 1976 statute does away with common law copyright for all practical purposes. The only kinds of works protected by the common law are works like extemporaneous speeches and sketches which have not been fixed in a tangible medium. They are still protected from the point of their creation by common law copyright. Once they are written down, recorded, filmed, or fixed in a tangible medium in any way, they come under the protection of the new law.

obvious limits." Even the least pretentious picture can be an original Holmes noted in reference to the posters involved in this case. Likewise, novelty is not important to copyright: the author doesn't have to be the first person to say something in order to copyright it. "All that is needed to satisfy both the Constitution and the statute is that the 'author' contributed something more than a merely trivial variation, something recognizably his own," one court ruled (*Amsterdam* v. *Triangle Publishing Co.,* 1951).

The key is how much of the author's own work is invested. In 1946 the *Philadelphia Inquirer* printed a copy of a map in connection with publication of a historical article. The map had been copyrighted by the Franklin Survey Company, which promptly sued for copyright infringement. The survey company created the map by studying other maps; the company did no surveying itself. It obtained road numbers from the highway department and road names almost exclusively from other maps. There was no question that the Franklin Survey Company spent a good deal of time assembling this material, but the fact was that the company did not create much of the material by its own labor. The court ruled that the survey company's copyright was invalid because the creative work by the plaintiff was not sufficient to make the map original (*Amsterdam* v. *Triangle Publishing Co.,* 1951). There must be at least a modicum of creative work in the map, the court said. Hadn't Franklin assembled this information in an original or unique fashion? This fact was immaterial, the court ruled. A map is protected only when the publisher gets some of the material "by the sweat of his brow." Originality is therefore the key; whether the work is novel or of artistic quality is not important.

News Events

Can an event be copyrighted? Suppose a reporter is standing next to a building which suddenly and violently collapses, killing scores of people trapped inside. Suppose the reporter is the only one who saw the building collapse. Can she write a news story about this disaster, copyright it, and then prohibit others from writing about the event as well? The answer is no.

This point was established in an interesting case. In 1917 the *New York Tribune* published a copyrighted story about the first large-scale use of submarine warfare by the Germans in World War I. The New York paper sold the republication rights for the story to the *Chicago Daily News.* Before the *Daily News* could print the story, the *Chicago Record-Herald* printed its own version of the story. The initial paragraph of the *Herald* version began, "The *Tribune* this morning in a copyrighted article of Louis Durant Edwards, a correspondent in Germany, says that Germany to make the final effort against Great Britain has plunged 300 or more submersibles into the North Sea."

The remainder of the *Herald* story was comprised of five additional paragraphs, each of which was almost an exact duplication of a paragraph from the much longer *Tribune* story. The *Tribune* sued for infringement of copyright. The *Herald* answered by saying that a newspaper cannot copyright the news. Lawyers for the defendant argued that all the newspaper did was made use of facts which were in the public domain.

The circuit court of appeals agreed that as such news is not copyrightable. If the *Herald* story had been merely a summary or statement of the *Tribune* story, the *Tribune* would then have no case. However, the *Herald* did not stick to just a summary of the facts, but used parts of the article including the literary style and quality. The article itself, the way the words were organized, the style—the creative aspects of the report—can be (and in this case were) protected by copyright. The court said (*Chicago Record-Herald* v. *Tribune Association*, 1921):

> This is plainly more than a mere chronicle of facts or news. It reveals a peculiar power of portrayal and a felicity of wording and phrasing, well calculated to seize and hold the interest of the reader, which is quite beyond and apart from the mere setting forth of facts. But if the whole of it were considered as stating news or facts, yet, the arrangement and manner of statement plainly discloses a distinct literary flavor and individuality of expression peculiar to the authorship, bringing the article clearly within the purview and protection of the copyright law.

The court ruled that the fact that the *Herald* gave the *Tribune* credit did not alleviate the theft. On the contrary, the court said, it might have conveyed to the public the incorrect idea that the *Herald* had got permission from the *Tribune* to use the story.

News cannot be copyrighted. But the style or manner of presentation can be protected. Consider the imaginary building-disaster story again. If reporter Jane Adams is the only one to witness the building collapse and publishes a copyrighted story it, no one else can publish that story without permission. Other news media can report that Jane Adams reported in a copyrighted story that a building collapsed, killing many people. These news media can also summarize—note, summarize—the facts given by Adams in her story. This summary is not an infringement of copyright.

As a matter of fact, most newspapers don't bother to copyright what they publish. A few do; each edition of the *New York Times* is copyrighted, for example. But the chances are better than one thousand to one that the newspaper in your town is not copyrighted, except for occasional scoops or big stories. Most newspapers feel that to copyright each edition is too much bother or hassle. In addition, newspapers see little purpose in it. Who would want to reprint an old newspaper? Remember the cliché, Nothing is older than yesterday's news. When this fact is kept in mind, an obvious question comes to mind. If a newspaper is not copyrighted, what prevents local radio and television stations from simply clipping articles from newspapers and reading them over the air? A broadcasting station could dismiss its entire news staff and read stories published in the daily papers during their news broadcasts. (It might be noted parenthetically that more clipping and reading go on than might be expected. Newspaper editors also listen to the radio and watch television to get story ideas. However, this fact is not the answer to the question.) The legal basis for stopping such practice is found in another, unrelated area of the law entitled misappropriation or unfair competition. Despite the fact that it has little to do with copyright, this area deals directly with news gathering, and a brief discussion of it is therefore appropriate.

Misappropriation

In 1918 the Supreme Court of the United States was asked to resolve a dispute between the Associated Press (AP) and the International News Service (INS), a competitive press association owned by William Randolph Hearst. (INS merged with the United Press in 1958 and today represents only the *I* in *UPI*.) The Associated Press charged that the International News Service pirated its news, saying that INS bribed AP employees to gain access to news before it was sent to AP member newspapers. The press agency also charged that the Hearst wire service copied news from bulletin boards and early editions of newspapers which carried AP dispatches. Sometimes INS editors rewrote the news, and other times they sent the news as written by AP. Copyright was not the question because AP did not copyright its material. The agency said it couldn't copyright all its dispatches because there were too many and they had to be transmitted too fast. The International News Service argued that because the material was not copyrighted it was in the public domain and could be used by anyone.

Justice Mahlon Pitney wrote the opinion in the seven-to-one decision. He said there can be no property right in the news itself, the events, the happenings, which are publici juris, the common property of all, the history of the day. However, the jurist went on to say (*Associated Press* v. *International News Service*, 1918):

> Although we may and do assume that neither party [AP or INS] has any remaining property interest as against the public in uncopyrighted matter after the moment of its first publication, it by no means follows that there is no remaining property interest in it as between themselves.

Pitney said there was a distinct difference between taking the news collected by AP and publishing it for use by readers and taking the news and transmitting that news for commercial use, in competition with the plaintiff. This action is unfair competition, he said—interference with the business of the AP precisely at the point where profit is to be reaped.

The decision in the *AP* case was based on the doctrine of unfair competition, or misappropriation. Courts have applied the doctrine in various instances of fraudulent or dishonest competitive business practices, but particularly in those instances where one seller attempts to substitute his own products for those of a well-known competitor by counterfeiting a trade name, package design, or trademark. For example, the owner of the Acme Motel remodels his building in the guise of a Holiday Inn, calls his remodeled creation Holiday Inn, and attempts to lure weary travelers into his establishment on the basis of the reputation of the real Holiday Inn. This practice is considered unfair competition.

In *Associated Press* v. *International News Service* the Hearst wire service attempted to pass off Associated Press news as its own, and the court said the deception was unfair. This law prohibits radio station KWAK from reading an early edition of the *River City Sentinel* over the air to its listeners, thereby interfering with the business of the newspaper. As a result, people would not have to subscribe to the newspaper to get the news, circulation would drop, advertisers would leave the newspaper, and the ultimate result could be the demise of the *Sentinel*.

DURATION OF COPYRIGHT PROTECTION

As far as authors and copyright owners are concerned, the most significant change in the new copyright law is the substantial increase in the duration of copyright protection. Under the old law, a work was protected for a maximum of fifty-six years: a twenty-eight-year initial term plus a twenty-eight-year renewal. Because in the late twentieth century authors live longer it was not unusual for the copyright on a work to expire before the author died. The work then became part of what is called the public domain, which means that any individual can copy it without infringing upon the copyright.

Under the new law copyright duration begins when the work is created and lasts for the author's life plus fifty years. The extended protection allows authors' heirs to reap the fruits of the work of their fathers, mothers, sisters, or brothers.

The 1976 law also provides extended terms for those works which are currently copyrighted. If the work is in its initial term of copyright, it is protected for the remainder of that term plus forty-seven years. That is, the owner of the copyright on a book which expires in 1985 can retain ownership of that book from the present time until 1985 plus forty-seven years.

If the copyrighted work is in its renewal term—the second twenty-eight years under the 1909 law—the work is protected for a total of seventy-five years. For example, a book which is in the fifteenth year of its second or renewal term has already been protected for one full term, twenty-eight years, and for fifteen years of the renewal term—a total of forty-three years. That book is protected for thirty-two more years from today, or a total of seventy-five years.

LIMITATIONS ON COPYRIGHT PROTECTION

Under the 1909 law all copying of a copyrighted work was against the law. This absolute prohibition on copying constituted a hardship for scholars, critics, and teachers seeking to use small parts of copyrighted materials in their work. A judicial remedy for this problem was sought. It was argued that since the purpose of the original copyright statute was to promote art and science the copyright law should not be administered in such a way as to frustrate artists and scientists who publish scholarly materials. In 1879 the United States Supreme Court ruled in *Baker* v. *Selden*:

> The very object of publishing a book on science or the useful arts is to communicate to the world the useful knowledge which it contains. But this object would be frustrated if the useful knowledge could not be used without incurring the guilt of piracy of the book.

A doctrine of "fair use" emerged from the courts, and under this judicial doctrine small amounts of copying were permitted so long as the publication of the material advanced science, the arts, criticism, and so forth.

Fair Use Standards

The 1976 copyright law contains the common law doctrine of fair use. Section 107 of the new measure declares, "the fair use of a copyrighted work . . . for purposes such as criticism, comment, news reporting, teaching (including multiple copies for classroom use), scholarship or research is not an infringement of copyright."

In determining whether the use of a particular work is a fair use, the 1976 statute says that courts should consider the following factors:

1. The purpose and character of the use, including whether such use is of a commercial nature or is for nonprofit educational purposes
2. The nature of the copyrighted work
3. The amount and substantiality of the portion used in relation to the copyrighted work as a whole
4. The effect of the use upon the potential market for or value of the copyrighted work

These, then, are the factors that judges will take into account in determining if a use is an infringement or a fair use. Fair use is perhaps the most confusing and complex part of the law, and the section of the law dealing with fair use became a major battleground for disputes between librarians and publishers. The librarians and other persons interested in photocopying of published works sought liberal rules under fair use. Publishers and copyright holders wanted tight rules against photocopying. The law seems to be a compromise, allowing for the photocopying of a single copy of a work for library use, but with several qualifications to the general rule.

Interestingly, the criteria included in the statute and just listed (1 through 4) for determining fair use are pretty much the same criteria that courts used under the old common law fair use doctrine. It is therefore instructive to consider how courts looked previously at the criteria.

In 1938 in *Holt* v. *Liggett & Myers Tobacco Co.* a federal court ruled that the use in a pamphlet of three sentences from a book published by Henry Holt & Company was not a fair use. The pamphlet was designed to induce people to smoke the defendant's cigarettes. The use was purely for commercial gain by the tobacco company, the court said.

In 1940 a columnist in the *New York Magazine* quoted twelve lines from a song. When the song publisher sued, the court ruled that the quotation was a fair use because it was clearly incidental to the article— it was a small part of the column—and clearly did not damage the plaintiff in any way. He lost no sales of his song because of the publication (*Broadway Music* v. *F-R Publishing Co.*, 1940).

In 1941 a publisher prepared a study guide for a French examination that was quite similar to one already published and copyrighted. In this case, the court ruled that the study guide exceeded fair use. In one examination the defendant's book contained ninety-six percent of the grammar items in the plaintiff's list and eighty-two percent of the plaintiff's items in a second examination. Despite the fact that the word lists comprised only fifteen percent of the entire book, the court said that because both books sought the same market the second book substantially interfered with the first (*College Entrance Book Co.* v. *Amsco Book Co.*, 1941).

In 1869 in *Lawrence* v. *Dana* a United States court ruled against a defendant on the grounds that a book didn't contain enough of his own original work to justify the defense of fair use. And in 1841 Justice Story wrote that fair use is exceeded if enough of the plaintiff's work is taken to diminish the value of the original work. He said the courts must "look to the nature and the objects of the selections made, the quantity and value of the material used, and the degree in which the use may prejudice the sale, or diminish the profits, or supersede the objects, of the original work" (*Folsom* v. *Marsh*, 1841).

A court of appeals ruled that a novelist who copied twenty-four passages from a biography of the life of Hans Christian Andersen exceeded fair use. The passages were translations of Danish documents, and while the documents were in the public domain, the biographer had translated them into English. The court ruled that the defendant, who used the material in a novel based on the life of Andersen, appropriated too much material to be considered fair use. By using the fruits of the biographer's labor, the translation of the Danish documents, the novelist was able to finish her work in far less time. Thus, she got much value from the plaintiff's work (*Toksvig* v. *Bruce Publishing Co.*, 1950).

A group of song writers once sued *Mad* magazine for publishing parody song lyrics of their compositions. The publication appeared in the special bonus to the *Fourth Annual Edition of Mad* and was described by the magazine as "a collection of parody lyrics to fifty-seven old standards which reflect the idiotic world in which we live." The parody lyrics were written in the meter of the original songs and were to be sung to the melody of the standard versions. The parody lyrics to the song "The Last Time I Saw Paris" concerned a sports hero turned television pitchman, and the song was called "The First Time I Saw Maris." A song about a woman hypochondriac was sung to the tune of "A Pretty Girl is Like a Melody" and was called "Louella Schwartz Describes her Malady."

The judge asked, How were the songwriters hurt? In a negligible way, the court concluded. The parody of lyrics was not a theft. They were not about the same topic and did not have the same rhyme scheme. The parody lyrics were in the same meter as the original lyrics, which was necessary if the original songs were to be recognized and the lyrics were to fit the melodies. "We doubt," the court added, "that even so eminent a composer as plaintiff Irving Berlin should be permitted to claim a property interest in the iambic pentameter." The use by *Mad* of the song titles and references to their melodies was fair use the court ruled (*Berlin* v. *E. C. Publications, Inc.* 1964).

Parody has often been the cause for copyright suits. The author of a parody must use enough of the material to suggest the original to the audience, but can't use too much or an infringement suit will stand. Jack Benny was sued for doing a parody on the movie *Gas Light* which he called *Auto Light*. In 1945 Benny gained permission from the movie producer to do a fifteen-minute parody on the radio. In 1952 he did a thirty-minute burlesque of the film on television, but this time did not obtain permission. Comparing the parody and the original, the court found that the locales and time settings were the same, the main sets were the same, the characters were the same, the points of the stories were identical, and the development of story, points of suspense, climax, and even much of the dialogue were the same. The primary difference was that Benny's version was a parody. The television version was not fair use, the court said. When the part that Jack Benny added to the movie for his parody was removed, the movie remained. However, when the motion picture was removed from the parody, little of the television presentation was left. The court ruled that creation of a comedy out of a serious work does not automatically constitute a fair use. In this case the license to borrow was grossly exceeded (*Benny* v. *Loew's*, 1956).

At about the same time Columbia Pictures sued the National Broadcasting Company for Sid Caesar's parody of the movie *From Here to Eternity*. In this case, however, the differences between the film and the television parody were significant. Entitled "From Here to Obscurity" the parody had substantial differences in style, incidents and characters. Caesar's production was much sillier than the movie. The court then suggested these guidelines for parodies (*Columbia Pictures* v. *NBC*, 1955):

1. Fair use is not as likely to apply when the work stays in the same style, drama to drama, as opposed to drama to comedy.
2. The parody may take locale, theme, setting, situation, basic plot, and even bits of dialogue.
3. When the parody goes farther, it is not a fair use.

Public Interest Standard

In addition to the four standards for criteria for fair use previously discussed (p. 221) courts developed another standard while fair use was part of the common law. This standard is the "public interest." Not until 1966 did a court opinion argue that use of copyright material should be permitted under fair use because such publication is in the public interest. The second circuit court of appeals ruled in a complex copyright suit that serving a public interest can be a compelling reason to allow fair use, in the absence of other traditional considerations such as furthering the arts and sciences. Random House planned to publish a biography of the late Howard Hughes in which a series of articles about Hughes in *Look* magazine were quoted rather extensively. When he learned of the Random House project, Hughes, who manifested almost a compulsion about his privacy, formed a corporation called Rosemont which bought the rights to the *Look* magazine story. Rosemont then sued Random House for using material from the series. All these events took place even before the book was published.

Judge Lumbard ruled in favor of Random House, noting that the purpose of the copyright laws was not to stop dissemination of information about publicity-shy public figures. It would be contrary to the public interest, he said, to allow a man to buy up the rights to anything written about him to stop authors from using the material. Lumbard said that at least the spirit of the First Amendment applied to the copyright laws, and that the courts should not tolerate the use of the copyright laws to interfere with the public's right to be informed regarding matters of general interest. Rosemont (Hughes) protested that such copying might be appropriate if the work in question were a scholarly biography of Hughes, but that the Random House venture was commercial. Judge Lumbard said this fact was immaterial (*Rosemont v. Random House,* 1966):

> Whether an author or publisher reaps economic benefits from the sale of a biographical work, or whether its publication is motivated in part by desire for commercial gain, or whether it is designed for the popular market, i.e., the average citizen rather than the college professor, has no bearing on whether a public benefit may be derived from such a work. . . . Thus, we conclude that whether an author or publisher has a commercial motive or writes in a popular style is irrelevant to a determination of whether a particular use of copyrighted material in a work which offers some benefit to the public constitutes a fair use.

The decision in *Rosemont* represented a bold new step forward in copyright law, a step which many authorities felt was long overdue. On its face the case could not have been equitably decided any other way. Hughes' attempt to buy up his own life story was so patently obvious that the entire suit was really a farce—a mild diversion for the idle rich. Many persons asked, will the public interest ruling stand?

Two years later a federal district court used the standard to allow the copying of several frames of very famous motion-picture film. An amateur photographer named Abraham Zapruder happened to be filming President John F. Kennedy when he was shot by an assassin in Dallas in 1963. The film is crude, but is the only film available. *Life* magazine bought the rights to the film from Zapruder for $15,000 with the stipulation that the magazine would allow government agencies to use it in connection with investigation of the president's death. *Life* had a tendency to buy the rights to important events, for example, signing contracts with all the astronauts for exclusive stories. The Zapruder film became (and remains) a central piece of evidence in the death of John Kennedy, and many persons who believe that the Warren Commission was wrong, that there was a conspiracy, that there was more than one gunman, use the Zapruder film to attempt to prove their thesis. In this case the defendant wanted to publish several frames of the film in his book proposing a multiassassin theory. When *Life* refused permission to use the film, the author used the frames anyway. Was this fair use?

Life said no, but the court disagreed. The judge said that there was little damage to the magazine as a result of publication of the pictures, that customers purchased the book because of its thesis, not because of its pictures, and that without the photographs the author's thesis was at best difficult to explain. "There is a public interest in having the fullest information available on the murder of President Kennedy. Thompson [the author] did serious work on the subject and had a theory entitled to public consideration." The public interest won out over the magazine's property rights (*Time, Inc.,* v. *Bernard Geis Associates,* 1968).

Most recently the federal courts ruled that the public interest in medical research is important enough to permit rather widespread use of copyrighted material. The case of *Williams & Wilkins Co.* v. *United States* was decided in 1973 by the United States Court of Claims, and the decision has since been affirmed by the Supreme Court by virtue of a four-to-four vote. The copying in question was done by various federal agencies such as the National Institute of Health Library and the National Library of Medicine. These agencies are recipients of large numbers of medical journals and periodicals, some of which are published by the plaintiff. It is the practice of these libraries to make photocopies of these articles, upon request, for scholars and doctors and researchers. The copying is restricted in the sense that only one copy of each article is made for each request, and the libraries do not copy articles exceeding fifty pages. During a year these various agencies duplicate about 200,000 copies of articles, the average length of which is ten pages. Two million pages are copied, and virtually all of this material is copyrighted.

The plaintiff, a publisher of medical journals, argued that this copying is damaging its business. To the defendant's argument that the copying is fair use the plaintiff asserted that copying an entire article can never be construed as fair use. It has generally been held that scholars can make a handwritten copy of an entire article for their own use, but photocopying is different, the plaintiff argued. Photocopying is just too easy.

The Court of Claims disagreed and called it a fair use. The plaintiff was not really harmed by this copying; there was no loss in business. The government libraries proved that. Just as important, however, is the fact that medical research can be severely hurt if the photocopying is stopped. The copying is restricted, the court noted; the libraries make no financial gain from it. All these factors added up to compelling reasons to allow this use to continue.

In 1975 the nation's high Court split four to four on the case, with Justice Blackmun abstaining. Hence the opinion of the Court of Claims remains law.

In 1973 researcher Jeanne Gross reported in *Journalism Quarterly* that by the spring of that year eighteen reported copyright cases cited the Rosemont case, and in five instances the public interest doctrine was used to some extent. So the standard remains for courts to confront in cases in which fair use is raised as a defense for infringement.

In light of the fact that the public interest was not included among the criteria listed in the 1976 copyright law, what are the chances that such an argument will continue to be accepted by the courts? This is an important question. It is also a question difficult to answer.

If judges approach the new copyright law using the traditional strict rules of statutory construction, a strong argument can be made that we have seen the last of the public interest criterion. Under traditional rules of statutory construction, when a part of the common law becomes a statute, and the legislature or the Congress leaves out specific principles which were a part of the common law, these actions should be taken as good evidence that the legislative body does not want these principles incorporated into the new law. The courts should follow the will of the legislature, which is supposed to be the voice of the people.

Nevertheless two counterarguments to this position can be made. First, the public interest criterion can become an important part of the first statutory criterion, the purpose and character of the use. It can be argued that publishing copyrighted material to serve an important public purpose weighs heavily in the favor of fair use. Second, and perhaps more important, it can be argued that the public interest standard is really a constitutional standard, a First Amendment standard, and despite the Congressional mandate to exclude the public interest criterion, the Constitutional imperative of freedom of expression must take priority.

Remember, all is speculation at this point. Whether courts continue to include the public interest as one aspect of fair use will be one of the most interesting questions which the judiciary will have to answer about the new law in the future.

HOW TO COPYRIGHT A WORK
Proper Notice

In order for a work to be protected under the copyright law, it must contain what is called a copyright notice. The new law specifically prescribes the kind of notice required and states that it consists of three parts.

The first part of the notice contains the word *Copyright*, or the abbreviation *Copr.*, and the symbol © (the letter *C* within a circle). The second part gives the year of publication. For periodicals the date supplied is the date of publication. For books the date is the year in which the book is first offered for sale (e.g., a book printed in November or December 1978 to go on sale January 1979 should carry a 1979 copyright). The third part gives the name of the copyright holder or owner. Most authorities recommend that both the word *Copyright* and the symbol © be used since the use of the symbol is required to meet the standards of the international copyright agreements. The symbol © protects the work from piracy in most foreign countries. A copyright notice should look something like this:

Copyright © 1979 by Jane Adams

The courts will be very strict with regard to the composition of the notice. Any old notice will not do. For example, a notice saying: "This book was written by Jane Adams and is her property until 2005" will not qualify as proper notice. The new statute is virtually identical with previous statutes in prescribing the composition of the notice. In 1903 the Supreme Court ruled that since the statute states a specific way to give the reader proper notice that is what the courts will demand. "In determining whether a notice of copyright is misleading, we are not bound to look beyond the face of the notice, and inquire whether under the facts of the particular case it is reasonable to suppose an intelligent person could actually have been misled" (*Mifflin* v. *H. H. White,* 1903).

However, the new statute made significant changes with regard to the failure of an author to put the required notice on a copy of the work. Previously, if copyright notice was not put on a publication, the work was for all practical purposes lost forever. Years ago, for example, Oliver Wendell Holmes (the father of the great Supreme Court justice) published twelve installments of a serial entitled the "Autocrat of the Breakfast Table" in the *Atlantic* magazine. The magazine was not copyrighted, and the story was not copyrighted. About a year later Holmes brought out a book version of the *Autocrat of the Breakfast Table* which he properly copyrighted. Several years later another publisher printed copies of the book, taken word for word from the version published in the *Atlantic.* Holmes sued on the grounds that the book was copyrighted. The Supreme Court of the United States agreed that the book was copyrighted, but since the original serialized version published in the *Atlantic* was not copyrighted, the author forfeited ownership of that version and it fell into the public domain (*Holmes* v. *Hurst,* 1899).

Also under the old law, the notice had to be in a specific place, and if it wasn't the copyright protection was lost. Congress was more liberal in 1976. In the first place, under current law the notice may be placed anywhere that it "can be visually perceived." Also, the 1976 law provides that omission of the proper notice does not destroy copyright protection for the work if the notice is omitted from only a relatively small number of copies, if an effort is made within five years to correct the omission, or if the notice is omitted in violation of the copyright holder's express requirement that as a condition of publication the work carry a copyright notice.

At the same time the law protects persons who copy a work on which the copyright notice was inadvertently omitted. Such an innocent infringer incurs no liability—cannot be sued—unless this infringement continues beyond the time he receives notice that the work has been copyrighted.

Registration

Proper notice is the only requirement that an author must fulfill to copyright a work. The work is then protected from the moment of creation for the life of the author plus fifty years. However, before a copyright holder can sue for infringement under the law, the copyrighted work must be registered with the federal government. The law specifically says that registration, the deposit of two complete copies of the work with the United States Register of Copyrights plus the payment of a $10 fee for most works, is required prior to institution of an infringement suit. Also, the law provides that the Register of Copyrights can require a copyright holder to make this deposit. Failure to comply can result in a fine.

Certainly for any published work, it is best to get into the habit of registering a work as soon as the work comes off the presses or is broadcast. This practice can save an immense hassle later should an infringement occur.

The requirement of notice is a very important one. It allows all the works which no one wants to copyright to fall into the public domain immediately. It also tells the reader whether a work is copyrighted, was ever copyrighted, or is still copyrighted. It also identifies the owner of the work and the date of publication. The change in the law which protects authors who accidently forget to include a copyright notice on their works is healthy and worthwhile. But writers and broadcasters should get into the habit of putting the notice on all material which they believe to be valuable, whether it is published or not.

COPYRIGHT INFRINGEMENT

It is important for authors to know how to protect their own work. It is equally important to know how to avoid being sued for stealing someone else's copyrighted material. Such theft does not always result in a successful suit or even in a suit at all. Many times the owner of the copyrighted matter is unaware of the theft. Other times the harm to the copyright holder is insignificant. In copyright, as in other areas of mass media law, who you are is often more important than what you stole. For example, if the *East Ames Morning Dispatch and World Advertiser* publishes in its entertainment section, without permission, one complete act of a Neil Simon play, the newspaper might get a nasty letter from Simon's attorney, but probably not much more. But if the American Broadcasting Company presents the same act on *Wide World of Entertainment* it will surely get slapped with a copyright suit. Publication of the play in a small newspaper hasn't harmed the playwright significantly, and in addition the paper probably doesn't have much money. But presentation of even a single act of the play on ABC can diminish Simon's future royalties since it would probably lessen the number of future stage productions of the play.

The United States copyright statute does not really define infringement. The law states that anyone who violates any of the "exclusive rights" of the copyright holder is an infringer of the copyright. That statement is of little help to courts attempting to determine whether an infringement has taken place. Consequently, it is expected that the courts will continue to rely upon the definition of infringement forged during the past one hundred fifty years. Most judges who seek to determine whether a copyright has been infringed upon look to four separate elements, or criteria. Normally, all four must be proved before plaintiffs can win their suit. The four elements are originality, access, copying, and substantial similarity. Copying and substantial similarity are quite alike and in some instances are considered a single element.

Originality

If a defendant in a copyright suit can demonstrate to the court that his work, supposedly an infringement, is substantially an original work he might succeed in stopping the infringement suit. On the other hand the plaintiff will seek to prove that the work in question is not really original, that the new material is not really a new work, that the additions by the infringer are really only trivial additions. In other words, if the pirate takes a copyrighted work and makes only trivial changes, the work is not original. The bulk of the work must be original. In 1921 a suit resulted when the publisher of a directory of jewelers sued another publisher for what he claimed was copyright infringement. The defendant in the case published a similar directory. Both directories, in addition to carrying names and addresses of jewelers, contained photographs of the jewelers' trademarks. The plaintiff prepared the photographs. The defendant clipped the pictures from the plaintiff's directory, sent them to the various jewelers, asked if the pictures were accurate representations of the trademarks, and then republished the plaintiff's pictures when the jewelers gave their approval. In a few instances jewelers sent new pictures for use in the directory. The court ruled that in this case the defendant's work was not original enough, that he was bound to make independent pictures of the trademarks, not merely obtain the jewelers' approval to use the plaintiff's photographs. The addition of a few new pictures was really only a trivial change (*Jeweler's Circular Publishing Co.* v. *Keystone Publishing Co.,* 1921).

Access

The second dimension of an infringement suit is access: the plaintiff must convince the court that the defendant had access to the copyrighted work. An opportunity to copy has to exist. If the plaintiff cannot prove that the so-called literary pirate had a chance to see and read the work, she is hard pressed to prove piracy. As Judge Learned Hand once wrote (*Sheldon* v. *Metro-Goldwyn-Mayer Pictures,* 1939):

> . . . if by some magic a man who had never known it were to compose anew Keat's "Ode on a Grecian Urn," he would be an 'author' and if he copyrighted it, others might not copy that poem, though they might of course copy Keat's.

Here in contemporary terms is what Judge Hand said. If through some incredible coincidence a young composer were to write and publish a song called "Alfie" which was an exact duplicate of the song by Burt Bacharach and Hal David, it would not be an infringement of copyright. Publishing a song exactly like a copyrighted song is not infringement; copying a copyrighted song is infringement. Moreover, if the young composer could prove that he had lived in a cave since birth, had never listened to the radio or records, and had never watched television or gone to the movies, and if Bacharach and David could not prove that the defendant had had access to "Alfie," they would lose their suit. It must be obvious that such a coincidence can never occur, but this illustration nevertheless makes the point. The plaintiff must prove access to the stolen work. The smaller the circulation of the copyrighted matter, the harder it is to prove access.

Copying

Copying is really the other side of the originality coin. When looking at the first element the court will ask, Did the defendant do his own work? In evaluating the element of copying the court will ask, Did the defendant copy the plaintiff's work? Copying has many aspects and is perhaps the hardest of the elements to deal with. If the defendant's work is a word-for-word replica of the plaintiff's work, copying is highly probable. Such cases are rare. More typical are cases like one which occurred in the 1940s when the publication *Racing News* sued a New England newspaper for stealing its handicapping information. The *Racing News* is the bible of the fans of thoroughbred racing and publishes daily comprehensive data on horses running at tracks around the nation. Newspapers usually publish smaller amounts of information on horses running in a few well-known races or at local tracks. The *Racing News* contended that the defendant newspaper took its published material on the past performances of horses, rewrote it, and published the information as its own. The newspaper argued that while it did use material from the *Racing News,* it used other information as well and that it rewrote all material that it published. Does paraphrasing a copyrighted work protect one from an infringement suit? Not at all, the court said. District Judge Wyzanski ruled that copying need not be ipsissma verba, that material stated in equivalent words is also infringement. "*Soule's Dictionary of English Synonyms* is not a licensed sanctuary for literary pirates," he added (*Triangle Publishing Co.* v. *New England Newspaper Publishing,* 1942).

In a more recent case a group aptly named Air Pirates copied Walt Disney characters for posters and T-shirts. Instead of portraying Mickey and Donald and Pluto and the gang as their lovable Disney selves, the company translated the characters into what the court called "awful characters." Changing the nature of the character did not excuse the infringement, the court said (*Walt Disney Productions* v. *Air Pirates,* 1972). Disney still owned the characters. Changing the medium doesn't work either. A toy manufacturer cannot make a plastic doll in the likeness of a comic strip character without first getting permission of the copyright owner of the comic character.

Substantial Similarity

The courts seem to have the most trouble in dealing with infringement cases involving dramatic works or adaptations of dramatic works. Imagine that John Smith gets an idea for a play about an elderly storekeeper in rural Georgia who is dying of cancer and decides to give his store to the nicest person in town. The play depicts the storekeeper trying to determine who is the nicest person in town. The play is copyrighted and produced. Jane Adams then writes a play about a young woman in New York who discovers she is dying of a brain tumor and decides she wants her two children to be adopted by the nicest person in her neighborhood. The play depicts the woman attempting to determine who is the nicest person in the neighborhood. Is Adam's play an infringement? That's a tough question. While an idea cannot be copyrighted, the pattern or the action of a play can be copyrighted. Courts look at each such case individually, and substantial similarity is an important factor in these cases. More than just minor similarities must be present: the two works must be substantially alike. Most authorities suggest it is safest to determine the fundamental theme of the work and see whether it has been appropriated.

In *Folsom* v. *Marsh,* a very old copyright case involving the letters and documents of President George Washington, Justice Story wrote, "if enough is taken to diminish the value of the original or the labors of the original author are substantially appropriated" piracy has occurred (*Folsom* v. *Marsh,* 1841). To make this judgment is not always an easy task. Sometimes courts invite experts—authors or playwrights—to testify whether they think a pattern or theme in a work was appropriated, or whether the defendant just added trivial details to a plot he stole. Sometimes the court will require that such theft be obvious to the average person. This requirement makes sense because if the audience is unaware of the theft, the copied work will probably not financially hurt the original author of the play or book or whatever. People will likely buy both works or attend both plays.

The simplest way to avoid an infringement suit is for authors to make certain that a substantial portion of their work is original, and that the borrowed portion is not the heart of their article or script.

DAMAGES

The plaintiff in a copyright suit can ask the court to assess the defendant for any damage she has suffered, plus the profits made by the infringer from pirating the protected work. Damages can be a little bit or a lot. In each case the plaintiff must prove to the court the amount of the loss or of the defendant's profit. But, rather than prove actual damage, the plaintiff can ask the court to assess what are called statutory damages, or damage amounts prescribed by the statute. The smallest statutory award is $250, although in the case of an innocent infringement the court may use its discretion and lower the damage amount to $100. The highest statutory award is $10,000. However, if the plaintiff can prove that the infringement was committed willfully, the maximum damage award can be as much as $50,000.

In addition the courts have other powers in a copyright suit. A judge can restrain a defendant from continued infringement, can impound the material which contains the infringement, and can order the destruction of these works. Impoundment and destruction are rare today.

A defendant might also be charged with a criminal offense in a copyright infringement case. If the defendant infringed upon a copyright "willfully and for purposes of commercial advantage or private financial gain" he could be fined up to $10,000 and jailed for not more than one year. The fines for pirating phonograph records and motion pictures are much higher: $25,000 and one year in jail for the first offense and $50,000 and up to two years in jail for subsequent offenses. Criminal actions for copyright infringement are rare today.

COPYRIGHT AND THE PRESS

The law of copyright is not difficult to understand and should not be a threat to most creative persons in the mass media. The law simply says to do your own work and not to steal from the work of other persons. Some authorities argue that copyright is an infringement upon freedom of the press. In a small way it probably is. Nevertheless most writers, most authors, and most newsmen—persons who most often take advantage of freedom of the press—support copyright laws which protect their rights to property which they create. Judge Jerome Frank once attempted to explain this apparent contradiction by arguing that we are adept at concealing from ourselves the fact that we maintain and support "side by side as it were, beliefs which are inherently incompatible." Frank suggested that we keep these separate antagonistic beliefs in separate "logic-tight compartments."

The courts have recognized the needs of society as well as the needs of authors and have hence allowed considerable latitude for copying material which serves some public function. Because of this attitude, copyright law has little, or should have little, impact upon the information-oriented mass media. No new law changes this situation.

BIBLIOGRAPHY

Here are some of the sources that have been helpful in the preparation of chapter 5.

Books   Ball, Horace. *The Law of Copright and Literary Property*. New York: Banks & Co., 1944.

Cambridge Research Institute. *Omnibus Copyright Revision*. Washington, D.C.: American Society for Information Science, 1973.

Kaplan, Benjamin, and Brown, Ralph S., Jr. *Cases on Copyright* . . . 2d ed. Mineola, N. Y.: Foundation Press, 1974.

Nimmer, Melville B. *Nimmer on Copyright*. New York: Matthew Bender & Co., 1963.

Pilpel, Harriet F., and Goldberg, Morton D. *A Copyright Guide*. 4th ed. New York: R. R. Bowker Co., 1969.

Ransom, Harry. *The First Copyright Statute: An Essay on An Act for the Encouragement of Learning, 1710*. Austin: University of Texas Press, 1956.

Wittenberg, Philip. *The Protection of Literary Property*. 2d ed. Boston: Writer, Inc., 1968.

Articles   Goldstein, Paul, "Copyright and the First Amendment," 70 *Columbia Law Review* 983 (1970).

Gross, Jeanne. "Rosemont v. Random House and the Doctrine of Fair Use," 50 *Journalism Quarterly* 227 (1973).

Holbrook, Lanny R. "Copyright Infringement and Fair Use," 40 *University of Cincinnati Law Review* 534 (1971).

Nimmer, Melville B. "Does Copyright Abridge the First Amendment Guarantees of Free Speech and Press?" 17 *UCLA Law Review* 1180 (1970).

Schulman, John. "Fair Use and the Revision of the Copyright Act," 53 *Iowa Law Review* 832 (1968).

Yankwich, Leon R. "What Is Fair Use?" 22 *University of Chicago Law Review* 203 (1954).

Cases   *Amsterdam* v. *Triangle Publishing Co.*, 189 F. 2d 104 (1951).

Associated Press v. *International News Service*, 248 U.S. 215 (1918).

Baker v. *Selden*, 101 U.S. 99 (1879).

Benny v. *Loew's*, 239 F. 2d 532 (1956).

Berlin v. *E. C. Publications, Inc.*, 329 F. 2d 541 (1964).

Bleistein v. *Donaldson Lithographing Co.*, 188 U.S. 239 (1903).

Broadway Music v. *F-R Publishing Co.*, 23 F. Supp. 302 (1938).

Chicago Record-Herald v. *Tribune Association*, 275 F. 797 (1921).

College Entrance Books Co. v. *Amsco Book Co.*, 119 F. 2d 874 (1941).

Columbia Pictures v. *NBC*, 137 F. Supp. 348 (1955).

Donaldson v. *Beckett*, 4 Burr. 2408 (1774).

Estate of Hemingway v. *Random House*, 244 N.E. 2d 250 (1968).

Folsom v. *Marsh*, 2 Fed. Cas. 342, No. 4901 (C.C.D. Mass. 1841).

Holmes v. *Hurst*, 174 U.S. 82 (1899).

Holt v. *Liggett & Myers Tobacco Co.*, 23 F. Supp. 302 (1938).

Jeweler's Circular Publishing Co. v. *Keystone Publishing Co.*, 274 F. 932 (1921).

King v. *Miser Music Corp.*, 224 F. Supp. 101 (1963).

Lawrence v. *Dana*, 15 Fed. Cas. 26, No. 8136 (C.C.D. Mass. 1869).

Lipman v. *Commonwealth*, 475 F. 2d 565 (1973).

Mifflin v. *H. R. White*, 190 U.S. 260 (1903).

Patterson v. *Century Products*, 93 F. 2d 489 (1937).

Rosemont v. *Random House*, 366 F. 2d 303 (1966).

Sheldon v. *Metro-Goldwyn-Mayer Pictures*, 81 F. 2d 49 (1939).

Time, Inc., v. *Bernard Geis Association*, 293 F. Supp. 130 (1968).

Toksvig v. *Bruce Publishing Co.*, 181 F. 2d 664 (1950).

Triangle Publishing Co. v. *New England Newspaper Publishing*, 46 F. Supp. 198 (1942).

Walt Disney Productions v. *Air Pirates*, 345 F. Supp. 108 (1972).

Washington Publishing Co. v. *Pearson*, 306 U.S. 30 (1939).

White v. *Kimmel*, 193 F. 2d 744 (1952).

Williams & Wilkins Co. v. *U.S.* 487 F. 2d 1345 (1973), affd. 95 S. Ct. 1344 (1975).

CHAPTER 6

Contempt

The work of a reporter can hardly be called a hazardous occupation when compared with the work of test pilots, race drivers, and structural steel workers. But occasionally, recently more often it seems, journalists face a special occupational peril—a term in jail. And the sentence comes not from robbing a bank or shooting someone, but for having written an article which a judge finds offensive, for refusing to disclose the name of a news source to a grand jury, or for violating a gag order (restrictive order). While a term in jail is not a common occurrence, the kinds of problems which can ultimately push the reporter into a jail cell are a common part of the daily routine for some journalists.

RELATIONSHIP BETWEEN REPORTER AND COURTS

The problems fall under two general headings, both of which concern the reporter's relationship with courts and judges. The first area concerns the publishing of material about cases which are before the courts or enroute to the courts. Involved is the so-called free press-fair trial dilemma, or fair trial-free press dilemma if you will. In any case, it is a problem. The second area concerns what is popularly called the shield law controversy, which properly should be called the controversy surrounding the privilege protecting reporters who refuse to answer legitimate questions of judges, grand jurors, and legislators about the names of news sources or about confidential information gained in the process of gathering news.

Both areas are special concerns for the reporter because in both instances what the reporter does or does not do can have a direct impact upon the success or failure of certain aspects of the legal process. The publication of certain kinds of information before a trial begins might seriously harm the defendant's chance of getting a fair hearing from an unbiased jury or judge. In addition, legitimate criminal investigations might be seriously hampered by a reporter who refuses to disclose vital names or facts.

Because of the serious consequences for the judicial system, the reporter who runs afoul of the law in these areas faces a serious consequence: a jail term and/or a fine. The consequence stems directly from the extraordinary power of judges. A mayor might have you tossed out of his office if you get nasty or belligerent, a city council might go into executive session, but a judge has the power to put you in jail. Reporters disciplined by an angry judge have probably not faced such absolute authority since confronting their mother as a small child or their drill sergeant in the army.

The dimensions of these problems are outlined in chapter 6, 7, and 8. In chapter 6 the awesome contempt power which has accrued to United States judges during the past several centuries is explored. Since the contempt power makes little sense without some understanding of its history, development of the power is also reviewed. Also discussed are the full consequences of actions which provoke threats from the judicial system, which reporters should understand. In chapter 7 the so-called free press-fair trial controversy is discussed, and both problems and proposed remedies are outlined. Finally, in chapter 8, the dimensions of the privileges often used by journalists to be exempt from testifying before grand juries and at trials are sketched.

Reporters who find themselves in the middle of court-press conflicts frequently attain celebrity status among their peers, having their pictures and stories published nationwide in newspapers and magazines. It is a heady experience, an experience that not only can challenge the best in journalists, but also can leave long-lasting scars.

CONTEMPT

In 1631 in England a British subject was convicted of a felony, not a very uncommon event. This particular subject was angered at being found guilty, and after the sentence was read he threw a brickbat at the judge. The brickbat missed the judge, but the man was quickly seized, his right hand was cut off and nailed to the gallows, and he was immediately hanged in the presence of the court (this story is recounted by Ronald Goldfarb in *The Contempt Power*).

While such judicial retribution is an uncommon exercise of the contempt power, it nevertheless is a representative example of the power of judges to control what goes on in their courtrooms. Even as the end of the twentieth century is approached, disobedience or disrespect of the court is normally put down swiftly by exercise of the power of contempt.

Any act which interferes with the orderly processes of justice is usually promptly stopped and the offender is quickly punished. While other governmental bodies (legislative bodies, for example) can use the contempt power, its use by judges, which is the subject of this chapter, is far more common today.

Doesn't it seem odd in what are supposedly representative democracies like the United States and Great Britain, countries in which the guarantee of civil liberties has long been part of the national heritage, that a single individual like a judge can wield such awesome power? The answer to that question is yes. Courts are an indispensable part of our governmental system. The courts make freedom of the press, freedom of speech, freedom of religion, and other civil liberties meaningful rights by protecting these constitutional guarantees. If the court system is impeded in some way, if judges are waylaid in their trek toward justice, society then suffers.

Even this rationale does not explain why judges and justices retain such extraordinary powers, powers which include summary punishment, when justice is stripped of many of the basic constitutional guarantees which the courts are supposed to protect. Nor does this rationale explain why supposedly intelligent men can believe that our court system, or any court system, can be infallible and should be free from citizen scrutiny and comment. The answers to these questions are, once again, found in the past.

British Heritage

In 1927 British legal scholar John Fox wrote in the *History of Contempt of Court*, "Rules for preserving discipline . . . came into existence with the law itself, and contempt of court has been a recognized phase of English law from the twelfth century to the present time." Order has always been essential to the administration of justice. Courts, after all, are where rational decision making must prevail. Yet the contempt power is peculiar to the common law nations. Judges in France or Holland or Italy do not enjoy such extraordinary latitude in dealing with disturbance, disobedience, and disrespect. The common law judges were able to assume such power because the first common law judge was the king himself. He was the administrator of justice. As Ronald Goldfarb points out in his important study of the contempt power (mentioned earlier), the people revered the king. Goldfarb writes, "This was but another, though not different, step from the sanctity of the medicine man, the priestly character of primitive royalty, and the Christian concepts of obedience." This legal scholar adds that the contempt power is clearly understandable, then, when viewed from the perspective of the age of its inception, "an age of alleged divinely ordained monarchies, ruled by a king totally invested with all sovereign legal powers and accountable only to God."

In some instances resistance to the king was a sin, punishable by damnation. Being jailed or fined or tortured for being contemptuous of the king was really rather unimportant when compared to the fate offenders faced on judgment day in the hereafter.

When the king became too busy to hear all the cases coming before his court, he appointed ministers to sit in judgment throughout the realm. Logically, disrespect toward one of the king's judges should not be a serious offense since the discourtesy was aimed at a mere mortal, not at a person divinely ordained to rule. But that was not the case, because while the king was not physically present in the courtroom, he was assumed to be there spiritually, guiding the hand of justice. Surely this assumption sounds like nonsense, but men will believe almost anything if the belief is important to them. In any case, disrespect or disobedience of the judge were considered to be disrespect or disobedience of the king or of the spiritual presence of the king. Punishment by the judge was as swift and as sure as punishment by the king would have been.

As representative democracy developed in England and royal influence on the government diminished, judges retained the contempt power. Through a major judicial blunder in eighteenth-century England, whose discussion will only delay our journey toward an understanding of the modern contempt power, the contempt power became institutionalized in common law courts in both Great Britain and the United States. (The judicial blunder just referred to is explained in Fox's *History of Contempt of Court* in the discussion of the case *Rex* v. *Almon.*)

Courts today rarely justify the exercise of the contempt power on the grounds that it protects the integrity of the judge. Today protection of the authority, order, and decorum of the court is the usual reason given for the use of the contempt power, and sometimes it is protection of the rights of the litigants using the court to settle a dispute.

Kinds of Contempt   Historically, legal scholars have tried to classify the various kinds of contempt power judges have at their disposal, but contempt seems to defy classification, or at least to defy consistent classification. Goldfarb refers to the "chameleonic characteristic" of contempt: that is, an action considered civil contempt in one court may be viewed as criminal contempt in another. Writing in the *Tennessee Law Review* (1971), Prof. Luis Kutner notes the problem:

> The distinction between civil and criminal contempt is not clear-cut. The same act in different situations may be regarded as either civil or criminal. Contempt has been regarded criminal if the purpose is to punish the contemnor for his misconduct in the presence of the court or for conduct out of the court's presence challenging its authority, and the contemnor is fined a fixed amount or imprisoned for

a definite term; it is regarded as civil if the primary purpose is to coerce compliance with a court order, usually for the benefit of an injured suitor, and the contemnor is imprisoned only until he complies. Whether the contempt is civil or criminal is determined by the judicial decision maker.

Despite the "chameleonic" nature of the contempt power, scholars frequently use the following method of classification. The classification is based on the purpose of the punishment: (1) punishment exacted to protect the rights of a private party in a legal dispute before the court and (2) punishment exacted to vindicate the law, the authority of the court, or the power of the judge. When the punishment is exacted for the first reason, the contempt is normally called a civil contempt. When the punishment is exacted for the second reason, the contempt is usually considered a criminal contempt. Here is a brief discussion of the types of contempt based on this classification scheme.

Civil Contempt   A civil contempt is not an affront to the court itself, but is more likely failure or refusal to obey a court ruling, decision, or order made to protect the rights of one of the litigants in the case. Normally, the punishment in a civil contempt suit is a jail sentence which is terminated when the contemnor agrees either to do something or to stop doing something. For example, John Smith wins a libel judgment from the *River City Sentinel*. The publisher of the *Sentinel* refuses to pay the judgment. A judge can find the publisher in contempt of court and put him in jail until he is willing to pay. The publisher's refusal to pay is a civil contempt: the newspaper publisher disregards the rights of the plaintiff in the case and disregards the ruling by the court. Civil contempt, then, is charged to obtain obedience to judgments, court orders, and court processes designed to protect the rights of the litigants in a case.

Criminal Contempt   Criminal contempt, on the other hand, is charged to protect the court itself, to punish a wrong against the court. Obstruction of court proceedings or court officers, attacks on court personnel, and deliberate acts of bad faith or fraud are all examples of criminal contempt. There are two kinds of criminal contempt, direct contempt and indirect contempt.

Direct Criminal Contempt   A direct criminal contempt is an action committed "in the presence of the court," that is, in the courtroom or near the courtroom. Generally two conditions underlie a direct contempt: first, the judge has actual personal knowledge of what occurred, and second, the act or action had a significant impact upon the judicial proceedings. The key seems to be the judge's personal knowledge. In the instance of a direct criminal contempt the judge is normally empowered to use what is called his summary power. When the judge exercises his summary power he acts as prosecutor, jury, and judge. Suppose that in the midst of the trial the defendant jumps on a table and begins to play an accordian. The judge can use his summary power. "I accuse you of disrupting this trial by playing an accordian [the prosecutor's role], I find you guilty of disrupting the trial [the jury's role], and I fine you $200 [the judge's role]."

Summary punishment is the most onerous aspect of the contempt power, for the citizen is not allowed to exercise some of the basic constitutional guarantees which are normally a part of the criminal process. There is no jury trial. The accuser is also the judge and jury. The accused has no right to call witnesses in his behalf. Many authorities argue that because the summary power can normally be exercised only in a direct criminal contempt, an instance in which the judge has direct personal knowledge of what took place, the summary power is really not a threat to civil liberty. But this argument is questionable. Anytime one person can wield such power, a threat to civil liberties exists. Any contempt conviction can be appealed, but the only record of the behavior or action which prompted the contempt citation is prepared by the judge. The appeal is based upon this factual record, the facts as seen by the judge.

The press infrequently gets involved in direct criminal contempt. However, if a photographer were to snap a flash picture in the midst of a trial, he would undoubtedly find himself in direct criminal contempt.

Indirect Criminal Contempt   Indirect criminal contempt is sometimes called constructive contempt and can be described as misconduct which occurs apart from the trial or apart from the court, but which still interferes with the proceeding.

Another definition of indirect criminal contempt is that it is a contempt about which the court or the judge has no firsthand knowledge. Comments published in a newspaper about the conduct of the court or of the judge in the midst of the trial can be constructive contempt. When during a trial a television station broadcasts the details of the defendant's confession after the judge suppressed the information the station commits an indirect contempt. Publication of false or grossly inaccurate stories about the proceedings of a court can be considered a constructive contempt. Any action which interferes with the administration of justice, but which occurs away from the courtroom, can be considered an indirect criminal contempt.

LIMITATIONS ON CONTEMPT POWER

Before the limits of the contempt power are discussed, it should be noted at this point that truth is not a limitation. That is, truthful criticism of the court, publishing truthful comments about a pending case, can be and frequently is regarded as contempt. As one author puts it, any adverse comment by the mass media, no matter how true, can interfere with the administration of justice and can be punished as contempt. The Supreme Court established this principle in the early years of this century when it upheld a Colorado court decision to punish the editor and publisher of a Denver newspaper for printing articles which questioned both the motives of the state's high court and the manner in which two of the supreme court judges had been seated. The criticism was published as part of a commentary on a case pending before the state high Court. Justice Oliver Wendell Holmes, writing for the United States Supreme Court, said the comments were inappropriate because the case was being considered by the court. "When a case is finished," he wrote, "courts are subject to the same criticism as other people, but the propriety and necessity of preventing interference with the course of justice by premature statement, argument or intimidation hardly can be denied" (*Patterson* v. *Colorado*, 1907). Holmes added that the fact that the criticism is truthful is immaterial in a case of constructive contempt. While many legal scholars and civil libertarians lament this decision, it remains the law today. The law is perhaps less important today because of other kinds of limitations upon the contempt power.

The contempt power, which was largely a creature of judicial development, has long bothered many persons who question the need for such arbitrary and absolute authority in courtrooms. The early years of the twentieth century must be regarded as a high watermark for the contempt power because since that time the opponents of this power have succeeded in placing rather severe limitations upon its use. Make no mistake. It is not a sterile power. Judges can and still do use their contempt power.

But as we embark upon the last quarter of this century, judges throughout the United States have far less freedom in how they use this power than they had in the first quarter of this century.

Legislative Limitations

One important limitation upon the power of the court to use contempt comes from legislatures. For example, for more than sixty years the Congress has passed laws which limit use of the summary power by federal judges to dispose of contempt citations. The 1914 Clayton Antitrust Act, for example, requires that judges provide a jury trial in a contempt case when the contemptuous action is also a crime under federal or state law. In 1932 as a part of the Norris-LaGuardia Act, the Congress mandated jury trials for all constructive contempts arising out of labor disputes. The 1957 civil rights law provided for a jury trial for contempts when the sentence imposed exceeds forty-five days in jail. The 1964 civil rights law contains the same provision.

Court-Imposed Limitations

The bench itself imposes limitations upon the use of the summary power. The *Federal Rules of Criminal Procedure* requires that in indirect contempts notice be given the contemnor and a hearing be allowed. In addition, there are the right to counsel, the right to cross-examine witnesses, the right to offer testimony, and in many instances the right to a jury trial. If the contempt citation is based upon criticism or disrespect of a judge, that judge is disqualified from the proceeding. Bail is also allowed. The courts and legislatures in many states also deem that a jury trial is a requirement in an indirect contempt.

In the instances just noted, the legislature or the bench itself grants the right to a jury trial. Is there a constitutional right to a jury trial in such cases? The United States Supreme Court has been grappling with this question since the 1960s.

In 1964 the high Court ruled that there is no constitutional right to a jury trial in a contempt case, in upholding the contempt conviction of the governor of Mississippi, Ross Barnett, who willfully disobeyed an order of the Fifth Circuit Court of Appeals. As one might expect at that time and in that place, the substantive question involved was civil rights. However, a footnote in the court's opinion states, "Some members of the Court are of the view that, without regard to the seriousness of the offense, punishment by summary trial without a jury would be constitutionally limited to that penalty provided for petty offenses" (*U.S.* v. *Barnett*, 1964).

Petty offenses generally carry a sentence of six months or less. What the court seemed to be hinting at is that a jury trial is required constitutionally if the penalty exceeds more than six months in jail. A few years later in *Cheff* v. *Schnackenberg* (1966) the high Court specifically said what it implied in the Barnett case—that sentences exceeding six months cannot be imposed in cases of criminal contempt without giving the accused a jury trial. Then in 1968 in *Bloom* v. *Illinois* the high Court took the last step and ruled that criminal contempt is a crime in the ordinary sense, and that since the United States Constitution guarantees the right to a jury trial in criminal cases, prosecutions by state courts for serious criminal contempts (those with more than a six-month penalty) must be heard by a jury.

One of the most interesting court-imposed limitations upon the power of contempt concerns judicial interpretation of the 1831 Federal contempt statute. One of the first acts of the first United States Congress in 1789 was to establish a federal judiciary system. In doing so it gave federal judges the power "to punish by fine or imprisonment, at the discretion of said courts, all contempts of authority in any case or hearing before the same."

This broad authority to use the contempt power remained unchanged until the 1830s when federal Judge James H. Peck arbitrarily punished an attorney who published an article critical of the judge. The judge's action resulted in his own impeachment. He was acquitted by a vote of twenty-two—twenty-one, but the trial prompted Congress to place a limit on the summary power. The 1831 law strictly limited federal judges' use of summary punishment to those contempts committed in the presence of the court, "or so near thereto" as to obstruct the administration of justice. The change in the law, then, was designed to limit the power of federal judges. But by the Civil War this law had been forgotten, and federal judges once again used their summary power to punish a wide variety of contemptuous behavior.

Typical of this attitude was a decision by the Arkansas Supreme Court in 1855 which rejected a state statute limiting use of the contempt power and ruled that the power in courts to punish for contempt springs into existence upon the creation of the courts, that it is a part of the court's inherent power (*State* v. *Morrill*).

In 1918 a question over interpretation of the 1831 law came before the Supreme Court. Toledo, Ohio, was in the throes of a major dispute over a change in the transit fares. While a federal judge deliberated over the constitutionality of the change in the price of a streetcar ride, a local newspaper, the *News-Bee*, published unflattering remarks about him. After the judge ruled that the change in fare was unconstitutional, he found the newspaper in contempt and summarily fined the publisher. The newspaper appealed the action on the grounds that the judge lacked the authority to invoke a summary punishment, that summary punishment could only be used in cases in which the contempt is committed in the presence of the court, or "so near thereto" as to create an administration of justice. The *News-Bee* was published miles from the courthouse, not in the presence of the Court nor "so near thereto." In other words, the *News-Bee* said that the 1831 law placed a geographic limitation upon the judge's use of the summary punishment. The high Court disagreed. It ruled that the 1831 limitation placed a causal, rather than a geographic, limitation upon the use of the summary power (*Toledo Newspaper Co.* v. *U.S.*, 1918). Chief Justice Edward F. White wrote that *so near thereto* meant that any action that was in "close relationship" to the administration of justice could be punished summarily. In this case, the newspaper articles critical of the judge surely had a relationship to the case at hand.

The matter appeared settled, albeit wrongly. In 1928 Walter Nelles and Alice King, legal researchers, looked into the history of the 1831 law ("Contempt by Publication in the United States"). By their research these writers demonstrated that the 1831 measure was designed to limit the power of federal judges, not to enlarge it, as a majority of the Supreme Court contended in the Toledo newspaper case in 1918.

In 1941 the Supreme Court had the opportunity to apply these research findings (*Nye* v. *U.S.*) in a case that didn't involve the press. Instead the case originated in a civil suit filed in federal district court against a patent medicine company. The plaintiff claimed that his son died as a result of drinking the medicine. Agents from the patent medicine maker plied the father with liquor one night and cajoled him into writing a letter to the judge, asking that the suit be dismissed. The judge was suspicious, investigated the request, and discovered the skullduggery by the drug company. He summarily fined the two men for their contemptuous behavior, despite the fact that their meeting with the plaintiff took place more than one hundred miles from the Court. In an appeal to the Supreme Court the convictions were overturned. Justice William O. Douglas, citing the legal research published by Nelles and King, noted that "so near thereto" has a geographic meaning, that before the summary power can be used the misbehavior must be in the vicinity of the courtroom, that is, in physical proximity to the proceedings.

Justice Douglas did not indicate how close, but most experts today believe that a federal judge's right to use his summary power probably extends to the hallway outside the courtroom and perhaps even to the lobby of the building when a disturbance occurs. Conceivably a demonstration on the sidewalk outside the building can also be ruled to be in physical proximity if the disturbance is noisy and disturbs proceedings.

Through various means, then, during this century the summary power of judges has been limited, and in turn the limitations have reduced the contempt power. Through statutes which explicitly limit the use of the summary power and through court rulings which limit the severity of punishment which may be applied in the absence of a jury, the absolute power of judges has been trimmed. Nevertheless, the summary power is still a threat. And even six months in jail is a long time!

First Amendment Limitations

The First Amendment was not raised as a barrier to contempt conviction until relatively modern times, in 1941 to be exact. In 1941 and again in 1946 and 1947 the United States Supreme Court ruled that freedom of the press to comment on the judiciary must be protected except in those circumstances in which the commentary presents a serious threat to the proper functioning of the legal process. These three decisions, *Bridges* v. *California* and *Times Mirror Co.* v. *Superior Court, Pennekamp* v. *Florida,* and *Craig* v. *Harney,* stand as the bedrock support for the argument that the First Amendment protects the press in writing about the judiciary.

The first case, *Bridges* v. *California* and *Times Mirror Co.* v. *Superior*

Court, 1941, actually consisted of two appeals from decisions by California courts, and the cases were decided together as one case. In the first instance a newspaper, the *Los Angeles Times,* was ruled in contempt for publishing a series of antilabor editorials which the trial court claimed were aimed at influencing the disposition of cases before the court concerning labor unionists. In the second case, labor leader Harry Bridges was held in contempt of court when he publicly threatened to take the dockworkers out on strike if the courts attempted to enforce a judicial ruling going against Bridges and his union. While the specter of a militant antilabor union newspaper and a militant labor leader arguing on the same side of this question is remarkable, it is not as remarkable as the high Court's decision which voided both contempt citations.

In a five-to-four decision the high Court repudiated the idea that the contempt power is valid because it is deeply rooted in English common law. Justice Hugo Black wrote that even if this were the case, the idea ignores the generally accepted historical belief that "one of the objects of the Revolution was to get rid of the English law on liberty of speech and press." Black said that before a judge can use his contempt power to close off discussion of a case there must be a "clear and present danger" that the discussion will produce interference with the proper administration of justice. In applying Holmes' famous World War I clear and present danger sedition test to contempt Black meant that only those threats to justice which are imminent or immediate can be punished. The substantive evil must be extremely serious and the degree of imminence extremely high before utterances can be punished, he wrote.

The government argued in these cases that commentary on a case is clearly proper, but only *after* the case is completed so that the course of justice cannot be influenced. Black rejected this notion, saying that it is while a trial is underway that the public interest about a case is highest. He wrote:

> We cannot start with the assumption that publications actually do threaten to change the nature of legal trials and that to preserve judicial impartiality it is necessary for judges to have a contempt power by which they can close all channels of public expression to matters touching on the pending cases.

It should be noted parenthetically that in using the clear and present danger test to block contempt convictions, Justice Black made better use of those four words than did the high Court in its application of the test in sedition trials. For the clear and present danger test indeed became an effective means of stopping contempt convictions against the press.

This concept was reinforced five years later when in the second case, *Pennekamp* v. *Florida,* 1946, the high Court reviewed an appeal from the Florida Supreme Court involving a contempt citation against the *Miami Herald.*

The *Herald* had been highly critical of the trial courts in Dade County, Florida, for many months. In at least two editorials the editors argued that the courts worked harder to protect the criminals than they worked to protect the people. But the editors' evaluation of the courts' performance was founded on serious misstatement of facts. The court found both the editor, John D. Pennekamp, and the newspaper in contempt and levied fines against them both.

The Supreme Court overturned the convictions, noting, "We are not willing to say under the circumstances of this case that these editorials are a clear and present danger to the fair administration of justice in Florida." Justice Stanley Reed wrote that while he couldn't precisely define clear and present danger, certainly the criticism of a judge's actions in a nonjury trial would not affect the legal process. What about the factual errors in the editorials? Justice Reed said the errors were quite immaterial. Free discussion, Reed said, is a cardinal principle of Americanism. Discussion after a trial ends might be inadequate and can endanger the public welfare. Freedom of discussion should be given the widest range compatible with the essential requirement of the fair and orderly administration of justice. "We conclude," Reed wrote, "that the danger under this record to fair judicial administration has not the clearness and the immediacy necessary to close the door of permissible public comment. When that door is closed, it closes all doors behind it."

The following year, the high Court once again reinforced the First Amendment barrier to the use of the contempt power in its decision in *Craig* v. *Harney,* 1947, the third case. In this case a Texas newspaper had been highly critical of a judge who directed a jury to return a verdict against a well-liked citizen in a civil suit. The *Corpus Christi Caller-Times* was found in contempt of court, and again the high Court struck down the conviction. Justice William O. Douglas admitted that in the court's opinion the critical articles were unfair because they contained significant errors about what actually occurred at the trial. "But inaccuracies in reporting," he wrote, "are commonplace. Certainly a reporter could not be laid by the heels for contempt because he missed the essential point in a trial or failed to summarize the issues to accord with the views of the judge who sat on the case."

Douglas wrote that it took more imagination than the court possessed to find "in this sketchy and one-sided report of a case any imminent or serious threat to a judge of reasonable fortitude. . . ." Douglas added, "Where public matters are involved, the doubts should be resolved in favor of freedom of expression rather than against it."

The three cases just discussed, *Bridges, Pennekamp,* and *Craig,* represent three strong statements in favor of a broad discussion of judicial matters, of trials, and of the legal process. To some degree they also represent a limitation upon the contempt power of the courts. The clear and present danger test is a formidable hurdle for any judge to clear before punishing a newspaper or television station with a contempt citation. However, lest we get swept away by the court's rhetoric, it is important to look at what was involved in each of these cases, or rather what was not involved. In none of the cases did the judge first issue an order banning certain kinds of publicity about the case. In none of the cases could a jury have been influenced by the media publicity. In none of the cases did the press publish or broadcast evidence or statements prohibited at the trial. As a matter of fact, all three cases involved the same thing—commentary or criticism directed toward a judge. From these cases it is clear that the Supreme Court expects the nation's judges to be strong, not to bend in the wind of public opinion, not to be influenced by journalistic commentary. But the Court has never indicated that it has the same expectations with regard to juries. It has never said that a judge must allow the press free rein in its comments on a pending case with regard to material evidence or the credibility of witnesses. The caution, then, is not to read more into these decisions than is actually there. *Bridges, Pennekamp,* and *Craig* stand for almost unlimited discussion of pending nonjury cases. That is about as far as we dare go, however.

Other Limitations

A few other limitations upon the contempt power also exist. At times judges have been prone to use contempt rather than libel as the means of defending their reputation from press criticism. Appellate courts are sensitive to this tactic and routinely overturn such contempt convictions. Courts are also prohibited from stopping publication of certain material in advance on the grounds that publishing it constitutes a contempt of court. This is another instance in which prior restraint is forbidden.

CONTEMPT POWER TODAY

In spite of limitations upon contempt, it is still a serious threat to the press. As we will see in chapters 7 and 8, regardless of extension of the jury trial to more and more cases, and regardless of the clear and present danger test, judges possess and use their contempt power in dealing with newspapers and broadcasting stations. Even when the use of the power seems apparently wrong, both morally and legally, the tradition of British common law sometimes raises its ugly head and plays havoc with honest, hardworking editors. To wit is James Turner, the publisher of a news magazine called *Today,* in Livingston County, Michigan.

Turner was a novice newsman, but he knew enough to recognize a good story when he saw one. When he discovered, quite by accident, serious irregularities in the way the county courts probated wills, he began to investigate. What he found was that a local attorney exercised an inordinate amount of control over a few county judges. Martin J. Lavin was a kind of political boss in the county and by controlling judges was able to charge immense probate fees. In one case he received a $20,000 fee for assistance in settling a half-million dollar estate, and in another instance he took money from the sale of a client's land without telling her he had sold the land. The woman died a public welfare charge while Lavin collected nearly $50,000 for the sale of the property.

Jim Turner wrote about these events in his magazine. "Martin J. Lavin exercised control over the courts of Livingston County which was more vicious than the control exercised by the Mafia in New York and Chicago." Turner also charged that Lavin "almost totally corrupted the entire judicial system in Livingston County. We believe the judges and most of the attorneys either live in fear of this man or for some reason are afraid or won't speak out against him."

A local circuit judge took exception to Turner's charges and found him in contempt of court. Turner asked for a jury trial, but was refused. He was summarily convicted by another judge, fined $150, and sentenced to fifteen days in jail. The response of the legal community, then, was not to investigate the problem, but to jail the editor.

Turner appealed and won the case. The Michigan Court of Appeals ruled that Turner had been wrongfully punished for his admittedly disparaging statements (in re *Turner,* 1969). In the end the people also were winners. Martin Lavin was disbarred, and criminal charges and charges of income tax evasion were filed against him. Seven of the eighteen active members of the Livingston County Bar Association, including four judges or former judges, were disciplined by the state bar association for misconduct.

During the appeal Turner incurred a $70,000 debt for his magazine. It was many months before the people of the community rallied to his side. However, Jim Turner took a philosophical outlook:

> There's nothing but heartaches and expense in a true, honest involvement. And you're classified as a radical and an idiot. My involvement was just like walking out into quicksand. I got out so far that everytime I wiggled I went down, down. . . . The press has a responsibility to the people. What the hell is a newspaper for? It's not to

report the social news and not to report the sports. Sure, that's part of it, but 90 percent of the responsibility of the press is to protect the people from what can hurt them.

The contempt power is alive and well, despite the fact that an appellate court may overturn a conviction if an individual can afford to take his case that far. Contempt is a power that just doesn't seem to fit in a democracy.

Writing in "Contempt Power: The Black Robe—A Proposal for Due Process," Luis Kutner states the issue best:

> The contempt power, which arose as an extension of monarchial power, is incongruous in a nation dedicated to the principles of popular democracy . . . all contempts are examples of unlimited and arbitrary powers remaining as historical accidents and anomalies, inconsistent and incompatible with individual liberties and rights.

BIBLIOGRAPHY

Here are some of the sources that have been helpful in the preparation of chapter 6.

Books Fox, John. *The History of Contempt of Court.* Oxford: Clarendon Press, 1927.

Goldfarb, Ronald. *The Contempt Power.* New York: Columbia University Press, 1963.

Articles Kutner, Luis. "Contempt Power: The Black Robe—A Proposal for Due Process," 39 *Tennessee Law Review* 27 (1971).

Nelles, Walter, and King, C. W. "Contempt by Publication in the United States," 28 *Columbia Law Review* 401 (1928).

Cases *Bloom* v. *Illinois*, 391 U.S. 194 (1968).

Bridges v. *California* and *Times Mirror Co.* v. *Superior Court*, 314 U.S. 252 (1941).

Cheff v. *Schnackenberg*, 384 U.S. 373 (1966).

Craig v. *Harney*, 331 U.S. 367 (1947).

Nye v. *U.S.*, 313 U.S. 33 (1941).

Patterson v. *Colorado*, 205 U.S. 454 (1907).

Pennekamp v. *Florida*, 328 U.S. 331 (1946).

State v. *Morrill*, 16 Ark. 384 (1855).

Toledo Newspaper Co. v. *U.S.*, 247 U.S. 402 (1918).

In re *Turner*, 174 N.W. 2d 895 (1969).

U.S. v. *Barnett*, 376 U.S. 681 (1964).

CHAPTER 7

Free Press and Fair Trial

People have complained about the abundance of crime news in American newspapers almost as long as American newspapers have existed, at least since the 1830s and 1840s when the newspaper evolved from being primarily a political journal to being a chronicler of public occurrences. For some as yet untold reason, both the press and the public seem to share a continuing fascination with the troubles and travails of humankind, especially the plight of persons caught up in the web of the law. For better than one hundred fifty years the press has provided Americans with a daily, weekly and/or monthly diet of crime news. Sometimes there was more crime news than at other times. Persons who complain that today reporters spend too much time writing about murder and kidnapping surely cannot remember the four decades between 1890 and 1930 when crime news was a staple of most American newspapers and the police reporter was the most important, envied man in the city room. Ben Hecht's remembrances in his play *Front Page* and his autobiography *A Child of the Century* are far more truthful than most journalists like to admit.

While some persons object to the publication of crime news because they believe it to be in bad taste, because they think such information is not relevant to present-day existence, or because they think the press should spend its time pursuing other news, other persons object to publication of crime news for another reason. Many people believe that the press—newspapers and broadcasting stations—interfere with the judicial process by the publication of such information.

The argument goes something like this: Every person accused of a crime has the right to a fair trial. According to the Sixth Amendment to the United States Constitution, a fair trial includes the right to an "impartial jury." Juries are selected from members of the community who read newspapers and watch television and listen to the radio. The trial process has built-in safeguards that protect accused persons. Certain kinds of information cannot be used as evidence against a suspected criminal. A past criminal record, for example, is immaterial in most trials. So are the results of examinations using the so-called lie detector. The court keeps this kind of information from the jury during the trial. What happens if the jurors read about these circumstances before the trial begins? What if they read, for example, that the defendant has a long record of convictions? What if they read that she refused to take a lie detector test? What if they read that he is an army deserter or that she operates a brothel? Doesn't the publication of such facts tend to prejudice jurors against the defendant? Many people believe that it does.

What is the solution? To stop the press from publishing such facts? After all, the Sixth Amendment guarantees a fair trial, an impartial jury. This solution is fine—except for one problem: the First Amendment, which guarantees a free press, an unimpeded press, a press at liberty from governmental restrictions.

If this situation strikes you as a dilemma, it is. It may be an insolvable problem. Justice Felix Frankfurter stated the problem quite succinctly in 1946 in his concurring opinion in the case of *Pennekamp* v. *Florida:*

> A free press is not to be preferred to an independent judiciary, nor an independent judiciary to a free press. Neither has primacy over the other; both are indispensable to a free society. The freedom of the press in itself presupposes an independent judiciary through which that freedom may, if necessary, be vindicated. And one of the potent means for assuring judges their independence is a free press.

The recent history of the free press-fair trial controversy in the United States has been the attempt to discover a way to balance these two very important constitutional rights. The attempt has not been completely successful. In those communities which solved the problem best, courts are forced to take extra care in shielding juries from publicity and in protecting defendants. The press also has to demonstrate its responsibility by exercising caution in publishing and broadcasting material about criminal and civil cases.

In this chapter the dimensions of both the problem and its solutions are sketched. First, the kinds of publicity many persons believe to be harmful to defendants is discussed, along with evaluation of the extent to which the mass media can in fact interfere with the trial process. In the remainder of the chapter the many schemes and ideas either proposed or enacted to solve the problem are outlined. It must again be remembered that in the free press-fair trial controversy fifty-one different judicial systems are involved. That is, while the problem is clearly national, the solutions tend to be local or regional in scope. Consequently, generalizations about such a complex issue can sometimes be misleading. Reporters and broadcasters are urged to investigate the specific rules applicable to their state regarding publication of material about the judicial process. A simple way to do this is to talk to judges, members of bar associations, and veteran court reporters.

KINDS OF DAMAGING STORIES

There is more agreement on the kinds of materials that *might* be damaging than on whether news stories can prejudice a jury. Unfortunately it isn't necessary to look very far to find instances illustrating this fact. For example, the *Los Angeles Times* ran a story a few years ago beginning this way:

> A television sportscaster, Stan Duke, shot and killed a radio commentator, Averill Berman, early Sunday at the Wilshire District home of Duke's estranged wife, police reported. Duke was booked on suspicion of murder.

Readers probably wondered why Duke was arrested for suspicion of murder when it was patently obvious from reading the lead that Duke had committed the crime—or had according to the *Los Angeles Times*. Under the American system of justice a man is presumed innocent until it is proved he is guilty. In other words the state had to prove that Duke shot and killed Berman.

A newspaper in Washington State ran a far less sensational story, but in its own way it could have been even more damaging. The *Yakima Herald-Republic* headlined the story: Innocent not Tried, Claims Prosecutor. The first sentence stated, "Because of the screening process built into the criminal justice system in this country, innocent men never go to trial, John Moore, Yakima County Deputy Prosecutor, said Wednesday." The people of that county probably spent a considerable amount of time wondering why they had courts at all if only the guilty went to trial. All that was really needed was an administrator of some kind to hand out sentences and fines.

The first story was written in a flush of journalistic excitement brought on by a sensational murder. The second story was written by a reporter who should have challenged the outrageous statement on the spot. Numerous other specific examples can be cited, but probably a better idea is to summarize the kinds of information many people agree can possibly interfere with the defendant's right to a fair trial. The following list was taken from lists published by the American Bar Association and various state press-bench-bar committees.

1. Confessions or stories about the confession that a defendant is said to have made, including even alluding to the fact that there may be a confession. The Fifth Amendment says that a person does not have to testify against himself. Therefore a confession given to police may be subsequently retracted and usually cannot be used against the defendant at the trial.

2. Stories about the defendant's performance on a test using a polygraph, or lie detector, or similar device, and about the defendant's refusal to take such a test. Most of this information is not permitted at the trial.

3. Stories about the defendant's past criminal record or that state he was a former convict. This information is not permitted at the trial. It may seem entirely logical to some people that when a man has committed ninety-nine robberies and is again arrested for robbery he probably did commit the crime. As a matter of fact, past behavior is immaterial in his current trial for robbery. The state must prove that he committed *this* robbery. The situation is a lot like the odds in the flip of a coin. If a penny is flipped ninety-nine times and each time comes up heads, the odds that it will come up tails on the hundredth flip should be very high. As a matter of fact, they are fifty-fifty. Every flip is a new flip, totally separate from all other flips. And every crime is a separate crime as far as the law is concerned.

4. Stories which question the credibility of witnesses and which contain the personal feelings of witnesses about prosecutors, police, victims, or even judges. To illustrate: in the Sam Sheppard case, which will be discussed a little later, the judge was quoted as telling a reporter—before the trial started—that he thought Sam Sheppard was "guilty as hell," and the remark was published (*Sheppard* v. *Maxwell*, 1966).

5. Stories about the defendant's character (he hates children and dogs), his associates (he hangs around with known syndicate gunmen), and his personality (he attacks people on the slightest provocation).

6. Stories which tend to inflame the public mood against the defendant. Such stories include editorial campaigns which demand the arrest of a suspect before sufficient evidence has been collected; man-on-the-street interviews concerning the guilt of the defendant or the kind of punishment he should receive after he is convicted; televised debates about the evidence of the guilt or innocence of the defendant. All these kinds of stories put the jury in the hot seat, as well as circulate vast quantities of misinformation.

This list is not exhaustive. There are other kinds of stories which many people agree can interfere with the judicial process. A study conducted by Prof. Fred Siebert in Michigan a few years ago (in *Free Press and Fair Trial,* ed. Chilton R. Bush) reported that judges believed publication of criminal records, performance on tests, and information about confessions were potentially the most damaging kinds of stories. They felt further that publication of such stories was inappropriate in nearly every case.

One positive note should be made at this point. Stories like these are less common today. Prof. George Hough (in *Free Press and Fair Trial,* ed. Chilton R. Bush) at Michigan State University recently documented a fact that most journalists have long believed: Newspapers today carry less crime news than most critics claim. After studying both court records and newspapers in Detroit for a six-month period Hough found that of all the felony cases in which warrants were issued only 7 percent were even reported in the newspapers. Hough also found that during a one-year period in which 9,140 felony warrants were issued only 3.4 percent of the cases ever came to jury trial. These statistics seem to argue that the press ignores most cases, and that the chance of interfering with a jury trial is quite small since so few arrests result in jury trials.

A recent study by Prof. J. Edward Gerald reported in *Journalism Quarterly* ("Press-Bar Relationships: Progress Since Sheppard and Reardon") reinforces Hough's findings. A majority of the prosecutors in the two hundred seventy-six urban counties surveyed by Gerald said that newspapers and broadcasting stations have sharply curtailed publication and broadcast of prejudicial news.

Even editors are beginning to realize that readers are really not as interested in crime news as they perhaps once were. One editor commented, "We don't get any calls for the gory stuff anymore. Most people who call in want to know why there isn't more good news."

One more point needs to be made. Intelligent and otherwise reasonable people still argue that the press publishes gory, sensational crime news to sell newspapers. Anyone familiar with the newspaper business knows that this argument is nonsense. News content has very little to do with the sale of newspapers. The day of newsboys loudly hawking newspapers on busy street corners is long since dead. Most newspapers are home delivered today—90 to 95 percent of most dailies are dropped on doorsteps or in the bushes next to doors. The few street sales are usually to businessmen seeking final stock market returns or looking for something to read during the train ride home. People buy newspapers for a lot of reasons, but there is no evidence anywhere suggesting that people buy one paper as opposed to another on the basis of sensational crime news headlines. Most people don't even have a choice of newspapers anymore since most communities have only one newspaper. This kind of logic only demonstrates to journalists that lawyers and judges really don't understand the true function of the press and often convinces editors that to cooperate with such "dunderheads" is unthinkable.

PREJUDICIAL NEWS   Despite the fact that there is less crime news in the press today than say, forty years ago, newspapers and television stations still have a tendency to publish and broadcast "prejudicial" information about defendants in some cases. Usually such cases are the big, sensational ones: Ax Murderer Confesses, Ex-Con Nabbed for Mass Murder, Sex Killer Arrested at Rape Scene. Does this kind of story endanger a defendant's right to a fair trial?

Before that question can be answered, another question must be first considered: Will such stories influence jurors who read this news in their deliberations on the guilt or innocence of defendants? Consensus on the answer to this question is slight.

Both attorneys and judges are in disagreement. Many say that this kind of publicity destroys the possibility of impartiality in potential jurors. Others agree with this opinion, but argue that screening processes (which are discussed later) will keep biased persons out of jury boxes. Still others argue that even when jurors are biased they follow the judge's admonition to decide the case on the facts presented in the courtroom, not on information from the press (Pember, Don R., "Pre-Trial Publicity in Criminal Cases: A Case Study").

For years we have looked to social science for the answer to this question, and various experiments regarding the impact of prejudicial material on jurors have been conducted. All of the studies had one factor in common—the use of mock juries and mock trials. A successful experiment using a real jury at a real trial has also been done. This kind of investigation was initiated thirty years ago when researchers bugged certain jury rooms. The research had just got underway when the bugging was made public, and the outcry from the bench, the bar, and the people quickly stopped the testing.

In the tests using mock jurors generally two sets of "jurors" hear a mock trial. One set is given prejudicial news accounts to read before the mock trial, and the other set is given unbiased accounts. After the trial the jurors are polled on the question of guilt or innocence, and it is not uncommon that a higher proportion of jurors who read the prejudicial material vote guilty than of those who did not read it. Critics of this kind of test accurately point out that using mock juries and mock trials is a far cry from using real jurors and real trials. While some circumstances can be simulated, the mystique of a courtroom—the majesty of the proceedings, the robed judge, the "hear ye's, hear ye's," the flags, the uniformed bailiffs—cannot be simulated properly. The mock jurors know they are mock jurors: they know that the defendant's fate does not rest in their hands. Another dimension of a real trial lacking in experimental trials is the judge, whom most jurors see as a high-authority figure. At a legitimate trial the judge admonishes jurors to ignore extraneous evidence, to consider only the facts presented at the trial. Although the judge admonishes the jurors in an experimental trial, the admonition does not carry the same weight.

The importance of this last factor cannot be discounted. Before the experiment using real jurors was aborted so abruptly, some data were gathered. Using the evidence from that experiment, Harry Kalven, project coordinator, drew this conclusion:

> We do . . . have evidence that the jurors take with surprising seriousness the admonition not to read the paper or discuss the case with other people. . . . Our overall impression . . . is that the jury is a a pretty stubborn, healthy institution not likely to be overwhelmed either by a remark of counsel or a remark in the press.[*]

One additional point needs to be made about the research by social scientists regarding publicity and prejudice. If the previous caveats are disregarded and the research is considered on its own terms, the findings remain inconclusive. Prof. Walter Wilcox recently studied this research data and arrived at the following conclusion (in *Free Press and Fair Trial,* ed. Chilton R. Bush):

> Communication research with all its advances and sophistication has not given us instruments to determine precisely the impact of a crime story upon the reader in terms of knowing and feeling, let alone acting. . . .
> As pretrial publicity was traced through the jury trial, the most noticeable overall phenomenon was a kind of flaking (or flaying) process, of dead ends, of self-cancelling propositions, of one concept confounded by another. The results do not add up to a neat and logical and defensible summary conclusion.

After citing with approval Harry Kalven's conclusion just given, Wilcox asks, "Could it be that the American jury confounds all the subtle nuances of the behavioral sciences and simply does its duty?"

[*]Harry Kalven: personal communication (to Director, American Law Institute).

THE LAW AND PREJUDICIAL NEWS

While social science shuffles about attempting to prove or disprove theories regarding prejudicial information, the law takes the only outlook it can, assumes that prejudicial publicity can affect the minds of jurors, and acts accordingly. This does not mean, however, that the law regards a potential juror as biased because he has seen prejudicial material or admits to having a slight bias. As recently as 1975 the United States Supreme Court ruled, "Qualified jurors need not . . . be totally ignorant of the facts and issues involved in a case" (*Murphy* v. *Florida,* 1975).

The definition of an impartial juror used by the courts in the United States is over one hundred seventy years old and stems from a ruling by Chief Justice John Marshall in the trial of Aaron Burr. Charges that the jurors were biased were made at the trial. In 1807 Marshall proclaimed that an impartial juror was one free from the dominant influence of knowledge acquired outside the courtroom, free from strong and deep impressions which close the mind. "Light impressions," Marshall wrote, "which may fairly be supposed to yield to the testimony that may be offered, which leave the mind open to a fair consideration of that testimony, constitute no sufficient objection to a juror . . ." (*U.S.* v. *Burr,* 1807).

While this definition is fairly precise, modern courts nevertheless have to cope with the problem of applying the definition to specific situations. It is appellate courts that most often must apply Marshall's definition to cases in which convicted defendants ask for a reversal on the grounds that the jury is not impartial, as guaranteed by the Sixth Amendment. Indeed, reversal is one important, if costly, remedy the judicial system uses to cope with prejudicial publicity, that is, to simply reverse the guilty verdict and require that the defendant be retried.

In looking at some of the instances in which appellate courts ruled on prejudicial publicity, one does not gain comfort from their consistency. Here are a few representative cases.

A copy of a newspaper containing information about the trial found its way into the jury room. The appellate court ruled that this fact in and of itself was not a sufficient reason to assume prejudice. The judge had told the jury to disregard the contents of the news story and it should be assumed that they followed these instructions unless there is evidence to the contrary (*Leviton* v. *U.S.,* 1951).

Three young black men were accused of raping a white girl. The local newspaper set about to inflame public opinion against the defendants. It published one article which said the men had confessed to the crime. They were convicted, but the conviction was overturned by the Supreme Court because blacks had been deliberately excluded from the grand jury which indicted the trio. Justice Robert Jackson noted, however, that he could not think of anything more prejudicial to the defendants than news of the confession (*Shepherd* v. *Florida*, 1951).

Wide publicity was given to the murder of a six-year-old girl by an elderly man. Reports that he had confessed were published, as well as comments by the district attorney that sex offenders (the defendant had such a background) should be handled like mad dogs. The Supreme Court chastised the trial court for permitting such publicity, but affirmed the conviction (*Stroble* v. *California*, 1952).

During a trial two newspapers containing stories about the defendant's prior criminal record were found in a courtroom. Jurors told the judge they had looked at the stories but vowed they could decide the case solely on the evidence presented in court. The Supreme Court overturned the conviction on the grounds that the jurors could not be impartial in such circumstances (*Marshall* v. *U.S.*, 1959).

Leslie Irvin was arrested in connection with a series of six murders. Statements that Irvin had confessed to all six killings received widespread publicity. At the trial, of four hundred thirty persons called as potential jurors, three hundred seventy-five told the judge that they believed Irvin was guilty. Of the twelve jurors finally selected, eight told the court they thought he was guilty before the trial started. The Supreme Court overturned the conviction, noting that in this case, in which so many persons, so many times, admitted prejudice, statements of impartiality could be given little weight (*Irvin* v. *Dowd*, 1961).

Wilbert Rideau was arrested and charged with robbing a bank and killing a bank employee. He confessed to these crimes while being questioned by the sheriff, an interrogation session that was filmed and shown on local television on three successive days. The Supreme Court overturned the conviction noting, "Any subsequent court proceeding in a community so pervasively exposed to such a spectacle could be but a hollow formality" (*Rideau* v. *Louisiana*, 1963).

Louis Van Duyne was arrested and charged with killing his wife. After his conviction he sought a reversal on the grounds that newspaper publicity had prejudiced the jury. One newspaper story cited by the defendant quoted Van Duyne as telling the police, "You've got me for murder." Newspapers were found in the jury room and there was evidence that the jury read other prejudicial accounts of the case. The New Jersey Supreme Court affirmed the conviction, ruling that there was no evidence that the defendant had not received a fair trial, there was no evidence that the jurors were overwhelmed by the prejudicial publicity (*People* v. *Van Duyne*, 1964).

Jack (Murph the Surf) Murphy appealed his conviction in Florida state courts for robbery and assault on the grounds that the jury had been prejudiced by extensive publicity about his previous criminal record and his other extralegal exploits. The Supreme Court disagreed and ruled that while the Constitution requires that the defendant have "a panel of impartial, indifferent jurors" they "need not, however, be totally ignorant of the facts and issues involved." It is sufficient that a juror can lay aside his impressions and opinions and render a verdict based on the evidence presented in court. The court did not find the hostility in the jury toward the defendant that was found, for example, in the Irvin case. Only twenty of the seventy-eight potential jurors indicated that they believed Murphy was guilty as they were questioned prior to being seated (*Murphy* v. *Florida,* 1975).

It is apparent from these few cases that judges disagree on how much publicity a juror can absorb without becoming biased toward a defendant. Nevertheless, judges seem more willing to trust the honorable instincts of the jurors than do many social scientists who have done research in this area. Reversal of a conviction is but one remedy to offset prejudicial publicity. There are many others.

The remedies discussed in the remainder of this chapter come from many sources. Some are centuries-old legal traditions which in the course of time were adopted to fight the impact of prejudicial publicity. For example, in the *Irvin* case just discussed the Supreme Court cited both voir dire and change of venue as procedural safeguards that can and should be used to cope with potentially damaging publicity. Other solutions are newer. The restrictive order resulted from both a Supreme Court decision, *Sheppard* v. *Maxwell,* and a set of proposals from the American Bar Association known as the Reardon Report. Other remedies are the result of studies by the American Bar Association and of agreements arrived at between the bench, the bar, and the press.

Two basic but distinct principles underly all the remedies developed over time to offset the damage from prejudicial publicity. The first principle is directed at stopping the publicity before it starts by issuing a specific court order or by shutting off the sources of such information so that the press has nothing to publish. The second principle, far less traumatic for both the press and the legal system, is to compensate within the judicial system itself for the prejudicial publicity. Screening of potentially prejudicial jurors is one such procedure.

Within the two basic principles a wide range of specific devices and procedures are available. We will discuss devices and procedures designed to compensate for the publicity first because they are noncontroversial, have little impact upon the press, and can be discussed quickly.

COMPENSATORY JUDICIAL REMEDIES

Reversal of Conviction

One of the most drastic and least productive solutions to the problem of pretrial publicity is to simply hold the trial without considering the impact which the news reports might have upon the jurors. If the defendant chooses to argue that the trial was unfair, an appellate court reviews the case and overturns the conviction if bias is found in the jury. This, obviously, puts an immense burden upon the defendant who must bear the cost of an appeal as well as the hardship of a second trial if the conviction is overturned. Also, if the defendant is in jail the delay between a trial and a successful appeal can impose an extreme, and in many cases, unnecessary hardship. Reversal of the conviction should be viewed as the last possible solution, to be used only when all else has failed.

Voir Dire

Before prospective jurors finally make it to the jury box, they must pass a series of hurdles erected by both the attorneys in the case and the judge. These hurdles are designed to protect the judicial process from jurors who have already made up their mind about the case or who have a strong bias toward one litigant or the other. In a process called voir dire each prospective juror is questioned prior to being empaneled in an effort to discover bias. Pretrial publicity is only one source of juror prejudice. If the defendant is on trial for shooting a police officer and if the prospective juror is the mother of a police officer, she is likely to be biased. Perhaps the juror is a business associate of the defendant. Possibly the juror has read extensively about the case in the newspapers and believes the police are trying to frame the defendant.

Both sides in the case question the jurors and both sides can ask the court to excuse a juror. This procedure is called challenging a juror. There are two kinds of challenges: challenges for cause and peremptory challenges. To challenge a juror for cause an attorney must convince the court that there is a good reason for this person not to sit on the jury. Deep-seated prejudice is one good reason. Being an acquaintance of one of the parties in the case is also a good reason. Any reason can be used to challenge a potential juror. All the attorney must do is to convince the judge that the reason is proper. There is no limit on the number of challenges for cause that both prosecutor and defense attorney may exercise.

A peremptory challenge is somewhat different. This challenge can be exercised without cause, and the judge has no power to refuse such a challenge. There is a limit, however, on the number of such challenges that may be exercised. Sometimes there are as few as two or three and sometimes as many as ten or twenty, depending upon the case, the kind of crime involved, the state statute, and sometimes the judge. This kind of challenge is reserved for use against persons whom the defense or the prosecution doesn't want on the jury, but whom the judge refuses to excuse for cause. For example, in the various Watergate trials, attorneys for John Mitchell, H. R. Haldeman, John Erlichman, and other Nixon associates sought jurors who were strong believers in law and order. Potential jurors were asked subtle questions about crime in the streets, the kinds of television programs they liked, the types of movies they enjoyed, and so forth. It was felt that people who thought that criminals were pampered and who liked cop shows on television and John Wayne blood-and-guts movies were "Nixon people" and might be more favorable to the defendants in the trial. The defense used its peremptory challenges to excuse the opposite kind of persons: typical "bleeding heart liberals" who looked at crime as a social disease, abhorred violence on television, thought George Patton was an authoritarian kook, and couldn't stand John Wayne movies. Obviously, this account is an oversimplification, but psychologists did draw up such profiles for the defense. The scheme worked in the first trial in which John Mitchell, Maurice Stans, and a few other defendants were acquitted. At the end of that trial the federal prosecutor said the government hadn't paid enough attention to selecting the jury.

Is voir dire a good way to screen prejudiced jurors? Seventy-nine percent of a large group of judges surveyed by Professor Emeritus Fred Siebert of Michigan State University said (in *Free Press and Fair Trial*, ed. Chilton Bush) that the questioning process was either highly effective or moderately effective in screening biased jurors. Most trial lawyers also agree, to a point. It is difficult, however, to argue with critics who say that voir dire uncovers only the prejudice that the prospective juror is aware of or is not too embarrassed to admit. Biased jurors can lie when questioned about their bias. They may not even know their mind is made up about the defendant's guilt. These kinds of objections are at the root of the entire jury system. The only way to find jurors who are not biased in even a small way is to lock up babies when they are born and raise them as jurors, isolate them from the rest of the world until they are adults, and then release them to act only as jurors at trials. Nobody wants this kind of system. The faith that most persons have in the effectiveness of voir dire is comparable to their faith in the entire jury system.

Change of Venue   Many judges and legal authorities describe a change of venue as an effective means of dealing with massive pretrial publicity. Imagine for a moment that John Smith is arrested for a series of six brutal murders committed in River City over a period of six weeks and highly publicized by the local press. When Smith is arrested, the local news media saturate the community with stories about the killings, about the arrest, and about Smith. Day after day the newspapers and broadcasting stations focus on one new angle after another. Soon most of the people in River City know more about the suspect's past than even the police and his parents know. One means to compensate for such publicity about a defendant in the community in which the crime takes place is to move the trial to another community. This procedure is called a change of venue. While the people in River City may be prejudiced against Smith by virtue of the reports in the news media, the people across the state in Ames have hardly heard of the matter. Therefore, the trial, including the prosecutor, the defendant, the judges, the witnesses, and assorted other trial participants is moved to Ames for the month or two of the trial. The jury is selected from a panel of people who live in Ames. Seventy-seven percent of the judges surveyed think a change of venue is highly effective or moderately effective in controlling prejudicial publicity (*Free Press and Fair Trial*). However, the procedures has serious drawbacks.

Change of venue is costly. The state must pay for housing and feeding all of the trial participants while they are in Ames. Also, the defendant must give up his constitutional right to trial in the district in which the crime was committed. Finally, there is no assurance that by the time the trial begins in Ames the newspapers and broadcasting stations in that town will not have saturated the community with prejudicial publicity. While the Ames press might not have been interested in murders across the state in River City, the slayings suddenly become a hot local story when the trial is moved to Ames. So the change of venue may or may not be effective. Probably effectiveness depends upon the magnitude of the crime. A simple homicide is really not a big story today, and a change of venue might effectively shield the defendant. But mass murder and assassination are quite different. Generally the interest is great and extends far beyond the community in which the crime was committed. (Was there a community in which the names Lee Harvey Oswald and Jack Ruby were not known?)

Continuance

A continuance is somewhat like a change of venue. But the time of the trial, instead of the location, is changed. That is, the trial is postponed. Back to John Smith for a moment. A delay of six to nine months in his trial might have pushed the slayings to the back of the mind of the community. People rapidly forget information not vital to their lives. It is probably far easier to empanel an unbiased jury after a continuance of six months. But again there are problems. The defendant sacrifices his right to a speedy trial. While the right to a speedy trial is one of the myths we are content to live with in the United States, continuance nevertheless means an even longer delay than normal. If the defendant can't make bail or if bail is not permitted, he spends the six months of the continuance in jail. Also, this scheme assumes that there will be little or no further publicity about the case. This assumption is wrong. Invariably, the week before the trial is scheduled to start (after the six-month delay) the press gives the community the information: Smith Murder Trial to Begin Monday. The gory details are rehashed to remind people of what happened.

Like a change of venue, continuance probably works best in those cases in which the crime is not too spectacular and the original publicity not too heavy. It can be very effective in cases of accidental publicity. A judge told of how just as he was scheduled to begin hearing a malpractice suit on a Monday morning the Sunday paper, quite innocently, carried a long feature story on the skyrocketing costs of physicians' malpractice insurance because of large judgments handed down in malpractice suits. The article pointed out that physicians passed the additional charges along to patients. The story was widely read. Jurors, who also pay doctors' bills, might hesitate to award a judgment to an injured patient knowing that it would raise insurance rates and ultimately cost patients more. The judge therefore continued the case for two months to let the story fade from the public mind.

While publicity before a trial can damage a defendant's chance for a fair trial, publicity during the trial can be equally dangerous. A significant portion of what occurs at a trial takes place while the jury is out of the courtroom. Imagine that Jane Adams is on trial for murder for stabbing her best friend with a kitchen knife. During the trial Ms. Adams' attorney calls a witness who testifies that the victim had been terminally ill with cancer when the killing occurred. The prosecutor objects, declaring that this testimony is irrelevant. The defense attorney disagrees. Before the judge can rule on the relevancy of the testimony he must hear it. So the jury leaves the courtroom, the witness gives the testimony, and the judge decides whether it is relevant and admissible evidence. The jury then returns to the courtroom. If the material is relevant, the witness goes through the testimony again, this time for the jury. If the material is not relevant, the next witness is called.

Reporters and the public usually remain in the courtroom while the judge evaluates the testimony of the witness. Assume that the judge in this case declares the material inadmissible. But that night the *River City Sentinel* runs the story anyway: Victim Terminally Ill Before Stabbing. What is to stop jurors from reading in the newspaper or watching on television what they were not allowed to see and hear in the courtroom?

Judges have two legal means, admonition to and sequestration of juries, to cope with the problem.*

Admonition to Jury

At almost every trial the judge admonishes the jury not to look at newspapers, to watch or listen to news reports, or to talk to other people about what happens at the trial. The following admonition, which is from the standard instructions which judges of the superior court in King County, Washington, give jurors, is typical:

> Do not discuss this case or any criminal case or any criminal matter among yourselves or with anyone else. Do not permit anyone to discuss such subjects with you or in your presence. . . .
> Do not read, view or listen to any report in a newspaper, radio or television on the subject of this trial or any other criminal trial. Do not permit anyone to read about or comment on this trial or any criminal trial to you or in your presence.

Jurors are warned that a violation of the order might result in a personal penalty against them and in a mistrial for the case. Judges who exhibit a strong faith in the jury system rate admonition to juries an important means of coping with publicity about trials.

Sequestration of Jury

For cases in which a high level of publicity is expected, publicity which might prove hard for a jury to avoid, the court has another device: sequestration of the jury, which means that once it is empaneled, the jury is locked up. Jurors eat together, are housed at state expense at a hotel or motel, and are not permitted to visit with friends and relatives. Phone calls are screened, as is contact with the mass media. Jurors are allowed to read newspapers only after court officials delete stories which could be objectionable.

Sequestration is a costly process for both the state and the jurors. Sequestration for three or four days might be a lark, but the trials in which juries are normally sequestered are long trials sometimes lasting as long as six months. Life can be seriously disrupted. The number of people who can afford the loss of income involved in such a task is limited.

Although sequestered jurors are free from prejudicial publicity, attorneys fear the long quarantine produces a different kind of prejudice—prejudice against one or the other of the two sides in the case—wrought from keeping jurors away from friends and family for so long. Defense

*Judges also have a third means: to forbid the press to report the happenings when the jury is not in the courtroom. Recently in Washington State when the judge used this means, the state supreme court ruled that the method constitutes prior restraint and is in violation of freedom of the press (*State* ex rel. *Superior Court* v. *Sperry,* 1971). Supreme courts in a few other states such as Ohio have ruled similarly.

attorneys express this fear most often, feeling that the jurors will come to look upon the defendant as the person responsible for the inconvenience or hardship and be prone to vote for conviction. At this time, however, there is no evidence to support this notion.

The fairly simple ways just discussed of coping with publicity both before and during a trial are timeworn and generally effective in the average criminal case. However, in recent years many persons argue that such simple solutions are simply inadequate to cope with sensational, widely publicized cases: mass murder, assassination, gory sex killings, and so forth. Consequently, new modes of control have been developed. Instead of coping with the publicity, the new controls are designed to cut it off, to stop it, to prohibit it. These schemes vary from the heavy-handed, authoritarian restrictive court order to the formal bench-bar-press agreements which have increased so rapidly in number during the seventies.

OPEN COURT VERSUS CLOSED COURT

Before restrictive orders are discussed and evaluated, a subsidiary procedure should be considered: closed judicial hearings, which have much the same impact as restrictive orders.

Traditionally some kinds of court hearings are frequently closed: juvenile court hearings, divorce hearings, certain pretrial hearings, bail hearings, and so forth. The law varies from state to state, and reporters must look to the authorities in their own state for guidance. Courts can also rule that in certain circumstances any trial can be closed. For example, when spectators are hostile to a witness the trial can be closed, and when a witness fears for his life and refuses to testify in public a trial can also be closed.

To whom does the right of a public trial belong? to the defendant? to the public? to the press? The answer to this question is not clear. In 1949 a federal court ruled that the safeguard of a public trial belongs to the public as well as to the accused and that courts are duty bound to enforce the right to a public trial in every criminal case (*U.S.* v. *Kobli*). In 1954, however, when the United Press Association sought access to a closed trial in New York, an appellate court ruled that the news-gathering organization lacked standing to sue in the case. The right to public trial belongs to the accused, the court said, not to the press. The press therefore has no legal right to sue in court to open such a trial (*United Press Association* v. *Valente*, 1954).

The most recent open-trial controversy occurred in New York in 1972 and involved the prosecution of Carmine Persico, a reputed underworld figure. Shortly after the trial started the *New York Times* and the *Daily News* both published stories stating that Persico had a criminal record and underworld connections. Persico asked for a mistrial on the grounds that these reports prejudiced the jury. Upon being polled by the judge, jury members said they had not seen the stories, and the motion for mistrial was denied. But the judge warned reporters that if more stories were printed the journalists would be found in contempt. The newspapers published additional reports and Justice Postel closed the courtroom to press and public.

The state high court ruled that the trial should not have been closed, stating that the purpose of Judge Postel's order was to punish the news media for publishing the stories. There was no evidence that the news reports jeopardized the defendant's chance for a fair trial. Chief Judge Stanley Fuld of the court of appeals (the state's high court) wrote (*Oliver* v. *Postel*, 1972):

> In short, then, it is our conclusion that the respondent's order was an unwarranted effort to punish and censor the press, and the fact that it constituted a novel form of censorship cannot insulate or shield it from constitutional attack. In the area of "indispensible" First Amendment liberties, the Supreme Court has been careful "not to limit protection to any particular way of abridging it."

The question of whether a judge can close a trial to the press and to the public is still open, but the 1972 decision in *Oliver* v. *Postel* goes a long way toward removing closure of trials as a means of punishing the press.

RESTRICTIVE ORDER

As mentioned earlier, the restrictive court order came into being as the result both of the Supreme Court decision in the sensational murder case of Dr. Samuel Sheppard and of the so-called Reardon Report, a set of standards relating to the problem of fair trial and free press published by the American Bar Association.

The Sam Sheppard Case

In the 1960s there was a popular television series called "The Fugitive." The show told the story of a doctor wrongly convicted of killing his wife. The train carrying Dr. Richard Kimble to prison derailed and he escaped, becoming a fugitive in search of a mysterious one-armed man who he claimed had actually done the killing.

Probably few people know that the genesis of the television series was a real criminal case, the case of Dr. Samuel Sheppard. On the morning of July 4, 1954, the dead body of Sam Sheppard's pregnant wife Marilyn was found by authorities in the upstairs bedroom of their Bay Village, Ohio, home. She had been bludgeoned to death. Dr. Sheppard told police that he was awakened as he slept on the downstairs couch by screams coming from his wife's bedroom. He hurried upstairs and saw a "form" standing over his wife's bed. He said he struggled with the form and was knocked unconscious. He told police that when he awoke his wife was dead. A few weeks later he was charged with murder.

The Sam Sheppard case caught the imagination of the nation during that hot summer of Eisenhower Republican normalcy. Before Sheppard was finally arrested Cleveland newspapers were asking in bold front-page headlines why the suburban doctor wasn't in jail. The publicity between the time of the killing and the trial was fantastic. Newspaper clippings alone filled five volumes. The coroner's inquest was held in a school gymnasium and broadcast live to the community. Debates were held, witnesses were interviewed by the media, and man-on-the-street interviews concerning Sheppard's guilt or innocence were broadcast. The trial was no better. The press dominated the courtroom. Lawyers had difficulty talking to the defendant without being overheard by newsmen who crowded close to the defense table. All participants—police, prosecutor, defense counsel—made extraneous statements, often outrageous statements, which found their way into print or onto television and radio. An appellate court finally described the trial as a Roman holiday, an orgy of sensationalism, for the press. Sheppard was convicted.

An appeal on the grounds that pretrial publicity had made a fair trial impossible was made to the Supreme Court. The high Court refused to hear the case. Sheppard went to prison. Several years later the press again entered the case when *Argosy* magazine used its column "Court of Last Resort" written by mystery writer Earl Stanley Gardner to publicize Sam Sheppard's plight. Finally, in 1966 the United States Supreme Court heard Sheppard's appeal and reversed his conviction. The state of Ohio chose to reprosecute the middle-aged doctor, and this time he was acquitted.

Justice Tom Clark wrote the high Court's opinion in the *Sheppard* case. The Supreme Court came down hard on the press, noting that bedlam reigned during the trial and that "newsmen took over practically the entire courtroom, hounding most of the participants in the trial, especially Sheppard. . . ." Justice Clark saved his sharpest criticism for Judge Blythin, who conducted the trial, and the other officers of the court for allowing the publicity about the case and the coverage of the trial to get out of hand. Here are some excerpts from Clark's opinion (*Sheppard* v. *Maxwell*, 1966).

> Bearing in mind the massive pretrial publicity, the judge should have adopted stricter rules governing the use of the courtroom by newsmen . . . the court should have insulated witnesses [from the media]. . . . The court should have made some effort to control the release of leads, information and gossip to the press by police officers, witnesses and the counsel for both sides. . . . And it is obvious that the judge should have further sought to alleviate this problem by impos-

ing control over the statements made to the news media by counsel, witnesses, and especially the coroner and police officers. . . . The trial court might well have proscribed extrajudicial statements by any lawyer, party, witness or court official which divulged prejudicial matters . . . the court could also have requested the appropriate city and county officials to promulgate a regulation with respect to dissemination of information about the case by their employes. In addition, reporters who wrote or broadcast prejudicial stories could have been warned as to the impropriety of publishing material not introduced in the proceedings.

The Supreme Court made it quite clear in the *Sheppard* decision that it holds the trial judge responsible for ensuring that the defendant's rights are not jeopardized by prejudicial press publicity. While the court was critical of the press' behavior, no suggestion was made that the judicial system launch an attack on the press. Nevertheless, at a meeting following the decision, a professor of law, in explaining the high Court's opinion in *Sheppard,* suggested that the Court proposed that judges use the contempt power to control the press. Justice Clark, who was at the same meeting, told the assembled trial lawyers that the professor misinterpreted the court's ruling (Friendly and Goldfarb, *Crime and Publicity*):

> The Court never held up contempt and it may well be that it will never hold up contempt because the restraint is too stringent. . . . The Court's opinion never mentioned any guidelines for the press. . . . I am not proposing that you jerk a newspaper reporter into the courtroom and hold him in contempt. We do not have to jeopardize freedom of the press.

As we will see shortly, this aspect of the Sam Sheppard controversy is frequently forgotten.

The Reardon Report   The ink was barely dry on the opinion in the *Sheppard* case when the American Bar Association (ABA) published the first draft of its "Standards Relating to Fair Trial and Free Press." The association, working under the leadership of Paul Reardon, Chief Justice of the Massachusetts Supreme Judicial Court, had begun its study of the free press-fair trial problem in 1965. The final draft of the so-called Reardon Report was published in 1967 and adopted by the House of Delegates of the ABA in 1968.

The Reardon Report quickly became the focus of the free press-fair trial debate. The guidelines in the document were aimed primarily at attorneys and judges. Its message was fairly simple: Don't talk about cases outside of court. If the prosecutor tells the police to keep quiet, if the defense attorney keeps quiet, and if the court tells the witnesses to keep quiet—if nobody says anything—the press then can't publish prejudicial information because it won't have any information to publish.

The report had one other aspect. The last guideline suggested circumstance in which judges should use the contempt power:

> . . . [against] a person who, knowing that a criminal trial by jury is in progress or that a jury is being selected for such a trial:
> (i) disseminates by any means of public communication an extra-judicial statement relating to the defendant or to the issues in the case that goes beyond the public record of the court in the case, that is willfully designed by that person to affect the outcome of the trial, and that seriously threatens to have such an effect; or
> (ii) makes such a statement intending that it be disseminated by any means of public communication.

The report also recommended that judges use the contempt power against persons who knowingly violate a valid judicial order not to disseminate information until completion of the trial, specific information referred to either in a closed pretrial hearing or in an open-court proceeding at which the jury is not present.

While many people believe that these specific limitations on the use of the contempt power ultimately offer the press more protection than does the clear and present danger test in *Bridges, Pennekamp,* and *Craig,* the news media do not see it this way, and perhaps for good reason.

Two things turned the press against the Reardon Report almost immediately. The first is obvious—the threat of contempt. The second reason is more subtle. Alfred Friendly and Ronald Goldfarb note in their book *Crime and Publicity* that a major thrust of the Reardon recommendations is the notion that criminal justice is a monopoly of the legal profession and the less said about the criminal justice system the better. The two authors suggest that this philosophy, more than any other factor, turned the press against the recommendations. The press saw the report as tending to encourage secrecy, to sanction the maintenance of silence about even the basic facts in a case.

Friendly and Goldfarb also rather prophetically point out one other fact: the danger that the media could be punished as an indirect result of a judicial punishment directed at someone else for disclosing information. Such an event did happen. In California a young reporter published a story containing information given to him by an attorney in the *Charles Manson* case. The court specifically prohibited the lawyers from revealing such information to the press. The judge asked the reporter the name of the attorney who provided the material, but the reporter refused to divulge his name. Reporter William Farr was found in contempt of court and went to jail for forty-six days (this case is discussed more fully in chapter 8).

Before the Reardon Report could become so-called law of the land, it had to be adopted by the judiciary of the various states, which did not happen. Not a single state chose to adopt these rules officially. This does not mean, however, that the Report did not make an impression. The Reardon Report, along with the *Sheppard* decision, had an immense impact upon the press. *Sheppard* told judges that it was up to them to keep the lid on publicity and the Reardon Report told them how to do it. Many states did adopt rules similar to those proposed in the Reardon Report, but without the contempt provision.

How Restrictive Orders Are Used

Beginning in the late sixties and continuing today courts throughout the nation hand down specific restrictive orders at the beginning of many newsworthy trials. These orders directly limit what the trial participants can say publicly, what the police can say publicly, and even what the press can publish. In the January 1976 issue of the *American Bar Association Journal* Jack C. Landau, who covers the Supreme Court for the Newhouse chain of newspapers, writes that at least one hundred seventy-four restrictive orders have been handed down since the *Sheppard* case in 1966 ("The Challenge of the Communications Media"). In sixty-one instances the court proceedings or records were closed, in sixty-three limitations were placed upon statements by participants, in thirty-nine prior restraints were put upon publication of material by the press, and in eleven specific restraints were placed upon photographers. In addition, Landau points out, eighty of the ninety-four federal district courts have standing restrictive orders which can be enforced by a contempt citation in most cases. In addition, numerous states have adopted voluntary bench-bar-press guidelines which contain many of the provisions in the Reardon Report.

The restrictive order, which carries out the Supreme Court's ruling in *Sheppard* that trial judges are responsible for safeguarding defendants' Sixth Amendment rights and includes guidelines laid down in the Reardon Report, is colored somewhat by a remarkable lack of sensitivity to the meaning of the First Amendment shared by a large number of trial judges in the United States. While most restrictive orders have been directed at silencing the participants in a trial, some have also been directed at the press. A book entitled *Courts and the Community* is published by the Judicial Administration of the American Bar Association for use at the National College of the State Judiciary, where judges are taught to evaluate the "totality of circumstances" in a case before issuing a restrictive order. This book, which could be called a textbook for trial judges who attend the college's course in judicial administration, advises judges, "cases of contempt by newsmen will be fewer if judges make their restrictive orders apply to the sources of news and not to the newsmen." Unfortunately most judges don't attend this school, and consequently the press becomes the recipient of gag orders.

Sometimes the orders are relatively harmless, and one can readily see the need for the restriction. In 1975 in California before the trial of Lynette Fromme for attempting to shoot the president, trial judge Thomas McBride banned the showing of a ninety-minute documentary about the Charles Manson family in any of the twenty-six counties around Sacramento where the trial was held. Miss Fromme was a member of the Manson family and the judge feared that jurors seeing the motion picture might be prejudiced against the defendant. As soon as the jury was sequestered, the ban was lifted.

In many more cases the restrictions are far more severe and not so obviously needed. Here a few such cases are summarized.

In Minnesota recently the press was ordered not to print a word about the sentencing of young car thieves. The judge passed sentence in open court on December 7, but the press was barred from reporting the matter until December 9. Why? One of the defendants' brothers was getting married on December 8 and the family wanted the news kept out of the newspapers until after the wedding. The judge agreed.

A judge in Monterey County, California, issued an order barring release of certain information about a pending case to the press. When a motion to vacate the order was made, the judge removed the press and the public from the courtroom while the motion was debated. He then forbade all public comments about the order and required that further motions made to the court about the secrecy order be made secretly, not in public.

A case recently decided by the United States Supreme Court was prompted by a judicial order by Judge Hugh Stuart in North Platte, Nebraska, in the trial of Erwin Simants who was accused of killing six persons. Judge Stuart barred the press from reporting much of the information revealed during the preliminary hearing for the defendant. Judge Stuart said he feared that news reports of information disclosed at the preliminary examination might so prejudice the community that he would be unable to find jurors who could give Simants a fair and impartial trial. The press sought an immediate review of the ban on publicity and asked Justice Harry Blackmun to lift the order until an appellate review could be conducted. Justice Blackmun modified Judge Stuart's order, giving the press the right to publish some details of the Simants' case, but still barred the press from disclosing information concerning confession and other statements which could harm the accused. Included in the ban was information that had been disclosed in open court. The high Court eventually ruled that the judge's order violated the First Amendment (*Nebraska Press Association v. Stuart,* 1976). (The implications of this case are discussed on pp. 279-280.) As noted, the case was appealed despite the fact that the issue was moot. Simants was convicted in early 1976.

These are the kinds of horror stories journalists tell each other. While such instances are not typical of the behavior of the judiciary, they are not uncommon either.

Typical Restrictive Order

There really is no such thing as a typical gag order. The reason judges favor such orders is because they can be tailored to the specific circumstances of the case at hand. In spite of this, a fairly typical restrictive order is presented on pages 274 and 275 so that you can see what one looks like. This one was issued by Judge William B. Keene in the murder trial of Charles Manson. Note how comprehensive such a regulation is.

Appellate Court Action

How do the appellate courts respond to such orders? Those orders that blatantly violate the First Amendment are struck down. Those that don't are generally affirmed. Let's consider a few representative cases.

A superior court judge in Phoenix, Arizona, attempted to stop publication of all information about a hearing on the petition for a writ of habeas corpus held before the jury was selected to hear the case. The state supreme court said the court action was censorship and struck down the order (*Phoenix Newspapers, Inc., v. Superior Court,* 1966).

In 1967 the United States Court of Appeals for the Fifth Circuit upheld the contempt conviction of a photographer who violated a standing order against taking pictures in the hallway outside the courtroom. "A defendant in a criminal proceeding should not be forced to run a gauntlet of reporters and photographers each time he enters or leaves the courtroom" (*Seymour* v. *U.S.,* 1967).

In 1969 when two reporters violated a federal court order prohibiting the publication of certain information, the court of appeals upheld their contempt conviction, noting that there was a reasonable likelihood that the publication of the prejudicial news would make it difficult to empanel an impartial jury and might result in an unfair trial (*U.S.* v. *Tigerina,* 1969). Note that the test the court used was "reasonable likelihood," not clear and present danger.

In Washington State a trial judge ordered the press to refrain from publishing reports about anything that occurred at a public trial when the jury was not in the courtroom. Two reporters for the *Seattle Times* violated the order and were found in contempt. The state's high court overturned the conviction, ruling, "The trial court's earnest effort to secure and maintain a fair trial for the defendant . . . had resulted in a deprivation of the appellant's constitutional right to report to the public what happened in the open trial." The court said that if the judge feared the newspaper reports might prejudice the trial he should have sequestered the jury. (*State* ex rel. *Superior Court* v. *Sperry,* 1971)

In 1972 an Arkansas trial court ordered the press not to report the verdict in a rape case, a verdict announced by the jury in a public trial. A Texarkana newspaper published the verdict anyway, and the editor

Superior Court of the State of California
for the County of Los Angeles

People of the State of California
Plaintiffs,

vs.

Charles Manson, et al.,
Defendants

No. A 253156

ORDER RE PUBLICITY

It is apparent, and this Court is going to take judicial notice of the fact, that this case has received extensive news media coverage as a direct result of its apparent public interest; further, it is equally apparent to this Court by reading various newspapers and weekly periodicals that this news media coverage is not limited to the County of Los Angeles, but has been extensive not only in the entire State of California but in the Nation as well, and of this fact the Court now takes judicial notice. This Court is of the firm conviction that the impossible task of attempting to choose between the constitutional guarantees of a free press and fair trial need not be made, but that they are compatible with some reasonable restrictions imposed upon pretrial publicity. It further appears to the Court that the dissemination by any means of public communication of any out-of-court statements relating to this case may interfere with the constitutional right of the defendants to a fair trial and disrupt the proper administration of justice. Some of the defendants now being for the first time before this Court, this Court now exercises its jurisdiction and assumes its duty to do everything within its constitutional powers to make certain that each defendant does receive a fair trial, and now issues the following orders, a violation of which will be considered as a contempt of this Court and will result in appropriate action to punish for such contempt.

It is the order of this Court that no party to this action, nor any attorney connected with this case as defense counsel or as prosecutor, nor any other attorney associated with this case, nor any judicial attache or employee, nor any public official now holding office, including but not limited to any chief of police or any sheriff, who has obtained information related to this action, which information has not previously been disseminated to the public, nor any agent, deputy, or employee of any such persons, nor any grand juror, nor any witness having appeared before the Grand Jury in this matter, nor any person subpoenaed to testify at the trial of this matter, shall release or authorize the release for public dissemination of any purported extrajudicial statement of the defendant relating to this case, nor shall any such persons release or authorize the release of any documents, exhibits, or any evidence, the admissibility of which may have to be determined by the Court, nor shall any such person make any statement for public dissemination as to the existence or possible existence of any document, exhibit, or any other evidence, the admissibility of which may have to be determined by the Court. Nor shall any such persons express outside of court an opinion or make any comment for public dissemination as to the weight, value, or effect of any evidence as tending to establish guilt or innocence. Nor shall any such persons make any statement outside of court for public dissemination as to the weight, value, or effect of any testimony that has been given. Nor shall any such persons issue any statement for public dissemination as to the identity of any prospective witness, or his probable testimony, or the effect thereof. Nor shall any such person make any out-of-court statement for public dissemination as to the weight, value, source, or effect of any purported evidence alleged to have been accumulated as a result of the investigation of this matter. Nor shall any such persons make any statement for public dissemination as to the content, nature, substance, or effect of any testimony which may be given in any proceeding related to this matter, except that a witness may discuss any matter with any attorney of record or agent thereof.

This order does not include any of the following:

1. Factual statements of the accused person's name, age, residence, occupation, and family status.

2. The circumstances of the arrest, namely, the time and place of the arrest, the identity of the arresting and investigation officers and agencies, and the length of the investigation.

3. The nature, substance, and text of the charge, including a brief description of the offenses charged.

4. Quotations from, or any reference without comment to, public records of the Court in the case, or to other public records or communications heretofore disseminated to the public.

5. The scheduling and result of any stage of the judicial proceeding held in open court in an open or public session.

6. A request for assistance in obtaining evidence.

7. Any information as to any person not in custody who is sought as a possible suspect or witness, nor any statement aimed at warning the public of any possible danger as to such person not in custody.

8. A request for assistance in the obtaining of evidence or the names of possible witnesses.

Further, this order is not intended to preclude any witness from discussing any matter in connection with the case with any of the attorneys representing the defendant or the People, or any representative of such attorneys.

It is further the order of the Court that the Grand Jury transcripts in this case not be disclosed to any person (other than those specifically mentioned in Penal Code Section 928.1) until 10 days after a copy thereof has been delivered by this Court to each defendant named in the indictment; provided, however, that if any defendant, during such time, shall move the Court that such transcript, or any portion thereof, not be available for public inspection pending trial, such time shall be extended subject to the Court's ruling on such motion.

It is further ordered that a copy of this order be attached to any subpoena served on any witness in this matter, and that the return of service of the subpoena shall also include the fact of service of a copy of this order.

This order shall be in force until this matter has been disposed of or until further order of Court.

Dated: December 10, 1969

William B. Keene
Judge of the Superior Court

was held in contempt. The state supreme court overruled, noting that no court has the power to prohibit the news media from publishing that which transpires in open court (*Wood* v. *Goodson,* 1972).

An identical order by a trial court in Florida was also struck down by the Florida Court of Appeals (*Miami Herald* v. *Rose,* 1972).

An order which forbade the press from publishing the names of the jurors during a murder trial was upheld in 1972 by a federal district court in Nevada (*Schuster* v. *Bowen,* 1972).

In 1973 a California trial judge issued an order prohibiting the press from publishing the true names and photographs of state prison inmates scheduled to be called as witnesses at a trial. The California Court of Appeals ruled that there was not sufficient evidence to establish that such a prior restraint is necessary to guarantee a fair trial (*Sun Company of San Bernardino* v. *Superior Court,* 1973).

Perhaps the most perplexing recent case is the 1972 decision in *U.S.* v. *Dickinson.* In this case, although the restrictive order of the trial court was struck down, the federal court of appeals refused to reverse the reporters' contempt conviction on the ground that the order should have been obeyed whether or not it was unconstitutional. The facts in this case are as follows.

In November 1971 a hearing was underway in federal court in Baton Rouge, Louisiana. A VISTA worker had been indicted by the state on charges of conspiring to murder the mayor of Baton Rouge. The defendant complained that the state had no evidence in the case and that prosecution was merely an attempt to harass him. The hearing in federal court was to determine the motives of the state in the prosecution. Since it was possible that the charges would be substantial and that the VISTA worker would be tried later in criminal court, the federal judge ruled that there could be no publicity about what took place during the hearing. The press could report that such a hearing was taking place, but that was all. Reporters Gibbs Adams and Larry Dickinson of the *Baton Rouge Morning Advocate and State Times* ignored the order, published a story about the hearing, and were found in criminal contempt and fined $300 each.

Upon appeal, the United States Court of Appeals for the Fifth Circuit struck down the trial court's no-publicity order, but at the same time upheld the contempt convictions. The court cited a 1967 Supreme Court ruling—*Walker* v. *Birmingham*—as precedent. In that case Martin Luther King and seven other clergymen were arrested and held in contempt for violating a Birmingham, Alabama, court injunction banning all marches, parades, sit-ins, and so forth. The high Court ruled that while the ban on marches and parades was unconstitutional Dr. King and the other defendants should have challenged the ban in court rather than just violate it. The contempt citations stood.

The same logic was applied in the *Dickinson* case. Judge John R. Brown wrote (*U.S.* v. *Dickinson,* 1972):

> The conclusion that the District Court's order was constitutionally invalid does not necessarily end the matter of the validity of the contempt convictions. There remains the very formidable questions of whether a person may with impunity violate an order which turns out to be invalid. We hold that in the circumstances of this case he may not.

This decision perplexes many persons who cannot understand why the press or anyone else for that matter should be punished for not obeying an order that is not legal in the first place. It is probably best to have Judge Brown explain by quoting a lengthy passage from his opinion in the *Dickinson* case:

> We begin with the well-established principle in proceedings for criminal contempt that an injunction duly issuing out of a court having subject matter and personal jurisdiction *must be obeyed,* irrespective of the ultimate validity of the order. Invalidity is no defense to criminal contempt. "People simply cannot have the luxury of knowing that they have a right to contest the correctness of the judge's order in deciding whether to wilfully disobey it. . . . Court orders have to be obeyed until they are reversed or set aside in an orderly fashion. . . ."
> The criminal-contempt exception requiring compliance with court orders, while invalid nonjudicial directives may be disregarded, is not the product of self-protection or arrogance of judges. Rather it is born of an experience-proved recognition that this rule is essential for the system to work. Judges, after all, are charged with the final responsibility to adjudicate legal disputes. It is the judiciary which is vested with the duty and power to interpret and apply statutory and constitutional law. Determinations take the form of orders. The problem is unique to the judiciary because of its particular role. Disobedience to a legislative pronouncement in no way interferes with the legislature's ability to dischage its responsibilities [passing laws]. The dispute is simply pursued in the judiciary and the legislature is ordinarily free to continue its function unencumbered by any burdens resulting from the disregard of its directives. Similarly, law enforcement is not prevented by failure to convict those who disregard the unconstitutional commands of a policeman.
> On the other hand, the deliberate refusal to obey an order of the court without testing its validity through established processes requires further action by the judiciary, and therefore directly affects the judiciary's ability to dischage its duties and responsibilities. Therefore, "while it is sparingly to be used, yet the power of courts to punish for contempts is a necessary and integral part of the independence of the judiciary, and is absolutely essential to the performance of the duties imposed upon them by law. Without it they are mere boards of arbitration whose judgments and decrees would be only advisory."

While most members of the press accept this logic to a point they argue that the press presents a special case because time is a crucial factor in news gathering. Had the reporters in the *Dickinson* case, for example, not disobeyed the order but instead appealed the decision to a higher court, the trial which they were covering would have been over before the restrictive order could have been declared invalid.

Judge Brown said that timeliness is an important aspect of news and that an appellate court should grant a speedy review of such orders. "But newsmen are citizens too," he wrote. "They too may sometimes have to wait. They are not yet wrapped in an immunity or given the absolute right to decide with impunity whether a judge's order is to be obeyed or whether an appellate court is acting promptly enough." Although Judge Brown seemed to see the need for speed, nine months elapsed between the original contempt citation and his ruling in the court of appeals.

The reporters appealed the ruling to the Supreme Court, but the high Court declined to hear the matter. Many authorities interpret the refusal as approval by the Court of the Fifth Circuit Court decision (*Dickinson v. U.S.*, 1973).

The implications of *Dickinson* are rather frightening. In a paper entitled "Judicial Restraints on the Press," Prof. Donald Gillmor quotes Dickinson's attorney:

> If the heavy burden which must be borne by the government to support any prior restraint can be met merely by the assertion of the possibility of a conflict . . . between constitutional rights, then freedom of the press as we know it would be held hostage to the fertile imagination of judges.

Many experts predicted that the precedent in *Dickinson* would be an open invitation to abuse by trial courts, and such prophecies were quickly realized.

In the summer of 1972 several persons were arrested on charges of conspiring to disrupt the 1972 Republican Convention in Miami. It is normal procedure in most courts to prohibit photography in the courtroom (more about this in a later section). Many newspapers and television stations use artists to make drawings of the proceedings. In the trial of the conspirators the judge told the press that sketching would not be permitted in the courtroom if the sketches were intended for publication. As a way around the court order, an artist for the Columbia Broadcasting System attended the trial (without pad and pencil) and sketched scenes from memory after the court session. Four sketches were broadcast by the network, which was immediately held in contempt for violating the order. The trial court then issued an order that banned sketching both inside and outside the courtroom and forbade publication of any sketch of the courthouse "regardless of the place where the sketch is made." The Columbia Broadcasting System appealed the order and the contempt citation.

The court of appeals struck down the ban on sketching, but upheld the contempt citation. Citing the *Dickinson* ruling, Judge Dyer wrote (*U.S. v. CBS*, 1974).

> That case stands for the proposition that before a prior restraint may be imposed by a judge, even in the interest of assuring a fair trial, there must be "an imminent," not merely a likely threat, to the administration of justice. The danger must not be remote or even probable, it must immediately imperil.

Despite the fact that the district court made no showing whatsoever that the sketching was obtrusive or disruptive or an imminent threat to the administration of justice, the court said the order should have been challenged rather than disobeyed.

The *Dickinson* and *CBS* cases exemplify two important propositions. First, Federal judges must be cautious in their application of restrictive orders on the press. There must be a serious threat to the fairness of the trial before such an order is used. Although the recommendation is good, the bench appears to ignore it. Second, the press had better obey restrictive orders whether they are constitutional or not, and challenge such censorship in court, not on the front page of a newspaper or during a news broadcast. These are the two important facts that emerged from the rulings of the court of appeals.

The *Dickinson* case leaves one additional residue, according to attorney Dan Paul, who represents the *Miami Herald* and several broadcasters in the southeastern United States. What happens is that as the media appeal restrictive orders to appellate courts, the upper courts frequently take months to reach a decision. Usually by that time, Paul reports, the trial has ended and the appellate court refuses to issue an opinion because the question is moot.

In 1976 as the restrictive order controversy escalated to the point that in many regions the press and the bench were in what United States district judge Walter Hoffman described as "perpetual conflict," the Supreme Court handed down its first word on this subject since the *Sheppard* case (*Nebraska Press Association* v. *Stuart*). In June of that year the high Court seemingly put an end to the worst kind of gag order. As noted previously, courts in Nebraska in an effort to control the publicity about a sensational murder trial in which defendant Erwin Simants was charged with six murders, forbade the press to report the existence and nature of the confession of Simants or to publicize any other material "strongly implicative" of the accused.

The high Court struck down the order (several months after the end of the Simants' trial), ruling that it was in violation of the First Amendment. In a narrow ruling which was constructed carefully around the facts in the case, Chief Justice Burger ruled that restrictive orders placed against the press are in most circumstances unconstitutional. After reviewing a considerable number of First Amendment rulings by the high Court, Burger wrote, "The thread running through all these cases is that prior restraints on speech and publication are the most serious and least tolerable infringement on First Amendment rights."

Justice Burger added, however, that under certain extraordinary circumstances (which he did not specify) such gag orders against the press might be permissible, provided that the state could bear the heavy burden of proving that there was no other way for the defendant to receive a fair trial. Joining Chief Justice Burger in his opinion were Justices Harry Blackmun and William Rehnquist. Three other members of the Court, Justices William Brennan, Potter Stewart, and Thurgood Marshall, said that they could conceive of no circumstance under which such a gag order might be permitted. Finally, Justices Byron White, Lewis Powell, and John Paul Stevens wrote that they were not prepared to decide at that time whether gag orders against the press might be constitutional under specific conditions.

Despite the unanimous victory for the press in *Nebraska,* there was little cause for dancing in the street. The high Court made it clear that trial judges are still empowered to close courtrooms to keep information secret, and it was clearly implied, if not explicitly stated, that trial judges can continue to gag the trial participants—news sources like the police, prosecutor, defense attorney, and so forth—in order to protect the rights of the accused.

American Bar Association Guidelines

For several years the American Bar Association has been preparing a set of guidelines for application of restrictive orders in trials of great public interest. The Association's Legal Advisory Committee on Fair Trial and Free Press, headed by United States Court of Appeals Judge Paul H. Roney, offered a first draft of its proposals in the summer of 1975, *Proposed Court Procedure for Fair Trial-Free Press Judicial Restrictive Orders.* These guidelines were heavily criticized by both journalists and lawyers as being too restrictive. The title of and language in the document led many persons to believe that the committee recommended that restrictive orders be directed specifically against the news media. The first draft also instructed judges to enter restrictive orders "punishable by contempt" in cases "where there is a reasonable likelihood that prejudicial publicity will prevent a fair trial."

In late summer of 1975 this draft was revised and retitled *Recommended Court Procedure to Accommodate Rights of Fair Trial and Free Press*. The original language was modified, and cautions recommending against issuance of orders imposing direct restraints upon the press were added. The expression "reasonable likelihood that prejudicial publicity will prevent a fair trial" was replaced by a statement urging use of "proper constitutional standards" to make the determination. It was also recommended that judges allow members of the press and other interested persons to discuss proposed restrictive orders before they are made public. While the second draft is only slightly more popular with the press than the first draft, it is likely that the House of Delegates of the American Bar Association will adopt this draft or something very like it. The assembly was scheduled to consider adoption of the rules at its February 1976 meeting, but action on the measure was postponed until the Supreme Court announced its decision in the *Nebraska* gag-order case.

Value of Restrictive Order

There is no question that the nation, the judicial system, and the press cannot tolerate another fiasco like the Sam Sheppard trial. Restrictive orders do stop such circuses. But restrictive orders not only solve certain problems, but also create others. Many critics compare the use of such orders to hunting mice with elephant guns. Here is a summary of the criticism.

Evelle J. Younger, for many years prosecutor in Los Angeles County, argues that the premise for using a restrictive order is that jurors are "inherently unable" to disregard news reports. "It has been my experience and the experience of the staff of my office that quite the contrary is true." Younger asks, "Who is to say that the juror is less concerned with seeing justice done in a particular case than is the United States Supreme Court?"

Younger also points out that muzzling of responsible sources of information often creates a vacuum that can only be filled by irresponsible sources. He notes that during the trial of Sirhan Sirhan for the murder of Robert Kennedy the courts clamped a lid on the dissemination of most information about the trial. The press turned to other sources, Younger says, and raised issues that the public prosecutor could not comment upon. One witness told the press she had seen a girl in a polka-dotted dress running from the scene of the shooting saying "We got Kennedy." Younger says that investigation by both the police and his office showed that the witness fabricated the story to get publicity. But because of the gag order Younger could not release this information to the public. At another time Younger was asked whether it was true that President Nasser of the United Arab Republic was behind the assassination. By virtue of the court order the prosecutor was forced to respond No comment, and his response led to speculation that such a link might have substance.

Judge Harold Medina is also critical of restrictive orders, noting that while they prevent a carnival atmosphere in a sensational trial, the price is too high:

> Without such activities (pretrial reporting), how are corruption and incompetency to be brought to light—let alone a deliberate but covert desire to impede or frustrate criminal procedures against guilty politicians, radicals, or those involved in racial disputes and other violence. This sort of muzzling strikes at the roots of our most precious freedoms—all this with the avowed purpose of preventing prejudicial publicity.

People in the press complain that the requirement that each such order be appealed is both costly and time-consuming. It frequently takes days or weeks to get a review and often the news is stale by then. Also, small newspapers cannot afford the legal expense of appealing each order that comes down the pike. Finally, many persons point out that these orders deny the public legitimate information, that the courts belong to the people and are not the sole province of either the legal profession or the judiciary.

For reporters there is but a single rule to remember with regard to restrictive orders: It is best to obey them until they are stricken or reversed. If reporters do not, a contempt citation will probably head their way. Sometimes disobedience is a proper way to gain review. However, in light of *Dickinson* and *CBS*, it is also an expensive way.

Writing in the *Southern California Law Review* ("Free Press-Fair Trial; The Gag Order: A California Aberration"), Robert S. Warren and Jeffrey M. Abell point out that when judges issue such orders they assume the role of the legislature, of the Supreme Court, of the executive head of local government, of the promulgator of rules of professional conduct, and of a censor of speech. "One can imagine the outcry from the legal community at comparable restraints emanating from the executive or legislative branch," they note.

But in some states the courts have taken a decidedly different route from the restrictive order. In these states most of the parties concerned think their idea is better.

BENCH-BAR-PRESS GUIDELINES

In nearly half of these United States members of the bench, the bar, and the press have attempted to alleviate the problems in press coverage of the judicial system by reaching agreement on the kinds of events that the press can publicize and the kinds of occurrences it should not publicize. Some states have had such guidelines for more than ten years. However, on record is an agreement between the City Court and the press in Burlington, Vermont, that was adopted in 1927:

> The City Court in a special way represents law and order in the community. The press can render large service in helping maintain general observance of law by wielding the power of its influence in creating and maintaining due respect for the City Court.

The free press-fair trial agreements of the 1970s are far more sophisticated than that statement. The Statement of Principles and Guidelines for the Bench-Bar-Press Committee of the State of Washington is one of the first free press-fair trial agreements and has worked exceptionally well during the past ten years. It is therefore a good example to consider in discussion of these agreements. The Washington State bench-bar-press agreement is a twelve-page booklet of guidelines for the reporting of criminal proceedings, grand jury proceedings, juvenile court proceedings, and civil proceedings. The guidelines for criminal proceedings are typical and demonstrate the thrust of the committee's work.

The guidelines open with a discussion of the role of the press in the proper administration of criminal justice. Specific suggestions are then presented. The committee states that is is appropriate for the press to make public the following kinds of information:

1. Biographical facts about the defendant including name, age, address, occupation, etc.
2. Substance or text of the charge
3. Identity of the investigating agency
4. Circumstances surrounding the arrest including time and place of arrest, resistance, pursuit, possession and use of weapons, and description of items seized by police.

These recommendations are followed by the suggestion that release of certain kinds of information can seriously prejudice a defendant's case without adding significant information to the public knowledge:

1. Opinions about the defendant's character, guilt, or innocence
2. Admissions, confessions, or alibis.
3. References to investigative procedures such as fingerprinting, ballistic tests, polygraph examinations, etc.
4. Statements about the credibility of witnesses
5. Opinions concerning evidence or arguments in the case

Finally, the guidelines suggest that publication of information about a prior criminal record can be highly prejudicial without adding significantly to the public's need to be informed. There are also suggestions regarding photographing the defendant, covering the trial, and using sensationalism in general.

The chief criticism levied against such guidelines is that they don't work, or that they don't work all of the time. This criticism is probably true. A recent study by the American Bar Association, however, suggests that guidelines may work better than their critics charge. The ABA reported that a substantial majority of newspaper editors, radio and television news directors, and bar association officials find the agreements are effective "in helping to protect the guarantees of fair trial and free press in crime news reporting."

Undoubtedly the guidelines don't work all the time nor in all states. In some states the bench, the bar, and the press meet to hammer out an agreement, and then disband and go their separate ways. Without any enforcement mechanism—and none of the guidelines have one—the guidelines are quickly ignored and become rather useless. In some states where the bench and the bar and press view their task as a continuing one the agreements are very effective. Again, Washington State is a good example to study.

The Bench-Bar-Press Committee in Washington has been a viable organization since 1966. It meets regularly to discuss problems in the general area of free press and fair trial. In addition, the committee periodically sponsors day-long seminars around the state to educate attorneys, reporters, and judges in application of the guidelines. The Washington Supreme Court is very active in its support of the committee, and the chief justice sits as chairman of the committee. This has the distinct effect of getting both trial lawyers and other judges to attend the seminars. Support by the state's leading newspapers is also helpful in getting reporters to attend. Discussion of libel and related press law problems is also a device used to lure the press to meetings so that a dose of free press-fair trial guidelines can be administered as well.

Also a subcommittee—called the liaison committee—of the state's bench-bar-press committee composed of a judge, an attorney, and a journalist acts as a special education group. The job of the committee is to respond quickly to immediate free press-fair trial problems. For example, a Seattle judge informed the press at the beginning of a trial that reporters would be excluded from certain portions of the trial. The reporters became angry, and the managing editor of one of the daily papers in Seattle immediately called the chairman of the bench-bar-press committee who in turn activated the liaison committee. The entire chain of events took about four hours. The judge who sat on the liaison committee called his colleague on the bench who had announced the trial closure. The committee member asked the judge if he realized that by closing the trial he violated provisions of the bench-bar-press agreement. He then informed the judge that it was his experience that the press can be trusted in situations like those and need not be excluded from a trial. The peer pressure worked. The trial judge called reporters into his chambers, told them he had changed his mind, and the trial would be open. But he asked the press to refrain from reporting certain sensational details of the testimony. The reporters honored his request. In other instances judges complained about newsmen, and the journalist on the liaison committee successfully applied the same kind of educational pressure on his colleagues.

This continuing work among the bench, the bar, and the press makes the Washington guidelines very effective. There are success stories in other states as well. The key factor which usually distinguishes between success and failure in application of guidelines is whether the dialogue and educational process among members of the group is continuing. Only one restrictive order has been handed down in Washington in the last seven years and it was overturned by the state supreme court, which urged the judge to read the guidelines. People in states in which guidelines work think their idea is a better solution.

CAMERAS AND TAPE RECORDERS IN COURTROOMS

In all but a handful of states in the United States the mass media are not allowed to bring cameras and tape recorders into courtrooms. Some states which are exceptions to this rule are Colorado, Oklahoma, Texas, Alabama, and Washington. The judicial rule against allowing photographic and sound equipment in courtrooms was passed in the 1930s when picture taking was a disruptive process. Flash equipment was needed, cameras were big and bulky, and photographers generally were rude and unruly. The American Bar Association adopted Canon 35, a canon of judicial ethics, which barred such equipment from courtrooms during trials. The bar in Colorado, Oklahoma, and Texas did not adopt Canon 35, and in Washington, Alabama and a few other states the rule was recently modified. In a handful of states the judge is allowed some discretion in permitting limited use of cameras. But basically the rule stands: No cameras in courtrooms.

By the sixties many journalists began to grouse about the regulations, arguing that photography with small 35-mm cameras using available light made the rule obsolete. The television industry argued that broadcast of a trial could be handled unobtrusively and was a First Amendment freedom. In 1962 in a big trial in Texas the press got its chance to show what it could do. As might be expected, the news media blew it.

The defendant was Billie Sol Estes who was accused of very fancy but illegal financial dealings. The story was a big one in the Lone Star

State and therefore television was permitted at the initial pretrial hearing and still photographers were permitted throughout the trial. The disruption was considerable. Twelve cameramen crowded into the tiny courtroom, cables and wires snaked across the floor of the room, lots of microphones were used, and distraction was significant. For the trial a booth to house the television and film equipment was built at the back of the courtroom. The situation improved, but not enough. Estes appealed his conviction on the ground that the picture taking denied him a fair trial. The question which finally confronted the United States Supreme Court was, Does the First Amendment give the press the right to take pictures—television, motion pictures, and still pictures—in a courtroom?

The high Court said no, at least not at the present time. "While maximum freedom must be allowed the press in carrying out this important function [informing the public] in a democratic society, its exercise must necessarily be subject to the maintenance of absolute fairness in the judicial process," wrote Justice Tom Clark for the majority (*Estes* v. *Texas,* 1965). Clark, who also authored the Sheppard decision the following year, said that this does not mean that cameras would always be banned from a trial. When technology permits cameras to be used without causing the present hazards to a fair trial, the situation will be different, Clark said.

These are the hazards Clark pointed out:

1. Interference with the jury—jurors might act differently if they know they are going to be televised and have to face community pressure.
2. Interference with witnesses—the quality of testimony could be impaired and witnesses might be embarrassed, frightened, intimidated, or demoralized. Witnesses who testify late in the trial could hear what witnesses who testify before them said.
3. Impact on the trial judge—he will have an extra burden in keeping photographers under control.
4. Impact on defendant—in its present form television can be a form of mental, if not physical, harassment resembling a police lineup or third degree.

Four justices dissented. Justice Potter Stewart wrote a dissent in which he said, "I cannot say at this time that it is impossible to have a constitutional trial whenever any part of the proceeding is televised or recorded on television film." But the 1965 decision in *Estes* v. *Texas* put the kibosh on cameras in courtrooms for the present except in those states which do not subscribe to Canon 35.

In 1972 the American Bar Association revised its *Canons of Judicial Ethics,* calling the new document the *Code of Judicial Conduct.* Section 3A(7) of the new code, which most states have adopted, suggests "a judge should prohibit broadcasting, televising, recording, or taking photographs in the courtroom. . . ." Nevertheless, the code permits the use of television equipment for presenting evidence, for making a trial record, and for other judicial administration purposes. Section 3A(7) also suggests that judges allow closed-circuit television broadcast of a trial to other rooms for press or spectators or to the defendant's cell if she refuses to behave in the courtroom. Closed-circuit broadcast can also be used for educational purposes.

By adopting this rule the ABA seems to acknowledge a fact that the press has argued all along, that photographing and recording a trial don't necessarily have to disrupt the proceedings. Experiments in both Colorado and Washington state demonstrated that photographic equipment is generally unobtrusive, and trial participants don't feel threatened, intimidated, or demoralized. The experiments were tightly controlled: the number of cameras allowed in the courtroom at any one time was limited and specific ground rules agreed to by the media were adopted.

Success in these experiments raises the hope that more states will begin to allow photographing and recording in courtrooms during trials. Nevertheless in the vast majority of the states in which the courts subscribe to Section 3A(7) of the *Code of Judicial Conduct* movie and still cameras, television cameras, and tape recorders are still banned from trials. Any attempt to use such devices can result in a swift contempt citation.

A good deal of space has been devoted to the free press-fair trial problem because it is an important problem and because it continues to be a problem. Within both the press and the law sharp divisions regarding solution of the problem remain. Many years ago during a battle over a free press-fair trial issue in one Southern state, the national office of the American Civil Liberties Union filed an amicus curiae (friend of the court) brief supporting a free and unfettered press while the state chapter of the same civil liberties group filed a brief in favor of the court's position supporting a fair trial.

Most journalists probably agree that we need more, not less, reporting on the justice system in the United States. In *Crime and Publicity* Friendly and Goldfarb write:

> To shackle the press is to curtail the public watch over the administration of criminal justice. . . . The press serves at the gate house of justice. Additionally, it serves in the manorhouse itself, and all

along the complicated route to it from the police station and the streets, to the purlieus of the prosecutor's office, to the courtroom corridors where the pressures mount and the deals are made.

The two authors also point out that we do not want a press that is free, more or less, just as we should not tolerate trials that are almost fair. "And to complicate the issue," they note, "it is evident that a free press is one of society's principal guarantors of fair trials, while fair trials provide a major assurance of the press's freedom."

Reporters dealing with the courts and the court system must be extremely sensitive to these issues. They should not be blinded as they clamor for news to the sensitive mechanisms which operate in the courts to provide justice and fairness. At the same time they should not let the authoritarian aspects of the judicial system block their effort to provide the information essential to the functioning of the democracy.

BIBLIOGRAPHY

Here are some of the sources that have been helpful in the preparation of chapter 7.

Books Advisory Committee on Fair Trial and Free Press. *Standards Relating to Fair Trial and Free Press.* New York: American Bar Association, 1966.

Advisory Committee on Fair Trial and Free Press. *Approved Draft Standards Relating to Fair Trial and Free Press.* New York: American Bar Association, 1968.

Bush, Chilton R., ed. *Free Press and Fair Trial: Some Dimensions of the Problem.* Athens: University of Georgia Press, 1971.

Friendly, Alfred, and Goldfarb, Ronald. *Crime and Publicity.* New York: Random House, Vintage Books, 1968.

Gillmor, Donald M. "Judicial Restraints on the Press." Freedom of Information Center, University of Missouri, 1974.

Judicial Administration Division. *Courts and the Community.* Salt Lake City: American Bar Association, 1973.

Pember, Don R. Pre-Trial Publicity in Criminal Proceedings: A Case Study. Master's thesis, Michigan State University, 1966.

Articles Gerald, J. Edward. "Press-Bar Relationships: Progress Since Sheppard and Reardon," 47 *Journalism Quarterly* 223 (1970).

Kline, Gerald, and Jess, Paul. "Prejudicial Publicity: Its Effect on Law School Mock Juries," 43 *Journalism Quarterly* 113 (1966).

Landau, Jack C. "The Challenge of the Communications Media," 62 *American Bar Association Journal* 55 (January, 1976).

Riley, Sam. "Pre-Trial Publicity: A Field Study," 50 *Journalism Quarterly* 17 (1973).

Simon, Rita. "Murders, Juries and the Press," May-June *Transaction* 40 (1966).

Warren, Robert S., and Abell, Jeffrey M. "Free Press-Fair Trial, The Gag Order: A California Aberration," 45 *Southern California Law Review* 51 (1972).

Cases *Estes* v. *Texas*, 381 U.S. 532 (1965).
Irvin v. *Dowd*, 366 U.S. 717 (1961).
Leviton v. *U.S.*, 193 F. 2d 848 (1951).
Marshall v. *U.S.*, 360 U.S. 310 (1959).
Miami Herald v. *Rose*, 271 So. 2d 483 (1972).
Murphy v. *Florida*, 95 S. Ct. 2031 (1975).
Nebraska Press Association v. *Stuart*, 96 S. Ct. 2791 (1976).
Oliver v. *Postel*, 282 N.E. 2d 306 (1972).
Pennekamp v. *Florida*, 328 U.S. 331 (1946).
People v. *Van Duyne*, 204 A. 2d 841 (1964).
Phoenix Newspapers Inc., v. *Superior Court*, 418 P. 2d 595 (1966).
Rideau v. *Louisiana*, 373 U.S. 723 (1963).
Schuster v. *Bowen*, 347 F. Supp. 319 (1972).
Seymour v. *U.S.*, 372 F. 2d 629 (1967).
Shepherd v. *Florida*, 341 U.S. 50 (1951).
Sheppard v. *Maxwell*, 384 U.S. 333 (1966).
State ex rel. *Superior Court* v. *Sperry*, 483 P. 2d 608 (1971).
Stroble v. *California*, 343 U.S. 181 (1952).
Sun Company of San Bernardino v. *Superior Court*, 29 Cal. App. 3d 815 (1973).
United Press Association v. *Valente*, 123 N.E. 2d 777 (1954).
U.S. v. *Burr*, 25 Fed. Cas. 49 No. 14692g (1807).
U.S. v. *CBS*, 497 F. 2d 102 (1974).
U.S. v. *Dickinson*, 465 F. 2d 496 (1972).
U.S. v. *Kobli*, 192 F. 2d 919 (1949).
U.S. v. *Tigerina*, 412 F. 2d 661 (1969).
Walker v. *Birmingham*, 388 U.S. 307 (1967).
Wood v. *Goodson*, 485 S.W. 2d 213 (1972).

CHAPTER 8

Journalists, Broadcasters, and Their News Sources

Imagine for a minute that you are the editor of a newspaper which has just published a thorough, revealing series of stories about conditions at a local hospital. Among the facts uncovered by your reporters are the filthy condition of the hospital, use of expired medications, excessive charges for services, use of untrained personnel to perform duties of registered nurses, and presence of three foreign physicians who are not licensed to practice medicine in the state, but who see patients, diagnose illness, and prescribe treatment.

Prosecutor John Smith announces that a grand jury will investigate the possibility of criminal negligence at the hospital. When you arrive at your office one day a process server hands you a subpoena requesting the pleasure of your company at the grand jury session Monday morning. Along with the summons is a note from the prosecutor telling you the panel is interested in knowing the sources of the information used in your series of stories on the hospital.

While some of the material was gathered firsthand by your staffers, hospital personnel provided much of the material. These people will likely lose their jobs if their identities are revealed. In fact your reporters promised the hospital employees that they would remain anonymous if they provided the information for the stories. What can you do?

1. Walk into the jury room with a copy of the Bill of Rights, read the First Amendment, and walk out.
2. Tell the grand jury that you won't be able to meet with it for several months because of pressing tennis engagements.

3. Tell the grand jury that you're no stoolie and that you're not going to help the cops.
4. None of the above.
5. All of the above.

The answer is number four. You must appear before the grand jury and in all likelihood answer all questions, or you can be held in contempt of court and jailed until you are willing to cooperate.

American journalists are no strangers to the confines of jail cells and prisons. In 1722 James Franklin, the less-publicized older brother of Benjamin Franklin, was jailed in a small cell for publishing a newspaper without the consent of the government of Massachusetts. He was the first of many journalists to see the inside of a jail cell. Until recently it was a fairly uncommon occurrence for a reporter to be imprisoned. Not true today. It seems that every few months a reporter or editor is jailed for refusing to cooperate with a grand jury or refusing to testify at a trial.

Why does the problem seem more acute today? Two or three factors are probably responsible. First is the changing social climate in the United States. The agitation and violence first of the civil rights movement, then of the antiwar movement, and now of the various radical movements have led to an increase in grand jury probes and secret investigations. The drug culture which blossomed during the last decade or so placed new pressures on the police and other law enforcement agencies. They were pushed to control the consumption of substances which many people believe to be harmless.

The press plays a key role in these controversies. The press can often gain access to information that law enforcement officials cannot. Reporters frequently are in direct contact with persons the law defines as fugitives or criminals. To the government, reporters frequently appear to be prime sources of potentially useful information in solving crimes, capturing felons, and stemming violence.

To some extent the press itself changed. Some newspapers—small underground papers—actually took a role in promoting drug use and radicalism. Other newspapers publicized such activities widely. Many reporters seemed less content to report only what the authorities told them; they felt compelled to talk to the persons who made the news—radicals, demonstrators, rioters, bomb throwers, and drug sellers and users. The press gained the confidence of these societal outs and became a valuable channel of information for the public. Again, legal authorities saw reporters as being able to get information that was denied to them.

Therefore the press, which had long enjoyed its imagined role as spectator of the legal process, suddenly became a participant with increasing regularity. Reporters throughout the United States were told to reveal what they knew about the activities of radicals or potheads or bombers, and the choice was most often to talk or to go to jail.

The interests involved in this problem are very basic to our system of government. No easy solutions are at hand. After his Senate committee had studied the issues involved in the controversy surrounding the reporter's claim of privilege for more than two months, former Senator Sam Ervin said that never had he dealt with a more difficult problem during his years in Congress.

It is every citizen's duty to testify before the proper authorities. This concept was so well established by the early eighteenth century that it had become a maxim. Wigmore, in his classic treatise on evidence (*A Treatise on the Anglo-American System of Evidence*), cites the concept thus: "the public has a right to everyman's evidence." The right to have witnesses and to compel them to testify is one of our cherished constitutional guarantees. The Sixth Amendment states, "In all criminal prosecutions, the accused shall enjoy the right to be confronted with the witnesses against him; and have compulsory process for obtaining witnesses in his favor." This is an important guarantee.

Suppose you were arrested for a crime you did not commit and that you had a witness who could prove you were fifty miles away at the time the crime was committed. How would you feel if your witness decided that he really didn't have time to go to court and testify? that he was too busy? that he didn't want to get involved? Your right to compel his testimony could be crucial to your freedom.

The Supreme Court has said on many occasions that it is a citizen's duty to testify. In 1919 the Court wrote as follows on the duties and rights of witnesses (*Blair* v. *U.S.*):

> [I]t is clearly recognized that the giving of testimony and the attendance upon court or grand jury in order to testify are public duties which everyone within the jurisdiction of the government is bound to perform upon being properly summoned, . . . the personal sacrifice involved is a part of the necessary contribution to the public welfare.

Most journalists do not dispute the immense societal value of the power to compel testimony, but they do argue that in most cases involving a reporter's sources society will benefit more if the reporter is not compelled to testify. Briefly the argument is this. The press is the eyes and ears of the people. Nothing should interfere with this role. The people must be informed; they must have access to the fullest information possible in order to operate properly as citizens in a democracy. Sometimes the only way a reporter can gain crucial information is to get it from an anonymous source. Why should there be anonymity? Take, for example, a defense department employee who discovers that a major defense contractor is bilking the government. His superiors seem unconcerned. He feels the people should know and therefore he tells the press. If his identity is revealed, he will probably be fired or demoted for making his superiors look foolish or for releasing classified information. If the press reveals the identity of this source not only will he be hurt, but also chances are great that the other employees will hesitate to step forward to reveal similar information in the future. The press argues that in this case the public loses a great deal just for revelation of the name of a single source.

Are news sources becoming reticent to talk for fear of exposure later? Studies by several researchers seem to indicate that they are. The Reporters Committee for Freedom of the Press conducted a study in 1973. The survey found that of the one thousand journalists surveyed one half said they used confidential sources regularly, and that a significant number of the reporters (nearly 40 percent of reporters covering the courts, for example) responded that their news sources were beginning to dry up because of the fear of exposure. In a study published in 1969 in the *Northwestern University Law Review* ("The Constitutional Argument for Newsmen Concealing Their Sources"), Mike Wallace, a reporter for the Columbia Broadcasting System, gave these reasons why a source might be reluctant to have his identity known: "fear of incurring the wrath of a superior, fear of losing a job, fear of losing a contract, and unwillingness to submit to the censure of colleagues for the expression of unpopular or unorthodox views."

The issue is quite simple: the right of the public to everyman's testimony versus the right of the public to full access to the news. This is not an easy choice by any means. The remainder of this chapter focuses upon the efforts of the press to gain a kind of exemption or privilege from the requirement of testimony. There are three sources in which such a privilege can be found. First is the common law, which will be studied to determine what, if any, precedents there are for a reporter's refusal to testify. Second is the constitutional provision of freedom of the press, which will be examined to see if it contains the exemption that journalists seek. Third are the efforts by state legislatures and the Congress to provide an exemption for journalists. After these sources of the privilege are examined, the policies of law enforcement agencies regarding the calling of journalists and witnesses are considered.

COMMON LAW RIGHTS

In some states the common law offers the privilege of refusing to testify to parties in various relationships. For example, spouses don't have to testify against their spouse. The attorney-client relationship is also privileged. In some states the privilege exists between a physician and a patient and between a clergyman and a penitent. The legislatures in many states have statutes to reinforce these common law rights.

While journalists often assert that such common law rights also exist for the press, I know of no court decision in which that right was accepted. In a case in New Jersey in 1913 a newsman made such an assertion in an effort to avoid revealing the name of a source for a story about graft in the village board of trustees. But the court wouldn't hear of such a thing (in re *Grunow*):

> In effect he pleaded a privilege which finds no countenance in the law. Such an immunity . . . would be far reaching in its effect and detrimental to the due administration of justice.

Somewhat more recently a United States federal court of appeals said about the same thing in the case of Marie Torre, a gossip columnist, who refused to reveal the source of a libelous remark about performer Judy Garland. "The privilege not to disclose relevant evidence obviously constitutes an extraordinary exception to the general duty to testify. . . . To recognize the privilege asserted here would poorly serve the cause of justice" (*Garland* v. *Torre*, 1958).

In truth, the privilege sought by journalists is somewhat different from the privilege granted in other instances. The privilege between a lawyer and a client, for example, is stated in such a way that the attorney cannot testify, not that he doesn't have to testify. Reporters have always sought the opportunity to choose not to testify, not a mandate forbidding testimony.

In other cases the privilege belongs to the client or the patient or the penitent. She can waive it and allow the attorney or physician or clergyman to testify. With regard to the journalist, the privilege belongs to him, not to the source. In the case of the privilege between lawyer and client or doctor and patient, both parties are known to the court; the communication between these parties is what remains confidential. In the case of journalists, normally the communication between the parties is known—it has been published or broadcast—it is the identity of the second party which is unknown. Such is not always the case, for journalists are called into court and before grand juries with increasing frequency to reveal not only who said something, but also what was said in addition to what was printed in the newspaper or broadcast on television.

These differences make the argument against common law recognition of the privilege for journalists fairly persuasive. If journalists are to get help for their problem, it is going to have to come from elsewhere.

**CONSTITU-
TIONAL
RIGHTS**

The First Amendment to the Constitution guarantees the freedom of the press. A very narrow view of that right is that it guarantees the right to publish, and no more. For at least the past half century journalists have argued for a broader interpretation: that the First Amendment includes the right to publish, the right to be free from discriminatory taxes, the right to freely distribute, the right to criticize the government, and so forth. In most instances journalists have won their arguments in courts, except for one very important issue—the right to gather the news. Until very recently there was but one reported decision supporting the notion that the right to gather the news is one of the First Amendment freedoms. It was a 1950 federal district court ruling in Providence, Rhode Island (*Providence Journal Co.* et al. v. *McCoy* et al., 1950).

The argument that the First Amendment grants to journalists a privilege to refuse to testify before grand juries and in courts is based on the rather tenuous legal principle that the First Amendment protects the reporter's right to gather the news. The argument is this. If a reporter is forced to reveal the names of confidential sources or other confidential information, his ability to use such sources in the future will be damaged. In turn his ability to gather the news will be impeded, which is a violation of the freedom of the press guaranteed by the First Amendment. While ancillary arguments are also used, this is the basic position taken by journalists who seek to use the First Amendment as justification for refusing to testify.

Marie Torre (mentioned earlier) used this argument in 1958 when she refused to name the source of a libelous remark about Judy Garland which she published in her gossip column in the *New York Herald Tribune*. The federal court of appeals pushed the argument aside, writing (*Garland* v. *Torre*, 1958):

> The concept that it is the duty of a witness to testify in a court of law has roots fully as deep in our history as does the guarantee of a free press. It is at the very foundation of the Republic. This duty sometimes impinges on the First Amendment freedoms of the witnesses. In these instances the First Amendment liberty must give way to a paramount interest in the fair administration of justice.

Other courts say basically the same thing, and reporters who use this argument go to jail until they agree to testify or are freed by the court. How long is a jail term? The jail sentences are usually open-ended. If the reporter refuses to testify before a grand jury, the jail sentence can last until the grand jury is dismissed, that is, for six months or a year. Moreover there is nothing to prevent the judge from calling a new grand jury, asking the reporter the same questions, and rejailing him for refusal to talk. If the reporter is in violation of a court order, the jail term can technically last until the judge leaves the bench or dies. Such a prospect faced William Farr, a young California journalist who refused to tell a Los Angeles Superior Court judge which of Charles Manson's attorneys had given him material which violated the court's restrictive gag order. A California appellate court finally ruled that if Farr could convince the trial judge that keeping him in jail would not force him to change his mind and testify the judge should then release the reporter. Farr did this, and Judge Older fined him and sentenced him to five additional days in jail, after which he would be free. Farr appealed the additional sentence. Despite the fact that sentencing is open-ended, reporters rarely serve more than thirty days in jail. Farr's forty-six-day term is the longest on record. But any jail time is hard time, especially when you are in jail only for doing what you believe is your job. (The *Farr* case is also discussed from the standpoint of the shield law on pp. 306-307.)

Not until recently has the press had limited success in using the First Amendment argument in newsman's privilege cases—even though the Supreme Court ruled that the privilege has no First Amendment right. If this state of affairs seems strange, it is. To understand it we must first focus on the ruling of the high Court.

Branzburg Ruling　　The most important ruling of the decade on the newsman's privilege was handed down by the Supreme Court in 1972. The case was really three cases, *Branzburg* v. *Hayes,* in re *Pappas,* and *U.S.* v. *Caldwell.* Today, the Court's decisions are referred to collectively as the *Branzburg* ruling.

Paul Branzburg was a staff reporter for the *Louisville Courier-Journal.* In 1969 and 1971 he wrote two stories about drug use in Jefferson County, Kentucky. In the first story he described in detail his observations of two young men synthesizing hashish. When he was called before a grand jury, he refused to identify the two individuals in his story, citing both the Kentucky reporters' privilege statute which he claimed exempted him from having to give testimony and the First Amendment. A Kentucky appellate court rejected his First Amendment argument and ruled that while the state's statute afforded a reporter the privilege of refusing to divulge the identity of a confidential source it did not give the reporter the right to refuse to testify about events he had witnessed personally. The second story was about drug use in Frankfort County, Kentucky, and the court rejected Branzburg's arguments a second time when he refused to testify before a Frankfort County grand jury. He appealed to the Supreme Court.

Paul Pappas was a reporter for a New Bedford, Massachusetts, television station. In July 1970 he was assigned to cover civil disturbances in an area near the headquarters of the local Black Panther organization. That afternoon he gained access to the Panther's headquarters and recorded and photographed a prepared statement read by one of the Black Panthers. He returned to Panther headquarters that evening and was allowed to spend three hours with members of the black militant organization as they waited for an anticipated police raid upon their headquarters—a raid which failed to materialize. As a condition of entry into Panther headquarters Pappas agreed not to disclose anything he saw or heard there. He was called to testify before a Bristol County grand jury, but he refused to answer questions about what took place inside the Panther headquarters, citing his privilege under the First Amendment. Massachusetts courts rejected his argument.

Earl Caldwell worked for the *New York Times* in 1970, an era in which there was significant public concern about the militancy of the Black Panthers. The press succeeded in fueling this fear by publishing masses of misinformation. Earl Caldwell, who was black, had gained the confidence of Black Panther leaders in Oakland, California, and consistently provided readers of the *Times* with accurate, illuminating accounts of the organization. It was probably natural, then, that when a federal grand jury began investigating the Panthers Earl Caldwell was subpoenaed and told to bring his notes and audiotapes. Caldwell refused, arguing that giving information to the government would destroy his ability to report on the Black Panthers, that none of the leaders would ever again take him into their confidence or even talk with him.

A federal district court partially supported Caldwell's plea. It said that he would not have to answer questions unless in each case the government could demonstrate that "a compelling and overriding national interest" would be served by Caldwell's answer to a question and that no alternative means of getting the information was available. The court based its ruling on the strong First Amendment interests which it said were at the core of the issue.

Caldwell and the *New York Times* were not satisfied, for the ruling still required the reporter to answer some questions. Since the proceedings were secret, the Panthers would never know which questions Caldwell answered and which questions he did not answer. Caldwell appealed to the Ninth Circuit Court of New York and again won. This time the court ruled that when it is shown that the public's First Amendment right to be informed will be jeopardized by requiring a journalist to submit to a secret grand jury interrogation the government must respond by demonstrating a compelling need for even the witness's presence before attendance can be required. The court added that this case was very unusual since most news sources aren't as sensitive as the Black Panther organization and most reporters don't enjoy such unique trust and confidence of news sources. Still, the ruling was a significant First Amendment victory for the press. Such a victory, in fact, that the government appealed the ruling to the Supreme Court.

The Court was badly split in its decision on the three cases. Four justices voted against the constitutional privilege, four voted in favor of the constitutional privilege, and Justice Lewis Powell voted in favor of the constitutional privilege in some circumstances, but not in these cases. Let us look first at the votes against the privilege.

Justice Byron White wrote the opinion of the court to which Chief Justice Warren Burger, Justice William Rehnquist, and Justice Harry Blackmun subscribed. White said that while the Court was sensitive to First Amendment considerations the case did not present any such considerations. There were no prior restraint, no limitations on what the press may publish, and no order for the press to publish information it did not wish to. No penalty for publishing certain content was imposed. White wrote (*Branzburg* v. *Hayes*, 1972):

> The use of confidential sources by the press is not forbidden or restricted. . . .
> The sole issue before us is the obligation of reporters to respond to grand jury subpoenas as other citizens do and answer questions relevant to an investigation into the commission of crime. Citizens generally are not constitutionally immune from grand jury subpoenas; and neither the First Amendment nor other constitutional provisions protects the average citizen from the disclosing to a grand jury information that he has received in confidence.

Reporters are no better than average citizens, White concluded.

The four dissenters differed sharply with the other justices. Justice Potter Stewart wrote, "The Court's crabbed view of the First Amendment reflects a disturbing insensitivity to the crucial role of an independent press in our society."

Justice Douglas took the view that the First Amendment protection provides the press with an absolute and unqualified privilege. But Justice Stewart, Justice William Brennan, and Justice Thurgood Marshall offered a kind of qualified privilege. They said that before a reporter can be forced to testify the government should fulfill the following requirements:

1. Show that there is probable cause to believe that the reporter has information that is clearly relevant to a specific probable violation of the law.
2. Demonstrate that the information sought cannot be obtained by alternative means less destructive of First Amendment rights.

3. Demonstrate a compelling and overriding interest in the information.

When the government cannot fulfill all three requirements, Justice Stewart wrote for the dissenters, journalists should then not be forced to testify.

Justice Lewis Powell's enigmatic concurrence with White, Burger, Blackmun, and Rehnquist left most observers puzzled. Powell said that his decision to support the requirement to testify was limited to legitimate grand jury probes. He said that no harassment of newsmen will be tolerated and that where legitimate First Amendment interests require protection the Court should protect them. The associate justice said that a balance must be struck between freedom of the press and the obligation of all citizens to give relevant testimony. "The Court," Powell added, "does not hold that newsmen, subpoenaed to testify before a grand jury, are without constitutional rights with respect to the gathering of news or in safeguarding their sources."

What did Justice Powell mean? In this case the Supreme Court said at the very least that news gathering is protected by the First Amendment, according to Justice White. Many observers, however, see far greater implications. They argue that Justice Powell's cryptic comments suggest that in circumstances other than legitimate grand jury probes he will join the four dissenters to support a qualified constitutional privilege for journalists.

For those of you who like to have loose ends tied up: By the time the Supreme Court had heard the appeals the grand juries in both California and Massachusetts had been dismissed and Caldwell and Pappas were out of trouble. Kentucky still wanted Branzburg, however, but he had gone to work for the *Detroit Free Press,* and the state of Michigan refused to extradite him to Kentucky.

Lower Court Rulings

One way to look at the meaning of a Supreme Court opinion is to see how the lower courts interpret it. Such examination is only somewhat helpful in the *Branzburg* v. *Hayes* opinion. The lower courts also seem to be confused. The important factor, however, is that the lower courts do not hesitate to quash subpoenas and grant the constitutional privilege. This action suggests that the courts seem to take seriously the notion just outlined that five members of the high Court favor a qualified privilege. First, let's look briefly at a few cases in which the courts upheld the reporter's request for the privilege.

In 1973 the Democratic party brought a civil action to win damages for the Watergate break-in. Ten reporters from the *New York Times, Washington Post, Washington Star-News,* and *Time* magazine and other publications were subpoenaed and told to bring their tapes, notes, letters, documents, and all other materials obtained during their reporting of the Watergate break-in. Upon a motion by the reporters the district court quashed the subpoena, noting that the press is entitled to at least a qualified privilege under the First Amendment (*Democratic National Committee* v. *McCord*, 1973):

> There has been no showing by the parties that alternative sources of evidence have been exhausted or even approached as to the possible gleaning of facts alternatively available from the Movants [reporters] herein. Nor has there been any positive showing of the materiality of the documents and other materials sought by the subpoenas.

A Florida state court cited the *McCord* decision a few weeks later when it quashed a subpoena against the *Miami News* in which the defendants in a civil suit sought confidential materials used by the newspaper to prepare an editorial blast against them. In *Spiva* v. *Francouer* (1973) the court said enforcement of the subpoena has a chilling effect on freedom of the press and can cause the newspaper's sources to dry up.

Finally, in *U.S.* v. *Calvert* (1974) a federal court quashed the subpoena of a Columbia Broadcasting System newscaster in St. Louis who correctly predicted in advance that a grand jury would indict a local man for mail fraud. The defendant in the mail fraud case sought the name of the reporter's source, but the court refused to grant the request.

The privilege has also been held to apply in a few libel cases too. Perhaps the best known is *Cervantes* v. *Time* (1972) which involved a $12-million libel action against *Life* magazine for publishing a story which suggested that the mayor of St. Louis, Alfonso Cervantes, had underworld connections. The mayor wanted to know the names of the sources in the Federal Bureau of Investigation and Justice Department who supplied the information to reporter Denny Walsh. Cervantes said he could not prove malice without these names.

However the information about the mayor was a small part of the story, which was extremely well documented. The charges against Cervantes comprised only four paragraphs of the eighty-seven-paragraph story. The court of appeals ruled, "To compel a newsman to breach a confidential relationship merely because a libel suit has been filed against him would seem inevitably to lead to an excessive restraint on the scope of legitimate newsgathering activity." The court said that if the plaintiff was able to provide persuasive evidence that this information was crucial to the question of malice the privilege might then have to give way. However, in this case "The mayor has wholly failed to demonstrate with convincing clarity that either the defendant acted with knowledge of falsity or reckless disregard of the truth." There was just no reasonable probability that the plaintiff would succeed in proving malice.

The same conclusion was reached in *Baker* v. *F & F Investment* (1972). In this case Alfred Balk, a former writer on the *Saturday Evening Post*, had written an article on blockbusting in Chicago. In an action filed in federal court charging a real estate firm with discrimination, Balk was called as a witness and asked to reveal the sources of information for his article. He refused, and the federal court of appeals upheld his refusal. The court said the plaintiff in the civil suit had not exhausted other sources of information, that the disclosure by Balk was not essential to protection of the public interest, and that the material sought did not go to the heart of the matter at issue in the case. Judge Kaufman wrote (*Baker* v. *F & F Investment*, 1972):

> While we recognize that there are cases—few in number to be sure—where First Amendment rights must yield, we are still mindful of the preferred position which the First Amendment occupies in the pantheon of freedoms. Accordingly, though a journalist's right to protect confidential sources may not take precedence over that rare overriding and compelling interest, we are of the view that there are circumstances, at the very least in civil cases, in which the public interest in non-disclosure of a journalist's confidential sources outweighs the public and the private interest in compelled testimony.

The supreme courts in both Vermont and Virginia ruled that the First Amendment grants a limited privilege to journalists. In the Vermont case (*State* v. *St. Peter*, 1974) reporter John Gladding refused to reveal the confidential source who tipped him off in advance about a police drug raid. The Virginia Supreme Court upheld a reporter's refusal to reveal a confidential source of a story he wrote about a murder case. The defendant in the case wanted to use the reporter's source in an attempt to impeach a witness for the state. The court said that since the information sought was not at the heart of the issue in the trial the First Amendment took precedence (*Brown* v. *Commonwealth*, 1974).

Decisions such as these cheer the heart of most journalists. Unfortunately the lower courts are not always so accommodating.

Brenda Presley and Sherrie Bursey were reporters for the Black Panther newspaper. They wrote a story about a speech by Panther leader David Hilliard in which he either did or did not threaten former President Richard Nixon. They were called to testify before several grand juries. Although the reporters always answered some of the questions, they refused to answer all queries regarding confidential information and information regarding management of the Panther paper. The government presented sufficient evidence to convince the district court that there was a compelling and overriding national interest, and the women were called to testify. They refused to answer fifty-six different questions. On appeal, the Ninth Circuit Court of Appeals of California ruled that the two reporters had to answer seventeen of the fifty-six questions (*Bursey v. U.S.*, 1972). The court said the women did not have to answer queries about the people who worked at the newspaper or about how the paper was edited, but they did have to answer questions about whether they had seen firearms and explosives at Panther headquarters and about whether the Panther leaders conducted discussions concerning violent activities. The government interests were legitimate and compelling, the court said, and infringement upon the First Amendment was incidental.

In another Watergate-related case, *U.S. v. Liddy* (1973), defendant G. Gordon Liddy subpoenaed a taped interview conducted by the *Los Angeles Times* with Alfred Baldwin, a minor player in the Watergate conspiracy. Liddy sought to use the tape to impeach Baldwin's testimony at the trial. A federal district judge refused to quash the subpoena, saying the defendant's right in this case to attempt to impeach testimony against himself outweighed the First Amendment.

In a case related to the disappearance of Patty Hearst, the manager of radio station KPFK in Los Angeles was held in contempt for refusing to surrender to a grand jury investigating the matter the original tapes and letters received from the Symbionese Liberation Army. Will Lewis gave authorities copies of the tapes and letters, but refused to surrender the original tapes. The Ninth Circuit Court of Appeals of California ruled that the grand jury was conducting a legitimate law enforcement investigation and that fact outweighed the First Amendment considerations (in re *Lewis*, 1974).

The privilege has also failed in libel suits. In 1974 Edward Carey, a former general counsel for the United Mine Workers, sued Jack Anderson for libel in regard to a column in which Anderson alleged that Carey and former United Mine Workers president Tony Boyle were seen taking records improperly from Boyle's office. Britt Hume, one of Anderson's reporters, testified that he had got the information from an employee of the United Mine Workers, but refused to reveal the employee's name. The court of appeals said in this case the information went to the heart of the plaintiff's suit and was critical to the claim of malice. The court said it was unreasonable to ask the plaintiff to interview all the United Mine Workers employees to get the information (*Carey v. Hume*, 1974). In distinguishing this case from the *Cervantes* case the court said it was not unlikely that Mr. Carey would win his suit.

Finally, in a libel suit against the *Wall Street Journal*, the Massachusetts Supreme Judicial Court ruled that there was no privilege to protect the newspaper from revealing the name of the source of its story charging that a local land developer had a bad reputation because he wanted to build an apartment house in an area zoned residential. The court ruled in *Dow Jones* v. *Superior Court* (1973), "The obligation of newsmen, we think, is that of every citizen, viz., to appear when summoned, with relevant written or other material when required, and to answer relevant and reasonable inquiries."

What is the meaning in all of these cases? One would have to agree with Prof. David Gordon who believes that even several years after the Supreme Court ruled on the issue of the newsman's privilege, "The status of the constitutional law, and the law in general on this topic, is much less than totally clear."

In 1975 in the *Hastings Law Journal* ("Branzburg v. Hayes and The Development of a Qualified Privilege for Newsmen") attorney James Goodale suggests these generalizations about the status of the constitutional privilege:

1. If reporters have witnessed a crime, the courts will usually require their testimony.
2. If reporters have possible criminal evidence in their possession, courts will frequently require them to produce that evidence.
3. In the context of other criminal matters, the matter of privilege depends upon the case and the other sources available.
4. In civil cases, reporters are generally excused from having to testify unless their information goes to the heart of the issue.

Many persons feel that the constitutional privilege is not strong enough for the press to rely upon. These persons think the answer to protecting the press is to pass comprehensive shield laws, or statutes which guarantee the privilege.

LEGISLATIVE RIGHTS (SHIELD LAWS)

In 1896 Maryland granted journalists a limited privilege to refuse to testify in court proceedings. Since then more than half of the fifty states have passed what the press refers to as a shield law. These laws set down in specific terms what the privilege entails, who may use it, and when it may be used. Some laws are nearly absolute. For example, the Alabama Shield Law provides:

> No person engaged in, connected with, or employed on any newspaper (or radio broadcasting station or television station) while engaged in a news gathering capacity shall be compelled to disclose, in any legal proceeding or trial, before any court or before a grand jury of any court, or before the presiding officers of any tribunal or his agent or agents, or before any committee of the legislature, or elsewhere, the sources of any information procured or obtained by him and published in the newspaper (or broadcast by any broadcasting

station or televised by any television station) on which he is engaged, connected with, or employed.

The laws in some states are qualified far more and prohibit use of the privilege in libel suits, for example, where the information might be material to the proof of malice. The privilege might also be denied in cases in which it is essential to prevent justice going astray, in which an overriding public interest is at stake, and in which reporters witness a crime. In some states the statutes are so filled with exceptions that at best the protection is of minimal value.

While shield laws can be effective in warding off unwanted and unnecessary subpoenas, they often create problems rather than provide protection. On the pages that follow some of the problems besetting state shield laws are set out.

1. The existing state shield laws are not very consistent from state to state. In California, for example, the manager of an FM radio station refused to answer questions before a grand jury concerning the murder of Marcus Foster, Oakland school superintendent. The station became involved in the case when it received a letter from the Symbionese Liberation Army claiming credit for the killing. The California Supreme Court ruled that the state's shield law protected the broadcaster and he did not have to testify (in re *Foster*, 1974). In a similar case in New York radio station WBAI was forced to give up a letter it had received from a radical group. The New York court said the state's shield law did not protect the station employees (in re *WBAI-FM* v. *Proskin*, 1973).

Enactment of a federal shield law is one way many people suggest to solve the problem of inconsistency. Congress would pass a law displacing all state laws in order to ensure protection of Fourteenth Amendment rights, that is, freedom of the press. This solution seems unlikely, however, since Congress has been considering a shield law which covers only federal courts and other federal proceedings for four or five years and has not yet voted on the law. In the early 1970s when reporters first started going to jail in droves, several bills were introduced in the House and Senate, but there was little consensus on a single bill. Moreover the press hasn't done a very good job of selling the idea of a shield law to the Congress, as discussion of the second problem of shield laws will show.

2. Much of the public and many journalists remain unconvinced of the need for laws which guarantee the newsman's privilege. A considerable number of journalists take the position that regardless of the Supreme Court position at the moment the First Amendment does protect reporters and the protection is absolute. They believe it is foolish to ask Congress for a qualified privilege when the guarantee of freedom of the press already gives the reporter an absolute protection.

A large segment of the public views the privilege as exactly that—a privilege for newsmen that other people are denied. If a citizen refuses to testify, she goes to jail. Why shouldn't a journalist also be jailed? The press, or perhaps journalists, has not done a good job of explaining the purpose of such laws to the public. Average citizens see the "shield" only as a law which protects journalists. The shield should also be viewed as a law which conceals sources of information, which protects anonymous informers from retribution from colleagues, employers, enemies, and even friends. The fundamental purpose of the law is to keep information flowing to the public. Secrecy of the source must be assured so that journalists will never have to make the decision to testify or to go to jail. Sources must be able to give information to reporters regardless of whether journalists have an iron constitution to withstand legal attack or are somewhat faint of heart, choosing to testify rather than to face a cold, dark jail cell. A shield law ensures that reporters will never have to face such a choice. The general public does not understand this aspect of the legislation and fails to see that in the end it will also benefit.

3. Shield laws suffer from definitional problems. That is, what a specific section of a law means depends upon the court interpreting it. Look at the Alabama law, for example. In the first sentence note the reference to newspapers: "No person engaged in, connected with or employed on any newspaper." What is a newspaper? The *New York Times* is a newspaper. A suburban weekly which covers the village government and schools is a newspaper. What about a militant propaganda sheet published by a radical group? Is it a newspaper? In Los Angeles among the requirements to qualify as a newspaper and have reporters get police press passes, according to the police and sheriff's departments, a publication must undertake "regular gathering and distribution of hard-core news generated through police and fire activities." The police say that the coverage of what they call "sociological news—riots, demonstrations, assassinations, news conferences" does not qualify a publication to be a newspaper.

Not all communities define a newspaper so narrowly. Defining a newspaper and its function is a real issue, however. Is the man who mimeographs a four-page newsletter and distributes it on street corners once a week publishing a newspaper? What about pamphlets? Do they qualify as newspapers? Many people say no before they remember the important role of pamphlets in our history, especially during the revolutionary period.

4. Even the so-called absolute shield laws are rarely absolute. Exceptions that can trap journalists are always present. Most shield laws protect reporters only with regard to information gained while they are

engaged in a "news-gathering capacity." If reporters are given information on their day off, or if someone approaches them with a tip after working hours, the law probably would not protect them. Doctors may be on duty twenty-four hours a day, but reporters are generally not believed to be that dedicated.

Frequently reporters are protected by the law only when they receive information secondhand. Reporters who are witness to criminal activity are required by law to testify.

In Maryland, home of the nation's oldest shield law, a reporter wrote a story about being offered a joint of marijuana by a clerk in a store. He was called by the grand jury and asked the name of the clerk and of the store. He refused to give the names and argued that the shield law protected him. The court said no, that in this case he had witnessed a crime and *he* was the source. The story was based on his firsthand account (*Lightman* v. *State*, 1972). Paul Branzburg got into trouble the same way, for Kentucky had a shield law. The courts ruled that Branzburg was a witness to a crime when he watched the hashish being synthesized. There was no other source. Two reporters in New York found out the same thing. Stewart Dan and Roland Barnes of television station WGR-TV were inside Attica during the prison riots in 1972. They were questioned by a grand jury and asked what they saw. They refused to tell, using the state's shield law as a defense. They lost. The court said the New York law protects news sources, not reporters who witness crimes (*People* v. *Dan,* 1973).

5. The fifth problem concerning shield laws is perhaps the most serious of all. Many courts don't like shield laws and therefore interpret the laws as narrowly as possible to force reporters to comply with subpoenas or with judges' instructions. For example, in New Jersey reporter Peter Bridge was called before a grand jury and ordered to give the unpublished details of his interview with a housing commissioner in Newark, New Jersey, who claimed she had been offered a bribe. Bridge attempted to use the state's shield law, but was unsuccessful. The court said that since the source of the story was already known and since Bridge had already revealed some information about the interview he had waived his right to use the privilege. Bridge spent twenty days in jail (in re *Bridge,* 1972).

One of the most perplexing of all the shield law cases is one mentioned earlier, the case of William Farr. The case is a classic example of how a shield law can sometimes prove to be absolutely worthless. In 1970 Farr, a reporter for the *Los Angeles Herald-Examiner,* was assigned to cover the trial of Charles Manson and his followers. A restrictive order was in effect during the trial prohibiting trial participants from releasing the contents or nature of all testimony given at the trial. During the trial a witness gave a member of the prosecution a written statement that one of the defendants in the case, Susan Atkins, had confessed to the crimes for which she and the rest of the Manson clan were being tried. Copies of the statement were prepared and given to each of the attorneys in the trial. One of them gave a copy to Farr who published it as part of a story in the *Herald-Examiner.* At the conclusion of the trial the judge convened a special hearing to determine the source of Farr's story. Called as a witness, Farr refused to identify the attorney who had given him the copy of the statement. Farr argued that he did not have to testify because of the California shield law, but the court ruled that the privilege did not apply to Farr because at the time of the hearing he was no longer a reporter but worked as a press aide to the Los Angeles district attorney. In addition, the California district court of appeals ruled that even though Farr was a working journalist the shield law was inapplicable because its use would interfere with the right of the trial court to enforce its edicts and control the conduct of participants at the trial: "To construe the statute as granting immunity to petitioner, Farr, in the face of the facts here present would be to countenance an unconstitutional interference by the legislative branch with an inherent and vital power of the court to control its own proceedings and officers" (*Farr* v. *Superior Court,* 1971). In other words, the people of California have no business giving journalists this privilege if it interferes with the work of the courts.

Farr went to jail. His appeal to the federal courts failed. In 1974 the California court of appeals, in an effort to keep the reporter out of jail but still uphold the judges contempt power, ruled that at some point Farr's imprisonment would become punitive rather than be likely to force disclosure of his source. At that point California law limits the prison term to five days (in re *Farr,* 1974). So Farr returned to the trial court and convinced the judge that more time in jail would not overcome his refusal to testify. Because there was no substantial likelihood that Farr would disclose his sources he was sentenced to five additional days in jail, fined $500 on each contempt count, and no longer held in contempt.

Shield laws are obviously not the be-all and end-all to the problem. Such laws are probably better than nothing, but not much better in some states.

SUBPOENA GUIDELINES

While it can hardly be called a satisfactory solution to the problem faced by journalists who seek to protect the identity of sources, the federal government has made an attempt to at least placate the press on the problem reporters and their news sources. In the early 1970s the Department of Justice issued guidelines which United States attorneys must follow before they can subpoena journalists. A summary of the guidelines follows.

---

1. There must be prior negotiation with the journalist before the subpoena is issued.

2. If the negotiations fail (if the reporter won't provide the material voluntarily) the attorney general must approve the subpoena based on the following guidelines:

    a. There must be sufficient evidence of a crime from a nonpress source. The Department does not approve of using reporters as springboards for investigation.

    b. The information the reporter has must be essential to a successful investigation—not peripheral or speculative.

    c. The government must have unsuccessfully attempted to get the information from an alternative nonpress source.

    d. Great caution must be exercised with respect to subpoenas for unpublished information or where confidentiality is alleged.

    e. Even subpoenas for published information must be treated with care because reporters have encountered harassment on the grounds that information collected will be available to the government.

    f. The subpoena must be directed to specific information.

The guidelines have worked fairly well. In a thirty-month period following initiation of the guidelines the justice department sought thirteen subpoenas. The attorney general denied their request seven times because of noncompliance with the guidelines. The guidelines have weaknesses as well. They can be canceled at any moment by the Attorney General, and probably would be if major social upheaval were to erupt again as in the late 1960s when push came to shove. There are definitional problems, for example, who is a reporter? The guidelines apply only to criminal cases, not to civil suits and not to legislative and administrative hearings. Nevertheless, they are better than nothing. In several states, local prosecutors have also adopted similar rules to guide the issuance of subpoenas in their communities.

Despite the subpoena problem, in most areas there is a good deal of cooperation between the press and the police on these kinds of matters. At the federal level, for example, a public information officer in the Department of Justice said that in 1972 of the twenty-eight subpoenas issued by the department in the previous three years, twenty-six were requested by journalists who were willing to testify, but wanted to be subpoenaed so that it would not appear they were overly cooperative. In some local communities newspapers and broadcasting stations routinely supply the police with photographs and information—in exchange, of course, for favors in news gathering such as tips on breaking cases.

For working reporters about the only really important point to remember is that chances are better than fifty-fifty that when they are called to give evidence they will either have to cooperate or face a jail sentence. While this truth is not very comforting, conditions can always be worse. Some small progress has been made during this decade in providing protection for journalists in certain situations. Of course there is always the chance that the Supreme Court will react differently to the next privilege case it decides and will determine that there is a limited constitutional privilege.

Until that time, however, journalists must live with the fact that news gathering can at times be hazardous.

BIBLIOGRAPHY
These are some of the sources that have been helpful in the preparation of chapter 8.

Books Gordon, David. *Newsman's Privilege and the Law.* Columbia, Mo.: Freedom of Information Center, 1974.

Wigmore, John Henry. *A Treatise on the Anglo-American System of Evidence in Trials at Common Law.* 2d ed. Boston: Little, Brown & Co., 1934.

Articles Blasi, Vince. "Press Subpoenas: An Empirical and Legal Analysis," 70 *Michigan Law Review* 229 (1971).

Goodale, James C. "Branzburg v. Hayes and the Development of a Qualified Privilege for Newsmen," 26 *Hastings Law Review* 709 (1975).

Guest, James, and Stanzler, Alan. "The Constitutional Argument for Newsmen Concealing their Sources," 64 *Northwestern University Law Review* 18 (1969).

Cases *Baker* v. *F & F Investment,* 470 F. 2d 778 (1972).

Blair v. *U.S.,* 250 U.S. 273 (1919).

Branzburg v. *Hayes,* 408 U.S. 665 (1972).

In re *Bridge,* 295 A. 2d 3 (1972).

Brown v. *Commonwealth,* 204 S.E. 2d 429 (1974).

Buchanan v. *Cronkite,* Civ. No. 1087-73 (DDCE, 1974).

Bursey v. *U.S.,* 466 F. 2d 1059 (1972).

Carey v. *Hume,* 492 F. 2d 631 (1974).

Cervantes v. *Time,* 446 F. 2d 986 (1972).

Democratic National Committee v. *McCord,* 356 F. Supp. 1394 (1973).

Dow Jones v. *Superior Court,* 303 N.E. 2d 847 (1973).

Farr v. *Superior Court,* 99 Cal. Rptr. 342 (1971).

In re *Farr,* 111 Cal Rptr. 649 (1974).

In re *Foster* (Alameda County, California Superior Court, March 28, 1974).

Garland v. *Torre,* 259 F. 2d 545 (1958).

In re *Grunow,* 85 Atl. 1011 (1913).

In re *Lewis,* No. 74-2170 (9th Circ. July 19, 1974).

Lightman v. *State,* 294 A 2d 149 (1972).

In re *Pappas,* 266 N.E. 2d 297 (1971).

People v. *Dan,* 41 App. Div. 2d 687 (1973).

Providence Journal Co. et al. v. *McCoy,* et al., 95 F. Supp. 186 (1950).
Spiva v. *Francouer,* 39 Fla. Supp. 49 (1973).
State v. *St. Peter,* 315 A 2d 254 (1974).
U.S. v. *Calvert,* No. 74-107 (ED Mo. April 26, 1974).
U.S. v. *Liddy,* 345 F. Supp. 208 (1973).
In re *WBAI-FM* v. *Proskin,* 42 App. Div. 2d 5 (1973).

CHAPTER 9

Obscenity, Pornography, and Other Dirty Words

311

The contemporary journalist rarely takes on a censor over a question of obscenity. Erotic material is just not a large part of the mainstream mass media in the United States today. About the sexiest things in most newspapers are the movie advertisements, and such display advertisements are frequently liberally doctored by newspaper artists who are adept at painting clothing on naked females and by rewrite men who clumsily revise film titles to excise naughty words or double entendres. Occasionally, however, a journalist, usually a loner, the publisher of an underground newspaper or a counterculture magazine, runs afoul of obscenity laws. Sometimes in such cases "professional journalists" have little sympathy for the plight of their "less respectable" colleagues: "After all, if he hadn't published that junk in the first place, he wouldn't be in trouble. And what does that have to do with news anyway." To those journalists and to other persons who think that journalists shouldn't be worried about obscenity convictions, the words uttered by Judge Cuthbert Pound more than fifty years ago are appropriate, "Although the defendant may be the worst of men . . . the rights of the best men are secure only as the rights of the vilest and most abhorrent are protected" (*People* v. *Gitlow,* 1921).

Perhaps more salient is Harry Clor's question concerning obscenity and pornography in *Obscenity and Public Morality.* "Why," Clor asks, "in an age which is not lacking in life-and-death issues must we continue to wrestle with this one?" The author goes on to answer his own question by arguing that vital issues lurk beneath the surface of this seemingly nonsensical dilemma. And, he noted, the problem of obscenity "manifests a strange capacity to arouse the interest, engage the passions, and enlist the efforts of large numbers of Americans." How right Clor is, for even today in a so-called age of reason it is very difficult to engage in a discussion of obscenity and pornography without the conversation quickly descending to the level of emotionalism and witless jabber.

The problem of obscenity is truly interesting, at least for a while. We do not intend to present an exhaustive report on the subject in these few pages. Instead, a brief introduction to the issue is provided, the history of the law of obscenity in the United States is highlighted, and the ways in which the Supreme Court has defined obscenity are discussed. Then we will consider how the law operates in real life at the local level and briefly note some aspects of both postal censorship and film censorship.

OBSCENITY DEFINED

There is great disagreement about what is and what is not obscene. A flower child who papers his walls with photographs of nude couples in various states of recline might consider war and violence obscene. To a man who thinks that shooting at kids who try to steal melons from his patch is big sport and who likes his killing in slow motion at the drive-in movie, any nudity at all is degenerate. While the university student might think the profits made by oil companies are "obscene," a stockholder in an oil company might think it obscene for a student to live in a commune with six other men and women. And so it goes.

Definitions for obscenity can be found in many places. In reputable dictionaries among the meanings for the word *obscene* is "indecent, lewd, or licentious." In turn, we will find *licentious* to mean "lewd or lascivious." Further research shows that *lascivious* means "inclined to be lewd or lustful." *Lustful* proves to mean "having lewd desires." Finally, *lewd* turns out to mean "indecent or obscene." We have come full circle.

The courts themselves have been in a constant state of confusion over the matter of obscenity. In 1948 the Ohio Court of Common Pleas wrote (*State* v. *Lerner*):

> Obscenity is not a legal term. It cannot be defined so that it will mean the same to all people, all the time everywhere. Obscenity is very much a figment of the imagination—an indefinable something in the minds of some and not in the minds of others, and it is not the same in the minds of the people of every clime and country, nor the same today that it was yesterday and will be tomorrow.

Former Justice of the United States Supreme Court John Marshall Harlan expressed a similar kind of frustration when he warned, "Anyone who undertakes to examine the Supreme Court's decisions since *Roth* which have held particular material obscene or not obscene would find himself in utter bewilderment" (*Ginsberg* v. *New York*, 1968). Harlan referred at least partially to the fact that between the Roth case in 1957 and 1968 when he wrote that comment the high Court had published signed opinions in thirteen obscenity cases. Fifty-four separate opinions were published in those thirteen cases!

Social scientists also recently entered the definitional fray. Some persons believe that sociologists and psychologists have the correct answers today. Probably the most well-known definition of pornography was made by Eberhard and Phyllis Kronhausen in their study *Pornography and the Law.* The researchers said that the main purpose of pornography is to stimulate an erotic response. They also listed several characteristics of pornography, among which were heavy emphasis on the physiological responses of participants, heavy emphasis on aberrant or forbidden forms of sexuality, heavy sadism and passive submission, and unrealistic presentation of both sexual activities and sexual capacities. Anthropologist Margaret Mead defined pornography as "words or acts or representations that are calculated to stimulate sex feelings independent of the presence of another loved and chosen human being." But even these kinds of definitions contain little precision and little agreement. Sexual aberrations which stimulate some persons nauseate others. The clothed body is far more erotic to some people than is naked flesh.

The general governmental response to obscenity and pornography (whatever these words mean, they are used interchangeably in this chapter) has been to pass laws against it. There are federal laws, state laws, city laws, county laws, township laws, and so forth. There are laws against importing obscenity, transporting it in interstate commerce, mailing it or broadcasting it over the radio and television. There are laws against publishing it, distributing it, selling it, displaying it, circulating it, and even possessing it if you plan to distribute it, sell it, display it, or circulate it.

The fact that obscenity is such an elusive concept to define makes prosecution extremely difficult sometimes. An obscenity case is not like a bank robbery, or like most other crime for that matter, where everyone agrees that a criminal act has occurred (i.e., a bank robbery) and the legal debate is about whether the defendant is the robber. In an obscenity case there is usually agreement that the defendant did commit the act (i.e., sold a book or showed a movie). The debate is over whether what the defendant did was a criminal act, whether the book was obscene or not.

The ambiguities in the law also make life less than certain for book-sellers and theater operators. They really can never be certain whether a local jury will rule that the books in the morning mail are obscene, and whether selling a copy of such books is a criminal act.

Why is obscenity banned? For many persons this is the $64 question. Many police believe that pornography is somehow tied to sexual crimes although there is very little evidence to support the notion. Many persons argue, as we will note later in this chapter, that dissemination of pornography and obscenity has a deleterious impact upon communities. This argument also has really little scientific evidence to support it. At the same time there is little evidence to support the argument of persons who oppose obscenity laws that distribution of the material has no impact at all. In fact, one of the interesting little quirks that pop up in academe on occasion relates to this problem. Some of the same people who insist that publication or broadcast of obscene material is harmless also insist that broadcast of violence on television is harmful.

Probably the best reason to explain why obscenity is banned is that it has been banned for more than one hundred years, and once a good suppression is started it is hard to stop. Once an obscenity law goes on the books it usually stays there, often virtually unenforced. Nevertheless, legislators rarely vote for repeal of an obscenity law. To many constituents a vote for repeal is a vote for obscenity. That could be a heavy cross to bear during an election.

HISTORY OF OBSCENITY LAW

The Puritans weren't the first to pass laws against obscene books and pictures. There is some confusion about obscenity laws during the colonial period because many persons argue that pre-Revolutionary laws against blasphemy also prohibited obscenity. However, the best evidence available doesn't support this argument.

Some of the other facts we know, or don't know, about pornography in the eighteenth and early nineteenth centuries are these.

Substantial amounts of pornography were in circulation at that time, some of it homegrown, much of it imported. As busy as he was, Benjamin Franklin still had time to write erotic literature.

We don't know whether the drafters of the First Amendment ever considered including obscenity within the First Amendment protections. Justice William Brennan of the Supreme Court says obscenity is not included in the protection of freedom of the press. Unfortunately, he is the only one who knows that fact for certain.

We know that the law was not too concerned about the circulation of such matter. The first obscenity prosecution in the history of the United States didn't occur until 1815 when a man named Jesse Sharpless was fined for exhibiting a picture of a man "in an imprudent posture with a woman." Earlier, other persons were tried for offenses tied to obscenity, but they were tried under the common law for theological crimes against God, not for merely displaying erotic pictures. In 1821

Peter Holmes was convicted for publishing an edition of John Cleland's *Memoirs of a Woman of Pleasure,* better known to us as *Fanny Hill.* Although the book was first published in 1740, the prosecution in Massachusetts was based not on the original version, but on an edition in which Holmes added both more explicit text and pictures.

In the late 1820s and 1830s the nation experienced the first strong attack on obscenity when several states passed laws limiting the distribution and sale of such material. Why should obscenity laws be passed at that particular period in our history? No one knows for certain, but numerous contemporary events and conditions may have been factors. This was a period of popular reform movements such as abolition, prohibition, and women's rights. This was also a time in which universal free education made great strides and more people were able to read, thereby increasing the market for erotic literature. The changes in printing technology which made publishing of books and magazines less expensive could also have resulted in wider distribution and visibility of erotic material. The more visible and widespread such material became, the better target it also became for reformers. Laws were the result.

The first of dozens of federal laws was passed in 1842. It was a customs law and prohibited importation of obscene paintings, lithographs, engravings, and so forth. The law was amended many times to prohibit more and more kinds of materials. The first postal law was passed in 1865, but it was an ineffective measure because the government had no authority to exclude material from the mails, only to bring a prosecution after the shipment was delivered. In 1873 a more effective law was adopted. This was largely the handiwork of Anthony Comstock, whom some authorities have described as a psychopathic reformer who got a thrill from suppressing what other people liked. First it was liquor that Comstock sought to snuff out. Then he attacked prostitution. To him there was no such thing as erotic art, only pornography. With the help of the Protestant leaders in New York and the Young Men's Christian Association, Comstock succeeded in gaining passage first of a New York law against obscenity and then in 1873 of a federal law, the so-called Comstock Law. After passage of the bill Comstock was named a special agent for the Post Office Department, and he worked with his Committee for the Suppression of Vice for more than forty years to stamp out smut. As a kind of incentive the government gave Comstock a percentage of all the fines collected on successful prosecutions based on his work. It has been suggested that he may be the first man to make a million dollars from pornography.

The 1873 law was simple: All obscene books, pamphlets, pictures, and so forth, were declared to be nonmailable. Violation of the law could result in a fine of $5,000 and five years in jail for the first offense and $10,000 and ten years for each offense thereafter. The Congress did not define obscenity, however, but left that to the courts.

After passage of this spate of laws in the late nineteenth century the country underwent a terrible seventy-year period of censorship of erotic material. The censors tended to lump all erotic work into one huge pile of prohibited material. They made no attempt to distinguish art from smut—Boccacio's *Decameron* from *The Dance with the Dominant Whip* or from other junk literature. The Post Office Department banned books on sex education as well as medical journals which dealt with sexual problems. The *American Journal of Eugenics* (the study of hereditary improvement) was declared nonmailable at one point because it carried an advertisement for a book entitled *The History of Prostitution*. The *Journal* wasn't obscene, but the book advertised in its pages was considered offensive. The *Journal* therefore was not allowed to be sent through the mails.

In the 1930s the Post Office Department banned among other books John O'Hara's *Appointment in Samara,* Hemingway's *For Whom the Bell Tolls,* and nearly everything that Erskine Caldwell wrote. In the forties the list included *From Here to Eternity, Butterfield Eight,* and *Memoirs of Hecate County.* Lots of girlie magazines, humor magazines, scandal magazines (e.g., *Confidential*), and even a skin diver's manual (because it contained pictures of several female divers with breasts exposed) were barred from the mails, and the publishers were often prosecuted.

The postal service used various devices in addition to prosecution as means of controlling pornography. It attempted to strip some publications of their second-class mailing subsidy because they failed to publish work that was for the public good. Obscenity was not for the public good, postal officials claimed. This ploy failed after a time (see *Hannegan* v. *Esquire,* 1946). The Post Office Department also used the mail block against publishers whose magazines contained solicitations for erotic materials. For example, if a magazine advertised that a reader could order an erotic book by sending $2 to the publisher, the postal service stopped delivering mail to the publisher in order to deprive him of those book orders. He received no mail at all! Not his electric bill, his bank statement, nothing. The courts declared this action illegal, but the post office continued the practice for several years (*Walker* v. *Popenoe,* 1945). According to Patricia Robertus in her study of the Post Office Department ("Postal Control of Obscene Literature, 1942-1957"), postal regulations were so restrictive that in the early 1940s a magazine with the power of *Esquire* took advance copies of both stories and layouts to postal authorities to see whether they met postal standards of mailability. In some instances postal officials asked for changes and got them. This is informal prior censorship at its boldest.

Laws against importation were also prosecuted vigorously, and customs agents, until the 1930s at least, rarely discriminated between works that were art and works that were trash. Consequently, there are scores of horror stories of customs officials destroying art works, art catalogs, religious works, and other materials which they believed to be obscene.

This can only be described as an awful period in the cultural history of the United States. Closely parallel is the struggle for freedom of the press that radicals and labor leaders endured (recounted earlier in this book), with one exception: whereas the Supreme Court grew more tolerant of aberrant political and economic philosophy, it showed little tolerance for erotic materials. Except for striking down some of the Post Office department's most outrageous censorship techniques, the high Court stayed out of the fray, leaving the lower courts to work out the definition of obscenity and construct constitutional guidelines. That is, the Supreme Court stayed out until 1957 when it entered the controversy wholeheartedly (*Roth* v. *U.S.*) and has been there ever since, attempting to explain to judges, lawyers, censors, writers, artists, filmmakers, and other people what the term *obscenity* means when used by the Court. As you will no doubt conclude after reading the next section, the efforts of the Court in this endeavor have not been terribly effective.

FEDERAL STANDARDS   It has been left to the American courts to define what is and what is not obscene. The Supreme Court alone has been at this job for more than twenty years, and in the view of many observers the Court hasn't really succeeded. Often in public but nonjudicial statements, members of the high Court express growing disenchantment with becoming what Justice Robert Jackson once called "the high Court of obscenity." As long as there are laws which prohibit sale, distribution, publication, and so forth, of obscenity, someone must decide what is and what is not obscene. Since the Supreme Court decided twenty years ago that the First Amendment protection of freedom of the press was never intended to include obscenity (*Roth* v. *U.S.*, 1957) it is perhaps fitting and proper that the high Court, like the ancient mariner, be plagued by the albatross of defining obscenity.

The Supreme Court borrowed and devised various tests in the past century in its frequent attempts to describe obscenity definitively. None of the tests have been satisfactory, but some were worse than others. The fatal defect in each test is that it is made up of words, words which mean different things to different people. For example, the test in use today declares that if a work has serious literary value it is not obscene. What does serious literary value mean? A comic book may have serious literary value for some people. At the other end of the spectrum, even professors of English literature haggle among themselves about whether some of the classics really have serious literary value. What we are faced with, therefore, is a dispute over not only the kinds of works which are obscene, but also the meaning of the words which the courts use to define obscenity.

In this section while the main focus is on the three primary tests fashioned by the Supreme Court for use in obscenity prosecution—the *Hicklin* rule, the *Roth-Memoirs* test, and the *Miller-Hamling* test—a number of secondary tests as well as the President's Commission on Obscenity and Pornography are discussed.

The Hicklin Rule   The first widely-used American test of obscenity was the Hicklin rule. The U.S. Supreme Court borrowed the Hicklin rule from British law when it was called upon to undertake an early interpretation of the 1873 postal statute on obscenity. Benjamin Hicklin was the recorder of London who presided over an obscenity trial in that city in the 1860s. He ruled that the pamphlet in question was not obscene, but on appeal by the government, a higher court reversed the decision. Lord Chief Justice Alexander Cockburn handed down a ruling which included a definition of obscenity, a definition which poor Benjamin Hicklin's name has been attached to ever since (*Regina* v. *Hicklin*, 1868).

The *Hicklin* rule says that a work is obscene if it has a tendency to deprave and corrupt those whose minds are open to such immoral influences and into whose hands it might happen to fall.

Look at the elements of this test for a moment. First, a work is obscene if it has a tendency to deprave and corrupt. It doesn't have to deprave and corrupt, but only a tendency to deprave and corrupt is required; that is, it might deprave and corrupt. You can decide for yourself what *deprave* and *corrupt* mean. The second aspect of the test was even deadlier for authors and painters. Whom must the work have a tendency to deprave and corrupt? Those whose minds are open to such influences, in other words, anyone who runs across the book or drawing. Children's minds are obviously open to depravation and corruption from obscenity. Children might also run across such works in a library or at a bookstore. Therefore, the Hicklin rule comes down to this: If a book might have an impact upon a child or an extremely sensitive person, it is obscene and no one can read it. The *Hicklin* rule reduced the population of the nation to reading what was fit only for children.

In adopting the *Hicklin* rule American courts also decided that if any part of a book or play or magazine or whatever was obscene, the entire work was then obscene. Selected passages which might be harmful to children could result in an entire book or magazine being banned. While the tests that the Supreme Court developed in the past twenty-five years cannot be called extremely liberal, compared to the *Hicklin* rule they provide virtually absolute freedom. The *Hicklin* rule was an extremely onerous test which was used for about seventy-five years. This test was what made prosecution of obscenity so easy in the twenties, thirties, and forties, and success in prosecution made government censors even more aggressive in rooting out "filth" and "smut."

In 1957 the Supreme Court wrote the obituary for the *Hicklin* rule when it declared that condemning the adult population to read only what children might safely read was unconstitutional (*Butler* v. *Michigan*, 1957). Various lower courts had tentatively reached this conclusion in the preceding fifty years, but the *Hicklin* rule remained law in most jurisdictions.

Roth-Memoirs Test

The 1957 decision in *Butler* was the first of a long series of high Court rulings which by 1966 had fashioned a new test for determining obscenity. Although it wasn't apparent in the beginning, the key cases, *Roth* v. *U.S.* in 1957 and *A Book Named John Cleland's Memoirs of a Woman of Pleasure* v. *Massachusetts* in 1966 (and a dozen or so lesser decisions in between) resulted in liberalizing the law with regard to obscenity (see, for example, *Manuel Enterprises* v. *Day*, 1962 and *Jacobellis* v. *Ohio*, 1964).

In 1957 the high Court announced definitively that obscenity is not protected by the First Amendment. Justice William Brennan, who was to be the chief architect of the high Court's new obscenity standards during the next nine years, wrote that while all ideas which have even the slightest redeeming social importance are entitled to the full protection of the First Amendment obscenity and pornography were not included within this protection. In the *Roth* decision Brennan wrote, ". . . implicit in the history of the First Amendment is the rejection of obscenity as utterly without redeeming social importance."

By placing obscenity beyond the pale of First Amendment protection the Court silenced those persons who believed the clear and present danger test should be used for determining obscenity as well as for determining dangerous political speech. Since obscenity is not guaranteed the protection of freedom of the press, the clear and present danger test does not apply. What is obscene then? In the *Roth* case Brennan said that a work is obscene if, to the average person, applying contemporary community standards, the dominant theme of the material taken as a whole appealed to prurient interest. The Court continued to reshape this test slightly until 1964 when in the *Memoirs* case the test evolved into the three-part definition which was used for nearly seven years. Under the *Roth-Memoirs* test, before a court can rule that a work is obscene, three requirements must be met.

First, the dominant theme of the material taken as a whole must appeal to prurient interest in sex. Implicit in this part of the test is the concept that the prurient (erotic) appeal of a book or film is determined by its impact upon the average man or woman, not upon a child or an extremely sensitive person. Also, the dominant theme of the work, not just selected passages or a few pages, must have this prurient appeal.

Second, a court must find that the material is patently offensive because it affronts contemporary community standards relating to the description or representation of sexual matters. Something that is patently offensive is something that is clearly indecent, and while we are hesitant to use this term, some people have argued that *patently offensive* means hard-core pornography. By contemporary standards the Court meant current standards, but the Court did not define what it meant by community: were the standards local, state, or national?

Third, before something can be found to be obscene it must be utterly without redeeming social value. That means to have no social value at all.

Two aspects of this test should be noted: First, all three of these elements had to be present before something was obscene. Something that was patently offensive and had a prurient appeal was still not legally obscene if it had redeeming social value. All three elements must coalesce. Second, it was not a balancing test. Social value was not weighed against prurient appeal. If there was any social value at all, the material was then not obscene. And this fact, probably more than any other, made prosecution of obscenity cases very difficult. Utterly without redeeming social value is a difficult standard to prove. Some appellate court judges believed that if even only one or two persons found some value in a book or movie it was not *utterly* without redeeming social value. Consequently, the typical tack taken by defense attorneys was to bring in expert witnesses—psychiatrists, English professors, art critics, and the like—to testify that the work had some value as sexual therapy or as an example of a certain type of literature or art.

As liberal as the *Roth-Memoirs* standard was, it was not liberal enough for some civil libertarians. Absolutists argued that because of the First Amendment the government had no business telling people what they could read or watch. The First Amendment prohibition which says there is to be no law abridging freedom of speech and press means no law. Judge Jerome Frank, who heard the *Roth* case in the court of appeals, argued that restrictions against obscenity were extremely dangerous (*U.S. v. Roth,* 1956):

> If the government possesses the power to censor publications which arouse sexual thoughts, regardless of whether those thoughts tend probably to transform themselves into anti-social behavior, why may not the government censor political and religious publications regardless of any causal relation to probably dangerous deeds?

Justice Brennan, who constructed the *Roth-Memoirs* test, dismissed such criticism. There is no social value to obscenity, he said, and therefore society loses little if it is banned. But by 1973 Brennan appeared to have changed his mind. In a long dissent from the high Court's rulings in a series of obscenity cases Brennan wrote that in 1957 he had assumed "incorrectly, as experience has proven, that obscenity could be separated from other sexually oriented expression without significant cost either to the First Amendment or to the judicial machinery charged with the task of guarding First Amendment freedoms." Brennan said that attempts to define obscenity one way or another and exclude it from the protection generally accorded to speech and press "cannot bring stability to this area of the law without jeopardizing First Amendment fundamental values." The Justice added that no formulation or test can reduce vagueness to a "tolerable level while at the same time striking an acceptable balance between the protection of freedom of speech and press on the one hand, and on the other the asserted state interest in regulating the dissemination of sexually oriented materials." (*Paris Adult Theatre I* v. *Slaton,* 1973.)

Between 1957 and 1973 a majority of the high Court argued that obscenity should be restricted because it lacks social value. In 1973 and 1974 the high Court took a more aggressive position and ruled for the first time that obscenity should be banned because it may be harmful, as discussion of the *Miller-Hamling* test will shortly show.

Commission on Obscenity and Pornography

Strangely enough, also between 1957 and 1973 a presidential commission studied the questions of whether obscenity should be banned and specifically whether evidence exists that pornography might be harmful, might produce antisocial behavior.

In 1967 the Commission on Obscenity and Pornography was established, at least in part, because of the judicial and scientific uncertainty regarding the effects of obscenity on persons who consume it. The commission, which was made up of social scientists, religious leaders, and government officials, spent two million dollars and two years studying what some observers called the puzzle of pornography. At the end of the study a majority of the commission—twelve of the seventeen members—concluded that there is no evidence that viewing obscenity produces harmful effects and recommended that all laws restricting the consumption of such materials by consenting adults be repealed. Three members of the commission field a vigorous dissent and two others said they believed the evidence, but didn't think it was sufficient to warrant the repeal of all laws.

The study was roundly criticized by persons who disagreed with its conclusions—rightly so in some cases. There were no long-range studies on the effects of exposure to pornography, for example, and no in-depth clinical studies. In some of the surveys people were asked blatantly foolish questions. For example, one survey asked people if they had experienced a breakdown in morals or had gone "sex crazy" from viewing explicit sexual material. Who would say yes to those questions? Patients at mental hospitals were questioned regarding the influence of pornography on sex crimes they had committed.

The single survey which received the widest publicity was the one which discovered that 60 percent of the persons questioned believed that adults should be able to read and watch whatever they want. However to another question in the same survey, 73 percent of the respondents said that sex scenes in movies that merely titillate should be censored. Moreover, in 1969 both the Harris and Gallup polls found that about 80 percent of the people wanted stiffer controls on obscenity and pornography.

Regardless of what the commission found or of the flaws in its research, its recommendations were never adopted. The Senate rejected the report out of hand and Richard Nixon, who was president at that time, vowed that so long as he was in the White House there would be no relaxation of the national effort to control and eliminate smut from our national life. Nixon noted that despite the commission's scientific evidence to the contrary, "centuries of civilization and ten minutes of common sense tell us otherwise. . . . American morality is not to be trifled with."

In 1973 and 1974 a majority of the Supreme Court apparently agreed with the president. In a series of five, five-to-four decisions, the high Court reshaped the test for obscenity and forged various other rulings that will have an impact upon the law for years to come.

Miller-Hamling Test

The most important impact of the case law during 1973 and 1974 is the new obscenity test. In his opinion in the case of *Miller* v. *California* (1973), Chief Justice Warren Burger made much of the fact that it was the first time a majority of the Supreme Court had agreed upon a test for obscenity since the *Roth* case in 1957. The new test has three parts, just as in the former test.

First, a court must find that an average person applying contemporary community standards would find that the work taken as a whole appeals to prurient interest. This is quite similar to the previous test, with one important exception: in the *Miller* case the Court said that the community standards to be applied are local community standards, not an imaginary national standard. Before examining the implications of this change let's look briefly at the next two parts of the test.

The second element a court must find before material can be deemed obscene is that the work depicts or describes in a patently offensive way sexual conduct specifically defined by the applicable state law. This part also has implications which are noted shortly.

Third, the work in question must lack serious literary, artistic, political, or scientific value. The utterly without redeeming social value test was junked.

The high Court's definition of community standards is one of the key elements of *Miller* v. *California*. Although the Court has never subscribed to a national standard, many persons believed that only a national standard was workable.* The issue here is complex. How is it possible for Hollywood to make a movie, for example, to play in various cities across the United States if each town has a different standard for obscenity? On the other hand, some persons argued that it is silly to suggest that the people in a small town in New Mexico share the same values or standards as people in New York City.

The issue was solved in *Miller*. The following year the Court amplified its 1973 decisions and clarified the community standards question somewhat. In *Hamling* v. *U.S.* (1974), Justice William Rehnquist wrote that the jurors are entitled to rely on their own knowledge of standards in their community in determining community standards. Rehnquist added:

> This Court has emphasized on more than one occasion that a principal concern in requiring that a judgement be made on the basis of contemporary community standards is to assure that the material is judged neither on the basis of each juror's personal opinion nor by its effect on a particular sensitive or insensitive person or group.

The jurors, then, are not supposed to use their own standards. Each juror is instead to draw on his own knowledge of the standards of the average person in that community.

This ruling does not really clarify the problem to any significant extent and has been criticized by some authorities. For example, although

---

*In 1964 in *Jacobellis* v. *Ohio*, as author of the Court's opinion Justice Brennan subscribed to the idea of a national standard, but Justice Arthur Goldberg was the only justice joining Brennan in subscribing to this standard. The other seven members of the Court either rejected the standard or did not comment on it at all.

it might make sense for different states to have different standards, how can federal law be applied? In prosecutions for importation of obscene material, can a federal court in Detroit apply one definition of obscenity based on the community standards in that city and a federal court in Los Angeles apply a different standard based on the mores of that community? Federal Judge Harold Leventhal, writing in the *American Bar Association Journal,* fears the growth of what he calls "fiefdoms of intolerance," noting:

> Since *Miller* permits a state option to prohibit distribution, the proper construction of federal law is to prohibit only those items as obscene that could not be vindicated in *any* [author's emphasis] substantial community market. That materials would pass muster in, say, New York and California, if established by evidence of persons knowledgeable as to their standards, would be enough to avoid federal interdiction without prejudice to prohibition by other states. . . .

Another commentator, Richard Shugrue, believes that whatever community standards are used the government should be forced to introduce evidence of those standards at the trial. Writing in the *Creighton Law Review* ("An Atlas for Obscenity: Exploring Community Standard") he cites a California case in which the conviction of a topless dancer was overturned because the state failed to show that the defendant's conduct exceeded the customary limits of candor as to affront the standards in the community. The court said (in re *Giannini*, 1972):

> To sanction convictions without expert evidence of community standards encourages the jury to condemn as obscene such conduct or material as is personally distasteful or offensive to the particular juror.

Shugrue went on to argue that since appellate courts must make independent decisions as to the obscenity of the material and do not constitute a cross section of a community (may not even be located in the same community), it is impossible for them to carry out their responsibilities without evidence directed toward proof of the community mores.

Rulings 1973-1974

In its 1973-1974 opinions the Supreme Court did not head in the direction of the in re *Giannini* ruling just noted by Shugrue. In fact the Court seems to be heading in a different direction altogether.

In two of the 1973 cases, *Kaplan* v. *California* and *Paris Adult Theater I* v. *Slaton,* the high Court ruled that the prosecution need not introduce expert testimony as to the obscenity of the material in question. Chief Justice Burger said that the materials themselves are the best evidence of what they represent. This new approach which places heavy emphasis on the jury in obscenity cases assumes that the jurors know the prevailing standards in the community as well as have the needed exposure to what one commentator calls "all manner of descriptions or representations of sexual matters, whether spoken, written or performed." Both of these assumptions are probably wrong and can be dangerous.

Still, the jury does not have complete control, as the high Court indicated in *Jenkins* v. *Georgia* in 1974. This decision relates directly to the second element of the *Miller-Hamling* test, that the material must describe or depict in a patently offensive way sexual conduct specifically defined by applicable state law. Several factors are involved here. First, censorship is limited to materials depicting sexual conduct, sexual conduct which is patently offensive. Some people say that this means hard-core pornography and they are probably right. Shortly after the *Miller* decision was handed down, a jury in Georgia found the movie *Carnal Knowledge* to be obscene and the high court of that state upheld this ruling.

The United States Supreme Court reversed the ruling, saying that the Georgia courts obviously misunderstood the *Miller* decision. The jury did have the right to determine local standards, but only those descriptions or depictions of sexual conduct that are patently offensive can be censored, regardless of local standards. Justice Rehnquist noted that in the *Miller* case Chief Justice Burger gave two examples of the kind of patently offensive material he was talking about. These examples included "representations or descriptions of ultimate sexual acts, normal or perverted, actual or simulated," and "representations or descriptions of masturbation, excretory functions, and lewd exhibition of the genitals." Rehnquist said that while this catalog of descriptions was not exhaustive, it was "intended to fix substantive constitutional limitations . . . on the type of material . . . subject to a determination of obscenity" (*Jenkins* v. *Georgia*, 1974). Therefore, under the second part of the *Miller* test, the jury is limited in what it can find to be obscene to what some commentators call hard-core pornography. In fact the National Data Center on the Law of Obscenity, a federally funded organization in California which advises local prosecutors on obscenity prosecutions, issued bulletins to prosecutors to the effect that the *Miller-Hamling* test limits district attorneys to proceeding against material which can be legitimately classified as hard-core pornography.

The second aspect of the test to be noted is this: Chief Justice Burger said the descriptions or depictions of sexual conduct which are banned have to be specifically defined by the applicable state law as written or authoritatively construed. This sounds as though before a state can prohibit a description of a certain kind of sexual conduct the state must pass a specific law defining that kind of material.

How specific does the applicable state statute have to be? Not very.

The high Court approved an Ohio statute which defined material as being obscene if it contained a display or description of nudity, sexual excitement, sexual conduct, bestiality, extreme or bizarre violence, cruelty, brutality, or human bodily functions or eliminations.

What if a state law does not define obscenity? What if it merely prohibits "obscene materials"? This is really not a problem, according to Justice Burger, who ruled that it is sufficient in such states if the state supreme court rules that the term *obscene materials* in the law means specific descriptions of sexual conduct. By mid-1975 nearly twenty state supreme courts had ruled that the obscenity statutes in their states were specific enough to meet the *Miller* standards, either as written by the legislature or as construed by the courts. In six states, courts held that the laws were too vague and ruled them unconstitutional under the *Miller* test (Illinois, Indiana, Iowa, Louisiana, New Jersey, and Wisconsin).

In *Miller-Hamling* by abandoning the utterly-without-redeeming-social-value test the high Court makes it much easier for the government to ultimately win cases. Bringing in evidence that something lacks serious value is far easier than proving that it is utterly without redeeming social value, as we shall see.

Of the important aspects of recent high Court rulings, none is more important than the clarification by the high Court of the very ambiguous 1969 *Stanley* v. *Georgia* ruling. There is some question whether the *Stanley* case is really an obscenity case. Police officers, armed with a search warrant which allowed them to look for gambling paraphernalia, entered the home of Robert Stanley and found three reels of pornographic film in a desk drawer. Stanley was convicted for possession of obscene material and sentenced to one year in prison. The case was appealed to the Supreme Court. During the oral argument it became apparent that the justices were troubled by several aspects of the case. First was the severity of the penalty. Also troubling was the lack of evidence that Stanley had ever shown the films to anyone. His unrefuted testimony was that a friend gave them to him and suggested that he look at them sometime. There was no evidence that he knew what kind of movies they were, except that they were stag films. There was no way for police to determine that the movies were pornographic without showing them, and this exceeded police authority under the search warrant. Only the title of one of the films, *Youngblood,* was on the cannister.

The Supreme Court ruled in Stanley's favor, saying that a person has a right to possess and use obscene materials in the privacy of his own home.

While this ruling might make good sense, it did raise more questions than it answered. To wit: If a man has a constitutional right to possess obscenity for his own use, can he buy it for his own use, and can he import it so long as it is only for his own use? Furthermore, if a person has a right to view obscene movies in the privacy of his own home, what about the privacy of adults-only motion-picture theaters? Aren't they private places? Lower courts began to acquit obscenity defendants on the basis of such logic (see, for example, *U.S.* v. *Articles of Obscene Merchandise,* 1970 and *Stein* v. *Batchelor,* 1969). But the Supreme Court halted that practice in 1973. In *U.S.* v. *Orito* (1973) the high Court said that transporting films across state lines is illegal and a defendant in such a case cannot claim the special considerations given to one's home. Congress has a right to prevent obscenity from entering the stream of commerce, Chief Justice Burger said. The same is true of importation, according to the decision in *U.S.* v. *12 200-ft. Reels of Super 8 mm. Film* (1973). What about the privacy of adult theaters? No, Chief Justice Burger said, theaters have always been regarded as public places, not private places (*Paris Adult Theatre I* v. *Slaton,* 1973). In fact the Civil Rights Act of 1964 defines motion-picture houses as places of public accommodation.

Justification

What justification can there be for such decisions? This leads us to perhaps the most interesting part of the 1973-1974 decisions—the high Court's defense of its rulings limiting the circulation of obscene material.

In contrast to the Warren Court which fashioned the *Roth-Memoirs* test and justified the censorship of obscenity on the grounds that it is of no value to society, the Burger Court has become more aggressive and asserted that not only is obscenity valueless, but it also may in fact be harmful. In the *Paris Adult Theatre* case Chief Justice Burger said there is a clear justification for banning adults-only theaters, even if they do not intrude upon the privacy of others and even if patrons are properly warned of the kind of film they will see. The justification is, he said, "the interest of the public in the quality of life and the total community environment, the tone of commerce in the great city centers and, possibly, the public safety itself."

Ignoring the majority report from the President's Commission on Obscenity and Pornography, Burger noted that the minority report states that there is an arguable correlation between obscene material and crime. Even if there were no scientific evidence, the Chief Justice wrote, "We do not demand of legislatures 'scientifically certain criteria of legislation,' for unprovable assumptions underlie much lawful state regulation of commercial and business affairs." There need not be conclusive proof of a connection between antisocial behavior and obscene material for a state legislature to reasonably conclude that such a connection exists or might exist, Burger said.

The basic thrust of the Burger argument is a kind of quality-of-life argument which many thoughtful scholars have made for several years. In the *Paris Theatre* opinion Burger in fact quoted Prof. Alexander Bickel, who represented the *New York Times* in the *Pentagon Papers* case. In 1971 in *The Public Interest* concerning justification for regulation of obscenity Bickel writes:

> It concerns the tone of the society, the mode, or to use terms that have perhaps greater currency, the style and quality of life, now and in the future. A man may be entitled to read an obscene book in his room, or expose himself indecently there. . . . We should protect his privacy. But if he demands a right to obtain the books and pictures he wants in the market, and to foregather in public places—discreet, if you will, but accessible to all—with others who share his tastes, then to grant him his right is to affect the world about the rest of us, and to impinge on other privacies. Even supposing that each of us can, if he wishes, effectively avert the eye and stop the ear (which in truth we cannot) what is commonly read and seen and heard and done intrudes upon us all, want it or not.

Perhaps the most literate spokesman for this point of view is Harry M. Clor in his book *Obscenity and Public Morality* (1969). The book came out at a time when the Warren Court was pushing the limits of permissibility farther and farther, and Clor was chided for even thinking about a change of direction by the Supreme Court. Now it appears that the Court has adopted his logic, if not his standards.

Clor argues that some kind of common ethos is needed in order to have a community and that the agencies which formerly provided this ethos—schools, churches, families—don't do it any longer. The law should set the example, he says. "It must be a task of modern government and law to support and promote the public morality upon which a good social life depends."

To enforce his argument Clor quotes Aristotle (in *Politics*):

> The education of a citizen in the spirit of his constitution does not consist in his doing the actions in which the partisans of oligarchy or the adherents of democracy delight. It consists in his doing the actions by which an oligarchy or a democracy will be enabled to survive.

He also cites Walter Berns (in *Freedom, Virtue, and the First Amendment*):

> Since the way of the community depends upon citizens of a certain character, it must be the business of the law to promote that character. Thus, the formation of the character is the principal duty of government.

Clor concludes his argument:

> It is generally understood that, whatever other purposes such laws may have, they are also designed to implement community ethical standards.

This is a thoughtful argument, and while many authorities may disagree, it seems to make some sense in the chaotic 1970s. There is another side to the coin, however, and perhaps Justice Brennan expresses it best in his dissent in the *Paris Theatre* (1973) ruling:

> I am now inclined to argue that the Constitution protects the right to receive information and ideas, and that this right to receive information and ideas, regardless of their social worth . . . is fundamental to our free society. . . . This right is closely tied, as Stanley recognized, to the right to be free, except in very limited circumstances, from unwarranted governmental intrusions into one's privacy. . . . It is similarly related to the right of the individual, married or single, to be free from unwarranted governmental intrusion into matters so fundamentally affecting a person as the decision whether to bear or beget a child . . . and the right to exercise autonomous control over the development and expression of one's intellect, interests, tastes, and personality.

Regardless of whether one agrees with Clor or Brennan, there is probably unanimous agreement that only a major change in the composition of the high Court can bring about a change in the *Miller-Hamling* standards handed down in 1973 and 1974. Such a change in the Court's composition is not a likely prospect at this time.

Counterpoints (Special Standards)

In the years between the *Roth-Memoirs* test and the *Miller-Hamling* test the Supreme Court also devised three other "obscenity" tests which have been used from time to time and may still remain viable. At least whether they were overruled in the 1973 and 1974 opinions is unclear. All three tests are designed to cope with pornographic material which does not meet the standard of hard-core pornography, but which may still be suppressed. In 1966 in *Ginzburg* v. *U.S.*, the Supreme Court ruled that the manner in which material is marketed, advertised, and displayed can be a factor in determining whether a work is obscene or not. This case was the result of publisher Ralph Ginzburg's efforts to sell three different publications. In marketing these publications, Justice Brennan said, Ginzburg emphasized their erotic nature and thus was engaged in "pandering"—that is, in "the business of purveying textual or graphic matter openly advertised to appeal to the erotic interest of customers." This action can be a key factor in determining whether a publication or a film is obscene or not Brennan said. Ginzburg's conviction was affirmed.

Richard Kuh, in *Foolish Figleaves,* defines pandering in this sense as using a provocative cover, using advertisements that list the previous bannings of the work, displaying the work along with other borderline items, or in various ways promoting the erotic, deviant, or scatological appeal of the material. Since both the *Ginzburg* case and a 1967 decision, *Redrup* v. *New York,* few courts have used this standard. However, persons who deal in pornography took the broad hint and usually make an effort to avoid "pandering" in their marketing schemes.

The second counterpoint to the primary obscenity tests comes from the just mentioned *Redrup* case. In this case the court said the distribution of otherwise protected (not obscene) erotic material might become a criminal act if the distribution of such matter is in a manner that is an assault upon individual privacy because it is impossible for an unwilling recipient to avoid exposure to it. In other words, a work which is not hard-core pornography can still be deemed to be obscene if it is marketed or displayed in such a way that persons who do not wish to see such material cannot avoid it. Imagine, for example, a motion-picture theater which mounts huge posters depicting erotic scenes from X-rated movies on its marquee. The pictures are thrust upon all passersby, some of whom may not want to see them. Like the earlier pandering test, this test has also been used sparingly. In fact the high Court used it in but a single obscenity case, *Rowan* v. *Post Office* in 1970, in which it upheld the postal regulation which gives persons the right to stop unwanted solicitation for erotic material from being delivered in their mail.

Finally, the high Court ruled that states may apply variable obscenity standards for juveniles and for adults. That is, material acceptable for sale to adults may not be acceptable for sale to children. In addition a bookseller or a theater owner can be prosecuted for providing obscene material to young people. This standard emerged from the *Redrup* case and from *Ginsberg* v. *New York* in 1968. States and cities around the country have adopted statutes which strictly limit the material available to juveniles. This standard explains why there are adult bookstores, and why magazine shops and arcades have adults-only section. The variable obscenity concept is also at the basis of the motion-picture rating code which the industry and most theater owners have adopted voluntarily.

COMPLIANCE AND NON-COMPLIANCE

Somebody once wrote that battles are planned by generals using maps, but are won by soldiers fighting in the trenches. The same thing is true of obscenity cases. Regardless of what the Supreme Court rules about obscenity, the tough issues are resolved at local levels by police, prosecutors, and defense attorneys at criminal trials. This point should be remembered. Also to be remembered is that an obscenity case is a criminal case. In our rush to discuss the lofty principles of freedom of speech and freedom of the press we sometimes forget that obscenity statutes are criminal statutes, and the same factors that work in resolving all criminal disputes—police discretion in making arrests, prosecutor discretion in bringing charges, plea bargaining, selecting a favorable jury, and so forth —also apply in obscenity trials.

Political scientists have proven "scientifically" a fact that good lawyers and judges have known for some time: that simply because the United States Supreme Court says something is "the law" doesn't mean that it is "the law" at local levels, at least not right after a decision. Local noncompliance with Supreme Court rulings is not a new phenomenon, but it has become more apparent during the last quarter century. It is a function of the fact that a lawsuit is a dispute between two parties, and the resolution of that dispute by the courts technically affects only those two parties, not everyone else in a similar situation. If the Supreme Court rules that it is unconstitutional for the state of Maine to print a prayer on its license plates, the other forty-nine states would undoubtedly follow that ruling without being forced to because it is really not a very important issue. However, if the Supreme Court tells Maine it cannot ban certain kinds of hard-core pornography, many other jurisdictions would probably be reluctant to follow that ruling until a court stops them from doing the same thing. Why? Because this issue is important. Technically the states do not have to comply unless they are forced to by a court.

In a study of compliance with obscenity rulings in Oregon Stephen L. Wasby wrote recently that one of the reasons for lack of compliance is the lack of agreement on what the court intends by its opinion on the subject. "The development of Oregon obscenity policy," Wasby added, "gives evidence that the impact nationwide of a Supreme Court decision is by no means uniform. If there is a much variance in interpretation *within* one state as occurred in Oregon, certainly considerable variation must exist across the nation as a whole." ("The Pure and the Prurient: The Supreme Court, Obscenity and Oregon Policy.")

What are the factors involved in compliance and noncompliance? Wasby identified several: role of the lawyers, legitimacy ascribed to the decision, direction of the decision, sentiment of the public, precision or ambiguity of the decision, decisiveness of the ruling, number of relevant opinions, and so forth.

Noncompliance in obscenity law is probably as high as in any area of the law. Obscenity is an emotional issue, and while only a few people are active in seeking to clean up "smut," they are very vocal, are frequently influential and represent a large segment of the population.

Prosecutors must be reelected periodically and nobody likes to be labeled soft on pornography. There are on record very few prosecutors who win reelection because they take a strong stand in defense of freedom of the press; there are, on the other hand, many who have won a new term in office by cleaning up filth and jailing "smut peddlers."

Regardless of how the Supreme Court defines obscenity, the best definition of what is obscene in a local community is what a jury says is obscene. While occasionally an appellate court overturns a conviction as being too restrictive, most individual defendants have neither the time, the money, nor the inclination to appeal their conviction. Hence, what the Supreme Court says is not too important.

FACTORS INFLUENCING OBSCENITY PROSECUTION

Many factors influence the final decision to initiate obscenity prosecution including the attitude of local authorities and local standards. After a charge is brought, another set of elements comes into play. Will the prosecutor decide to use plea bargaining? What kind of jury will hear the case?

Local Attitudes and Standards

The general trend in most big cities in the United States today is to isolate pornographic activity in a specific part of town, maybe a few blocks in size, and then generally ignore it most of the time. Some cities have gone so far as to use zoning ordinances to isolate purveyors of pornography in a single area. In 1976 the city of Detroit adopted such a law and the United States Supreme Court ruled the law to be constitutional (*Young* v. *American Mini Theatres,* 1976). These "erogenous zones" are normally located in the less desirable part of the central city. Adult movie theaters, adult bookstores, peep shows are all located there for the convenience of customers. The rest of the community can ignore these activities. Police keep an eye on them, make occasional raids to keep everybody honest, but are not very aggressive in enforcement so long as (1) things don't get too gross, (2) citizens lodge no serious complaints, (3) shop owners confine themselves to the so-called safe zone, and (4) other criminal laws are not violated as a result of the pornographic traffic. Concerning point four, increases in prostitution or homosexual crime in the area can bring a crackdown on the shop owners since many people believe (without evidence) that obscenity breeds such criminal activity.

In some cities both police and prosecutors are more aggressive. In Los Angeles, for example, a center of pornographic production, police have often taken the offensive in tracking down both producers and distributors. Recently undercover police in that city organized an adult-film talent agency. Actors and actresses who specialize in pornographic films flocked to the agency, signed contracts with the "talent agents," and then unwittingly gave the police references, names of producers of pornographic films for whom they had worked. Using this information the police arrested several filmmakers.

Los Angeles undercover police also organized an agency for the distribution and publication of obscene books, magazines, films, and so forth. Pornographers came to the agency and displayed their wares to the "distributors" in the hope of getting a contract. Police found it quite easy to get indictments against such persons based on this information. Such aggressive action does not seem to be the norm in the 1970s. The *New York Times* reported recently that nationwide the fight against pornography is lagging. "Residents appear to be apathetic," reporter James Sterba wrote. "The police say they have more important crimes to fight. Many local prosecutors contend that they have neither the time nor the money to spend cracking down on smut dealers."

What impact has the 1973 court rulings had on the prosecution of pornographers? There has been some impact, but probably not as much as you might think. Police officers who work the vice detail are fairly candid in reporting that their standards of obscenity have changed little because of the *Miller-Hamling* rulings. Police officers are usually guided by two factors in deciding whether they think material is obscene: their individual judgment, and, more important, knowledge of the kinds of materials that have been successfully prosecuted in the past in the community. One officer told the author that court tests are useless to beat detectives. He added, "After you have been on the porno detail for awhile and come into contact with enough of this stuff you get sort of a gut feeling as to what is or what is not obscene."

Bringing a Charge   When the police officer thinks a work is obscene does he make an arrest? In most larger cities the answer is no. The officer buys a copy of the material and takes it to the prosecutor. If it is a film, he asks members of the prosecutor's staff to view the picture. Most prosecutors believe that since the obscenity guidelines are vague and somewhat airy it is better to have several opinions on the suspected material before bringing charges. In Seattle, Washington, for example, three members of the prosecutor's staff review the material independently before a decision is made. What standards are used? The court tests are one consideration, but more important is the type of material successfully prosecuted in the past. One prosecutor noted, "By paying attention to what juries have already said appeals to the prurient interest, is patently offensive and has no serious literary, artistic, political or scientific value, you can predict with some certainty success in a prosecution."

Why worry so much about successful prosecution? Why not just arrest those persons the prosecutor believes are selling obscenity? For better or worse one of the ways many people determine at election time whether their prosecutor has been doing a good job seems to be his percentage of convictions. And one way for a prosecutor to have a high conviction rate is to only prosecute sure cases.

Plea Bargaining   Once charges are brought against a bookseller or theater owner, other elements of the criminal justice system then go to work. One is plea bargaining. To plea bargain means that the defendant is willing to plead guilty to a charge less serious than the one for which he is arrested. If he is charged with five counts of violating the state law and faces a possible two-year jail term, the state might be willing to reduce the charge and merely fine the defendant if he is willing to plead guilty. Why would a defendant agree to this? This is what a good defense attorney who specializes in obscenity cases says:

> All these defendants are ready and willing to fight the charges against them, but you must understand that regardless of how tough or easy they might think the law is it always boils down to a matter of balancing their concerns over free speech with their financial interests and truthfully, most of them are not in the business to crusade for the First Amendment but more simply just to make a living. Therefore, since they are first and foremost businessmen, who contrary to popular belief operate within a tight profit-loss margin, it is hard for them to justify facing the cost of going to trial and even the slightest chance of incurring the stiff fine and jail sentence that a formal conviction will most likely bring if the opportunity presents itself to avoid, or at least minimize these hardships. . . .

One prosecutor told University of Washington researcher, Kirk Anderson, that he is willing to plea bargain with pornography dealers because "it is not my business to put people in jail, but rather to stop public distribution of certain obscene materials." If he can get the same results through a plea without going to trial, so much the better.

The Jury   If a case goes to trial it is the judge and the jury who must define obscenity. Some defense attorneys believe that the most important part of an obscenity trial is selecting the jury. At the Practicing Law Institute in New York, where defense lawyers can take courses about various kinds of legal problems, attorneys Michael Kennedy and Gerald Lefcourt presented what their experience and research had showed were the characteristics of ideal defense jurors and ideal prosecution jurors in obscenity trials.

According to Kennedy and Lefcourt, defense attorneys should seek jurors who are under thirty years of age, have some college background, preferably a liberal arts background, come from a middle-income economic stratum, are irreligious, have some exposure to pornography, tend to be independent in their life-style, and are employed in a nonauthoritarian occupation. Prosecutors, according to the two attorneys, should look for men jurors more than fifty years of age if possible, since men tend to be more conservative than women. They should seek jurors with less than a high school education or with more than a college education—technical training is desirable. Those persons who have a very low or very high income, are religious, have no exposure to pornography, and have an authoritarian employment (a supervisor) make the best jurors for the state. Kennedy and Lefcourt have also found that Asians tend to be more tolerant of pornography than are other groups, and that while blacks are generally antiprosecution they are rarely sympathetic to rich white pornographers. Persons with an artistic background tend to be more tolerant of pornography, persons with Spanish surnames usually have a religious bias, the closer jurors live to the place where the obscenity is distributed the less sympathetic they are to the pornographer. A jury made up of all one kind of jurors—all male, all old, all black, all college graduates—is bad for the defense. ("Trial Strategy in an Obscenity Case.")

Judge's Instructions   In addition to the jury members the instructions given the jury are vitally important to the outcome of an obscenity case. The instructions, of course, tell the jury what the law is—in other words, how to determine whether the material is obscene or not. A trial judge generally bases his instructions both on his personal reading of the law and on personal experience. Judge David Soukup of the Washington State Superior Court, who has tried numerous obscenity cases, told researcher Anderson this about jury instructions:

> Basically the matter of deciding what to include in a set of instructions depends on what the judge himself feels is necessary such that the jury can make a knowledgeable and legally sound determination, a judgement that is predicated upon his own interpretation of the law and what it requires, in combination with what his practical experience tells him jurors need in order to best understand the criteria they must apply to the facts at hand. The result of this highly individualized process which is also influenced by the judge's philosophy of his role under the law and his feeling about pornography in general, is that some judges will stick pretty close to the Miller test and the definitions of it provided by the Supreme Court, while others will attempt to embellish them by adding varying degrees of explanation arising from their own interpretations of the law. . . .

In addition to determining whether the material is obscene or not, jurors are also called upon to answer the question of whether or not the defendant was knowledgeable about the contents of what he was selling or distributing or publishing. This is called scienter, or guilty knowledge. In a 1959 case, *Smith* v. *California*, the United States Supreme Court ruled that before a person can be convicted for selling obscene books, the state has to prove that the seller was aware of the contents of the books, that he knew what they were about. The reason for this ruling is quite simple. As Justice William Brennan wrote nearly twenty years ago, "If the bookseller is criminally liable without knowledge of the contents, . . . he will tend to restrict the books he sells to those he has inspected; and thus the state will have imposed a restriction upon the distribution of constitutionally protected as well as obscene literature . . ." (*Smith* v. *California,* 1959).

There has always been some confusion about exactly what the state or other jurisdiction must prove. For example, does the bookseller have to know the books were obscene? In the *Hamling* decision the Supreme Court tried to clarify this point by repeating that scienter merely means proving that the defendant had a general knowledge of the material in question, that it was a book about homosexuals, for example, or that the movie contained sadistic scenes. It is not necessary that the bookseller or the theater operator know that the material is legally obscene. Normally a prosecutor can demonstrate scienter without much trouble, but it is another question which the jury must decide.

IMPACT OF MILLER-HAMLING

What do local prosecutors, defense attorneys, and judges think about the impact of the 1973-1974 decisions on obscenity prosecution? Prosecutors think that the loss of the utterly-without-redeeming-social-value standard is the most significant part of the rulings. Pressure was formerly on prosecutors to show that the material had not even the slightest hint of merit, and defendants could often easily offset this proof by introducing expert testimony to the contrary. Some defense lawyers in the past argued that if a film or book was entertaining it had social value. "If people would pay five bucks to see a film, it must have some value to them," one attorney said.

Defense attorneys now have to spend more time arguing that the work has some specific value in the areas outlined by the court—literary, political, scientific, or artistic. This is not going to be easy for most materials prosecuted during this era. One defense attorney says that he will probably spend most of his time arguing that the prosecution has failed to demonstrate that the books or movies lack such value, rather than proving that the material has such value.

Most local officials queried still do not think the law has the precision desired, that the *Miller-Hamling* test for obscenity is just about as vague as the old *Roth-Memoirs* test. This is bad. Prosecutors must spend many hours ascertaining whether something is legally obscene, and can still be wrong. Dealers and sellers are forced to take day-to-day risks, not knowing whether the material they sell is protected or not.

So the battle will continue. The new test is not really better nor worse than the old one. It is just different. Local officials will continue to use their own interpretation of the law—which means what local juries will accept—in their decision on whether or not to prosecute.

The government moves against pornography in various kinds of ways. While all we have written thus far in this chapter applies to postal censorship and film censorship, regulation of the mails by the federal government and regulation of movies by states and cities are unique in some aspects. Consequently some discussion of these points is merited.

POSTAL CENSORSHIP

Using the postal service to censor obscenity has a long tradition in the United States. In fact, it is through the postal system that the federal government becomes involved in the regulation of obscenity. The Post Office Department has long been an insensitive and moralistic censor of all sorts of material. Armed with congressional authority as well as a nineteenth-century Supreme Court ruling which designated use of the mails a privilege and not a right (ex parte *Jackson,* 1878), the postal service has worked hard to keep the mails free of "smut," even smut in plain brown wrappers. While the government cannot tamper with first-class mail legally, publishers of magazines of all kinds—girly, nudist, art, anthropological, crime, true confessions—have long been plagued by postal inspectors. While the loss of much of this material would not be a severe blow to the nation's cultural heritage, it is still highly frustrating to publishers who must depend upon the postal service to deliver their wares. For most publications the Post Office Department runs the only game in town.

The Post Office Department has traditionally been plagued with administrative slovenliness which causes it to run afoul of the law. Federal courts have for years been telling the postal service that it cannot do this or that: institute mail blocks, for example, or deny due process of law in obscenity hearings, ban publications which don't contribute to "the public good," or force patrons to come to the post office to pick up mail from Communist countries. In 1968 the postal service took a new tack in regulating certain kinds of obscene material, a tack designed to take the service off the legal hot seat. What is known as the Anti-Pandering Law or Section 3008 of Title 39 of the United States Code was put into effect by Congress. It was designed to stop the delivery of unwanted obscene solicitations to mail patrons' homes. This had been a problem for years, a real problem in many cases. Mailers were indiscriminate in sending out such material, and it was not uncommon for youngsters to receive lurid solicitations from magazines, books, and pictures.

Section 3008 allows postal patrons to remain free from such solicitations, but only after they have received such an advertisement. It works this way. Imagine that John Smith finds an advertisement for La Femme french postcards in his mailbox and is properly shocked. Under Section 3008 John can fill out a postal form which is sent by the Post Office to the La Femme company advising the mailer that Mr. Smith does not want to receive such solicitations in the future. If La Femme were to send John a subsequent mailing, the company could be subject to prosecution.

The interesting aspect of this law concerns the definition of obscenity—there is none. Postal patrons decide for themselves what is obscene. When they don't like the material, the dislike then is all that is needed. Once the notice is sent to the mailer, *any* subsequent mailing is a violation of the law. John might decide that a *Time* magazine solicitation or an advertisement for seat covers, or a record club is obscene. There must be solicitation, but that is the only requirement.

The distributers of erotic material challenged this law since to remove a name from a mailing list is quite costly. Also they argued that the law violated their First Amendment rights, and because the law did not define obscenity, it was too vague and therefore a violation of Fifth Amendment rights. But the Supreme Court unanimously supported the law. The Court said that Congress intended to give the postal patron the right to decide on the obscenity of an advertisement and this right eliminates the Post Office Department from a censorship role.

As far as the First Amendment right to communicate (if there is such a right) is concerned, the high Court ruled that the right of privacy is also guaranteed by the Constitution. This law does impede the flow of ideas, information, and so forth. However, Chief Justice Burger wrote (*Rowan* v. *Post Office,* 1970):

> . . . today everyman's mail is made up overwhelmingly of material he did not seek from persons he does not know. And all too often it is matter he finds offensive. It seems to us that a mailer's right to communicate must stop at the mailbox of an unreceptive addressee. . . . We categorically reject the argument that a vendor has a right under the Constitution or otherwise to send unwanted material into the home of another.

A more recent addition to the postal laws operates on somewhat the same principle, and has caused the pornography distributors even more headaches. Section 3010 of Title 39, United States Code, called the Goldwater Amendment to the Postal Reorganization Bill, allows mail patrons the opportunity to get off pornographers' mailing lists even before they receive their first solicitation. Under this law John Smith can fill out a form at his local post office which asserts that he does not want to receive any sexually oriented advertising. The postal service periodically publishes computerized lists of the names and addresses of persons who have signed this form. After a person's name has been on the list for thirty days, it is illegal to send that individual sexually oriented advertising matter. Mailers who ignore this are subject to both criminal and civil penalties.

Where do the mailers get the lists of names? They have to buy the lists from the government. When the law went into effect a few years ago the cost of a master list was more than $5,000. Of course supplements are published periodically and they must be purchased as well.

Section 3010 is different from Section 3008 in that it defines sexually oriented material whereas the Anti-Pandering Law lets the postal patron decide on his own.

Here is how the statute defines sexually oriented material:

> . . . any advertisement that depicts in actual or simulated form, or explicitly describes, in a predominantly sexual context, human genitalia, any act of natural or unnatural sexual intercourse, or any act of sadism or masochism, or any other erotic subject directly related to the foregoing.

The law does not pertain to materials in which the sexually oriented advertisement comprises only a small and insignificant part of a larger catalog, book, or periodical. This statute was also upheld by the federal courts (*Pent-R-Books* v. *U.S. Postal Service*, 1971). This law also provides that any envelope containing an advertisement which falls within the definition just given must carry a warning on the outside as to the nature of the contents.

Both of these statutes have been widely used and have solved one of the most serious problems relating to pornography—its shipment to people who don't want it. However, neither of these laws preclude the possibility of criminal obscenity prosecution against advertisers for sending out such material, even to people who want it. The 1974 *Hamling* case was based on just such an advertisement.

**FILM
CENSORSHIP**

Courts have always treated movies differently than they treat books, magazines, and artwork. Initially the Supreme Court refused to include films under the protection of the First Amendment. In 1915 in the case of *Mutual Film Corp.* v. *Industrial Commission of Ohio*, Justice Joseph McKenna wrote for the court that while, indeed, movies may be mediums of thought so are many other things such as circuses and the theaters. "It cannot be put out of view," the justice wrote, "that the exhibition of moving pictures is a business, pure and simple, originated and conducted for profit, like other spectacles, not to be regarded . . . as part of the press of the country or as organs of public opinion."

This was the law until the 1950s when the high Court ruled that film is a medium protected by the First Amendment and cannot be censored by the state, except in cases of obscenity (*Burstyn* v. *Wilson,* 1952). This seemed to put moviemakers on the same footing as magazine publishers, with one exception. The courts permitted prior censorship with regard to motion pictures; that is, a theater owner or film distributor could constitutionally be required to present his film to a board of censors for approval before showing it in the theater. In 1961 a film distributor challenged this practice and lost. In a five-to-four ruling the high Court said that there is no complete and absolute freedom to exhibit, even once, any and every kind of motion picture (*Times Film Corp.* v. *Chicago*).

While approving prior censorship for motion pictures, the high Court also demands procedures within the censorship sysem which protect the rights of theater owners. As such the high Court struck down several film censorship systems (for example, in Maryland and Dallas) which took too long to reach a decision, placed the burden of proof on the theater owner rather than on the government, and so forth (*Freedman* v. *Maryland,* 1965 and *Interstate Circuit* v. *Dallas,* 1968). In 1965 when the Court struck down the Maryland censorship law in *Freedman* v. *Maryland* it outlined the constitutional requirements of a permissible film ordinance. But the Court was unable to find an ordinance that passed muster until 1974 when it summarily affirmed the judgment of a three-judge panel which approved the revamped Maryland law.

The Maryland law which was approved in *Star* v. *Preller* (1974) had these provisions.

1. Every film, including those in coin-operated loop machines, must have a license from the state board of censors before it can be shown. Showing a film without a license is a crime, regardless of whether it is obscene or not.
2. Once a film is submitted to the censorship board, the board must either issue a license or initiate an action in court against the film within eight days.
3. In the court action to determine whether or not the film is obscene, the censorship board must prove the film is obscene. The film distributor does not have to prove that it is not obscene.
4. Hearing must be held in court within five days after the action is filed.

5. The court must issue a ruling within two days after the hearing is over. There is also a provision for expedited appeals.
6. The film cannot be shown until the hearing is completed.

Given the fact that prior restraint is allowed, the benefits of this ordinance are that a film must be licensed or declared obscene in a maximum of fifteen days. Moreover the state bears the burden of proof in any hearing that results. Perhaps this seems like crumbs for a starving man, but this system is nevertheless far superior to those of yesterday in which motion pictures were often tied up for months with the censors and the theater owner or film distributor was forced to go into court and try to prove a negative, that a movie was not obscene.

Many communities no longer operate film censorship boards. They are costly, and because the censors frequently abused the system they have a bad name. In Chicago, for example, the censorship board, which was comprised of police officers and the proverbial little old ladies in tennis shoes, once cut a scene showing the birth of a deer from a Walt Disney nature movie. Most communities proceed against obscene movies much as they do against obscene books—case-by-case prosecution.

Film prosecutions also present problems. In the case of an obscene book, an undercover officer can buy a copy of the suspect edition, and it can be scrutinized and later used as evidence if a criminal action results. But the price of a movie ticket only includes the right to look, not to take. So the police and the courts experienced many years of pushing and shoving over what was and was not legal. For a while the police merely seized all copies of the film. But the courts didn't approve of that because whether the film was obscene or not was for the courts to decide. If the jury decided the film was not obscene, seizure then constituted a clear case of prior restraint. So the police were forced to use other means. In some cities the police videotaped portions of the movie for use as evidence in a trial. But the quality of the tape was poor and often theater owners who were arguing about the high technical quality of a film complained that the police copy made the picture look worse than it actually was.

In 1973 in *Heller* v. *New York,* the Supreme Court handed down rules which clarified the matter, even though the new policies didn't satisfy many people on either side. Under the *Heller* rules a film cannot be seized by police as evidence until a warrant is issued by a neutral judge or magistrate who has viewed the film and has ruled that it is obscene. The hearing in which the judge issues the warrant is not an adversary hearing because the theater owner is not represented. This warrant is called an ex parte warrant. Only the state is represented, and all that the warrant says is that one judge has seen the film and thinks it is obscene.

Following seizure, an adversary hearing is held—a trial—to determine whether the film is in fact obscene. During the period between seizure and final judicial determination of obscenity, the theater owner can continue to show the motion picture if he has a second copy. If no second copy is available, the state must then permit the exhibitor to make a copy of the film that was seized so that exhibition of the movie can go on. Therefore, the police get their evidence and the theater owner can keep showing the movie until the trial is over. The only serious problem is that it is expensive for the theater owner to make a second copy of the movie. *Heller* and a companion case, *Roaden* v. *Kentucky* (1973), make it clear that a police officer cannot seize a motion picture even as evidence incidental to an arrest unless a judge first sees the movie (at the theater, of course) and declares it to be obscene.

In the end, one question seems to always pop up: Why is there so much ado about nothing? Of course there are persons who argue that obscenity is not "nothing"; it is something, something very important. The morality of the community is at stake. And maybe it is.

The First Amendment hasn't worked very well with regard to obscenity. The eloquent vagueness of the drafters of the Bill of Rights has not served us at all well in this issue. Both sides use the silence of the First Amendment with regard to obscenity to bolster their opposite arguments.

One does not get a great deal of satisfaction from studying the obscenity problem for any length of time. Often it appears that in this dispute no one is right. The trash that is normally peddled as erotic art seems not much worse than nonerotic trash, but it costs much more. Society wastes an immense amount of money, and police, prosecutors and courts waste an immense amount of time trying to control "the obscenity problem." In one recent term 10 percent of the case load of the United States Supreme Court were obscenity cases. The debate on both sides is rarely lofty; the principles at stake are often obscure. It is troublesome that in an age which is rife with problems we spend so much time on this controversy.

BIBLIOGRAPHY
Here are some of the sources that have been helpful in the preparation of chapter 9.

Books   Berns, Walter. *Freedom, Virtue and the First Amendment.* Chicago: Henry Regnery Co. Gateway Editions, 1965.

Clor, Harry M. *Obscenity and Public Morality.* Chicago: University of Chicago Press, 1969.

Kennedy, Michael, and Lefcourt, Gerald. "Trial Strategy in an Obscenity Case." In *Obscenity and the Law.* New York: Practicing Law Institute, 1974.

Kronhausen, Eberhard, and Kronhausen, Phyllis. *Pornography and the Law.* Rev. Edit. New York: Ballantine Books, 1964.

Paul, James C. N., and Schwartz, Murray L. *Federal Censorship: Obscenity in the Mail.* Glencoe, Ill.: The Free Press, 1961.

Robertus, Patricia. "Postal Control of Obscene Literature, 1942-1957." Ph.D. dissertation, University of Washington, 1974.

Sunderland, Lane. *Obscenity, The Court, The Congress and The President's Commission.* Washington, D.C.: American Institute for Public Policy Research, 1974.

Wasby, Stephen L. "The Pure and the Prurient: The Supreme Court, Obscenity and Oregon Policy." In *The Supreme Court as Policy Maker,* edited by David Everson. Carbondale, Ill.: Public Affairs Research Bureau, Southern Illinois University, 1968.

Articles   *Amicus: Bimonthly Newsletter for Prosecutors.* Thousand Oaks, Calif.: National Legal Data Center for the Law of Obscenity, 1973-76.

Bickel, Alexander. "On Pornography: Concurring and Dissenting Opinions." *The Public Interest* 22 (1971), p. 25.

Leventhal, Harold. "1973 Round of Obscenity-Pornography Decisions." *American Bar Association Journal* 59 (1973).

Shugrue, Richard. "An Atlas for Obscenity: Exploring Community Standard." 7 *Creighton Law Review* 157 (1974).

Teeter, Dwight L., and Pember, Don R. "The Retreat from Obscenity: Redrup v. New York." 21 *Hastings Law Journal* 175 (1969).

Teeter, Dwight L., and Pember, Don R. "Obscenity, 1971: The Rejuvenation of State Power and the Return to Roth." 17 *Villanova Law Review* 211 (1971).

Cases   *Burstyn* v. *Wilson,* 343 U.S. 495 (1952).

Butler v. *Michigan,* 352 U.S. 380 (1957).

Commonwealth v. *Claflin,* 298 N.E. 2d 888 (1973).

Detco, Inc., v. *McCann,* 365 F. Supp. 176 (1973).

Ebert v. *Maryland,* 313 A 2d 356 (1973).

Freedman v. *Maryland,* 380 U.S. 51 (1965).

In re *Giannini,* 72 Cal. Rptr. 655 (1968).

Gibbs v. *State,* 504 S.W. 2d 719 (1974).

Ginsberg v. *New York,* 390 U.S. 629 (1968).

Ginzburg v. *U.S.* 383 U.S. 463 (1966).

Hall v. *Commonwealth,* 505 S.W. 2d 166 (1974).

Hamling v. *U.S.,* 418 U.S. 87 (1974).

Hannegan v. *Esquire,* 327 U.S. 146 (1946).

Harmar Theaters v. *Cryan,* 365 F. Supp. 1312 (1973).

Heller v. *New York,* 413 U.S. 483 (1973).

Interstate Circuit v. *Dallas,* 390 U.S. 676 (1968).

Ex parte *Jackson,* 96 U.S. 727 (1878).

Jacobellis v. *Ohio,* 378 U.S. 184 (1964).

Jenkins v. *Georgia,* 418 U.S. 153 (1974).

Kaplan v. *California,* 413 U.S. 115 (1973).

Keating v. *Vixen,* 301 N.E. 2d 880 (1973).

Manuel Enterprises v. *Day,* 370 U.S. 478 (1962).

Memoirs v. *Massachusetts,* 383 U.S. 413 (1966).

Miller v. *California,* 413 U.S. 15 (1973).

Mohney v. *State,* 300 N.E. 2d 66 (1973).

Mutual Film Corp. v. *Industrial Commission of Ohio,* 236 U.S. 230 (1915).

Paris Adult Theatre I v. *Slaton,* 413 U.S. 49 (1973).

Pent-R-Books v. *U.S. Postal Service,* 328 F. Supp. 297 (1971).

People v. *Enskat,* 109 Cal. Rptr. 433 (1973).

People v. *Gitlow,* 195 App. Div. 773 (1921), dissent.

People v. *Heller,* 307 N.E. 2d 805 (1974).

Price v. *Commonwealth,* 201 S.E. 2d 798 (1974).

Redlich v. *Capri Cinema, Inc.,* 349 N.Y.S. 2d 697 (1973).

Redrup v. *New York,* 386 U.S. 767 (1967).

Regina v. *Hicklin,* L. R., 3 Q. B. 360 (1868).

Rhodes v. *State,* 283 So. 2d 351 (1973).

Roaden v. *Kentucky,* 413 U.S. 496 (1973).

Roth v. *U.S.,* 354 U.S. 476 (1957).

Rowan v. *Post Office,* 397 U.S. 728 (1970).

Slaton v. *Paris Adult Theatre I,* 210 S.E. 2d 456 (1973).

Smith v. *California,* 361 U.S. 147 (1959).

Stanley v. *Georgia,* 394 U.S. 557 (1969).

Star v. *Preller,* 95 S.Ct. 217 (1974).

State v. *Bird,* 499 S.W. 2d 780 (1973).

State v. *Bryant,* 201 S.E. 2d 211 (1973).

State v. *J-R Distributors, Inc.,* 512 P. 2d 1049 (1973).

State v. *Lerner,* 81 NE 2d 282 (1948).

State v. *Shreveport News Agency, Inc.,* 287 So. 2d 464 (1973).

State v. *Wedelstedt,* 213 N.W. 2d 652 (1973).

Stein v. *Batchelor,* 300 F. Supp. 602 (1969), vacated and remanded sub. nom. *Dyson* v. *Stein,* 401 U.S. 200 (1971).

Times Film Corp. v. *Chicago,* 365 U.S. 43 (1961).

U.S. v. *Articles of Obscene Merchandise,* 315 F. Supp. 191 (1970).

U.S. v. *Bennett,* 24 Fed. Cas. 1093 (N.Y.S.D., 1879).

U.S. v. *Orito,* 413 U.S. 139 (1973).

U.S. v. *Roth,* 237 F. 2d 796 (1956).

U.S. v. *Thevis,* 484 F. 2d 1149 (1973).

U.S. v. *12 200 Ft. Reels of Super 8 mm. Film,* 413 U.S. 123 (1973).

Walker v. *Popenoe,* 149 F. 2d 511 (1945).

Young v. *American Mini Theatres,* 96 S.Ct. 2440 (1976).

CHAPTER 10

Regulation of Advertising

Americans are treated to scores of advertisements daily. Someone has estimated that each of us is exposed to at least one hundred ten advertisements per day, and at least seventy-six of them register in our consciousness. People in the business tell us that advertising is the cornerstone of our capitalistic economic system. Low prices for consumers are dependent upon mass production, mass production is dependent upon volume sales, and volume sales are dependent upon advertising. Many economists support this theory. Critics of advertising argue that while people probably would pay more for some products without the savings wrought by mass production and advertising they would pay less for many more products such as cosmetics and patent medicines half of whose purchase price pays for large advertising expenditures. Critics also argue (not without challenge) that people buy more than they really need because of advertising. Regardless of who is right, about $29 billion was spent in 1976 for advertising. About four cents of every dollar spent by every man, woman, and child for goods and services went to pay for advertising costs. Some companies in this country spend one dollar for every three dollars they earn in sales on advertisements for their products. Proctor & Gamble Co. spent almost $300 million on advertising in a single year. Far more money is spent for advertising than for many social needs, a fact which makes advertising controversial.

Regulation of advertising is also controversial. There are persons who consider that publication and broadcast of advertising are First Amendment rights, that advertisements are speech or press protected from censorship to the same extent as are editorials and news broadcasts. Our capitalistic system is based upon a laissez-faire economic theory in which consumers must compete in the marketplace like everyone else. Within bare limits (such as laws against selling dangerous medicines or tainted meat), the consumer must learn to shop carefully, read advertising closely, be skeptical about any claim: caveat emptor—let the buyer beware.

On the other hand there are persons who consider purely commercial messages, those designed to convince consumers to purchase products, undeserving of First Amendment protection. Freedom of the press is designed to protect ideas, not the trivialities of advertising. Consumer information is the basis of our capitalistic system, they argue, and only those advertisements which inform truthfully and accurately should be published or aired. Each time they make a purchase consumers should not have to worry that they are being lied to or deceived by the manufacturer. The government should police unfair and deceptive advertising just as it polices other fraudulent conduct such as extortion and phony land sales. Caveat venditor—let the seller beware.

As the last quarter of the twentieth century gets underway, advertisers find themselves somewhere between the two positions, but closer to the second position than to the first. A measure of regulation has been built into the law, as this chapter will show. We will take a brief look at the history of advertising regulation in the United States and consider some of the conditions making regulation necessary. Then we will consider the protection the First Amendment affords advertising claims and get a brief perspective of the means available to regulate unfair and deceptive advertising including industry and governmental regulation. Most of the chapter, however, is given over to consideration of the Federal Trade Commission, the primary watchdog of advertising in this country. Its jurisdiction, its standards, its remedies to correct bad advertising, and its procedures are discussed. Finally, the various kinds of deceptive advertising are identified and discussed briefly, and the defenses an advertiser can use in a false advertising suit are outlined.

HISTORY OF REGULATION

From a historical standpoint, the regulation of advertising is a fairly recent phenomenon in this country because advertising as we know it today is a relatively modern practice. True, the first American newspaper published more than two hundred and seventy-five years ago contained advertisements, but they were really announcements by merchants that goods had arrived or that certain merchandise was now in stock. The announcements were embellished somewhat, of course, but the modern advertising pitch did not become a common affair until the last part of the nineteenth century. Advertising depended upon the mass marketing of goods, which depended upon the so-called industrial revolution and modern modes of transportation.

In the past one hundred years or so the nation has moved gradually from having no regulations upon advertising to having hundreds of different kinds of laws whose purpose is to regulate advertising. While in this chapter we are primarily concerned with how untrue and deceptive advertising is policed, it must also be noted that today there are scores of other laws applicable to commercial messages of which advertisers and advertising agencies must be aware.

In the wake of the civil rights movement of the past two decades, a whole range of regulations whose purpose is to make advertisements comply with equal rights provisions have been adopted. In employment and housing advertisements, for example, it is illegal under federal as well as under many state laws to discriminate against persons because of sex, race, national origin, or marital status. The publication, as well as the advertiser, can be held liable for the violation of such laws. The Truth in Lending Law placed various credit disclosure requirements upon advertisers. There are numerous laws at both federal and state levels which prescribe certain rules for political advertising. The rates for political advertising are frequently limited. In many states newspapers and broadcasting stations must file the names of political advertisers with public disclosure commissions. In most states the name of the sponsor of a political advertisement must be included in the advertisement. Political party labels must also be conspicuous.

Other laws dictate what can and cannot be said in specific kinds of advertisements. For example, strict regulations apply to liquor advertising. The law requires the publication in a conspicuous type size of alcoholic content (86 proof) and kind (bourbon) of whiskey.

The provisions just given are but a few examples of how advertising laws have evolved to meet changing political and social conditions in the United States. It is sufficient to say that the advertiser must be both cautious and knowledgeable when preparing advertisements.

NEED FOR REGULATION

The first fact an advertiser must remember is that he must obey the laws which specifically regulate advertising messages *in addition* to all the other laws which regulate the mass media. In other words, an advertisement can be libelous and the advertiser can be sued for defamation. An advertisement can be obscene and can invade the privacy of a person. It can violate copyright law or violate the Federal Communications Act. It can violate a federal, state, or local advertising regulation.

The basic thrust of advertising regulation at all levels is to outlaw deceptive advertisements, unfair advertisements, advertisements which are dishonest or untruthful. Here is where the first—perhaps the biggest—problem arises. Whose standard of truth do we use? While this question is considered in greater detail later in the chapter, it is important to note at this point that there are persons who think that most advertising is dishonest, that the concepts of truth and advertising are antithetical in most instances. To demand advertising to be truthful, some argue, would be to stop most advertising. This argument is worth exploring for a moment.

Were a man to invent a truly unique product—such as an automobile which can be powered by tap water—advertising for such a product could simply be informative and tell consumers that this product is available. But if there were such a product, advertisements would not really be needed for long. Changes in the product might require new advertising, but consumers rarely have to be convinced to buy a product with such obvious advantages. However, if you watch television closely and read the advertisements in newspapers and magazines, you will find that most advertising is not about products like the water-powered car. Most advertising dollars are spent on products which are not unique—headache remedies, toothpastes, automobiles, cosmetics, detergents, soda pop, and so forth. Because the differences between various brands of these products are usually marginal, the consumer must be given reasons to buy Bufferin rather than Bayer Aspirin or Anacin, Seven-Up rather than Pepsi-Cola. Those who argue that there is little truth in advertising point to such advertisements and say that these advertisements manufacture differences that don't exist or aren't important. One product is called "the un-cola," another claims it "quenches your thirst" yet another contains "the taste of *lymon*" and the fourth is "the real thing." They ask who cares about such differences? and say that to promote them is dishonest.

There is considerable truth in such an argument, but not enough to halt a $29-billion-per-year industry. The regulators of advertising in the United States find it fairly easy to rationalize that such advertisements really don't hurt anybody because consumers are smart enough to realize that their only purpose is to catch the attention, not to inform. What harm is done when one cigarette advertises that it is milder, another that it is longer, another that it is cooler, another that it is more masculine, and another that it is more feminine? No one believes these advertisements anyway. But can we be sure that consumers are skeptical of advertisements? As we will see, the law does not require that advertising actually inform, only that it doesn't deceive.

FIRST AMENDMENT PROTECTION

What about the First Amendment? Does it protect advertising? The answer is unclear at this point in light of recent court rulings which will be discussed shortly. Perhaps one author put his finger on it best when he wrote, "Commercial advertisements are at least less rigorously protected than other speech."

As in its continuing involvement with defining obscenity, the Supreme Court has only partially provided a final answer to whether the First Amendment extends its protection to advertising. In 1942 the high Court ruled that advertising does not fall under the protection of the Amendment, but other federal courts moved away from this ruling, at least to a limited extent. And the Supreme Court itself moved away from this position following decisions in 1975 and 1976. Let us first consider the 1942 ruling.

Valentine v. Chrestensen

A man named Chrestensen bought a used Navy submarine, moored it at a pier in New York City, and began distributing handbills on the city streets advertising his attraction. The New York police told him that it was against the law to distribute commercial and business advertising matter on the streets. Only handbills devoted solely to "information or public protest" could legally be passed out on city streets. Chrestensen reprinted his handbills so that one side contained a protest that the city refused him permission to dock his submarine at a city pier, and the other side contained a commercial message advertising the submarine. Police stopped him from passing out the material. Chrestensen went to court and got an injunction which restrained New York police from banning his handbills. The city appealed the ruling to the Supreme Court which reversed the lower court ruling. Justice Owen Roberts wrote the majority opinion and noted that the court had previously unequivocally held that the streets were the proper place for the exercise of rights of freedom of the press and freedom of speech, and that states could not unduly burden or proscribe the freedom of expression with unreasonable regulations. However, Roberts added, "We are equally clear that the Constitution imposes no such restraint on government as respects purely commercial advertising." (*Valentine* v. *Chrestensen*, 1942).

What about the fact that a protest was printed on one side of Chrestensen's handbills? Didn't that represent an informational purpose? Roberts said that while the court would not indulge in any appraisal of its position based on subtle distinctions at that time it was clear enough that the use of the protest on the opposite side of the advertisement was done "with the intent, and for the purpose, of evading the prohibition of the ordinance."

New York Times v. Sullivan

A series of decisions since 1942 have led the courts in a step-by-step movement away from the rule in the *Chrestensen* case. In 1964 the Supreme Court ruled in *New York Times* v. *Sullivan* that editorial advertising, that is, advertising to promote an idea such as "Save the Whales," "Stop the War," or "Ban Pesticides" rather than a product like used cars or spaghetti is protected by the First Amendment.

Pittsburgh Press v. Human Rights Commission

In 1973 the high Court again had a chance to consider whether the guarantees of free speech and press apply to commercial advertising in a case involving help-wanted advertising in the *Pittsburgh Press*. In its columns of help-wanted classified advertising the newspaper used male and female designations. The city human relations commission issued a cease and desist order on the grounds that the practice violated a city ordinance prohibiting employment advertising which discriminated on the basis of sex. In deciding the case, the Supreme Court did not say that the advertisements were protected by the First Amendment. But as P. Cameron Devore and Marshall Nelson point out in the *Hastings Law Journal* ("Commercial Speech and Paid Access to the Press"), neither did the high Court say that commercial advertising remains outside the realm of First Amendment protection.

The *Pittsburgh Press* raised two arguments in an attempt to rebut the rule that commercial advertising is not protected under the First Amendment. The newspaper argued that advertising dollars provided fully 75 percent of the newspaper's revenue and limitation on advertising could damage the *Press*. The high Court did not reject this contention. It merely noted that in this case the city ordinance did not significantly impair the ability of the newspaper to publish.

Attorneys for the *Press* argued that the newspaper exercised considerable editorial judgment in the acceptance and placement of advertising and that the ordinance interfered with that. The Court agreed that editorial judgment was a factor in the publication of commercial advertising, but in that case the degree of judgment was insufficient to separate it from the commercial character of the advertisement. In its decision the high Court noted that discrimination in employment is an illegal commercial activity per se (*Pittsburgh Press Co.* v. *Pittsburgh Commission on Human Rights*, 1973):

> Any First Amendment interest which might be served by advertising an ordinary commercial proposal and which might arguably outweigh the governmental interest supporting the regulation is altogether absent when the commercial activity itself is illegal and the restriction on advertising is incidental to a valid limitation on economic activity.

While there are many ways of reading such a decision, DeVore and Marshall argue persuasively that the court may have placed some limitations on its outright declaration that commercial advertising is beyond the pale of the First Amendment. It can be argued, they say, that if regulation of commercial advertising were shown to endanger the economic base of the press, if it were shown that advertising is a basic content of the media because of the basic editorial judgments involved, or if it were shown that the advertisements are for otherwise lawful activity, then the court might be willing to grant First Amendment protection to purely commercial messages.

Bigelow v. Virginia

Two years after the *Pittsburg Press* ruling the Supreme Court reversed the conviction of a Virgina newspaper editor who had been found guilty of publishing an advertisement which offered assistance to women seeking abortion. Abortion was illegal in Virginia in 1971 when the advertisement was published. The Woman's Pavilion, a New York group, urged women who wanted an abortion to come to New York. As if to emphasize the argument made by Devore and Marshall in analyzing the *Pittsburg Press* case Justice Blackmun wrote for the Court that speech does not lose the protection of the First Amendment merely because it appears in the form of a commercial advertisement. Blackmun distinguished this ruling from the high Court's ruling in *Chrestensen* by arguing that in that instance the Supreme Court merely upheld the New York ordinance as a reasonable regulation *of the manner in which commercial advertising can be distributed* (author's emphasis). Blackmun refused to open the door completely or to state explicitly how far this ruling opened the door. "We need not decide in this case," he wrote, "the precise extent to which the First Amendment permits regulation of advertising that is related to activities the state may legitimately regulate or even prohibit" (*Bigelow* v. *Virginia*, 1975). Following on the heels of the *Bigelow* case a federal court in Seattle recently struck down a state law which prohibited margarine manufacturers from using the word *butter* in their advertising messages, on the ground that the law violated the First Amendment.

Board of Pharmacy v. Citizens' Consumer Council

Finally, in 1976 the Supreme Court seemed to provide a much clearer answer in the case of *Virginia State Board of Pharmacy* v. *Virginia Citizens' Consumer Council, Inc.* The high Court ruled that a Virginia statute which had the effect of prohibiting pharmacies from advertising the price of prescription drugs violated the guarantee of freedom of expression in the First Amendment. Justice Harry Blackmun wrote:

> Advertising, however tasteless and excessive it sometimes may seem, is nonetheless dissemination of information as to who is producing and selling what product, for what reason, and at what price. So long as we preserve a predominantly free enterprise economy, the allocation of our resources in large measure will be made through numerous private economic decisions. It is a matter of public interest

that those decisions in the aggregate be intelligent and well informed. To this end, the free flow of commercial information is indispensable.

The high Court made it clear, however, that government was completely free to continue to regulate commercial speech which is false, misleading, or deceptive and which proposes illegal transactions. It therefore appears that the Court has come virtually full circle from the 1942 *Valentine* case. At the same time, the high Court remains reluctant to grant to advertisers the broad protection given to political speech and other public-affairs-oriented discussion.

WAYS TO REGULATE UNFAIR AND DECEPTIVE ADVERTISING

The regulation of unfair and deceptive advertising is a most difficult task, for as previously noted disagreement about what is and what is not unfair and deceptive is frequent. Society uses various means to control this kind of advertising. The industry—the advertisers, the advertising agencies, and the mass media—polices itself. Both competitors (of errant advertisers) and consumers use the courts to seek redress for false or unfair advertising. Cities and states also have laws which prohibit untrue and deceptive advertising. Regardless of all these efforts, the federal government is the primary agent in regulation of advertising. To understand why this is so, we must first examine the controls just mentioned.

Self-Regulation

A great many people place considerable stock in self-regulation of advertising. The advertising industry has various codes and boards which proscribe certain unfair and deceptive advertising practices. The mass media, the newspapers and broadcasting stations, usually have policies on the kinds of advertising they will and will not accept. Normally, legal counsel for the advertiser, for the advertising agency, and for the medium scrutinize every national advertisement published or broadcast. In *The Law of Advertising* George and Peter Rosden report that advertising censors at the Columbia Broadcasting System reject or request changes in one of every five advertisements submitted to the network. Still, self-regulation does not seem to meet all the needs of a society seeking freedom from false and deceptive advertising. Louis Engman, former chairman of the Federal Trade Commission (FTC), said in a speech to the American Bar Association in 1974, "The voluntary approach (to regulation) yields far more satisfactory progress in the development of compliance mechanisms than it does in the development of substantive standards." In other words, the industry sets up codes and panels and boards, but has not been successful in establishing hard rules on what is and what is not deceptive advertising. Staff consultants to the Federal Trade Commission were even more critical in 1973 in the *Staff Report to the Federal Trade Commission*:

> . . . from the advertiser's perspective the purpose of marketing communications is ultimately to sell the product or the service. Thus, to the extent that the provision . . . [information which educates the consumer] conflicts with the ability of the advertiser to sell the product it is unlikely that he will indulge voluntarily in such "informational" communication.

At the very basis of self-regulation is the assumption that the advertiser and the consumer agree upon standards of deception and honesty, that they share a value system regarding the sale of consumer goods. Such agreement is perhaps beyond human facility at this point in its evolution. While newspapers and the broadcasting stations do not necessarily share the advertisers' point of view, they tend to be more sympathetic to advertisers since they are after all the ones paying the bills.

Most economic theories are based on the presumption that if all things are equal such and such will result. Self-regulation is based on the assumption that all sellers and advertisers are honest and fair and look out for the good of the consumers who buy their products. However, all things are not equal; and all advertisers are not honest and scrupulous. Hence, self-regulation does not work very often.

Competition

One school of thought holds that the best watchdogs of dishonest and unfair advertising are competitors of dishonest and unfair advertisers. While initially this theory sounds quite plausible, probably it contains much less truth than meets the eye. Given a market structure with many manufacturers of the same product, all with about an equal share of the market, an advertiser might be concerned about his competitor getting the edge by using false or misleading advertisements. Much of the market today does not meet this criterion, however. The Eastman Kodak Company, which sells most of the film bought in the United States today, would probably be quite unconcerned about exaggerated product claims of a small film manufacturer with but a tiny portion of the market. This is not an unrealistic portrait of a large segment of the marketplace.

But let's say Ford Motor Company does get angry at General Motors. What can Ford do? Really, very little by itself. There is no deceptive advertising tort at common law. Only business torts such as unfair competition apply. It is difficult, if not impossible, for a competitor to sue for unfair competition on the basis of simply a false advertisement. Both courts and legislatures have been hostile to the development of competitor suits. The courts have enough work without being burdened by hundreds of false-advertising suits.

A competitor can sue for disparagement of property, which is sometimes known as trade libel (see chapter 3). But this action applies only to advertisements which make false and harmful statements about a competitor's product, and the burden of proof upon the plaintiff is heavy since proof of falsity, malice, and damages must be presented.

One course open to a competitor is to alert legal authorities such as the FTC to the existence of the deceptive advertising. This practice is common. When Standard Oil of California was taken to task recently for its advertisements for F-310, competing oil companies were the ones who put pressure on the Federal Trade Commission to take action. The companies even provided test results from their own laboratories which they asserted proved the falsehoods in the claims in the Standard Oil advertisements.

Consumer Action

Consumers are also left in the lurch when it comes to policing false advertising. They too can report false and deceptive advertising to the authorities, but as individuals they have virtually no remedy at law for a deceptive advertisement. As the Rosdens point out in their massive compendium, *The Law of Advertising,* historically common law courts have not been receptive to protecting consumers. "During the most formative period of common law," they write, "only a few goods in the marketplace were manufactured products so that the buyer was in an excellent position to judge for himself goods offered to him." Dairy products could be judged by their smell and texture; vegetables, meat, and fruit, by their looks. Judgments about wine, beer, and cloth were also easy to make. Protection was really necessary only in case of fraud such as watered beer. The basic slogan in those days was caveat emptor—buyer beware.

While today consumers are far better protected—they must be because of the thousands of consumer products about which they know little or nothing—there is little consumers can do themselves to attack the dishonest advertiser short of reporting the advertisement to the proper authorities. Even if the law allowed a suit to redress an injury wrought by a false advertisement, where can a consumer find a lawyer to handle the case? Let's say you buy a certain toothpaste because the advertisements claim it will brighten your teeth and stop formation of cavities. If your teeth don't get brighter and you sue, your damages are for 73 cents. On a contingency fee the lawyer gets 40 percent or about 29 cents. Even suit over a $150 dental bill doesn't give an attorney-at-law much to work for, especially when a malpractice victim who wants to sue for $200,000 may lurk around the next corner.

The Rosdens point out that it is possible for a consumer to sue under product liability laws, but in such a case the advertisement must contain a commitment about the product which is not fulfilled after purchase by the consumer. For example, a carpet cleaner advertises that it will not damage carpets, but after a consumer uses it, a large hole appears in the rug. The consumer would be able to sue (if she could find a lawyer) for a new carpet. Products rarely make such a claim today. Hedging is much more common. That is, the advertisement states that in normal use the cleaner will not harm a carpet, but also suggests that the cleaner be tested first in an inconspicuous area of the carpet. Then, if the cleaner makes a hole in the carpet, the only problem for the manufacturer is a small hole in a carpet, which is not very serious. At least that may be the court's opinion in awarding the consumer only $15 in damages.

Consumers and competitors are marvelous snitches for attorneys general and the Federal Trade Commission. Unhappily our legal system is just not designed to allow individual attack on a false advertisement. A new law makes it possible for the Federal Trade Commission to sue on behalf of consumers to get back money wasted because of false promises. How often the FTC sues under this law and how well the law works remain to be seen.

State and Local Laws

State regulation of advertising predates federal regulation by several years. This fact is not surprising when you consider that at the time the public became interested in advertising regulation—around the turn of the century—the federal government was a minuscule creature relative to its present size. Harry Nims, a New York lawyer, drafted a model law called the *Printers' Ink* Statute (it was *Printers' Ink* magazine that urged passage of the law) in 1911. Nearly every state adopted one version or another of this law. Here is the text of the original law:

> Any person, firm, corporation or association who, with intent to sell or in any way dispose of merchandise, securities, service, or anything offered by such person, firm, corporation or association, directly or indirectly, to the public for sale, or distribution, or with intent to increase the consumption thereof, or to induce the public in any manner to enter into any obligation relating thereto, or to acquire title thereto, or an interest therein, makes, publishes, disseminates, circulates, or places before the public, or causes, directly or indirectly, to be made, published, disseminated, circulated, or placed before the public, in this State, in a newspaper or other publication, or in the form of a book, notice, handbill, poster, bill circular, pamphlet, or letter, or in any other way, an advertisement of any sort regarding merchandise, securities, service, or anything so offered to the public, which advertisement contains any assertion, representation or statement of fact which is untrue, deceptive or misleading, shall be guilty of a misdemeanor.

The general verdict is that these statutes have been fairly ineffective in dealing with false advertising. Enforcement, which is in the hands of attorneys general or local prosecutors, has been weak because these legal officers have many other statutes to enforce. When people are being murdered or robbed or maimed or kidnapped, the fact that you or I have been deceived by an advertisement from a local furniture store seems relatively unimportant.

However, because of the consumer revolution of the last decade, cities, counties, and states have all strengthened their laws and their enforcement of false and deceptive advertising. In some areas prosecution is quite vigorous. In others it is not. The laws vary from state to state, even from city to city. It is advised that persons involved in advertising obtain copies of all relevant laws regarding statutes in the area in which publication is made. There is no way possible for a single chapter on advertising to cover all laws in all areas. It is possible, however, to state a few generalizations.

First, in addition to general consumer protection laws directed at stopping misleading advertising, most states have an increasingly large number of specific laws with regard to advertising. Most of these laws were passed to protect businessmen, not consumers, and hence strike an unusual chord. For example, state laws proscribe the members of various professions from advertising—doctors, lawyers, dentists, and so forth. (It should be noted that at this time (1977) attorneys across America are urging the American Bar Association to change its rules and permit lawyers to advertise—at least to advertise legal specialties and typical fees.) These laws were passed at the urging of medical societies, legal societies, and dental societies to discourage patients from shopping around and to maintain the dignity of the profession. Other state laws limit what financial institutions like banks and savings and loan associations can advertise.

While laws like these are fairly well policed, most states don't do nearly so well in policing false advertising statutes. There are exceptions like Washington and Wisconsin. Prosecuting false advertising is a rigorous, time-consuming chore. Big companies can afford good legal counsel to defend their advertising practices. The suits are complicated. In the time needed to begin a prosecution, the offensive advertising campaign has usually long since ended. Victory really brings little satisfaction. Outright fraud—used cars being sold as new—is usually promptly policed. However, it is costly, time-consuming, and of not much interest to the general public to take an automobile dealer to court for claiming that a car gets 22 miles to a gallon of gasoline when it actually gets only 15 miles.

It is probably unfair to dismiss state and local regulation of deceptive advertising as handily as is done here. In some areas, cities and state attorneys general really do a superior job of protecting consumers. But that is not the norm. Unfortunately, the consumer's best friend when it

Federal Regulation

comes to stopping false and misleading advertisements is also a distant friend, the federal government.

Here is the advertiser, surrounded by industry codes, media regulations, and state and city laws, confused at best. But the worst is yet to come. The primary agent of the federal government which regulates advertising is, of course, the Federal Trade Commission, which has a general mandate to police unfair and deceptive advertising. In addition to the Federal Trade Commission Act, federal regulations on advertising can be found in at least thirty-two other statutes. To name a few: the Communication Act, Federal Drug and Cosmetics Act, Consumer Credit Protection Act, Copyright Acts, Consumer Products Safety Act, Federal Cigarette Labelling and Advertising Act, Wool Products Labeling Act of 1939, and Plant Variety Protection Act. In addition, regulations can be found in the Age Discrimination Employment Act, Federal Seed Act, National Stamping Act, Savings and Loan Act of 1952, Securities Act, and Aid to Blind and Handicapped Act. Also postal regulations contain numerous provisions regarding the mailability of advertising matter. There is a law which states that the United States flag cannot be used for advertising purposes. There is a criminal statute which makes it illegal to use the name of the Federal Bureau of Investigation, or FBI, in an advertisement without permission from the bureau. Also, the likeness of United States currency and securities can't be used in advertising.

These laws are fairly clear. A law degree isn't required to understand a regulation which says the likeness of a dollar bill shouldn't be published in an advertisement. Advertisers do a fairly good job of not running afoul of these regulations. The general FTC mandate that bans false and deceptive advertising is not so simple, however. For instance, just what is false and deceptive advertising?

The remainder of this chapter focuses on this problem, defining false and deceptive advertising within the context of the Federal Trade Commission. We will discuss the jurisdiction of that agency, its standards, remedies at its disposal, and its procedures. By the end of the discussion the dimensions of such terms as *unfair, misleading,* and *deceptive* should be clearer.

**FEDERAL
TRADE
COMMISSION**

The Federal Trade Commission, or "the little gray lady of Pennsylvania Avenue" as its detractors once called it, was created in 1914 to police unfair methods of competition. As Congress conceived the agency the FTC was to make certain that Company A did not engage in practices which gave it an unfair advantage over its competitive rival Company B. One method of unfair competition was deceptive advertising. If Company A advertised that its widgets were four times quieter than any other widgets and they weren't, this claim gave Company A an unfair competitive advantage. What about the consumers, the people who bought widgets? As originally conceived the FTC was not to worry about the effect of advertising on buyers, only on competitors.

Jurisdiction

In the 1920s the agency began to flex its muscles illegally and cracked down on all kinds of deceptive advertising: advertising that endangered competition and advertising that merely cheated customers. Until 1931, that is, when the Supreme Court ruled in *FTC* v. *Raladam* that the FTC could not stop a false advertisement unless there was proof that the advertisement had unfairly affected the advertiser's competitors. While the ruling did not totally destroy the efficacy of the agency, it did slow it down and made action against false and deceptive advertising more difficult.

In 1938 Congress bolstered the FTC when it passed the Wheeler-Lea Amendment to the Trade Commission Act giving the agency the authority to proceed against all unfair and deceptive acts or practices in commerce, regardless of whether they affected competition. This amendment gave the commission the power it had been seeking.

Today the FTC is one of the largest of the independent regulatory agencies, having a staff of more than 1,600 and an annual budget of about $35 million. In addition to policing false advertising the agency is charged with enforcing the nation's antitrust laws, the Flammable Fabrics Act, the Truth in Lending Law, the Fair Credit Reporting Act, and various labeling laws. The five members of the commission are appointed by the president and confirmed by the Senate for a term of seven years. No more than three of the commissioners can be from the same political party. The chairman, one of the five members of the commission, is named by the president. While the agency is located in Washington, D.C., it has regional offices in Atlanta, Boston, Chicago, Cleveland, Dallas, Kansas City, Los Angeles, New Orleans, New York, San Francisco, and Seattle.

The aggressiveness of the FTC has been a matter of controversy for many years because of its reluctance to investigate and prosecute—hence the nickname "the little gray lady of Pennsylvania Ave." Consumer advocates argue that the agency languished until the successive appointments as chairman of Casper Weinberger and Miles Kirkpatrick in the late sixties and early seventies. After four or five go-go years the agency again slowed down somewhat under the chairmanship of Louis Engman. In 1974 a staff report of the House Subcommittee on Commerce and Finance complained that the FTC lacked leadership, made fewer investigations, issued fewer rules, and brought fewer cases. Still, even the critics of the agency admit that the contemporary commission is a good deal more active than the 1950s-early 1960s commission.

Perhaps the most significant difference between the current FTC and the earlier Weinberger-Kirkpatrick model concerns the kind of advertisers being challenged. Both Chairman Weinberger and Chairman Kirkpatrick had a propensity to attack leading advertisers such as Standard Oil, Coca Cola Company, Firestone Tire and Rubber Company, ITT Continental Baking Co., and so forth. Such suits are rare today. The commission seems instead to direct its action against smaller regional advertisers. The lessening of the attack upon major manufacturers could be due to the commission's reluctance to act or to its relative lack of success against bigger advertisers.

Before going further, we must understand the term *advertising* as defined by the federal government. According to FTC practice and legal custom, *advertising* is defined as any action, method, or device intended to draw the attention of the public to merchandise, to services, to persons, and to organizations (see, for example, *Rast* v. *van Deman & Lewis Co.*, 1916, and *State* v. *Cusick*, 1957). Included in the definition in addition to the obvious products advertised are trading stamps, contests, freebies and premiums, and even labels on products.

Does the FTC regulate all advertising? Legally, no, it cannot. Practically, it regulates almost all advertising. Because the agency was created under the authority of Congress to regulate interstate commerce, products or services being offered must be sold in interstate commerce, or the advertising medium must be somehow affected by interstate commerce. While many products and services are sold locally only, nearly every conceivable advertising medium is somehow affected by or affects interstate commerce. All broadcasting stations are considered to affect interstate commerce. Most newspapers ship at least a few copies across state lines. If they aren't, it is very likely that some of the news in the newspaper comes across state lines, or that the paper on which the news is printed, the ink and type used to print the news, or parts of the printing machinery travel across state lines. The federal government became quite adept at demonstrating that businesses affect interstate commerce or are affected by interstate commerce as it learned to enforce laws like the Public Accommodations Act. The motel owner who declared that he didn't have to abide by the federal law because his business was a local operation soon discovered that if the chickens or apples he served in his restaurant were shipped in from out of state the courts were willing to say that his motel operation was a part of interstate commerce.

There are some other requirements which must be met before the FTC can act. It must be shown that the agency is acting in the public interest, which is really not too difficult since false advertising generally has an impact upon the public. If the FTC says it is acting in the public interest, courts usually take its word for it.

The advertisement must be unfair or deceptive before the FTC can act. Although deceptive advertising is discussed more fully later in the chapter and specific words and types of advertisements are considered, a few general facts about deceptive advertising must be given at this point. An advertisement is deceptive if it has a tendency to deceive (see *FTC v. Raladam,* 1942). The FTC does not have to show that any person has been deceived. In fact, the commission can rule that an advertisement is deceptive even if the advertiser presents as witnesses consumers who testify that the advertisement is not deceptive.

There are really four aspects of the determination that an advertisement is deceptive. First, the meaning of the advertisement must be determined—that is, what promise is made. Second, the truth of the message must be determined. Is the promise kept? Third, when only part of the advertisement is false, it must be determined whether the false part is a material aspect of the advertisement, that is, capable of affecting the purchasing decision of consumers (*Moretrench Corp. v. FTC.,* 1942). The Chevron F-310 advertisements illustrate this point very well. A spokesman for the company claimed he was standing in front of the Standard Oil research laboratories when in fact, he was standing in front of a county courthouse. This was a false statement. But was the statement a material aspect of the advertisement as a whole? A hearing examiner said no, that the location of a spokesman is irrelevant to a consumer making a purchasing decision.

The fourth aspect of determining deception concerns the level of understanding and experience of the audience to which the advertisement is directed. This aspect, in turn, has several dimensions.

If the advertisement is directed toward a special group—children—it is judged by the ordinary perception of that group. In 1974 when the FTC announced that advertising directed at children which focused on premium offers (such as advertisements for breakfast cereals) was banned, Chairman Engman said:

> The child who makes or participates in a purchasing decision faces an already taxing and complex task. Even so simple a decision as the rational selection of a breakfast cereal involves the weighing of price, taste, nutritional value, convenience and promotional devices designed to create distinctiveness. The injection of a premium offer cannot help but multiply the difficulties of choice. When that factor is irrelevant to the merits of the product, it can only increase the likelihood of confusion.

The same special consideration is given advertisements directed to specialists. An advertisement prepared for publication in a technical magazine read by engineers need not be meaningful to average consumers. However, the FTC might consider an advertisement written for a special audience but published in a magazine for the general public to be deceptive.

Standards

How does the FTC evaluate the intelligence of that great mass audience to which you and I belong? For years the commission took the approach of the lowest common denominator. The FTC really didn't think we were very bright or cautious. In a 1942 case, *Aronberg* v. *FTC*, a federal judge outlined the prevailing standard:

> The law is not made for experts but to protect the public—the vast multitude of which includes the ignorant, the unthinking, and the credulous who are making purchases, do not stop to analyze but too often are governed by appearances and general impressions.

This was, perhaps still is, the standard the FTC uses in judging advertising. However, experts in this area recently noted a swing away from this standard to a standard based on "the average man." The first clue cited in the change of attitude is a ruling by the FTC in 1963. Commissioner Elman, speaking for the agency, said (*Heinz* v. *Kirchner*):

> Perhaps a few misguided souls believe, for example, that all "Danish pastry" is made in Denmark. Is it therefore an actionable deception to advertise "Danish pastry" when it is made in this country?

The commission said no. An advertisement is not false and deceptive merely because it is "unreasonably misunderstood by an insignificant and unrepresentative segment" of buyers.

Ten years later the Federal Trade Commission seemed to have changed its mind when it rejected the argument of its staff that advertisements for Hi-C fruit drinks implied that the beverages (which contain about 10 percent fruit juice) were as good as or better than fresh orange juice. The FTC ruling implied (it did not specifically say) that the average consumer is smart enough to tell the difference between Hi-C and real fruit juice (in re *Coca-Cola Co.*, 1973). Commissioners dissenting from this point of view argued that the agency was changing its definition of consumers, that it was beginning to assume they were discriminating, knowledgeable, skeptical, and incredulous. One dissenter said, "This consumer knows that fruit drinks are not the same as citrus juices despite what Hi-C ads say." Whether the Federal Trade Commission has adopted a new standard remains to be seen.

When it comes down to the bottom line most lawyers who represent advertisers before the FTC have a simple, if cynical, definition of deceptiveness. An advertisement is deceptive, they say, if the FTC says it is. This assertion seems to contain substantial truth. A finding of deceptiveness by the FTC does bind courts which must often hear appeals from commission decisions, as will become obvious in the discussion of commission procedures.

Remedies

In 1973 in a study of the Federal Trade Commission by the American Enterprise Institute for Public Policy Research, law professor Richard A. Posner concludes that the cardinal weakness in the FTC is in the area of remedies. "To be sure," Posner writes, "it is possible that even though the commission's constructive activity is very small in any given year the very existence of the commission serves to deter a great deal of unlawful conduct. But it is unlikely that the FTC's power to deter is very great, given the limitations of its sanctions." (*Regulation of Advertising by the Federal Trade Commission.*)

The commission's greatest enemy in dealing with false advertising is time, the time needed to bring an action against the advertiser. Advertising campaigns are ephemeral—here today, gone tomorrow. The average campaign doesn't last more than six or eight months. It normally takes the commission much longer than that to catch up with the advertiser, to comply with all the due-process requirements involved in a hearing, and to ultimately decide whether there has been a violation of the law. By that time everybody has forgotten about the advertisement, and the advertiser is promising people a new pot of gold at rainbow's end. Even the commission recognizes this problem. Chairman Engman noted in a speech to the American Bar Association in 1974 that while good law is more important than fast law the commission's proceedings nonetheless have too often "had a Nuremberg quality providing the public with more moral compensation than meaningful protection."

The Federal Trade Commission has a wide range of what might be called remedies for, or means to attack, deceptive advertising. Recent remedies were specifically directed at providing more meaningful protection.

Guides (Advisory Opinions)

At the top of the list of remedies is the power of the commission to issue industry guides, which are really policy statements by the commission about potential problems. For example, if a cigar company wants to know whether it can legally advertise its cigars as "the coolest burning cigar in town" it can ask the FTC for an opinion before launching the campaign. Normally the FTC will advise companies about the legality of proposed claims. In some cases the FTC issues an industry guide, which is merely an advisory interpretation of what the FTC believes the law to be on the subject. For example, the FTC has issued a guide on the use of the word *free* and similar representations in advertising. It has issued a guide for advertising private vocational schools and home study courses. It has issued a guide for the decorative wall paneling industry. There are many, many other guides. In a guide the commission tells the advertiser that statement X can be made, statement Y cannot be made, statement Z cannot be made without substantiation, and so forth. The purpose of the guides is to help advertisers stay within the law. What happens when an advertiser fails to comply with the provisions of a guide? The FTC must proceed against the advertisement as it would against any other advertisement. The guides do not have the force of law. They are merely FTC opinions about what the law says. Deceptiveness still has to be proved in an FTC hearing.

Voluntary Compliance

Industry guides and advisory opinions apply only to prospective advertising campaigns, events that haven't yet occurred. The next remedy on the ladder is voluntary compliance and is used for advertising campaigns that are over or nearly over. Imagine that the cigar company is nearing the end of its coolest-burning-cigar-in-town campaign. The FTC believes that the claim is deceptive. If the advertiser has had a good record in the past and if the offense is not too great, the company can voluntarily agree to terminate the advertisement and never use the claim again. In doing this, the advertiser makes no admission and the agency no determination that the claim is deceptive. There is just an agreement not to repeat that particular claim in future advertising campaigns. Such an agreement saves the advertiser considerable legal hassle, publicity, and money, all especially desirable since the advertising campaign is over or almost over.

Consent Order

The next remedy seems to be similar to voluntary compliance, but is more complicated and more binding. The remedy is called a consent order and is a written agreement between the commission and the advertiser in which the advertiser again makes promises concerning future advertising. The advertiser is asked to agree not to do certain things and may also be asked to do certain other things. If the advertiser signs the agreement, the FTC takes no further action.

Here are some recent consent orders which were published in FTC consumer bulletins. In 1974 the Ford Motor Company agreed to stop claiming that its LTD cars ran quieter than a glider in flight. Why was this claim a problem? Apparently a glider is really quite noisy in flight, and the FTC believed that the advertisement in which the announcer said "Nobody has to convince you how quiet a glider is" was misleading. In 1975 the Morton Salt Company agreed to stop advertising its product Lite Salt in such a way as to lead buyers to believe that it was more healthful than ordinary salt. The company also agreed that all future advertising of Lite Salt would contain the statement "Not to be used by persons on sodium or potassium restricted diets unless approved by a physician." The company which makes Gaines Burgers dog food agreed recently to stop claiming that Gaines Burgers contain nutrient ingredients unless the ingredients are present in a nutritionally significant amount. The firm also agreed to stop advertising that pets have a need for a nutrient that in fact they do not need and to stop making representation about the nutritional quality of its dog food unless it has evidence to support the claim.

General Foods Corp. also agreed to stop its advertisements for Post Grape Nuts which depicted the late Euell Gibbons picking and eating, or pointing to, wild plants and bushes and stating that this vegetation was edible and tasty. The FTC said that the advertisements could influence children to eat plants and shrubs most of which are not edible and may be poisonous.

As will be noted in the discussion of FTC procedures, there is considerable pressure on the advertiser to agree to a consent order. The chance of winning a case before the FTC is usually slim. The litigation is also costly. Finally, the publicity that results from such litigation often does the product more harm than any FTC sanction now in captivity.

If after accepting the consent order the advertiser then violates the agreement the company is subject to a severe fine, up to $10,000 a day while the violation continues (i.e., while the advertising campaign continues).

Cease and Desist Order

What happens if the cigar company really believes that its cigar is "the coolest burning cigar in town" and doesn't want to sign a consent order? The commission issues a cease and desist order. The advertisements must stop or the advertiser faces severe civil penalty: again, a fine of up to $10,000 a day. In the long-running (eleven years) Geritol case, for example, the commission issued an order in 1965 prohibiting the J. B. Williams Company from implying in its advertising for Geritol that its product can be helpful to persons who are tired and rundown (in re *J. B. Williams Co.*, 1965; *J. B. Williams Co.* v. *FTC*, 1967). The commission contended that medical evidence demonstrates that Geritol, a vitamin-and-iron tonic, helps only a small percentage of persons who are tired and that in most persons tiredness is a symptom of ailments for which Geritol has no therapeutic value. The J. B. Williams Company violated the cease and desist order (at least, that is what the commission alleged) and in 1973 was fined more than $800,000. A court of appeals threw out the fine in 1974 and sent the case back to district court for a jury trial, which the advertisers had been denied the first time around (*U.S.* v. *J. B. Williams*, 1974). The jury was to decide whether the Geritol advertisements did in fact violate the cease and desist order. At a second hearing in 1976 the FTC won a $280,000 judgment against the patent medicine manufacturer. This is a good example of what violating such an order can ultimately cost the advertiser.

Standard Oil of California was ordered recently to stop claiming that its Chevron gasolines with F-310 produce pollution-free exhaust. The commission banned television and print advertisements in which the company claimed that just six tankfuls of Chevron will clean up a car's exhaust to the point that it is almost free of exhaust-emission pollutants.

Few advertisers are willing to carry a case as far as the cease and desist order, and those that go that far frequently go beyond to a court of appeals to challenge the FTC's ruling. The appeal process is explored in the discussion of FTC procedures (pp. 371-372).

The pressure is heavy upon advertisers to voluntarily comply or to sign a consent order, especially since in neither case is there admission of wrongdoing and in both instances the legal processes will take so long that the offensive advertising campaign will probably be finished before the case is heard. Many people feel that the FTC does its job if it gains compliance voluntarily, for the mission of the agency is, after all, to stop deceptive advertising, not to punish advertisers. Other observers disagree, however, and argue that without stronger sanctions the advertiser is not motivated to refrain from future illegal acts. This kind of argument prompted the FTC to undertake new regulatory schemes, which we will now examine.

Substantiation

Substantiation of an advertisement at first glance hardly seems like an important regulatory scheme, but it is a very important one. The program began in 1971 and had only limited success. Since then it has been modified and reportedly now works better. The basis of the program is simple: the FTC asks advertisers to substantiate all claims in their advertisements. There is no assertion that a claim is false or misleading. The government merely tells advertisers to prove what they say.

At first the FTC chose an entire industry—like the soap and detergent makers—and gave all companies in the industry sixty days to provide documentation for all their claims: claims that Ivory Soap is pure, that Clorox is able to do what detergents alone cannot do, and that Pine-Sol kills household germs.

The firms then supplied the FTC with support for their claims if they could, and most of the companies could. If they could not, through a consent order the FTC usually asked them to stop making the claim. All kinds of industries were included in substantiation orders: the automobile industry; the air-conditioning manufacturers; the makers of shampoos, electric shavers, cough and cold remedies, and antiperspirants; and so forth. However problems arose. About 90 percent of the material submitted as documentation was too technical for a layman to understand, and since one of the goals of the project was to allow consumers to study the proof offered by the advertisers, this aspect of the program was a failure. In 1974 the FTC ordered that when documentation is in technical or scientific language it must be accompanied by a summary in lay language.

Another problem was the amount of information submitted. When an entire industry, or industries, had to submit documentation there was just too much material. Now the FTC uses a committee of experts to screen advertising claims and target those advertisements which seem the most suspect for substantiation. Also, the time the advertiser has to submit material was cut from sixty to thirty days.

Finally, the FTC changed its policy concerning publicity about substantiation. In the past the agency publicly announced that all automakers, for example, had been asked to document their claims. Advertisers complained that many consumers incorrectly presumed that the claims were somehow deceptive. Why else would the government seek documentation? Now, no announcement is made until after the commission receives the material and places it on the public record. This policy seems to satisfy advertisers.

On its face substantiation seems a fairly innocent little process. Nevertheless from a legal standpoint it has had a major impact on regulation because it shifted the burden of proof in a great many advertising cases from the commission, which in the past had to prove that an advertisement was deceptive, to the advertiser who must now prove it is true. If the case goes to litigation and a hearing, the FTC must still prove that the advertising claim is deceptive. Since most problems are solved short of this stage by consent agreement, substantiation has reduced considerably the work load of the FTC. The FTC no longer has to convince advertisers prior to getting their assent to an agreement that it can prove the advertisement is deceptive. By not being able to substantiate its claim, the advertiser accomplishes the proof himself.

Corrective Advertising

Corrective advertising is a highly controversial scheme which the FTC first used in 1971 against the ITT Continental Baking Company. The scheme is based on the premise that to merely stop an advertisement is in some instances insufficient. If the advertising campaign is successful and long running, a residue of misleading information remains in the mind of the public after the offensive advertisements have been removed. Under the corrective advertising scheme the FTC forces the advertiser to inform the public that in the past it has not been honest or has been misleading. One commentator called the scheme "commercial hara-kiri." In truth, the remedy sounds a lot worse than it really is, but advertisers fought tooth and nail against it.

The FTC first attempted to force what it calls affirmative or corrective disclosures in 1950, but a court of appeals ruled that it lacked the power to do so under the Federal Trade Commission Act. The court ruled in *Alberty* v. *FTC* (1950) that the agency lacked the authority to encourage or require informative advertising. Ten years later, however, in *Feil* v. *FTC* (1960), the courts reversed the *Alberty* decision. The FTC threatened to use the remedy against the Campbell Soup Company to correct the misperception created when the company put clear marbles in the bottom of a bowl of vegetable soup to force the vegetables to the top (Campbell Soup Co., 1970). The first corrective advertisement didn't appear until 1971. As mentioned earlier, it was the result of a consent order signed by the ITT Continental Baking Company with regard to its advertising for Profile Bread. The television version of the advertisement was this:

> I'm Julia Meade for Profile Bread. And like all mothers I'm concerned about nutrition and balanced meals. So I'd like to clear up any misunderstanding you may have about Profile Bread from its advertising or even its name. Does Profile have fewer calories than other breads? No, Profile has about the same per ounce as other breads. To be exact Profile has seven fewer calories per slice. But that's because it's sliced thinner. But eating Profile Bread will not cause you to lose weight. A reduction of seven calories is insignificant. It's total calories and balanced nutrition that counts. And Profile can help you achieve a balanced meal. Because it provides protein and B vitamins as well as other nutrients.

This corrective advertisement was in response to a Profile campaign that led some people to believe that one could lose weight by eating Profile Bread.

The commission required that corrective advertisements like this one constitute 25 percent of the advertising for Profile Bread during the year following the agreement. This is the typical percentage in a corrective-advertising agreement, although at times the FTC has agreed to allow advertisers to allot only 15 percent of their advertising budget for corrective advertisements.

Only a few other manufacturers of well-known nationally advertised products have been forced to make corrective disclosures. One was the company making Ocean Spray Cranberry Juice which for years advertised that its cranberry juice had more food energy than other juices. Since food energy is really only another way of saying caloric value, the FTC ordered the juice maker to tell people that fact in a corrective ad (*Ocean Spray Cranberries, Inc.*, 1972). Neither the Profile advertisement nor the cranberry juice advertisement pleased all consumer advocates. Many thought the advertisements were too weak. In fact, studies showed that sales of Profile Bread were not hurt by the corrective campaign.

The FTC has been both tougher and more prepared to use the corrective advertising device against small advertisers. Some corrective advertisements even have to include what lawyers dub "the Scarlet Letter," a statement by advertisers that the FTC found previous advertising to be deceptive. An example of such an order is the one agreed to by Wasem's Drug Store in Clarkston, Washington. The store marketed vitamin pills under its own name in advertising which the FTC deemed to be false and misleading. In the consent order the firm agreed to devote 25 percent of its advertising for one year to corrective advertising, to refrain from using the word *super* in the trade name of the vitamins, and to broadcast seven, sixty-second corrective advertisements on seven consecutive days on local television stations. This is the corrective ad, including the Scarlet Letter:

> This advertisement is run pursuant to an order of the Federal Trade Commission. I have previously been advertising Wasem's Super B Vitamins and have made various claims which are erroneous or misleading. Contrary to what I told you previously, Super B will not make you feel better nor make you better to live with nor work with on the job. There is no need for most people to supplement their diet with vitamins and minerals. Excess dosages over the recommended daily adult requirement of most vitamins will be flushed through the body and be of no benefit whatsoever. Contrary to my previous ads, neither the Food and Drug Administration nor the Federal Trade Commission nor anyone else has recommended Super B or approved our prior claims. Super B Vitamins are sold on a money-back guarantee, so if you are not fully satisfied, then return them to me at Wasem's Rexall Drug Store in Clarkston for a refund.

Nobody really knows whether these kinds of advertisements really are effective in ridding the consumer's mind of the falsity. Probably many buyers retain an unfavorable impression of the advertiser. If this is true, corrective advertising will probably constitute an important deterrent for exaggerated claims.

Injunctions
When Congress passed the Trans-Alaska Pipeline Authorization Act in 1973 attached to that piece of legislation was a bill which authorized the FTC to seek an injunction to stop advertisements which it believed violated the law. Attorneys for the FTC can seek these restraining orders in federal court. An injunction is clearly a drastic remedy and one which the agency has said it will not use often. Spokesmen for the FTC have said that the agency will use the power only in those instances in which the advertising can cause harm, in those cases where there is a clear law

violation, and in those cases where there is no prospect that the advertising practice will end soon.

The first time the FTC used its new power was in 1973 when it sought and got a restraining order against several West Coast travel agents who promoted trips to the Philippines for "psychic surgery." The FTC said that many Americans were being fleeced by so-called psychic surgeons who supposedly performed bloodless operations on patients by using their mind rather than scalpels. The agency won its case.

Trade Regulation Rules

In January 1975 President Ford signed the Magnuson-Moss Warranty —Federal Trade Commission Improvement Act, the most significant piece of trade regulation legislation since the Wheeler-Lea Amendment in 1938. The new law did many things, but basically it greatly enlarged both the power and the jurisdiction of the FTC. Until the bill was signed the FTC was limited to dealing with unfair and deceptive practices which were "in commerce." The new law expanded the jurisdiction to practices "affecting commerce." The change of a single word gave the FTC broad new areas to regulate.

Three sections of the act expanded the remedies of the FTC. First, the agency was given the power to issue trade regulation rules defining and outlawing unfair and deceptive acts or practices. The importance of this power alone cannot be overestimated. In the past the agency had to pursue deceptive advertisements one at a time. Imagine, for example, that four or five different breakfast cereals all advertise that they are good for children because they contain nine times the recommended daily allowance of vitamins and minerals. Medical experts argue that any vitamins in excess of 100 percent of the recommended daily allowance are useless, therefore these advertisements are probably deceptive or misleading. In the past the FTC would have had to issue a complaint against each advertiser and in each case prove that the statement was a violation of the law. Under the new rules the agency can issue a trade regulation rule—as it had done for nutritional claims—which declares that claims of product superiority based on excessive dosage of vitamins and minerals are false and misleading. If advertisers make such a claim they are in violation of the law. All the commission must prove is that the advertiser had actual knowledge of the trade regulation rule, or "knowledge fairly implied from the objective circumstances."

The advantages of the trade regulation rules, or TRRs as they are called, are numerous. They speed up and simplify the process of enforcement. Advertisers can still litigate the question, challenge the trade regulation rule, seek an appeal in court, and so forth. In most cases they probably will not go to that expense. Trade regulation rules should have a great deterrent effect as they comprehensively delimit what constitutes an illegal practice. In the past after the commission issued a cease and desist order, businesses frequently attempted to undertake practices which fell just outside the narrow boundaries of the order. The TRRs are much broader and will make it much harder for advertisers to skirt the limitations. Finally, via TRRs the FTC will be able to deal with problems most evenhandedly. An entire industry will be treated similarly, and just one or two businesses will not be picked out for complaint.

While the FTC has issued TRRs since 1962, it has done so sparingly since it was unsure of its power to take this action. In 1974 a court of appeals upheld the right of the agency to promulgate such rules (*National Petroleum Refiners Association* v. *FTC,* 1974). This court decision was made law by Congress in the FTC Improvement Act. Since that time, according to one FTC representative, the commission has been busy promulgating rules so that this aspect of regulation is more visible now.

The two other aspects of the new law which improved FTC remedies are these. The FTC may now seek civil penalties against any one who knowingly violates the provisions of a cease and desist order, even if that person was not originally the subject of the order. To wit: A Chemical Company sells a spray paint which is toxic if used in a closed area, but the product is advertised as being completely harmless. The FTC moves against the company and issues a cease and desist order that states that in the future the firm must not advertise the product as being completely harmless. B Chemical Company also sells a spray paint which has the same toxicity and is advertised the same way. If it can be shown that B Company was aware of the provisions of the order against A Company and continued to advertise its product as being completely safe, B can be fined up to $10,000 per day for violating the order, even though the order is not directed against B.

Finally, the new law gives the FTC the right to sue in federal court on behalf of consumers who have been victimized by practices that are in violation of a cease and desist order or by practices that are in violation of a TRR.

These new remedies give the FTC more muscle. Their greatest strength will be as a deterrent, giving advertisers something to think about before beginning a questionable advertising practice.

Procedures

In order to understand both the regulation of advertising and the problems faced by the FTC, it is necessary to have at least a sketchy understanding of how the agency operates in a deceptive advertising case. Most cases come to the attention of the FTC from letters written either by consumers or by competitors of the offending advertiser. The legal staff of the agency then does a preliminary investigation. If the complaint counsel, an FTC staff attorney, feels there is no substance to the charge, the case ends. But if he believes there is a provable violation, he writes a memorandum to the commission. A proposed complaint and a proposed consent order accompany the memorandum.

The agency takes a vote, and if it agrees with staff lawyers—it usually does—the advertiser is notified that a complaint is about to be issued. The advertiser is given the opportunity to sign the consent order or to negotiate a more favorable consent order. At this point there can be three results. First, the advertiser can agree to the consent order and the commission can vote to accept the consent order. Second, the commission can vote not to accept the order. Third, the advertiser could reject the consent order. If the first happens the order is published and sixty days later is made final.

If either the commission or the advertiser rejects the consent order, a complaint is issued and a hearing is scheduled before an administrative law judge, who works within the FTC and officiates at commission hearings. At the hearing that follows—which is a lot like an informal trial—the burden of proof rests upon the FTC staff lawyers—complaint counsels—to show a violation of the law. In a criminal trial for robbery or murder, the evidence must show "beyond a reasonable doubt" that the defendant is guilty. In a civil case liability must be established by "preponderance of evidence." In a hearing before an administrative law judge all the complaint counsel must show is that there is "substantial evidence" of a violation of the law. While what substantial evidence is, is hard to define, it is less evidence than is required in either a criminal suit or a civil suit. After the hearing the judge either orders the case dismissed or issues a cease and desist order. The decision is final unless either the complaint counsel or the advertiser appeals. If that happens the entire commission decides the matter. Overruling an administrative law judge is not uncommon. For example, after the hearing on Chevron F-310 the commission overruled the judge's decision to dismiss the charges. More recently the commission overruled a judge's cease and desist order against several television advertisements for Dry Ban spray deodorant. The judge agreed with complaint counsel that the advertisements implied that the spray "went on dry," but in fact was wet when it hit the skin. The FTC disagreed and said that all the advertisement implied was that Ban went on the skin drier than other antiperspirant sprays. A court of appeals must finalize either a consent order or a cease and desist order, but it is a routine matter.

If the FTC dismisses the cease and desist order, the matter ends there. If it supports the order, the advertiser can still appeal to the courts for relief. This is not a common practice, however. It is difficult for courts to reverse an FTC ruling. There are only a handful of reasons which a judge can use to overturn the commission decision. The case goes to the court of appeals and there is no new finding of fact: what the FTC says is fact, is fact. If the court finds "convincing evidence" that the agency made an error somewhere in the proceeding, if there is no evidence at all to support the commission's findings, if the agency violated the Constitution (did not provide due process of law, for example), if the FTC goes beyond its powers, if the facts relied upon by the FTC are not supported by substantial evidence, and if the agency acts arbitrarily or capriciously are all instances in which the court can overturn the ruling. Such an event is an extreme rarity. An appeal of an adverse ruling by a circuit court can be taken to the Supreme Court, but only if certiorari is granted.

The enforcement powers of the FTC are limited, but can be nevertheless effective. Violation of either a cease and desist order or a consent order can result in a penalty of $10,000 per violation per day. A fine such as this can add up fast! As a result of the Geritol case the agency can be forced into district court to prove to a jury that in fact the orders were violated. This action impedes the enforcement procedure, for a jury trial is time-consuming and costly. As an alternative the agency can go back to the court of appeals which finalized the consent order or the cease and desist order and seek a civil contempt citation against the advertiser. The penalty is then up to the judge and will probably be much smaller since civil contempt damages are considered remedial and are not intended as a deterrent.

Enforcement is a complex and sometimes confusing process. This fact at least partially explains why FTC procedures often move so slowly. It also explains why the agency works so hard to gain compliance with consent orders since voluntary compliance alleviates many bureaucratic hassles. It is easier to enforce TRRs, and the use of this remedy probably will become more common in light of the decision in the Geritol case.

DECEPTIVE ADVERTISING

It must be obvious that advertising regulations are fairly clear on one point: deceptive, unfair, misleading, untruthful advertising is not permitted. But what is deceptive, unfair, misleading, untruthful advertising? It is the same kind of question we confronted when defining what is obscene and what is libelous. There is no great scroll in the sky providing a complete and comprehensive list of advertisements that are permitted and those that are not permissible. An advertiser is expected to use common sense to some extent and to supplement his common sense by examining what the various regulatory agencies in the past have deemed to be deceptive. In this section we will talk about the regulatory guidelines, but you are cautioned that this discussion is by no means exhaustive or complete. Scores of deceptions which have been prohibited are not included here, and scores and scores are yet to be created. So be forewarned.

Concept of Truth

Just because an advertisement is untruthful does not mean that it is deceptive or illegal. When a supermarket advertises that the Easter Bunny left lots of good grocery buys in the produce section or a gasoline company advertises that you can put a tiger in your tank, most people realize that they are being kidded. These kinds of fanciful nonmaterial untruths are generally acceptable so long as the advertiser doesn't get carried away. All other kinds of untruths including explicit untruths (big lies), half-truths, and more subtle deceptions are problems.

If you advertise a watch as being waterproof and it isn't, that is a lie and is a violation of the law. An advertiser can't qualify a lie appearing in one part of an advertisement by providing a sneaky list of exceptions elsewhere in the advertisement (*Giant Food, Inc.,* v. *FTC*, 1963). For example, it is deceptive to claim in a prominent headline that your brand of watch is waterproof and then in a footnote in small type at the bottom of the advertisement indicate that the watch is waterproof except when immersed in water for more than 14 seconds.

Not telling the whole truth is also deceptive. To claim that 93 percent of all your watches sold since 1952 still keep perfect time is a half-truth unless you also state that the watches have only been on the market for the last three years. Deceptive mock-ups and demonstrations are also considered illegal if the mock-up is used as proof of an advertising claim (*FTC* v. *Colgate-Palmolive Co.*, 1965). More explanation is needed. For many years a shaving cream company claimed that its product was so good that it could be used to shave sandpaper. In a television commercial an actor put Rapid Shave on sandpaper and a few minutes later was shown shaving off the sand. While the claim was apparently true (if the shaving cream was left on the sandpaper long enough, that is), the demonstration was phony. What the actor shaved was not sandpaper but loose sand sprinkled on glass. The government said this was deceptive advertising and the courts—including the United States Supreme Court—agreed, despite advertiser pleas that it had tried to shave real sandpaper in the commercial, but because the sand and the paper were the same color, and because the ads were in black and white, viewers could not see that the sand really came off. In other words, as one author wrote, a mock-up cannot overcome the shortcomings of the medium, even were the claims true.

In its decision the Supreme Court did not rule that all fake demonstrations or mock-ups are illegal, only those in which the faked portion is supposed to prove a product claim (*FTC* v. *Colgate Palmolive Co.*,

1965). For example, let's say that in a television commercial packaged ice cubes are the product being sold. The film must be shot under hot lights. Since the ice cubes would melt in the heat, plastic cubes are used. A pile of the plastic cubes are put on a table, and while the cameras grind away an announcer extolls the virtues of these marvelous, uniform-size, crystal-clear ice cubes. This device is illegal because the plastic cubes are used to prove the advertising claims. Let's now say that soda pop instead of ice cubes is being sold, and the actor drops three or four plastic cubes into a glass before he pours in "the mouth-watering, cool, and refreshing" soda. It is permissible to use the plastic cubes in this situation because they are not being used to demonstrate a product claim.

What about advertisements that have a double meaning, a truthful meaning and one that is not? Here is a classic example. "We will put a new motor in your old car for $35 dollars." What does this statement mean? It can be read to mean that the advertiser will sell you a new motor and install it in your car for $35. That is a good deal. However, the statement can also mean that if you have a new motor for your old car the advertiser will install it for $35, which is not such a good deal. In such situations the government presumes that people believe the misleading meaning, and such advertising is deceptive (*FTC* v. *Sterling Drug Co.*, 1963).

The entire problem of half-truths, partial truths, double meanings, and so forth, is one of the most serious problems the government faces. Complaints against such advertisements are common. More than twenty years ago the FTC challenged an advertisement for Old Gold cigarettes which quoted an independent survey finding Old Golds to be low in nicotine and tar (*P. Lorillard Co.*, 1950). This claim was true, but the group which did the research also concluded that none of the cigarettes tested—including Old Gold—had sufficiently low nicotine-and-tar content to be safe. The cigarette maker didn't disclose this fact, making the advertisement deceptive. More recently the government has pressured the company that makes Wonder Bread for advertising that its product contains vitamins and minerals which will help young people to grow up to be big and strong. The government says that nearly all commercially baked bread is fortified with vitamins and minerals and will help young people to grow up to be big and strong. The FTC argues that by not disclosing that Wonder Bread is no different from any other bread, the company tells only half the story (in re *ITT Continental Baking Co.*, 1973). The makers of Geritol, by not saying that Geritol does not help most people who are tired, and the Ford Motor Company, by comparing the quietness of their car to that of a glider and not saying that a glider is noisy

Testimonial

in flight, were guilty of the same kind of deception. This kind of deceptive advertising is probably the most common problem today.

The testimonial, ranging from Joe Namath advertising panty hose to "the average man" promoting a pain reliever, is a large part of the advertising business. Before 1932, when a company paid for a testimonial—any testimonial—that fact had to be revealed in the advertisement. This hasn't been the law for more than forty years, however (*Northam Warren Corp.* v. *FTC*, 1932). Today, within certain limits, paid testimonials are allowed. The testifier must have in fact endorsed the product (*Eastern Railroad Presidents' Conference* v. *Noerr Motor Freight, Inc.*, 1961). It is deceptive, as well as an invasion of privacy, for an advertiser to assert that astronaut Neil Armstrong eats X brand of breakfast cereal if Armstrong does not, in fact, endorse the product. A testimonial cannot be altered to change the meaning (see *FTC* v. *Standard Education Society*, 1937). Suppose this is a movie review: "This is the worst movie of the year. You can see it—but only if you want to make yourself ill." Now here is an advertisement for the movie citing the review: "The critics loved it. '. . . the movie of the year. See it . . .'" The quotation is used out of context and its use is deceptive. An advertisement can note that a testimonial is unsolicited, but only if it is unsolicited (*FTC* v. *Inecto, Inc.*, 1934).

The Federal Trade Commission adopted a new set of rules for testimonial advertising in 1975. Experts who endorse products must now have the expertise to evaluate the products. They must have used a product before evaluating it. When stating that a product is superior, the expert must in fact have found it to be equal or superior to all other products with which it is compared. When an organization endorses a product, the endorsement must be the result of the collective judgment of the organization. If a ski manufacturer says that the Western United States Ski Association endorses his product, he must have polled the members of that association on the question. An endorsement from the executive director of a group cannot be represented as an endorsement from the group.

An endorser cannot make any statement that an advertiser cannot make; that is, the endorser also must have support for his conclusions. The makers of a cough syrup cannot honestly say that their product cures a cough. A housewife who endorses the cough syrup cannot make that statement either. If an endorser changes his view and decides the product is no good, the advertiser must stop using his testimonial.

Endorsements which claim to be from typical consumers must be made by consumers, not by actors playing the part of consumers. Laymen cannot endorse the effectiveness of drug products. If an endorser says she removes facial hair safely with a depilatory, her experience must be typical of most consumers. She cannot be the exception to the fact that the product damages the skin of most women who use it.

Finally, a connection between the endorser and the seller which might materially affect the weight or the credibility of the endorsement must be noted. The fact that a movie actress owns the perfume company must be noted in her endorsement of the product. However, the FTC rules are that under most circumstances mere payment of money to a person for an endorsement is not a material connection, unless the endorser is not a celebrity or an expert. When a typical consumer is paid for pushing a product, this fact must be disclosed.

The new rules go a long way toward ridding testimonial advertising of deceptive practices. How well the rules are enforced will be interesting to watch.

Puffery

Under the common law a distinction between an advertiser's assertions of factual claims and his assertion of opinion developed. Dean William Prosser in *Handbook of Law of Torts* writes that it is a seller's privilege to "lie his head off" so long as nothing specific is said about the product. A reasonable man knows that these generalities are merely subjective puffery or hyperbole about the product. Therefore under the common law, statements claiming that a sport coat is all wool, or is made in England, or is the lowest-priced coat in town have to be true because they give specific facts about the product. However, it is all right to say that the coat is the best-looking sport coat in town, or that it is the best buy today, or that girls will really notice men when they wear the coat. These claims are puffery which reasonable people do not tend to believe. Objective statements must be true. Opinion or subjective statements can be exaggerated.

Today there is very little common law adjudication of false advertising claims. The FTC and state and local agencies which police advertising are not as receptive to puffery as is the common law. In a ruling in 1957 the commission noted, "*Puffing* . . . is a term frequently used to denote exaggerations reasonably to be expected of a seller as to the degree of quality of his product, the truth or falsity of which cannot be precisely determined" (in re *The Matter of Better Living,* 1957). Since that time the agency has shown little inclination to allow puffery. In the 1974 *Staff Report to the Federal Trade Commission* prepared by John Howard and James Hulbert, the two researchers write, "The traditional common law distinction between misrepresentation of fact and of opinion—the latter not being considered actionable—has to a large extent been rejected under the FTC Act." In the *Law of Advertising* Rosden and Rosden argue, "Advertisers who do not want to risk a proceeding before the

Commission will have to be exceedingly careful in using hyperbole in their advertising." The Rosdens note that the test must be whether ordinary consumers of the advertised goods or service can recognize hyperbole for what it is or will be deceived by it (*Western Radio Corp* v. *FTC*, 1965).

Bait-and-Switch Advertising

One of the classic false advertising games is what is called bait-and-switch advertising. Here is the general idea. An appliance store advertises in the newspaper that it is selling a brand-new washing machine for $57. The advertisement is the bait, to get customers into the store. When customers come to the store to grab up this bargain, the salesmen are very honest about the advertised washer and say that it is a pile of junk (and it probably is!): it has no dials, it tears fine fabrics, it tends to leak, its motor is loud, and so forth. However, over in a corner is a really good buy, a snappy model for only $395, for only a few days. This high-pressure selling is the switch. If customers insist on buying the bait, chances are they will be told the machines have all been sold. The merchant had never intended to sell that model. The whole idea is to use the bait to lure into the store people who are in the market for washing machines, and then skillful, if not honest, salesmen switch customers to a more costly model via high-pressure selling—convenient monthly payments, and so forth.

Bait-and-switch advertising is illegal. Technically the law says that it is deceptive to advertise goods or services with the intent not to sell them as advertised or to advertise goods and services with the intent not to supply reasonably expected public demand, unless limitation on the quantity is noted in the advertisement (see Title 16 C. F. R. 238).

Bait-and-switch advertising is not the same as loss-leader advertising, which is legal in many places, in which a merchant offers to sell one item at below cost (the leader) in order to get customers into the store who in turn then buy (he hopes) additional merchandise at regular cost. Supermarkets use this scheme and so do other retail outlets. Those states which outlawed this practice did so because of pressure from small merchants who cannot afford to sell anything at a loss and don't want to be put at a marketing disadvantage with high-volume sellers.

Other Deceptions

Advertising can be deceptive in any number of ways. Let's look at a few.

Price Deception

It is deceptive to be untruthful about matters of cost and price: to say that the price of an item is reduced when it is not; to advertise a factory discount price when it is not; to advertise a special introductory price when it is not. The use of the word *free* causes many problems. If a merchant gives a free toothbrush to all persons who come into the store he can advertise that he is giving away free toothbrushes. The word *free* may be used in connection with mail-order giveaways, even if the customer is charged a small fee for postage and handling, fifteen or twenty-five cents. However, to advertise a free set of drinking glasses and then require people to pay three dollars postage and handling is illegal.

The word *free* can be used even when the customers are required to buy another item before getting the free item so long as this fact is made clear in the advertisement: a free toothbrush with every purchase of a tube of toothpaste. However, this rule applies only so long as the price of the toothpaste is not inflated to cover even partial cost of the toothbrush. The toothpaste must be sold at the regular price. The same limitation applies to two-for-one sales: the first item must be sold at regular price, not at inflated price.

Seller Deceptions

A vendor can't advertise his business as wholesale if it is really retail. He can't advertise his operation as a nationwide distributor if it is really only local in scope.

Merchandise Deceptions

A seller cannot falsely advertise the origin of merchandise, that is, say it is imported when it is not or claim cheese is Wisconsin cheese when it is really Vermont cheese. A seller can't exaggerate about the quantity, that is, advertise a bushel of apples that is really only a peck or label a small can of coffee giant economy size when in fact the price per ounce of the coffee is higher than the regular-size can.

Deceptions about the quality of merchandise are also prohibited. A merchant can't advertise a chair as an antique unless it meets strict government definition of what is and what is not an antique. Under the 1931 Tariff Act only furniture made before 1830 is considered antique. The same is true for porcelain and silver. A rug made after 1701 is not an antique. A violin made before 1801 is. And so on. Unless the item meets these standards it cannot be advertised as antique.

Something advertised as homemade has to be made at home. Home style is another matter. "Home style" cottage cheese can be manufactured in a dairy plant. *Colorfast* means that the fabric colors won't run or fade. The word *cure* implies that a permanent solution to a problem is offered. Most medicines give temporary relief, and then only for the symptoms of a specific medical problem. The word *permanent* means just that—permanent. Hair dye cannot be advertised as *permanent* because hair continues to grow, and new undyed roots will always appear. A product advertised to be "fireproof" must be fireproof, not merely fire resistant. A paint advertised to be easy to apply and to clean up must be easy to apply and clean up. The word *remedy* also implies a permanent cure: there is no such thing as a headache remedy since these words imply that users will have no more headaches. There are products, however, which temporarily relieve headaches. A product that is advertised to be safe must be safe for ordinary use. If a painter must wear a gas mask to avoid toxic fumes when he applies a paint the paint is not safe since people normally don't paint wearing gas masks.

If a company has sold its maple syrup for twenty-five years using 20 percent real syrup in each bottle and then suddenly eliminates the real maple syrup and substitutes chemically flavored corn syrup, it must announce the change on the label. Any change in a product detrimental to the product must be noted on the label. This kind of change is not often advertised. For instance the syrup manufacturer would be better off to discontinue selling the old brand of syrup and introduce a new brand, "with that old-fashioned maple flavor." He can then sell his corn syrup and only inveterate readers of package labels will know that they are buying chemically adulterated corn syrup.

Results
Deception

An advertiser can't claim that a product is capable of something it can't do. If a spot remover cannot remove oil-base spots, it it illegal to advertise that it can remove all kinds of grease and grime from rugs. Antiperspirants cannot be advertised as such unless they really prevent perspiration.

By the same token, the harmful effect of a product must also be disclosed. If a laxative can be damaging to kidneys, that fact must be disclosed on the label. If an aerosol cleaner can irritate the eyes, that fact must be acknowledged.

The list is endless. Probably, the Federal Trade Commission or another regulatory agency will find a way to interpret as misleading almost any claim capable of being seen in that light.

Irrelevant
Claim

At times—but not consistently—the FTC has said that advertising which invokes an irrelevant factor to win sales is deceptive. Health products are especially vulnerable to this interpretation. What is an irrelevancy? For example, an advertisement based on sex appeal. The FTC recently issued a complaint against Vivarin, a patent medicine which contains both an analgesic and a stimulant, for advertising which implies that use of the product makes persons more exciting and attractive, improves their personality, marriage, and sex life, and solves mental and personal problems. These benefits are irrelevant (as well as exaggerated) to the primary purpose of the product, to relieve a headache (*J. B. Williams*, 1972).

DEFENSE

The basic defense in any false advertising suit is truth, that is, proving that a product does what the advertiser claims it does, that it is made where he says it is made or that it is as beneficial as it is advertised to be. While the burden is upon the government to disprove the advertiser's claim, it is always helpful for an advertiser to offer proof to substantiate advertising copy.

Another angle which advertisers can pursue is to attack a different aspect of the government's case rather than try to prove the statement true. For example, an advertiser can argue that the deceptive statement is not material to the advertisement as a whole, that is, it will not influence the purchasing decision, or that the advertisement does not imply what the government thinks it implies. For example, to say that a deodorant "goes on dry" does not mean that it is dry when it is applied, merely that its application is drier than that of other antiperspirants.

The success rate in defending false advertising cases is not high. As for most legal problems, it is best to consult legal counsel before a problem arises and not after a complaint has been issued.

Advertising law is complicated, involved, and constantly changing. Even advertisers who set out to honestly follow the straight and narrow run into difficulty once in a while. The best way to cope with these problems is thorough understanding of both the law and the way the law operates.

BIBLIOGRAPHY
Here are some of the sources that have been helpful in the preparation of chapter 10.

Books   Alexander, George. *Honesty and Competition.* Syracuse: Syracuse University Press, 1967.

Howard, John A., and Hulbert, James. *A Staff Report to the Federal Trade Commission.* Washington, D. C.: Federal Trade Commission, 1974.

Posner, Richard A. *Regulation of Advertising by the Federal Trade Commision.* Washington: American Enterprise Institute for Public Policy Research, 1973.

Prosser, William L. *Handbook of Law of Torts.* St. Paul, Minn.: West Publishing Co., 1964.

Rosden, George E., and Rosden, Peter E. *The Law of Advertising.* New York: Matthew Bender & Co., 1975.

Articles   Devore, Cameron, and Nelson, Marshall. "Commercial Speech and Paid Access to the Press," 26 *Hastings Law Journal* 745 (1975).

"Note: Corrective Advertising and the FTC," 70 *Michigan Law Review* 374 (1971).

Cases   *Alberty* v. *FTC,* 182 F. 2d 36 (1950).

Aronberg v. *FTC,* 132 F. 2d 165 (1942).

Bigelow v. *Virginia,* 95 S. Ct. 2222 (1975).

Campbell Soup Co., 77 FTC 664 (1970).

In re *Coca-Cola Co.,* Docket No. 8839 (1973).

Eastern Railroad Presidents' Conference v. *Noerr Motor Freight, Inc.,* 365 U.S. 127 (1961).

FTC v. *Colgate Palmolive Co.,* 380 U.S. 374 (1965).

FTC v. *Inecto, Inc.,* 70 F. 2d 370 (1934).

FTC v. *Raladam*, 283 U.S. 643 (1931).

FTC v. *Raladam*, 316 U.S. 149 (1942).

FTC v. *Standard Education Society*, 302 U.S. 112 (1937).

FTC v. *Sterling Drug Co.*, 317 F. 2d 669 (1963).

Feil v. *FTC*, 285 F. 2d 879 (1960).

Giant Food, Inc., v. *FTC*, 322 F. 2d 977 (1963).

Heinz v. *Kirchner*, 63 FTC 1282 (1963), aff'd. sub. nom. *Kirchner* v. *FTC*, 337 F. 2d 751 (1964).

In re *ITT Continental Baking Co.*, 79 FTC 248 (1971).

P. Lorillard Co., 46 FTC 735, aff'd 186 F. 2d 52 (1950).

In re *The Matter of Better Living*, 54 FTC 648 (1957).

Moretrench Corp. v. *FTC*, 127 F. 2d 792 (1942).

National Petroleum Refiner's Association v. *FTC*, 340 F. Supp. 1343 (1972), rev'd 482 F. 2d 672 (1974).

New York Times v. *Sullivan*, 376 U.S. 254 (1964).

Northam Warren Corp. v. *FTC*, 59 F. 2d 196 (1932).

Ocean Spray Cranberries, Inc., 70 FTC 975 (1972).

Pittsburgh Press Co. v. *Pittsburgh Commission on Human Rights*, 413 U.S. 476 (1973).

Rast v. *van Deman & Lewis Co.*, 240 U.S. 342 (1916).

State v. *Cusick*, 84 N.W. 2d 544 (1957).

U.S. v. *J. B. Williams Co.*, 498 F. 2d 414 (1974).

Valentine v. *Chrestensen*, 316 U.S. 52 (1942).

Virginia State Board of Pharmacy v. *Virginia Citizens' Consumer Council, Inc.*, 96 S. Ct. 1817 (1976).

Western Radio Corp. v. *FTC* 339 F. 2d 937 (1965).

In re *J. B. Williams Co.*, 68 FTC 481 (1965).

In re *J. B. Williams Co.* v. *FTC*, 381 F. 2d 884 (1967).

In re *J. B. Williams Co.*, 79 FTC 410 (1971).

In re *J. B. Williams Co.*, 81 FTC 238 (1972).

CHAPTER 11

Broadcasting Regulation

When the regulation of broadcasting is first considered, we must temporarily set aside many of the principles encountered in earlier chapters of this book. Although they must observe all the other laws concerning such issues as libel and invasion of privacy, in both theory and practice, broadcasters face a regulatory scheme totally different from that faced by their counterparts in the print media. In 1966 Chief Justice Warren Burger, then a judge in the United States Court of Appeals for the District of Columbia, wrote (*Office of Communication, United Church of Christ* v. *FCC*, 1966):

> A broadcaster seeks and is granted the free and exclusive use of a limited and valuable part of the public domain; when he accepts that franchise it is burdened by enforceable public obligations. A newspaper can be operated at the whim or caprice of its owners; a broadcast station cannot.

There was a time in the United States when the only requirement confronting broadcasters was to request a license before broadcasting. Newspaper publishers and broadcast station owners were on almost equal terms. However, this scheme didn't work very well, or at least most people seemed to think that it didn't. The era of almost regulation-free broadcasting was a failure: neither broadcasters nor listeners were satisfied. Both listeners and broadcasters therefore asked the government to step in and impose order on the chaos, and regulation was the result.

Why didn't freedom work? One reason is the nature, or physical limitations, of the transmission of radio signals. Only a small number of radio (or television) signals can be transmitted in one place at one time.

Each signal must be carefully guided along its own private roadway or it will interfere with other signals. This is where the problem of the "spectrum," or the "ether" as some old-timers still call it, arises. The airwaves are capable of carrying only a limited number of signals; that is, the spectrum is limited.

Still, even limited-spectrum, regulation-free radio broadcasting could have worked had the broadcasters cooperated with each other in sharing the valuable airwaves and in using caution when transmitting their signals to avoid interference with other broadcasters. Many broadcasters, however, were not willing to cooperate. More people wanted to own a broadcasting station than could be accommodated, and usually each owner wanted the best and strongest signals for his station. When two or more broadcasters attempted to transmit simultaneously on the same frequency there was chaos, and listeners were often treated to what might be charitably called gobbledygook. Regulation seemed to be the only answer. Regulation—some observers say overregulation—is what we have today.

The purpose of this chapter is not to train lawyers for the Federal Communications Commission or general counsels for the networks. Rather, the focus of the chapter is the Federal Communications Commission (FCC) *and* its influence on all aspects of broadcasting. We begin by briefly reviewing the origins of the commission by considering the development of radio and the federal laws resulting from its development. We then move on to the commission itself and take a quick, overall look at its procedures and powers. Next, the most important of these powers, licensing, renewal of licenses, and program regulation are discussed in depth, as are two of the sometimes controversial powers of the commission, the equal time rule and the Fairness Doctrine. Finally, the other segment of the electronic media, cable television, is explored.

Considerable controversy exists today over whether regulation of broadcasting should continue at its current level, or whether broadcasting should be regulated at all. While this chapter was being written the Congress undertook a study of the regulation of broadcasting with an eye to possible major revisions in the broadcast laws. But this issue—whether or not broadcasting should be regulated at all—is beyond the scope of this chapter. Therefore, when controversy exists over certain rules it will be noted, but the urge to explore will be resisted. This is a book about mass media law and the law is basically what *is*, not what should be.

DEVELOPMENT OF RADIO

Radio is not the invention of a single individual. Rather, it represents an accumulation of many ideas that emerged during the last years of the nineteenth century. At first only simple radio signals were transmitted.

But gradually transmission of more complicated voice signals became possible. The basic hardware of radio had been developed by 1910, but the medium grew far differently than did the print medium. Remember, printing came at a time when people were groping for a means of spreading propaganda, and the printing press became a major weapon in the battle for religious freedom in England. The press was used as a means of spreading information and ideas. Radio has never really been dedicated to those ends. Initially it was a gadget which tinkerers built as a plaything to talk to friends and neighbors and to listen to strangers in distant places. The military was first to see the practical value of radio. The navy used radio as a means of keeping track of its ships out of port and for transmitting messages to captains on the high seas. The army too saw radio as an effective device for improving military communications. After World War I the armed forces made one concerted push to have the government take control of all radio communication, but the effort failed.

Aside from the military, few persons could see the practical side of radio, especially of radio broadcasting. The giant radio manufacturers were the first to reason that if they used radio to broadcast entertainment people would want to buy radio sets. Commercialism took a bigger step forward in the early twenties when the concept of broadcasters selling broadcast time to sponsors developed.

RADIO ACT OF 1912

The regulation of broadcasting in the United States dates from 1910 when Congress ruled that all United States passenger ships must carry a radio. Two years later the lawmakers passed the Radio Act of 1912 in response to considerable pressure from the army and navy which asserted that increasing numbers of amateur broadcasters interfered with military transmissions. The 1912 law required that all radio transmitters be licensed by the federal government and that operators of the transmitters be required to have a license. The secretary of labor and commerce, who was delegated the job of administering the law, was given authority to assign specific broadcast wavelengths to specific kinds of broadcasting (military wavelength, ship-to-shore wavelength, etc.). The secretary also had the power to determine the time periods when broadcasts could be carried, but he had no discretionary power to license. Anyone walking in the door and filling out an application could get a license.

Part of the problem in the early 1920s was the proliferation of licenses. Too many people wanted a license and too many radio stations wanted to transmit at the same time. In 1923 Secretary of Commerce Herbert Hoover decided to take things into his own hands when he refused to grant a license to an applicant, claiming that this discretion was inherent in the 1912 law. A federal court disagreed with the secretary, however. "The duty of issuing licenses to persons or corporations coming within the classification designated in the act reposes no discretion whatever in the Secretary of Commerce. The duty is mandatory," Judge Van Orsdel wrote (*Hoover v. Intercity Radio Co., Inc.*, 1923).

While Hoover was defeated in the courts, conscientious broadcasters and other persons concerned with the future of radio continued to urge the secretary to set up regulations to control broadcasting. At the Fourth National Radio Conference in 1925 (Hoover called yearly meetings to draft broadcasting regulations which Congress annually rejected) the secretary of commerce outlined his philosophy with regard to broadcast regulation. This philosophy remains today the basic foundation for the regulatory scheme:

> We hear a great deal about freedom of the air, but there are two parties to freedom of the air, and to freedom of speech for that matter. Certainly in radio I believe in freedom for the listener. . . . Freedom cannot mean a license to every person or corporation who wishes to broadcast his name or his wares, and thus monopolize the listener's set. We do not get much freedom of speech if one hundred fifty people speak at the same time at the same place. The airwaves are a public medium, and their use must be for the public benefit. The main consideration in the radio field is, and always will be, the great body of the listening public, millions in number, countrywide in distribution. There is no proper line of conflict between the broadcaster and the listener. Their interests are mutual, for without the one the other could not exist.

Under pressure from elements in the broadcasting industry and somewhat flush with the consensus which the annual radio conferences seemed to indicate, Hoover continued to act beyond his legal authority in regulating broadcasting. In 1926 his actions were again challenged by Eugene F. McDonald who operated station WJAZ in Chicago on an unauthorized wavelength, and at times not authorized by his license. His challenge to Hoover was joined in federal district court and Hoover lost. Judge Wilkerson ruled, "There is no express grant of power in the [1912] Act to the Secretary of Commerce to establish regulations" (*U.S. v. Zenith Radio Corp.*, 1926).

Hoover insisted that the attorney general appeal the ruling, but in a lengthy opinion Acting Attorney General William J. Donovan stated that he agreed with Wilkerson's interpretation of the law. Donovan wrote that while stations were required to have licenses to operate the secretary of commerce had no authority to assign specific stations to specific wavelengths, to limit hours of operation, or to place limitations on the amount of broadcast power used by a station. Donovan added (35 Op. Attyns. Gen., 1926):

> It is apparent from the answers contained in this opinion that the present legislation is inadequate to cover the art of broadcasting, which has been almost entirely developed since the passage of the 1912 Act. If the present situation requires control, I can only suggest that it be sought in new legislation, carefully adopted to meet the needs of both the present and the future.

Hoover capitulated, and the chaos which the secretary's illegal regulations had somewhat abated returned to the airwaves. Finally, Congress could no longer ignore the mounting pressure and adopted federal legislation by passing the comprehensive Radio Act of 1927.

RADIO ACT OF 1927

The nation had operated without substantial regulation of broadcasting for about twenty years, but nonregulation didn't work. A traffic cop was obviously necessary to make certain that broadcasters transmitted on assigned wavelengths, that they operated during assigned hours, and that they operated at assigned levels of power. Only with this kind of regulation could listeners use the medium. The Radio Act of 1927 created much more than a traffic cop however. As FCC Commissioner Glen Robinson notes in *The Administrative Process,* "Even a cursory examination of the Act, however, indicates that the regulatory powers granted to the Federal Radio Commission (and later to the FCC) exceeded those minimally required to avoid electronic interference." The new law governed programming, licensing and renewal, and many other aspects of radio not associated with broadcast signals and electronic interference.

The years immediately following the passage of the new law brought order to broadcasting. The courts upheld the power of the federal government to regulate the broadcast media, and the system of regulations which exist today began to take shape. The 1927 act also provided the basic philosophical foundation for broadcasting regulation. The law asserted that the radio spectrum, the airwaves, belong to the public and that broadcasters merely use this public resource while they operate a licensed station. The law established that the broadcaster must operate in "the public interest, convenience or necessity" at all times. This was the standard of conduct which would be used to evaluate licensees at renewal time. An independent agency, the Federal Radio Commission, was also established to supervise the regulation of broadcasting.

While the 1927 legislation was satisfactory in dealing with the problems of broadcasting, it became evident following a study initiated by

President Franklin D. Roosevelt in 1933 that the radio industry and the telephone and telegraph industries were interdependent. In 1934 Roosevelt urged Congress to adopt a new law which would be broad enough in scope to govern all these media. After extensive hearings and debates the federal Communications Act of 1934 was approved. This law has been amended frequently since 1934, but it stands as the basic regulation of the broadcast industry today (47 U.S.C., Sec. 151, 1970).

FEDERAL COMMUNICATIONS COMMISSION

In the federal Communications Act of 1934 the 1927 law with regard to broadcasting was basically reenacted and provision for regulating the telephone and telegraph industries—the common carriers—was also included. The five-member Federal Radio Commission was replaced by a seven-member Federal Communications Commission. Members of the FCC are appointed by the president, with the approval of the Senate, to serve a seven-year term. One member is selected by the president to be Chairman. The law also provides that not more than four members of the agency can be from the same political party.

Like all administrative agencies, the FCC is guided by broad Congressional mandate—in this case the federal Communications Act. The agency has the power to make rules and regulations within the broad framework of the Communications Act and these regulations carry the force of the law. With regard to some matters the 1934 law is very specific. For example, Section 315—the equal opportunity provision (or equal time rule)—details regulations concerning the use of the broadcast media by political candidates. But in other areas Congress was eloquently vague. The mandate that broadcasters operate their stations in "the public interest, convenience or necessity" can mean almost anything a person wants it to mean. Consequently, the FCC developed rules like the Fairness Doctrine and the ascertainment rules (we will talk about these rules in detail later) in its effort to implement the public interest requirement.

Procedures

The commission employs a large staff and is divided into various divisions. The Broadcast Bureau, for example, deals exclusively with broadcasting problems. Other divisions work with telephone and telegraph problems and with safety and special services. Administrative law judges, which are assigned to the FCC by the Civil Service Commission, are independent of control and direction by the agency. The administrative law judges are responsible for conducting inquiries for the agency and have powers which are normally incident to conducting trials and hearings. Their decisions on matters, such as controversy involving alleged violation of the Fairness Doctrine and license revocation, are final unless an exception is filed by any of the parties in the case. If there is an exception the FCC commissioners themselves normally hear the dispute and render a decision. Here is an example of this procedure.

Imagine that the National Rifle Association accuses television station KLOP of violating the Fairness Doctrine in presentation of material on gun control. The Fairness Doctrine requires that when a broadcaster presents a discussion of a controversial public issue all sides of the issue be fairly presented. The National Rifle Association files a complaint with the FCC which the Broadcast Bureau then investigates. Assume that after its investigation the Broadcast Bureau concludes that the station did violate the Fairness Doctrine. It then files a complaint with KLOP. The administrative law judge then conducts the hearing in the dispute. The Broadcast Bureau argues that the Fairness Doctrine was violated, and the station argues that it was not. Imagine that the judge decides that the station did not act fairly and rules against KLOP. This decision is final unless the station files an exception within thirty days. If the judge rules that the station did not violate the doctrine, the Broadcast Bureau can file an exception. The issue of whether KLOP violated the Fairness Doctrine then goes before the seven commissioners where oral argument is held and a decision is reached.

What happens if the FCC rules against KLOP? Is the matter finished? No. The station can ask a United States court of appeals (not the district court since the FCC has already conducted its fact finding) to review the decision.

As was noted in chapter 2 a court cannot substitute its own judgment for that of the Federal Communications Commission. The judges do not review the factual record to see if they would reach the same conclusion. FCC decisions, like the decisions of all administrative agencies, cannot be overhauled except for quite specific reasons. The court can check to see whether the petitioner (the party who brings the appeal) has been afforded due process of law. It can investigate various other issues. Were there procedural irregularities? Did the FCC make an adequate finding of the facts? Did the commission state the reasons for its decision? Are the findings of the agency supported by the evidence in the record? Did the action by the FCC conform to its Congressional mandate or did it go beyond the authority granted in the Communcations Act?

While theoretically these are the only kinds of issues a court can examine, courts on occasion have gone beyond these limits to examine the factual questions. Some judges have been reluctant to refrain from examining the substantive issues involved and sometimes have even reached conclusions different from those reached by the FCC. The United States Supreme Court is available for the final appeal.

We have briefly reviewed how the FCC operates. Other aspects of

Powers

FCC procedures are considered when licensing and programming controls are discussed in detail. Let us next take a quick look at FCC powers as invested by the Communications Act of 1934.

An important aspect of the 1934 law was an affirmation of the philosophy in the 1927 measure which established a privately owned broadcasting system operating over the public airwaves. This was a kind of compromise between establishing complete government control of broadcasting, as in most nations, and allowing the broadcasting industry to operate like most other industries, that is, with no government regulation.

Control of the Airways

The Congress approved the 1934 law under the authority of the commerce clause of the United States Constitution which gives the federal legislature the exclusive power to regulate interstate commerce. Under the 1927 act the question had arisen of whether this clause meant that the federal government lacked power to regulate broadcasters whose signals did not cross state lines, stations that were not engaged in interstate commerce. In 1933 in *FRC* v. *Nelson Brothers* the United States Supreme Court ruled that state lines did not divide radio waves and that national regulation of broadcasting was not only appropriate, but also essential to the efficient use of radio facilities. However laws must be based on the Constitution, not just on efficiency. What legal logic did the Court use to back up its opinion? Simply this: While a radio station's signal may not cross state lines, it can interfere with the signal from a radio station which does cross state lines. Consequently, regulation of intrastate broadcasting is "ancillary" to the regulation of interstate broadcasting. In order to properly regulate the vast majority of broadcasting which falls within interstate commerce, the federal government must have the power to regulate all broadcasting. Later in this chapter we will see that this is the same rationale used to justify federal regulation of cable television.

Licensing of Broadcasters

While the Communications Act branded telephone and telegraph companies common carriers (because they are monopolies they have to be common carriers; that is, they must accept business from anyone who wishes to use their services), broadcasting stations were not so designated. Because broadcasters are not common carriers they may refuse to do business with anyone or any company. Broadcasters do not have to make their facilities available to all members of the public. In addition the commission lacks the power to set rates for the sale of broadcasting time. Broadcasting is founded on the basis of free competition among holders of broadcast licenses.

The Communications Act makes it clear that while broadcasters may freely compete they in no way assume ownership of a frequency or wavelength by virtue of using it for three years or for three hundred years. When a license is granted, the broadcaster must sign a form in which is waived any claim to the perpetual use of a particular frequency.

While the FCC has direct control over all broadcasting stations, there is nothing in the Communications Act which gives the agency authority to control the broadcast networks. The National Broadcasting Company, the broadcast network, does not really broadcast anything itself. The network transmits programs to its affiliate stations which in turn do the broadcasting. Technically, therefore, the FCC has no power over the networks because they do not "broadcast."

But as is often the case, in this instance the technical truth is not the real truth. The FCC does in fact exercise considerable authority in spite of the Communications Act. How? First, since each of the networks owns several radio and television stations, the FCC controls the networks to a considerable extent by controlling the programming and practices of these "owned-and-operated" stations. Second, by controlling the actions of stations affiliated with the networks, the FCC can in fact regulate the networks. The infamous "prime time rule" is a good example. Several years ago the FCC was convinced by an assortment of groups that the networks dominated the program schedules of their affiliated stations. So the FCC adopted a rule that a network cannot provide more than three hours of programming for its affiliates during the prime evening viewing hours from 7 P.M. to 11 P.M., thereby giving local stations and other independent producers a chance to get programs into prime time. The fact that this rule has failed miserably is immaterial to us at this point. Because the FCC has no direct authority to control the networks, it is unable to rule that the National Broadcasting Company, The Columbia Broadcasting System, and The American Broadcasting Company cannot provide more than three hours of programming. But the agency can and did rule that the affiliated broadcasting stations cannot accept more than three hours of network programming. These are two ways in which the FCC can regulate broadcasting networks.

Recently, however, the FCC went a step beyond these means and made regulations aimed directly at the networks. The agency ruled, for example, that networks can no longer syndicate old television programs, but have to sell them to someone else for syndication. This was a direct regulation and was challenged in court. But the United States Court of Appeals for the District of Columbia upheld the right of the FCC to take such actions. In *Mt. Mansfield Television* v. *FCC* (1971) the court ruled that the fact that the Communications Act vested no explicit authority in the FCC to regulate the networks is not conclusive. The court said the rules passed by the agency, though they are direct regulation of the networks, are within the commission's statutory power if they are "reasonably ancillary to the effective performance of the Commission's various responsibilities for the regulation of television broadcasting."

Censorship

Technically the FCC lacks the power to censor broadcasters. Section 326 of the Communications Act states:

> Nothing in this act shall be understood or construed to give the commission the power of censorship over radio communications or signals transmitted by any radio station or condition shall be promulgated or fixed by the commission which shall interfere with the right of free speech by means of radio communication.

No censorship then. At least that is what Section 326 states. But that is not the way this section has been interpreted. The FCC has chosen to interpret Section 326 (with the approval of the courts) to mean that it may not censor specific programs, that is, forbid a broadcaster to carry programs on radical politicians or programs which picture members of a minority group in a derogatory fashion. However at license renewal times the agency can consider the kind of programming the licensee broadcasts and if the agency finds the programming objectionable this fact can be held against the licensee. Most people would call this censorship. Section 326, then, has limited meaning and is of limited value to broadcasters.

Other Powers

The commission has broad-ranging powers in dealing with American broadcasters. Section 303 of the Communications Act outlines some of the basic responsibilities of the agency which include classification of stations, determination of the power and technical facilities licensees must use, and specification of hours during the day and night stations can broadcast. The FCC also regulates the location of stations, the area each station can serve, the assignment of frequency or wavelength, and even the designation of call letters. There are not many things that broadcasters can do without first seeking the approval or consent of the Federal Communications Commission. For the purpose of this chapter the most important FCC powers are the licensing power, the renewal power, and the authority to regulate programming and program content.

LICENSING

Issuing and renewing broadcast licenses are perhaps the most important functions of the FCC. These functions are very important to broadcasters as well, for without a license there can be no broadcasting. Virtually everything the broadcaster does is tied in some way to having the license renewed. In addition to getting a license for a new station, the broadcaster must also seek FCC approval for most operational changes such as increasing power, changing the antenna height or location, selling the station, transferring ownership, and so forth.

The original licensing process is very complex and loaded with small but important details. Mountains of paperwork must accompany the license application. The first thing the potential licensee seeks is a construction permit, permission to start building the station. Obtaining this permit is actually the biggest hurdle. If the permit is granted, if construction of the station conforms to technical requirements, and if the work is completed within the time specified in the permit, the license is routinely issued for three years of operation.

What kinds of qualifications must the prospective licensee meet? The applicant must be a United States citizen, must be capable of building and operating the station for one year without taking in any revenue, and must possess (or be able to hire people who possess) the technical competence to construct and operate a broadcasting station. The applicant must also be honest and open, in dealing with the commission and must have generally good character. The applicant must meet the qualifications under the multiple ownership rules which prohibit one individual from owning more than seven television stations, two of which must be ultrahigh frequency (UHF) stations, seven amplitude modulation (AM) radio stations, and seven frequency modulation (FM) radio stations. There are additional rules which limit ownership of multiple broadcasting properties and newspapers and broadcasting stations within a city or market area. The applicant has to endeavor to ascertain the needs and interests of the people in the community to be served by the station and then prepare a programming scheme which will serve those needs and interests. If the applicant shows the commission that he is in compliance with these requirements, and if there is no competing applicant or community protest against granting the permit, the permit to construct the station will be granted. The license then follows when construction is completed.

Challenges

License applicants can face two kinds of challenges, the first from other applicants and the second from already licensed stations. Let us consider challenges from other applicants first. One such challenge comes when two applicants apply for the same license. When this occurs, the commission is required to compare the qualifications of both applicants. This type of challenge is considered more fully when license renewal is discussed.

Another challenge occurs when two applicants apply for separate licenses, but the proposed stations are mutually exclusive. For example, one applicant plans to build a station in a city just four miles away from the city in which the other applicant wants to build a station. Since only one frequency remains in the spectrum in that area, the two stations are mutually exclusive. In this case the FCC must grant both applicants a hearing. The commission cannot arbitrarily choose one applicant and ignore the other.

The second kind of challenge applicants for a new license may face comes from an existing station in the area where the new station is proposed to be located. The challenger usually argues that there is no room in the spectrum for the addition of another signal, that it will damage the quality of his own signal. Also in the past, existing broadcasters argued that they would be damaged economically by addition of a new station, that the total advertising dollars available in the community would have to be shared by an additional station, that there was not enough business to go around. Is this a legitimate argument? To a point it is. In 1940 the United States Supreme Court ruled, "Resulting economic injury to a rival station is not, in and of itself, . . . an element the FCC must weigh" in granting a new license (*FCC* v. *Sanders Brothers Radio Station,* 1940). In 1958, however, the United States court of appeals weakened this proposition somewhat by pointing out that in the 1940 decision the high Court added that economic injury can become a relevant factor if reduced revenues *will adversely affect program service.* Whether a station makes a big profit should not be of interest in such a case, the Court ruled (*Carroll Broadcasting Co.* v. *FCC,* 1958):

> . . . [but] if the situation in a given area is such that available revenue will not support good service in more than one station, the public interest may well be in the licensing of one station rather than two stations. To license two stations where there is revenue for only one may result in no good service at all.

Cost

How much does a license cost? Licenses used to be practically free until 1970 when the FCC instituted a new fee schedule which substantially increased the cost of obtaining and renewing a license. In addition broadcasters were charged an annual fee for the privilege of using the airwaves. All charges were based on the kind of broadcast station in question—radio, television, cable television, frequency modulation, and so forth—as well as on the revenues the station earns. For example, the cost of filing an application for a construction permit for a VHF television station in one of the nation's top fifty markets was $5,000. A $45,000 fee was charged when the license was granted. In addition, the station had to pay an annual fee which was twelve times the highest amount the station charged for a thirty-second commercial or a minimum fee of $144, whichever was more. If the station's highest thirty-second spot sold for $2,000, the annual fee was $24,000. A small AM radio station on the other hand paid a filing fee of $25, a grant fee of $225, and an annual fee of twenty-four times the highest rate charged for a one-minute spot or $52, whichever was more.

However, in December 1976 a United States Court of Appeals declared the entire fee schedule to be invalid on the grounds that it was not based solely on the "value to recipient" standard as required by the Independent Office Appropriation Act (31 U.S.C. Sec 483a). The Commission was forced to refund all fees collected under the schedule that exceeded the legally permissible amount (*NAB* v. *FCC*, 1976). While this chapter was being written the agency was drafting a new fee schedule which would comply with the law.

Licenses cost money today. But lest ye weep for the poor broadcaster, remember that the radio and television business is generally very lucrative, especially for the larger radio and television stations which normally earn huge profits.

RENEWAL OF LICENSES

The process of having a broadcasting license renewed is one of the most odious tasks ever devised by man. Perhaps it should be, for after all the broadcaster usually reaps grand profits through use of the public airwaves. Every three years the license of each station comes up for renewal. Renewals are staggered so that every two months the FCC receives a batch of between three and five hundred renewal applications. The broadcaster must provide the FCC with volumes of data, which points out an important facet of renewal: the FCC does not conduct an independent investigation of the licensee. Rather, the licensee (and sometimes other interested persons) provides the commission with nearly all the relevant material.

Program Information

At renewal time in addition to wanting a considerable amount of technical data, the commission seems most interested in programming information, that is, in the kinds of programs the licensee carried during the past three years. The FCC establishes what is called a composite week, taking a Monday from one month, a Tuesday from another month, perhaps a Wednesday from the following year, and so forth. The licensee must report what programs were broadcast on those days. Licensees must break down other program data into categories such as news and public affairs, religion, and so forth and must also show that they have provided programs on local needs and interests, all of which will be discussed in some detail further on. If the FCC is not satisfied with what it sees, it can schedule a formal hearing on the renewal application. A formal hearing is prerequisite to both nonrenewal and revocation of a license before expiration.

Theoretically, at least, the renewal process is supposed to be a rigorous examination of whether the broadcaster is serving the public interest. While the process is odious because it does entail a great deal of work for the broadcaster, the examination is rarely rigorous. The FCC is too small, too understaffed, to give renewal applications much more than a cursory examination. Unless there are serious citizen complaints, renewal is generally automatic. Between 1935 and 1969 less than fifty renewal applications were denied. Since 1969 the number of denials has increased somewhat, but the increase is due to challenges to renewal from citizen groups, as we shall soon see.

Another problem fundamental to the entire spectrum of broadcast regulation is that while the Communications Act and the FCC both frequently refer to "public interest, convenience or necessity," there exists no specific definition of these words. Instead of defining the words for broadcasters, over the years the FCC has developed a rather extensive set of policies and rules—broadcasters must do this, broadcasters cannot do that. If licensees follow the rules it is assumed that they are serving the public interest. Of course this may or may not be true.

Inertia is another reason why the renewal process is less than a rigorous examination of the licensee. The FCC, which is a bureaucracy on the grand scale, takes too long to begin meaningful action. In 1976 the agency was still in the process of deciding whether to strip a Tacoma, Washington, radio station of its license even though the hearings had begun four years earlier. In 1975 the commission voted to strip the licenses from all the public television stations in Alabama because they had discriminated against blacks in the late 1960s. Their renewal applications were denied in spite of the fact that by 1975 the stations had solved discrimination problems of the 1960s and offered a broad range of programming for the black citizens of the state. In fact many persons looked to public television in Alabama as a model for a broadcasting operation which both employed minority group members and served the minority community with high-quality programming. The FCC had taken more than five years to get up enough steam to correct a serious problem. By the time the agency reached a solution the problems were solved. Also in 1975 the FCC denied Don Burden the renewal of licenses for his five radio stations for among other reasons improperly using newscasts to promote political candidates in 1964 and 1966, almost ten years earlier, a long delay.

Clearly the sanction of nonrenewal can be a valuable sanction. No broadcaster wants to lose a license, nor do broadcasters want to face the prospect of a costly renewal hearing. However, the threat is worse than fact since examination is generally cursory. So long as broadcasters can convince the FCC that they have followed agency rules, renewal is usually automatic. Former FCC commissioners Nicholas Johnson and Kenneth Cox once described the renewal process this way: "a sham—a ritual in which little review of performance actually takes place."

**Nonrenewal
Standards**

However, there have been cases in which licenses were not renewed, and these cases established principles which are now law. A York, Nebraska, radio station had a renewal application rejected for broadcasting advertisements and information for fraudulent business enterprises and false and misleading statements about medical products. The owner of the station was apparently involved in the crooked businesses. Broadcasting fraudulent advertising, then, can result in nonrenewal (*May Seed and Nursery Co.* et al., 1936). A Georgia station was threatened with nonrenewal for broadcasting a contest which was a lottery, a violation of federal law. The station changed its errant ways and got its license renewed (*WRBL Radio Stations,* 1936). A station cannot be used solely to promote causes of the owner—even religious causes. "Where the facilities of a station are devoted primarily to one purpose and the station serves as a mouthpiece for a definite group or organization it cannot be said to be serving the general public," the FCC ruled (*Young People's Association for the Propagation of the Gospel,* 1938).

In the *Trinity Methodist Church* case in 1932 the former Federal Radio Commission was faced with a situation in which a station owner used his broadcast facilities for sensational attacks upon the Catholic Church. The licensee also had been convicted of using his radio station to obstruct justice and was held in contempt of court. When the commission refused to renew the license, the Reverend Dr. Shuler argued that this violated his First Amendment rights. The court of appeals issued what probably remains the definitive ruling on this question. Acknowledging the First Amendment considerations, the court nevertheless ruled (*Trinity Methodist Church, South* v. *FRC,* 1932):

> . . . this does not mean that the government, through agencies established by Congress, may not refuse a renewal of license to one who has abused it to broadcast defamatory and untrue matter. In that case there is not a denial of the freedom of speech, but merely the application of the regulatory power of Congress in a field within the scope of its legislative authority.

The previous year another court of appeals judge had ruled that the commission had a perfect right to look to past programming practices of a renewal applicant to determine whether the license should be renewed. Invoking the Biblical injunction By their fruits ye shall know them, the court affirmed that past programming is a central issue in consideration of service in the public interest (*KFKB Broadcasting Association* v. *FRC,* 1931). Past programming, then, is an important element in the renewal scheme. Another important element today is what is called ascertainment, which we will consider for a moment.

Ascertainment

The commission has always insisted that the broadcaster attempt to find out what is on the people's mind in the community. Ascertainment was first mentioned formally in the commission's 1960 programming statement. "From this relatively modest application," writes Commissioner Glen Robinson, "the local needs ascertainment policy has been crystallized into an increasingly formalized and elaborate requirement for community surveys and reporting to the FCC both the survey efforts and how the station's programming is responsive to the ascertainment needs and interests."

The definitive policy on the problem is the FCC "Primer on Ascertainment of Community Needs" issued in 1971 and amended the following year. With the exception of a handful of very small radio stations (10 watts or less) all stations—including public broadcasting stations—must fulfill the ascertainment requirements.

When ascertaining community needs and interests the broadcaster is required to consult with leaders of significant groups in the area, as well as with members of the general public. The applicant must also report to the commission on the minority or ethnic population in the community and the various economic, governmental, and public service concerns in the area. It is expected that top-level persons of the station will consult with the public on these kinds of questions. While sample surveys can be (and frequently are) used to communicate with the general public, personal meetings with leaders of community groups are required.

A significant number of persons must be contacted as well as all leaders from significant groups reflecting the economic, social, political, and racial compositions of the area. Ascertainment must be undertaken six months before the application for license or renewal is filed with the commission.

According to the FCC Primer, ascertainment is not designed to elicit program suggestions from the people. Rather, it is to discover community problems which broadcasters then must attempt to deal with in their programming. Must programming cover all community problems? "Not necessarily," according to the Primer. "However, he [the broadcaster] is expected to determine in good faith which of such problems merit treatment by the station." Programming can take form of public service announcements, editorials, segments of news casts, and special programs. Ascertainment is a distinct improvement over the days when the station manager had lunch with the mayor and the bishop, requested the presidents of the Kiwanis and Exchange clubs to write letters about local needs, and called these activities investigating community needs.

The Public Interest

Prior to 1966 the license renewal process was generally a two-party process between the license holder and the commission. Information about the broadcaster's performance came from the broadcaster and from the FCC's Broadcast Bureau, which maintained minimal surveillance of the licensee. All letters of complaint which the commission received about the licensee were also included in the record. But citizens, listeners or viewers, were not permitted to officially bring forth evidence or testimony either in support of or against renewal of the broadcast license. In order to participate in a license renewal hearing "standing" was needed, according to the FCC. *Standing* is a five-dollar legal word meaning some kind of direct and substantial interest in the outcome of the hearing. *Standing* was frequently defined as "economic interest." Since viewers and listeners of a broadcasting station stood to gain or lose no money regardless of the results of a renewal hearing, the FCC just did not allow participation by these kinds of people.

This policy was reversed in 1966 by the United States court of appeals. A group of citizens from Mississippi wanted to protest the renewal of a license for television station WLBT which they claimed had discriminated against blacks both in programming and in hiring. The FCC refused to hear the Mississippians because they lacked standing. The challengers went to the United States court of appeals which ruled that the commission's action was improper. The action of the FCC, Judge Warren Burger wrote (*Office of Communication, United Church of Christ* v. *FCC,* 1966),

> . . . denies standing to spokesmen for the listeners, who are most directly concerned with and intimately affected by the performance of a licensee. . . . The theory that the commission can always effectively represent the listener interests in a renewal proceeding without the aid and participation of legitimate listener representatives . . . is one of the assumptions we collectively try to work with so long as they are reasonable and adequate. When it becomes clear, as it does to us now, that it is no longer a valid assumption which stands up under the realities of actual experience, neither we nor the commission can continue to rely on it.

The effect of allowing citizens to challenge the renewal of broadcast licenses has had a significant and sometimes intimidating impact on broadcasters. The statistics themselves are not very impressive. From 1970 until 1974, two hundred forty-seven citizen petitions to deny license renewal were filed with the FCC. Sixty-seven were unsuccessful, forty-eight were withdrawn, and at the time of this writing 131 were still unresolved. Only one license renewal application was denied.

The true story is found in the category labeled "petitions withdrawn," for in most cases the petitions were withdrawn only after the broadcaster agreed to important concessions in hiring, programming, and public service. In order to get a citizen challenge withdrawn when it purchased television stations in four cities, McGraw-Hill, Inc., agreed to meet minority employment quotas, set up minority advisory councils, and increase the amount of minority programming. These are typical of the kinds of concessions broadcasters have been forced to make to get licenses renewed and, more important, to avoid costly renewal hearings. While the results of these challenges seem socially desirable, there is something basically unhealthy about a situation in which broadcasters are "blackmailed" into making changes to keep from losing a license or to defend a challenge. There is no way to know whether the challenging groups really represent the public interest any better than broadcasters do. A far more desirable system would be to force the FCC to exert this kind of pressure on broadcasters when it is needed. But in such a system the FCC would be forced to take a far more active role in the renewal process than it currently takes. Renewal roulette, as it is called by broadcasters, is better than the old system in which no citizen voice was allowed. However, any system which places a premium on pressure by organized, but not necessarily representative, groups is suspect.

Competing Applicants

The license renewal challenges discussed to this point have concerned citizens seeking to have the broadcaster stripped of the license, but not seeking the license themselves. However, there are also persons seeking to have the renewal denied because they want the license. In other words, the challengers have a proposal to operate a broadcasting station on the same frequency used by the current license holder. Since only one of the applicants can use the frequency, the FCC faces a problem.

Historically, the commission has maintained the illusion that all renewals will be granted on what is called a comparative or competitive basis. That is, if station KLOP seeks a license renewal, all other applicants for the use of that frequency will be considered at the same time before the renewal is granted or denied. Indeed, in 1928 in the *Second Annual Report of the Federal Radio Commission* the agency noted that it applied a comparative, not an absolute, standard to broadcasting stations:

> Since the number of channels is limited and the number of persons desiring to broadcast is far greater than can be accommodated, the commission must determine from among the applicants before it which of them will, if licensed, best serve the public.

Theoretically, at least then, all applicants for the license should be evaluated at the same time. In 1965 the FCC issued a policy statement on comparative hearings which involved regular renewal applicants. To obtain the best service for the public and the maximum diffusion of control of the mass media, the commission said it would consider at least seven items in regard to each applicant for license or license renewal.

1. Diversification of control of the media: Persons holding existing media (like a newspaper or a second broadcasting station) in the area or having significant media holdings elsewhere will not be considered as favorably as those without or with fewer media holdings.

2. Full-time participation in station operation by the owners: The FCC will favor working owners over absentee owners.

3. Proposed program service: What does the applicant propose to do with the frequency? Supposedly, applicants who plan to devote more time to programs on public affairs and education and information will be favored over those who plan to program heavily with entertainment.

4. The past broadcast record of the current license holder as well as the record of other broadcasters who seek the license: If the past record is average it is disregarded. If it is exceptional with unusual attention to public needs and interests, or if it is especially poor with regard to serving the public interest, the past record then becomes a factor.

5. Efficient use of the frequency. This is a technical question and has to do with judicious use of the spectrum.

6. Character of applicants. Does the applicant have a record free of criminal prosecutions; is he considered honest and trustworthy, and so forth.

7. Other factors. The report did not outline these additional factors.

Theoretically, then, based on the above criteria, the best applicant will be given the license, regardless of who previously held the license.

Despite the rhetoric and the policy of the FCC, the notion of a comparative hearing at renewal time was an illusion in 1965 and had been since the middle 1940s. Despite the fact that nothing in the Communications Act states that the license holder should get preference, that is exactly what the FCC based its decisions on. In cases in 1951 (Hearst Radio, WBAL) and 1963 (Wabash Valley Broadcasting Co., WTHI-TV) the FCC publicly stated it gave the incumbent licensee preference. In the 1963 *Wabash Valley Broadcasting Co.* ruling the commission said that a newcomer seeking to oust an incumbent license holder must make a showing of superior service and must be higher on other comparative criteria as well. In other words, when the incumbent was average, the challenger had to be superior in several criteria before it can gain the license.

In a very strange case—*WHDH-TV* case—in 1969 the FCC reversed its policy of favoring the incumbent and stripped the television license from the Boston-Herald Traveler Corporation and gave it to a challenger,

Boston Broadcasters, Inc., which proved to be superior to the license holder in the diversification and owner participation categories (in re *WHDH, Inc.,* 1969). This decision shocked the industry and left the nation's broadcasters in a state of apoplexy. At stake, of course, were billions of dollars in invested capital and the licenses of more than one hundred twenty television stations in the nation's top fifty markets with the same problems of diversification and owner participation as WHDH-TV. It was therefore not surprising that by the end of June 1969 nearly sixty bills had been introduced in Congress which would have the effect of prohibiting the FCC from making similar rulings in the future. The power of the broadcasting lobby in Washington is legendary since the destiny of many office holders depends to some extent upon their gaining access to the broadcast media in local communities. Unhappy television station owners can make access difficult. Also, some congressmen and senators themselves own broadcasting stations or stock in companies which own broadcasting properties.

The intensity of Congressional interest pushed the FCC to reconsider its position on the matter, and in January 1970 the commission issued a new policy, with but a single dissent, that in the future license holders would be given a controlling preference in any renewal hearing if they could demonstrate that their past performance had had no "serious deficiencies," and that they had been substantially attuned to meeting the needs and interests of the community. Only if incumbents failed to meet these criteria would the challengers or competing applicants be given an opportunity even to present their proposals. In other words, so long as the licensee met the minimum requirements for service to the community, there was no chance of the license being taken away, even when challengers were prepared to provide service that was a hundred times better.

This policy—which resembled many congressional proposals—effectively killed comparative renewal. There was not a single challenge to a license renewal by a competing applicant during the first eighteen months the policy was in effect. In June 1971 the FCC policy was reversed, not by the commission, but by the courts (*Citizens Communication Center* v. *FCC*). A group called the Citizens Communication Center challenged the 1970 renewal policy. The group argued that the commission's policy violated the federal Communications Act as it had been interpreted by the Supreme Court and other courts. The Court ruled that every applicant must get at least a hearing. Judge Skelly Wright, writing the unanimous opinion for the United States Court of Appeals for the District of Columbia, said that when two or more applicants for a license are mutually exclusive—that is, only one can have the license—the commission must conduct a full comparative hearing. This ruling applied to renewals as well as to original applications. The court recognized that in a comparative renewal hearing the challenger can be required to demonstrate qualifications superior to those of the incumbent. Under the law, however, challengers must be given the chance to present their proposal, a right denied them by the commission's 1970 policy.

In a footnote to that decision the court urged the FCC to formulate in both qualitative and quantitative terms a definition of superior service or superior qualifications. The following year the same court outlined some aspects of what it believed to be superior service, noting such things as elimination of excessive advertising, delivery of quality programs, reinvestment of profits in the station to improve service to the public, diversification of media ownership, and independence from governmental influence in promoting First Amendment objectives (*Citizens Communication Center* v. *FCC*, 1972).

The FCC has been slow to take the court's suggestion, preferring to operate on a case-by-case basis. In addition, both the executive branch and some members of Congress are working to change the Communications Act so that incumbent license holders will not have to undergo comparative hearings. One bill, which would extend the licensing period from three to five years, requires broadcasters to set aside specific amounts of time for certain kinds of programming, such as news and public affairs. If a station meets these requirements and if there are no other serious deficiencies, it will not have to face a comparative hearing. This idea is very popular in the industry. Many other bills have similar objectives. As seemingly benign as the comparative hearing requirement is, broadcasters still don't like it and want to be rid of it. They have many allies in Congress.

Licensing and renewal are two of the most important tasks that the FCC undertakes. These jobs bear some resemblance to the role envisioned for the agency by policy makers in the 1920s. But regulation of programming is something else altogether. Deep doubts remain in the minds of many authors over whether the Congress in 1927 and again in 1934 envisioned programming regulations of the kind now enforced by the commission.

PROGRAM REGULATION

The Federal Communications Commission has extensive control over programming matters. Regulations range from specific federal statutes such as the law which prohibits broadcast of obscenity to vague general guidelines such as the recent policy statement regarding broadcasters' responsibility for phonograph records played over the air. Each rule or policy promulgated by the FCC is tied to the Communications Act of 1934, many by that tenuous and wispy thread "public interest, convenience or necessity."

Some rules are simple. Stations, for example, are required to identify themselves periodically. Broadcasters must announce when the station or program receives a gratuity in return for an advertising plug on the air. It is illegal for a station to broadcast a lottery. A station may not knowingly carry fraudulent advertising. A few stations are periodically charged with violating one of these rules. Sometimes the station license is revoked and sometimes its renewal is denied. The license for station WWBZ in Vineland, New Jersey, was not renewed in 1955 at least partially because it had broadcast information on lotteries—in this case horse races. Giving the race results from the local track as a part of the evening news is one thing, but broadcasting up-to-the-minute race results from racetracks around the country is something else altogether. At least the FCC thought so and ruled that such information is useful primarily to persons involved in illegal gambling (in re *Community Broadcasting Service, Inc.*, WWBZ, 1955).

At one time the FCC tried to ban two nationally broadcast game shows which were constructed around participation by viewers and listeners at home. A band played a melody and the emcee called randomly selected listeners. If the listeners could "name that tune" or tell the band to "stop the music" they won a prize. The commission said that the games were lotteries and were illegal for broadcast purposes. The Supreme Court disagreed, ruling that while the FCC may indeed regulate the broadcast of lotteries, these games were not lotteries (*FCC* v. *American Broadcasting Co.* et al., 1954). To qualify as a lottery a contest must have three elements. First, there must be a prize for the winner. Second, the prize must be awarded to a person chosen wholly or partly by chance. Finally, winners must be required to furnish something of value—called consideration—in order to participate in the game. When participants must buy a product before they are allowed to play the game, have to ante up money, or have to send in a box top, they are furnishing consideration. The third element was missing from the musical game shows and is missing from nearly all televised game shows today. (Tickets to the show to get the chance to play the game are always free.)

Revocation of a license is not a typical FCC response to a programming violation. Regulation by what some writers call "lifted eyebrow" is more common. The broadcaster receives a letter from the commission in which the agency indicates its concern over a particular programming practice. The letter or phone call requests the station to justify what it is doing, and before you know it the practice has stopped. The closer the station is to license renewal time the more powerful this kind of "sanction" can be. A station can receive a fine, or when renewal time does come around, it can receive what is called a short-term renewal, a one-year renewal. This is how the FCC says "We don't like some of the things you have been doing. You have a year in which to shape up."

Before some important specific programming regulations are explored in depth, the FCC's general programming policies should be noted. Although the FCC is not supposed to tell broadcasters what to broadcast, when renewal time comes the kind of programming the station has carried becomes an important factor in determining whether the broadcaster has served the public interest, convenience, or necessity. In lieu of saying specifically what is to be broadcast, the FCC has issued two important sets of general guidelines.

Blue Book Guidelines

The first set of guidelines, a report issued by the commission in 1946, is remembered in the industry as the Blue Book. The Blue Book, which was neither vigorously enforced nor officially repudiated, covered a wide variety of topics including public service programming. The document said that broadcasters have the responsibility to carry sustaining programming (programming which is not sponsored or paid for) to provide listeners and viewers with a well-balanced radio or television diet. The commission said that certain kinds of programs such as programs on politics, religion, and education are not appropriate for sponsorship, and should be carried on a sustaining basis. So should programs required to meet the tastes and interests of minority groups, programs which are a service to nonprofit groups, and experimental programs which typically cautious advertisers will be likely to avoid.

The Blue Book also suggested that broadcasters carry programming which features local talent and reflects local needs and issues. "The public interest clearly requires that an adequate amount of time be made available for the discussion of public issues," according to the Blue Book. Finally, broadcasters were told to avoid advertising excesses such as too many advertisements, advertisements that are too long or offensive, and fraudulent advertisements.

en Banc Programming Inquiry

Fourteen years after the Blue Book was issued the FCC issued a second general programming policy which is usually called the Commission's en Banc Programming Inquiry. This policy was milder than the Blue Book, has been more effectively enforced than the Blue Book, and is the law today. The en Banc Inquiry is a long, often thoughtful report. "In view of the fact that a broadcaster is required to program his station in the public interest, convenience and necessity," the commission notes, "it follows that despite the limitations of the First Amendment and Section 326 [no censorship] of the Act, that his freedom to program is not absolute." Broadcasters must afford a reasonable opportunity for the discussion of conflicting views on issues of public importance. They should consider the tastes, needs, and desires of the public in the community which is served by the station. The Commission then notes:

> The major elements usually necessary to meet the public interest, needs and desires of the community in which the station is located as developed by the industry, and recognized by the commission have included:

1. Opportunity for local self-expression
2. Development and use of local talent
3. Programs for children
4. Religious programs
5. Educational programs
6. Public affairs programs
7. Editorialization by licensees
8. Political broadcasts
9. Agricultural programs
10. News programs
11. Weather and market reports
12. Sports programs
13. Service programs for minority groups
14. Entertainment programs

The commission noted that these elements are not all-embracing, that they are not constant, and that they provide no rigid mold to which all stations must conform. The ascertainment of local needs is the responsibility of the broadcaster. Despite these caveats and although it was issued in the hope of improving diversity in broadcasting, the 1960 en banc programming statement has had the opposite impact. It has reinforced the inherent tendencies of the broadcasters to conform to safe, established patterns of operation and programming. The FCC fosters this conformity in large measure by checking at renewal time to see how many of the fourteen little boxes (the elements just listed) the broadcaster has checked. Only recently have some radio stations, primarily FM stations in metropolitan areas, been able to program solid music and news, for example, and ignore the other twelve categories, and then only because the commission is assured that other stations in the community fulfill the other twelve elements.

Broadcasters are terribly conservative and seize upon any suggestion that might facilitate renewal of their valuable broadcasting licenses. They want to be able to say to the FCC, "You see how well we have been serving the public interest. We program in all fourteen categories." And so they do, despite the fact, for example, that not one farmer or anyone else interested in agricultural programming is within four hundred miles of the station. Whether the programming is good, bad, or indifferent is immaterial. The station broadcasts material in all fourteen categories. License renewed! Next case, please.

The commission's en banc policy on programming was challenged in 1962 in a federal court of appeals (*Henry* v. *FCC,* 1962). The court upheld the agency and ruled that the guidelines did not violate the First Amendment. Citing a nineteen-year-old decision handed down by the United States Supreme Court (*NBC* v. *U.S.,* 1943). Judge David Bazelon ruled that the commission may impose reasonable restrictions upon the granting of licenses to assure programming designed to meet the needs of local communities.

Obscenity

Broadcasters have a special set of problems concerning pornography. Section 1464, Title 18, of the United States Code gives the Federal Communications Commission the power to revoke any broadcast license if the licensee transmits obscene, indecent material over the airwaves. No station, however, has ever had its license revoked for broadcasting obscenity. Nor has the FCC denied renewal of a license solely on the grounds that the licensee broadcast pornographic or indecent material. The commission is quite hesitant to use its big guns in this area because of the immense constitutional questions involved. It is clearly a free speech issue. Yet stations have been put on short-term renewal and have been fined, as will be noted momentarily.

Generally, when the FCC receives a complaint from a listener or viewer about a broadcast believed to contain obscene language or pictures, the agency responds with a form letter which includes the following statement:

> The broadcast of obscene, indecent or profane language is prohibited by a federal criminal statute. Although the Department of Justice is responsible for prosecution of federal law violations, the commission is authorized to impose sanctions on broadcast licensees for violation of this statute, including revocation of the license or the imposition of a monetary forfeiture. However, both the commission and the Department of Justice are governed by past decisions of the courts as to what constitutes obscenity, and the broadcast of material which may be offensive to many persons would not necessarily be held by the courts to violate the statute.

In terms you and I understand, this is a cop-out. The FCC is saying to the viewer "We'd like to help you but we are powerless" when this is not in fact the case. Offensive programming may not be obscene, but it may not be in the public interest either. While the courts decide what is obscene, the FCC decides what is in the public interest.

Although the FCC approaches the problem of obscenity cautiously, the mere fact that it sends out even a form letter has an impact upon

conservative broadcasters. In 1975 the National Association of Broadcasters (NAB), claiming all the while that it only wanted to stave off
stricter federal regulation, informed broadcasters who subscribe to the
NAB Code of Good Practices (nearly all broadcasters do) that the hours
from seven o'clock to nine o'clock each night were to be considered
family-viewing time on television, which was all the excuse the blue-
pencil pushers (censors) at the networks and the local stations needed.
No violence and no sex in the early hours! was the cry. Under such a
banner the word *virgin* was cut from one program (*innocent* was substituted). Censors began to look anew at Cher's navel and a braless guest
star on the "Phyllis" show was "re-dressed" before filming began. Much
more was done, of course, to stave off a federal regulation which the
FCC seemed reluctant to exercise in the first place. When writers and
directors challenged this rule, a federal court in Los Angeles in the fall
of 1976 declared that while the family hour itself was not illegal or unconstitutional, it was illegal for the three networks to conspire together
to institute a family hour. The networks denied that they had done this
in the first place and indicated individually their intention of continuing
the policy (*Writers Guild* v. *FCC*, 1976). Law professor Harry Kalven
wrote almost ten years ago in the *Michigan Law Review* that while a
regulation may not directly interfere with free speech "in operation it
may trigger a set of behavioral consequences which amount in effect to
people censoring themselves in order to avoid trouble with the law."
Or what people believe will be trouble with the law. Such is the case
with the regulation of obscenity in broadcasting.

By looking at several cases we can see exactly how the FCC operates
in the matter of obscenity.

1. A country-western disc jockey on radio station WDKD was accused of habitually telling off-color or indecent jokes on the air. The FCC
chose to call the material coarse, vulgar, suggestive, and susceptible of
a double meaning rather than obscene or indecent to avoid having to
cope with the voluminous case law on obscenity. The commission nevertheless refused to renew the license for WDKD on the grounds that these
incidents were not isolated occurrences but constituted a fairly substantial portion of the broadcast time. This practice was inconsistent with the
public interest and an intolerable waste of the only operational broadcast
facility in the community, the commission said (in re *Palmetto Broadcasting Co.*, 1962).

2. In a discussion program on KPFA the topic of academic freedom
was considered by two recently fired college English instructors. A poem
in which four-letter words are used to ascribe sexual acts to God was read
and then discussed by the two professors and other panel participants.

Complaints resulted in a hearing at renewal time. The FCC ruled that the management of KPFA neglected to follow the guidelines imposed by the Pacifica Foundation, the station owner. A short-term renewal was granted, and the commission noted, "At the expiration of this period you will be afforded the further opportunity to demonstrate adherence to your program supervisory representations" (in re *Pacifica Foundation*, 1964).

3. The radio station WUHY-FM was found guilty of broadcasting vulgar four-letter words on two different programs in January 1970. One of the programs was an interview with Jerry Garcia of the rock group the Grateful Dead. Garcia used such words frequently, as did a local announcer who later discussed the interview. The FCC ruled that the words were indecent, not obscene. Since it was a noncommercial educational station, WUHY was fined only $100. In its ruling the FCC made this comment (in re *WUHY-FM, Eastern Educational Radio*, 1970):

> And here it is crucial to bear in mind the difference between radio and other media. Unlike a book which requires the deliberate act of purchasing and reading (or a motion picture where admission to public exhibition must be actively sought) broadcasting is disseminated generally to the public . . . under circumstances where reception requires no activity of this nature. Thus, it comes directly into the home and frequently without any advance warning of its content. Millions daily turn the dial from station to station. While particular stations or programs are oriented to specific audiences, the fact is that by its very nature thousands of others not within the "intended" audience may also see or hear portions of the broadcast. Further, in that audience are very large numbers of children.

4. WGLD-FM in Oak Park, Illinois, was one of many stations in 1973 which adopted a current fad format called topless radio. The format features call-in programs in which the host and the callers have "frank" discussions about sex over the air. On one particular segment of the "Femme Forum" the announcer and his callers tediously discussed oral sex in a generally adolescent fashion. Complaints resulted in a hearing, and for the first time on record the FCC finally called a broadcast obscene, as opposed to indecent, vulgar, suggestive, or what have you. Using the *Roth-Memoirs* test (which was the law at that time) the commission ruled that the comments on the program were patently offensive, appealed to prurient interest, and lacked any redeeming social value. The station was fined $2,000. While many persons in the industry urged the Sonderling Corp. to appeal the ruling, others believed that it was best to keep the courts out of the matter for the time being to avoid setting a bad precedent, one that would have a greater impact than the FCC ruling. What the FCC ruling accomplished was to kill topless radio across the

nation. Were it not for its negative First Amendment implications, this ruling would stand as one of the best things the agency has ever done (*Sonderling Broadcasting Corp.*, 1973).

5. WBAI in New York broadcast a recording of a monologue by George Carlin in 1973. The recording, which was played in mid-afternoon after the announcer warned listeners that it might be offensive to some, contained seven four-letter words which were used many times. The record was played as a part of a program on society's attitude toward language. The FCC got one complaint, and as a result took action against the station on the grounds that it had broadcast indecent language. It defined indecent language as "language that describes in terms patently offensive as measured by contemporary community standards for the broadcast medium, sexual or excretory activities and organs, at times of the day when there is a reasonable risk children may be in the audience." The FCC said the WBAI broadcast met this definition.

Pacifica Foundation, which owns and operates the station, challenged the ruling and in March 1977 the United States Court of Appeals overturned the FCC action, ruling that the Commission's order was overbroad and vague. The Court said that it was not deciding whether or not, because of the unique characteristics of radio and television, the FCC may prohibit the broadcast of non-obscene speech or speech that would otherwise be protected. However, in this case the FCC ruling would prohibit the broadcast of many great works of literature or drama, even Shakespearian drama, because it does not consider the context in which such "indecent" words are used. Also, the ruling did not define "children." Was the Commission talking about someone under ten, under 14, under 17, or who? The court said, "the order sweepingly forbids any broadcast of the seven words irrespective of context or however innocent or educational they may be . . . clearly every use of the seven words cannot be deemed offensive even to minors . . ." (*Pacifica Foundation* v. *FCC*, 1977).

In practical terms there is little government censorship of broadcast obscenity. The broadcasters censor themselves too well for obscenity to be much of a problem. The cases that do pop up tend to be from stations which are not in the mainstream of broadcasting—little educational stations, offbeat FM stations, and the like. The managers of these kinds of stations tend to believe the First Amendment means what it says and aren't afraid to rock the boat. The vast majority of station owners and managers, however, are reluctant to even get into the boat. To see how shock waves can reverberate through the industry let's look briefly at the controversy over drugs and song lyrics.

In the early 1970s as the United States tried to put its finger on the reason why so many young people were turning to drugs to find salvation and happiness, someone, somewhere, suggested that popular music was probably a factor. The reasoning was that all those muscians and singers used dope and talked about dope and drugs in all their songs. They were undoubtedly Pied Pipers leading little Billy and Sally astray. Peter G. Hammond, the executive director of the National Coordinating Council on Drug Abuse and Education, as well as numerous other experts on drug use and drug abuse, testified that they found no evidence whatsoever of a cause-and-effect relationship between song lyrics and drug abuse. Nevertheless in March 1971 the FCC issued Public Notice 71-205 regarding *Licensee Responsibilities to Review Records Before Their Broadcast*. On its face it was a harmless enough document: it merely reminded licensees that they were responsible for material broadcast over their station—including songs whose lyrics promoted the use of drugs. When it hit the rock stations the notice literally caused an explosion. Most broadcasters saw it as an effort by the FCC to exclude certain kinds of songs from air play, but they complied with what they believed to be the wishes of the commission. One station owner confiscated the entire record library and then eliminated all Bob Dylan songs because he could not understand the lyrics.

The disc jockeys were told not to play any songs which mentioned drugs and were threatened that if they violated this rule the station would change from a rock station to an easy-listening format. Do Not Play Lists, common at all radio stations even before the public notice, suddenly expanded from listing a few records to listing often hundreds. Some of the records put off limits included "With a Little Help from My Friends" by the Beatles, "White Rabbit" by the Jefferson Airplane, the Beatles' "I Am the Walrus" and "Lucy in the Sky with Diamonds," "One Toke Over the Line" by Brewer and Shipley, and "Mr. Tambourine Man" by Bob Dylan and the Byrds. Even "Puff the Magic Dragon" by Peter, Paul, and Mary was banned at many stations. Some station owners read the notice to mean that all drug-related songs, not just songs which glorified or suggested the use of drugs, were banned. Songs like "The Pusher" and "Snowblind Friend" by Steppenwolf, both of which had strong antidrug lyrics, were also banned by many stations.

Because of the vast number of songs issued each week, and because the lyrics of many rock songs are unintelligible or subject to various interpretations, many songs were banned from the airwaves because there wasn't time to give them a careful screening or because the screeners found it impossible to understand either the words or the meaning of the lyrics. Some songs were banned at one station, but not at another station in the same community. Record companies began to distribute copies of the lyrics with the records and sometimes tossed in an explanation of what the words meant if it was needed. One record company fired most of its artists—those who would admit they used drugs or those who were suspected of using drugs—and promoted its new "clean" image to radio stations and record buyers. All these events took place within the span of about one month.

Five weeks after the initial notice the situation was so bad that the FCC had to publish an explanation of its original notice. In the explanation the agency said that it was not suggesting that radio stations ban certain records, but were merely pointing out that the licensee's responsibility for the material broadcast over his facilities extends to phonograph records. The agency added that the broadcaster must make the judgment. At renewal time, the explanation continued, the commission will look at the broadcaster's overall programming record, not at whether he broadcast this song or that song. Serving the public interest is the key, the memorandum noted.

The explanation lowered the blood pressure in the industry by thirty or forty points and since then things have cooled off. But this incident remains an interesting case study of the sensitivity of the broadcast industry to any little twitch by the regulatory agency.

News Programs

The FCC treads a bit softer when it comes to dealing with news programming. The commission normally gets involved in news programming through its enforcement of the Fairness Doctrine, which we shall consider shortly. There have been instances, especially recently, in which charges were made that stations and networks falsified the news. Congress also gets into such debates as it did in the controversy over the Columbia Broadcasting System broadcast "The Selling of the Pentagon," but usually takes no action. The FCC is also reluctant to act in such cases. The only difference is that the FCC astutely seeks to avoid confronting the issues involved in the charge of news falsification, whereas inaction by Congress results from both sensitivity to the First Amendment and inertia.

Complaints were made to the commission about such programs as "The Selling of the Pentagon" and "Hunger in America." The Columbia Broadcasting System was accused of careless editing in the program on the Pentagon, editing which took quotes from various parts of a speech and made it appear that these separate statements were actually one statement. There were other questionable editing practices as well. In "Hunger in America" the same network showed viewers a baby which it claimed had died of malnutrition. While many babies do die each week of malnutrition, the one photographed by the network had in fact died of other causes. The response of the FCC in "The Selling of the Pentagon" case is typical of how that agency handles such complaints. "Lacking evidence or documents that on their face reflect deliberate distortion, we believe that this government licensing agency cannot properly intervene," the commission ruled. "As we stated in the *Hunger in America* ruling, the commission is not the national arbiter of truth." While taking a hands-off action itself, the agency reminded broadcasters, "The licensee must have a policy of requiring honesty of its news staff and must take reasonable precautions to see that news is fairly handled. The licensee's investigation of substantial complaints . . . must be a thorough, conscientious one, resulting in remedial action where appropriate." From this one can glean that obvious and blatant staging of news will be considered a disservice to the public interest, but that the FCC is not in a position to evaluate or monitor the editing techniques of thousands of news departments. Errors will have to be fairly serious and well documented before the commission intervenes.

The two most widely discussed programming controls exercised by the FCC are the Fairness Doctrine and what is known as the equal time rule. The Fairness Doctrine is a creature of the commission based on an interpretation of the 1934 act, but the so-called equal time rule is Section 315 of the Communications Act. While the commission has interpreted this rule frequently, it remains primarily a rule designed by Congress. Let us look first at the equal time rule.

EQUAL TIME RULE

Section 315 is not really difficult to understand. If a broadcasting station permits one legally qualified candidate for public office to use its facilities, it must afford equal opportunity to all other such legally qualified candidates for the same office. Section 315 also specifically prohibits the station from censoring material in broadcasts by political candidates.

What does equal opportunity mean? It means equal time, equal facilities, and comparable costs. If John Smith buys one half hour of television time on station KLOP to campaign for the office of mayor, other legally qualified candidates for that office must be allowed to purchase one half hour of time as well. If Smith is able to use the station's equipment to prerecord his talk, other candidates must have the same opportunity. If the station charges Smith $100 for the half hour of time, the station must charge his opponents $100.

The station does not have to solicit appearance by the other candidates; it merely must give them the opportunity to use the facilities if they request such use within one week of Smith's appearance. Finally, Section 315 clearly states that the broadcaster does not have to allow any political candidates the use of his facilities if he so chooses. However, if he allows one candidate to use the facilities, he must allow the same use to all who are seeking the same office.

Federal Election Campaign Act

In 1971 the Congress passed The Federal Election Campaign Act which instituted revisions of Section 315, but only as they applied to federal elections. Under the new law the broadcaster cannot institute an across-the-board policy refusing all candidates the opportunity to use his station. The new law states that it is a ground for revocation of a license for a licensee willfully or repeatedly to fail "to allow reasonable access to or to permit purchase of reasonable amounts of time for the use of a broadcasting station by a legally qualified candidate for federal elective office on behalf of his candidacy." Therefore, in regard to candidates for federal office, the broadcaster's right to refuse use of station facilities does not really apply. However, broadcasters can still refuse the use of facilities to candidates for state and local office.

The 1971 law also specified the highest rate which a broadcaster can charge a candidate for federal office for using station facilities. Forty-five days before a primary election and sixty days before a general election the charge to a candidate cannot exceed the lowest rate the station charges local advertisers for that particular time slot. At other times the rate must be "comparable" to what the station charges other advertisers.

This ruling effects the equal time rule in this way. Candidate John Smith appears on KLOP 61 days before the election. He is charged $300 for 30 minutes. Candidate Jane Adams asks for equal opportunity and appears on KLOP for 30 minutes 51 days before the election. Under the old rule Adams would have to pay a comparable price—$300. Under the new rule, however, she may pay less. Because it is within 60 days of the general election, the station must bill Ms. Adams at its lowest rate for that time slot, which may be $200. In that case she pays only $200. What if the price that Smith paid—$300—is below the station's lowest rate for that time slot? Then Ms. Adams pays $300. She will pay either what Smith pays or the station's lowest rate—whichever is less.

Use of the Airwaves

Section 315 states that "use" by one candidate of a broadcast facility entitles his or her opponents to "use" that facility as well. A key question then is, What does the word *use* mean? What constitutes an appearance by a candidate in the eyes of the law? It is easiest to begin by listing those things which do not constitute a "use."

1. The appearance by a candidate in a bona fide or legitimate newscast does not constitute use of the facility in the eyes of the law. Section 315 will not be triggered.

2. The appearance of a candidate in a bona fide news interview program does not constitute a use. The key words are *bona fide*. An ap-

pearance on "Meet the Press," which is a bona fide news interview show, is not use of a broadcasting facility. But an appearance on "Meet the Candidates," a public-affairs show created by a television station for the express purpose of interviewing candidates prior to the election is use because it is not a bona fide news interview show. The show was created especially for the election campaign by the station and is not broadcast when electioneering is not in progress.

3. The appearance of a candidate in the spot news coverage of a bona fide news event is not use. When candidate Smith is interviewed at the scene of a bad fire about the problems of arson in the city it is not use in terms of Section 315. Political conventions are considered bona fide news events; therefore an appearance by a candidate at the convention can be broadcast without invoking Section 315.

4. The appearance of a candidate in a news documentary is not use if the appearance is incidental to the presentation of the subject of the program. Example: During the spring months of the 1968 political campaign, the Columbia Broadcasting System broadcast a documentary on reform of the federal income tax laws. An interview with Sen. Robert Kennedy, who was leading a fight in the United States Senate for tax reform, was included in the program. At that time Kennedy was a candidate for the presidency, but his appearance in the documentary did not activate the equal opportunity rule because the program was about tax laws. Kennedy's appearance was incidental to that subject. A news documentary about Kennedy would have been a different story and would have triggered Section 315. In the documentary the network was merely talking to Kennedy about a national problem on which he was an expert.

Press conferences held by political candidates, as well as debates between political candidates, are bona fide news events and the broadcast of these events will not initiate Section 315, according to an FCC ruling in 1975. The only qualification for a debate to be exempt is that the debate must be under the control of someone other than the broadcaster or the political candidates. If the Rotary Club sponsors the debate or if the Press Club sponsors the debate, it is considered a news event and can be broadcast without invoking the equal opportunity rule.

With these exceptions, all other appearances by a candidate are considered use in the meaning of Section 315. A paid political broadcast, a spot announcement, and even a five-minute interview on the "Tonight Show" are all appearances that will invoke Section 315. Opposing candidates would have the right to ask for equal opportunity. When Ronald Reagan was running for president in 1976 stations had to refrain from showing his old movies and segments of "Death Valley Days" in which he appeared as the host. Pat Paulsen's quadrennial run for the

White House forces television stations and networks to pull movies in which he appears out of their libraries until the election is over. Once, Johnny Carson entertained the mayor of Burbank, California, on his program in recognition of the fame that town gained by being the butt of a joke on Rowan and Martin's "Laugh-In." But Carson's staff hadn't done its homework, for the mayor was in the midst of a campaign for reelection. The National Broadcasting Company affiliate in Los Angeles was forced to give each of the mayor's dozen or so opponents equal time.

Legally Qualified Candidates

One of the most confusing aspects of Section 315 regards the FCC's definition of a legally qualified candidate. It is a long definition filled with lots of *ands* and *ors* and needs clarification.

A legally qualified candidate is any person (1) who publicly announces that he or she is a candidate for nomination or election to any local, county, state, or national office, *and* (2) who meets the qualifications prescribed by law for that office, *and* (3) who qualifies for a place on the ballot or is eligible to be voted for by sticker or write-in methods, *and* (4) who was duly nominated by a political party which is commonly known and regarded as such or makes a substantial showing that he or she is a bona fide candidate.

There should be no question about number one in the definition: the candidate must be an announced candidate. Number two merely states that the person must be eligible to hold the office to which he or she aspires. A ten-year old girl, for example, is not eligible to be president (because of her age). Despite the fact that she may be an announced candidate for that office, she is not a legally qualified candidate. Number three is self-explanatory: the person's name must appear on the ballot or he must be an eligible write-in or sticker candidate. It is number four which is confusing. Who knows what a substantial showing really is? What is a political party "commonly known and regarded as such"? Answers to these questions are judgment calls, and broadcasters with questions can solicit answers from the FCC. In fact, it is through the solicitation of such questions that the agency makes most of its Section 315 rulings.

Equal opportunity cases are rare. Normally the broadcaster asks the agency for guidance and then follows the recommendations of the commission. If there is a valid Section 315 complaint, the FCC usually just informs the licensee that candidate Adams is entitled to equal opportunity time and the station provides the time.

Many critics charge that a smart politician can refrain from announcing his candidacy for reelection, for example, and just make many television appearances and not be in violation of Section 315. That is true. But stations should be able to see what the candidate is doing and can

Exceptions

refuse to allow appearances by the unannounced candidate, especially appearances which are clearly political in nature. A station which is not careful in this regard can be subject to problems at renewal time.

The FCC has granted two exceptions to the application of the equal opportunity doctrine, one of which appears much more important than it really is. The first exception is broad: In primary elections, Section 315 applies to intraparty contests rather than to interparty contests. In a primary election, the situation is not Republicans versus Democrats, it is Republican versus Republican and Democrat versus Democrat. Only opponents can get equal opportunity. Imagine Jane Adams is a Republican candidate for governor. She is one of four Republicans seeking to win the primary. Six Democrats are also seeking to win the primary election and gain the nomination for the governorship in their party. Ms. Adams appears on KLOP for fifteen minutes. What are the station's obligations? The station is obliged to give equal opportunity to the other three Republican candidates since they are the ones against whom Jane is running. The Democrats are not running against Ms. Adams at this time. While this exception to the rule is broad, it makes a good deal of sense.

The second exception turns out to be not much of an exception at all although it appears to be one on its face. The only appearance that triggers Section 315 is an appearance by the candidate. Under Section 315 appearances by friends, relatives, supporters, and so forth, do not require the station to give equal opportunity to opponents. However (this is an important however), the FCC has decided that such noncandidate appearances do require the station to provide an opportunity for appearances by supporters of the other legally qualified candidates.

This is known as the Zapple rule and was formulated a few years ago in response to a letter from Nicholas Zapple, formerly a staff member of the Senate Subcommittee on Communications. It was restated in the FCC's 1972 *Report Regarding the Handling of Political Broadcasts*. This is what the FCC said:

> The commission held in "Zapple" that when a licensee sells time to supporters or spokesmen of a candidate during an election campaign who urge the candidate's election, discuss the campaign issues, or criticize an opponent then the licensee must afford comparable time to the spokesmen for an opponent. Known as the quasi-equal opportunity or political party corollary to the fairness doctrine, the "Zapple" doctrine is based on the equal opportunity requirement of section 315 of the Communications Act; accordingly, free reply time need not be afforded to respond to a paid program.

The Zapple Rule is a fairly specific formulation of one part of what had been vague FCC policy for some time, that is, that during political campaigns programs that do not invoke Section 315 fall under the ambit of the fairness doctrine. This means that licenses are required to play fair with all candidates. Broadcasters are therefore obliged to scrutinize even those programs which are exempt from Section 315 such as newscasts to ensure that a balance of some sort is maintained.

Two last points need to be made about Section 315. First, since broadcasters are not permitted to censor the remarks of a political candidate, they are immune from libel suits based on those remarks. In 1959 the Supreme Court ruled that since stations cannot control what candidates say over the air they should not be held responsible for the remarks. The candidate, however, can still be sued (*Farmers Educational and Cooperative Union of America* v. *WDAY*, 1959). Second, ballot issues like school bond levies, initiatives, and referendums do not fall under Section 315, but are treated as controversial issues under the Fairness Doctrine.

FAIRNESS DOCTRINE

There is no aspect of broadcast regulation that is more controversial than the Fairness Doctrine. Some authorities consider it a flagrant affront to the First Amendment's guarantee of freedom of expression; others argue that the Fairness Doctrine is the only thing which makes freedom of expression a reality in broadcasting. In addition to being controversial, the doctrine is confusing. Even many broadcasters really don't have a good grasp on what the doctrine means. No wonder! While on the face the doctrine appears patently simple, one needs a clear mind and a pure heart to wade through the hundreds of FCC rulings which interpret one or another aspect of this infamous doctrine.

The Fairness Doctrine is a broad doctrine, affecting advertising (as will be noted later in this chapter) political campaigns, and political candidates, as was just noted briefly. Its primary thrust, however, is aimed at public affairs programming and controversial public issues. In barest essentials the Fairness Doctrine involves a two-fold duty for broadcasters. First, broadcasters must devote a reasonable percentage of their broadcast time to the coverage of public issues. Second, the coverage of these issues must be fair in the sense that an opportunity for presentation of contrasting points of view is provided. That is it, period. What's so hard about that? Well, it's little words like *reasonable* and *public issues* and *fair* and *contrasting* that are troublesome. These are the words that need to be clarified.

A quick look at the origin of the Fairness Doctrine is in order first. Examination of the Communications Act will not reveal a single word about it because the Fairness Doctrine is a creature of the FCC, which is one reason making it controversial.

In 1927 and again in 1933 members of Congress tried to include a kind of Fairness Doctrine in federal legislation regulating broadcasting. All attempts failed, stopped either by the Congress itself or by presidential veto. In 1947 another attempt was made when a Senate bill to adopt a legislative Fairness Doctrine was introduced, but again the effort failed.

With or without a law, however, first the Federal Radio Commission (FRC) and later the Federal Communications Commission ruled that balance and fairness were requirements of broadcasting which serves the public interest, convenience, and necessity. In 1929 in the *Great Lakes Broadcasting* case the FRC ruled, "insofar as a program consists of discussion of public questions, public interest requires ample play for the free and fair competition of opposing views and the commission believes that the principle applies not only to addresses by political candidates but to all discussion of issues of importance to the public" (in re *Great Lakes Broadcasting Co.*, 1929). Sixteen years later in the *United Broadcasting* case the FCC echoed the FRC. The commission agreed with the broadcaster's contention that a radio station is not a common carrier, but noted also (in re *United Broadcasting Co.*, 1945):

> These facts, however, in no way impinge upon the duty of each station licensee to be sensitive to the problems of public concern in the community and to make sufficient time available, on a non-discriminatory basis, for a full discussion thereof. . . .

The first "official" announcement of what we know as the Fairness Doctrine was made in 1949 when the FCC issued the long report *In the Matter of Editorializating by Broadcast Licensees.* The report was the result of an extensive study that the commission undertook after broadcasters and other persons protested a 1941 ruling by the agency that licensees could not editorialize on their stations (in re *Mayflower Broadcasting Corp., WAAB*, 1941). The editorialization report stated that broadcasters had an affirmative responsibility to provide a reasonable amount of time for the presentation of programs devoted to the discussion and consideration of public issues. The report added that it was the licensee's responsibility to afford a reasonable opportunity for the presentation of all responsible positions on the matters discussed. The commission said that a licensee would not be meeting his fairness doctrine responsibility when he refused to broadcast all controversial matter. The FCC also noted:

> . . . it is clear that any approximation of fairness in the presentation of any controversy will be difficult if not impossible of achievement

unless the licensee plays a conscious and positive role in bringing about balanced presentation of the opposing viewpoints.

To the question that would surely be raised about the commission's role as censor in applying the fairness doctrine, the agency noted, "The duty to operate in the public interest is no esoteric mystery, but essentially a duty to operate a radio station with good judgment and good faith guided by a reasonable regard for the interests of the community to be served."

This, then, is the origin of the Fairness Doctrine. Congress never directly approved nor disapproved of the policy. In 1959, however, while passing an amendment to the Communications Act which excluded news programming from the ambit of the Section 315 equal opportunity requirement, the Congress approved language in the bill which said that nothing in the amendment should be construed to relieve broadcasters "from the obligation imposed upon them under this Act to operate in the public interest and to afford reasonable opportunity for the discussion of conflicting views on issues of public importance." Is this a sanction of the Fairness Doctrine? The FCC has argued that it is. But in 1975 when the chairman of the commission suggested that perhaps enforcement of the Fairness Doctrine should be relaxed with regard to some broadcasters (AM radio stations in large cities), he argued that the Fairness Doctrine is a creature of the commission and can be changed by the commission. This argument prompted Sen. John Pastore, an author of the 1959 amendment just mentioned, to state that the Fairness Doctrine is a Congressional policy, approved in 1959. The issue remains unresolved.

Before the application of the doctrine is discussed, one point needs to be further emphasized. Broadcasters have an affirmative responsibility to make certain that all sides of a public question are presented. That is, broadcasters must either find spokesmen or make the presentation themselves. Merely allowing persons who have a different viewpoint to use the station is not sufficient. Broadcasters are obliged to seek out spokesmen for divergent viewpoints.

Meaning   In 1971 the FCC decided to review the Fairness Doctrine. Did it work? Should it be replaced? be modified? be abandoned? In 1974 the commission issued its findings in a report entitled *Fairness Doctrine and Public Interest Standards*. To sum up what the agency said in a single sentence is quite simple: The Fairness Doctrine is needed and it works just fine. The commission justified the need for the doctrine by the nearly fifty-year-old argument of scarcity. There are not enough frequencies for all to have one, and therefore owners who do must make certain that all points of view are thoroughly aired. Critics of this rationale have argued for years that scarcity is no longer a problem since cable television now provides an unlimited number of channels. In the report the commission quite properly refuted this argument:

> The effective development of an electronic medium with an abundance of channels (through the use of cable, or otherwise) is still very much a thing of the future. For the present we do not believe that it would be appropriate—or even permissible—for a government agency charged with the allocation of the channels now available to ignore the legitimate First Amendment interests of the general public.

The commission went on to assert that the net effect of the Fairness Doctrine has been to enhance the volume and quality of the coverage of issues of public importance, which is important in the complex era in which we live. Quoting from an earlier opinion it had issued, the commission alerted broadcasters, "We regard strict adherence to the Fairness Doctrine—including the affirmative obligation to provide coverage of issues of public importance—as the single most important requirement of operation in the public interest, the *sine qua non* ["the indispensable requisite"], for grant of a renewal of license."

In addition to defending the Fairness Doctrine in this report, the FCC outlined and provided an interpretation of the doctrine. If this interpretation is used as a guide, it is possible to gain a good understanding of what the Fairness Doctrine means today.

Question one: What is adequate time for the discussion of public issues? This determination is up to the broadcaster, according to the FCC. Some persons—even some members of the FCC—suggest that the agency set a minimum standard for public affairs programming. For example, former Commissioner Nicholas Johnson suggested that at least 5 percent of a station's programming be devoted to the discussion of public issues. However the FCC has resisted adopting such a scheme. "It is the individual broadcaster who, after evaluating the needs of his particular community, must determine what percentage of the limited broadcast day should be devoted to news and discussion or consideration of public issues," the FCC said.

The debate is somewhat meaningless since this aspect of the Fairness Doctrine is not rigidly enforced anyway. Broadcasters must have some public issue programming, but even a minimal amount will protect a broadcast license.

Question two: What is a reasonable opportunity for opposing viewpoints? The Fairness Doctrine does not require—as does Section 315—one-to-one precision in granting time for opposing viewpoints. So long as all sides of the issue are reasonably aired (this is terribly vague) the strictures of the Fairness Doctrine will have been met. Do all viewpoints have to be aired? What about the fellow in the valley whose ideas are different from those of everyone else? No, that would be unreasonable. The commission requires an airing only of viewpoints which have a significant measure of support or viewpoints which reflect the ideas of a significant segment of the community. But remember, it is the duty of broadcasters to make certain that these views are publicly aired. They have an affirmative duty to find someone to raise these points or have someone at the station present these ideas.

Question three: What is a controversial issue of public importance? In actual practice (as will be noted shortly) the broadcaster decides what is controversial and what is not. Some of the factors which the FCC suggests that the licensee take into consideration when determining whether an issue is controversial or not include the following:

1. The degree of media coverage of the issue
2. The degree of attention the issue receives from government officials and other community leaders
3. The impact the issue is likely to have on the community at large

By and large it comes down to whether the broadcaster believes that an issue is important, is controversial, and does stimulate debate within the community.

How It Works   If our discussion of the Fairness Doctrine were stopped at this point, the doctrine would indeed appear imposing. It is really far from that, despite what broadcasters say. Yes, it is disconcerting—even frightening— to receive an inquiry from a government agency, the government agency which grants your license, asking whether you have been fair in dealing with a community issue. However the mechanics of the process are such that broadcasters really have little to fear if they have only attempted to do their job.

The FCC does no monitoring for violations of the Fairness Doctrine itself, but depends instead upon viewer and listener complaints. Organizations like Accuracy in Media (AIM) which take the pose of "professional media monitors" are popping up across the nation. Usually these groups have an axe to grind of one sort or another. Nevertheless, they do make complaints, and have created problems for broadcasters.

The FCC requires that a fairness doctrine complaint contain the following items:

1. The name of the particular station involved
2. The particular issue of a controversial nature discussed over the air
3. The date and time when the program was carried

4. The basis for the claim that the station presented only one side of the question
5. Whether the station afforded or has plans to afford an opportunity for presentation of contrasting viewpoints

Numbers one and three are simple to accomplish. Number two can be a problem, however, for the station may define the issue aired during the program somewhat differently than does the complainant, as we shall soon see. Number five requires that the complainant talk to the station before making a complaint, which is the only way the question can be answered. It is number four, however, that is the primary problem for unhappy viewers. The Fairness Doctrine does not require that a station present all sides of an issue within the context of a single program. What is required is that in its *overall programming* it make a balanced presentation of the issues. This month the station might present a program which is against abortion, and next month it may present one which is for abortion. Overall, the station has been fair. Therefore, in alleging that the station has only presented one side of an issue, the complainant has to have a pretty good idea of the station's overall programming—what has gone on in the past as well as what is going to happen in the future. This is a heavy burden for persons who seek to complain. Imagine seeing a one-sided gun-control program on television tonight. How certain are you that somewhere along the line in the past few months the station did not present the other side of the issue? maybe in a documentary? maybe during the news? maybe on a Sunday afternoon while you were watching a football game on another channel? While complaints are not foreclosed, they are difficult to make.

What happens to the complaints the FCC does receive? According to the commission, nothing in most cases. The FCC reports in "Fairness Doctrine and Public Interest Standards" that of approximately 2,400 Fairness Doctrine complaints received in 1973, only 94 were forwarded to the licensee for comment. That is about 5 percent. If the complaint is forwarded to the station, the FCC letter asks the broadcaster these two questions:

1. Is the issue of controversial public importance in your viewing area?
2. Have you fulfilled your Fairness Doctrine obligations by presenting balanced programming on that issue?

If the broadcaster says that the issue is not controversial or not of public importance, the FCC must accept the answer unless there is evidence that the broadcaster is arbitrary or capricious in his determination. So long as the broadcaster makes a good faith judgment that the issue is not controversial, there is nothing the FCC can do. The broadcaster has the discretion to decide what is and what is not controversial. Furthermore the FCC cannot substitute its judgment for that of the broadcaster. Clearly if the broadcaster ignores overwhelming evidence that the people are interested, if he ignores the fact that a vigorous public debate is underway, the FCC can then rule that the determination is not made in good faith. But this is a very rare kind of ruling. Generally the agency takes the licensee's word.

In 1972 *The National Broadcasting Company* broadcast a program entitled "The Broken Promise," a docucentary about private pension plans. It was very critical of certain private pension plans and graphically showed how millions of Americans had been ripped off and cheated. Narrator Edwin Newman told viewers *that most private pension plans are good,* that they provide a real benefit to the workers. Most of the NBC program however dealt *with bad pension plans.*

A Fairness Doctrine complaint was lodged against the network by AIM. The FCC asked The National Broadcasting Company whether the program dealt with a controversial issue. The network said no, and this was its reasoning. The program talked about bad private pension plans. There were no allegations that all pension plans were bad. In fact, quite the opposite: it was stated that most plans are good. The National Broadcasting Company focused on the bad plans. Everybody agrees that some plans are bad. There is no controversy about that. Since the program focused only on the bad plans, it did not deal with a controversial issue.

The FCC didn't accept this logic. But when the decision was appealed to the court of appeals, the agency had its hand slapped. The court said that so long as the network had made a good faith judgment, the National Broadcasting Company was to exercise the discretion as to whether the issue was controversial (*NBC* v. *FCC,* 1974). The FCC could not come to a different conclusion on the basis of the same evidence. That was not permitted. What the agency must ask was this: Was there any evidence that could lead the network to decide that the issue was not controversial? And if there was, then NBC's determination was made in good faith.

Because the case took so long to get through the courts, the rulings by both the FCC and the court of appeals were in the end moot. The controversy disappeared when Congress passed its pension reform bill. So the *Broken Promise* case is not a precedent. However the rules have not changed. The case was cited to show how the rules work. If another case were to come along tomorrow, the same kinds of restrictions upon the FCC would exist. It is basically the broadcaster's decision whether the issue at hand is controversial and important.

If the licensee says the issue is controversial, the station must then tell the commission how it has fulfilled the Fairness Doctrine requirements, or how it plans to fulfill its responsibilities. Here the FCC has a bit more discretion. However the key is still whether broadcasters *make a good faith effort to provide balanced programming*, rather than whether they *provide balanced programming*. Unless the licensee is really out in left field, the commissioners are usually satisfied. It is only in outrageous cases that the FCC demands a hearing, or demands that the broadcaster provide time for opposing viewpoints. Remember also that the initial burden of proof is upon the complainant to convince the FCC that a violation of the doctrine did indeed occur. Before the FCC even sends out a letter to the station the complainant must provide "a reasonable basis for the conclusion that the license has failed in its overall programming to present a reasonable opportunity for contrasting views."

What happens if the FCC finds there has been a violation? A request may be made that the station provide time for airing opposing viewpoints, or a fine may be levied against the broadcaster. In extreme cases the broadcast license may not be renewed (see *Brandywine-Main Line Radio, Inc.*, v. *FCC*, 1972). Denial of renewal generally results only when a pattern of flagrant abuses of the Fairness Doctrine can be shown. Few fairness complaints result in action of any kind against the station. Still, the time and trouble involved in answering such a complaint, especially one which evolves into a hearing and a court case like The National Broadcasting System case just discussed, are quite onerous. Typical complaints may cost from $500 to $1,000 to answer. When a hearing is involved, expenses can easily reach into the tens of thousands of dollars. A West Coast television station won a Fairness Doctrine hearing which cost the broadcaster $20,000 to defend.

Advertising

The Fairness Doctrine has been applied to advertising as well as to other subjects. In 1967 in response to a petition from a young attorney named John Banzhaf, the commission ruled that stations which carried advertisements for cigarettes must carry free public service messages showing the dangers of smoking as well (*WCBS-TV; Applicability of the Fairness Doctrine to Cigarette Advertising*, 1967). Cigarette smoking was a controversial subject. Later, of course, Congress passed a law which banned cigarette advertisements from the airwaves completely.

Following the *Banzhaf* ruling other public interest groups sought to have broadcasters balance advertisements for gasoline and automobiles with messages about environmental protection. But the FCC did not agree to these proposals. The commission argued that the smoking decision was unusual, that smoking is a habit that can disappear, that the government urged the discontinuance of cigarette smoking, that government studies showed the danger of smoking, and so forth. In other words the problem of smoking is different from the problem of pollution. So the Friends of the Earth went to court, and in 1971 the court of appeals reversed the FCC ruling. The court said it could not see the distinction between the cigarette case and that case (in re *Wilderness Society and Friends of the Earth*, 1971):

> Commercials which continue to insinuate that the human personality finds greater fulfillment in the larger car with the quick getaway do, it seems to us, ventilate a point of view which not only has become controversial but involves an issue of public importance. Where there is undisputed evidence, as there is here, that the hazards to health implicit in air pollution are enlarged and aggravated by such products, then the parallel with cigarette advertising is exact and the relevance of *Banzhaf* inescapable.

The court said, however, that stations do not have to broadcast anti-big-car advertising, as in the cigarette advertisements case. The key is overall programming. If the licensees carry programming which discusses the environmental dangers of pollution and the dimunition of resources, the Fairness Doctrine will be satisfied.

In its 1974 report the FCC discussed the application of the Fairness Doctrine to advertising. The commission said that it would apply the doctrine to editorial advertising—commercials which consist of direct and substantial commentary on important public issues—but not to product advertising, not even to controversial products. It said that the cigarette decision was a mistake, that if it had to decide the case today it would not make the same decision. "We believe that standard product commercials," the commissioners wrote, "make no meaningful contribution toward informing the public on any side of any issue." The commission also rejected a proposal by the Federal Trade Commission that the FCC require stations to offer rebuttal time to public interest groups to answer commercials which raise controversial issues, commercials which make claims which are based on disputed scientific premises, and commercials which are silent about the negative aspects of the advertised products (like too many aspirin can be harmful). The FCC said that almost all commercials raise controversial issues for some people, that such a "counteradvertising proposal" could have an adverse economic effect on broadcasting, and that it did not believe that the Fairness Doctrine was an appropriate vehicle with which to correct false and misleading advertising.

**Personal
Attack Rules**

The 1974 report states the rules as they exist today. Remember, a court can overturn these rules as in the *Friends of the Earth* case in 1971. The FCC may wish to stay out of the product advertising controversy, but some product advertisements are controversial and as such may become the legitimate target of a Fairness Doctrine complaint.

While the Fairness Doctrine remains a nebulous policy which has been outlined almost on a case-by-case basis, the commission has drafted specific rules with regard to one portion of the doctrine—what are known as the personal attack rules. The personal attack rules are a subsection of the doctrine (see 32 Fed. Reg. 10303; 11531; and 33 Fed. Reg. 5362; 1967) and deal with one specific kind of one-sided presentation. Here are the rules:

Personal attacks; political editorials.

(a) When, during the presentation of views on a controversial issue of public importance, an attack is made upon the honesty, character, integrity or like personal qualities of an identified person or group, the licensee shall, within a reasonable time and in no event later than one week after the attack, transmit to the person or group attacked (1) notification of the date, time and identification of the broadcast; (2) a script or tape (or an accurate summary if a script or tape is not available) of the attack; and (3) an offer of a reasonable opportunity to respond over the licensee's facilities.

(b) The provisions of paragraph (a) of this section shall not be applicable (1) to attacks on foreign groups or foreign public figures; (2) to personal attacks which are made by legally qualified candidates, their authorized spokesmen, or those associated with them in the campaign, or other such candidates, their authorized spokesmen, or persons associated with the candidates in the campaign; and (3) to bona fide newscasts, bona fide news interviews, and on-the-spot coverage of a bona fide news event (including commentary or analysis contained in the foregoing programs, but the provisions of paragraph (a) of this section shall be applicable to editorials of the licensee).

NOTE: The Fairness Doctrine is applicable to situations coming within [(3)], above, and, in a specific factual situation, may be applicable in the general area of political broadcasts [(2)], above.

(c) Where a licensee, in an editorial, (i) endorses or (ii) opposes a legally qualified candidate or candidates, the licensee shall, within 24 hours after the editorial, transmit to respectively (i) the other qualified candidate or candidates for the same office or (i) the candidate opposed in the editorial (1) notification of the date and time of the editorial; (2) a script or tape of the editorial; and (3) an offer of a reasonable opportunity for a candidate or a spokesman of the candidate to respond over the licensee's facilities: *Provided, however,* That where such editorials are broadcast within 72 hours prior to the day of the election, the licensee shall comply with the provisions of this paragraph sufficiently far in advance of the broadcast to enable the candidate or candidates to have a reasonable opportunity to prepare a response and to present it in a timely fashion.

The personal attack rules stem from FCC rulings in 1962 stating that when licensees broadcast what amounts to a personal attack upon an individual or group within the community they have an affirmative obligation to notify the target of the attack of the broadcast and offer the target an opportunity to respond. In 1967 these earlier decisions were clarified and made more specific with the publication of the personal attack rules.

As you can see from the rules the licensee's obligations are quite specific. It is important to remember that just naming someone in an editorial or commentary does not necessarily constitute a personal attack. On the other hand the rules apply to attacks made by everyone, not just by the station itself.

Paragraph (b) of the rules exempt attacks made by candidates and their followers upon other candidates and their followers. Newscast, news interviews, and on-the-spot news coverage are also exempted from the personal attack rules, but not from the more general provisions of the Fairness Doctrine. Paragraph (c) outlines licensee obligations with regard to editorial endorsements of candidates.

Soon after the personal attack rules were published they were challenged in court. A small radio station in Pennsylvania challenged an FCC ruling requiring it to provide free time to Fred Cook, an author, who had been attacked by right-wing evangelist Billy James Hargis. The United States Court of Appeals for the District of Columbia upheld the constitutionality of both the personal attack rules and the Fairness Doctrine (*Red Lion Broadcasting Co.* v. *FCC*, 1967). While this case was being litigated the Radio and Television News Directors Association and other broadcasting organizations petitioned the United States Court of Appeals for the Seventh District in Chicago to review the constitutionality of the Fairness Doctrine. In this case the court of appeals struck down both the personal attack rules and the Fairness Doctrine as being in violation of the First Amendment (*Radio and Television News Director's Association* v. *U.S.*, 1968). With two circuit courts at odds on the question, the Supreme Court had to decide the issue.

The argument made by opponents of the Fairness Doctrine, more specifically of the personal attack rules, was two pronged. First, it was asserted that by forcing broadcasters to carry material, that is, the reply by the target of the attack, the government interfered with the First Amendment rights of broadcasters. Second, it was claimed that the Fairness Doctrine amounts to prior restraint as well. Here is the argument.

A station has a public affairs budget of $5,000, just enough to produce and air a documentary opposing mandatory busing of children. The Fairness Doctrine requires the licensee to present both sides of the issue; therefore the station has to produce a second documentary which outlines the favorable aspects of busing. But the station has no money for that and therefore cannot air the first documentary opposing busing. This government interference amounts to restraining the broadcast of the documentary opposed to busing. Hence, there is a violation of the First Amendment, there is prior restraint.

Whatever merit you may find in these arguments, the Supreme Court found little to recommend them. In a unanimous decision in 1969 the high Court upheld the constitutionality of both the personal attack rules and the Fairness Doctrine with the argument that the First Amendment operates as a command to the government to protect the public from one-sided presentations of public issues. Going back to the original Congressional mandate that the broadcaster operate in the public interest, the Court said the public interest is served only when the community receives exposure to all sides of controversial matters. As far as the First Amendment is concerned, wrote Justice Byron White, the licensed broadcaster stands no better off than those to whom the licenses are refused (*Red Lion Broadcasting Co.* v. *FCC*, 1969):

> A license permits broadcasting, but the licensee has no constitutional right to be the one who holds the license or to monopolize a radio frequency to the exclusion of his fellow citizens. There is nothing in the First Amendment which prevents the government from requiring a licensee to share his frequency with others and to conduct himself as a proxy or fiduciary with obligations to present those views and voices which are representative of his community and which would otherwise, by necessity, be barred from the air waves.

Later in the opinion Justice White asserted, "It is the right of the public to receive suitable access to social, political, esthetic, moral and other ideas and experiences, which is crucial here. That right may not constitutionally be abridged either by the Congress or by the FCC."

This case, *Red Lion Broadcasting* v. *FCC*, stands as the leading declaration that the First Amendment is for the people, not for the media, that the purpose of the First Amendment is to ensure that the public obtains the information needed to act as knowledgeable voters and citizens. The Court is willing to stand behind this philosophy with regard to broadcasting, but rejects these ideas with regard to the printed press in the *Tornillo* case discussed earlier in the book. How strong the high Court will stand behind the Fairness Doctrine today as it is battered from all sides is an important question. In 1973 at least some of the nine justices hinted that perhaps they were pulling back somewhat from their earlier unanimous declaration in a case involving the obligation of a broadcaster to sell, note the word *sell,* time to persons seeking to air controversial public issues.

First Amendment Implications

Broadcasting stations are not common carriers. That is, they have the right to refuse to do business with anyone they choose. During 1969 and 1970 two groups, the Democratic National Committee and a Washington, D. C., organization known as Business Executives Movement for Peace sought to buy time from television stations and networks to solicit funds for their protest of the Vietnam War and to voice their objections to the way the war was being prosecuted by the government. Broadcasters rebuffed these groups on the grounds that airing such controversial advertisements and programming would evoke the Fairness Doctrine and then they would be obligated to ensure that all sides of the controversy were aired. Such action was a nuisance and could be costly. The broadcasters told the Democratic committee and the businessmen that one of their basic policies was not to sell time to any individual or group seeking to set forth views on controversial issues.

When this policy was challenged before the FCC, the commission sided with the broadcasters, noting that it was up to each individual license to determine how best to fulfill Fairness Doctrine obligations. But the United States Court of Appeals for the District of Columbia reversed the FCC ruling, citing the *Red Lion* decision that the right of the public to receive information is deeply rooted in the First Amendment. A ban on editorial advertising, the court ruled, "leaves a paternalistic structure in which licensees and bureaucrats decide what issues are important, whether to fully cover them, and the format, time and style of coverage. . . ." This kind of system, the court ruled, is inimical to the First Amendment (*Business Executives Movement for Peace* v. *FCC,* 1971):

> It may unsettle some of us to see an antiwar message or a political party message in the accustomed place of a soap or beer commercial. . . . We must not equate what is habitual with what is right or what is constitutional. A society already so saturated with commercialism can well afford another outlet for speech on public issues. All that we may lose is some of our apathy.

The victory of the businessmen and Democrats was shortlived, for by a seven-to-two vote, the United States Supreme Court overturned the appellate court ruling (*CBS* v. *Democratic National Committee,* 1973). Stations have an absolute right to refuse to sell time for advertising dealing with political campaigns and controversial issues. To give the FCC the power over such advertising runs the risk of enlarging government control over the content of broadcast discussion of public issues.

In response to the argument that by permitting broadcasters to refuse such advertising we place in their hands the power to decide what the people shall see or hear on important public issues Justice Burger wrote:

> For better or worse, editing is what editors are for; and editing is the selection and choice of material. That editors—newspaper or broadcast—can and do abuse this power is beyond doubt, but that is no reason to deny the discretion Congress provided. Calculated risks of abuse are taken in order to preserve high values.

The court was badly fractured on this case and Justices Brennan and Marshall dissented. Only two other justices—Stewart and Rehnquist—joined the chief justice in his opinion. The remainder joined in overturning the court of appeals ruling, but for their own reasons. It could be said that the issue is not completely resolved, but in light of the unanimous Tornillo decision the following year the matter probably is settled (*Miami Herald Co.* v. *Tornillo,* 1974). Broadcasters are required to present programming on public issues and to do so in such a manner as to ensure that all sides get a fair hearing. How this is to be accomplished is the business of the broadcaster. The Fairness Doctrine does not provide right of access to television or radio.

CABLE TELEVISION

Cable television, in which wires are used to relay radio and television into homes, offices, schools, and public buildings, is different from broadcasting, in which radio and television signals are transmitted through the airwaves. Therefore we could ask, How did the FCC happen to get jurisdiction to regulate cable television? Regulation had to be done by someone (according to many people), and the FCC turned out to be the someone.

Despite unclear jurisdiction in the field (notwithstanding court opinions), the FCC takes a strong hand in the regulation of cablecasting. Cable television (CATV) is really a hybrid of broadcasting and wire (telephone and telegraph) communications. It might therefore be argued that since the FCC has Congressional authority to regulate both broadcasting and wire communications it has the authority to regulate cablecasting.

The first move toward regulation occurred in 1958. In the *Frontier Broadcasting* case the commission ruled that since cable television is neither common carrier nor broadcast system the agency would not regulate cable television directly (*Frontier Broadcasting Co.* v. *Collier,*

1958). However, the agency did say that one of its concerns was to control excessive electromagnetic radiation emissions by cable systems which might interfere with other communication systems. It therefore intended to keep an eye on happenings.

Four years later in 1962 the commission changed its mind somewhat and asserted indirect jurisdiction over cable systems. Cable systems often use microwave relay towers to pick up television signals and move them along to the cable system. This practice smacks of broadcasting and the FCC ruled that it has the power to deny a permit for a relay system if the existing broadcasting stations and thus the public interest will be injured by increased competition from the cable system. This ruling, known as the *Carter Mountain Transmission Corp.* decision, was affirmed by both the court of appeals and the United States Supreme Court. The FCC was well on its way to controlling cable under the justification of serving the public interest by protecting existing broadcasters from competition (in re *Carter Mountain Transmission Corp.*, 1962, 1963).

In 1965 the FCC issued its *First Report and Order on Microwave-Served CATV.* The agency adopted a series of operating rules for cable television and said it would grant microwave relay permits only to those cable systems which agreed to abide by the FCC rules. The rules included an agreement by the cable operator to carry local as well as distant stations, to not duplicate local programming by bringing in distant stations carrying the same network programming as the local station, and so forth. At the same time the commission issued a notice that it planned to apply these rules to all cable systems some time in the future.

The future was 1966, the following year, when the FCC issued its *Second Report and Order.* It applied the rules formerly directed at those systems seeking microwave relay permits to all cable systems. This action was challenged by the Southwestern Cable Co. and ultimately the case came before the Supreme Court. In 1968 the high Court backed the FCC in its newly asserted power to control all cable systems. Justice Harlan wrote for the court (*U.S.* v. *Southwestern Cable Co.*, 1968):

> The commission has been charged with broad responsibilities for the orderly development of an appropriate system of local television broadcasting. . . . The commission has reasonably found that the successful performance of these duties demands prompt and efficacious regulation of community antenna television systems. [cable systems] We have elsewhere held that we may not, "in the absence of compelling evidence that such was Congress' intention . . . prohibit administration action imperative for the achievement of an agency's ultimate purpose. . . ." There is no such evidence here, and we therefore hold that the commission's authority over "all interstate . . . communication by wire or radio" permits the regulation of CATV systems.

Justice Harlan added that the FCC can regulate cable television at least to the extent "reasonably ancillary to the effective performance of the commission's various responsibilities for the regulation of television broadcasting."

It was at this point that the FCC shifted its posture from regulation of cable systems in order to protect broadcasters to regulation of cable systems in order to enhance communication by improving the nature of communication media available to the public. The agency imposed equal time rules, sponsor identification rules, and the Fairness Doctrine upon all programming originated by cablecasters. In addition, the FCC ruled that all cable systems having more than 3,500 subscribers would have to operate "to a significant extent as a local outlet by originating cable-casting." In other words, the cable operators could no longer merely scoop the signals of other broadcasting stations out of the air and send them into a home via wire. They had to create programs themselves, which required programming facilities far beyond the needs of the simple automated services thus far originated by cable operators.

The Midwest Video Corp. challenged this rule. Again the Supreme Court upheld the authority of the FCC. In a five-to-four decision the court ruled (*U.S.* v. *Midwest Video Corp.*, 1972):

> The effect of the regulation, after all, is to assure that in the re-transmission of broadcast signals viewers are provided suitably diversified programming. . . .
>
> In sum, the regulation preserves and enhances the integrity of broadcast signals and therefore is "reasonably ancillary" to the effective performance of the commission's various responsibilities for the regulation of television broadcasting.

Cable television operators argued, as did Justice Douglas in a strong dissent, that the FCC was forcing them into the broadcasting business when they did not want to be licensed for that business. A majority of the court disagreed, however, noting that the cable operators voluntarily engaged themselves in providing that service and that "the commission seeks only to ensure that it satisfactorily meets community needs within the context of their undertaking."

Given this broad, sweeping power, the FCC issued a comprehensive set of cable regulations in 1972, the *Fourth Report and Order on Cable Television Service*. We should say comprehensive *and* controversial, for the outcry from cablecasters forced the agency into rethinking its position on some questions. Some minor changes were made by the FCC, but as of spring 1977 the rules remain basically the same.

FCC Rules

One can see by the 1972 rules that the FCC plans to regulate cable systems in a comprehensive fashion. First, the rules specify which signals can and cannot be carried by cable systems. A cable system must carry the signals of all stations licensed within thirty-five miles of the system. There is a complex formula for importation of distant signals, depending upon the size of the community in which the cable system is located. Nonduplication, or program exclusivity, rules prohibit cable systems from carrying network programs (on another station) which duplicate those carried on a local network affiliate at the same time. For example, if local station KLOP carries "The Rockford Files," the cable system can transmit KLOP's broadcast of the show, but cannot transmit station KUTZ's (located 150 miles away) broadcast of "The Rockford Files" within a week of KLOP's broadcast. With regard to syndicated and nonnetwork programs, cable operators may have to wait as much as two years to duplicate the programming of local stations.

The 1972 rules require that a cable system which is located in one of the top one hundred (based on size) television markets must have a minimum twenty-channel capacity. For each broadcast channel there must be one nonbroadcast channel. One channel must be dedicated to public access, one for use by schools and colleges, and one for use by local governments. The cable system must also have the facilities to originate programs.

The FCC also set down guidelines which are to be used by local authorities for franchising cable systems. These guidelines set up construction timetables, franchise duration, installation and subscription rates, complaint procedures, and franchise fees. The rules do not designate which local authority shall control cable systems. Consequently in some areas state public utility commissions act as franchising agencies, and in other areas the city or county government provides the service.

Despite the entry of the FCC into the regulation of cable television (perhaps because of it) much confusion still reigns in cable control. The FCC has often used the prerogative administrative agencies enjoy to change their mind. While the commission seems to know what it is doing, few other people seem that assured.

Copyright Obligations

Cable companies have been a prime target for the scorn and anger of motion-picture producers, television networks, and other groups who hold copyright to material which is broadcast over television. When a local television station broadcasts a motion picture owned by Paramount Pictures, for example, it must pay Paramount royalties for broadcasting the film in compliance with the copyright laws. But in the past when a cable company picked up the signal from the local station (which is broadcasting the movie) and relayed the broadcast of the motion picture to its subscribers via cable, it was not obligated to pay royalties to the owner of the motion picture. On two different occasions copyright owners took their case all the way to the United States Supreme Court in an effort to change this rule. Both times they failed.

In 1968 United Artists Television, Inc., brought suit against the Fortnightly Corp., a CATV operator in West Virginia. United Artists Television argued that to cablecast programs produced and owned by United Artists and broadcast over local television stations without having a license and paying royalties was a violation of the federal copyright laws. By a vote of five to four the Supreme Court disagreed. Justice Potter Stewart wrote that television viewing results from the combined activities of the broadcaster and the viewer. A broadcaster takes programming and converts it into electronic signals which are then broadcast. The viewer sets up an antenna, buys a receiver to rearrange the electronic signals, and then consumes the pictures and sounds. When television is looked at in this way, Stewart says, it is clear that cable television is of benefit to the viewers' side and simply enhances viewers' capacity to receive the broadcast signals. To relay programs originally broadcast by a television station is not considered "broadcasting" or "performing" in terms of the copyright laws (*Fortnightly Corp.* v. *United Artists Television, Inc.,* 1968).

More recently The Columbia Broadcasting System brought a similar suit against Teleprompter, one of the nation's largest cable operators. The network made the same argument that United Artists Television made, but stressed that today cable systems are far more than mere "relay" stations. Cable companies import signals from distant cities, originate their own programs, cablecast advertising messages, and so forth. The court again ruled in favor of the cable companies, this time by a six-to-three vote. Even relaying programs originally broadcast in distant cities does not constitute a violation of the copyright law. Justice Stewart also pointed out that Teleprompter did not sell advertising on the basis of the network programs, nor did it use copyrighted material in its program origination. The associate justice suggested that by its lawsuit the Columbia Broadcasting System was really trying to change the FCC regulations on cable broadcasting through the copyright laws. Stewart said changes in regulations should properly come from the FCC or Congress (*CBS* v. *Teleprompter; Teleprompter* v. *CBS,* 1974).

Congress did take action. The 1976 Copyright Act established that cable operators must pay a royalty fee for the programs carried on their systems. The fee is based on the number of subscribers and the income earned by the cable operator.

The regulation of broadcasting is not something that is either easy to grasp or fun to hold. It is a mess. One final point should be recalled.

It must be remembered that broadcasters must obey all the rules and regulations on broadcasting in addition to all the other rules and regulations discussed in this book. The television station manager must worry about libel, privacy, access, contempt, and Federal Trade Commission rules in addition to the Federal Communication Act of 1934 and the several thousand Federal Communications Commission edicts issued since that time.

BIBLIOGRAPHY
Here are some of the sources that have been helpful in the preparation of chapter 11.

Books   Geller, Henry. *The Fairness Doctrine in Broadcasting.* Santa Monica: Rand Corp., 1973.

Media and the First Amendment in a Free Society. Amherst: University of Massachusetts Press, 1973.

Pember, Don R. *Mass Media in America,* 2d edition. Chicago: Science Research Associates, 1977.

Robinson, Glen O., and Gellhorn, Ernest. *The Administrative Process.* St. Paul, Minn.: West Publishing Co., 1974.

Articles   Botein, Michael. "Access to Cable Television." 57 *Cornell Law Review* 419 (1972).

———. "CATV Regulation: A Jumble of Jurisdictions." 45 *New York University Law Review* 816 (1970).

Houser, Thomas J. "The Fairness Doctrine: An Historical Perspective." 47 *Notre Dame Lawyer* 550 (1972).

Johnson, Timothy P. "Regulating CATV: Local Government and the Franchising Process." 19 *South Dakota Law Review* 143 (1974).

Marks, Richard D. "Broadcasting and Censorship: First Amendment Theory After Red Lion." 38 *The George Washington Law Review* 974 (1970).

Robinson, Glen O. "The FCC and the First Amendment: Observations on 40 Years of Radio and Television Regulation." 52 *Minnesota Law Review* 67 (1967).

Wheeler, Tom. "The FCC and the First Amendment." 5 *Loyola of Los Angeles Law Review* 329 (1972).

Cases and Reports   *Brandywine-Main Line Radio, Inc.,* v. FCC, 24 FCC 2d 2218 (1970), 473 F. 2d 16 (1972).

In re *Business Executives Movement,* 25 FCC 2d 216 (1970).

Business Executives Movement v. FCC, 450 F. 2d 642 (1971).

Carroll Broadcasting Co., v. FCC, 258 F. 2d 440 (1958).

In re *Carter Mountain Transmission Corp.,* 32 FCC 459 (1962), affd 321 F. 2d 359 (1963), 375 U.S. 951 (1963).

CBS v. *Democratic Nation Committee,* 412 U.S. 94 (1973).

CBS v. *Teleprompter,* 415 U.S. 394 (1974); *Teleprompter* v. *CBS,* (1974).

Citizens Communication Center v. FCC, 447 F. 2d 1201 (1970).

Citizens Communication Center v. FCC, 463 F. 2d 822 (1972).

Commission en Banc Programming Inquiry, 20 P. & F. Rad. Regs. 1901 (1960).

In re *Community Broadcasting Service, Inc., WWBC,* 20 FCC 168 (1955).
In re *Complaint Concerning CBS Program "Selling of the Pentagon,"* 30 FCC 2d 150 (1971).
In re *Democratic National Committee,* 25 FCC 2d 216 (1970).
In re *Editorializing by Broadcast Licensees,* 13 FCC 1246 (1949).
Fairness Doctrine and Public Interest Standards—Handling of Public Issues, 39 Fed. Regs. 26372 (1974).
Farmers Educational and Cooperative Union of America v. *WDAY,* 360 U.S. 525 (1959).
FCC v. *American Broadcasting Co.* et al., 347 U.S. 284 (1954).
FCC v. *Sanders Brothers Radio Station,* 309 U.S. 470 (1940).
Federal Election Campaign Act, 47 U.S.C. Sec. 801-805 (1972).
FRC v. *Nelson Brothers,* 289 U.S. 266 (1933).
First Report and Order on Microwave Served CATV, 38 FCC 683 (1965).
Fortnightly Corp. v. *United Artists Television, Inc.,* 392 U.S. 390 (1968).
Fourth National Radio Conference, Recommendations for Regulation of Radio (Washington, D. C., Oct. 6-10, 1924).
Fourth Report and Order on Cable Television Service, 37 Fed. Regs. 3251 (1972).
Frontier Broadcasting Co. v. *Collier,* 24 FCC 251 (1958).
In re *Great Lakes Broadcasting* v. *FRC,* 3 FRC Ann. Rep. 32 (1929), 37 F. 2d 993 (1930).
Hearst Radio, WBAL, 15 FCC 1149 (1951).
Henry v. *FCC,* 302 F. 2d 191 (1962).
Hoover v. *Intercity Radio Co., Inc.,* 286 F. 1003 (1923).
KFKB Broadcasting Association v. *FRC,* 47 F. 2d 670 (1931).
In re *Mayflower Broadcasting Corp.,* 8 FCC 333 (1941).
May Seed and Nursery Co. et al., 2 FCC 559 (1936).
Miami Herald Co., v. *Tornillo,* revd 94 S. Ct. 2831 (1974).
Mt. Mansfield Television v. *FCC,* 442 F. 2d 470 (1971).
N.A.B. v. *FCC,* U.S. Court of Appeals, D. C., No. 75-1618, March 1, 1977.
NBC v. *FCC,* 516 F. 2d 1101 (1974).
NBC v. *U.S.,* 319 U.S. 190 (1943).
Office of Communication, United Church of Christ v. *FCC,* 359 F. 2d 994 (1966).
In re *Pacifica Foundation,* 36 FCC 147 (1964).
Pacifica Foundation v. *FCC,* U.S. Court of Appeals, D. C., No. 75-1391, March 16, 1977.
In re *Palmetto Broadcasting Co.,* 33 FCC 250 (1962).
Policy Statement on Comparative Broadcast Hearings, 1 FCC 2d 393 (1965).
Policy Statement on Comparative Hearings Involving Regular Renewal Applications, 22 FCC 2d 424 (1970).
Primer on Ascertainment of Community Needs, 27 FCC 2d 650 (1971).
Public Notice 71-205 re Licensee Responsibility to Review Records Before Their Broadcast, 28 FCC 2d 409 (1971), *Explanatory Memorandum and Order 71-428,* 31 FCC 2d 377 (1971).
Public Service Responsibility of Broadcast Licensees, 1946.
Radio and Television News Director's Association v. *U.S.,* 400 F. 2d 1002 (1968).
Red Lion Broadcasting v. *FCC,* 381 F. 2d 908 (1967).
Red Lion Broadcasting v. *FCC,* 395 U.S. 367 (1969).

Second Annual Report of the Federal Radio Commission (1928).

Second Report and Order on Microwave Served CATV, 2 FCC 2d 725 (1966).

Sonderling Broadcasting Corp., 27 P. & F. Rad. Regs. 285 (1973).

Suburban Broadcasters, 20 P. & F. Rad. Regs. 951 (1961), affd *Henry* v. *FCC,* 302 F. 2d 191 (1962).

Trinity Methodist Church, South v. *FRC,* 62 F. 2d 650 (1932).

In re *United Broadcasting Co.,* 10 FCC 515 (1945).

U.S. v. *Midwest Video Corp.,* 406 U.S. 649 (1972).

U.S. v. *Southwestern Cable Co.,* 392 U.S. 157 (1968).

U.S. v. *Zenith Radio Corp.,* 12 F. 2d 616 (1926); 35 Op. Attys. Gen. 126 (1926).

Wabash Valley Broadcasting Co., WTHI-TV, 35 FCC 677 (1963).

WCBS-TV, 8 FCC 2d 381 (1967), affd *Applicability of the Fairness Doctrine to Cigarette Advertising,* 9 FCC 2d 921 (1967), affd *Banzhaf* v. *FCC,* 405 F. 2d 1164 (1971).

In re *WHDH, Inc.,* 16 FCC 2d 1 (1969), affd *Greater Boston Television* v. *FCC,* 444 F. 2d 841 (1970).

In re *Wilderness Society and Friends of the Earth,* 30 FCC 2d 643 (1971), revd *Friends of the Earth* v. *FCC,* 449 F. 2d 1164 (1971).

WRBL Radio Stations, 2 FCC 687 (1936).

Writers Guild v. *FCC, U.S.D.C.,* Calif. No. CV-75-3710-F, November 4, 1976.

In re *WUHY-FM, Eastern Educational Radio,* 24 FCC 2d 408 (1970).

Young People's Association for the Propagation of the Gospel, 6 FCC 178 (1938).

CHAPTER 12

Access to Information

If there is a battle cry among journalists, a call to arms that brings even aged copy readers to their feet, it is The Right To Know. The right to know, is a phrase whose elegance is exceeded only by its vagueness. Whose right to know? The right to know what? When do we have the right to know? Why should there be the right to know? Generally many more questions than answers are raised by this issue.

Surely the people have the right to know, to know what their government is doing at all times, in order to be better equipped to exercise the duties of citizenship. Madison stated the need well (Padover, *The Complete Madison*), "A people who mean to be their governors must arm themselves with the power which knowledge gives. A popular government, without popular information, or the means of acquiring it, is but a prologue to a Farce or Tragedy; or perhaps both." The fourth president added that the right to freely examine public characters and measures and the right to discuss them openly are the only effectual guardians of every other right.

Conditions were simpler in the early nineteenth century than they are today. While writing years earlier, Professor William E. Hocking expressed the reality of the seventies when he wrote, "We say recklessly that [readers and listeners] have a right to know; and yet it is a right which they are helpless to claim, for they do not know that they have the right to know what as yet they do not know."

It is a function of the press in the United States to act as the eyes and ears of the people with regard to their government, a function often referred to as "the watchdog role." It is the responsibility of journalists, then, to tell people that they do have the right to know, and what it is they should know. It is a responsibility, however, which each day is more and more difficult to carry out. Today, attempts to scrutinize the activities of government bump headlong into two increasingly persistent propositions: government secrecy and the right of privacy.

Interest in the right of privacy is just beginning to burgeon, partly because of the recent revelations of government snooping into private lives, partly because of the increased government involvement in nearly everyone's private business, and partly because of the slowly diminishing privacy which each of us enjoys. The Privacy Act of 1974, The Family Educational Rights and Privacy Act of 1974 and the Law Enforcement Assistance Administration rules on access to criminal records are manifestations at the federal level of the increased concern for the individual's right of privacy. These measures are discussed more fully later.

GOVERNMENT SECRECY

Government secrecy, an idea older than the right of privacy, has blossomed with new vigor since World War II. The revelations of secret government actions which emerged in the backwash of Watergate should frighten every citizen. The fact that such misuses of power are being exposed offers little comfort because little is lost in telling what happened in the past. Our real concern should be for what still goes on.

In his classic analysis of bureaucracy as a form of social organization, Max Weber argues that preoccupation with secrecy is an inherent characteristic of administrative organizations. Weber asserts that this preoccupation is partially based on a functional need to keep certain phases of administrative operations secret to maintain a competitive edge over rival administrative units. Weber also notes that while secrecy is a legitimate behavior in some agencies—those which deal with defense or diplomacy—secrecy is often transformed into obsession. Secrecy which begins as a means to achieve organizational objectives often becomes an end in itself.

Much has happened to impel secrecy in government in the United States since 1945. The cold war, which has since cooled off, provoked men and women in government to actions totally inconsistent with an open, democratic society. One such action in the name of national security was to designate all measure of material classified information. In late 1974 the *New York Times* reported that in the federal government seventeen thousand persons were still empowered to stamp documents classified. The group was of course headed by the president, but also included (at the bottom of the list) were Navy ensigns (very junior officers). Many persons considered such circumstances as big power diplomacy, détente, strategic weapons talks, secret missiles, war in Indochina, and many more good reasons to expand secrecy in government. Horror stories abound, but are too numerous to mention here.

The expanded scope of government regulation of business, industry, schools, health agencies, and financial institutions has created another morass of hidden information. Regulation requires enforcement, and the numerous government regulatory agencies like to operate in secret during investigation of "regulatees." Premature disclosure might damage an innocent person or an otherwise substantial case.

As government touched the private life of more and more persons by means of welfare payments, loans, social security, and other programs, more and more personal data about private citizens—information which should remain private—was assembled. Many sins of secrecy were committed under the guise of privacy. The government itself employs millions of persons, and maintains extensive personnel records on each employee.

Finally, in addition to keeping things secret, government at all levels erects a sophisticated public relations screen to thwart the press in its attempt to ferret out data. While press aides and public affairs officers ostensibly provide information to both press and people, the important part of their job is to keep information from getting out. Public relations people are a buffer between the people and the government officers who conduct the public's business.

The catalog of reasons for increased secrecy in government given here is not complete. The mere fact that government each day grows a little larger means that there are more people to be secretive and more things about which to be secret. Reporters who cover government—federal, state, and local—carry on a running battle with officials and their employes in the attempt to gain information which they believe should be made public. There are lots of tricks to this game, and most good reporters will tell you that using the law is sometimes the least effective way to gain information. The old saw You catch more flies with honey than with vinegar is applicable. Cultivating a news source is a fine art in the business of journalism. Often the reporter's ability to laugh at awful jokes, buy a cup of coffee for the right person, or to provide a government official with favorable (if undeserved) publicity will accomplish more in gaining access to government information than any law on the books.

There comes a time however when such tactics won't work, and recourse to the law is the only option left. Quite honestly, the law is also frequently found wanting.

Our discussion of the law regarding access to government information must be in generalities because of the hundreds of different state rules and laws as well as the morass of federal regulations. What is provided instead are clues, clues which you can use to determine the status of access laws in your state. We can be somewhat more specific in discussing federal law, but even there a team of highly competent lawyers is needed to sort out all the ramifications and manifestations of the United States law on this subject.

COMMON LAW RIGHTS

Persons unacquainted with the problems of access to government information are usually startled to discover that there is neither clear common law nor constitutional right to gather news. While it is perhaps not completely accurate to assert that there is no common law right of access whatsoever, the common law provides only bare access to government documents and to meetings of public agencies. In Great Britain, where the common law developed, complete and total access to Parliament was not guaranteed until 1874, and even then the House of Commons could exclude the public by a majority vote. Initially the public was excluded because members of Parliament feared reprisal from the crown for statements made during floor debate. Later this fear subsided, but secret meetings continued in order to prevent voters from finding out that many members of the legislative body were not faithful in keeping promises to constituents.

Secrecy in England had a direct impact upon how colonial legislatures conducted their business. The Constitutional Convention of 1787 in Philadelphia was conducted in secret. The public and the press had almost immediate access to sessions in the United States House of Representatives, but it was not until 1794 that spectators and reporters were allowed into the Senate chambers. While today access is guaranteed to nearly all sessions of Congress, much (maybe even most) congressional business is conducted by committees which frequently meet in secret. The common law, then, has just not provided the wedge needed to pry open meetings and records.

CONSTITUTIONAL RIGHTS

The Constitution does not offer much more. Despite the fact that the United States was conceived as a representative democracy, and despite the fact that the nation's founders professed an apparently sincere belief in the right of the people to govern themselves, the Constitution contains no provision stating that the public's business shall be conducted in public.

First Amendment Protection

While the First Amendment has been interpreted to mean many things including the right to publish without prior restraint, the right to circulate what has been printed, and the right to be free from arbitrary and unfair taxation which can inhibit circulation, the courts in the United

States have been very reluctant to state flatly that the First Amendment guarantees the right of access to government records and meetings.

In 1950 in Rhode Island a federal district judge ruled that when public records are restricted from examination and publication "the attempt to prohibit their publication is an abridgement of the freedom of the speech and press" (*Providence Journal Co.* et al. v. *McCoy* et al., 1950). The case involved two newspapers seeking to examine tax cancellation and abatement records. The Pawtucket city council gave permission to one newspaper (the paper which supported the city government in power), but refused to give similar access to an opposition newspaper. In addition to ruling that denial of access was an abridgement of freedom of the press, the federal court ruled this kind of action to be a denial of equal protection of the law. The court of appeals upheld the lower court ruling, but solely on the grounds of equal protection. The lower court ruling that denial of access is a violation of the First Amendment is therefore of limited value. Yet this case stands as one of the very few times when a court of any kind ruled that freedom of the press is somehow diminished when access to information is denied.

There are obvious reasons why courts are reluctant to interpret the First Amendment as permitting a broad right of access to meetings and public records. The consequences of establishing such a principle, it is thought, would be to arm the press with a key which it would use to unlock *all* doors and thereby gain access to material restricted for the welfare and protection of society. This is a very weak argument and is based on the notion that the press is totally irresponsible and that the law is the only factor keeping newspapers and broadcasting stations from destroying this country.

There is a better argument, however, for the judiciary's reluctance to establish a constitutional right of access. Perhaps it is merely a more logical argument.

"The reluctance of the courts to recognize distinctly a news-gathering right in the press," writes Lynn C. Malingren in the *Villanova Law Review* (1974), "stems from a valid concern with the administrative problems and from the logical necessity of making the determination of what constitutes the press for the purposes of constitutional protection." If the right of the press to gather news is merely the same as the right of the public to gather news, the commentator adds, then the press may go only where the public may go. ("First Amendment: Freedom of the Press to Gather News.") But if the press has a special right, reporters would have access to many more areas than does the public. The problem then is this: Who is a reporter? or What is the press? As noted in the discussion of the shield law controversy, there is a long tradition that freedom of the press protects everyone, that its provisions apply equally to a citizen who publishes a mimeographed newsletter and to the publisher of the *New York Times*. If the courts declare that the press has the constitutional right of access, they must either also delineate what comprises "the press" or be prepared to face the potential onslaught of all the citizenry seeking access to records and meetings. The courts have found it far easier just to refuse to acknowledge that the First Amendment protects the right to gather the news.

In 1964 the Supreme Court ruled in a case concerning the right of a United States citizen to travel to Cuba in violation of a State Department ban on such travel that the right to speak and publish does not carry with it the unrestrained right to gather information (*Zemel* v. *Rusk,* 1964). This decision was generally regarded to be the law until the early 1970s when a few lower courts suggested that the First Amendment might indeed protect the right to gain access to information. In *Branzburg* v. *Hayes* (1972), a newman's privilege case, the high Court itself dropped a kind of bombshell. "Nor is it suggested that newsgathering does not qualify for First Amendment protection; without some protection for seeking out the news, freedom of the press could be eviscerated," the majority opinion stated.

The Supreme Court faced the problem of the constitutional right of access almost head-on in what have become known as the prison-interview cases in 1974.

Access to Prisons   Two cases in which the facts in each were virtually the same came before the Court. In *Pell* v. *Procunier* (1974) reporters in California attempted to interview specific inmates at California prisons. In *Saxbe* v. *Washington Post* (1974) reporters from that newspaper sought to interview specific inmates at federal prisons at Lewisburg, Pennsylvania, and Danbury, Connecticut. In both instances the press was barred from conducting the interviews. The United States Bureau of Prisons rule, which is similar to the California regulation, states:

> Press representatives will not be permitted to interview individual inmates. This rule shall apply even where the inmate requests or seeks an interview.

At issue was not access to the prison system. The press could tour and photograph prison facilities, conduct brief conversations with randomly encountered inmates, and correspond with inmates through the mails. Outgoing correspondence from inmates was neither censored nor inspected, and incoming mail was inspected only for contraband and statements which might incite illegal action. In addition, the federal rules had been interpreted to permit journalists to conduct lengthy interviews with randomly selected groups of inmates. In fact, a reporter in the *Washington Post* case did go to Lewisburg and interview a group of prisoners.

The argument of the press in both cases was that to ban interviews with specific inmates abridged the First Amendment protection afforded the news-gathering activity of a free press.

The Supreme Court disagreed in a five-to-four decision in both cases. Justice Stewart's opinion was subscribed to by the chief justice, and Justices Blackmun, White, and Rehnquist. Justice Stewart wrote that the press already had substantial access to the prisons and that there was no evidence that prison officials were hiding things from reporters. Stewart rejected the notion that the First Amendment gave newsmen the special right of access to the prisons. "Newsmen have no constitutional right of access to prisons or their inmates beyond that afforded the general public," the Justice wrote. Since members of the general public have no right to interview specific prisoners, the denial of this right to the press does not infringe upon the First Amendment.

The high Court did not disagree with the findings of the District court in the *Saxbe* case that face-to-face interviews with specific inmates are essential to accurate and effective reporting about prisoners and prisons. What the Court seemed to say was that while the First Amendment guarantees freedom of expression it does not guarantee effective and accurate reporting. In fact, about five months after the *Saxbe-Pell* decisions on November 2, in a speech at the Yale Law School Sesquicentennial Convocation. Justice Stewart made this exact point:

> The press is free to do battle against secrecy and deception in government. But the press cannot expect from the Constitution any guarantee that it will succeed. There is no constitutional right to have access to particular governmental information, or to require openness from the bureaucracy. The public's interest in knowing about its government is protected by the guarantee of a free press, but the protection is indirect. The Constitution itself is neither a Freedom of Information Act nor an Official Secrets Act. The Constitution, in other words, establishes the contest, not its resolution.

It is important to note that in these cases the high Court did not distinguish between the right of journalists to gather information and the right of the public to be informed. In other recent decisions, most notably in the *Red Lion Broadcasting* case discussed in chapter 11, the high Court has made a point of separating the two rights. While the high Court has shown little indication that it wants to give special rights to journalists, it has demonstrated—again, most notably in the *Red Lion* case—a sincere concern for the public's need for information.

In summing up the results of the prison interview cases Robert Taft writes in "Prisons and the Right of the Press to Gather Information":

> Saxbe makes clear that the public's right to know is not unlimited, but rather subject to reasonable constraints when confronted with competing governmental interests. It also makes clear that the freedom of the press to gather information is not absolute. When the sole limitation imposed on news gathering in prisons applies equally to newsmen and the general public, the First Amendment freedom of the press is not abridged.

This comment also summarized fairly well the constitutional right of access. It is clearly a narrow and limited right, one which hasn't been fully defined and one that may, in the end, not really exist. In attempting to gain access to both records and information and to meetings of public bodies and agencies, the press has found the First Amendment of little value. Of far greater value is specific legislation which guarantees such access.

We must remember that there are really fifty-one different legislative systems—the federal system and the fifty state systems—as we discuss legislative rights of access to information. In the states with laws guaranteeing access to records and meetings, each legislature approached the problem somewhat differently. Furthermore, none of the state laws mirror federal legislation on the subject. We will first examine the federal laws and then consider in general terms the important kinds of state laws.

FEDERAL LEGISLATIVE RIGHTS

Freedom of Information Act

Between 1789 and 1966 access to the records of the federal government was largely an unsettled question. Various housekeeping laws, administrative procedure statutes, had been passed by Congress, but none were aimed at providing the kind of access to government records that both the press and a large segment of the population believed necessary to the efficient operation of our democracy. Before 1966 the laws Congress passed were really laws authorizing information to be withheld, rather than laws forcing government agencies to open their files. Also, reporters could do little when requests for information were denied. In 1966 after many years of hearings and testimony and work, Congress adopted the Freedom of Information Act (FOIA) which was ostensibly designed to open up records and files long closed to public inspection. One can write an open records law in two basic ways. The first way is to declare that all of the following kinds of records are to be open for public inspection and then list the kinds of records which are to be open. The second way is to proclaim that all government records are open for public inspection except the following kinds of records and then list the exceptions. Congress approved the second kind of law in 1966 and it went into effect on July 4, 1967.

In broad language the measure ensured that all persons will have access to all records except those listed in nine categories of exemptions. Exemption categories one and seven were altered by a 1974 amendment to the law. Exemption category three was changed by the Congress in 1976. (The reasons for these changes will be discussed shortly.) The Freedom of Information Act, as it stood after these amendments, provided access to all records in the executive branch of the Federal government except the following (comments in parentheses are my clarification of the records designated as exempt):

1. Matters specifically authorized under criteria established by an Executive order to be kept secret in the interest of national defense or foreign policy and in fact properly classified pursuant to such an Executive order (defense and diplomatic secrets).

2. Matters related solely to the internal personnel rules and practice of any agency (vacation schedules, coffee break rules, parking lot assignments, etc.).

3. Matters specifically exempted from disclosure by statute (other than section 552b of this title) provided that such statute requires that the matters be withheld from the public in such a manner as to leave no discretion on the issue, or establishes particular criteria for withholding or refers to particular types of matters to be withheld (social security and income tax records).

4. Trade secrets and commercial and financial information obtained from any person and privileged or confidential (financial data from homeowners the Federal Housing Administration needs before guaranteeing loans, patent applications, etc.).

5. Interagency and intraagency memorandums and letters which would not be available by law to a private party in litigation with the agency (working papers, not final decisions).

6. Personnel and medical files the disclosure of which would constitute a clearly unwarranted invasion of personal privacy.

7. Investigatory records compiled for law enforcement purposes, but only to the extent that the production of such records would (a) inter-

fere with enforcement proceedings, (b) deprive a person of the right to a fair trial or an impartial adjudication, (c) constitute an unwarranted invasion of personal privacy, (d) disclose the identity of a confidential source and, in the case of a record compiled by a criminal law enforcement authority in the course of a criminal investigation, or by an agency conducting a lawful national security intelligence investigation, confidential information furnished only by the confidential source, (e) disclose investigative techniques and procedures, or (f) endanger the life or physical safety of law enforcement personnel.

8. Matters contained in or related to examination, operating, or condition reports prepared by, on behalf of, or for the use of any agency responsible for the regulation and supervision of financial institutions (reports on financial condition of banks for agencies like the Federal Reserve Board).

9. Geological and geophysical information and data (including maps) concerning oil wells.

Before the major revisions in the Freedom of Information Act in 1974 and 1976 the law probably did not fulfill the expectations of its original sponsors. In 1969, two years after the law had been in effect, Kenneth Culp Davis, a leading authority on administrative law, in "The Information Act: A Preliminary Analysis" writes:

> The overall conclusion . . . is that the press, which was the principal political force behind the enactment, will benefit only slightly. Members of the bar and their clients will be the principal beneficiaries of the law. . . .
> To find what information is subject to required disclosure, we begin with that small portion and subtract what the Act exempts, the largest chunks being information about national defense or foreign policy, with the first exemption, personnel and medical and similar files within the sixth, and investigatory files within the seventh. Not much is left. Even if we make the false assumption that the Act will be fully obeyed, the information the Act opens up that would otherwise be closed is minimal.

Davis's assessment was generally right. Federal agencies waffled considerably because they were reluctant to release material previously held secret. The "big stall," a device for defeating the intent of the measure, developed. Delay often followed delay, often followed by more delay. Going to court to force disclosure was cumbersome. Litigation was expensive and time-consuming. The latter point was especially crucial since news by definition is very perishable—it loses its value quickly. In addition, courts misread the legislative history of the act and interpreted the law in a fashion making it far easier for the government to keep its records secret. The philosophy and spirit of the law—to open up the processes and files of government—was ignored. As so often the case, bureaucracy emerged the victor. While the law was sometimes effective in assisting specific citizens to get government information, it was of little use to the press. One reason has been stated, but another important factor is press ignorance of how the law operated. In a study of the effectiveness of the law conducted in 1973 Robert D. Smith reported that familiarity with the law among members of the press was "disturbingly low." Smith blamed the ignorance in large part upon the professional journalism associations "which seem to have passed up an opportunity to aggressively educate their members on the use of the law." ("The 1966 Freedom of Information Act: The Executive, The Congress, and The Press.")

Smith's conclusion is this:

> The press can make effective use of the Freedom of Information Act when it wishes to. Congress can effectively influence the information practices of the Executive when it wants to. At this time, the most important variable in gaining access to federal information does not seem to be the excellence of the legal tools at hand; the important variable seems to be the determination on the part of the actors involved [the press] to use those legal tools effectively.

Over the strenuous objections of both President Ford and most agencies in the executive branch of government Congress amended The Freedom of Expression Act in the autumn of 1974. Ford vetoed the amendments, but Congress repassed the measures by two-thirds vote, overriding the veto. The changes in the law were strong ones directed at implementing the spirit of open government as was intended when the measure was adopted eight years earlier. Significant alterations in the procedures by which citizens and the press can seek material from the government were made, and two of the nine original exemptions were changed.

Procedural Amendments

Departments must now answer requests for records and documents within ten days. If an appeal is filed after a denial the agency has only twenty days to rule upon the appeal. Each agency must publish quarterly, or more frequently, an index of the documents and records it keeps. If an agency charges for searching out records or for duplicating them it must have a uniform schedule of fees (everyone is charged the same amount) and the charges must be fair and reasonable. Agencies must report to Congress each year and include a list of the materials to which access was granted and to which access was denied and the costs incurred. If a citizen or reporter has to go to court to get the agency to release materials and the agency loses the case, the agency may be assessed the cost of the complainant's legal fees and court costs. Finally, agency personnel are now personally responsible for granting or denying access, a requirement federal agencies object to strenuously. An employee of an agency who denies a request for information must be identified to the person who seeks the material, and if the access is denied in an arbitrary or capricious manner, the employee can be disciplined by the Civil Service Commission. A preliminary evaluation of these changes suggests that they are quite effective in opening access to many governmental records and documents.

Exemption
Amendments

In addition to providing the procedural changes, Congress also took aim at two of the exemptions which interfered the most with open access: exemption one, the national security exemption and exemption seven, the law enforcement files exemption.

As passed in 1966 the national security exemption stated "Matters specifically required by Executive order to be kept secret in the interest of the national defense or foreign policy" will not be open to inspection. The intent of the exemption was good, but in practice the exemption was badly abused, especially by the Nixon administration. In simple translation the exemption meant that any material classified confidential, secret, or top secret did not have to be revealed. In March 1973 when former President Nixon realized that testimony at the trial of Daniel Ellsberg in Los Angeles would reveal that White House security agents had rifled confidential files in the office of Ellsberg's psychiatrist, Nixon and his aides decided to cloak the raid in a national security label, classifying all information about the break-in and thereby ensuring that it could not be revealed. This action was clearly a violation of the spirit, if not of the letter, of the Freedom of Information Act. Furthermore the courts provided small recourse.

Federal courts took the position that once information is classified the classification cannot be challenged. In 1970 when scholars attempted to gain access to classified files on Operation Keelhaul, the forced repatriation of anti-Communist Russians after World War II, the court of appeals ruled that it did not have the authority to review an agency's decision to classify material (*Epstein* v. *Resar,* 1970). No justification for the classification was needed: all the agency need do was to go to court and assert that the material was confidential or secret. The United States Supreme Court took the same position three years later in *EPA* v. *Mink* (1973) when Congresswoman Patsy Mink sought classified documents from the Environmental Protection Agency that supposedly justified the decision to conduct a nuclear test on Amchitka Island, Alaska. Congresswoman Mink argued that the Court should review the documents in private and determine whether they were classified properly or whether the government was merely attempting to hide controversial material from the public. Justice White, and a majority of the high Court, disagreed, stating that in wording exemption one as it did Congress specifically precluded judicial inspection of the contents of classified documents:

> We do not believe that Exemption 1 permits compelled disclosure of documents . . . that were classified pursuant to this Executive Order. Nor does the exemption permit in camera [private or something that is done in the judges chambers] inspection of such documents to sift out so-called "non-secret" components. Obviously, this test was not the only alternative available. But Congress chose to follow the Executive's determination in these matters and that choice must be honored.

Once a document is classified, the Court argued, no further inquiry can be made into its contents. By spring 1973 the time was ripe for amendment of the law. As one commentator said, "The Nixon administration was subjecting the national security label to abuse, the courts hesitated to expand their own scope of review, and the Supreme Court hinted in *Mink* that an appropriate solution would have to come from the legislative branch." It may not be readily apparent by looking at the amended first exemption (page 446), but the 1974 change in the law accomplished two results. First, courts now have the power to inspect classified documents in private to determine whether they are classified properly. That is, the executive branch must establish criteria for classification (for example, it may declare that all material dealing with United States troop strength in Europe will be classified), and the court can then determine whether the classified documents meet the criteria set down by the government. The new law also permits a court to review decisions by government agencies to withhold requested material to determine whether decisions were properly arrived at or whether they are arbitrary and capricious.

It is important to note in respect to these changes that they are actions courts *can* take, not actions they *must* take. The Fourth Circuit Court of Appeals has already turned down a request that it privately examine specific secret materials to see whether the documents were classified properly. The court claimed it lacked the expertise to make such a judgment and told the complainant to file a complaint with the agency denying access originally (*Alfred A. Knopf* v. *Colby,* 1975). This action can hardly be considered an auspicious beginning for the new law. One hopes that other judges will view their responsibility to open access more seriously.

The changes in the seventh exemption are not quite as spectacular.

Former exemption seven precluded from inspection "all investigatory files compiled for law enforcement purposes except to the extent available by law to a private party." Clearly within such files is considerable information which should probably remain secret, but also within the files is a significant amount of information for which the classification of secret cannot be justified and to which the public should have access. On the authority of exemption seven, agencies were prone to keep all information in their files closed. However, amended exemption seven permits agencies to limit access only to the information whose release will interfere with the investigation, endanger the right of fair trial, constitute an unwarranted invasion of privacy, reveal a confidential source, disclose investigative techniques, endanger law enforcement personnel, and so forth.

What the new law means is that law enforcement agencies and departments which conduct law enforcement investigations (like the Federal Trade Commission) will not be allowed to deny access to an *entire* file on the basis that *some* of the information in the file must remain secret. Only that information which meets the criteria laid down by Congress in the exemption can remain secret. The remainder of the information in the file and in other files maintained by the agency must be released. The new law will prevent such events as the following. Suppose that the Federal Trade Commission is investigating claims made by the makers of cold remedies. It conducts its own tests on these products, hoping to bring legal action against manufacturers whose advertising claims exceed their product's capabilities. A consumer group which is also testing cold remedies seeks to compare its findings with those of the commission. The agency refuses access to these files on the grounds that release of some of the information may interfere with the investigation. Release of *some* information may interfere with the enforcement proceedings, but clearly release of government data on the effectiveness of the cold remedies will not. In the past the agency was able to refuse such a request. Now it will have to segregate the test findings from the secret material and allow access to those findings when requested.

In 1976 Congress revised the third exemption as well in response to what that legislative body believed to be an erroneous interpretation of the exemption by the Supreme Court. Originally, exemption three forbid the disclosure of "matters specifically exempted from disclosure by statute." A freedom of information case arose when a citizen sought access to some system's worthiness analysis reports kept by the Federal Aviation Administration. Some statutes permit the FAA to withhold some data. In this case the agency argued that it did not have to permit access to the reports on the basis of these statutes. The FAA claimed that exemption three allowed the agency administrator to withhold data when in his judgment disclosure would adversely effect the submitter and is not in the public interest. The Supreme Court supported this interpretation in *Administrator, FAA,* v. *Robertson,* 1975.

Congress believed this was too broad an interpretation of the exemption and rewrote it to its current form as presented on page 446. Under the new exemption, three criteria exist for withholding material. There must be a statute that authorizes or requires the withholding of information. The statute must designate specific kinds of information which fit the criteria for withholding. And the information requested under the Freedom of Information Act must fit within the scope of the information which is authorized to be withheld.

Supreme Court Decision 1974

While the amendments to the law are significant and were fairly comprehensively discussed, we must also note that a Supreme Court decision in 1974 has had an important impact upon exemption five (*U.S.* v. *Nixon*). Exemption five protects from disclosure interagency or intra-agency memorandums and letters. Since the Freedom of Information Act does not affect either the judicial branch nor the legislative branch of government, we must keep in mind that the agencies referred to here are the executive branch and the numerous independent regulatory commissions like the Federal Trade Commission, the Federal Communications Commission, and the Securities and Exchange Commission.

Since 1794 beginning with President George Washington, American chief executives have asserted that the president enjoys a common law privilege to keep presidential papers, records, and other documents secret. This right is called executive privilege. Washington asserted the privilege when Congress called for all papers and records in the possession of the president which would facilitate its investigation of the negotiation of the Jay Treaty, a controversial agreement with Great Britain. Washington refused to comply with the congressional demand, citing executive privilege. Andrew Jackson refused to give Congress information relating to a boundary dispute in Maine. Millard Fillmore refused a request from the Senate that he provide that body with information regarding negotiations with the Sandwich (Hawaiian) Islands.

In modern times, however, the heads of agencies within the executive branch have asserted that they also enjoy a kind of limited executive privilege. Exemption five covered the kinds of documents—working papers, memorandums, and so forth—traditionally claimed exempt from public scrutiny by executive privilege. The purpose of the exemption was to protect the confidentiality of the decision-making process. However exemption five was used as a shield to avoid disclosing all manner of material totally unrelated to decision making. Legal memorandums, correspondence, minutes and transcripts, staff analyses, interpretations and opinions, and recommendations of experts and consultants have all been at one time or another declared to fall within the boundaries of exemption five.

In 1974 in *U.S.* v. *Nixon*, the Supreme Court sharply limited the boundaries of the traditional executive privilege. In this case several of the famous White House tapes were subpoenaed by the special prosecutor for use in the criminal trial of some of the Nixon aides. The former president argued that the tapes were protected by executive privilege. He said that revelation of the material on the tapes would damage the integrity of the decision-making process, and that under our system of separation of powers the courts were precluded from reviewing his claim of privilege. He also argued that even if his claim of absolute executive privilege should fail the court should at least hold as a matter of constitutional law that his privilege superseded the subpoena.

However, in an unanimous opinion (eight to nothing since Justice Rehnquist did not participate in the decision) the Burger Court rejected the notion of absolute privilege in this case. The Court said that an absolute privilege can only be asserted when the material in question consists of military or diplomatic secrets. When other kinds of information are involved, privilege of the president must be balanced against other values, in this case, against the operation of the criminal justice system. The need for the privilege must be weighed against the need for the information. Courts will have to make these decisions from private examination of the materials in question.

How does this decision affect exemption five? Since exemption five is based on the notion of the executive privilege, and since the courts have said such an absolute privilege does not exist in the absence of military or diplomatic secrets, agencies which claim exemption five as reason to deny access will have to allow the courts to scrutinize the material in question and evaluate whether the need for secrecy outweighs the benefits of disclosure. The mechanical process of the past under which agencies could gain the exemption merely by asserting that the material in question fell under the purview of the fifth exemption is probably gone. Now, when they are challenged, agencies will have to prove to a judge that the material does in fact come within the fifth exemption. Disclosure of much such material withheld in the past should be ensured.

The Freedom of Information Act is not the be-all and end-all of access legislation. Certainly stronger bills could be written. But the act isn't bad when we consider that Congress was under extreme pressure from the executive branch of the government to pass no bill at all. What is perhaps needed now is a concerted educational campaign within the press to teach journalists how to use the law. In addition, the press will need to put its money where its mouth is for a few years and take some of its access problems to court to build a satisfactory body of case law supporting access. Faced with the real chance of going to court and probably losing, aloof Washington bureaucrats who often give the impression of having a proprietary interest in this material will be less likely to deny the press access to it.

Open Meeting Laws

There are no open meeting laws per se at the federal level. While it is traditional for Congress to meet in public, the body can close a session when it wants to.

Prior to 1970 a congressional committee could enter into an executive session by mere consensus or by declaration of a committee chairman that a meeting would be closed. In 1970 Congress ruled that a majority vote of the committee or subcommittee is needed to close a meeting, but what can (and does) happen is that the committee votes at its first meeting of the year to close all subsequent meetings during the legislative session. In 1973 the House of Representatives adopted a rule that the vote of each committee member on a motion to close a session be made public. The Senate has no such rule.

Government in the Sunshine Act

In 1976 Congress passed and the president signed into law the Government in the Sunshine Act, a law which opens up hitherto often-closed hearings and meetings of the more than fifty federal boards, commissions, and other agencies with two or more heads or directors. Included are the many regulatory agencies such as the Securities and Exchange Commission, the Federal Power Commission, and the Federal Trade Commission.

While the law does not require these agencies to open all their meetings to public observation, the agencies are required to keep transcripts of what takes place during closed sessions. The law also prohibits informal communication between officials of an agency and representatives of companies or other interested persons with whom the agency does business.

This law is a small step forward in opening up meetings within the federal government. Of course, the most meaningful step that the national government could take is also the most unlikely step: to open meetings of the legislative branch to wider scrutiny. However this is a beginning.

STATE LEGISLATIVE RIGHTS

It is not as easy to talk about access at the state level as it is at the federal level, for we are dealing with hundreds of different statutes. (Most states have multiple laws dealing with access to meetings, access to records, and other access problems.) We can at best make a few generalizations. Harold Cross made some of the most astute generalizations in 1953 in his pioneering book *The People's Right to Know*. Cross was really the first scholar to present a comprehensive report on access problems. In his book he listed four issues or questions common to every case of access.

1. Is the particular record or proceeding public? Many records and meetings kept or conducted by public officers in public offices are not really public at all. Much of the work of the police, though they are public officers and work in public buildings, is not open to public scrutiny.

2. Is public material public in the sense that records are open to public inspection and sessions are open to public attendance? Hearings in juvenile courts are considered public hearings for purposes of the law, but they are rarely open to the public.

3. Who can view the records and who can attend the meetings open to the public? Many records, for example, might be open to specific segments of the public, but not to all segments. Automobile accident reports by police departments are open to insurance company adjusters and lawyers, but such records are not usually open to the general public.

4. When records and meetings are open to the general public and the press, will the courts provide legal remedy for citizens and reporters if access is denied?

The last question is probably not as important today as it was when Cross wrote his book in 1953, for at that time access to many public records and meetings in the states was based on the common law. Today this fact is no longer true. Access to meetings and records is nearly always governed by statute, and these statutes usually, but not always, provide a remedy for citizens who are denied access. This provision is more widespread in open meeting laws, which tend to be more efficient in providing access, than in open records laws, which are still weak and vague in many jurisdictions.

Depending upon how an open meeting is defined, forty-six or forty-eight of the fifty states have open meeting legislation. West Virginia and Mississippi don't have any kind of open meeting legislation, New York has no open meeting law, but has legislative rules which mandate open meetings for legislative committees, and Rhode Island has an administrative procedures law which speaks indirectly to the problem of open meetings. In the remaining forty-six states the laws range from good to awful.

The need for open meeting laws is obvious. There never was a solid common law right to attend the meetings of public bodies, and as stated earlier, the constitutional provisions regarding freedom of expression have proved inadequate with regard to access.

Many states have good laws with strong sanctions to be used against public officials who fail to live up to the legislative mandate.

William R. Wright II, writing in a recent edition of the *Mississippi Law Review* ("Open Meeting Laws: An Analysis and a Proposal"), outlined the basic provisions of state open meeting laws. According to Wright, the most vital provision of such a law is a strong, clear statement by the legislature to open up the deliberations and actions of the government to the people. If a provision of the law is questioned in court, a strong legislative declaration in favor of open access can be used to persuade a judge that if a section of the law is vague it should be interpreted to grant access rather than to restrict access since that is what the legislature wants.

In Washington the state's open meeting law begins as follows:

> The legislature finds and declares that all . . . public agencies of this state and subdivisions thereof exist to aid in the conduct of the people's business. It is the intent of this chapter that their actions be taken openly and that their deliberations be conducted openly.

State legislatures have usually written their open meeting laws in one of two ways. Some state legislatures have declared that all meetings will be open except specific meetings and then list the meetings to be open. Other states list the agencies which must hold open meetings. Generally excluded from the provisions of an open meeting law in either case are meetings of the legislature itself, of legislative committees, of parole and pardon boards, of law enforcement agencies, of military agencies like the national guard, of public hospital boards, and so forth.

Wright says that a good law should specifically define a meeting by giving the number of members of the board or commission who must be present to constitute a public meeting (a quorum? at least two? etc.), by stating that all deliberative stages of the decision-making process are considered meetings and must be open to the public, and by stating that social gatherings and chance encounters are not considered meetings and are therefore excluded from the provisions of the law. Some laws are not this specific and merely refer to all meetings, all regular or special meetings, all formal meetings, or whatever.

The exclusion of chance meetings and social gatherings is often troublesome to the press, especially in small towns. It is not uncommon that all members of the school board or the city council happen to have dinner at the same restaurant just before a meeting. If the dinner is obviously a ploy to avoid the law, a suit can be brought against the members. Often it is difficult to prove that the dinner is anything other than a chance encounter or a social gathering.

Most open meeting laws provide for closed or executive sessions in certain kinds of cases. Meetings at which personnel problems are discussed is an obvious example. A public airing of a teacher's personal problems could be an unwarranted invasion of privacy. The discussion of real estate transactions is another obvious example. When a school board considers buying a parcel of land for a new high school, premature public disclosure of this fact could cost the taxpayers money should the owner raise the price of the property or speculators buy it and force the school district to pay far more than it is worth. Meetings involving public safety are also often best conducted in private rather than in public. Virtually every open meeting law has the provision that no final action can be taken at an executive session, that the board or commission must reconvene in public before a final determination can be made on any issue.

Most open meeting statutes require not only that meetings be open to the public, but also that the public be notified of both regular and special meetings far enough in advance that they can attend if they wish. Time requirements vary, but normally a special meeting cannot be held without an announcement a day or two in advance.

The laws in twenty-one states provide procedures for enforcement. In other states complainants must muddle through on their own in the courts. In fourteen states any action taken at a meeting which was not public, but should have been public, is null and void. The action must be taken again at a proper meeting. Most laws provide fines and short jail terms for public officers who knowingly violate the law, but prosecution is rare.

While a few laws date from the nineteenth century the open meeting laws in most states are a relatively new phenomenon. Such laws, which owe their passage to strong, forceful pressure from the press, have developed largely since 1950. In 1959 only twenty states had such laws. Formation in the early 1970s of the public lobby Common Cause gave great impetus to the passage of open meeting laws. In 1972 and 1973 alone nine states passed such statutes. But after it had evaluated all of the nation's open meeting laws in 1973, the organization concluded that only eight states have laws which are adequate. Common Cause defined an adequate law as one which covers both the legislative and executive branches, permits executive sessions only in extremely limited circumstances, and also includes provisions which void actions taken at illegally closed sessions. (See model open meeting statute in Appendix.)

One commentator recently noted that the lack of effectiveness of these laws "means that the reporter's most marketable skill is still very much in demand for covering local government. His or her special talent has been to ferret news from unexpected or well-cultivated sources. . . ." There is much truth in this statement with regard to open meeting laws. Despite open meeting legislation, one informal remedy is still very effective: to subject the commission or board which decides to meet in secret to public embarrassment. Reporters should never voluntarily leave a meeting which they believe should be public. Rather, they should force public officials to escort them to an exit. Resistance is not advised, for criminal charges then might be levied against the reporter. If possible, a photographer should record the removal from the meeting. The photograph and the story can then be prominently featured on page one the next day. Public officials don't really like to meet in public, but they like even less to be pictured conducting "the public's business" behind closed doors. Voters begin to wonder what goes on in secret meetings.

Public Records Laws

Laws regarding access to public records are far less easy to categorize than are open meeting laws. Only two states—Rhode Island and West Virginia—don't provide some kind of statutory right to inspect public records. This is not to say that public access to documents and records is guaranteed in the other forty-eight states, for the laws vary widely and are sometimes ineffectual. Common law rules regarding access still play a large role in many jurisdictions. In some states access laws are limited to only a few kinds of public records and access to other documents is available only through the courts. In other states, statutes pretty much reflect the old common law rules on access. The basic common law principle regarding access to records was well stated in 1961 by the Oregon Supreme Court in the case of *MacEwan* v. *Holm:*

> In determining whether records should be made available for inspection in any particular instance, the court must balance the interest of the citizen in knowing what the servants of government are doing and his proprietary interest in public property against the public interest in having the business of government carried out efficiently and without undue interference.

Why a person wants to see a record is often a key element in the case, and normally the burden rests upon the state agency to prove that the record should not be disclosed.

Generally, access laws either follow the federal formula—all records are open except the following—or list the kinds of records which the public does have a right to inspect. Some laws merely define what constitutes a public record, but fail to provide for the specific right of inspection. Some statutes merely provide for the right of inspection of public records, and fail to outline what constitutes a public record. In most states when access to records is denied the complainant has to go to court.

But two states, Connecticut and New York, have introduced innovations which could improve access to records.

Connecticut has established an independent commission to handle citizen appeals on denial of information requests. The three-member commission must meet within twenty days after receiving an appeal, hear the matter, and issue a ruling within fifteen days. The body can uphold the denial or make the agency provide access to the material. Either citizens or government agencies can appeal any decision by the commission to a court.

In New York the state's new access law establishes a Committee on Public Access to Records. This committee is given wide authority to issue regulations for the use of records and implementation of the new statute. There are seven members on the committee—three government officials and four persons appointed by the governor, two of whom must be from the media. The committee's function is different from the Connecticut commission which act as a review board. In New York the committee advises agencies and local government on access questions through guidelines, opinions, and regulations. It is supposed to recommend changes in the law when problems arise. In addition, to make the new law work more efficiently the commission issues rules and guidelines: rules regarding the time and place records must be available, fees for copying, persons responsible for divulging records, and so forth. Finally, it is the job of the committee to ensure that the right of privacy of New York citizens is protected in connection with public access to the state's records. Some people criticize this last function, arguing that it makes little sense to make the same agency in charge of facilitating public access responsible for protecting the right of privacy. Something about foxes guarding chicken houses was mentioned. The law is so new that it is difficult to assess whether this potential conflict will develop.

New York has chosen not to follow the model of the Freedom of Information Act, and instead its law lists the kinds of records which must be available for public inspection. In summary, the law requires the following kinds of records to be open:

1. Final opinions and concurring and dissenting opinions in litigation
2. Policy statements and supporting factual data
3. Minutes of meetings and hearings
4. Audits and supporting data
5. Staff instructions and manuals
6. Name, address, title, and salary of government officers, except law enforcement officers
7. Final determinations and dissenting opinions of governing bodies.

This trend toward establishing public committees or commission to handle access problems, to help interpret the law, and to issue guidelines is a very good one. It is far easier to complain to a commission when access is denied than to file a court suit. Committees like the New York Committee on Public Access to Records will make a state law far more meaningful and useful when a local government is dealt with. Access laws passed by states are often ignored at the local level because of ignorance or because citizens and press are unlikely to complain until a big issue arises. By providing guidelines and rules for local communities a committee on public access immediately breathes life into an access law.

It is incumbent on all journalists and broadcasters to be as familiar as possible with the laws regarding access in their state. Knowledge of these kinds of laws is vital to efficient and complete reporting on government activities. Employees of public agencies are often as uninformed as average citizens about their responsibility to provide access to meetings, especially to records. Because of the normal adversary relationship between press and government, the natural tendency is to want to keep the reporter out of public documents and public meetings. Too often reporters are buffaloed by stubborn, uninformed, untruthful public employees who insist that they are not permitted by law to allow public inspection of certain records. If reporters know the law they can recognize such bluffs on the spot and fulfill their responsibility to keep the public fully informed on the business and activities of government.

THE FUTURE

Despite the gains, and there have been many gains in the past decade with regard to access, the future does not look particularly bright. That enormous mess Watergate has left not only a bad taste regarding secrecy in government, but also a terrible paranoia about government snooping into private lives. Consequently, whereas Watergate in some respects prompted a more open government, the backwash seems to be spawning legislation to close doors. One such law is considered in the discussion that follows. It should be noted that the discussion can in no way be considered comprehensive, but rather serves only to point out the kinds of problems that may lie ahead.

Law Enforcement Assistance Administration Guidelines

One of the programs started by the Nixon administration, the Law Enforcement Assistance Administration (LEAA), was a comprehensive aid plan for local police agencies. In addition to providing large sums of money to police agencies for equipment and education, the LEAA also provided the framework for a centralized record-keeping system. The computerized system gave local law enforcement agencies access to the records of virtually all other police departments in the country, and at the same time gave all other police departments in the country access to the records kept by local police departments.

Concern for the right of privacy led the Law Enforcement Assistance Administration to draft guidelines for release of law enforcement records to the public and the press. Guidelines were published in May 1975 and immediately provoked an outcry from the press and many other citizens who were concerned that the guidelines seriously limited the public's right to know. All access to an individual's past criminal record was virtually closed. Law enforcement officers could be fined up to $10,000 for giving out information regarding past convictions, trials, and arrests. Police could release information about a current case so long as the information was reasonably contemporaneous with the crime. Court records remained open, but were to be kept chronologically rather than alphabetically. If a reporter knew that a person had been convicted of theft on January 15, 1971, he could confirm it by checking the chronological court records. Similarly the police blotter or arrest index was kept open on a chronological basis so that a reporter could confirm an arrest if he knew the exact date it occurred.

The outcry against these guidelines provoked public hearings in November and December 1975. New, less-stringent guidelines were announced in March 1976. While the new rules seem like a breath of fresh air when compared with the first set of guidelines, they still represent less access to public records than reporters had prior to the adoption of the first LEAA guidelines.

Here is a brief summary of the new rules.

1. Data regarding convictions may be disseminated by police agencies and other law enforcement organizations without limitation, a significant change in the original rules.

2. Criminal justice agencies can also disseminate without limitation criminal history record information relating to the offense for which an individual is currently within the criminal justice system. That is, material regarding arrest, detention, indictment, charge, and so forth, can be given out freely regarding an offense for which an individual is currently being detained by police, or for which he has been charged, or for which he is awaiting trial. But police and other law enforcement agencies are limited to confirming specific inquiries regarding the criminal history on other offenses. Reporters have to ask specifically, Was John Smith arrested or charged with murder on December 15, 1964? Police and prosecutors can say yes or no. Also, access to nonconviction criminal history must be authorized by a state statute such as an open records law.

3. Court records are no longer covered by the regulations and can therefore be maintained either chronologically or alphabetically.

Also, we should note that local police agencies are not required to follow the guidelines, but they are precluded from getting assistance from the Law Enforcement Assistance Administration or using its records if they do not, which means, of course, that virtually all police agencies will adopt the rules.

In addition to the LEAA rules, Congress adopted two broad privacy laws in 1974. The first, the Privacy Act of 1974, went into effect in the fall of 1975. Another law, the Family Educational Rights and Privacy Act of 1974, took effect about the same time. Both of these bills are directed at protecting the privacy of American citizens, but indirectly could result in lessening the accessibility to information traditionally open to the press.

There are provisions in the Privacy Act of 1974, Section b (2), which states that the new Privacy Law does not take precedence over the Freedom of Information Act. The section states that no agency shall disclose any record which is contained in a system of records "unless disclosure of the record would be required under section 552 [the Freedom of Information Act] of this title." In a report of the House and Senate staff conference on the Privacy Act, the conferees made a point of stating that subsection b(2) was designed to preserve the status quo as interpreted by the courts regarding the disclosure of personal information under the Freedom of Information Act. So the new law should not have an impact upon the federal government's open records law.

The Privacy Act of 1974 also created a Privacy Protection Study Commission to examine the problem of invasion of privacy in both the public and private sectors and to recommend new legislation if necessary. One of the issues that the new commission is studying is whether records kept by newspapers—the so-called newspaper morgue which contains extensive clippings from past editions—constitutes an invasion of privacy.

As government gets more complex and touches the lives of American citizens more directly, access to information will probably be harder and harder to obtain. But access has never been easy to obtain. The access to public meetings and public records that the press now enjoys is not a gift from a benevolent government, but the product of much fighting and arguing and persistence. It is a battle worth fighting, and one that must ultimately be won.

In the dissenting opinion in re *Mack* (1956) the late Pennsylvania Supreme Court Justice Michael Musmanno seems to sum up the entire issue of freedom of the press, access to information, and the right of the public to know:

> Freedom of the press is the right of the people to be informed through the press and other media of communication. . . . Freedom of the press is not restricted to the operation of Linotype machines and printing presses. A rotary press needs raw material like a flour mill needs wheat. A print shop without material to print would be as meaningless as a vineyard without grapes, an orchard without trees or a lawn without verdure. Freedom of the press means freedom to gather the news, write it, publish it and circulate it. When any one of these integral operations is interdicted, freedom of the press becomes a river without water.

BIBLIOGRAPHY
Here are some of the sources that have been helpful in the preparation of chapter 12.

Books Adams, John B. *State Open Meeting Laws: An Overview.* Columbia, Mo.: Freedom of Information Foundation, 1974.

Cross, Harold. *The People's Right to Know.* New York: Columbia University Press, 1953.

Gerth, H. H., and Mills, C. Wright, eds. *From Max Weber: Essays in Sociology.* New York: Oxford University Press, 1946.

Marwick, Christine M., ed. *Litigation Under the Amended Freedom of Information Act,* 2d edition. Washington, D. C.: American Civil Liberties Union and The Freedom of Information Clearing House, 1976.

Padover, Saul, ed. *The Complete Madison.* New York: Harper Brothers, 1953.

Smith, Robert D. "The 1966 Freedom of Information Act: The Executive, the Congress, and the Press." Master's Thesis, University of Washington, 1973.

Rourke, Francis E. *Secrecy and Publicity.* Baltimore: Johns Hopkins Press, 1961.

Articles Barton, Ansley B. "U.S. v. Nixon and the Freedom of Information Act: New Impetus for the Agency Disclosure." 24 *Emory Law Journal* 405 (1975).

Davis, Kenneth C. "The Information Act: A Preliminary Analysis." 34 *University of Chicago Law Review* 761 (1967).

Malmgren, Lynn C. "First Amendment: Freedom of the Press to Gather News." 20 *Villanova Law Review* 189 (1974).

"National Security and the Public's Right to Know: A New Role for the Courts Under the FOIA." 123 *University of Pennsylvania Law Review* 1438 (1975)

Scher, Jacob. "Access to Information: Recent Legal Problems." 37 *Journalism Quarterly* 41 (1960).

Taft, Robert A., II. "Prisons and the Right of the Press to Gather Information." 43 *University of Cincinnati Law Review* 913 (1974).

Wright, William R., II. "Open Meeting Laws: An Analysis and a Proposal." 45 *Mississippi Law Review* 1151 (1974).

Cases *Administrator, FAA v. Robertson,* 422 U.S. 255 (1975).

Alfred A. Knopf v. Colby, 502 F. 2d 136 (1975).

Branzburg v. Hayes, 408 U.S. 655 (1972).

EPA v. *Mink,* 401 U.S. 73 (1973).
Epstein v. *Resor,* 296 F. Supp. 214 (1969), affd. 421 F. 2d 930 (1970).
In re *Mack,* 126 A 2d 679 (1956).
MacEwan v. *Holm,* 359 P. 2d 413 (1961).
Pell v. *Procunier,* 94 S.Ct. 2800 (1974).
Providence Journal Co. et al. v. *McCoy* et al., 94 F. Supp. 186 (1950).
Saxbe v. *Washington Post,* 94 S.Ct. 2811 (1947).
U.S. v. *Nixon,* 94 S.Ct. 3090 (1974).
Zemel v. *Rusk,* 381 U.S. 1 (1964).

Common Cause Model Open Meeting Statute, An Act Requiring Open Meetings of Public Bodies

465

SECTION 1
PUBLIC POLICY

It is essential to the maintenance of a democratic society that public business be performed in an open and public manner and that the citizens be advised of and aware of the performance of public officials and the deliberations and decisions that go into the making of public policy. Toward this end, this act shall be construed liberally.

SECTION 2
DEFINITIONS

As used in this act:

a) "Meeting" means the convening of a quorum of the constituent membership of a public body, whether corporal or by means of electronic equipment, to discuss or act upon a matter over which the public body has supervision, control, jurisdiction, or advisory power.

b) "Public body" means any administrative, advisory, executive, or legislative body of the state or local political subdivision of the state, or any other entity created by law, that expends or disburses or is supported in whole or in part by tax revenue or that advises or makes recommendations to any entity that expends or disburses or is supported in whole or in part by tax revenue, including but not limited to any board, commission, committee, subcommittee, or other subsidiary thereof.

c) "Quorum," unless otherwise defined by applicable law, means a simple majority of the constituent membership of a public body.

SECTION 3
OPEN MEETINGS

Every meeting of all public bodies shall be open to the public unless closed pursuant to sections 4 and 5 of this act.

**SECTION 4
CLOSED
MEETINGS**

A public body may hold a meeting closed to the public upon an affirmative vote, taken at an open meeting for which notice has been given pursuant to section 6 of this act, of two thirds of its constituent members. A meeting closed to the public shall be limited to matters allowed to be exempted from discussion at open meetings by section 5 of this act. The vote of each member on the question of holding a meeting closed to the public and the reason for holding such a meeting, by a citation to a subsection of section 5 of this act, shall be recorded and entered into the minutes of the meeting. Nothing in this section or section 5 of this act shall be construed to require that any meeting be closed to the public.

**SECTION 5
EXCEPTIONS**

a) A public body may hold a meeting closed to the public pursuant to section 4 of this act for one or more of the following purposes:
1) discussion of the character, as opposed to the professional competence, or physical or mental health of a single individual provided that such individual may require that such discussion be held at an open meeting; and provided that nothing in this subsection shall permit a meeting closed to the public for discussion of the appointment of a person to a public body;
2) strategy sessions with respect to collective bargaining or litigation, when an open meeting would have a detrimental effect on the bargaining or litigation position of the public body;
3) discussion regarding the deployment of security personnel or devices; and
4) investigative proceedings regarding allegations of criminal misconduct.

b) This act shall not apply to any chance meeting or a social meeting at which matters relating to official business are not discussed. No chance meeting, social meeting, or electronic communication shall be used in circumvention of the spirit or requirements of this act to discuss or act upon a matter over which the public body has supervision, control, jurisdiction, or advisory power.

c) This act shall not apply to judicial proceedings, but shall apply to a court or other judicial body while exercising rule-making authority or while deliberating or deciding upon the issuance of administrative orders.

d) This act shall not prohibit the removal of any person or persons who willfully disrupt a meeting to the extent that orderly conduct of the meeting is seriously compromised.

SECTION 6
NOTICE

a) All public bodies shall give written notice of their regular meetings at the beginning of each calendar year. The notice shall include the dates, times, and places of such meetings.

b) All public bodies shall give supplemental written public notice of any regular, special, or rescheduled meeting no later than 72 hours before the meeting. The notice shall include the agenda, data, time, and place of the meeting.

c) Written public notice shall include, but need not be limited to:

1) posting a copy of the notice at the principal office of the public body holding the meeting, or if no such office exists, at the building in which the meeting is to be held, and in at least three other prominent places within the governmental unit; and

2) mailing a copy of the notice to any person who requests notice of such meetings; any such person shall be given notice of all special or rescheduled meetings in the same manner as is given to members of the public body.

SECTION 7
MINUTES

a) All public bodies shall keep written minutes of all of their meetings. Such meetings shall include, but need not be limited to:

1) the date, time, and place of the meeting;

2) the members of the public body recorded as either present or absent;

3) the substance of all matters proposed, discussed, or decided, and at the request of any member, a record, by individual member, of any votes taken; and

4) any other information that any member of the public body requests be included or reflected in the minutes.

b) The minutes shall be public records and shall be available within a reasonable time after the meeting except where such disclosure would be inconsistent with sections 4 and 5 of this act.

c) All or any part of a meeting of a public body may be recorded by any person in attendance by means of a tape recorder or any other means of sonic reproduction except when a meeting is closed pursuant to sections 4 and 5 of this act; provided that in so recording there is no active interference with the conduct of the meeting.

SECTION 8
VOIDABILITY

Any final action taken in violation of sections 3 and 6 of this act shall be voidable by a court of competent jurisdiction. A suit to void any final action must be commenced within ninety days of the action.

**SECTION 9
ENFORCEMENT**

a) The Attorney General and the public prosecutors of competent jurisdiction shall enforce the provisions of this act.

b) Any person denied the rights conferred by this act may commence a suit in a court of competent jurisdiction for the county or city in which the public body ordinarily meets or in which the plaintiff resides for the purpose of requiring compliance with or preventing violations of this act or to determine the applicability of this act to discussions or decisions of the public body. The court may order payment of reasonable attorney fees and court costs to a successful plaintiff in a suit brought under this section.

**SECTION 10
PENALTIES**

Any person knowingly violating any provisions of this act shall be guilty of a misdemeanor and upon conviction thereof shall be fined not more than $500 or imprisoned not more than six months, or be both fined and imprisoned.

**SECTION 11
CONFLICT
OF LAW**

If the provisions of this act conflict with any other statute, ordinance, regulation, or rule, the provisions of this act shall control.

**SECTION 12
SEVERABILITY**

If any provision of this act, or the application of this act to any particular meeting or type of meeting is held invalid or unconstitutional, such decision shall not affect the validity of the remaining provisions or the other applications of this act.

**SECTION 13
EFFECTIVE DATE**

This act shall take effect thirty days after enactment into law.

Table of Cases

Index